TELEVISION AND AGGRESSION

A Panel Study

QUANTITATIVE STUDIES IN SOCIAL RELATIONS

Consulting Editor: Peter H. Rossi

UNIVERSITY OF MASSACHUSETTS
AMHERST, MASSACHUSETTS

In Preparation

Toby L. Parcel and Charles W. Mueller, **ASCRIPTION AND LABOR MARKETS: *Race and Sex Differences in Earnings***

Robert F. Boruch and Joe S. Cecil (Eds.), **SOLUTIONS TO ETHICAL AND LEGAL PROBLEMS IN SOCIAL RESEARCH**

Irving Tallman, Ramona Marotz-Braden, and Pablo Pindas, **ADOLESCENT SOCIALIZATION IN CROSS-CULTURAL PERSPECTIVE: *Planning for Social Change***

Published

J. Ronald Milavsky, Ronald C. Kessler, Horst H. Stipp, and William S. Rubens, **TELEVISION AND AGGRESSION: *A Panel Study***

Ronald S. Burt, **TOWARD A STRUCTURAL THEORY OF ACTION: *Network Models of Social Structure, Perception, and Action***

Peter H. Rossi, James D. Wright, and Eleanor Weber-Burdin, **NATURAL HAZARDS AND PUBLIC CHOICE: *The Indifferent State and Local Politics of Hazard Mitigation***

Neil Fligstein, **GOING NORTH: *Migration of Blacks and Whites from the South, 1900–1950***

Howard Schuman and Stanley Presser, **QUESTIONS AND ANSWERS IN ATTITUDE SURVEYS: *Experiments on Question Form, Wording, and Context***

Michael E. Sobel, **LIFESTYLE AND SOCIAL STRUCTURE: *Concepts, Definitions, Analyses***

William Spangar Peirce, **BUREAUCRATIC FAILURE AND PUBLIC EXPENDITURE**

The list of titles in this series continues on the last pages of this volume.

TELEVISION AND AGGRESSION

A Panel Study

J. RONALD MILAVSKY
Social Research Department
National Broadcasting Company
New York, New York

RONALD C. KESSLER
Social Research Department
University of Michigan
Ann Arbor, Michigan

HORST. H. STIPP
Social Research Department
National Broadcasting Company
New York, New York

WILLIAM S. RUBENS
Research Department
National Broadcasting Company
New York, New York

ACADEMIC PRESS
A Subsidiary of Harcourt Brace Jovanovich, Publishers
New York London
Paris San Diego San Francisco São Paulo Sydney Tokyo Toronto

ACADEMIC PRESS, INC.
111 Fifth Avenue, New York, New York 10003

United Kingdom Edition published by
ACADEMIC PRESS, INC. (LONDON) LTD.
24/28 Oval Road, London NW1 7DX

Library of Congress Cataloging in Publication Data
Main entry under title:

Television and aggression.

(Quantitative studies in social relations)
Includes index.
1. Television broadcasting--Social aspects--United States. 2. Violence on television--Social aspects--United States. 3. Aggressiveness (Psychology)
I. Milavsky, Ronald J. II. Series.
HE8700.8.T335 302.2'345'0973 82-6774
ISBN 0-12-495980-6 AACR2

PRINTED IN THE UNITED STATES OF AMERICA

82 83 84 85 9 8 7 6 5 4 3 2 1

Contents

PART III

SUMMARY AND CONCLUSIONS

CHAPTER 15

FOREWORD

Puzzled and frustrated by the lack of definitive research on the subject of television and violence, which became evident during the hearings of the Eisenhower Commission on the Causes and Prevention of Violence (1968), the management of NBC asked me—then serving as NBC's head of research—what sort of study could best be done to provide data that would be both rigorous and realistic on the issue of television and violence.

The key area in which research was lacking was the investigation of the long-term impact of exposure to television programs on aggressive behavior patterns under realistic conditions. It seemed to me the most promising approach to this issue would be to undertake a multiwave, multiyear panel study, in which the same children and teenagers would be interviewed repeatedly over a period of years so that changes in their behavior could be related to their prior television exposure.

The panel design was devised by Paul F. Lazarsfeld specifically for the study of social issues in real-life terms. NBC researchers applied the panel techniques to the problem of measuring television's effects in the commercial area—the effectiveness of television as an advertising medium—starting in the early 1950s.

A typical study of advertising effectiveness used panel data to follow the natural changes in levels of viewing and levels of purchase to discover their causal connections. The plan of analysis employed Lazarsfeld's 16-fold table, in which classifications of respondents, representing the "changers in viewing" and the "changers in purchasing," were cross-related to each other. The panel analysis clearly showed that changes in viewing behavior resulted in corresponding changes in buying behavior (NBC, 1953).

As a consequence of a decade of work with panel design, I knew that the technique worked and believed it to be effective in determining causality. In 1969, when I made a formal research proposal for a study of television and aggression, it took the form of a long-term panel design.

Throughout the earlier years of our panel studies, we had stayed in contact with Lazarsfeld and received helpful feedback and suggestions from him. He, in turn, had continued developing and refining techniques for the analysis of panel data. It was natural, therefore, to turn to him for suggestions on the new study. We were able to persuade him to become chief consultant on the study, and he remained so until his death in 1975.

And now, how has it all turned out?

After having served on the original Surgeon General's Scientific Advisory Committee on Television and Social Behavior and having followed the literature since then, I feel that our decision to conduct a long-term panel study was right—this indeed was the right kind of study to do.

And as I read the book, the outstanding impression it leaves is one of quality—of care, concern, and competence. Thanks to the caliber of staff and consultants we were able to assemble, the study was executed with meticulous care in the field, and the analytic techniques developed go far beyond anything I had imagined.

I hope the reader will conclude, as I have, that this has turned out to be the most thoughtful, technically sophisticated, and thoroughly documented study in its field, and that its findings will reshape the thinking about the relationship between television viewing and aggressive behavior.

THOMAS E. COFFIN

PREFACE

The following pages describe the most extensive study of television effects on childhood and adolescent aggression that has appeared in the scientific literature. It utilizes a panel design in which some 3200 young people were interviewed—many of them on up to six separate occasions over a 3-year period.

The main purpose of the study was to assess the impact of television viewing on subsequent aggression under realistic conditions. To do this, we measured real-life aggressive behavior as well as the amount and types of television programs the respondents watched.

We used state-of-the-art techniques to analyze the data. Several distinct television exposure measures were assessed for their predictive influence on subsequent aggression. The possibility that television effects may be magnified or attenuated by certain situational or individual predisposing influences was also tested.

This volume contains all the information and documentation that professional students of mass media effects expect from a research monograph. At the same time, we have tried to make this book accessible to lay readers. This allows the ultimate consumers—psychologists, sociologists, educators, broadcasters, government policymakers, or other interested readers—to have access to all the data they need to evaluate our work critically.

The book begins with brief reviews of the social context in which the issue of television's possible impact on aggression has been debated and the state of social research that led to this study. The introductory chapter also summarizes the organization of the volume.

PREFACE

This project was sponsored and supported by the National Broadcasting Company. Without NBC's sustained support over the 13 years since the pilot work for the first data collection began, it would have been impossible to complete so massive a project as this. Longitudinal research analyzing panel data is surely going to become increasingly important as investigations of social reality try to deal with the complexity of the world we live in.

While NBC supported the research reported in this book, the statements and interpretations of facts in it are the sole responsibility of the authors.

ACKNOWLEDGMENTS

A study that is as complicated and that extended over as long a period of time as this one owes debts to many people. Although we are not able to mention everyone, we particularly want to acknowledge the following:

Berton Pekowsky, who began working on the study soon after it started and helped in its design and execution. He also conducted analyses of the aggression measures and of television's effects on elementary school sample subgroups and prepared initial drafts of this material.

William Fishman, who established the initial computer processing system for the project and who trained Timothy Murphy, who remained in charge thereafter. Murphy proved to be not only ingenious in being able to provide anything any analyst wanted from an extremely complex data set, but was and is so careful that he never lost a single record for any child.

Eleanor Singer, who helped with the organization of the book, edited early drafts, and in the process helped greatly to move the manuscript toward its present state. Charlotte Fisher and Barbara Collins, who converted all our scribbles to beautifully coherent type. Julia Hammett, who supervised the extensive data cleaning, assisted with computer work, organized the school record data, and wrote the scoring program for girls. Liivi Joe, who served in many different capacities, including supervising fieldwork, interviewing, keeping records, correspondence, and computer programming. Doris Katz, who provided us with the bibliographic material we drew upon in planning the study and in writing the results. Theodore Kneisler, who worked on LISREL analysis, Nancy Stedman, who worked on the analysis of effects within subgroups for teenagers, and Eric Cardinal, who contributed in a variety of important ways. George Fuchs, whose social concern led to the initiation of this project and David Adams, whose respect for knowledge provided an environment in which research could flourish.

George Bohrnstedt, William McGuire, George Comstock, Percy Tannenbaum, and Aimee Dorr, who read and commented on portions of earlier drafts.

Samson Tuchman, who worked with us during the development stage and who assisted in constructing the teen and parent questionnaires. John Meyer, Michael Hannon, and William Bowers, who first suggested the model for analysis of causal relations. Gerald Glasser and Gale Metzger, who advised us about our initial sampling plan. Richard Maisel, who advised us about testing for statistical significance in analysis of wave pairs. Blair Wheaton, who advised us in the LISREL analyses.

Jack Landis, Betty Roberson, Steven Levitt, Janis Smith Jeffers, and Jane Pelis of Marketing Evaluations, Inc. for their expert, efficient, and conscientious management of the fieldwork and for giving first priority to doing the job right. Rosalyn Amdur Baker of Twin Cities Interviewing Service, Inc., who supervised fieldwork in Minneapolis; Wanema Keeton, La Freida Norman, Jessie Dennis, and Mary Winters of Southwest Research, Inc., who supervised fieldwork in Fort Worth and who did all that was required, and more, to collect data of the highest quality and to achieve the highest possible response rates.

Richard Faunce, Research Director, Minneapolis Public School System and Charles Evans, Research Director, Fort Worth School System, who helped us obtain permission to conduct the study in their respective system's schools. Evans was assisted in this effort by Herbert LaGrone, Dean of the School of Education, Texas Christian University. Dean LaGrone also made facilities available to us for interviewing teenage boys. John Schwarzwalder, Executive Vice President and General Manager of KTCA, who encouraged teenage respondents and their parents to participate in the study and provided facilities for interviewing.

We also want to thank Meryl Alster, David Armor, Dennis Flaherty, Sam K. Ghosh, Selma Glick, David Kenny, Judith Langer, Joseph McDermott, Mark Penn, Arnold Simmel, Marti Stein, Dan Weiss, Robert Wirt, and all the others who took part in the fieldwork and data processing and who gave advice from time to time.

We want to thank the parents, the elementary school teachers and administrative staff, and especially the children.

TELEVISION AND AGGRESSION

A Panel Study

CHAPTER 1

INTRODUCTION

SOCIAL CONTEXT

The decade of the 1960s was one of violence in the United States. There was a wave of political assassinations, beginning with that of John F. Kennedy, and followed by those of Robert F. Kennedy, Martin Luther King, Medgar Evers, and Malcolm X. The effects of generations of discrimination, disadvantage, and poverty exploded in a series of civil disorders that culminated, in the summer of 1967, in riots in more than 23 American cities. Protest against the war in Vietnam climaxed in the demonstrations and riots accompanying the August 1968 Democratic National Convention.

In response to these events, the National Commission on Civil Disorders, more widely known as the Kerner Commission, was established in July 1967; its massive investigative report was issued in March 1968. Then, in June 1968, President Lyndon Johnson by Executive Order established the National Commission on the Causes and Prevention of Violence, headed by Dr. Milton Eisenhower. One of the volumes of the commission report, released in November 1969 under the editorship of Robert K. Baker and Sandra J. Ball, constituted an extensive examination of what was then known about the relationship between media practices and violence in society.

While the commission hearings were in progress, Senator John O. Pastore of Rhode Island, Chairman of the Senate Sub-Committee on Communications, issued a call to the Surgeon General to conduct an investigation into the effects of television, similar to the one carried out for smoking and health in 1962. That investigation culminated in 1972 in what has come to be known as the "Surgeon

General's Report on Television and Social Behavior," consisting of five volumes of findings from newly commissioned research and the interpretative report of a special advisory committee.

Thus, the climate of the 1960s—characterized by violence, protest, and investigative response—led to a substantial increase in research on the role of television as a possible contributor to violence. Broadcasters were part of this research effort and the study at hand is one of its products.

EXPERIMENTAL RESEARCH

From the beginning of television, there has been concern about its possible harmful effects, particularly on children. In the late 1950s, research by Himmelweit (1958) and Schramm (1961) found very little to justify such concern. But in the early 1960s, laboratory experiments on television's impact on aggressive behavior by Bandura, Ross, and Ross (1961) and Berkowitz and Rawlings (1963) provided some evidence of negative effects. When Congressional hearings were held about increasing violent crime in this country, academic researchers pointed to this experimental evidence as supporting the possibility of a link between television violence and social violence.

These laboratory experiments documented that exposure to filmed depictions of aggressive actions was associated with imitative reactions on the part of young children. Experiments with older children and adolescents showed increases in the commission of surrogate aggressive actions. Usually, the subjects in those experiments underwent a frustration experience before they were exposed to the aggressive (experimental group) or nonaggressive (control group) material.

Researchers in the television industry felt the results of these studies did not establish that television has similar effects in the real world on a number of grounds, centering on the artificiality of the studies' experimental conditions. For example, the experimental treatment was not exposure to actual television programs shown at the time but to material filmed by the experimenters or to clips from theater movies. The surrogate measures of aggression used in these experiments—hitting a plastic inflatable "Bobo" doll, or pressing a button that subjects believe inflicts an electric shock on another person—seemed removed from the sort of violence people were concerned about. Also, these studies covered only short time periods and did not address the issue of long-term effects.

Broadcasters who testified at Congressional hearings in the early 1960s expressed concern over social violence but did not accept the laboratory experiments as evidence of a link to television. They agreed to consider other kinds of research on the issue.

At that time, an effort was made to conduct research that would have the support of the entire industry. This effort was encouraged by the U.S. Department of Health, Education and Welfare. Beginning in 1962, the Department called meetings and conferences that brought industry and university researchers together.

One result of these meetings was the establishment in mid-1963 of a Joint Committee for Research on the Effects of Television on Children. Ultimately, membership consisted of the three major networks and the National Association of Broadcasters. The Joint Committee solicited and funded several proposals.

One study seemed so appropriate that other industry efforts were placed on hold to wait for its results. It was an experimental study proposed by Seymour Feshbach with random assignment and manipulated treatment. Unlike earlier studies, the setting was not a laboratory but live-in schools and homes for boys. Within each, boys were divided into two exposure groups, one allowed to watch only "action" programs, which contained depictions of violence, the other allowed to watch only "non-action" programs. Effects were sought over a 6-week period instead of just immediately after exposure as in the laboratory experiments.

When Feshbach reported his first results to the Joint Committee in 1967,[1] they seemed to favor what became known as the "catharsis hypothesis": Viewing television programs with violence was associated with a drop in aggression; boys who viewed the nonviolent fare became more aggressive. It became evident, however, that this result was questionable because of problems that had occurred in the conduct of the experiment. Indeed, the Feshbach study indicated that even the best designed realistic experiments could run into problems in execution.[2]

The problems with the Feshbach study were later discussed by his co-author Robert D. Singer and by Robert M. Kaplan:

> The major problem in interpreting the Feshbach and Singer field study concerns the fact that the aggression scores for some of the aggressive diet groups in the boys' homes were initially higher than those for the groups given the nonviolent diet. This was the sort of unfortunate chance happening described by Campbell and Boruch (1976) as "unhappy randomization." Because of this problem, the observed catharsis effect for these boys may have been due to regression toward the mean. For this reason we feel safest concluding that the Feshbach and Singer study supports a null rather than a catharsis view. Certainly

[1]The results were published in Feshbach and Singer (1971).

[2]These problems led the Joint Committee to fund a replication with several improvements by William Wells (1973). That study did not reproduce the "catharsis" finding, and it was equivocal on the issue of increased aggression.

> the study shows no support for the theory that viewing of aggressive TV increases real life aggression [1976:55].

Both the Feshbach study and the Wells replication alerted researchers to another basic problem with experiments in natural settings that try to alter normal viewing patterns. There are almost no people who do not watch television among whom the experimental treatment can be instituted randomly. The application of the "treatment" involves depriving some viewers of their normal television fare. That deprivation results in "side effects" that invalidate the experiment's results. In both the Feshbach and Wells studies, boys in the control group who were assigned the nonviolent programs became resentful and hostile as a result of their chance "deprivation" of programs they preferred to watch.

It thus seemed that laboratory experiments introduced artificialities and that field experiments produced ambiguous results. This meant that the industry was back to ground zero. It became clear that the work of the Joint Committee would not be enough and, in the late 1960s, each network began to consider alternative ways of conducting valid studies. The National Broadcasting Company (NBC) chose a panel study as the best way of providing relevant data on the issue.[3] At the time, no one else was considering that approach to study the question at hand.

THE PRESENT STUDY

The key elements of the design of the panel survey are repeat measurements of television viewing and aggression of the same individuals at multiple time points. These features enable the researcher to make inferences about television's possible causal role by studying change in aggression in relation to prior patterns of television viewing. Such a design is best suited to address a central question of concern to the public: does television violence play a discernible role in socializing young viewers to act aggressively.

Panel surveys have strategic advantages over experiments and other designs, even though they lack the one feature that in theory sets experiments apart from all other designs for the study of causation—random assignments of subjects to pure, manipulated treatments.

A panel survey design has a serviceable substitute for random assignment. It uses each individual in the study as his or her own control. Properly analyzed, this design controls for prior aggression and for any initial correlation between

[3]CBS funded field experiments by Milgram and Shotland (1973) and a cross-sectional survey by Belson (1978). ABC commissioned survey studies by Heller and Polsky (1975) and laboratory experiments by Lieberman Research, Inc. (1975).

viewing and aggression and therefore accomplishes much of what experiments do through randomization. And panel designs take the real world as it comes. They do not attempt the usually futile task of taming reality to meet the experimenter's demanding conditions. All these features, as well as the shortcomings of panel designs, will be discussed in this report.

The panel design also was chosen to fill a gap in research by assessing lasting, long-term effects of television programming on children's aggressive behavior in natural surroundings, and to do this while taking into account other factors identified by prior research as determinants of aggressive behavior.

This study was designed to relate patterns of normal television viewing behavior to changes in aggression over periods between a few months and 3 years. It focuses on the impact of a steady diet of television violence on the long-term development of aggressive behavior patterns among the children studied. Short-term arousal or modeling effects of the sort studied in the experimental literature are not addressed. Also, the study design cannot uncover effects of specific program segments in triggering unusual or rare acts of violence.

RECENT RESEARCH ON TELEVISION AND AGGRESSION

The decade since the study's inception has seen much new research and even more discussion—among social scientists and among the general public—on the relationship between television and aggression. The research included in the Surgeon General's Report (1972) was designed to advance scientific knowledge regarding the impact of television on the viewer. However, the studies in that report did not end the debate about the effects of television on aggression. With one exception, all of the studies were laboratory experiments or cross-sectional surveys. The experiments provided evidence similar to that obtained by previous experiments, which is mute on the question of long-term effects of real-life exposure. The surveys provided rather consistent evidence for the existence of cross-sectional correlations between television exposure and aggression. This evidence, of course, does not address the causal issue, since correlations can be produced by effects of aggression on viewing behavior or by third variables that antecede both viewing and aggression.

The one exception to those studies in the Surgeon General's Report was one by Lefkowitz, Eron, Walder, and Huesmann (1972) which assessed long-term developmental effects of the sort our study is designed to detect. That study documented a statistically significant relationship between preference for violent television programs and aggression measured 10 years later. However, the Surgeon General's Report regarded its findings "not conclusive" by virtue of several methodological problems with the data collected.[4] In fact, in its recommendations for future research, the report called attention to "the gap in longitudinal research on the effects of television programs on children," and emphasized: "This gap needs to be filled before we can learn something dependable about the long-term effects of repeated exposure to standard television fare [Surgeon General's Scientific Advisory Committee, 1972: 114]." We say more about this earlier study in Chapter 15.

A number of other studies concerning possible causal connections between television exposure and aggression have appeared since the inception of this study. Major projects include the field experiments by Milgram and Shotland (1973), testing imitation of specific television incidents under realistic conditions, and a cross-sectional survey of British boys by Belson (1978). The only longitudinal panel studies relevant to this topic that we know of are on preschoolers by Dorothy and Jerome Singer (1979) and on elementary school boys and girls by Huesmann, Fischer, and Eron.[5] As a result, a study like this continues to be of importance.

SUMMARY OF STUDY DESIGN AND ANALYSIS METHODS

In this introductory chapter, we sketch out the main features of the research. The research design is described in detail in Chapter 2 and the logic of the analysis in Chapter 5.

The study was conducted in two midwestern cities. Some 3200 young people—a sample of elementary school children and a sample of teenage boys—were surveyed over a 3-year period. Repeated measurement of the same children and adolescents allowed us to study the relationship between

---

[4]The summary report by the Surgeon General's Scientific Advisory Committee stated that the study's findings are "consonant with the interpretation that violence viewing leads to later aggression, but are not conclusive" (1972, p. 95). See also Chaffee's (1972, pp. 27–28) review of that study.

A relationship between a measure of preference for television violence and later peer-rated aggression was found. However, the earlier television measure was based on mother reports, which are of questionable validity, and the later television measure was based on self-reports, which are likely to be more reliable. There are also differences in the early and later aggression measure (in addition to questions about the validity of the later measure). The validity questions and the differences in reliability between early and later measures have the potential of distorting the results of the analysis. In addition, the researchers used an analysis technique (cross-lagged correlations) that frequently has been criticized.

[5]A report on that research (Eron, 1982) does not include any analysis of the panel data. It does cite four other studies showing a "relation between television violence and *subsequent* aggressive behavior in natural situations [1982: 197, emphasis added]." Three of these clearly do not show such a relationship because they do not provide measures of both television exposure and aggression at more than one point in time (e.g., Greenberg, 1975; Hartnagel, Teevan, & McIntyre, 1975; McCarthy, Langner, Gersten, Eisenberg, & Orzech, 1975).

developmental changes in antisocial behaviors and exposure to television violence under natural conditions.

The field work was conducted from May 1970 through December 1973. During that period, data were obtained at six different points in time from about 1200 boys and almost as many girls in the elementary school sample through questionnaires that were administered to the children in their classrooms. In addition, interviews were conducted with the parents (almost 400 mothers and almost 200 fathers) of some boys. Teachers' reports and student records were also collected for a large number of the respondents.

The other sample consists of about 800 teenage boys in Grades 7–12. These boys were also sampled with the cooperation of the school systems; however, they were not interviewed in their classrooms but at central interviewing locations. Data from teenage boys were obtained in five data collection waves over the same 3-year period in which the younger children were studied. As with elementary school boys, data were also obtained from mothers and fathers.

When the study was planned, public concern focused on boys' aggression; hardly anybody regarded aggressiveness among girls as a problem. As a result, it was decided to concentrate resources on a study of boys. Since the sample unit for elementary school boys was the entire classroom, data for girls in these classes were also collected and analyzed and are reported here. However, the girls' parents were not interviewed, and no data on teenage girls were collected.

Initial findings from this research project were reported in a paper read at the 1972 annual meeting of the American Sociological Association. Based on data from the first four of the six study waves, it addressed the question of the causal influences of television violence on aggression with methodology suggested by Lazarsfeld (1972). One of the main purposes of that paper was to elicit comments from experts in the field of television violence effects as well as from experts in methodology and to use their suggestions in the further analysis of data from the study. As it turned out, there were many conflicting suggestions. But it was clear from this initial analysis that the association between television and aggression was much smaller than could be analyzed with the methods we had planned to use (i.e., 8- and 16-fold tables). (We had no way of anticipating this at the onset of the study because the first correlations in the research literature appeared in the 1972 Surgeon General's Report.) This meant that we needed to find an analysis method sensitive enough to study small effects, one that would adjust for measurement error, and detect subtle patterns of association.

The search for a better analysis method than existed at the time we began the study, and the suggestions of methodologists about alternative approaches, set us off on a 3-year journey into deeper methodological and statistical waters than we had anticipated. After several decades during which Lazarsfeld's method was the only available approach for panel analysis, several new strategies were proposed in the 1960s and early 1970s: cross-lagged panel correlation analysis, path analysis, log-linear analysis, and several other approaches that were under development. Therefore, we found ourselves faced with many alternative approaches to analyze these panel data. After much consultation and evaluation of alternatives, and the fortunate development of a vastly improved approach to the estimation of measurement error in 1973 (Jöreskog, 1973), we selected the approach that we eventually used in this volume. Since that time, this approach has become the most widely adopted one among methodologists (Jöreskog & Sörbom, 1977; Rogosa, 1979; Sörbom, 1975) and is increasingly being adopted by substantive researchers (Kohn & Schooler, 1978, 1982; Mortimer & Lorence, 1979; Wheaton, Muthen, Alwin, & Summers, 1977). In Chapter 5, we present an assessment of the advantages and disadvantages of alternative approaches and the reasons we chose the method that was finally adopted.

Independent of the search for such an analysis method, the smallness of the observed relationships also prompted us to reconceptualize our measures of exposure to see if we could find one which showed a stronger relationship to aggression than the one we initially observed. None of these attempts to examine the data with greater resolution succeeded in detecting evidence that the small associations found in them were indicative of a caused connection from exposure to aggression.

Preliminary reports on the study were presented at three professional meetings during 1977.[6] A summary report was prepared for the "Update" of the 1972 Surgeon General's Report (Pearl *et al.*, 1982, Volume II). The present volume, with its fuller description of the measures, analyses, and findings, allows the reader to examine the conclusions in more detail than was possible in these summary reports.

ORGANIZATION OF THE BOOK

Because different methods were used to study the two age groups sampled, analyses and findings are reported separately in this volume. Chapters 2–8 deal with elementary school children, and Chapters 9–14 with teenage boys. Data for the two samples are presented in the same order.

[6]The first report, read at the annual meeting of the American Association for Public Opinion Research, focused on the basic question of effect (Milavsky, 1977a). The second paper, read at the annual meeting of the American Psychological Association, focused on whether the basic findings would remain unchanged if exposure to television violence were conceptualized in different ways (Milavsky, 1977b). The third paper was read at the annual meeting of the American Sociological Association and reported analyses of television effects among subgroups of the sample (Milavsky, 1977c).

The first chapter of the elementary school section, Chapter 2, describes the design of the young children's study. This is followed by two chapters that present the basic measures used in the analyses: aggression and exposure to television violence (Chapters 3 and 4).

The analysis of the relationship between television and aggression starts in Chapter 5, which presents cross-sectional correlations and discusses strategies for causal analysis. Time-lagged causal analyses are presented in Chapter 6.

Chapter 7 reports a number of supplementary analyses. First, we examine whether the findings reported in Chapter 6 change when the exposure measure is conceptualized in different ways. The alternative conceptualizations examined include a measure of relative exposure to violent television, a measure of cumulative exposure, and a "favorite show" measure. Next, we examined specifications of the relationship between television and aggression among subgroups, testing the hypothesis that exposure effects are most likely to appear among children who are predisposed to act aggressively or are in situations that might facilitate aggression. Then we report two analyses that are smaller in scope. One shows that the analysis methods used to explore causal relationships between television and aggression are capable of detecting significant associations between other variables and aggression. The other examines mutual causes of television and aggression that were not controlled in our basic analysis model.

Chapter 8 reports data for elementary school girls as well as pooled data for girls and boys. All analyses reported are identical to those performed for boys. However, since fewer data were collected, some analyses are less extensive.

The second part of the book is devoted to the analysis of data for teenage boys. Chapter 9 describes the design, Chapter 10 the aggression measures, and Chapter 11 the measurement of television exposure. Cross-sectional data and the causal analysis strategy for the older boys are presented in Chapter 12; the findings, in Chapter 13. The additional analyses described for elementary school boys were also carried out for teenagers and are reported in Chapter 14.

The final chapter summarizes the study and its findings and attempts to put them in perspective by relating them to other studies of television violence and aggression.

Background on the selection of the study cities, on the sampling of programs, and some details of the subgroup findings are omitted here because of space limitations. Reports on these aspects are contained in a number of working papers that are available on request. (They are referred to at the appropriate places in the chapters.) The study generated a great deal of material on issues indirectly related to the central question of analysis—such as data on the respondents' family and personal characteristics and their relationships with aggression. We also assessed the characteristics of heavy television viewers. Those analyses, too, are available on request.

PART I

ELEMENTARY SCHOOL CHILDREN: ANALYSES AND FINDINGS

CHAPTER 2

DESIGN OF THE STUDY OF CHILDREN

The study design flows from the purpose outlined in Chapter 1: to conduct a longitudinal multiwave panel study, measuring young people's aggressive behavior and television exposure under natural conditions in the context of their family and other social environments. To accomplish this objective, data were collected for a period of over 3 years beginning in May 1970 and ending in December 1973.[1]

The study consists of two parts: an elementary school sample of second- through sixth-grade boys and girls, and a sample of teenage boys. When the study began, the younger respondents ranged in age from 7 through 12 years old, the older respondents from 12 through 16. Over the 3-year period, our data reflect the behavior of children and adolescents ranging in age from 7 through 19.

Different data-gathering techniques were used and different information was obtained for each sample, to take into account the respondents' age differences and the resulting disparities in maturity and skills. This chapter describes the design for the elementary school portion of the study..

Data on aggression and television exposure were collected on six different occasions from the same elementary school children in their school classrooms (see Table 2.1). With the exception of summer, when school is not in session,

[1]Marketing Evaluations, Inc., a private research company, was engaged to conduct the fieldwork. They, in turn, hired professional interviewing organizations in the two study cities. Marketing Evaluations was also responsible for the production and distribution of questionnaires and other materials. NBC's Department of Social Research designed the study, analyzed the data, and supervised data collection in the field.

TABLE 2.1
Dates of the Six Data Collection Waves for Elementary School Children

WAVE	DATE	
I	May–June	1970
II	October–November	1970
III	February	1971
IV	May	1971
V	May	1972
VI	May	1973

the waves covered all seasons, including fall and winter, when viewing levels are highest.[2] The time intervals between waves were varied purposefully. The list of time intervals is shown in Table 2.2. Fifteen pairs of waves are available for longitudinal analysis, permitting assessment of television effects over durations ranging from 3 months to 3 years.

All data collection took place more than 6 weeks after the beginning of the school year; most took place close to the end of the school year, to ensure that the children knew their classmates well and could give valid reports about their aggression.

The remainder of this chapter elaborates on the design features just outlined. First, an overview of data sources and methods of data collection is provided. Sampling is the topic of the next section. The final sections deal with attrition and with respondents who entered the sample after Wave I.

DATA SOURCES AND METHODS OF COLLECTION

Data were obtained from school children, their teachers and parents, and their school records. The data central to our study, pertaining to aggression and television exposure, were obtained directly from the children through questionnaires administered in school classrooms. This section first summarizes the methods used to obtain those data. (Detailed accounts are given in Chapters 3 and 4.) A description of the additional data sources follows.[3]

---

[2]This conclusion is based on data from commercial rating services. The respondents in our study also indicated higher exposure levels during fall and winter (Waves II and III). This topic is discussed further in Chapter 4.

[3]Copies of all instruments used in the collection of data—questionnaires for children, teachers, mothers, and fathers; school-record code sheets; and guides for questionnaire administrators—are available on request from the authors.

TABLE 2.2
Duration of Time Lags between Wave Pairs

NUMBER OF WAVE PAIRS	DURATION	WAVE PAIR
1	3 months	III–IV
1	4 months	II–III
1	5 months	I–II
1	7 months	II–IV
1	9 months	I–III
3	1 year	I–IV
	1 year	IV–V
	1 year	V–VI
1	1 year, 3 months	III–V
1	1 year, 7 months	II–V
2	2 years	I–V
	2 years	IV–VI
1	2 years, 3 months	III–VI
1	2 years, 7 months	II–VI
1	3 years	I–VI

Main Data Sources: Development of Aggression and Television Exposure Measures

Following a review of the literature and consultations with several experts in research on young children, on teenagers, and on problems of measuring aggression and delinquency, we undertook several pretests aimed at evaluating a number of different ways of collecting valid and reliable data on both of the study central measures. These included self-administered and peer questionnaires and in-home interviews using mothers as informants or as interpreters. Special care was devoted to the problems of how to communicate effectively with young children and with minority groups and disadvantaged children, to assure that they understood what we were asking and that we understood what they were replying.

As a result of this developmental work, which extended over a period of 8 months, we concluded that a measure of aggression utilizing a peer-rating technique, administered simultaneously to all children in a school classroom, would yield more valid and reliable data than either self-reports or reports obtained from mothers. In contrast, we found that a self-report measure of television exposure, administered in a similar manner, could also produce valid and reliable data provided special procedures were designed to accommodate the limited reading and writing skills and short attention span of young respondents.

CHILDREN'S QUESTIONNAIRE

Based on this developmental research, we constructed questionnaires to measure aggression and exposure. The questionnaires also included items about prosocial behavior, friendship patterns, and exposure to such other media as magazines, comic books, and theater movies. In some waves, additional items were included, such as questions about word-of-mouth discussions of television programs, reactions to violent and nonviolent movie scenes, and measures of "masculine" and "feminine" attitudes.[4] These questions not only provided additional information, but also served to diffuse attention from the central measures.

Administration of the questionnaires, which children answered during regular school hours, was supervised by a team of trained interviewers in each classroom while the teacher completed a questionnaire in another room. Interviewers read the instructions from specially prepared scripts to inform the children clearly and uniformly how to give their answers correctly.

Having several interviewers present ensured that attention could be given to individual children experiencing difficulties with the questionnaire. It also permitted continual checking to make sure all children were answering according to procedure. With few exceptions, the children were cooperative and answered questions carefully.

As soon as the questionnaires had been completed, they were reviewed and edited by the interviewers in a separate room. If omissions, uncertainties, or inaccuracies were found, interviewers went back to the classroom, spoke to the children involved, and clarified the responses. This immediate review procedure provided us with more complete and accurate data than would have been obtained without it.

Additional Data Sources

TEACHER QUESTIONNAIRE

The format of the teacher questionnaires, completed on each of the six data collection waves, was the same as that used for the behavior questions in the children's questionnaire.

The questionnaire contained between 21 and 27 questions, depending on the wave. It contained the same antisocial and prosocial items as the children's

[4]Most of these additional items were pretested in a special data collection preceding Wave V.

questionnaire; additional antisocial and prosocial items; and questions about each child's intellectual competence, emotional functioning, relationships with other class members, and comparative physical size.

SCHOOL RECORDS

School records were consulted immediately after the first data collection wave. The schools of the two study cities provided similar, though rarely identical, information about the children. In both cities the records were cumulative for each child, but even within a city some of the data were not available for all children.

Records from both cities contained information on school grades,[5] IQ and other aptitude and achievement test scores,[6] number of days absent, and number of days tardy. Both also indicated whether the child had repeated a grade and gave some information about the number of different schools the child had attended. Each city provided some measure of the child's deportment, through either a "citizenship" grade or teacher comments.

In addition, school records in one city contained information on the number of children in the child's family, the occupations and marital status of the parents, and the birthplaces of the child and parents. These records also contained comments about the child by each of his teachers, from which we obtained information about intellectual competence, peer relationships, and emotional functioning as well as indications of antisocial and prosocial behavior. These data must be considered soft, as they involve the teacher's subjective judgment. Further, teachers were not required to report systematically on any specific aspect of the child, but rather could comment on anything they chose. Indeed, most reports contained nothing about aggressiveness. However, those that did spontaneously mention aggressive behavior were useful in validating the peer-rating measure.

In order to derive measures that could be used with a substantial portion of the sample, it was necessary to combine original data from different sources. For example, we utilized scores on various IQ, aptitude, or achievement tests, depending on what was available for each child, to obtain a measure of intellectual ability. However, since somewhat different data were used in

---

[5]One city had a 3-point grade scale (average, above average, and below average), the other a 5-point scale (A, B, C, etc.). To make the scales comparable, we first averaged each child's grades and then ranked children, separately within each city, into six equally sized groups. Then these groups from both cities were combined into one 6-point scale.

[6]The school's IQ score (based on Wechsler, Stanford Binet, or other IQ tests) or, if these were not available, scores from other tests, such as SRA and Lorge-Thorndike, were used. Quartiles were computed and then combined into one 4-point variable.

deriving these variables, findings related to them should be interpreted with caution.

MOTHER INTERVIEWS AND FATHER QUESTIONNAIRES

Mothers of elementary school boys were interviewed twice during the course of the study. The first interviews (of approximately 90-min duration) were conducted in the spring of 1971, between Waves III and IV. The second interviews (of 60-min duration) were conducted in the summer and fall of 1973, after Wave VI.

The purpose of these interviews was to obtain information about family background, parent–child relationships, parental behavior, and parental attitudes, as well as additional information about the child's behavior considered relevant for the analyses. Some questions were asked in both interviews, but many were asked only once.

The mothers were contacted and later interviewed at home by female interviewers. If there was a father (natural or stepfather) in the household, the interviewer left a short questionnaire for the father to complete and mail back. The questionnaires contained items similar to those asked of mothers; question format was changed where necessary to conform to requirements of self-administration.

SAMPLING

Sample selection involved several stages:

1. Selection of the study location
2. Selection of respondents
3. Selection of mothers and fathers to interview.

Selection of Cities

To allow for a replication of results, the study was conducted in two locations rather than one.[7]

We decided to choose the two largest cities we could find which could be matched on demographic and economic factors, but which differed in crime rates. The difference in crime rates would provide an opportunity to detect any interaction between television fare and the larger social context, controlling for social and economic factors (Gastil, 1971). Large cities were where concern about crime and violence was greatest, and therefore would be more appropriate settings for the study of television's impact than either small towns,

[7]The analyses that led to the final selection are described more fully in a special documentation that is available upon request. (Documentation 2A, "Selection of Cities.")

suburban or rural areas. In addition, large cities also had the largest selection of television programming.

The optimal locations for research on television exposure were cities with at least four stations on the VHF band[8] that were located in the central time zone. There, prime time begins 1 hr earlier than in the rest of the nation, and many children watch programs not viewed by children in other time zones.[9] Much of the discussion concerning possible effects of television on children focused on prime-time programs. Therefore, this was considered an important criterion for the selection of study locations.

In considering additional criteria, we selected two cities that were fairly similar to each other and not atypical of the United States as a whole in social and economic characteristics.

We selected Fort Worth, Texas and Minneapolis, Minnesota on the basis of these criteria. They were similar in terms of the television programs shown, and both offered a large variety of programming. Furthermore, they were similar in size and in many social and economic characteristics. However, the murder and nonnegligent manslaughter rate in Fort Worth was considerably higher than in Minneapolis.[10]

Selection of Respondents

Because the study design called for data collection from children in classrooms, classrooms were the sampling units and all children in these classrooms were recruited as respondents.

Within the framework of this design we devised a sampling plan that would produce sizable numbers of groups of children considered relevant for this research: middle- and lower-income children, blacks and whites, and children of all ages from 7 to 12. The inclusion of middle- and lower-income children and blacks and whites would tend to result in greater heterogeneity with respect to other characteristics considered relevant to a study of television exposure and aggression—for example, family intactness, family size, punishment practices, and scholastic ability. The plan aimed for roughly 20% blacks and an evenly balanced sample with respect to socioeconomic status (SES) and age. We tried

[8]At the time of the study, many people could not watch UHF stations because their sets (and antennas) were not equipped to receive signals transmitted at those frequencies.

[9]A program shown in New York at 9:00 P.M. is seen in the central time zone at 8:00 P.M., and as a result, has a much larger audience of children. The same is true of the 10:00 P.M. programs, shown at 9:00 P.M. in the Midwest, even though the majority of the younger children in either time zone do not see those programs.

[10]In 1969 the FBI reported the following murder and nonnegligent manslaughter rates for the two cities: Fort Worth, 14.3 per 100,000 population; Minneapolis, 3.2 (FBI *Uniform Crime Reports*, 1969). For more details, see Documentation 2A on selection of cities.

to omit schools with residential mobility so high as to render a long-term panel study virtually impossible.[11] Schools in the wealthiest neighborhoods were also avoided.

As data were to be gathered from children in classrooms, a measure of "school SES" was used to select schools for the study. The school SES classification was based on assessments by principals and the school systems' research departments. In addition, we took the following criteria into account in selecting the schools: (*a*) very large schools (of which there were few) were excluded to prevent overrepresentation of any one type of child; (*b*) schools where a substantial number of the students could not read or comprehend English well enough to provide valid data were also excluded.

Fort Worth's schools were racially segregated. To include blacks there at all, therefore, meant choosing one school in which virtually all children were black. Ultimately, four schools were chosen, two in middle-income white neighborhoods, one in a low-income white neighborhood, and one in a low-income black neighborhood.

Once schools in Fort Worth had been selected, the director of research for the city's school administration in Minneapolis helped us to obtain comparable ones in that city. The schools selected corresponded fairly well to those in Fort Worth. In Minneapolis, where schools were somewhat more racially integrated, one low-income school consisted of about two-thirds black children.

After the schools had been selected, all classes within a given grade automatically became part of our sample. As described in the previous section, aggression scores for each child were based on the ratings of his or her classmates. Since the members of a class in one year usually disperse to many classes the following year, the only way to get the ratings on the original sample in a new school year without interviewing additional classes is to include all the classes in a grade initially. This means, for example, that all children in all third-grade classes in one year are followed by interviewing all fourth-grade classes the next year.

Even so, two factors led to increasing the number of schools and classrooms as the study progressed. In Fort Worth, after Wave I, the school system began the practice of moving children from elementary schools to middle schools after the fifth grade. To avoid losing such children, we followed them to the middle schools to collect data from them. In Minneapolis the schools contained a number of split-grade classrooms (fourth and fifth grades together in the same

[11]The dropout rate was indeed higher from the low-SES schools selected for the study, but not so high as to cause severe analysis problems. Unfortunately, we did not know that the area surrounding one school in Minneapolis was about to undergo urban renewal. As a result, we lost a relatively high percentage of respondents from that school after the first few waves, primarily from lower-income white families. (See also section on attrition.)

classroom). Because of such situations, we had to include additional classrooms in order to reinterview the same children the following year.[12]

The fact that the entire class was the sampling unit and that all members of a class were part of the study had another important consequence. Respondents who entered a grade after the initial selection at the time of Wave I became part of the sample. Therefore, the Wave II, III, IV, V, and VI samples all include a number of new children, that is, those who had not been part of the initial sample (see Table 2.5).

The instruments used in collecting aggression data required knowledge of the full names, including nicknames, of all the boys and girls in each classroom. Therefore, after classes had been selected, lists of all members of these classes were obtained from school records and from teachers. The initial sample of boys comprised 805 names.[13]

The following tables illustrate the results of these selection procedures. Table 2.3A shows the number of classes selected in each city for the initial sample by grade and the SES of the school. Among low-SES children, blacks were selected in grades three and five, whites in grades two, four, and six.[14]

Table 2.3B shows the number of boys in the initial sample resulting from the selection of classes described in Table 2.3A. Table 2.3B shows, for both cities separately, the number of boys in each grade by race. The uneven distribution of blacks across grades is clearly reflected in these data. There are practically no blacks among second and fourth graders, and very few among sixth graders. Among third and fifth graders in each city, blacks comprise one-third to one-half of the sample. Overall, the percentage of blacks in the two cities is almost identical: 21% in Fort Worth, 20% in Minneapolis.

The number of respondents in each grade is slightly different in the two cities. This is because we did not sample exactly the same number of classes in each city and because classes have different sizes. There are more second,

---

[12]In Waves V and VI, we did not follow a few respondents who moved into classes where they were the only ones who were part of our study. Following these boys would have meant increasing the sample by 10–25 respondents for each boy; the new respondents would have been of little value to the analyses, since they would have been in the study in only one or two waves.

[13]The names of 857 boys were on the questionnaire list. On the day of data collection in Wave I, 123 boys were not present and, therefore, did not report their television viewing behavior; 52 of these never showed up in any other study wave. We estimated that more than 30 of these boys, whom we could not identify, had already left the school by the time of the first data collection. Also, some of the 52 were sixth graders who graduated out of the elementary school sample after Wave I. Because such boys could not be included in any analyses linking television and aggression, we excluded all 52 from the initial sample.

[14]Low levels of racial integration, especially in Fort Worth, made it impossible to select within-grade samples of the size we planned that were distributed evenly by race. In the face of this difficulty we drew the sample in such a way that one race predominated in each grade.

TABLE 2.3

A: Number of Classes in Each City in Initial Sample by Grade and School SES

	FORT WORTH				MINNEAPOLIS			
	LOW-SES SCHOOL			MIDDLE-SES SCHOOL	LOW-SES SCHOOL		MIDDLE-SES SCHOOL	
GRADE	BLACK		WHITE	WHITE[a]	BLACK[b]	WHITE	WHITE[a]	TOTAL CLASSES
2			4	3		3	3	13
3	3			3	5		3	14
4			2	4		2	3	11
5	2			3	4		2	11
6		3[c]		3		2	2	10
Total classes:	5	3	6	16	9	7	13	59

[a] No black middle-SES schools were available.

[b] The classes in the "black" school contained approximately one-third white students.

[c] The sixth-grade low-SES classes were racially mixed.

B: Number of Boys in Initial Sample in Each City by Grade and Race

	FORT WORTH				MINNEAPOLIS			
	RACE			TOTAL NUMBER	RACE			TOTAL NUMBER
GRADE	WHITE	BLACK	OTHER[a]	OF BOYS	WHITE	BLACK	OTHER[a]	OF BOYS
2	98		1	99	64	1	3	68
3	41	40		81	75	38	3	116
4	80	1	4	85	54	1	6	61
5	44	33	1	78	57	39	1	97
6	60	13	1	74	55	1		56
Total:	313 (78%)	87 (21%)	7 (2%)	407 (101%)	305 (77%)	80 (20%)	13 (3%)	398 (100%)

[a] Includes respondents who are Native American, Spanish-surnamed, and Oriental.

fourth, and sixth graders in Fort Worth and more third and fifth graders in Minneapolis. Overall, 51% of the initial sample of boys lived in Fort Worth, 49% in Minneapolis. Finally, the number of respondents in each grade is unequal. In both cities combined, there are 157 second graders, 197 third graders, 146 fourth graders, 175 fifth graders, and 130 sixth graders.

Table 2.4 shows the sample size in each of the six waves. It can be seen that the sample size declines in Wave II, is more or less constant in Waves II–IV, which all took place in the same school year, then declines again in Wave V, and again in Wave VI.

TABLE 2.4
Size of Sample in Each of Six Waves

WAVE	DATE	TOTAL NUMBER OF BOYS IN WAVE
I	May–June 1970	805
II	October–November 1970	703
III	February 1971	704
IV	May 1971	713
V	May 1972	500
VI	May 1973	293

The decrease in sample size is not primarily due to attrition through mobility and refusals. Most of the children excluded from the later waves graduated out of elementary school into junior high school, and many of these were recruited into the teenage sample of the study. Attrition due to the graduation of sixth graders and other causes is discussed in detail in the next section.

Respondents entering the sample for the first time after Wave I are included in these figures. As in the case with the sixth graders who graduated, data for these additional boys are not available for analysis in all possible pairs of waves.

Table 2.5 shows how many of the respondents in Waves II–VI were in the initial Wave I sample and how many were added in later waves. As an example, the table should be read as follows: In Wave IV, the total sample size is 713. Of these boys, 548 had been part of the Wave I sample; 165 had not been part of the Wave I sample but entered the study in Wave II, III, or IV.

The percentage of respondents who were not part of the initial sample increases steadily until Wave V. In Wave VI we ceased efforts to follow up respondents who had participated in only one or two of the previous waves and were in new split-grade classes in Minneapolis. As a result, the percentage of new respondents decreased slightly.[15]

Because only two cities are involved, the sample cannot be representative of all children in these age groups throughout the United States. Still, we have indications that our sample is by no means atypical. We analyzed 12 sample characteristics—those we deemed relevant and were able to find comparable national data for—and found a surprisingly high degree of agreement between this sample and data representative of the total United States in 1970 with

[15]Many of the additional respondents in Waves IV, V, and VI had been in more than one previous wave; see Table 2.14 for the number of boys present for the first time in each wave. The total number of second- to sixth-grade boys who were included in at least one wave is 1151.

TABLE 2.5
Number of Boys from Wave I Sample and Number of New Respondents in Each of Six Waves

	TOTAL NUMBER OF BOYS IN WAVE		TOTAL NUMBER OF BOYS IN WAVE WHO WERE IN WAVE I SAMPLE		TOTAL NUMBER OF BOYS IN WAVE WHO ENTERED THE SAMPLE AFTER WAVE I	
WAVE	*N*	(%)	*N*	(%)	*N*	(%)
I	805					
II	703	(100)	575	(82)	128	(18)
III	704	(100)	556	(79)	148	(21)
IV	713	(100)	548	(77)	165	(23)
V	500	(100)	332	(66)	168	(34)
VI	293	(100)	204	(70)	89	(30)

respect to family structure (both natural parents present or not), race, family income, mother's employment, father's occupation, and mother's occupation.[16] Boys in our sample, on the other hand, come from larger families; the educational level of their fathers is higher; their fathers are somewhat more likely to be unemployed; they are more likely to come from families who own their own home and own a color television. Finally, as a result of the study locations chosen, there are more Lutherans and Baptists and fewer Catholics in the sample than in the total U.S. population.

Selection of Mothers and Fathers

Respondents for the first mother interview were selected according to a sampling plan that provided quotas for interviews with mothers of children who had participated in the first three waves and of those sixth graders who were recruited for the teen study.[17] Concentrating efforts on children who were in multiple waves maximized the opportunity of benefiting from the panel feature of the design.

In order to have the achieved sample of mother interviews match as closely as possible the sample of children recruited for the panel, sampling quotas were set up for city, SES, and grade. Given the purpose of the study, aggression was an even more important variable than age, SES, race, and city, and obtaining data from mothers of highly aggressive boys was considered essential. Since aggression scores were available at the time of selection of the sample of mothers, aggression was included in the sampling quota plan as well.

[16]For details see "Comparison of Sample Characteristics with U.S. Population Characteristics," available on request (Documentation 2B).

[17]The grades of the children used in the sampling were the grades at the time of Wave I. At the time the mother interview was done, respondents had moved to the next grade.

The quotas required that about half the interviews should be conducted in each of the two cities; half should be from middle-SES schools, the other half from low-SES schools; and equal numbers of interviews should be with mothers of boys in grades two through five. Mothers of all sixth graders to be included in the adolescent sample were to be interviewed. Finally, based on the median aggression scores in each grade in each school, respondents were classified as high- or low-aggression boys, and equal numbers of interviews were carried out with mothers of boys in these two groups.

Table 2.6 shows the quota plan for the selection of mothers for the first wave of interviews, which called for 362 interviews overall, 288 with mothers of boys who had been in the first three waves.[18] Note that in the low-SES schools the number of available respondents was sometimes below or just equal to the quota number. Overall, 96% of the quota was reached. However, completed interviews were slightly below the quota for low-SES boys and over it for high-SES boys.

Mother interviews for an additional 24 boys were obtained through pretest interviews. Because there were few differences between the data obtained from mothers in the pretest and in the main study, we combined them. Also, as might be expected, some boys had brothers or sisters in the school who were also included in our sample. Thus we obtained interviews with the mothers of 377 of all respondents, 315 interviews for respondents for whom aggression data were available in the first three waves.[19]

Table 2.7 examines the extent to which respondents for whom mother interviews were obtained are representative of the total sample of boys in Wave I (excluding sixth graders). The comparison is possible for three characteristics: city of residence, race, and average scholastic grade. There are virtually no differences with respect to city and race. The scholastic grades of those without mother interviews are somewhat lower, but the difference is not dramatic.[20]

We also compared aggression scores of the boys with and without mother data. (Aggression was a quota for the selection of the sample.) Mean aggression scores of boys with and without data from mothers are about the same.

Of the 377 boys for whom interviews with mothers were obtained, 303 had a natural father or stepfather living at home; of these, 184 (61%) returned a father

[18]The latter figure excludes 74 sixth graders who graduated out of the sample.

[19]The sampling plan shows 527 as "total available," that is, all boys for whom there were aggression data in the first three waves. Since card cleaning and other tasks necessary to prepare data for computer analysis had not been completed when the sampling plan was designed, this number deviates from the final number, which is 549.

[20]Also, there are no pronounced or systematic differences between the two groups in aggressiveness, as measured with the aggression measure discussed in the following chapter.

TABLE 2.6

Quota for Mother Interviews (Wave 1)[a]

	FORT WORTH							
	LOW SES				MIDDLE SES			
	LOW AGGRESSION		HIGH AGGRESSION		LOW AGGRESSION		HIGH AGGRESSION	
GRADE	QUOTA	NUMBER AVAILABLE	QUOTA	NUMBER AVAILABLE	QUOTA	NUMBER AVAILABLE	QUOTA	NUMBER AVAILABLE
2	9	9	9	12	9	20	9	12
3	9	16	9	14	9	16	9	12
4	9	7	9	13	9	31	9	10
5	9	12	9	6	9	21	9	11
6	All available = 19				All available = 19			

Quota = 182
Available = 260

	MINNEAPOLIS							
	LOW SES				MIDDLE SES			
	LOW AGGRESSION		HIGH AGGRESSION		LOW AGGRESSION		HIGH AGGRESSION	
GRADE	QUOTA	NUMBER AVAILABLE	QUOTA	NUMBER AVAILABLE	QUOTA	NUMBER AVAILABLE	QUOTA	NUMBER AVAILABLE
2	9	12	9	11	9	13	9	12
3	9	21	9	24	9	18	9	21
4	9	5	9	9	9	9	9	16
5	9	19	9	17	9	17	9	7
6	All available = 18				All available = 18			

Quota = 180
Available = 267

Both cities: Total quota = 362
Total available = 527

[a]The figures include sixth graders (see discussion).

TABLE 2.7
Characteristics of Respondents with and without Mother Questionnaire Data (Wave I)

	WITH MOTHER DATA (%)	WITHOUT MOTHER DATA (%)	INITIAL SAMPLE WAVE I (EXCLUDING SIXTH GRADERS) (%)
City			
Fort Worth	52	47	49
Minneapolis	48	53	51
Race			
Black	21	24	23
White	75	74	75
Other	5	1	3
Average scholastic grades[a]			
Low	30	39	34
Medium	32	27	29
High	39	35	37
N	(315)	(360)	(675)

[a]Not available for 5–10% of the respondents.

questionnaire.[21] An additional 12 questionnaires were returned by fathers who did not live at home or by other males close to the child, providing a total of 196 father questionnaires.

The target group for the second interview with mothers consisted of those who had participated in the first. Interviews were obtained from 85%, or 319 mothers. A high proportion of the remaining 15% had moved away; there were relatively few refusals.[22] Again, fathers and other close males were asked to return a father questionnaire. Such data were obtained for 63% of the 169 boys whose mothers were interviewed and who had a father living at home.

ATTRITION

Sources of Attrition

Like all panel studies, this one experienced sample attrition. Attrition reduces the number of cases available for analysis and can affect sample composition.

[21]Reminder postcards were mailed to those who did not return the questionnaire after the initial mailing.

[22]Self-administered questionnaires were mailed to parents who had moved away. The 85% includes respondents who had moved, and the 15% includes those who did not return mailed questionnaires.

TABLE 2.8
Loss of Respondents Due to Graduation of Sixth Graders[a]
(Initial Sample in Wave, I, N = 805)

WAVES	NUMBER OF RESPONDENTS LOST BETWEEN WAVES
I and II	130
II and III[b]	0
III and IV[b]	0
IV and V	184
V and VI	150
Total	474

[a]Figures indicate loss due to graduation only.
[b]Both waves conducted during the same school year.

The next sections discuss the nature of attrition found in the study and summarize their effect on sample composition. A detailed examination of the impact of attrition on sample composition appears in Appendix A.

GRADUATION OF SIXTH GRADERS

The main reason for attrition in this study was an inherent part of the research design: When a respondent graduated from the sixth grade, he "graduated" out of the sample of elementary school children. The aggression measure used in the peer study was designed for class members who spend most of the school hours together and know each other well. The other data collection methods were also designed for elementary school children, not for boys in junior high school. Therefore, sixth graders were excluded from the elementary school sample, and after 3 years, those who were sixth, fifth, and fourth graders in Wave I had left the sample.

Table 2.8 shows the loss of respondents due to the graduation of sixth graders. The loss of sixth graders from the elementary school sample meant that fewer children were available for analyses of longer-term effects. Alternate designs, which avoided this source of attrition, were considered but rejected.[23]

[23]For example, one possibility was to sample only second and third graders in Wave I (they would have been fifth and sixth graders after 3 years). This alternate design was rejected because it would have yielded an extremely narrow age range at any one point in time. The missing age groups could have been the very children affected by the kind of television programs shown at that time, and there was no way of knowing this in advance. We therefore chose a design that provided a wider age range in the first four waves, and elected to suffer the consequent attrition.

Another possibility considered was to employ a single set of administrative procedures and measuring instruments for the entire age span, 7–17, thus eliminating the division into an elementary school and a teenage sample. This alternative was rejected because literature reviews

(*Continued on next page*)

To lessen the impact of attrition due to the graduation of sixth graders, many of them were recruited into the sample of teenage boys (see Chapter 9 for details).

MOBILITY

The study experienced not only planned attrition through the graduation of sixth graders, but also unintended and uncontrollable "panel mortality"—that is, permanent loss of respondents through mobility.

This section describes losses due to two kinds of mobility that cannot be distinguished from one another. The first, and presumably most frequent, type is *residential mobility*—children leaving the school because their families move. The other type is *mobility between schools*—the child's family did not move, but the child entered a private or parochial school. Because the design of the study required interviewing entire classrooms of respondents, it was not possible to obtain aggression data from these respondents through mail questionnaires.

Table 2.9 shows the number of respondents lost because of mobility. The largest loss, 88 boys, occurred between Waves I and II. Additional large losses occurred between Waves IV and V and Waves V and VI. These three time periods represent 12-month lags between school years. Mobility losses were comparatively small during the short periods that fell within the same school year (II and III, III and IV). The total number of boys who left the study because of mobility is 226, 33% of those in the initial sample who could have participated in other waves ($N = 675$ second to fifth graders.) However, many of those who left because of mobility would have left the study in any event because of graduation from sixth grade.

TEMPORARY ABSENTEEISM

In each of the six waves, some sample children were absent on the day of data collection and consequently could not answer the television exposure questions, though they were rated on aggression by the other children present. Thus, temporary absenteeism caused incomplete data and a reduction in the number of cases available for analyses requiring exposure data. To minimize such losses, in Waves V and VI television questionnaires were left with teachers to be completed by the absent children when they returned to class. This could have been done in earlier waves, but it did not occur to us until after Wave IV. Table

---

and pretests showed that the differences between young children and teenagers demand different methodologies. Otherwise, either the younger respondents cannot understand their tasks or the questions, or the older respondents are bored or even insulted by "childish" questions.

Finally, we considered using parents as data sources. Pretests demonstrated, however, that many parents are not valid reporters of their children's aggression or television viewing (see Chapters 3 and 4 for a discussion).

TABLE 2.9
Loss of Respondents Due to Mobility (Initial Sample in Wave I, N = 805)

WAVES	NUMBER OF RESPONDENTS LOST BETWEEN WAVES
I and II	88
II and III[a]	21
III and IV[a]	10
IV and V	75
V and VI	32
Total	226

[a]Both waves conducted during the same school year.

2.10 shows the loss of television data due to temporary absenteeism in all six waves among respondents included in the initial sample.

Effects of Attrition on Sample Composition

Respondents who dropped out of the sample permanently or temporarily differed in several respects from those who stayed. However, the impact of these dropouts on sample composition was not great.

Respondents who were lost as a result of mobility tended to have lower grades, to be from lower-income families, to be less likely to live with their natural parents, and to have change residence more frequently before leaving the study.[24] (For a detailed analysis, see Appendix A.) These are the kinds of children a study such as this one should include, because circumstances associated with these characteristics may make them more vulnerable to television's effects. Fortunately, many children with similar demographic characteristics stayed in the sample for the duration of the study, allowing us to analyze these groups separately.

As attrition affected sample composition, there is a possibility that it will affect findings pertaining to television's effects. This is especially true of attrition due to mobility, which has the greatest impact. However, it is only a possibility: Attrition will alter findings only if the characteristics that differ between those who leave and those who stay are modifiers of television's effects. The direct impact of attrition on basic findings is investigated in Chapter 6 and Appendix B in Chapter 6. In addition, the role of attrition-related variables as modifiers of television's effect is addressed in Chapter 7.

[24]They were also more aggressive; see Appendix B in Chapter 6.

TABLE 2.10
Loss of Television Exposure Data Due to Temporary Absenteeism[a]
(Initial Sample in Wave I, N = 805)

WAVE	TELEVISION AND AGGRESSION DATA AVAILABLE (*N*)	NO TELEVISION DATA AVAILABLE BECAUSE OF TEMPORARY ABSENTEEISM (*N*)
I	734	71
II	575	42
III	556	36
IV	548	46
V	332	0
VI	204	3

[a]A small number of refusals is included.

Those analyses indicate that the impact of attrition on the findings was extremely small.

NEW RESPONDENTS

As a result of the research design, Wave II and subsequent waves contain some respondents who were not part of the original sample. Before using data from these respondents in the analyses, we investigated potential differences between them and the initial sample.

Such differences were examined in basically the same way as differences between the initial sample and those who left. However, only two of the characteristics used in the attrition analyses are available for new respondents: city of residence and race. None of the family data are available, since interviews were conducted only with mothers of respondents who were in the initial sample.

Data for the comparison are shown in Table 2.11. Column (1) shows the distribution of respondents in the initial sample; the distribution of respondents new for the first time in Waves II, III, IV, V, and VI, respectively, is shown in columns (2)–(6). Compared with the initial sample, new respondents were much more likely to live in Minneapolis, and they were more likely to be white.[25]

As previously noted, respondents were added to the sample when they entered a class that had been sampled initially and when respondents who were

[25]The new boys were also slightly more aggressive, thus counterbalancing the effect of mobility (see Appendix B in Chapter 6).

TABLE 2.11
Characteristics of Respondents Who Were in the Initial Sample and New Respondents

CHILD CHARACTERISTICS	INITIAL SAMPLE IN WAVE I (%) (1)	NEW RESPONDENTS WITH AGGRESSION DATA FOR FIRST TIME IN WAVE (%): II (2)	III (3)	IV (4)	V (5)	VI (6)
City of residence						
Fort Worth	57	27	29	33	20	46
Minneapolis	49	73	71	67	80	54
Race						
Black	21	9	9	10	9	3
White	77	88	91	90	88	95
Other	3	2	0	0	4	3
N	(805)	(128)	(35)	(30)	(104)	(37)

part of the sample moved into new classes. In Minneapolis, many respondents moved into split-grade classes, which resulted in the addition of about twice as many new respondents from that city as from Fort Worth. It appears that the main reason for the high percentage of whites among the new respondents is that the new children in split-grade classes were more likely to be white than those who had been in the sample initially.

However, since the number of new respondents is not large, their effect on the overall sample composition is small in most analyses. As a result, the possibility that new respondents affect the findings is slight.

APPENDIX A: THE EFFECTS OF ATTRITION

Chapter 2 reported on the nature and amount of permanent and temporary attrition from the sample. Such attrition has important consequences. First, it reduces the number of cases available for panel analysis. Second, attrition may change the sample composition, and this, in turn, may affect findings. This appendix examines the effects of attrition on the number of cases available for analysis and on sample composition. Effects on basic findings are reported in Chapter 6 and its Appendix B.

Attrition and Cases Available for Analysis

Table A.1 shows the effect of attrition, including the graduation of sixth graders, on the number of cases available for analyses that require both television and aggression data in two waves. (Two-wave models are at the heart

TABLE A.1
Number of Boys for Whom Aggression and Television Exposure Data Are Available in All Wave Pairs Beginning with Wave I (Initial Sample Wave I, N = 805[a])

WAVE PAIRS	N
I and II	473
I and III	456
I and IV	438
I and V	296
I and VI	175

[a]Includes sixth graders, who are unavailable for any panel analysis of elementary school children.

of our analysis plan, as discussed in Chapter 5.) The table shows all five pairs having Wave I data, and it is clear that the longer the time span, the smaller the number of cases available for analysis. As will be shown later, sample size also diminishes as the number of waves required for analysis increases. At the limiting end is the sample in which complete data, that is, television and aggression data, are available in all six waves. Here the sample size is 142.[26] As described in Chapter 2, the graduation of sixth graders accounts for the largest loss of respondents.

Attrition and Sample Composition

Sample composition is affected by attrition to the degree that respondents who leave the sample differ from those who stay. When differences are large, they could affect findings dealing with television's impact, because this may vary among boys with different characteristics. In this section, we examine the size and direction of differences between those who left the sample and those who stayed.

The present analysis focuses on the possible impact on sample composition of the two other causes of attrition—mobility and temporary absenteeism.

[26]This figure includes respondents with "less valid" television exposure data in one or more waves. (See Chapter 4 on the validity of the exposure measure.) Only 58 respondents have aggression and valid television data in all six waves.

Both analyses examine three characteristics available for practically all respondents: city of residence, race, and average scholastic grade (during the school year ending at the time of Wave I). In addition, some characteristics of the child's family, derived from interviews with mothers, are also examined. (As the loss of sixth graders after graduation was a design feature that simply determined that the sample consisted of boys aged 7–12, the impact on sample composition of this kind of "attrition" will not be investigated here.)

Mobility

We begin by comparing respondents in the initial sample (Wave I) with those who left the study because of mobility and those who stayed in the study throughout subsequent waves. Since we are primarily interested in over-time analysis of respondents, we focus on those who could have been present in more than one wave, that is, all second to fifth graders in the initial sample in Wave I.

Data will be presented separately for respondents in several grades: for second and third graders combined, for fourth graders, and for fifth graders (as of Wave I). This separation enables us to learn about the effects of attrition over increasingly longer periods of time, because a respondent's total possible stay in the study depended on his grade at the start. Second and third graders in Wave I could be in the study for its total duration of 3 years. Fourth graders graduated after Wave V and therefore could not be included in Wave VI. Fifth graders graduated after Wave IV and therefore could not be included in Waves V or VI.

Among second and third graders, we can compare respondents who stayed in the study for 3 years with those who dropped out permanently after 1 year or less, after 2 years, and after 3 years, respectively. Among fourth graders, we can compare those who stayed in the study for 2 years with those who dropped out after 1 year or less and after 2 years, respectively. Among fifth graders we can compare only two groups: those who stayed for a year and those who stayed for less than a year. In addition, we will compare the initial sample with those respondents who stayed for the longest duration possible. Such a comparison will provide information about the total impact of attrition due to mobility.

Tables A.2–A.7 present the relevant data. The tables are arranged as follows: The first columns (e.g., (1), (2), and (3) in Table A.2) show the comparison of samples of respondents who left permanently, starting with those who left earliest. Respondents who left at any time during the first year—that is, by Wave II, III, or IV—are combined, because there are too few cases in some of these groups to analyze separately. (About three-quarters of those who left during the first year left by Wave II.) The next column (e.g., (4) in Table A.2) shows those respondents who were part of the initial sample and stayed in all

TABLE A.2

Effect of Attrition through Mobility on Sample Composition for Second and Third Graders (Characteristics of Respondents Who Left the Study at Different Points in Time, Those Who Stayed in the Sample, and Those Who Were in the Initial Sample)

	RESPONDENTS WHO LEFT STUDY			RESPONDENTS WHO STAYED IN STUDY AS LONG AS POSSIBLE (WAVES I–VI) (%)[a]	INITIAL SAMPLE (%)[b]
	BY WAVE IV (%)	BY WAVE V (%)	BY WAVE VI (%)		
CHILD CHARACTERISTICS	(1)	(2)	(3)	(4)	(5)
City of residence					
Fort Worth	36	54	50	48	48
Minneapolis	64	46	50	52	52
Race					
Black	11	22	25	26	22
White	87	78	75	71	76
Other	2			3	2
Average scholastic grade[c]					
Low	48	39	13	20	27
Medium	23	28	33	36	33
High	30	33	54	45	40
N	(61)	(50)	(32)	(193)	(354)

[a]Definition of group: Aggression data available in all waves.
[b]Definition of group: Aggression data available in Wave I.
[c]Not available for 5–10% of the respondents.

TABLE A.3

Effect of Attrition through Mobility on Sample Composition for Fourth Graders (Characteristics of Respondents Who Left the Study at Different Points in Time, Those Who Stayed in the Sample, and Those Who Were in the Initial Sample)

	RESPONDENTS WHO LEFT STUDY		RESPONDENTS WHO STAYED IN STUDY AS LONG AS POSSIBLE	
CHILD CHARACTERISTICS	BY WAVE IV (%) (1)	BY WAVE V (%) (2)	(WAVES I–V) (%)[a] (3)	INITIAL SAMPLE (%)[b] (4)
City of Residence				
Fort Worth	45	68	58	58
Minneapolis	55	32	42	42
Race				
Black			2	1
White	91	88	93	92
Other	9	12	5	7
Average scholastic grade[c]				
Low	36	52	26	33
Medium	43	24	28	29
High	21	24	46	38
N	(22)	(25)	(96)	(146)

[a]Aggression data available in Waves I–V.
[b]Aggression data available in Wave I.
[c]Not available for 5–10% of the respondents.

TABLE A.4

Effect of Attrition through Mobility on Sample Composition for Fifth Graders (Characteristics of Respondents Who Left the Study at Different Points in Time, Those Who Stayed in the Sample, and Those Who Were in the Initial Sample)

CHILD CHARACTERISTICS	RESPONDENTS WHO LEFT STUDY BY WAVE IV (%) (1)	RESPONDENTS WHO STAYED IN STUDY AS LONG AS POSSIBLE (WAVES I–IV) (%)[a] (2)	INITIAL SAMPLE (%)[b] (3)
City of residence			
Fort Worth	53	42	45
Minneapolis	47	58	55
Race			
Black	39	42	41
White	61	57	58
Other		2	1
Average scholastic grade[c]			
Low	56	49	50
Medium	30	21	22
High	15	31	28
N	(36)	(134)	(175)

[a]Aggression data available in Waves I–IV.
[b]Aggression data available in Wave I.
[c]Not available for 5–10% of the respondents.

possible waves. The final column (e.g., (5) in Table A.2) shows all respondents included in the initial sample.[27]

Discussion of the tables begins with the three characteristics available for all children (shown in Tables A.2, A.3, and A.4). Then we discuss family data derived from interviews with mothers, available for only some of the respondents (Tables A.5, A.6, and A.7).

CHILD CHARACTERISTICS

Table A.2 reports city, race, and average scholastic grade[28] for second and third graders. Looking first at Column (4), showing the 193 children who

[27]Being part of the sample is defined as having aggression data. Leaving the sample permanently is defined as the absence of aggression data in a particular wave and all following waves. A very small number of respondents who left the sample and returned at a later point are excluded from the analyses. As a result, the sum of respondents who left permanently and those who stayed is a few less than the number of respondents who were part of the initial sample.

[28]Because one city had a 3-point scale, the other a 5-point scale, grades for different courses were averaged sextiles computed for each city separately. Then the results from cities were combined into one 6-point variable.

TABLE A.5

Effect of Attrition through Mobility on Sample Composition for Second and Third Graders (Comparisons of Family Data of Respondents Who Left the Study at Different Points in Time, Those Who Stayed in the Sample, and Those Who Were in the Initial Sample)

FAMILY DATA	RESPONDENTS WHO LEFT STUDY			RESPONDENTS WHO STAYED IN STUDY AS LONG AS POSSIBLE (WAVES I–VI) (%)[a]	INITIAL SAMPLE (%)[b]
	BY WAVE IV (%)	BY WAVE V (%)	BY WAVE VI (%)		
	(1)	(2)	(3)	(4)	(5)
Family income					
Low third (under $8000)	NA	38	20	19	30
Middle third ($8000–$11,999)		52	50	54	47
Top third ($12,000 and up)		10	30	27	24
Family structure					
Child lives with natural father and mother		59	70	84	73
Child does not live with natural father and mother		41	30	16	27
Previous residential mobility					
Child has lived in 1–3 homes		45	55	77	67
Child has lived in 4 or more homes		55	45	23	33
Total N	(61)	(50)	(32)	(193)	(354)
Family data available N	(7)	(29)	(20)	(105)	(165)

[a]Definition of group: Aggression data available in all waves.
[b]Definition of group: Aggression data available in Wave I.

TABLE A.6

Effect of Attrition through Mobility on Sample Composition for Fourth Graders (Family Data of Respondents Who Left the Study at Different Points in Time, Those Who Stayed in the Sample, and Those Who Were in the Initial Sample)

	RESPONDENTS WHO LEFT STUDY		RESPONDENTS WHO STAYED IN STUDY AS LONG AS POSSIBLE	
FAMILY DATA	BY WAVE IV (%) (1)	BY WAVE V (%) (2)	(WAVES I–V) (%)[a] (3)	INITIAL SAMPLE (%)[b] (4)
Family income				
Low third (under $8000)	NA	31	39	38
Middle third ($8000–$11,999)		62	43	47
Top third ($12,000 and up)		8	18	16
Family structure				
Child lives with natural father and mother		69	90	70
Child does not live with natural father and mother		31	10	30
Previous residential mobility				
Child has lived in 1–3 homes		50	61	59
Child has lived in 4 or more homes		50	39	41
Total *N*	(22)	(25)	(96)	(146)
Family data available *N*	(1)	(13)	(56)	(71)

[a] Aggression data available in Waves I–V.
[b] Aggression data available in Wave I.

TABLE A.7

Effect of Attrition through Mobility on Sample Composition for Fifth Graders (Family Data of Respondents Who Left the Study at Different Points in Time, Those Who Stayed in the Sample, and Those Who Were in the Initial Sample)

FAMILY DATA	RESPONDENTS WHO LEFT STUDY BY WAVE IV (%) (1)	RESPONDENTS WHO STAYED IN STUDY AS LONG AS POSSIBLE (WAVES I–IV) (%)[a] (2)	INITIAL SAMPLE (%)[b] (3)
Family income:			
Low third (under $8000)	NA	33	34
Middle third ($8000–$11,999)		36	35
Top third ($12,000 and up)		32	30
Family structure			
Child lives with natural father and mother		81	70
Child does not live with natural father and mother		19	30
Previous residential mobility			
Child has lived in 1–3 homes		58	56
Child has lived in 4 or more homes		42	44
N	(36)	(134)	(175)
Family data available *N*	(3)	(76)	(79)

[a] Aggression data available in Waves I–IV.
[b] Aggression data available in Wave I.

remained in the sample throughout the study, and comparing them with the initial sample of 354 in Column (5), we see that the total impact of attrition through mobility on these three sample characteristics was slight, but larger on scholastic grade than either of the others.

Tables A.3 and A.4 show the same breakdowns among fourth and fifth graders. Because there is less mobility among fourth and fifth graders, differences between those who left the sample and those who stayed have even less effect on sample composition. (Some of the differences between the groups compared in these tables are difficult to interpret because they are based on very small numbers of boys.)

In brief, the data shown in Tables A.2–A.4 suggest that attrition through mobility does have an effect on sample composition with respect to one of the child's characteristics: scholastic grade. The effect of attrition on racial composition is minimal, and there is no effect on city of residence. In addition, there is some indication that those who left the study early were more likely to be different from those who stayed in the study than those who left late.

FAMILY DATA

Investigating family data, derived from interviews with mothers, we selected three characteristics that describe the families in important respects. The first is family income, an indicator of socioeconomic status. Second is a measure of family structure—whether both natural parents are present in the household. (If they are not, it is the natural father who is not present in nearly all of the cases.) Finally, we examined a measure of past residential mobility, showing in how many homes the child has lived.

Tables A.5, A.6, and A.7 show the effects of mobility on these three characteristics. Note the two different entries for the number of cases in these tables. The second to last row, "Total *N*," refers to the total number of boys in each of the defined groups; these numbers are identical to those shown in Table A.2. The last row of the tables, "Family data available *N*," reports the number of boys in each group for whom family data are available. If the number of cases with family data is less than 10, data are not reported (indicated by "NA," not available).

Table A.5 presents data for second and third graders. It is apparent that attrition has an impact on the sample composition with respect to all three characteristics. Those who left the sample—and especially those who left early—were more likely to come from lower-income families, were less likely to live with both their natural parents, and had lived in more homes before they became part of (and left) this study.

Again, the impact of attrition is less among fourth and fifth graders than among younger respondents, because the proportion of those who dropped out

TABLE A.8

Effect of Attrition through Temporary Absenteeism on Sample Composition (Characteristics of Respondents Who Were Present and Those Who Were Temporarily Absent

CHILD CHARACTERISTICS	INITIAL SAMPLE WAVE I (%)[a] (1)	TEMPORARILY ABSENT IN WAVE I (%)[b] (2)	SECOND–FIFTH GRADERS: INITIAL SAMPLE WAVE I (%)[a] (3)	SECOND–FIFTH GRADERS: TEMPORARILY ABSENT: IN WAVE II (%)[c] (4)	SECOND–FIFTH GRADERS: TEMPORARILY ABSENT: IN WAVE III (%)[c] (5)	SECOND–FIFTH GRADERS: TEMPORARILY ABSENT: IN WAVE IV (%)[c] (6)
City of residence						
Fort Worth	51	56	49	57	33	61
Minneapolis	49	44	51	43	67	39
Race						
Black	21	20	23	29	33	26
White	77	80	75	69	67	72
Other	3		3	2		2
Average scholastic grade[d]						
Low	35	49	34	41	53	46
Medium	31	26	29	41	24	28
High	35	25	37	19	24	26
N	(805)	(71)	(675)	(42)	(36)	(46)

[a]Television and/or aggression data available.
[b]Aggression data only available. Children who are not part of any other wave are excluded.
[c]Aggression data only available.
[d]Not available for 5–10% of the respondents.

TABLE A.9

Effect of Attrition through Temporary Absenteeism on Sample Composition (Family Data of Respondents Who Were Present and Those Who Were Temporarily Absent)

FAMILY DATA	PRESENT IN WAVE I (%)[a] (1)	TEMPORARILY ABSENT IN WAVE I (%)[b] (2)	SECOND–FIFTH GRADERS: INITIAL SAMPLE WAVE I (%)[a] (3)	SECOND–FIFTH GRADERS: TEMPORARILY ABSENT: IN WAVE II (%)[b] (4)	IN WAVE III (%)[b] (5)	IN WAVE IV (%)[b] (6)
Family income						
Low third (under $8000)	31	21	30	54		35
Middle third ($8000–11,999)	46	53	47	31	NA	26
Top third (12,000 and up)	23	26	24	15		39
Family structure						
Child lives with natural father and mother	70	82	73	60		65
Child does not live with natural father and mother	30	18	27	40		35
Previous residential mobility						
Child has lived in 1–3 homes	59	68	63	69		61
Child has lived in 4 or more homes	41	32	37	31		39
Total *N*	(805)	(71)	(675)	(42)	(36)	(46)
Family data available *N*	(377)	(19)	(315)	(13)	(8)	(23)

[a]Television and/or aggression data available.
[b]Aggression data only available.

of the sample is much smaller (Tables A.6 and A.7). Thus, there is very little impact with respect to family income and previous mobility. However, even among fourth and fifth graders, attrition has a strong effect with respect to family structure, because respondents who left the study were less likely to live with both natural parents.

Before continuing, it is worth reflecting on one implication of these findings about attrition. Children who do not live with both their natural parents have higher mobility rates. The majority of such children live with their mother, not their father, and other studies have shown that father absence is related to aggression. However, as we shall show in Chapter 7, the effect of television on aggression does not differ in subgroups defined in terms of whether the father is present or not. Consequently, although the variance of aggression is reduced by the mobility of children from single-parent families, the measure of television's impact on aggression remains unbiased by this loss.

Temporary Absenteeism

The second cause of attrition we will examine is temporary absenteeism. As in the examination of permanent dropouts, we analyze groups of respondents who were in the initial Wave I sample and investigate sample composition with respect to child characteristics and family data.

As with the permanent dropouts, scholastic grade is the only child characteristic that clearly distinguishes respondents who stayed in the sample from temporary absentees, with absentees having lower grades (Table A.8).

With respect to family characteristics, the principal finding is that absentee respondents were less likely to live with both natural parents than were those in the total sample (Table A.9).

CHAPTER 3

AGGRESSION MEASURE

We decided that the most appropriate definition of aggression for studying the effects of televised violence was: physical or verbal acts intended or known in advance to cause injury to others. Intentional harm to others was the essential consideration, because this was and remains the key element in the social concern about violence. Other related constructs that do not involve intentional harm, for example, outbursts of rage that are merely expressive and not directed at others, or victimless criminal acts such as use of prohibited drugs, were thus excluded by definition.

Because the study sample included children between 7 and 12 years of age, we did not focus on serious, violent, or criminal aggression. Although these issues are of the utmost concern to the society, such acts are quite rare among preteen children. Among teenage boys, where delinquent acts are less rare, we did obtain measures of serious aggression (see Chapter 10).

In addition, we chose to focus on aggressive *behavior*, and not such related constructs as hostility, aggressive attitudes, attitudes about aggression, or aggressive self-image, all of which have been used in other studies (Comstock & Rubinstein, 1972; Surgeon General's Scientific Advisory Committee on Television and Social Behavior, 1972). In a very important sense, aggressive behavior is the single most important outcome of all the concepts above, and therefore the one most germane to social concern about television's effects.

Turning from conceptual issues to operational ones, we attempted to measure aggressive behavior in the context of daily life. Surrogate measures of aggression—such as hitting dolls, punching padded boards, or pressing buttons and turning dials that supposedly inflict noxious stimuli—were rejected as inadequate, primarily because the degree to which they accurately measure real antisocial aggression is open to question. For example, some of these measures do not involve intention to hurt, whereas others do not involve the possibility of punishment, both being important aspects of real-life aggression (Tedeschi *et al.*, 1974:541).

The aggression measure we used—developed by two psychologists, Walder, and Eron—is based on ratings given by children in the school classroom (Eron, Walder, & Lefkowitz, 1971; Walder *et al.*, 1961).[1] We believe it to be the most valid and reliable measure of all those available to us, even though it has some shortcomings. Because of the setting in which it is obtained, we cannot be certain of the extent to which it is a good indicator of antisocial aggression in other circumstances. Eron, Walder, and Lefkowitz (1971:42–45) present evidence that the peer-rating measure is indeed related to aggression in the home and to aggression occurring in experimental situations outside the classroom, and, as we discuss in the section on validity, we too have found evidence that it correlates with aggression outside the school, such as the mother's rating of her son's general aggressive behavior. However, despite this evidence, we do not know the exact degree of overlap, and it would therefore not be appropriate to generalize findings about this type of aggression to other types without further investigation.

Further, questions have been raised about the long-term social consequences of this sort of antisocial behavior. We do have some data indicating that scores on this aggression measure predict further antisocial behavior and not simply assertiveness. There are weak to moderate correlations between aggression as measured in childhood and aggression measured up to 30 years later (Block, 1971; Bloom, 1964; Kagan & Moss, 1962; Lefkowitz, Eron, Walder, & Huesmann, 1977; Robins, 1966). Research by Lefkowitz and his colleagues (Lefkowitz *et al.*, 1972) provides evidence that boys rated as highly aggressive were more likely to have been arrested 10 years later than the least aggressive boys, but the incidence of arrest in both groups was quite low and the difference between groups was not statistically significant. Peer ratings were weakly related to a measure of "potential for delinquent behavior" obtained 10 years later. Finally, in our data we find modest positive correlations between this aggression measure and a measure of serious criminal aggression obtained when the same children had become teenagers.[2]

---

[1]This kind of measure was also used in the longitudinal study done for the Surgeon General's report on television and aggression (Lefkowitz *et al.*, 1972).

[2]These data are based on samples of elementary school boys who took part in the teenage study. In two instances ($N = 36$ and $N = 60$, respectively) elementary school and teenage data were obtained from the same boys within a month. Correlations between the elementary school measure of mild aggression and the teenage measure of serious aggression that we call

These questions of generalizability deservê additional study. Still, irrespective of what it portends for future behavior, the kind of aggression measured here is a problem at the time it occurs and is worth studying on those grounds alone. Furthermore, even if our measure refers largely to school behavior, that, too is an important social problem whose study is worthwhile.

MEASURING AGGRESSION

Exploratory Work

We experimented with two ways of measuring aggression before deciding on the one ultimately used. One was to ask children directly about their aggressive behavior. Compared with peer ratings obtained for the same children, this method seemed to produce considerable underreporting.

The second method was to ask mothers to rate the aggressive behavior of their children. Again, these ratings did not agree well with ratings obtained from peers. There was evidence that mothers tended to underreport aggressive behavior and that using mothers as reporters might produce a biased sample, as mothers of boys who were rated as highly aggressive by classmates and teachers were less likely to cooperate. For these reasons, mother interviews, in addition to self-reports, were ruled out as a primary source of information about aggressive behavior.[3]

The classroom rating procedure developed by Eron and Walder seemed to work well. This technique had several important advantages: It could be used with relatively young children (those approximately 8 years old); information from large numbers of children could be obtained efficiently; and, most important, extensive methodological work by Eron, Walder and their colleagues demonstrated that the method yields highly reliable information that

---

"delinquency aggression" were .32 and .33, respectively (both were significant). Larger numbers of boys in the elementary school sample became part of the teenage sample at a later point. Most correlations between the two aggression measures, taken up to 3 years apart, were significantly positive (usually between .10 and .20). For additional details see Chapters 9 and 10.

[3]Direct observation, another possible research method, did not appear to be a workable approach in this study. Aside from the logistical problems associated with observing hundreds of children over periods of time sufficient to obtain stable ratings of aggression, we were dissuaded from this approach by several considerations. First, observations could not have been truly unobtrusive and would probably have affected the behavior we wanted to measure, especially the more serious forms of aggression. Then, reliable coding of the observed acts—distinguishing playful and aggressive punching, for example—appeared extremely difficult, especially since observations would have to be from a distance and since videotape technology was not well developed at the time of the study.

validly measures the aggressiveness of school children. Our own pretests of the method confirmed all of these advantages.

As adapted to the purposes of this study, the method involved obtaining information about each child's behavior from all children in a school classroom. Its basic element was a questionnaire containing "tell us who" questions that asked children to identify which members of the class fit descriptions of behavior or other characteristics—for example, "Who tries to hurt others by pushing or shoving?" The names or nicknames of all members of the class, which were obtained from the teacher, were listed for each question, and children drew lines through as many names as applied. Pretests indicated that drawing lines through names provided more accurate information about the intended nominees of young respondents than other methods, such as circling a name or making a check or cross next to it. Inclusion of a response category "no boys" and "no girls" enabled us to be certain that no question was omitted.

The names of the boys and girls were listed separately in alphabetical order by first name for every question. This meant that children's names were placed in the same position on the list for all questions. Eron and Walder had indicated that the position of names did not affect results.[4] Had we changed the name order after each question, the children would probably have become confused. This appeared to be a possible source of more error than order bias.

Administrative Procedures

Because of the potential difficulties of trying to obtain reliable information from young children, we instituted several procedures based on pretesting and on Walder and Eron's experience. In general, we followed their procedures for administration but deviated where we thought it would improve data collection.

The youngest children included in our study were at the end of their second year of elementary school—that is, 8 years old on average. Although Eron and Walder had obtained satisfactory data from third graders, we discovered in pretests that young children, in first grade or beginning second grade, could not cope adequately with this method. Therefore, we devised special administrative procedures to ensure valid data from the youngest children.

The questionnaire was administered to a designated class by a team of trained people: an interviewer and two or more monitors who were on hand to assist. Many of the interviewers and monitors were teachers or student teachers. They

---

[4]For an analysis of the effect of name order on aggression score in the present study, see "Boys' Aggression Measure: Possible Sources of Error," available on request (Documentation 3).

were trained by members of our staff as well as by professional interviewer supervisors, who also supervised the actual data collection.

To ensure that uniform procedures were used across all classrooms and across all waves, interviewers were given prepared guides with written scripts that carefully and clearly informed the children how to record their answers.[5]

To aid children who were not good readers, all questions were read aloud twice to the class. Each question was printed on a different colored sheet so that interviewers would be aware of which questions were being answered by the children at a particular time (see Figure 3.1). In addition, to help ensure that children would associate printed names with the right question, each child in the lower grades was asked to raise his or her hand as his or her name was read aloud before administration began.

The presence of an interviewer and two or more monitors during classroom administration allowed the team to pay attention to any individuals who were having difficulties with the questionnaire. It also permitted continual checking to make sure children understood the procedures. If any members of the team noticed that a child did not answer a question, he or she would be able to call this to the child's attention and try to get the child to answer. Likewise, if a team member noticed a child drawing lines through the names of all the children in the class, he or she would check to make sure the child genuinely believed that was the correct answer. Questionnaire administrators attempted to ensure that there was order in the classroom during the procedure, and also tried to ensure that each child gave his or her own independent answer.

During these data-gathering sessions, teachers were almost always out of their classroom because we felt the children would answer more truthfully without the teacher's presence. However, in a few cases teachers were present to help with classes that otherwise might have been unruly. With few exceptions, the children were cooperative and answered questions carefully.

Immediately after the questionnaires had been completed and collected, they were carefully reviewed by the interviewing team in a separate classroom. If omissions or inaccuracies were found, interviewers went back to the classroom to speak to the children responsible and corrected the questionnaire accordingly.

Finally, all data collection waves took place at least 6 weeks after the beginning of the school year. (In fact, most took place close to the end of the school year.) In this way we ensured that the children had had enough time to get to know their classmates and give valid and reliable reports based on their personal knowledge.

---

[5]These were called "Classroom Administrator's Guide" and "Monitor's Guide." Copies are available on request.

13. *Who tries to hurt others by pushing or shoving?*

No boys	No girls
Andy	Brenda
Bart	Sherrie
Robert	Cathy
Clanton	Lynley
Dean	Linda
Tim	Amy
David	Lori
Mike	Beverly
Vernon	Angela
Terry	Larie
Moody	Carrie
Miles	Sharon
John	Michelle
Kent	Cristy

FIGURE 3.1. *Example of aggression question (reduced from 8½ × 11 page).*

Aggression Items

In our initial pretests, we used all the aggression items Eron and Walder retained in their final index after systematically examining and testing over 200 items. The following were the items they used:

1. Who does not obey the teacher?
2. Who often says, "Give me that?" (asked with emphasis)
3. Who gives dirty looks or sticks out their tongue at other children?
4. Who makes up stories and lies to get other children into trouble?
5. Who does things that bother others?
6. Who starts a fight over nothing?
7. Who pushes or shoves children?
8. Who is always getting into trouble?
9. Who says mean things?
10. Who takes other children's things without asking?

In order to keep the total interview time to a manageable length (under 45 min), it was necessary to reduce the number of aggression items in the questionnaire. First, children, especially the younger ones, easily become restless and fatigued. In addition, the school administration did not want too much time taken up by activities related to our study. Further, in addition to collecting data about aggression, we had to ask questions about television exposure, use of other media, friendship patterns, and prosocial behavior. We also recognized the importance of administering the interview carefully, which required covering the material slowly.

A final consideration that limited the number of different types of aggression items included was a decision to measure behavior with and without reference to a specific time period. Thus, for each behavior there were two questions, one asking, for example, "Who pushes or shoves . . . ?" and the other "Who happened to push and shove yesterday?—that is, the day before the interview. These questions are discussed in more detail below.

As it turned out, reducing the number of items resulted in no real loss of information. Confirming Eron and Walder's findings, our pretests showed that the 10 aggression items were highly intercorrelated, which indicated that a subset of items would probably work as well as the whole set. We decided to include those items that asked about the more serious, seemingly more important forms of aggression, and excluded 5 items deemed less important.[6]

The types of aggression asked about initially were physical aggression (such as hitting and punching, pushing and shoving) and verbal aggression (such as saying mean things and lying). In one of the cities, school administrators were wary of asking sociometric questions about behavior, and we therefore avoided asking questions about more serious behavior (e.g., stealing). However, after the first two waves they had acquired confidence that the children were not being adversely affected by the procedure, and we were able to include questions about more serious aggressive behaviors, such as stealing and damaging property, beginning with Wave III.

In contrast to Eron and Walder, we included the concept of intention to hurt or injure in each item in an attempt to have it conform to our definition of violence. Although intention was thus built into each question, and presumably into the aggression measure itself, we cannot be certain that children effectively distinguished between intentional and accidental acts.[7] We did not attempt to

---

[6]The following items were excluded: Who does not obey the teacher? Who often says, "Give me that?" Who gives dirty looks or sticks out their tongue at other children? Who does things that bother others? Who is always getting into trouble?

[7]Eron and Walder felt that their measure fit a definition of "an act which injures another object," and not one involving intent to injure. They decided this on the basis of the fact that items excluding intention clustered with those presumably including it. However, they do not appear to have included items clearly delimiting intention, and this may have confounded their results. Furthermore, if items including intention cluster with those that do not, it may be because children cannot distinguish between the two, not because the two types of acts are truly related.

distinguish justified from unjustified aggression or provoked from unprovoked aggression, because we believed that this would introduce too much subjectivity into children's ratings.

The following six aggression items were included in the study:

1. Who tries to hurt others by saying mean things to them?
2. Who makes up stories or lies to get someone else into trouble?
3. Who tries to hurt others by pushing or shoving?
4. Who hits or punches other people to hurt them?[8]
5. Who takes things that do not belong to them?
6. Who purposely breaks other people's things or property?

The first four items were included in all six waves and became the basis for the major aggression index used in the study. The fifth and sixth items were used starting with Wave III, when other items were dropped to make room for them. All six items are phrased in terms of general behavior, with no time reference indicated.

Eron and Walder's work had left ambiguous the extent to which the aggression measure included elements of a general reputation for aggression, as opposed to measuring recent aggressive behavior. In order to be able to relate television viewing at an earlier time to aggression at a later time, however, we needed a measure of aggressive behavior during a specific, recent period. To make certain that we had such a measure, we decided to include additional parallel questions about behavior "yesterday" (i.e., the day before the interview). This would permit an examination of the relationship between the "yesterday" items and the more general items and would yield a time-specific measure in the event that the general measure proved to be reputational. The four time-specific items, which were asked immediately following the general aggression items, were as follows:

7. Who tried to hurt others by saying mean things to them yesterday?
8. Who happened to make up stories or lies to get someone else into trouble yesterday?
9. Who happened to try to hurt others by pushing or shoving yesterday?
10. Who tried to hurt someone by hitting or punching them yesterday?

Aggression Score

A standardized score for each aggression question was obtained for each boy by summing the nominations he received on it and dividing that total by the

[8]This item was somewhat different from the one used by Eron and Walder, which asked, "Who starts a fight over nothing?" The latter item might be interpreted as asking about who loses his temper easily, whereas ours asks more specifically about intended physical aggression.

number of children in the class who could possibly have nominated him (self-nominations were excluded). Thus a score for each question is a percentage: those who nominated of those who could have nominated.

The basis for the scoring procedure is the assumption that the higher the score, the more aggressive the child. This in turn is derived from the assumption that the more aggressive the child, the greater the number of children who will be aware of this through direct encounter with the aggression, through observing it done to others, or through reports by others.

There are at least two separate aspects of aggression that the method might measure without distinguishing between them. One is frequency; the other is intensity. The procedure cannot distinguish children who commit a great number of aggressive acts from those performing fewer but more serious ones. Either of these two aspects of aggressiveness could lead to more children noticing the behavior or deciding it qualifies as aggression. Nevertheless, although the precise referent of the measure is not clear, the result appears to be a valid measure of aggression, as indicated in the section on validity below.

Standardizing scores by the size of the class permits comparisons of scores for individuals over time as well as between individuals at a particular point in time. We will present evidence to indicate that overall the measure is reliable and valid and therefore class differences are probably not large, although we do not know the extent to which different classes perceived and therefore scored children's aggression differently.[9]

Table 3.1 shows the means of all aggression items in all waves for boys for whom scores were available,[10] arranged from highest to lowest. Note that whereas the possible score for each item can range from 0 to 100%, the means in all waves indicate that the great majority of boys scored at the low end of the scale.

Table 3.1 indicates that, in general, mean scores for particular items are similar across different waves, which is some evidence for the reliability of the measure. "Pushing," "saying mean things," and "hitting" have higher means than the other general items, suggesting that they are more common behaviors than the others. "Making up stories" and "taking things" are somewhat less common, and "breaking things" is least common.

Since a boy does not necessarily engage every day in behavior that is generally characteristic of him, we expected to find, and did find, that scores for the "yesterday" items (at the bottom of Table 3.1) are considerably lower than

[9]We also have evidence that certain variable aspects of the classes, such as their size and sex composition, do not seem seriously to impair reliability or validity. (See Documentation 3, "Boys' Aggression Measure: Possible Sources of Error," available on request.)

[10]Some boys did not receive aggression scores, either because they had permanently left the class between the time the class list was compiled and the time we interviewed, or because they entered the class after lists had been compiled.

TABLE 3.1
Means of Aggression Items

ITEM	WAVE I	II	III	IV	V	VI
Pushes and shoves	26.0	25.2	25.2	27.0	25.3	24.2
Says mean things	22.0	22.8	25.2	25.2	25.3	23.5
Hits or punches	22.9	21.6	24.2	24.2	24.1	22.7
Makes up stories or lies	19.3	19.2	17.5	18.8	17.5	16.6
Takes things			16.5	18.7	19.0	19.2
Breaks things			11.2	13.6	12.0	12.4
N	(805)	(655)	(685)	(713)	(490)	(289)
Pushed and shoved yesterday	13.4	13.9	9.8			
Said mean things yesterday	13.7	14.6	12.7			
Hit or punched yesterday	10.9	11.2	8.5			
Made up stories or lies yesterday	8.5	9.7	6.6			
N	(805)	(634)	(635)			

scores for the general items. This was true in all waves including such items, and it was true of data collected from teachers as well.

CONSTRUCTION OF THE AGGRESSION INDEX

In order to develop indices of aggression, the first question we addressed was which items were part of such a construct. Initially we wished to see not only which aggression items were related, but also whether or not prosocial items would be included.

To answer these questions, we performed exploratory factor analyses on those aggression and prosocial items that were included in all waves. These preliminary factor analyses, based on an iterative principal factors procedure, indicated that two significant factors existed in the data in each wave. After varimax rotation of the two-factor solutions we concluded that the factors represent aggressive and prosocial tendencies, respectively. Table 3.2 shows the factor loadings produced by the rotated two-factor solutions for the four general aggression items and the three prosocial items in all waves. Note the consistency in the results. In all waves, all the aggression items have loadings of .8 and .9, whereas the prosocial items have loadings of −.1 and −.2. The differentiation of aggression and prosocial behavior into two factors was not an

TABLE 3.2

Varimax Rotated Factor Loadings of Aggression and Prosocial Items[a]

	WAVE											
	I		II		III		IV		V		VI	
ITEM FACTOR:	1	2	1	2	1	2	1	2	1	2	1	2
Says mean things	.88	−.14	.91	−.18	.86	−.28	.89	.23	.89	−.25	.88	−.25
Pushes and shoves	.94	−.16	.94	−.17	.92	−.23	.94	−.18	.93	−.20	.92	−.24
Makes up stories or lies	.84	−.20	.86	−.16	.82	−.27	.87	−.21	.76	−.32	.84	−.28
Hits or punches	.90	−.13	.90	−.18	.90	−.22	.93	−.16	.90	−.14	.90	−.16
Says nice things	−.15	.76	−.12	.83	−.23	.81	−.20	.86	−.28	.76	−.25	.85
Helps others	−.14	.85	−.20	.83	−.25	.82	−.20	.86	−.15	.91	−.26	.85
Kind to you					−.22	.81	−.16	.87			−.15	.84
N	(805)		(655)		(685)		(713)		(490)		(289)	

[a]Varimax rotation of all factors with eigenvalues greater than or equal to 1.0. The same basic structure appeared when an oblique rotation was used.

artifact of question location, because these items were systematically alternated within the questionnaire.

The fact that the aggression items and the prosocial items did not load together indicated that our measure did not include this nonaggressive component. Had the two types of items loaded together highly, it would have meant that we did not have a pure measure of aggression, but something more general, such as a measure of "good boy–bad boy."

We next factor-analyzed antisocial behavior items only. Whereas the previous analyses used aggression items asked in all six waves, this analysis included additional items used in some of the waves only. Factor loadings presented in Table 3.3 indicate that there was no differentiation among types of aggression. Physical and verbal aggression, as well as aggression against property (stealing and damaging property), are all part of one factor. However, the "yesterday" items all had slightly lower loadings than the more general questions.[11]

We next sought to determine whether any differentiation among these types of aggression existed among older boys and younger boys separately. Essentially the same result was found among all age groups. Factor analysis yielded only one type of aggression.[12] This finding agrees with factor analyses reported by Eron and Walder (1971), who used most of the items we included as well as a few we did not.

Table 3.3 also indicates that there is no separate, specifically time-anchored aggression factor based on yesterday items in the waves in which they were included. This result also appeared among all different age groups.

Accordingly, the high correlation between yesterday and general items is consistent with the view that the general items are measuring current aggressive behavior and not merely a reputation for aggression or past behavior. The yesterday items were rather simple direct questions about behavior recent enough not to present recall problems. Therefore, the children were likely to have answered these questions fairly accurately.

---

[11]The yesterday items were dropped from questionnaires in Waves IV, V, and VI when it became apparent that they added nothing to the aggression measure obtained without them. Eliminating items permitted inclusion of additional questions not previously asked. Correlations between yesterday items and exposure to violent television do not differ from those between the general items and television.

[12]We did find differentiation between types of aggression among teenagers, a finding that will be discussed in the chapter reporting the analysis of the adolescent data. The difference between the two groups may be due in part to the difference in methods of measuring aggression (the teenage measure is based on self-report, and attempts to measure frequency and recency of various behaviors). However, it is also possible that aggression is genuinely more differentiated among adolescents. Greater differentiation in social roles and social status occurs as boys get older, and this may encourage and facilitate greater differentiation of all types of behavior, including aggression.

A minor distinction can be noted in Table 3.3 between the item "makes up stories and lies" and the other three indicators of aggression. For all waves this indicator is among those with the lowest loading on the aggression factor. Analyses reported in Appendix C in Chapter 6 show that this indicator is systematically biased over time to a very small degree. For most of the analyses reported here, however, this minor bias is ignored, owing to the fact that its influence on the results obtained is quite small.

The factor analyses indicated that we could combine aggression items in various ways to form a good index. It would have been possible to form an index based on all 10 aggression items, the 6 general aggression items, or the 4 general items excluding stealing and damaging property. Analyses involving correlations between the indices themselves, reliabilities of the different indices, and correlations between the indices and violent television viewing showed all three of these indices to be equally valid,[13], we decided to use the 4-item index for two major reasons.

First, the four general items, unlike other items, were present in all six waves. Therefore, precise comparisons over time, necessary in a panel study such as this, could be made only with the index using those items.[14]

Second, the use of "yesterday" items would have reduced the sample size somewhat, since some children were absent on that day and could not have been scored on "yesterday's" aggression.

The four items used in the aggression index were the following:

1. Who tries to hurt others by saying mean things to them?
2. Who makes up stories or lies to get someone else into trouble?
3. Who tries to hurt others by pushing or shoving?
4. Who hits or punches other people to hurt them?

The index was obtained by adding together the percentage scores on each of the separate items.

As scores on each of the individual items could range from 0 to 100, the composite index could theoretically extend from 0 to 400. Figure 3.2 presents the distribution of scores in all waves, grouped into 20-point intervals. Each of

[13]The major aggression measure, an index based on the four general items, is essentially the same as an index based on these four items plus the comparable four yesterday items. In Waves I, II, and III, the only waves where yesterday questions were asked, the correlation between the two indices is .98.

The basic four-item index is also nearly identical to an index based on the four items plus the stealing and property-damaging items. The correlation between the two indices is .99 in Waves III, IV, V, and VI, the only waves where comparisons could be made.

[14]In those waves available for such analyses, lagged associations between violent television exposure and yesterday items do not differ systematically or significantly from those between television and the aggression measure used in the study.

TABLE 3.3
Factor Loadings of Aggression Items

ITEM	WAVE I	II	III	IV	V	VI
Says mean things	.87	.91	.89	.91	.91	.90
Said mean things yesterday	.85	.89	.85			
Makes up stories or lies	.86	.88	.88	.91	.85	.89
Maded up stories or lies yesterday	.76	.82	.72			
Pushes and shoves	.93	.92	.90	.95	.93	.95
Pushed and shoved yesterday	.86	.91	.84			
Hits or punches	.90	.92	.91	.94	.90	.91
Hit or punched yesterday	.83	.84	.81			
Takes things			.84	.91	.88	.88
Breaks things			.85	.90	.88	.90
N	(805)	(634)	(635)	(713)	(490)	(289)

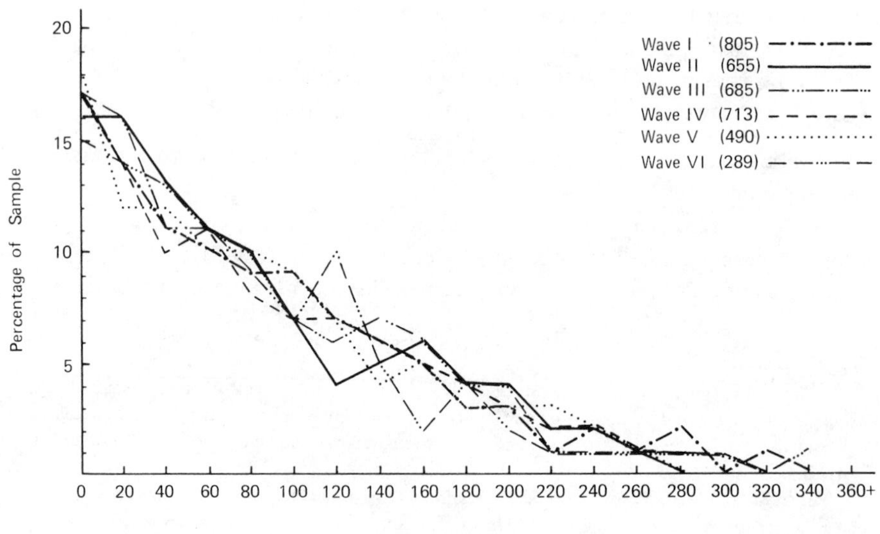

FIGURE 3.2. *Distribution of aggression in all six waves.*

the distributions approaches a J curve, with most boys scoring very low and only a few boys scoring very high. Eron, Walder, and Lefkowitz (1971:38, 175) also found this distribution of aggression and pointed out that as long ago as 1934, Floyd Allport had indicated that deviant behavior is often characterized by such a J curve. The distribution also indicates that there is a good deal of variation; there are boys all along the aggression continuum. Table 3.4 presents the means, standard deviations, and other statistics for the aggression measure in all six waves. Unlike Figure 3.2, these statistics are based on ungrouped data.

The statistics in each of the six waves are quite similar, suggesting that the measure is comparable across waves. They point up what Figure 3.2 shows: Most children score quite low on aggression. The median is always low, and the mean is always a little higher because of the outliers at the top of the score range. The mode is always 0. All this information indicates that aggression is relatively rare, and the more severe it is, the rarer it is.[15]

PROPERTIES OF THE INDEX

Reliability

Having decided on the four-item index as our basic measure of aggression, we undertook an extensive analysis of its internal consistency.[16] Using a reliability estimate based on the internal consistency of the four items (Heise-

---

[15]A comparison of means and medians in the six study waves shows that there is little variation in the amount of aggression reported as the sample grows older. This is confirmed by a longitudinal analysis presented in Documentation 5 ("Correlates of Aggression Among Elementary School Boys"). In that analysis aggression levels were found to be quite stable, but they were slightly lower in the sixth grade than in earlier grades. In general, these findings agree with research by Feshbach (1956) and Tuddenham (1959).

[16]Walder and his colleagues report two different checks on reliability, one involving test–retest reliability and the other involving interjudge agreement on items. In the former method the retest included some aggression items in the same context as the initial test and some in a different item context. The retest was done 2 weeks after the initial test, and there is good reason to suppose that true aggression did not change substantially in that interval. The authors found that correlations for nine different items, each of which was retested in the same and in different contexts, ranged from .70 to .92, with the great majority at least .80. Included among those items were some that were very similar to those we used. The authors concluded, "The range of .70 to .92 shows this method to be robust in the face of a two-week interval and context changes [Eron, Walder, & Lefkowitz, 1971:541]."

The second reliability check done by Walder and his colleagues involved a method that selected items based on their capacity to discriminate among subjects and, at the same time, reduce interjudge disagreement. They found fairly high reliabilities for individual items and exceedingly high reliabilities for clusters of items (Eron, Walder, & Lefkowitz, 1971:506–525).

TABLE 3.4
Aggression Descriptive Statistics for the Six Waves

STATISTIC	WAVE					
	I	II	III	IV	V	VI
Median	73.4	71.8	75.6	76.6	76.5	69.8
Mean	90.2	88.8	92.0	95.1	92.2	87.1
Mode	0	0	0	0	0	0
Standard deviation	75.0	73.0	70.4	77.2	74.9	72.2
Range	0–370	0–376	0–328	0–355	0–383	0–357
Skewness	1.0	1.0	0.9	0.9	1.0	1.2
N	(805)	(655)	(685)	(713)	(490)	(289)

Bohrnstedt, 1970),[17] we estimated reliability of the index to be at least .95 in all six waves. Reliability was also examined by comparing the scores of boys obtained from boy raters with those obtained from girl raters. We found that the two correlated very well: in Wave III .69; in Wave IV .76; in Wave V .73. These correlations are all about as large as the correlations between pairs of items making up the index, which suggests that boy and girl raters agree in their nominations

At least two factors may artificially inflate the reliability of the aggression index. One of these is method variance due to the nomination method of rating aggression. That is, there may be some tendency for raters to cross out the same names in the response to every question, regardless of its content. The second factor that may artificially raise reliability is a halo effect surrounding the ratings. Such an effect could stem from a generalized notion of either aggressive behavior or a more inclusive sort of improper behavior. Nominators who hold such generalized perceptions might nominate the stereotyped children for acts they did not in fact commit.

There is no way to estimate an effect of this sort empirically with the data collected from nominators. However, a related sort of bias was isolated in analyses of the stability of the aggression index over time. In this analysis, we estimated a complex measurement model based on an unmeasured variable approach to maximum-likelihood regression analysis (Jöreskog, 1973). The analysis is reported in detail in Appendix C in Chapter 6. The results suggested

[17]This measure assumes one or more underlying factors to a set of items and computes the reliability coefficient from factor analysis results. If a particular factor analysis yields a factor with high factor loadings and high communalities, the reliability coefficient for those items in the scale will be high. If the items in a factor are more weakly correlated, the reliability will be low.

We also estimated a six-wave measurement error model of aggression (see Appendix C in Chapter 6). Factor loadings from this analysis were used in the formulas and yielded reliability estimates that were very similar to those obtained from the traditional factor analysis results.

that one of the items in the aggression index, the one about lying to get others in trouble, was adding to the stability of the index, and thus to its estimated reliability, for reasons related to some source other than true aggression. Our suspicion is that children come to gain reputations as liars that persist longer than the lying behavior itself, thus leading to a reputational bias in the consistency with which the child is rated by his classmates.

It is reassuring that the extent of this particular bias, though significant when judged in terms of conventional statistical tests, was so small that the corrected reliability estimates of the aggression index were still above .90 in all six waves. Although we cannot believe the index is completely reliable, our analyses indicate that the reliability is very high indeed.

Validity

Evidence about systematic bias in the aggression index raises an issue we considered: the extent to which the index validly measured the real aggression of respondents rather than some related characteristic, such as popularity with students or perhaps undeserved typing as troublemakers. Although certain data have already been presented to suggest that the measure is valid in this sense—such as the differentiation of index items from prosocial behavior items in exploratory factor analyses[18]—this section discusses other bases for considering the measure a valid index of aggressive behavior.

We based our assessments of validity on the work of Eron, Walder, and their colleagues, who argued that the facts that (*a*) boys received higher scores than girls, (*b*) peer ratings correlated well with teacher ratings, and (*c*) the ratings formed a J-shaped distribution all argued for the validity of the index. In addition, they reported that their measure correlated with other variables, such as parental punishment, in meaningful and expected ways. They also found that a very high proportion of parents whose names appeared in newspapers for antisocial behavior had children with relatively high aggression scores, and that children with aggression problems who were seen by child guidance clinics also had relatively high aggression scores (Eron, Walder, & Lefkowitz, 1971, 39–41).

Our own tests support conclusions about the validity of the aggression measure. Thus, for example, the aggression of the children as rated by their teachers is very similar to their aggression as rated by classmates. Table 3.5

[18]It is worth noting that several friendship items, such as "Who are your closest friends in this class?" and "Who do you spend a lot of time with outside of school?" did not load with the aggression items either. This indicates that aggression was not simply a measure of which children were liked or disliked. It also suggests that friendship or the lack of it did not strongly influence the selection of aggressive children.

TABLE 3.5
Correlation[a] between Teacher Aggression Rating[b] and Aggression Score

	WAVE					
	I	II	III	IV	V	VI
	.58	.54	.55	.57	.56	.57
N	(737)	(591)	(624)	(631)	(425)	(231)

[a] Pearson correlations. (Linearity of relationships was tested; no significant deviations from linearity were found.)

[b] Data from a few teachers were not obtained in all waves. In Waves II–VI the missing data were for boys in the sixth grade in one of the cities. In Wave I the missing data did not come from any specific group.

shows the correlations between the two sets of ratings. Teachers were asked the same questions as children (e.g., "Who hits or punches other children to hurt them?"), and were provided with the same class lists so that they could draw lines through the names of those children they wished to nominate. However, as the teacher is a single rater, the score for any child on any item is either 0 (if not nominated) or 1 (if nominated).

The total teacher score is based on the same four items as the peer ratings and therefore ranges from 0 to 4. Despite the difference in scoring, the two measures are quite highly related. Table 3.5 indicates that the correlations are very stable, and average about .55.

Other teacher reports were also used to check on the validity of the aggression measure. In one of the two cities, the school records at the end of the year contained comments about the children by the teachers. The comments were open-ended, that is, the teachers could mention anything they wanted about the child, including ability, schoolwork, and behavior. These comments were coded and analyzed. One category of comments involved active antisocial behavior—the teacher indicated whether the child did such things as fight, steal, quarrel, disrupt, etc. Forty-five children were mentioned for such behavior in the 1969–1970 school year, the year in which Wave I was done. Of these 45 children, 84% scored above the median on the aggression measure in Wave I; over 50% fell within the highest sixth of the aggression distribution.

School records provided additional information on the child's aggressiveness in social worker or child guidance intervention reports and comments by the child's earlier teachers. Thirty children were coded into this category, of whom 93% were above the median on the aggression score and 57% were in the highest sixth of the aggression distribution.

Although the number of children involved in these instances of aggressive behavior is small, the pattern of their aggression scores lends support to the validity of the measure.

Another indication of validity was the moderately high correlation between the peer rating of aggression and the child's aggression reported by his mother. Although pretests had indicated that some mothers were not accurate reporters of their sons' aggression, and therefore should not be used as a primary source of information about this, they provided reasonably accurate data on the average. This led us to expect some correlation between mothers' ratings and those derived from peers, as indeed Eron and his colleagues had also found (1971:42). The mother's score, based on a single question about whether her son had gotten into physical fights with children outside the family during the past year "often," "occasionally," "seldom," or "never," correlated .38 with the classroom aggression measure in Wave II, .42 with the aggression measure in Wave III, and .41 with the aggression measure in Wave IV. (Those aggression measures were the most appropriate ones to use for comparison because they were closest in time to the interview with mothers.)

Like Eron and Walder, we found that the aggression scores of boys were significantly higher than those of girls. For example, in Wave IV, the mean aggression score for girls was 53, compared with a mean of 95 for boys.[19]

The evidence for reliability and validity is even more persuasive because a number of possible sources of error appear to have very little effect on the measure. Specifically, five such sources of error were considered: absenteeism; composition of junior high school classes, which differed from elementary school classes; number of raters in the class; position of name on the class list; and sex composition of the raters.[20]

The analyses undertaken indicated that none of the five possible error sources had a perceptible effect on either reliability or validity. After examining their separate effects, we tried to estimate the total contamination of the aggression measure from several of these error sources combined: number of raters in the class, position of name on the class list, and sex composition of the raters. To do this we computed multiple regressions that assayed the impact of the three factors on aggression in each of four different waves. Results from this analysis suggest that the errors are cumulative, but that the impact is small. The total variance in aggression accounted for by all three variables is 3.2% in Wave I, 3.5% in Wave IV, 2.8% in Wave V, and 5.9% in Wave VI. It should be noted that to the extent that these three facators are true correlates of

[19]Additional support for the measure's validity is derived from the correlations obtained between it and a host of other variables included in the study. These relationships are described in Chapter 5, but it is worth noting here that aggression as measured relates to other variables in theoretically predictable ways or in ways that have been documented by prior research (e.g., Feshbach, 1970).

[20]For details see Documentation 3, "Boys' Aggression Measure: Possible Sources of Error," available on request.

aggression rather than error, the true percentage of variance in aggression due to error is less than these figures indicate.

Stability

Since this is a panel study, it is important to see how much aggression itself changes over time. The greater the stability of aggression, the less the potential impact of television or any other factor.

Our interest in the stability of aggression also stems from our interest in the nature of aggression. Is it an enduring characteristic of a child, or is it temporary behavior, likely to increase or decrease rather easily?

In order to examine stability, the correlations between aggression at earlier and later points in time are presented in Table 3.6. The top half of the table, above the diagonal, presents the observed correlations, ranging from .84 over the shortest time span (3 months) to .54 over the longest span (3 years). These correlations are high enough to indicate that in general aggression is a fairly stable characteristic of the children studied here.

At the same time these stabilities show that the index is highly reliable, for not even the most stable behavior would have produced stabilities as large as this without also being very reliable. This is true because unreliability characteristically reduces the correlation between two measures of the same concept below what it might have been with perfectly reliable indicators. This means that, by adjusting for the small amount of unreliability in the index, we

TABLE 3.6
Stability of Aggression: Adjusted and Unadjusted Autocorrelations between all Wave Pairs[a]

WAVES	I	II	III	IV	V	VI
I		.659 (572)	.659 (556)	.651 (548)	.620 (329)	.540 (202)
II	.690		.841 (619)	.761 (607)	.695 (353)	.632 (212)
III	.693	.880		.844 (665)	.732 (381)	.678 (217)
IV	.681	.792	.883		.749 (389)	.688 (221)
V	.652	.727	.770	.784		.724 (246)
VI	.565	.658	.710	.716	.758	

[a]The unadjusted autocorrelations are given above the diagonal; the autocorrelations adjusted for measurement unreliabilities below. The reliability coefficient for the aggression measure in each wave is the Heise-Bohrnstedt Ω (Heise-Bohrnstedt, 1970). N's are given in parentheses.

TABLE 3.7
Aggression Stability (Autocorrelations)[a] and Length of Time between Waves

WAVE PAIRS	DURATION	AUTOCORRELATION	(*N*)
III–IV	3 months	.883	(665)
II–III	4 months	.880	(619)
I–II	5 months	.690	(572)
II–IV	7 months	.792	(607)
I–III	9 months	.693	(556)
I–IV	1 year	.681	(548)
IV–V	1 year	.784	(389)
V–VI	1 year	.758	(246)
III–V	1 year/3 months	.770	(381)
II–V	1 year/7 months	.727	(353)
I–V	2 years	.652	(329)
IV–VI	2 years	.716	(221)
III–VI	2 years/3 months	.710	(217)
II–VI	2 years/7 months	.658	(212)
I–VI	3 years	.565	(202)

[a]Adjusted for measurement unreliabilities. See footnote to Table 3.6.

might find the real stability of aggression to be even higher than that shown above the diagonal in Table 3.6.

The estimated stabilities of aggression, adjusted for the amount of unreliability we assume to exist in the aggression index, are shown below the diagonal in Table 3.6. As the estimated reliability is quite high, the adjustment does not increase the already high stabilities by very much. However we estimate that the true stabilities range from .57 to .88. The average of all 15 correlations is .73.

The correlations indicate the extent of relative stability in aggression. Since we have already shown that the mean aggression score for all children did not change much, the correlations indicate that there is considerable relative as well as absolute stability in aggression. In other words, children remain in a similar position on the aggression distribution over time and their absolute scores remain fairly similar.

To provide a better indication of the relationship between stability and length of time between periods, Table 3.7 presents the adjusted correlations, arranged from shorter to longer elapsed time periods. In general, the longer the time period between waves, the lower the correlation. (The average for the five shortest periods, those less than a year, is .79; the average for the five middle periods, those between 1 and 2 years, is .74; and the average for the five longest periods, those 2 years or longer, is .66.)

The implications of this degree of stability for our analyses of television's impact on aggression are discussed in greater detail in Chapter 6. Here it is sufficient to point out that in a 3-year period, aggression in children is slow to change.[21] There is some change, however, and, as will be shown in Chapters 5 and 6, this amount of change provides the possibility for determining television's impact on aggression.

---

[21]Bloom (1964) and Kagan and Moss (1962) have found moderate to high stability for aggression over roughly equal periods of time for children of similar ages. As mentioned above, Lefkowitz *et al.* (1972) found moderate correlations between aggression scores based on peer ratings taken 10 years apart.

CHAPTER 4

TELEVISION EXPOSURE MEASURE

Our intention was to investigate possible effects of television exposure under natural conditions using an exposure measure that reflected actual viewing behavior. In addition, hypotheses linking television viewing and aggression suggest that program content (e.g., violence) affects behavior. Hence, a measure of exposure that provided data on the total amount of viewing as well as viewing of specific programs was needed.[1]

A review of the literature, focusing on the various methods of measuring television-viewing behavior used in academic and commercial research, revealed that many were not suitable for this study for several reasons[2]:

1. Some methods yield inaccurate data (e.g., those that use general time estimates, such as "How may hours do you watch every week?" or unaided-recall measures).
2. Some methods (e.g., general time estimates) do not provide information about the kinds of programs that have been watched.
3. Some methods (e.g., repeated phone interviews) are very intrusive and are likely to sensitize respondents to the purpose of the research.

---

[1]Much of the material in this chapter is adapted from Stipp (1975).

[2]See Stipp (1975:247–250) for a discussion of all specific methods considered. In these investigations commerical television rating data and research by rating services were extremely useful. The term "ratings" refers to television exposure data collected by commercial services. These ratings are estimates of the size of a viewing audience for specific programs (in numbers or percentages) or of the total amount of viewing (in hours) by an audience during a week. In this context, the audience we speak of usually consists of children. See Stipp (1975:137–215) for a discussion of commerical ratings on children's television-viewing behavior.

4. Methods that require reading and writing skills and recall can present problems for young respondents who have limited skills of this sort and poorer recall than adolescents or adults.

We therefore endeavored to develop a method unencumbered by the shortcomings just discussed. Two aided-recall methods were pretested with a sample of children, their mothers, and siblings. The first, based on a method used by the Brand Rating Index (BRI) research service, used a program checklist to be filled out by the children. In the second method, a television diary was filled out by their mothers or older siblings[3] and personal interviews about programs viewed were conducted with the children. The program checklist was filled out in classrooms by almost 200 children. Fifty of these were interviewed daily for a week while their mothers kept a television diary on the children's viewing.

On the basis of comparisons among these separate data sources we concluded (*a*) that first graders, generally age 6, are not accurate reporters of their television viewing; (*b*) that mothers are often less accurate about their children's viewing than the children themselves, a conclusion that agrees with research by Greenberg, Ericson, and Vlahos (1972) and by Kay (1972); (*c*) that the classroom-administered aided-recall method, in which respondents are instructed to mark how often within a specified time period they have seen the programs listed, was well suited for this project.

On the basis of the pretest, we took great care in the design of the questionnaire to keep the lists of programs short, to space the titles of programs liberally, and to keep the question wording simple. Standardized adminstrative procedures were set up to ensure that all respondents understood the task and had enough time to fill out the checklist accurately.

The pretest also provided a method for identifying respondents whose data were suspect. In the pretest the titles of nonexistent "dummy" programs had been included in the checklists. We found that respondents who had problems recalling their viewing on the previous day in personal interviews were more likely to mark dummy programs. Thus, we decided to add such dummy items to the program checklists to be used in the study. Later analyses (discussed in the validity section of this chapter) showed that marking dummy programs did indeed indicate a more general pattern of reporting viewing behavior inaccurately.

---

[3]Commercial-rating services obtain television-viewing data for children by means of a diary. The diary lists day and time and requires the respondent to enter the name of the programs watched. Rating services ask the diary keeper to enter the viewing of all household members. We asked for information on the child's viewing only.

MEASURING TELEVISION EXPOSURE

This section describes the television exposure measure used in the six waves. The format of the checklists is described, the procedure for choosing samples of programs is explained, and the administration of the measure is discussed.

Format of Program Checklists

The television programs were listed on four pages in the questionnaire. The first page listed about 15 prime-time shows, the second about 11 weekend daytime programs, the third about 12 daily (Monday–Friday) programs, and the last page listed about 8 movies—a total of about 45 shows.

In addition to the sampled programs, all checklists contained dummy programs—about one per page. The titles of the dummy programs were made up arbitrarily, but we tried to avoid titles that could easily be confused with actual programs.

An example of a program checklist page is presented in Figure 4.1.[4] For a listing of all programs in all waves, as well as a listing of dummy programs, see Appendix A.

Respondents were asked to circle a number for each program to indicate how many episodes of that program they had watched in the last 4 weeks (in the case of weekly shows) or the last week (in the case of daily shows). In addition, respondents had to indicate whether or not they had watched the movies listed. The children's task, recalling their viewing behavior, was facilitated by the fact that all programs listed, with the exception of the movies, were regularly scheduled series shown every week or every day, Monday–Friday.[5] In addition, as detailed below, most programs sampled were quite popular with children; many were viewed by 20–30% of the respondents every time they were televised.

Sampling of Programs

We could not include all programs shown on television in the checklists of the exposure measure, and we had evidence that a complete list of the hundreds of programs shown during a month would not have produced accurate data. The checklists therefore sampled programs from all those shown on the stations in the study cities during the previous 4 weeks.

---

[4]Item L, *Terror Gangs*, is the dummy program on this list.

[5]At the time of this study, program turnover was low and preemptions through specials and mini-series were rare compared to recent programming developments.

After collecting as much commercial-rating information as possible on the viewing behavior of children and investigating the consequences of different procedures for the planned data analyses, the following criteria were used to select the sample of programs:

1. *Programs should be aired when children can view.* We sampled only programs televised at times when children could be expected to watch (i.e., programs shown during school hours were not included).

2. *Programs should be popular with children.* In order to ensure that the exposure scores were fairly representative of respondents' viewing, we needed a list of shows that had a reasonably high probability of being seen, as indicated by actual audience ratings. Only programs seen by at least 2% of 6- to 11-year-old children, according to the most recent ratings (about 2 months prior to Wave I), were selected.

3. *Violent programs should be overselected.* The analyses to be conducted required good data on respondents' exposure to different kinds of programs, but especially programs with violent content.[6] Thus, it was decided that close to 50% of the sample had to be made up of such shows.[7] On the other hand, since it is not known for certain which (if any) type of program can affect aggressive behavior, all types of programs watched by children had to be included in the sample.

4. *Program samples in the two cities should be matched.* Weekday afternoon shows, which comprise a large amount of children's television exposure, are local shows that, unlike network programs, differ from one city to another. To obtain comparable data, local shows in one city had to be matched as closely as possible—with respect to program type, violent content, and audience size—with local shows in the other city.

5. *Samples from wave to wave should be comparable.* Since this was a panel study, cross-wave analyses would compare exposure scores obtained at different times. In order to prevent artificial changes in scores as a result of sample variations rather than actual changes in viewing,[8] steps had to be taken to ensure the comparability of the sample of programs over time.

It was decided that most of the programs and movies in Wave I should be selected according to a stratified probability procedure in which the chances of

---

[6]It was particularly important to include violent programs shown five times a week, Monday–Friday, as such programs were likely to account for a very large portion of a respondent's diet of violent television.

[7]Ratings analyses showed that more than half of the programs popular with children had little or no violent content. As a result, shows with violence had to be oversampled. See subsequent sections for a discussion of the construction of the violence exposure measure and definition of violent content.

[8]Since data were collected at different times of the year, seasonal variations in the amount of viewing are to be expected. Commercial ratings show, for example, that viewing is higher during the winter. See Stipp (1975:137–215).

programs being chosen were proportional to their popularity with children.[9] However, some dummy shows were added to the sample, as were a few programs of special interest to us. In subsequent waves, a purposive selection procedure was used to match shows as closely as possible to those selected in Wave I, using the sampling criteria just listed.[10] Analyses reported below suggest that we were relatively successful in obtaining valid viewing reports that are comparable from wave to wave.

The number of programs selected varied slightly from wave to wave. Generally, the checklists contained between 40 and 50 items—about 85% series titles and 15% movie titles.

The television stations in each of the two study cities broadcast a total of over 500 hr of programming every week. During the hours when schoolchildren are able to watch television, they broadcast about 300 hr.[11] In general, the program samples cover about 65–75 hr of programming per week. That is less than 15% of all programs but close to 25% of programs shown when school children can watch. Because we oversampled popular programs, the sample covers at least one-third of the average child's amount of viewing, and because we oversampled violent programs, the sample covers about half of the average child's amount of violence viewing.[12]

Administrative Procedures

As mentioned in Chapter 3, the questionnaires were administered in classrooms by teams consisting of one administrator and one or more monitors

---

[9]Details of the procedure are given in "Procedures for Sampling TV Programs" (Documentation 4A), available on request.

[10]Many programs were retained on the checklists from one wave to the next. For example, the peer questionnaires for Waves V and VI both contain a list of 15 prime-time programs; 12 of these are identical.

[11]The calculation assumes children watch at these times: Monday–Friday, 7:00 to 8:00 A.M. and 3:00 to 11:00 P.M.; weekends, 8:00 A.M. to 11:00 P.M.. (The number of stations is four; thus all figures are multiplied by four.)

[12]These figures were determined by comparing the commercial ratings of the sampled programs with the total amount of viewing in this age group. We first obtained an estimate of the total amount of viewing by children (in the age groups we had sampled and during the weeks covered by our exposure measure) through commercial ratings. The ratings told us, for every half hour of every program, what percentage of children watched. Adding the ratings for every program half hour, we obtained an index of the children's total amount of viewing.

Then we performed the same calculation for those programs listed in the television questions. Adding the ratings for the half hours of programs listed, we obtained an index of the amount of viewing covered by the measure. The ratio of this index divided by the index of total viewing gives an estimate of the percentage of viewing covered by the sample of programs in the television exposure measure. (The percentage is an estimate because the ratings are subject to sampling error and because there are differences between the sample used by the rating service and our sample of respondents.)

in each class. The administrators were given a "Classroom Administrator's Guide" and the monitors a "Monitor's Guide," which detailed their tasks and spelled out exactly what to say.[13]

After the administrator and the monitor(s) had introduced themselves, the method of administration was explained to the children. Then the administrator read the questions, demonstrated the procedures, and clarified the concepts.

When the class reached the first page of the exposure measure, the classroom administrator said:

> Please listen very carefully to what I'm going to tell you. Don't start answering until I have finished explaining this question. This question is about television programs you may watch. This is a list of nighttime programs that are on television once a week. What you have to do is to tell us how many times you have seen each program out of the *last four* times it was on television. Now, this does not mean how many times you have *ever* seen the program.
>
> If a show is on Monday night, the last four times it was on would be the past Monday night, the Monday night before that one, the Monday night before that, and finally the one before that. So you see, you have to think carefully about each show, and about the last *four* times it was on, and decide how many of those last four programs you saw. Think only about the last four times it was on. Don't think about how often you saw the show before then.
>
> To answer this question you do not put a line through anything. You answer by drawing a circle. I'll show you how.

The administrator then went to the chalkboard and, after writing the name of the first show and the numbers 0, 1, 2, 3, and 4 as they appear on the list, he or she demonstrated the procedure:

> If you did not happen to see it at all the last four times it was on television, draw a circle around the zero—like this. Now, you may have seen it a lot a long time ago, but not in the last four weeks, so you have to circle zero.

The administrator continued:

> If you happened to see it just once of the last four times it was on television, draw a circle around the number one.

---

[13]Since the guides underwent only slight changes from wave to wave, the excerpts given here provide an accurate picture of the methods used in all waves. However, the emphasis on viewing during the last 4 weeks only was not present in the Wave I guide. It was added to the text of the guide after Wave I to ensure that all children understood that we were not interested in their general viewing, but only in their very recent viewing.

While explaining this, he erased the numbers, rewrote them, and circled the 1. The administrator continued until he had demonstrated all numbers from 0 to 4. Then the instructions for the other shows were given:

> Now, I'll read each program and you draw a circle around the right number for you. Each program should have one circle. *If you make a mistake, put an X through the number you circled and make a new circle around the correct number*. All those who understand please raise your hand.

If any child did not raise his or her hand, the procedure was explained again. In any case, the administrator was advised to remind the children to think carefully and not to rush. Children who asked for help or appeared to be having problems were given special assistance by the monitors.

After completion of the questionnaire, each was reviewed for errors by the monitors, and children who made mistakes were asked to correct them.

This standardized administration of the questionnaire, with its built-in training and checking features, was considered essential for obtaining good data from children as young as the respondents in our study. In fact, because of its elaborate administration procedure, the questionnaire for the elementary school respondents should be regarded as only part of a very complex procedure; this was not a self-administered questionnaire in the usual sense.

CONSTRUCTION OF EXPOSURE MEASURES

Total Television Exposure Index

The reported frequency of viewing weekly programs (prime-time and weekend shows) during the 4-week period covered by each questionnaire was multiplied by the program's duration. The shortest programs listed were a half hour long. Therefore, a half hour was used as the computation unit; 1-hr shows were weighted by 2.

A similar procedure was followed for daily (Monday–Friday) programs. The reported frequency of viewing those shows during the week covered by the questionnaire was multiplied by 4 to make that score comparable to the score of the weekly programs, which was based on a 4-week period.

Most of our television exposure measures include exposure to television movies. The reported viewing of movies was added in the following way: Each movie title marked as "seen" was weighted by its duration in half hours. Then the viewing score of all movies was multiplied by 2 to make it comparable to the 4-week viewing score for weekly television programs. This adjustment was

17. On this page is a list of *night time* programs that are on television once a week. Draw a circle aroung the number that tells how many times you have seen the program out of the last four times it was on television.

(14)	A. GUNSMOKE	0	1	2	3	4
(15)	B. BIRD'S EYE VIEW	0	1	2	3	4
(16)	C. JULIA	0	1	2	3	4
(17)	D. MOD SQUAD	0	1	2	3	4
(18)	E. ALL IN THE FAMILY	0	1	2	3	4
(19)	F. SMITH FAMILY	0	1	2	3	4
(20)	G. BEWITCHED	0	1	2	3	4
(21)	H. IRONSIDE	0	1	2	3	4
(22)	I. HIGH CHAPARRAL	0	1	2	3	4
(23)	J. BRADY BUNCH	0	1	2	3	4
(24)	K. PARTRIDGE FAMILY	0	1	2	3	4
(25)	L. TERROR GANGS	0	1	2	3	4
(26)	M. MISSION IMPOSSIBLE	0	1	2	3	4
(27)	N. MARY TYLER MOORE	0	1	2	3	4
(28)	O. FBI	0	1	2	3	4
(29)	P. BONANZA	0	1	2	3	4

FIGURE 4.1. *Example of program checklist page (reduced from 8½ × 11 page).*

necessary because the movie sample represented only 2, not 4, weeks of programming.[14]

The computations for each of these program types were summed across all programs listed to derive a total score, with a range of about 0–550, which was rounded and divided by 10 to make figures less cumbersome.

It is tempting to think of these exposure scores as the number of half hours of reported viewing during a 4-week period (divided by 10). The scores, however, do not represent precise viewing-time figures and the measure is not designed to supply such data.[15] Nevertheless, it does yield good estimates of relative amounts of viewing, and is treated as an interval scale in our analyses.

Table 4.1 shows the descriptive statistics of the total exposure measure for all six waves, for valid reporters.[16] The distributions of scores in each wave are presented in Figure 4.2. The means and medians in Table 4.1 show relatively

[14]Because of the large number of movies televised, a 4-week listing of movies would have been too long for young respondents, so a 2-week sample was used.

[15]For details see Stipp (1975:250–256). The findings are based on the validation research of the BRI measure on which our exposure measure is based (e.g., Simmons, 1969:13–23). In the analyses, BRI data were compared with validated commercial ratings. These ratings showed that viewers miss parts of most programs they watch and that programs are not seen as regularly as reported in the BRI measure. At the same time, the relative amount of viewing reported with the BRI measure was found to be quite accurate. Our own analyses support these findings.

[16]As already indicated and as discussed in detail later in this chapter, some children gave viewing reports of questionable accuracy. Table 4.1 is based on accurate, or valid, reporters

TABLE 4.1
Total Television Exposure: Descriptive Statistics for All Six Waves[a]

	WAVE					
STATISTIC	I	II	III	IV	V	VI
Median	16.1	18.4	19.2	14.2	13.2	15.0
Mean	17.2	18.8	19.6	15.2	13.7	14.9
Mode	12	22	13	11	15	14
Standard deviation	8.9	9.2	8.7	8.1	7.1	5.9
Range	0–44	0–43	0–44	0–38	0–35	0–31
Skewness	.5	.4	.2	.3	.4	.2
N	(553)	(428)	(510)	(546)	(406)	(236)

[a]Based on data obtained from valid reporters only.

little variation, especially among the spring waves, Waves I, IV, V, and VI.[17] However, they are higher in Waves II and III. Since those two waves were conducted in October–November and February, respectively, the higher means and medians accurately indicate seasonal variations in viewing: Commercial-rating services report higher viewing levels in those months (when outdoor play is less frequent) than in May, when all the other data were collected.[18]

only. Appendix C contains tables based on data from less valid reporters and total samples for the violence exposure measure used in most analyses.

[17]This is true despite the fact that our sample gets older from wave to wave. Commercial ratings suggest that there is little variation in the amount of viewing between the ages of 7 and 12. (A Nielsen [1974a] report shows a small decline from the 6–8 to the 9–11 group; 12- to 14-year-olds watch significantly less.) Our findings agree with these ratings. The slight decline from Wave I to IV, V, and VI is probably accentuated by the tendency for more of the heavier viewers to drop out of the sample (see Chapter 2).

[18]Seasonal variations in viewing are discussed in Stipp (1975: Chapter IV). Good agreement exists between our data and ratings data, as shown by comparing data from our respondents with ratings data collected at the times when our six waves were conducted (see table below).

Seasonal Variations in Viewing: Study Data and Nielsen Ratings

WAVE	TELEVISION EXPOSURE SCORES[a]	NIELSEN RATINGS[b]
I	100	100
II	120	120
III	120	140
IV	95	95
V	85	105
VI	100	105

[a]Valid respondents, fifth- and sixth-grade boys, blacks excluded.
[b]Nielsen, NTI/NAC reports; national sample, 6 to 11-year-olds (boys and girls).

Continued next page.

In interpreting the range and the standard deviation, it is important to keep in mind that the scores presented here have been divided by 10. Thus, the range on the raw scores is 0 to about 310–440, depending on the wave. The skew is always positive, with values indicating that the distributions are close to normal, with a slight skew toward the high scores. The values are much lower than the corresponding ones for the aggression variables, which are rather highly skewed. Range, standard deviation, and skewness are lowest in Wave VI.

Violent Television Exposure Index

Hypotheses linking television exposure and aggression do not suggest that watching television per se causes aggressive behavior. Rather, it is suggested that specific program content (i.e., violence) affects behavior. Consequently, a measure of exposure to violent content (rather than a measure of general exposure) was used for most analyses.

Construction of such a measure poses problems. First, there is little agreement among scholars about how violence should be defined. Second, even if a consensus definition of violent content existed, there are no studies that offer an objective measure of amount of violent content on a series-by-series basis.[19] However, studies had been conducted to determine which programs were perceived as violent by various segments of the population.

When we began the analysis of the data collected in the early waves of our study, we had obtained a preliminary report of a study by Greenberg and Gordon, later published in the Surgeon General's Report (Greenberg & Gordon, 1972), which offered violence ratings that could be used as violence weights for certain programs.

In March 1970, Greenberg and Gordon conducted a telephone survey in the Detroit area (*N* = 303 completed interviews) and sent questionnaires to newspaper and magazine television critics (*N* = 37 completed questionnaires). Both the general public and the critics samples were given program lists and

---

For this comparison, the Wave I exposure scores and the Nielsen ratings at the time of Wave I are made the standard; both are given the value 100. The variations in exposure scores are presented as percentages of the standard score; the variations in ratings as percentages of the standard rating. The analysis controls for two characteristics of the respondents: age and race. As age is only weakly related to amoung of viewing, the age control may not be necessary. However, without the race control, variations in viewing levels from wave to wave could be due to fluctuations in the racial composition of the samples. (It was not possible to apply such controls to the Nielsen samples. However, those samples are not panels; thus, the average age of respondents does not increase. Further, there is no evidence of pronounced fluctuation in the composition of the Neilsen samples.)

The comparison shows a remarkable degree of agreement, especially considering that the data were obtained from different samples with different methods.

[19]During the data collection period, George Gerbner published a "violence index" based on monitoring "violent acts" in one week of TV programs yearly (cf. Gerbner, 1972; Gerbner,

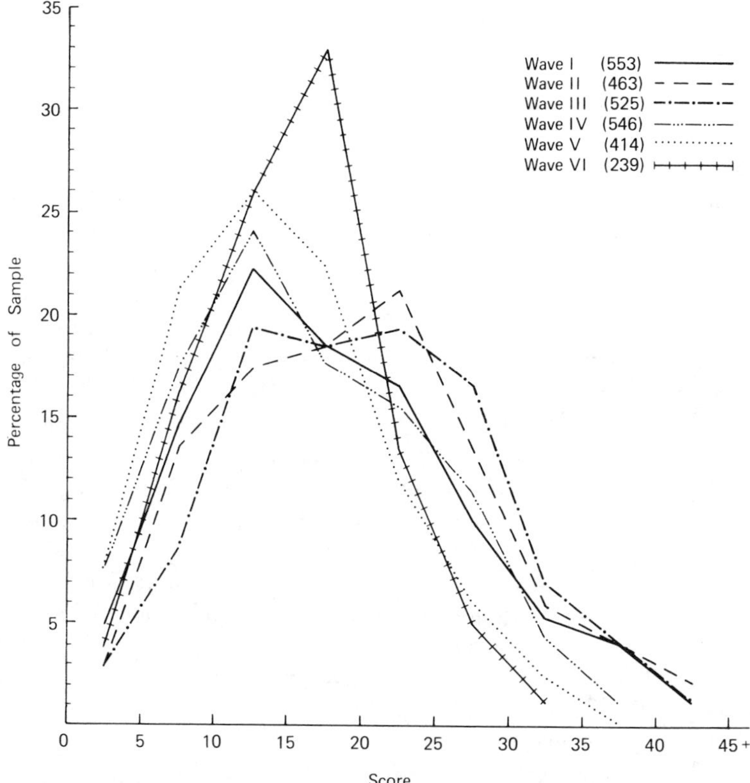

FIGURE 4.2. *Total television exposure measure: Score distribution in Waves I–VI. (Based on data obtained from valid reporters only.)*

Gerbner & Gross, 1976; Gross *et al.*, 1976). The Gerbner data were inappropriate for use in constructing a violence exposure measure for several reasons. First, although the definition of violence underlying his "index" may be appropriate for the theoretical issues he addressed, namely, power relations in American society, its suitability for a study of television as an instigator of aggressive actions among children is not apparent. Gerbner appears to count not only killings and fighting but also accidents, "acts of nature," slapstick play, and magical acts as "violence." Second, this study aimed at assessing whether television violence perceived as such by the public was harmful, and Gerbner's system produced program rankings which were at odds with those produced by public perceptions (Coffin & Tuchman, 1972–1973). Finally, since only one episode of each program was analyzed by Gerbner, and since the variation in the amount of violence between program episodes is considerable, this method is not suitable for rating multiple episodes of program series.

Violence ratings were also published by the National Association for Better Broadcasting and by the *Christian Science Monitor*. These approaches were deemed less appropriate than that of Greenberg and Gordon, in that both rated programs according to the opinions of raters who were not selected in a systematic manner.

instructions that asked them to rate the programs on a 5-point scale (1–5) according to the amount of violence in the program. Violent content was defined in this way: "By violence, I mean how much fighting, shooting, yelling, or killing there usually is on the show." The researchers obtained ratings on 66 prime-time programs (1969–1970 season).

Average program ratings ranged from 1.02 to 3.91. Probably the most important finding was that, even though the critics gave programs higher violence ratings than the general public, there was a high level of agreement on the rankings of programs, including those rated as violent. Using a very similar methodology, Murray, Cole, and Felder (1970) obtained violence ratings from 41 high school students, and the rankings of this group agreed very strongly with the rankings obtained from both the general public and the critics in the Greenberg and Gordon study.[20]

These findings suggest that there is a remarkable degree of agreement between diverse subgroups of the American public on what is generally referred to as "television violence." In the absence of violence scores that are widely accepted as objective, such rankings were used to construct a measure of exposure to violent television content.

McLeod, Atkin, and Chaffee (1972) used these violence ratings for a measure of exposure to violent television programs in a study of television violence and aggression. Rather than using average ratings such as 3.91, they collapsed the average scores based on the three surveyed groups (general public, critics, and high school students) to an 8-point scale, with 0 indicating the lowest and 7 the highest amount of violence.

On the basis of this reaseach, we constructed an index of violence exposure by applying the 0–7 violence scale to each program. The individual programs were then added according to the basic computation procedures just outlined for our measure of total exposure. Thus, like the total exposure measure, the scores obtained on the violence exposure measure do not represent hours of viewing.

Most programs included in our questionnaires in the six waves could not be weighted directly as they were not included in the Greenberg and Gordon or Murray, Cole, and Felder research. We tried to solve this problem by analyzing the violence ratings of the 68 programs listed by the researchers to see whether they followed a pattern that would make it possible to score programs not previously rated. We believed we found such a pattern, and more recent research indicates that it is possible to extrapolate from the rated programs to others on the basis of that pattern.

Violence ratings in these studies appear to depend on two elements: first, the

[20]The study was conducted in November–December 1970. Violence ratings were obtained for 59 of the 66 programs listed by Greenberg and Gordon and for 2 additional programs.

amount of serious physical injury portrayed (programs with a large number of very serious acts achieve a high rating) and second, the context in which the violence occurs—from dramatic, realistic, and contemporary to humorous, unrealistic, and noncontemporary (realistic contemporary dramas obtain a high rating).[21]

More recent research on public perceptions of television violence indicates that our estimates reflect the public view regarding the amount of violence in these programs quite accurately. Abel and Beninson (1976) as well as Banks (unpublished) obtained ratings on eight prime-time shows and several cartoons not rated by the Greenberg/Gordon and Murray samples, but estimated by us. All of our estimates were within one point of the ratings in these studies. A paper by Robinson, Hamernik, and Genova (1980) also confirms the violence rating estimates made by us.[22] Appendix A lists the violence weights of all programs in all waves.[23]

Table 4.3 summarizes the descriptive statistics and Figure 4.3 the full distribution of the measure of exposure to violent television in the six waves.

---

[21]The programs receiving the highest violence ratings are police dramas and mysteries, which frequently show violent acts in a realistic contemporary dramatic context. However, *Adam 12*, a realistic contemporary police drama that highlights nonviolent as well as violent police work, received a 4 rating in the studies, not 6 or 7 as the exclusively violence-oriented programs of this genre did. Westerns, such as *Bonanza*, which show violent action in a noncontemporary setting, generally were rated slightly lower than the contemporary crime dramas, usually 5. The ratings for *Mission Impossible* (6) and *Land of the Giants* (5) also support the interpretation that people perceive noncontemporary and unrealistic violence as generally less severe.

One of the programs listed, *Get Smart*, a spoof of serious spy-adventure dramas, shows violence in a humorous context. The program was rated 3, suggesting that slapstick is conceived by the public as much less violent than serious violence. Another program with humorous violence, *Hogan's Heroes*, also received a low rating (2). Since no cartoon programs with humorous violence were included in the list, it was decided that cartoons with a number of violent acts in a humorous context should be rated 2–4, depending on the extent of slapstick violence. A more recent study (Banks, unpublished), patterned after the Greenberg/Gordon/Murray research, suggests that these ratings do indeed reflect public perceptions. None of the cartoons in that study were rated higher than programs that received a "4" in the Greenberg/Gordon/Murray studies.

Other programs receiving violence ratings between 1 and 4 can be characterized as containing occasional violence in a dramatic context. They are adventure shows or medical dramas, which do not deal with violent crimes in most episodes but do contain occasional aggressive acts. Situation comedies, variety shows, and game shows were rated nonviolent (0). If *Laugh-In* is regarded as a variety show, it is the only exception. It was rated 1.

[22]For example, adult respondents, after seeing excerpts from a number of cartoon programs, rated *Johnny Quest* highest in violence. In our violence ratings *Johnny Quest* is the highest rated cartoon (see Appendix A).

[23]For more details on the violent television measure—such as distribution of programs in the six waves, types of programs listed, and viewing patterns—see Chapter 7, "Other Conceptualizations of TV Exposure."

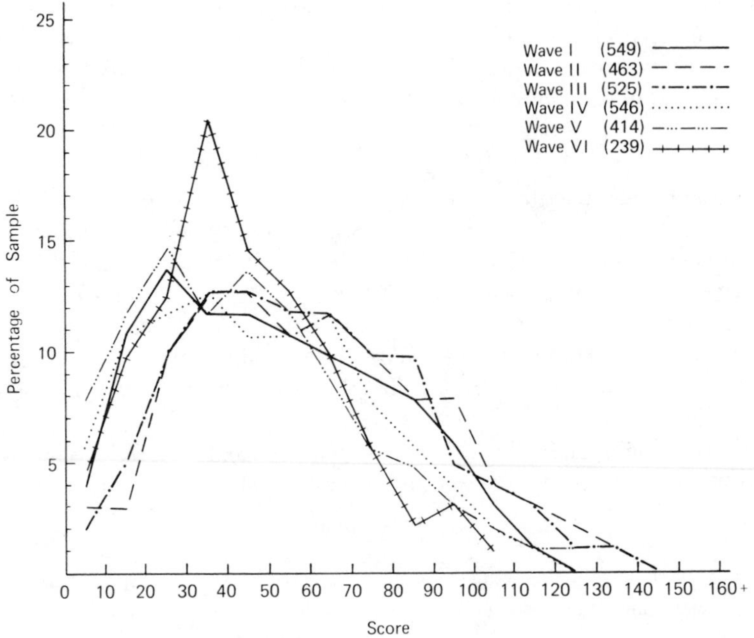

FIGURE 4.3. *Violent television exposure measure: Score distribution in Waves I–VI. (Based on data obtained from valid reporters only.)*

(Again, data are based on valid reporters only. Data based on less valid reporters and total samples are shown in Appendix C.) The measures of central tendency and dispersion are higher for the violence exposure index than for the total exposure index, because the former is weighted up and consequently has a larger scale than the latter (see Table 4.3). However, the distribution of the violence exposure index, given in Figure 4.3, closely matches that of the total exposure index.

The two indices of total exposure and of violence exposure correlate very highly, on average about .92 over the six waves (see Table 4.2). This correlation and other data (reported in Chapter 7) suggest that there is very little over- or underselection of violent programs by most viewers in our sample. Knowing how much television a child watches overall, tells us within a small margin of error how much violent television he watches.[24]

[24]As we shall see in Chapter 7, we were able to isolate a subset of respondents who watch predominantly violent television fare. But for the greater part of the sample, pronounced overselection of violent programs does not occur.

The substantial correlations we find between total viewing and violence viewing are much

TABLE 4.2
Correlations between Total and Violent Television Exposure Scores (Valid Reporters)[a]

WAVE	*N*	*r**
I	(553)	.936
II	(404)	.934
III	(525)	.923
IV	(546)	.931
V	(414)	.933
VI	(239)	.874

[a] All correlations are significant (.05 level).

PROPERTIES OF THE VIOLENT TELEVISION EXPOSURE INDEX

Reliability

Having decided on the violence exposure index as our basic measure of television viewing, we studied the internal properties of the scale. In the following section we investigate the presence of systematic error in the television data; in this section we consider the reliability with which exposure is measured.[25]

Two of the methods available for estimating the reliability of a score are directly applicable to the measure of television exposure. One is the split-half reliability estimation technique, in which parallel forms of a score are

---

higher than those reported in the Surgeon General's study that compared these types of viewing (McLeod, Atkin, & Chaffee, 1972:216). The size of these correlations may be inflated by our oversampling of violent programs. However, the low correlations found by McLeod *et al.* are based on measures of total and violence exposure very different from each other, one of which is, in addition, probably inaccurate. The "Overall Violence Viewing" scores are based on a program checklist similar to ours and the measure is computed similarly also. On the other hand, the "Total Viewing Time" measure used by McLeod, Atkin, and Chaffee is based on three questions that ask the respondent to estimate the amount of time he spends watching television. Such viewing time estimates are crude and inaccurate measures of television exposure.

However, correlations between viewing different program types, obtained with the same measure, are quite similar in McLeod *et al.*'s study and in ours. (Our data are reported in Chapter 7.)

[25]Unreliability in the exposure measure has the effect of reducing the observed correlation between it and other variables. If a great deal of unreliability exists, the observed results may underestimate the true relationship between exposure and these other variables unless a correction factor is introduced. Our purpose here is to evaluate the reliability of the measure of television exposure in order to be able to adjust observed correlations between this measure and our measure of aggression for the deflation due to measurement error.

TABLE 4.3
Violent Television Exposure Measure: Descriptive Statistics for All Six Waves[a]

	WAVE					
STATISTIC	I	II	III	IV	V	VI
Median	46.2	55.5	54.9	42.9	40.5	38.5
Mean	49.1	58.5	57.3	45.3	42.7	41.6
Mode	27	39,80	21,37	66	43	38
Standard deviation	27.2	29.3	28.4	27.2	26.5	21.6
Range	0–122	0–140	0–144	0–118	0–125	0–103
Skewness	.3	.3	.4	.4	.6	.5
N	(553)	(428)	(510)	(546)	(406)	(236)

[a]Based on data obtained from valid reporters only. For tables based on "less valid" reporters and the total sample, see Appendix C.

created for individuals by dividing the items on the basis of which the total score is computed (television programs in this case) into two groups. The correlation of these two half-scores estimates the reliability of the total score. In Wave II, for example, the split-half reliability estimate is .79 (valid reporter sample). The other method of estimating the reliability of the score is to develop a causal model of measurement error in which reliability is estimated as one of the unknowns.

Our estimate of television score reliability is based on the second of these two methods. The work of Werts and Linn (1975) suggests that the causal model approach gives a more accurate assessment of reliability than the split-half approach, if the assumptions necessary to compute the former can reasonably be met (which they can in our data).

In addition, we have selected the causal modeling approach because it generally gives a *lower* estimate of reliability than does the split-half method.[26] The lower estimate of reliability is preferred, as this maximizes the adjusted correlation between the television measure and its correlates, aggression being one of these. If there is an error in our estimate of reliability, we have chosen it to be on the side of observing a significant relationship between exposure and aggression where none really exists rather than in failing to see one where it might exist.

This approach, like that taken in our analysis of the aggression measure in the last chapter, was made possible by using a maximum-likelihood regression model for estimating unmeasured variables (Jöreskog, 1973). The reliability

[26]The split-half method includes any correlated error terms among the separate reports of viewing (for instance, a consistent tendency to overreport viewing all television shows) as part of the reliability of the index. The causal modeling approach eliminates this component, and therefore generally produces a lower estimate of reliability.

coefficients obtained by this method range from .60 to .77 and average .68 over the six waves.[27]

These coefficients, although lower than the split-half estimates, tell us that the index has good reliability for one collected in a field study. On the basis of these results we estimate that the observed relationship between the exposure score and the aggression index will be deflated on average by approximately 18% $(1-.68^{1/2})$ as a result of unreliability in the exposure measure. This deflation is not large relative to characteristic levels found in survey research and is certainly not large enough to mask any true causal relationship between exposure and aggression.

Validity: Sytematic Bias in Reporting Television Viewing

The pretests showed that many of the youngest respondents in the sample—second and third graders, and especially those from low-SES backgrounds—had rather limited reading and writing skills. We devised elaborate techniques which helped many of the children to produce accurate and valid data. Nevertheless, many of the young and those below average in reading and writing skills still appeared to be unable to provide such data about their viewing.

It was not possible to establish directly which respondents gave poor reports of their television viewing, because an independent measure of the exposure of individual respondents was unavailable. Special analyses appeared to identify groups of respondents who gave viewing reports of comparatively low accuracy. We call these respondents "less valid reporters." At the same time, the analyses suggest strongly that most respondents provided accurate data; we call those "valid reporters."

This type of inaccuracy presents a problem for this research because inaccurate reporting of television viewing is related to respondents' aggression. These children as a group are more aggressive than other respondents (see Chapter 5). Since they appeared to give strongly exaggerated reports of their viewing behavior, we risked biasing the findings by including them in the analysis. However, we also risked missing an important component of the television–aggression relationship by excluding them, since they were significantly more aggressive than the "valid reporters."

Our solution was to compute all central analyses of the television–aggression relationship twice, once including and once excluding these less valid

[27]The reliabilities reported here are all for the violence exposure index. Because of the high correlation between total exposure and violence exposure, the same reliabilities are found for total exposure. The coefficients reported here are for those described in the next section as "valid reporters" of viewing, but separate computations were also made for the total sample. Both sets of computations are described in detail in Appendix C in Chapter 6.

reporters.[28] As we shall see in subsequent chapters, analyses which include the biased, exaggerated viewing reports led to essentially the same conclusions as analyses based on valid reporters only. This makes it somewhat superfluous to discuss in great detail procedures isolating less valid reporters. But, even though the question of valid reporting turned out to have little significance empirically, it was of great concern in analyzing the data, and, therefore, we report the procedures in Appendix B.[29]

"VALID" AND "LESS VALID" REPORTERS

The two respondent groups, "valid" and "less valid" reporters, were classified on the basis of their scores on three indicators of less valid reporting. The first one is marking of "dummy" programs—claiming to have watched nonexistent programs that we inserted in the program checklists. The second indicator is what we call an "extremity response pattern"—marking primarily extreme values on the program checklists, indicating that most programs were either never viewed or were viewed every time they were shown. Finally, the third indicator is claiming to have regularly watched programs aired simultaneously. Appendix B provides explanations and additional details regarding these reporting patterns that indicate questionable accuracy.

Table 4.4 lists the number of valid and less valid reporters among boys in the six waves. There is a considerable amount of less valid reporting—between 25 and 30% in the early waves, and 17% in the later waves. As respondents grow older and acquire better reading and writing skills, they are somewhat less likely to be less valid reporters.[30] (The one exception is Wave I, where there are fewer less valid reporters than in Wave II. The Wave I figure is somehat understated, because one of the indicators of less valid reporting was less powerful in Wave I than in the other waves.)

---

[28]We entertained the possibility of adjusting the exposure scores of less valid respondents to reflect more accurately what we think their real viewing behavior might be. However, we decided that a better procedure would be to include their exaggerated viewing reports as a way of setting an upper bound on the influence they might have on the results.

As we show below, most of the internal checks used to pinpoint less valid reporters were checks on *over*reporting viewing habits. Therefore, we believe these children all actually watch less television then they report. However, since they are also more aggressive than other children, including these exaggerated viewing reports increases the estimated relationship between television and aggression beyond what we believe the true relationship to be.

[29]The validity analyses are described in detail in Stipp (1975:Chapter VI) and in Appendix B. The analyses were conducted primarily with Wave IV data, and girls were included to increase the sample size and to permit examination of sex differences in viewing behavior.

[30]Less valid reporting was not a problem among teenage boys.

TABLE 4.4

Number of Valid and Less Valid Reporters in the Six Waves[a]

WAVE	TOTAL SAMPLE N	TOTAL SAMPLE %	VALID REPORTERS N	VALID REPORTERS %	LESS VALID REPORTERS N	LESS VALID REPORTERS %
I	(734)	100	(553)	75	(181)	25
II	(603)	100	(428)	71	(175)	29
III	(639)	100	(510)	80	(129)	20
IV	(653)	100	(546)	84	(107)	16
V	(490)	100	(406)	83	(84)	17
VI	(283)	100	(236)	83	(47)	17

[a]Aggression and television data available for all respondents.

Most of the less valid reporters in one wave are valid in many other waves, and therefore are available for analysis in those waves. This is illustrated in Table 4.5, which shows those respondents with television aggression data in each of the six waves who are valid reporters in *all* waves in which they are present, valid in some and less valid in other waves in which they are present, or less valid in *all* waves in which they are present.

In all waves, the largest group is made up of respondents who are valid reporters in all waves in which they are present; in five out of six waves the size of this group is close to 60% of the sample. An additional 30 to 40% are valid in at least some waves. The group of those who are less valid in all waves is consistently the smallest by far; on the average it makes up 6% of the sample. In

TABLE 4.5

Number of Valid and Less Valid Reporters Across Waves[a]

WAVE	TOTAL SAMPLE N	VALID REPORTERS IN *ALL* WAVES WITH TELEVISION DATA N	VALID REPORTERS IN *ALL* WAVES WITH TELEVISION DATA %	VALID AND LESS VALID REPORTERS IN WAVES WITH TELEVISION DATA N	VALID AND LESS VALID REPORTERS IN WAVES WITH TELEVISION DATA %	LESS VALID REPORTERS IN *ALL* WAVES WITH TELEVISION DATA N	LESS VALID REPORTERS IN *ALL* WAVES WITH TELEVISION DATA %
I	734	468	64	199	27	67	9
II	603	345	57	219	36	39	6
III	639	367	57	219	38	32	5
IV	653	380	58	237	36	36	6
V	490	297	61	173	35	20	4
VI	283	139	49	130	46	14	5

[a]Aggression and television data available for all respondents.

TABLE 4.6

Stability of Violent Television Exposure: Adjusted and Unadjusted Autocorrelations between all Wave Pairs[a]

WAVES	I	II	III	IV	V	VI
I		.523 (291)	.542 (305)	.480 (294)	.277 (188)	.263 (98)
II	.832		.667 (393)	.527 (386)	.388 (239)	.278 (117)
III	.780	.960		.625 (439)	.447 (269)	.348 (131)
IV	.710	.779	.836		.507 (269)	.416 (143)
V	.452	.633	.660	.769		.494 (169)
VI	.429	.454	.514	.631	.827	

[a] The autocorrelations are based on data obtained from valid reporters only. For tables based on less valid reporters and the total sample (unadjusted only), see Appendix C. The unadjusted autocorrelations are given above the diagonal. The autocorrelations adjusted for measurement unreliabilities are given below the diagonal. For a discussion of the method used, see Appendix C in Chapter 6.

brief, although the loss of cases because of less valid reporting averages 21% in a given wave, the overwhelming majority of those excluded from the analysis in one wave are included—as valid reporters—in one or more of the other waves. This, too, reduces the chance that biased reporting alters the results.

Stability of Exposure over Time

Thus far we have examined the exposure measures at one point in time. It is also important to see how stable patterns of viewing are over the 3-year duration of this panel study. The more stable the measure, the less complex it will be to describe viewing patterns over the 3 years.

Our interest in the stability of television exposure also stems from concern with the nature of television watching and its effects on children. We want to know whether children are, in fact, characterized by relatively stable patterns of viewing that endure over time, or whether they change their viewing habits with little reference to past behavior.

Correlations between violence exposure scores at different points of the panel are presented in Table 4.6.[31] The coefficients above the diagonal are observed correlations. They range from .67 over 4 months to .26 over 3 years. The coefficients below the diagonal are adjusted for unreliability in the indexes, as computed by means of our measurement models (see Appendix C in Chapter 6). These range from .96 to .43.

[31] The stability of total exposure is very similar to that for violence exposure.

Violent television exposure exhibits some persistence over time, but it is substantially less stable than aggression. Most children change their viewing patterns over relatively short periods of time. In the causal analyses, this instability makes it easy to see if changes in viewing are followed by subsequent changes in aggression. It would be more difficult to detect exposure effects if viewing was highly stable.

APPENDIX A: LISTING OF PROGRAMS AND VIOLENCE WEIGHTS (ELEMENTARY SCHOOL BOYS AND GIRLS)

TABLE A.1
Prime-Time Programs[a]

	WAVE						VIOLENCE WEIGHTS
	I	II	III	IV	V	VI	
Mod Squad	X	X	X	X	X	X	7
Gunsmoke	X	X	X	X	X	X	6
Mission Impossible	X	X	X	X			6
Bonanza	X	X	X	X	X		5
Death Valley Days	X						5
Dragnet	X						5
Adam 12	X	X			X	X	4
Bewitched	X	X	X	X			0
Brady Bunch	X	X	X	X			0
Doris Day	X	X	X				0
Englebert Humperdinck	X						0
Family Affair	X	X					0
Hee Haw	X	X	X				0
Tom Jones	X						0
Wrestling		X					5
Matt Lincoln		X					4
Young Rebels		X					4
Arnie		X	X				0
Don Knotts		X					0
Headmaster		X					0
FBI			X	X	X	X	7
Ironside			X	X			5
Name of the Game			X				5
Men from Shiloh			X				4
Eddie's Father			X		X		0
Julia			X	X			0
Partridge Family			X	X	X	X	0

(Continued next page)

TABLE A.1 *(continued)*

	WAVE						VIOLENCE WEIGHTS
	I	II	III	IV	V	VI	
High Chaparral				X			5
Smith Family				X			2
All in the Family				X	X	X	1
Bird's Eye View				X			0
Mary Tyler Moore				X	X	X	0
Hawaii 5-O					X	X	7
Alias Smith & Jones					X		4
Cade's County					X		4
Emergency					X	X	2
Laugh-In					X	X	1
Flip Wilson					X	X	0
Mannix						X	7
Kung Fu						X	5
Rookies						X	5
Temperature's Rising						X	1
Number of programs listed in wave	14	16	16	15	15	15	

[a]All programs are listed in both cities.

TABLE A.2
Saturday–Sunday Programs (Exclusively Prime-Time)

	WAVE						VIOLENCE WEIGHTS
	I	II	III	IV	V	VI	
Invaders[a]	X	X	X				6
Time Tunnel[b]	X			X	X		6
Banana Splits	X						4
Perils of Penelope	X		X				4
George of the Jungle	X						3
Hot Wheels	X	X	X	X			3
Children's Hour	X						2
Archie	X	X	X	X	X	X	1
Here Comes Grump	X						1
Jetsons	X						1
Pink Panther	X			X	X		1
Wild Kingdom	X	X					1
Amateur Hour	X						0
Discovery 70	X	X	X	X			0
Patty Duke[b]	X						0

(Continued next page)

TABLE A.2 *(continued)*

	WAVE I	II	III	IV	V	VI	VIOLENCE WEIGHTS
Wagon Train[b]		X					6
Johnny Quest		X	X	X	X		5
Josie and the Pussycats		X	X	X	X	X	4
H. R. Pufnstuf		X	X	X			2
Dr. Dolittle		X	X	X	X		1
Hot Dog		X	X				0
Man from UNCLE[b]			X	X	X		6
Bugaloos				X			2
Lassie				X			1
Bugs Bunny					X	X	4
Lancelot Link					X		1
Jackson 5					X	X	0
Take a Giant Step					X		0
Rat Patrol						X	6
Land of the Giants						X	5
Underdog						X	3
Fat Albert						X	1
Roman Holidays						X	1
Talking with a Giant						X	0
Number of programs listed in wave	13	10	10	11	10	9	

[a]Programs listed only in Fort Worth.
[b]Programs listed only in Minneapolis.

TABLE A.3
Daily Programs (Monday–Friday)

	WAVE I	II	III	IV	V[c]	VI[c]	VIOLENCE WEIGHTS
Star Trek[a,d]	X	X	X	X	X	X	6
Dark Shadows	X	X	X				5
Run for Your Life[a]	X						5
Popeye[b]	X	X	X		X	X	4
Perry Mason[b]	X						4
Siegfried[a]	X						4
Little Rascals[b]	X						2
Bozo's Big Top[b]	X						1
Flintstones	X	X	X	X		X	1

(Continued next page)

TABLE A.3 *(continued)*

	WAVE						VIOLENCE WEIGHTS
	I	II	III	IV	V[c]	VI[d]	
Hobo Kelly[a]	X						1
Lunch with Casey[b]	X	X	X				1
News (CBS)	X	X	X	X	]X	]X	1
News (NBC)	X	X	X	X	]	]	1
10 O'Clock News	X	X	X	X	X	X	1
General Hospital	X						0
I Love Lucy[e]	X	X	X	X	X	X	0
Mr. Rogers	X						0
Sesame Street	X	X	X	X			0
Batman[f]		X	X	X			6
Big Valley[a]		X			X	X	5
Have Gun Will Travel[b]		X	X	X			5
Daniel Boone		X	X	X			4
Gilligan's Island[a,g]		X	X		X	X	1
Munsters[b]		X	X	X			1
Leave It to Beaver[b]		X	X	X	X	X	0
Lost in Space[a]			X				5
It Takes a Thief[a,b,h]				X	X	X	6
Fred & Friends[a]				X			1
Gomer Pyle				X			1
McHale's Navy[a]				X			1
Wild Wild West[a,b,i]					X	X	6
Dragnet					X		5
Virginian[a]					X		5
Electric Company					X	X	0
Flying Nun[a]					X		0
To Tell the Truth[a]					X	X	0
Truth or Consequences[b,j]					X	X	0
High Chaparral[a]						X	5
Rifleman[b]						X	5
I Dream of Jeannie[b]						X	0
That Girl[b]						X	0
Number of programs listed in wave	14	13	13	12	11	11	

[a]Programs listed only in Minneapolis.

[b]Programs listed only in Fort Worth.

[c]In Waves V and VI titles are listed that are not part of the regular exposure measures but were included for special analyses.

[d]Both cities in Wave I.

[e]Only in Fort Worth in Wave VI.

[f]Only in Fort Worth in Wave IV.

[g]Both cities in Waves V and VI.

[h]In Minneapolis in Wave V, in Fort Worth in Wave VI.

[i]In Fort Worth in Wave V, in Minneapolis in Wave VI.

[j]Both cities in Wave VI.

TABLE A.4
Television Movies

WAVE	VIOLENCE WEIGHTS	WAVE	VIOLENCE WEIGHTS
Wave I (8 movies)		*Wave IV* (7 movies)	
Corridors of Blood[a]	6	*Black Eagle of Sante Fe*[b]	6
Khartoum	6	*Phantom of the Opera*[a]	6
Denver and the Rio Grande	5	*Rough Night in Jericho*	6
Gorilla at Large[b]	5	*Stage Coach*	6
Rage	5	*Triple Cross*	4
Tarzan and the Valley of Gold	5	*Back Street*[a]	2
Missouri Traveler[b]	2	*Disorderly Orderly*	1
Operation Amsterdam	2	*Fortune Cookie*	1
Young Lawyers	2	*Lover Come Back*[b]	1
Rhubarb[a]	1	*Wave V* (6 movies)[c]	
Wave II (7 movies)		*Deadly Hunt*	6
Dirty Dozen	7	*Spartacus*	6
Tarzan's Great Adventure[b]	6	*Apache Uprising*	5
Tarzan Triumphs[a]	6	*Arrividerci Baby*	0
Tony Rome	6	*Enter Laughing*	0
Cast a Giant Shadow	5	*Gigi*	0
The Great Race	3	*Wave VI* (6 movies)[c]	
The Magnificent Men in Their Flying Machines	1	*Hornet's Nest*	6
The Russians Are Coming	1	*The Long Duel*	6
Wave III (9 movies)		*The Silencers*	6
		The Hired Hand	5
Chamber of Horrors	6	*Screaming Woman*[b]	5
Duel at Diablo	6	*Tick . . . Tick . . . Tick*[a]	5
In Like Flint	6	*Beg, Borrow, or Steal*[a]	2
Johnny Cool[b]	6	*Footsteps: Nice Guys Finish Last*[a]	2
Spartacus	6	*1,000 Clowns*[b]	1
Bridge on the River Kwai	5	*Three on a Couch*[b]	1
Tarzan's Hidden Jungle[a]	5		
The Invisible Man[b]	2		
Horse Feathers[a]	1		
American in Paris	0		
Marriage on the Rocks	0		

[a]Movies listed only in Fort Worth.
[b]Movies listed only in Minneapolis.
[c]In Waves V and VI titles are listed that are not part of the regular exposure measures but were included for special analyses.

TABLE A.5
Dummy Programs

WAVE	PRIME TIME	SATURDAY/SUNDAY	DAILY (MONDAY–FRIDAY)	TV MOVIES
I		*Sunday School Room/Battle of the Space Monsters*	*Happy Hiccups*	*What a Lovely Day*
II	*Shooters from Chicago*	*Rupert Trickshot*	*Killers from the Coast*	*The Deadly Flowers*
III	*Shooters from Chicago*	*Rupert Trickshot*	*Killers from the Coast*	
IV	*Terror Gangs*	*Lolly Popsickle*	*Five Funny Faces*	*Codeword: Kill*
V	*Adventures in the Fog*	*Slinky Lizards*	*Suicide Warrior*	*Downtown Taxi*
VI	*The Last Wave*	*Peewee the Pirate*	*Cooperation in Violence*	*The Computer Is Down*

APPENDIX B: "VALID" AND "LESS VALID" REPORTERS

Indicators of Less Valid Reporting

Three indicators of less valid reporting led to the identification of groups of respondents who gave television viewing reports of questionable accuracy. The indicator variables are described in more detail below.

One of the indicators of less valid reporting was based on the dummy programs inserted on each page of the program checklists. It was hypothesized that respondents who claim to view nonexistent programs may also err in the reporting of actual programs. Although most children did not claim to view such programs, some did, and some even claimed viewing all three of the dummy programs listed among television series every time they were on. It seemed likely that such children also claimed viewing actual programs they did not see. Analyses reported below suggest that this indeed was the case.

The second indicator was based on analyses showing that some people are likely to mark the extreme values on scales such as those used in the program checklists even though such answers do not correspond to their actual behavior. These respondents usually claim to watch programs every time they are shown over the period asked about when, in fact, they watch them only every other time or nearly every time they are shown.

We found that some children gave such undifferentiated viewing reports. In most cases, they checked primarily high extreme values, that is, they indicated that they watched most of the programs listed in the specific time period asked about every time they were aired.[32]

Since such a response pattern implies an exaggeration and distortion of viewing reports, checking high extreme values was also used as an indicator of less valid reporting.

The third indicator involved claims of viewing two or more programs shown at the same time nearly every time they are aired. This is only possible if the respondent starts watching one program and switches, at least once, to another. It is certainly possible that children do this some of the time. However, it seemed unlikely that many would do this nearly always. Starting in Wave II, we listed about five such situations in the program checklists and considered suspicious a response pattern in which at least three of these resulted in reports that both programs were seen just about every time they were aired.[33] In fact,

[32]A reasonable explanation for such a response pattern is that they have watched most of the programs listed at some time or other—not necessarily in the "past 4 weeks," the time period we asked about. This confusion about the time period leads to marking many more high values than zeros.

[33]There were a few simultaneously aired programs in the Wave I lists, but we had not included them with the purpose of identifying "less valid" reporters. As a result, this indicator is not as powerful in Wave I as in other waves.

we found some children reported such a viewing pattern for all program pairs in the television checklist. This response pattern, too, has the effect of exaggerating viewing level and was used as a third indicator of less valid reporting.

The three indicators are related, suggesting a reporting syndrome of invalidity. Marking dummy programs is weakly to moderately related to the other two indicators ($r = .34$, with high extremity response pattern; $r = .40$ with claimed viewing of simultaneously televised programs); the high extremity response pattern and claimed viewing of simultaneously televised programs are highly related ($r = .80$).[34]

Children who report such questionable viewing information tended to be younger, to have lower grades, and to score lower on measured IQ, and they were more often reported to be slow readers by their teachers (Stipp, 1975:323). It is not surprising, then, that the higher a child's score on the indicators, the worse the outcome on the validity tests described below.

Variables Indicating Less Valid Reporting

DUMMY PROGRAMS

As described, the dummy variable used as an indicator of less valid reporting simply counts the number of such programs selected on the checklists with television series. (The television movie dummy was not counted.)

The variable was dichotomized as follows: no dummy marked = "low," one, two, or three dummies marked = "high." Analyses indicated that even those who marked only one dummy but scored high on another indicator were less valid reporters.

Table B.2 shows the number of respondents—in Wave IV—who marked 0, 1, 2, or 3 dummy programs.

EXTREMITY RESPONSE PATTERN

A (high) extremity response pattern was identified by examining two types of information simultaneously: the number of programs reported seen and the proportion of high extreme values checked on those programs (that is, "fours" in the case of weekly and "fives" in the case of daily programs). The validity analyses indicated that marking a large proportion of high extreme values was indicative of less accurate reporting only when respondents reported viewing a large proportion of the programs listed (see Stipp, 1975:299–302; 455–480). Consequently, a questionable response pattern was indicated when a respondent claimed viewing half or more of the programs listed and marked high extreme values for three-quarters of those programs, or when he claimed

[34]All correlations are based on Wave IV, the wave in which the validity analyses were conducted.

viewing three-quarters of the programs and marked high extreme values for more than half of them.[35]

Table B.1 shows the definition of the "extremity response pattern." (See Table B.2 for the number of cases in each of these categories.) In the dichotomy 0 is "low" and 1, 2, and 3 are "high." Respondents who scored high on this and on another indicator were classified as "less valid." Most of those who scored high on this variable (including those who scored "1") also scored high on another indicator of less valid reporting.

VIEWING OF PROGRAMS TELEVISED SIMULTANEOUSLY

This variable was computed to indicate the extent to which the respondent claimed regular viewing of programs (of equal length) shown at the same time. Here, also, two types of information were considered: How many pairs of simultaneously shown programs the respondent claimed to have watched regularly, and the regularity with which these pairs of programs were viewed.

In Wave IV, eight pairs of programs were listed (giving a possible range from 0 to 8). On each of those pairs, the respondent could indicate that he watched both programs every time they were shown. (This would suggest that he constantly switched from one to the other program every time they were on.) The respondent was given a score of 3 for every pair marked in this way, the most suspicious reporting pattern, for a possible high score of 24 for the eight pairs. Respondents who marked one of two programs shown simultaneously as seen every time it was on and the other as seen three times out of four (in the case of weekly programs) are still indicating a rather unusual viewing pattern. But as they showed some discrimination by indicating that they watched one program more often than the other, this was regarded as less suspicious and it was decided to score this response pattern with a 1. (It was not possible to test whether another scoring system would have produced a significantly better indicator.) If a respondent indicated any lesser degree of regularity of watching such pairs of programs, he received a score of 0. (Ratings data indicate that there is some channel switching and that people do not watch the same programs every time they are shown.)

Validity analyses suggested that those who scored 0 on this variable gave valid reports, whereas those with a score of 6 or more—respondents who claimed to view regularly at least two of the eight pairs of programs—gave less valid reports. Those scoring 1–5 ("medium") were accurate reporters unless

[35]The exact cutoff point between a suspicious and a nonsuspicious response pattern could not be determined through the validity analyses because of the small number of cases between, for example, those marking 75% and 70% extreme values. However, the analyses suggest that this cutoff point is close to the optimal cutoff point.

TABLE B.1
Extremity Response Variables: Definition of Categories

	NUMBER OF SHOWS MARKED AS SEEN	PERCENTAGE OF SHOWS MARKED AS SEEN WHERE THE HIGH EXTREME VALUE IS MARKED
0 (low)	0–17	Any
	18–27	< 75
	28–38	< 51
1 (medium)	18–27	75–100
2 (high)	28–38	51–74
3 (extreme)	28–38	75–100

TABLE B.2
Distribution of Scores on Three Indicators of Less Valid Reporting[a]

VARIABLE	SCORE	DESCRIPTION OF CATEGORY	IN WAVE IV[b] *N*	%
Dummy shows	0 (Low)	No TV series dummy marked	(1026)	81
	1 (Medium)	One out of three TV series dummies marked	(152)	12
	2 (High)	Two or three out of three marked	(81)	6
Extremity response pattern	0 (Low)	Low or medium viewers, no high extreme response	(1028)	81
	1 (Medium)	Medium viewers, some high extreme response	(54)	4
	2 (High)	High viewers, medium high extreme response pattern	(99)	8
	3 (Very high)	High viewers and high extreme response pattern	(78)	6
Viewing of programs televised simultaneously variable	0 (Low)	Score of 0 out of 24	(758)	60
	1 (Medium)	Score of 1–5	(296)	24
	2 (High)	Score of 6–9	(102)	8
	3 (Very high)	Score of 10–24	(103)	8

[a]Dotted lines indicate how variables were collapsed.
[b]Sample includes boys and girls.

they also scored high on the dummy variable or on both other indicators (see Stipp, 1975: 302–304; 455–460). Thus, this indicator was collapsed into three categories: 0 ("low"), 1 ("medium"), and 2 and 3 ("high"). Table B.2 shows the number of cases in each of the categories.

CLASSIFICATION OF VALID AND LESS VALID REPORTERS

Respondents scoring low on at least two of the three indicators were classified as valid reporters. Those who scored high on at least two indicators were classified as "less valid."

Table B.3 gives a more detailed picture of the classification.

Validity Tests

Respondents were classified as "less valid reporters" if they scored high on at least two of the three indicators of less valid reporting. In this appendix section, we summarize results of a series of tests indicating that those classified as less valid reporters did, in fact, give less accurate information about their television viewing.

First, the reports about viewing of prime-time programs listed on the checklists were compared with commercial ratings in a number of tests. One of these tests compared Wave IV viewing reports with Nielsen ratings covering the same period (May 1971). Table B.4 shows the correlations between the two kinds of data for those scoring "low" on the three indicators of less valid reporting and for the total sample. Correlations with the ratings are higher for respondents scoring low on an indicator ($r = .93$, .92, .93 respectively) than for the total sample ($r = .89$). This is because reports by respondents scoring high on an indicator have much lower correlations with the ratings (between .44 and .68; see Stipp, 1975:318).[36]

Second, we conducted a test of sex differences in viewing patterns, again using ratings as criterion measures. Two exposure scores were computed for each respondent: one, exposure to "boys' programs," the other, exposure to "girls' programs." "Boys' programs" were those programs found by commercial research to be more popular with boys, "girls' programs" those found to be more popular with girls. Those children scoring low on each of the three indicators of less valid reporting exhibited distinctive viewing differences by sex: Boys watched relatively more boys' programs and girls watched relatively

[36]An additional test controlled for some of the differences between the Nielsen sample and our sample of respondents. Since the ratings services oversampled middle-class respondents to some extent, we compared ratings with respondents in our sample who attended middle-class schools ($N = 686$). Again we found that those scoring high on each of the indicators of less valid reporting agree less with the ratings than those who score low.

TABLE B.3
Classification of Valid and Less Valid Respondents

DUMMY PROGRAM	EXTREMITY RESPONSE	VIEWING OF PROGRAMS TELEVISED SIMULTANEOUSLY	CLASSIFICATION
0 (low)	0 (low)	0 (low)	Valid
0 (low)	1, 2, 3 (high)	0 (low)	Valid
0 (low)	1, 2, 3 (high)	1 (medium)	Valid
0 (low)	1, 2, 3 (high)	2, 3 (high)	Less valid
1, 2, 3 (high)	0 (low)	0 (low)	Valid
1, 2, 3 (high)	0 (low)	1 (medium) or 2, 3 (high)	Less valid
1, 2, 3 (high)	1, 2, 3 (high)	1 (medium) or 2, 3 (high)	Less valid

more girls' programs. Differences in viewing patterns were smaller in the total sample, which includes those presumed to be less accurate reporters.

Third, we converted the television exposure scores from Wave IV (May 1971) into rough hours-per-week estimates.[37] Data by ratings services and other research suggest that children watch about 20 hr per week in May. Table B.5 shows that the reported amount of viewing for those who score low on the indicators of less valid reporting is very close to these estimates. However, when those scoring high on the indicators are included in the sample, the mean is raised to about 27 hr per week. The reason is that those scoring high, the "less valid reporters," report suspiciously high viewing levels (about 50 hr per week on average) in addition to the other inaccuracies and inconsistencies.[38]

Fourth, one of the most conclusive validity tests compared questionnaire exposure reports with viewing data obtained through elaborate interviews probing the child's viewing on the previous day. Interviews conducted with a number of children who had received either high or low scores on the dummy

[37]See Stipp (1975:325–328). As pointed out above, the exposure measure was not designed to provide precise data on the number of viewing hours and minutes and, as a result, these hours-per-week figures are rough estimates. They are, however, useful to compare the reported viewing of different groups.

[38]Further, comparisons between the amount of viewing reported by our elementary school sample and our sample of teenage boys shows the same differences between children's and adolescents' viewing as reported by the ratings services. Overall, children watch more than teenagers, especially during the afternoon and Saturday mornings. However, they watch less than teens after prime time, 10 P.M. central time. (Since we did not use identical exposure measures for elementary school children and teens, a precise comparison is not possible. This comparison was made on the basis of the average amount of viewing reported per program in the various time periods.)

TABLE B.4

Correlations between Viewing Reports of Prime-Time Programs Based on Commercial Ratings[a] and on Respondents with Low Scores on the Three Indicators of Less Valid Reporting[b]

INDICATORS OF LESS VALID REPORTING	*r*	*N*
"Dummy" variable; 0 low	.93	(1026)
"Extremity response pattern" variable; 0 low	.92	(1028)
"Claimed viewing of simultaneously televised programs" variable; 0 low	.93	(758)
Total sample	.89	(1259)

[a]Nielsen, NTI/NAC report; May 1971 (children 6–11).
[b]Sample includes boys and girls.

variable supported the conclusion that "less valid" respondents' viewing reports are exaggerated and distorted (Stipp, 1975:346–349).

A comparison of interview data and questionnaire reports shows that those who score high on the indicators of less valid reporting do tend to be somewhat heavier viewers than other respondents. However, their questionnaire reports claim much higher viewing levels than the interviews suggest.[39] At the same time, these interviews supported the conclusion that reports by respondents who score low on the indicators are valid.

The results of this test are especially important, since in the tests just discussed it could not be ruled out that disagreements between ratings data and reports by our respondents were due to actual differences in viewing behavior. However, in this test, both types of data, questionnaire reports and interviews, were obtained from the same children.

Fifth, we conducted an analysis of the correlates of television exposure among valid reporters and compared our findings with those obtained in previous studies dealing with children's television behavior. The analysis revealed that relationships between viewing and more than a dozen variables (including socioeconomic background, parents' viewing, and the child's IQ and use of other media) agreed with other researchers' findings in practically all instances. These analyses represent another test of concurrent validity, though

[39]The interviews revealed that most of those who score high on indicators of validity had difficulty remembering yesterday's viewing and reported their viewing inaccurately. (We were able to determine this because of the design of the test: We asked respondents about the content of the programs seen and compared their description with the actual program content, which was usually known to us through monitoring the day before the interview most programs popular with children.) It was no wonder, then, that many of these respondents found it difficult to report their viewing accurately during the last 4 weeks in the questionnaire.

TABLE B.5

Amount of Viewing[a] Reported by Respondents with Low Scores on the Three Indicators of Less Valid Reporting[a]

INDICATORS	ESTIMATE OF HOURS OF VIEWING PER WEEK[b]	N
"Dummy" variable; 0 low	24	(1026)
"Extremity response pattern" variable; 0 low	22	(1028)
"Claimed viewing of simultaneously televised programs" variable; 0 low	18	(758)
Total sample	27	(1259)

[a] Sample includes boys and girls.
[b] Based on converted television exposure scores.

much weaker than the evidence just discussed. At the same time, the data provide an interesting portrait of the characteristics of high and low television viewers. For example, we found that high viewers tend to be from a low-income background and to have to low IQs, but they do not seem to have emotional problems or to be isolated.[40]

APPENDIX C: TELEVISION EXPOSURE: SUPPLEMENTARY TABLES

TABLE C.1

Violent Television Exposure Measure: Descriptive Statistics for All Six Waves (Data Based on Less Valid Reporters)

STATISTIC	WAVE I	II	III	IV	V	VI
Median	101.2	115.5	104.8	103.3	90.5	85.0
Mean	98.7	114.8	109.5	102.0	92.6	87.8
Mode	103	95	98	111	89	73
Standard deviation	23.1	24.3	26.0	15.4	23.8	23.8
Range	41–142	47–164	60–177	58–143	22–139	42–138
Skewness	—.3	—.3	.3	—.1	—.3	.2
N	(181)	(188)	(133)	(107)	(86)	(47)

[40]The findings of the analyses are reported in Documentation 4D, "Correlates of TV Exposure."

TABLE C.2
Violent Television Exposure Measure: Descriptive Statistics for All Six Waves (Data Based on Total Sample)

STATISTIC	WAVE I	II	III	IV	V	VI
Median	60.1	72.6	64.5	51.4	46.5	44.2
Mean	61.3	74.9	68.0	54.6	51.3	48.9
Mode	27	80	68	66	43	38
Standard deviation	33.8	37.6	34.9	33.1	32.1	27.9
Range	0–142	0–164	0–177	0–143	0–139	0–138
Skewness	.3	.2	.4	.3	.5	.7
N	(734)	(651)	(658)	(653)	(500)	(287)

TABLE C.3
Violent Television Exposure Measure Over-Time Correlations in All Six Waves (Data Based on Less Valid Reporters in Both Waves)

WAVE PAIR	DURATION	PEARSON CORRELATIONS	*N*
III–IV	3 months	.452	(65)
II–III	4 months	.462	(80)
I–II	5 months	.371	(74)
II–IV	7 months	.378	(61)
I–III	9 months	.175	(60)
I–IV	1 year	.318	(47)
IV–V	1 year	.256	(28)
V–VI	1 year	.269	(22)
III–V	1 year 3 months	.215	(36)
II–V	1 year 7 months	.244	(34)
I–V	2 years	.283	(30)
IV–VI	2 years	.313	(18)
III–VI	2 years 3 months	.650	(18)
II–VI	2 years 7 months	.650	(21)
I–VI	3 years	.211	(15)

TABLE C.4

Violent Television Exposure Measure Over-Time Correlations in All Six Waves (Data Based on Total Sample in Both Waves)

WAVE PAIR	DURATION	PEARSON CORRELATIONS	*N*
III–IV	3 months	.731	(592)
II–III	4 months	.707	(582)
I–II	5 months	.657	(474)
II–IV	7 months	.652	(559)
I–III	9 months	.629	(456)
I–IV	1 year	.614	(438)
IV–V	1 year	.611	(363)
V–VI	1 year	.624	(246)
III–V	1 year 3 months	.574	(369)
II–V	1 year 7 months	.533	(354)
I–V	2 years	.487	(298)
IV–VI	2 years	.544	(203)
III–VI	2 years 3 months	.444	(205)
II–VI	2 years 7 months	.502	(192)
I–VI	3 years	.432	(176)

CHAPTER 5

CROSS-SECTIONAL CORRELATIONS AND THE LOGIC OF CAUSAL ANALYSIS

In this chapter, we examine whether a systematic relationship exists between exposure to violent television and aggression. The argument that exposure to televised violence leads children to behave aggressively implies at a minimum that the two measures covary. Although the existence of a correlation does not imply that two variables are causally linked, the absence of a correlation would strongly suggest that they are not.

Most research in the area of children and television has found a cross-sectional relationship between exposure to television violence and aggression (Eron, 1979; Singer, 1979; Surgeon General's Report, 1972). We begin this chapter by showing that our measures of television exposure and aggression also are correlated. We then discuss the various possible interpretations of this finding and the necessity for over-time analysis to investigate causality. In that context we compare the strength of the television–aggression relationship with other correlates of aggression and show that these other correlates can influence the relationship between exposure and aggression. Finally, we describe the logic of our analysis of television's causal effects.

CROSS-SECTIONAL CORRELATIONS

Table 5.1 shows the cross-sectional correlations of two exposure measures—total exposure and violence exposure—with the aggression measure in each wave, for the total sample including "less valid" reporters. As described in Chapter 4, the total exposure measure is computed by summing the reported

TABLE 5.1
Cross-Sectional Correlations between Measures of Total and Violent Television Exposure and Aggression

	TOTAL SAMPLES		
WAVE	TOTAL TELEVISION EXPOSURE	VIOLENT TELEVISION EXPOSURE	*N*
I	.217*	.225*	(734)
II	.100*	.130*	(603)
III	.144*	.158*	(639)
IV	.161*	.176*	(653)
V	.156*	.167*	(490)
VI	.187*	.190*	(283)

*Significant at the .05 level (see footnote 1).

amount of exposure to episodes of a long list of programs, and the violence exposure measure multiplies each program by a "violence" weight before summing.

Table 5.1 shows that both measures of exposure are weakly but positively correlated with aggression in all waves.[1] Correlations between the aggression measure and the violence exposure measure are slightly higher (an average correlation of .17) than those between aggression and total exposure (an average correlation of .16).[2]

The correlations presented in Table 5.1 are based on the total sample, that is, with less valid reporters of television exposure included. As discussed in the previous chapter, there are a number of reasons to believe that those boys we refer to as less valid reporters considerably exaggerated the amount of television they watch. In addition, as shown in Table 5.2, they also score higher on the aggression measure. Their median aggression scores are, on the average, nearly 50% higher than those of valid reporters.

Because they score so high on violent television exposure, and at the same time are more aggressive, their inclusion in Table 5.1 has caused the cross-sectional correlations to be higher than they would be were less valid reporters excluded. To demonstrate the extent to which less valid reporters inflate the

[1] We do not have a probability sample of children from some target population. However, we make use of traditional tests of statistical significance to judge the probability with which our sampling of six time points from an ongoing continuous process might lead us to infer the existence of causal connections between television exposure and aggressive behavior when none actually existed in the process as a whole.

[2] Although previous studies have generally not found total exposure to be correlated with aggression (Comstock, 1976), violent shows were oversampled in the present study and make up a substantial part of the total exposure score. In fact, as noted in Chapter 4, the correlation between the two scores is over .90, and this probably accounts for the correlation between aggression and total exposure in the present study.

TABLE 5.2
Median Aggression Scores by Validity of Television Reporting in All Six Waves

	VALID REPORTERS		LESS VALID REPORTERS		TOTAL[a]	
WAVE	MEDIAN	*N*	MEDIAN	*N*	MEDIAN	*N*
I	64	(553)	107	(181)	72	(734)
II	61	(428)	82	(175)	71	(603)
III	69	(510)	94	(129)	75	(639)
IV	72	(546)	107	(107)	75	(653)
V	72	(406)	100	(84)	77	(490)
VI	64	(236)	101	(47)	69	(283)

[a]Respondents with television data (Table 3.4, Statistics for Aggression Measure, includes respondents without television data).

overall correlation, we present Table 5.3, which shows correlations between both total exposure and violence exposure and aggression, separately for valid and less valid reporters. The correlations between total exposure and aggression among valid reporters average .09, about 45% lower than in the total sample. The correlations between violence exposure and aggression average .11, about 35% lower than in the total sample.[3]

The correlations reported in Table 5.3 are uncorrected for measurement unreliability, and hence are smaller than estimates of true correlations. Table 5.4 shows the same correlations, for valid television reporters only, after correction for unreliability in both the exposure and aggression scores.[4] The effect is to raise the correlation for the total exposure measure from an average of .09 to .12 and for the violence exposure measure from an average of .11 to .15. Although such increases represent substantial percentages, the absolute values of the corrected coefficients are small.

On the basis of these calculations, we estimate that the true relation between violent television exposure and aggression in this study is somewhere in the range of .10–.20.

[3]Correlations in both subsamples are smaller than those in the total sample. This is so because knowing whether or not a respondent is a valid reporter is a better predictor of his aggression than his reported television exposure is. However, since less valid reporting and the exposure score are positively related to each other, failing to control for validity of reporting, as in the analysis of the total sample, artificially inflates the relationship between exposure and aggression. This suggests that in other studies of elementary school children, reported correlations between aggression and self-reported television exposure are probably much higher than the true correlations, since none of these studies have taken "less valid" reporting into account.

[4]No measurement adjustments were made for the total sample, which includes less valid reporters, because it would be inappropriate to make reliability adjustments for data of questionable validity. (See discussion in Chapter 4 and Appendix C in Chapter 6.)

TABLE 5.3
Cross-Sectional Correlations between Measures of Total and Violent Television Exposure and Aggression by Validity of Television Reporting in All Six Waves

WAVE	VALID REPORTERS			LESS VALID REPORTERS		
	TOTAL TELEVISION EXPOSURE	VIOLENT TELEVISION EXPOSURE	*N*	TOTAL TELEVISION EXPOSURE	VIOLENT TELEVISION EXPOSURE	*N*
I	.099*	.130*	(553)	.111*	.088	(181)
II	.039	.081*	(428)	−.096	−.061	(175)
III	.083*	.106*	(510)	.172*	.179*	(129)
IV	.065	.098*	(546)	.211*	.185*	(107)
V	.093*	.096*	(406)	.137	.226*	(84)
VI	.153*	.172*	(236)	−.031	−.001	(47)

*Significant at the .05 level.

It is difficult to compare these correlations with those reported in other research, since the measures of television viewing and indicators of aggression used in those studies vary considerably from those used here (Comstock, 1978). For example, even though Lefkowitz *et al.* (1972) used an aggression measure very similar to ours for their third-grade sample, their television measure was completely different (it was not an exposure, but a favorite show measure.) Showing that two measures are related, however, says very little about causal connections between them. The point-in-time correlations just stated could be generated by a variety of causes, but three general determinants may be postulated:

1. Exposure to televised violence leads children to behave aggressively.

TABLE 5.4
Cross-Sectional Correlations between Measures of Total and Violent Television Exposure and Aggression, Corrected for Measurement Unreliability,[a] Valid Reporters

WAVE	TOTAL TELEVISION EXPOSURE	VIOLENT TELEVISION EXPOSURE	*N*
I	.163*	.168*	(553)
II	.052	.104*	(428)
III	.099*	.124*	(510)
IV	.071	.117*	(546)
V	.137*	.127*	(406)
VI	.224*	.227*	(236)

[a] Reliability estimates for aggression are the Heise-Bohrnstedt Ω. Reliability estimates for television are discussed in Appendix C in Chapter 6.

*Significant at the .05 level.

2. Aggressive children differentially select violent programs on television.
3. Some unexamined third variable(s) lead(s) children both to select violent programs differentially and to behave aggressively.

It is also possible, of course, that two or more causal processes are at work simultaneously and that these build up to create the relationships observed in Table 5.4.

Later in this chapter, we discuss the logic of our analysis of these rival explanations. Before doing so, we present some evidence bearing on the possibility that some third variable(s) lead(s) children both to watch violent programs and to behave aggressively.

OTHER CORRELATES OF AGGRESSION

We carried out a series of analyses to see how the various background variables contained in the data set related to violent television exposure and to the aggression scale. We did this to learn something about the mutual correlates of television and aggression. This provided some insight into possible sources of spuriousness in the television–aggression relationship, and it also convinced us that the television and aggression scales behaved as would be expected in correlations with outside predictors (a test of concurrent validity). We report here some of the results of the aggression correlation analyses to place the television–aggression correlations just reported into better perspective.[5] Further, we can examine the extent to which these correlations are spurious—that is, attributable to the correlation of both television exposure and aggression to some antecedent variable(s).

Table 5.5 presents a rank ordering of all predictors we examined that have average correlations greater than or equal to .10 with aggression in the six waves [6] Some 34 variables or clusters of variables out of about 100 examined are presented. (The table also gives the strength of the relationship and indicates how many of the six correlations obtained for each variable are significant at the .05 level.)

One very important reason to examine Table 5.5 is that it gives us our first glimpse of what the antisocial aggressive boy is like. For example, we learn that he is more likely to be found in environments where there are many aggressive

[5]See Documentation 5, "Correlates of Aggression," for details. Correlations of television exposure are discussed in Documentation 4B.

[6]Most relationships under .10 are insignificant. For nominal variables the measure of association is the correlation ratio (η).

Average correlations—and also average partial regression coefficients—are adopted in this report to summarize extensive analyses. These averages should be interpreted only as measures of central tendency in the distributions of parameters.

TABLE 5.5
Correlates of Aggression (Summary Table)

	AVERAGE CORRELATION WITH AGGRESSION IN SIX WAVES	NUMBER OF SIGNIFICANT COEFFICIENTS IN SIX WAVES	RANK
Four measures of aggression of boy's friends[a] (highly aggressive)[b]	.56 to .38	(6)	1
Aggression of total class (highly aggressive)	.33	(6)	2
Emotional instability [teacher nominations] (unstable)	.33	(6)	2
Plays make-believe [peer nominations] (plays make-believe)	.32	(6)	4
Silly [teacher nominations] (silly)	.30	(6)	5
Average grade in school (high)	−.27	(6)	6
Need for approval from other children [teacher nominations] (needs approval)	.25	(6)	7
Mother's occupation/education (professional/college)	−.25/−.16	(6)(3)	7
Parents' feelings about raising boy when young (difficult)	.24	(6)	9
Father hits son (often)	.23	(6)	10
Parents' support for physical aggression (high)	.19	(5)	11
Father yells at son (often)	.19	(4)	12
Family income (high)	−.18	(4)	13
Mother yells at son (often)	.18	(6)	13
Mother takes away privileges (often)	.18	(5)	13
Violent television exposure/total sample	.17	(6)	16
Shared activities (family does many things together)	−.16	(6)	17
Family religiosity (religious)	−.16	(6)	17
Mother's frustration (high)	.16	(4)	17
Violent television exposure/valid sample/adjusted for error	.15	(6)	19
Enjoyment of violence in movie scenes (like violence)	.15	(5)	19
Family type (natural mother and father/natural parent and step parent/natural mother only)	.15	(4)	19
Family size (large)	.14	(5)	22
Parents' feelings about pregnancy (upset)	.14	(5)	22
Father's activities with boy during early years (many activities)	−.14	(3)	22

(Continued next page)

TABLE 5.5 *(continued)*

	AVERAGE CORRELATION WITH AGGRESSION IN SIX WAVES	NUMBER OF SIGNIFICANT COEFFICIENTS IN SIX WAVES	RANK
Father's acceptance of force in child rearing (pro-force)	.13	(2)	25
Exposure to violent theater movies (high)	.13	(4)	25
Mother/father act out frustrations (often)	.12/.12	(4/1)	Both 27
Violent television exposure/valid sample/not adjusted for error	.11	(6)	29
Exposure to violent comic books (high)	.11	(4)	29
Exposure to magazines (high)	.11	(5)	29
Sex of siblings (none/brothers/sisters/both)	.11	(0)	29
Need for approval from teachers [teacher nominations] (needs approval)	.11	(5)	29
Large for age [teacher nominations] (large)	.11	(4)	29

[a]Closest friends, boys with whom time is spent in/out of school, who boy would "like to be."

[b]End of scale with high numerical value is shown in parentheses. For nominal variables, all categories are listed. For more detail on many of these variables, see Chapter 7 (section on subgroups). Additional descriptions of the variables are available on request.

boys. He is identified by teachers as someone who is emotionally unstable and is seen by peers as engaging in fantasy and being silly. He is a poor student and is socially insecure. He has many siblings and both parents were upset when they first learned that the wife was pregnant. After his birth, they felt that he was difficult to raise. His father often hits him and both parents shout at him. His family has little money, is not religious, and does few things together. His mother would, if given the chance, prefer to live most of her life over again differently.

It is clear that the aggressive boy had problems even before he was born and that his present situation is decidedly unpleasant in a variety of ways.

We are also interested in the relative importance of television exposure as a correlate of aggression. This importance varies somewhat depending on which of our several estimates of exposure we consider. If we take the average correlation between violent television exposure and aggression in the total sample, television ranks 16th in correlation among the 34 in this table. If, instead, we take the adjusted correlation among valid reporters, television is

19th in importance. Or, if we consider the unadjusted relationship between television and aggression among valid reporters, television falls to 29th.[7]

MUTUAL CORRELATES OF AGGRESSION AND VIOLENT TELEVISION EXPOSURE

In this section, we present some evidence concerning the *cross-sectional* association between violent television exposure and aggression, controlling for some of the other predictors of aggression considered in Table 5.5. We do this to show the extent to which the basic relationships observed in Tables 5.1–5.4 are changed by introducing various controls.

We have limited ourselves in this exercise in two ways. First, even though we can see in Table 5.5 that a number of potential control variables are more highly related to aggression than television, we have considered only those that are most clearly possible *causes* of aggression rather than its effects or concomitants. And, second, we have limited ourselves within this restricted set to those variables that are clearly not caused by television exposure, even though they are empirically related to exposure. In this way, we can be sure that any change can be attributed to partial elimination of the spurious common causal influence of the controls on aggression and television. Here we will look at the relationship between television and aggression in the total sample.

The results of this analysis, presented in Table 5.6, are more complicated than they might otherwise be because we have made use of some control variables that are not available for every boy in the sample. The variables we consider are: (*a*) quality of television reporting, a dummy variable coded 1 if the respondent is a less valid reporter, 0 otherwise; (*b*) race, a dummy variable coded 1 if the respondent is white, 0 otherwise; and (*c*) SES, measured by family income and mother's occupation (including housewife). The two rows at the top of the table present the zero-order correlations between exposure and aggression, in each of the six waves, for the following samples: (*a*) the total sample, among whom we can assess the influence of reporting quality; (*b*) the sample consisting of boys with complete race and SES data, among whom we can assess the influence of reporting quality, race, and SES. The three rows at the bottom of the table present partial correlations between television exposure and aggression under various control conditions.

[7]Most of the other correlates examined were measured only once, and none of the correlations were adjusted. If other measures had been obtained in all six waves, and if all correlations had been adjusted, television would undoubtedly rank lower.

TABLE 5.6
Zero-Order and Partial Correlations between Exposure to Violent Television and Aggression (Total Sample)[a]

	WAVE						SIX-WAVE AVERAGE
	I	II	III	IV	V	VI	
Zero-order correlations							
Complete total sample (as shown in Table 5.1)	.23* (734)	.13* (603)	.16* (639)	.18* (653)	.17* (490)	.19* (283)	.17
Total sample with quality of reporting, race, and SES data	.15* (335)	.15* (278)	.14* (278)	.23* (261)	.24* (166)	.21* (95)	.19
Partial correlations							
Controlling for:							
Quality of reporting	.12* (731)	.04 (600)	.12* (636)	.10* (650)	.12* (487)	.14* (279)	.11
Quality of reporting and race	.11* (730)	.04 (599)	.11* (635)	.09* (649)	.09* (486)	.11* (278)	.09
Quality of reporting, race, and SES	.02 (331)	−.01 (274)	.01 (274)	.04 (257)	.22* (164)	.10 (91)	.06

[a]*N*s are given in parentheses.
*Significant at .05 level.

With the exception of Wave V, the results across columns are quite similar.[8] First, by controlling quality of reporting the observed relationships between exposure and aggression are reduced by a third, from an average of .17 to one of .11. Nonetheless, five of the six correlations remain significant. Next, in the more restricted sample of respondents for whom race and SES data are available, a further control for race along with quality of reporting reduces the observed relationship between television and aggression by about 50%, from an average correlation of .19 to one of .09. Here again, though, five of the six correlations remain significant. Finally, when we introduce a control for family SES along with quality of reporting and race, we reduce the average correlation even more, about 70%, from .19 to .06. Furthermore, only one of the six coefficients remains significant under this condition.[9]

These results indicate that a substantial part of the relationship between violent television viewing and aggression can be explained by the facts that

[8]We do not have an explanation for the Wave V finding.

[9]The results of this analysis based on the restricted sample of valid reporters leads to very similar conclusions.

nonwhites, respondents from lower SES backgrounds, and those who gave comparatively less valid viewing reports are both rated by their classmates as more aggressive and report watching more violent TV than other children in their classes. Once we control for the influence of these three variables, a significant cross-sectional association between television viewing and aggression remains only in Wave V.[10]

It appears, then, that subsequent causal analyses are based on very small and unstable associations. Still, there might be other mutual causes of television and aggression that work in a different way, being positively associated with one of the two variables and negatively with the other. Were we to find a control variable of this sort—which we did not in our examination of the control variables collected as part of the study—an adjustment for this mutual determination would *increase* the association between television aggression, not decrease it. Therefore, our ability to explain away a large part of the television–aggression relationship with these controls does not put an end to the question of whether or not television has a direct causal effect on aggression. It is this question to which we address ourselves in subsequent analyses.

MODEL OF CAUSAL ANALYSIS

As noted, the small remaining correlations between television exposure and aggression could be generated by three kinds of causal processes: Television exposure leads to increased aggressiveness; or aggressive children tend to select violent television programs; or some third variable(s)—still unexamined—lead both to aggression and television exposure.

In experimental research these various causal possibilities are sorted out by random assignment of respondents to experimental and control groups (thus assuring that initial characteristics unrelated to the experiment are distributed randomly across the various groups) and active manipulation of the experimental variables. For example, randomly composed groups of children might be differentially assigned to watch television programs that emphasize themes thought to influence their subsequent behaviors. If the groups differ

[10]McLeod *et al.* (1972), who used an exposure measure similar to ours, did not find that controls for SES and race reduced the cross-sectional correlations between television and aggression substantially. The reason may well be that there is little variation in the socioeconomic status of their respondents. Their Wisconsin sample, for example, was all white, and the researchers describe their Maryland sample as "atypical in being somewhat higher than average on various measures of socioeconomic status [1972, 174]." In contrast, our sample was selected in such a way that considerable variation in socioeconomic status was guaranteed. We have both lower-class blacks and affluent professional families. For example, 12% of our boys have fathers who did not go to school beyond the eighth grade, and 19% have fathers who graduated from college.

beyond chance on a criterion behavior measure, we could infer that exposure influenced this difference in behavior.

We rejected the use of an experiment to test a hypothesis about the influence of television violence on children's aggression because we could not think of one that would be both realistic and long term. Experiments on this subject tend to be so far removed from reality that the results can not be generalized to the real world. There is very little experimenters can do to redress this problem: the very procedures they use to build into their designs to rule out rival causal hypotheses, make the results dependable but unrealistic.[11]

Instead, the approach used in this study is a panel survey design. Here individuals are selected and followed over time in their natural environment. The key measures—in this instance, television exposure and aggression—are obtained at several points in time.

Although the controls possible in experimental research cannot be duplicated in panel research, the panel is a "quasi-experimental" design (Campbell & Stanley, 1963; Cook & Campbell, 1979), which means that it approximates an experiment. It does this by using over-time data to study the relationship between television exposure and later aggression and, at the same time, statistically controls for the initial relationship between exposure and aggression. Together these two features—over-time analysis and statistical control—approximate the controlled conditions and randomization that characterize an experimental design.

Basic Model

The basic model of this approach, expressed here in linear terms, is the following equation for respondent i:

$$A_{t_i} = a + b_1 A_{(t-1)_i} + b_2 TV_{(t-1)_i} + u_i \qquad (1)$$

In the equation, the lagged influences of violent television exposure (TV) and aggression (A) at time $t-1$ are studied, with the individual's prediction error indicated by u_i. The outcome of interest is aggression measured at time t.

Note that the lagged aggression measure, $A_{(t-1)}$, is included as a predictor along with the lagged exposure measure, $TV_{(t-1)}$. As a result, this model effectively rules out any influence on the television effect caused by the initial correlation between earlier television and aggression, and, hence, also the influences of the causal forces that created that initial correlation. This model also ensures that any observed television–aggression association cannot be due

[11]As discussed previously, the problem of artificial experiment conditions is especially pronounced in this field of research: It would be unethical to simulate serious aggression realistically in experiments.

to an influence from a tendency of previously aggressive children to self-select violent programs. Any such effect will be part of the initial correlation and thus will be controlled out. In the absence of any other causes of aggression that are related to $TV_{(t-1)}$, the coefficient b_2 thus yields an unbiased estimate of television's lagged causal influence on aggression.

This quasi-experimental panel analysis approach reduces considerably the ambiguity about the possible causal role of television exposure on aggression. Still, it does not eliminate it altogether.

Limitations of the Analysis Model

In this model, just as in cross-sectional surveys, unmeasured common causes of violent television exposure and aggression can spuriously affect results. Since we control earlier aggression in our time-lagged model, these possible influences form a more restricted class than in cross-sectional surveys: unmeasured factors can show earlier television to be spuriously related to later aggression only if they relate to the earlier level of exposure and affect change in aggression over the interval of the panel.

For example, consider the influence of a young boy's peer group in which action and adventure are stressed. As part of a syndrome of attitudes, values, and behaviors, the children in this group might both engage in aggressive acts and watch programs with violent content on television. An initiate in this group will be first influenced to take on the external trappings of membership—styles of dress, manner, or speech, and possibly exposure to certain popular television shows. Only at a later point in his socialization will he become engaged in the more serious behaviors characteristic of membership, including various types of aggressive behavior.

If such a child is considered in our basic model, we might spuriously conclude that television has influenced him to change his behavior in an aggressive fashion. After all, his change in behavior is preceded by exposure to violent television programs. In reality, of course, the influence of the peer group accounts for both the exposure and the subsequent change in behavior.

In the analysis, we have been attentive to the possibility that our results are influenced by such unmeasured common causes of television viewing and subsequent aggression. The lagged panel relationships reported in the following are analyzed with this caution in mind.

One other qualification of this research design is that it only addresses the possibility of television effects over specified time spans—ranging from 3 months to 3 years. It is possible to determine whether the influence of violence exposure has an impact on children only within the limits of this availability—that is, over a few months, over 1 year, over 2 years, or over 3 years, not longer than 3 years. One can investigate causal hypotheses dealing with television exposure before the first wave by using retrospective data, but not with the same rigor as within the study's time frame.

If the data are collected so as to misspecify the time period over which a predictor has its impact on a dependent variable, the estimates of causal impact will be biased. It can be shown, however, that when the dependent variable is relatively stable over time, as it is in the case of aggression in the 3 years of our panel, this dilution of the true causal impact will not be serious so long as the misspecification is not extreme. For example, if the true impact of television violence manifests itself after a 9-month delay, any longitudinal study that includes lags of 1 year, 2 years, and 3 years will not err by a large amount in estimating this true influence. Because we find that the stability of aggression is high over these 3 years, any true causal influence within these limits will not be drastically distorted. If, however, the true influence of television appears only many years after the exposure, our design will not capture this influence.[12]

In the analysis of elementary school boys and girls, presented in the following chapters, we use this approach to causal analysis in the form of the two-wave, linear–additive model described in Eq. (1). In addition, we consider certain nonlinear and nonadditive modifications. In the analysis of teenage boys, we use two somewhat different approaches; one is a multiwave linear–additive model, the other a two-wave log–linear model. These various models are discussed as they are introduced into the analysis (Chapter 12). For the moment, though, we are concerned more with their common logic than with their differences.

ALTERNATIVE ANALYSIS APPROACHES

In an effort to select the best possible method of analysis, we were guided by two considerations. First, our independent and dependent variables can be considered interval scales rather than ordinal or categorical.[13] Second, ours is an "asymmetric" question: that is, we are primarily concerned with the extent to

---

[12]Of course, transient aggressive reactions will not be captured by this design, either, unless they contribute to a pattern stable enough to be seen after 3 months. For a technical discussion of the statements on causal lags made in this section, see Pelz and Lew (1970:28–37) or Kessler and Greenberg (1981).

[13]The scale of exposure to televised violence measures frequency of exposure, a ratio scale, weighted by a "violence weight." Weighting procedures affect the interval nature of the measure, unless it is assumed that the weighting scheme itself is an interval scale. Clearly, this is not at all a certainty, and as a result the measure of exposure to violence is not strictly interval.

Two considerations make this problem tractable. First, children in the study population seem to watch television rather indiscriminately with respect to the violence weights used here, so that

(Continued next page)

which exposure to television violence influences the subsequent behaviors of children exposed. Although we are also interested in the reciprocal impact of aggressive behavior as a factor in determining the preferences of children for violent television programs, this is of secondary concern only.

Two widely known methods of panel analysis address the question of reciprocal influences of two variables on each other over time. These two methods begin with the premise that both causal processes are at work. They ask, in effect: Given the observed cross-sectional correlation between exposure and aggression, which one of the two variables was more powerful in bringing about the other? Is the stronger causal process one in which aggressive children seek out television fare that reinforces their previously acquired behaviors and values? Or is the opposite process stronger, so that television content changes previously nonaggressive children to aggressive ones?

Sixteen-fold Tables

The oldest technique for addressing this question is Lazarsfeld's 16-fold table technique (1948). This method makes use of a cross-classification of two dichotomized variables, each measured at two points in time. By comparing various combinations of cell counts, this method produces an "index of mutual effects," which describes the relative importance of each of the two variables in bringing about changes in the other.[14]

---

the overall correlations between the raw exposure counts and the weighted violence exposure scores in each wave average around .92. For all practical purposes, then, the weighted scores can be considered interval scales of raw exposure. And second, it has generally been found that some distortion of a true interval scale (in this case, the true scale of exposure to violence) will not have a substantial impact on the substantive results obtained if (*a*) the scale has a broad range of values and (*b*) the scale is only a minor distortion of the true interval scale (Labovitz, 1971, 1972; O'Brian, 1980). Our scale of exposure has a range of about 150 points in each wave and, as noted above, is highly related to a true interval scale (raw count of exposure to television). The scale is, then, clearly appropriate for treatment as an interval scale.

The scale of aggressive behavior is a sum of peer reports of four separate actions considered aggressive: hitting, pushing and shoving, lying, and saying "mean things." Exploratory factor analyses showed that these four behaviors do indeed occur together, and, as is demonstrated in the appendices to Chapter 6, confirmatory factor analyses showed that the data fit a model that assumes an unmeasured interval scale of "true aggression" to determine the pairwise correlations among the four ratings. The four items are themselves interval, based as they are on percentage nominations for each of the behaviors. The scale has been created by summing the four percentage nominations. This method of scale construction produces results effectively identical to those obtained by constructing factor-weighted scales.

The correlations between factor-weighted scores and the regular aggression scores are about 99 in each of the six waves. For a conceptual discussion of the distinction between the two methods of scale construction, see Alwin (1973).

[14]Lazarsfeld also developed an asymmetric version of his 16-fold table technique, the 8-fold table method, which is logically identical to the procedure we use here. The logic is asymmetric

Cross-Lagged Correlations

The second technique, cross-lagged panel correlation (CLPC), was developed by Campbell (1963) as a continuous-variable counterpart to Lazarsfeld's 16-fold table procedure. In it, zero-order correlations between the cross-lagged variables—A1B2 and B1A2—are compared to estimate the relative causal influences of the two variables in bringing about an observed correlation, A2B2, at a point in time.

A number of investigations of possible causal connections between television exposure and aggression have made use of the CLPC technique in drawing causal inferences. (For example, Eron, 1979; Lefkowitz *et al.*, 1972; Singer & Singer, 1979.) But Bohrnstedt (1969), Duncan (1969, 1972), Heise (1970), Lazarsfeld (1973), and most recently Cook and Campbell (1979) and Rogosa (1980), have criticized the CLPC approach, noting that simple comparison of zero-order cross-lagged correlations confounds the effect of differential stability with differential causal influence. For example, if a larger correlation between X_1Y_2 than between Y_1X_2 is found, this approach fails to discriminate the influence of X on Y and the greater stability of Y than X in accounting for the difference in the correlations. (For a detailed discussion, see Kessler and Greenberg, 1981.) Accordingly, it is not clear whether findings in studies using this approach reflect the causal connections between measures or reflect, at least partially, differences in the stability of the measures.

Campbell's work has stimulated a series of discussions that have produced new approaches directly relevant to our problem (Bornstedt, 1969; Duncan, 1969, 1972; Heise, 1970, Jöreskog and Sörbom, 1975; Kenny, 1975). To correct for the shortcomings of the CLPC approach, a linear regression approach has been suggested to adjust for differential stability of the two variables through time by computing the partial regression of each Time 2 variable on the Time 1 value of the other, over and above the influence due to stability and to the relationship between the two variables at the time the study started. This is the approach we have used; we turn next to a discussion of the findings.

---

because initial values of the dependent variable (aggression in this case) and the predictor variable (television exposure in this case) are simultaneously used to predict subsequent change in the dependent variable only. A measure of the later predictor variable is not used.

In an earlier analysis of this same data set, Milavsky and Pekowsky (1972) made use of 8-fold tables. More detailed study showed, however, that the continuous-variable models, path analysis and confirmatory factor analysis, have advantages over the dichotomous version of the same logic. They allow us to use more of the data at our disposal.

In order to employ the 8-fold table technique on continous data, it is necessary to dichotomize these variables into arbitrary "high" and "low" groups. Choice of the point of division can greatly influence the results obtained. And such a procedure ignores variation within both of the initial high and low groups, thus losing much of the power of the continuous variables. These drawbacks make the use of continuous-variable models attractive in comparison.

As we just mentioned, we have not limited ourselves to a two-wave, linear–additive regression approach in the analyses that follow. Because of attrition problems in the elementary school sample, we have used two-wave models, but we have also considered nonlinear models as well as linear ones, and nonadditive models as well as additive ones. In the analysis of teenage boys we have additionally considered multiwave models and also some that are log-linear. These specific approaches will be discussed more fully as they are used.

CHAPTER 6

THE EFFECT OF TELEVISION VIOLENCE ON AGGRESSION: FINDINGS FROM THE BASIC MODEL

In the previous chapter we introduced the model

$$A_{t_i} = a + b_1 A_{(t-1)_i} + b_2 TV_{(t-1)_i} + u_i \qquad (1)$$

in which aggression at a later time is predicted from earlier levels of exposure, controlling for earlier aggression.

The ideal way of estimating this model is to work with a full six-wave generalization and simultaneously examine the causal relationships among all the variables in the six waves. However, because of the graduation of sixth graders, attrition, and "less valid" reporting, only 58 boys have aggression and valid television data in all waves. Therefore, a full six-wave analysis would be precarious. Besides yielding estimates that would be unstable because of the small sample size, this procedure would waste the information available for a much larger number of boys for whom we have data in some of the waves. Therefore, we worked with Eq. (1) over each of the 15 logically possible wave pairs separately.

This use of wave pair models creates a certain amount of redundancy, because the 15 wave pairs are not all independent of one another. There are only five wave pairs in which the beginning and the end points of the lags do not overlap with other panels and are therefore independent. (Those are wave pairs I–II, II–III, III–IV, IV–V, and V–VI.) The other 10 lags are overlapping, not adjacent, and so are not mutually independent.

An analysis with 15 wave pairs, therefore, uses the same information more than once. For example, let us assume that the true causal impact of television exposure I on aggression over Waves II and III is as shown in Figure 6.1A, with

A : "Full" I–II–III model

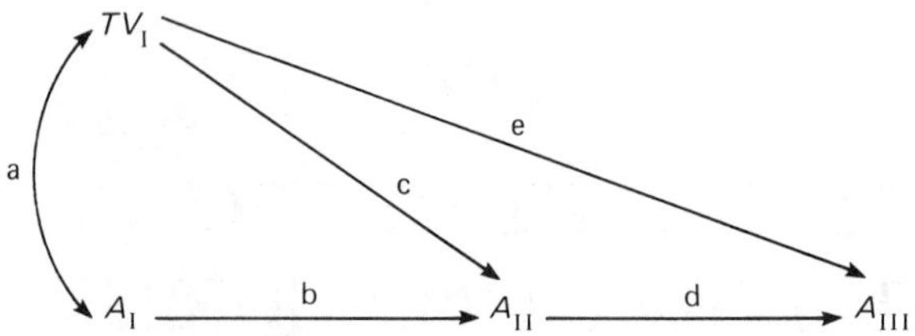

B : Reduced I–II model

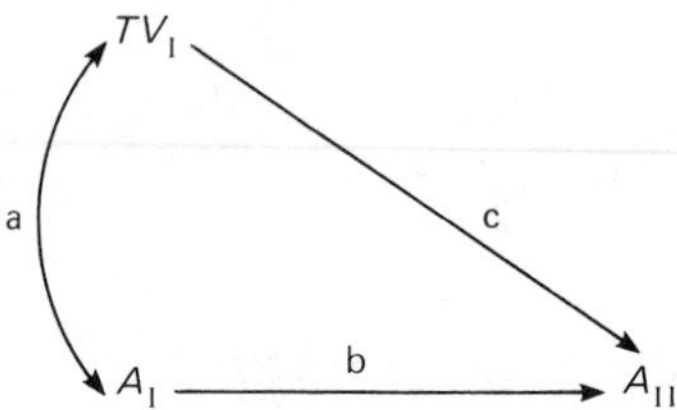

C : Reduced I–III model

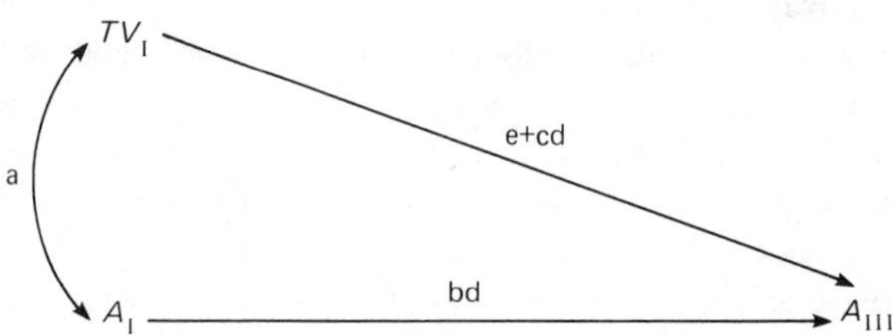

FIGURE 6.1. *"Full" and reduced models of the effect of television exposure on aggression.*

the impact (a standardized regression coefficient) on Aggression II equal to "*c*" and the impact on Aggression III equal to "*e*." A reduced two-wave model I–II (Figure 6.1B) would correctly capture the impact of *TV* I on Aggression II. However, the two-wave I–III model (Figure 6.1C) would not correctly express the causal impact of *TV* I on Aggression III, but instead add to it a part of the true impact of *TV* I on *A* II. Indeed, in this example, even if *TV* I had absolutely no independent impact on *A* III (that is, $e = 0$), we would still estimate an impact (*cd*) simply because of this redundancy.

Depending on the true causal structure relating the exposure scores and aggression scores measured over the full six waves of the study, various of the reduced two-wave models will contain redundant information of this type. However, without estimating the full six-wave model, which we are unable to do for practical reasons, we cannot know the extent to which this is the case. Nor can we reconstruct the full model from the 15 partial two-wave models, since identical values of the latter can be generated by quite different underlying values of the former.

A way of partially removing the redundancy from these models is to control all intervening measures of television exposure in each model separately. For instance, in the I–V model (which looks at the relationship between exposure in May 1970 and aggression in May 1972) we can control for television measured at times II, III, and IV, and focus on the relationship between *TV* I and Aggression V.

The results obtained in these models have removed from them the overlap effects of the television measures at the different waves of the panel.[1] However, these models also have a disadvantage: The television effect coefficients are less stable than the comparable parameter estimates in the two-wave models without controls since the sample sizes are reduced by missing data in the intervening television measures and since there is a potential for multicollinearity between the multiple television exposure measures in the regressions.

In order to obtain the most complete and conclusive data possible, we computed both models: the basic two-wave model without controls, the one that uses the largest number of boys available in each wave pair; and also the model with controls for intervening television variables that reduces the ambiguity caused by overlap in the 15 wave pairs.

The two sets of 15 wave-pair models were estimated separately for the sample of valid reporters of their viewing and for the total sample that includes less valid reporters. In both cases the overall set of model results was evaluated in an attempt to detect a *consistent* and *significant* association between television exposure and later aggression.

Consistency of the association was determined by whether the coefficients had

[1]Overlap among the aggression measures is not removed. Although we could have done this by controlling all intervening aggression scores, we chose instead to estimate the effect of the television exposure score on the total change over the wave pair. This approach maximizes our chances of finding television effects (as shown in Figure 6.1).

the same sign. When coefficients do not have the same sign, even though they may be statistically significant they are causally ambiguous.

To determine *significance* of the television–aggression associations in a set of 15 models of this sort, an overall analysis of the total set of models is required. Even if no causal connections are present, the probability of all 15 coefficients being insignificant is only 46%.[2] One or two out of 15 independent coefficients could easily reach the .05 level of statistical significance by chance alone. In fact, at least 3 of the 15 coefficients in the analysis controlling for overlap must be significant at the .05 level before the pattern as a whole is significant at this level.[3] In the models where the overlap in waves is not controlled, it is possible that an even higher number of coefficients would individually reach the .05 significance level entirely on the basis of chance.

In the following sections, we begin with a two-wave model that assumes (*a*) all variables are measured without error, (*b*) any relationships which exist between variables are linear, and (*c*) the multivariate relationships among the variables in the model are additive. Violation of any of these assumptions can have serious implications for the results obtained. In subsequent analyses these assumptions are all relaxed and examined empirically to be sure that the findings obtained in these basic analyses are in fact accurate.[4]

---

[2]The formula for computing the probability of all 15 coefficients being statistically insignificant is $.95^{15} = .46$ (46%), as each coefficient has a 95% chance of statistical insignificance at the .05 level.

[3]Again, if there were in fact no causal connections in the data, the probability of the number of significant coefficients in 15 independent wave pairs at the .05 level can be computed as follows:

The probability of finding exactly one of the coefficients significant is $.95^{14} \times .05 \times 15 = .37$ (37%). The probability of finding two significant coefficients is $.95^{13} \times .05^{2} \times 15 \times 14 / 2 = .14$ (14%). If we find 3 or more of the 15 coefficients statistically significant, there is only a .03 probability that this happened by chance (according to this formula: $1 - .46 - .37 - .14 = .03$ [3%]), where .46 is the probability of finding all coefficients insignificant, .37 the probability of finding one significant, .14 the probability of finding two significant).

[4]The first two assumptions are discussed in this chapter, with detailed results of our empirical examinations reported in appendices. The last assumption, concerning multivariate additivity, is addressed later in the text. First, in Chapter 7 we consider a special kind of nonadditivity, one in which a series of earlier television measures at times t–1, t–2, etc., nonadditively influence change in aggression over the time interval t–1 to t. The substantive interest here is in studying the possibility that "consistency" of high exposure over long periods of time has an effect on aggression that might not be observed in the models considered in the present chapter. A second sort of nonadditivity is considered in Chapter 7, when we consider the possibility that the influence of earlier television exposure on subsequent aggression is partially a function of initial aggression. The substantive consideration here is that television might have either an influence in "generating" aggression among previously unaggressive boys, or in "preserving" high levels of aggression among previously aggressive boys, but not both, in which case the meaningful causal effect in one subsample of boys would be obscured in the analyses presented in this chapter.

BASIC FINDINGS

Results of the 15 wave-pair regression analyses are reported in Table 6.1 (for the model without controls) and in Table 6.2 (for the model with controls).[5] The wave pairs are arranged by amount of elapsed time, from the pair with the shortest elapsed time (Waves III–IV, 3 months) to the pair with the longest elapsed time (Waves I–IV, 3 years).

Limitations Imposed by the Stability of Aggression and the Number of Cases

Change in the dependent variable over the time intervals measured is crucial for a fair test of the hypothesis that television exposure has a net impact on subsequent aggression, with initial aggression controlled. If initial aggression perfectly predicts later aggression, then, obviously, neither television nor any other predictor can possibly have an effect.

We therefore begin by examining aggression's stability, shown in Column (1b) of Tables 6.1 and 6.2. The pattern that emerges from these stability coefficients is the same in both tables and the same as was reported in Chapter 3: Aggression among these boys is quite stable, but the longer the elapsed time between waves, the lower the stability of aggression. Thus, there is change that provides the possibility for investigating possible television effects, especially in the longer lags.[6]

The number of cases available for analysis is reported in Column (7) of the two tables. In the wave pair of 3 months' duration, the number of boys is close to 500. As elapsed time between waves increases, however, the sample sizes decrease steadily, until for the wave pair representing the longest elapsed time there are only 112 cases in Table 6.1 and 70 in Table 6.2.

Both the stability of aggression and the number of cases available for analysis have implications for the analysis. First, as aggression's stability is high in the wave pairs representing short lags, there is relatively little absolute change for television or any other possible causal factor to explain. However, in the longer lags there is quite a lot of change to explain. Thus, an explanatory factor may

[5]Results for the total sample and a discussion of the findings can be found below in Tables 6.3 and 6.4.

[6]One way to think of this stability is in terms of the variance in later aggression uniquely due to the earlier aggression score: These coefficients, shown in Column 2 of Table 6.1, measure the amount of R^2 increase in the prediction of later aggression due to the addition of the earlier aggression score to a prediction equation that previously included only the earlier exposure score. The largest coefficient is .72, for wave pair III–IV, representing 3 months. This means that 72% of the variance in aggression in Wave IV was uniquely attributable to aggression measured 3 months earlier in Wave III. The lowest coefficient, representing the stability of aggression over 3 years' time, is .28 in Table 6.1 and .30 in Table 6.2.

TABLE 6.1

Basic Model Regression Coefficients Showing the Impact of Violent Television Exposure on Later Aggression for All Wave Pairs (Valid Reporters)

WAVE PAIR	DURATION	EARLIER AGGRESSION COEFFICIENTS		UNIQUE CONTRIBUTION OF EARLIER AGGRESSION TO TOTAL R^2	EARLIER VIOLENT TELEVISION EXPOSURE COEFFICIENTS		UNIQUE CONTRIBUTION OF EARLIER VIOLENT TELEVISION EXPOSURE TO TOTAL R^2	TOTAL R^2	VARIANCE OF CHANGE IN AGGRESSION EXPLAINED BY EARLIER TELEVISION	N
		b (1a)	β (1b)	(2)	b (3a)	β (3b)	(4)	(5)	(6)	(7)
III–IV	3 months	.921*	.857	.716	.167*	.063	.004	.748	.015	(497)
II–III	4 months	.852*	.844	.700	.091	.038	.001	.719	.003	(413)
I–II	5 months	.713*	.686	.447	−.070	−.026	.001	.467	.002	(364)
II–IV	7 months	.844*	.771	.584	.244*	.094	.009	.615	.022	(409)
I–III	9 months	.710*	.671	.427	−.016	−.006	.000	.450	.000	(356)
I–IV	1 year	.699*	.632	.379	.065	.023	.001	.403	.002	(349)
IV–V	1 year	.723*	.734	.522	−.070	−.026	.001	.533	.002	(301)
V–VI	1 year	.688*	.723	.508	.154	.058	.003	.533	.006	(188)
III–V	1 year/3 months	.727*	.734	.526	.016	.007	.000	.541	.000	(291)
II–V	1 year/7 months	.737*	.665	.435	.038	.016	.000	.446	.000	(240)
I–V	2 years	.685*	.594	.335	.176	.067	.004	.369	.006	(211)
IV–VI	2 years	.673*	.708	.485	.125	.049	.002	.519	.004	(161)
III–VI	2 years/3 months	.620*	.642	.402	.281(*)	.121	.015	.460	.026	(147)
II–VI	2 years/7 months	.765*	.677	.450	.152	.065	.004	.476	.007	(121)
I–VI	3 years	.644*	.543	.280	.306	.113	.012	.315	.018	(112)

*Significant at .05 level.
(*)Coefficient = 1.94 its standard error.

TABLE 6.2

Basic Model Regression Coefficients Showing the Impact of Violent Television Exposure on Later Aggression for All Wave Pairs with Controls for Intervening Television Exposure (Valid Reporters)

		EARLIER AGGRESSION COEFFICIENTS		UNIQUE CONTRIBUTION OF EARLIER AGGRESSION TO TOTAL R^2	EARLIER VIOLENT TELEVISION EXPOSURE COEFFICIENTS		UNIQUE CONTRIBUTION OF EARLIER VIOLENT TELEVISION EXPOSURE TO TOTAL R^2	TOTAL R^2	VARIANCE OF CHANGE IN AGGRESSION EXPLAINED BY EARLIER TELEVISION	N
WAVE PAIR	DURATION	b (1a)	β (1b)	(2)	b (3a)	β (3b)	(4)	(5)	(6)	(7)
III–IV	3 months	.921*	.857	.716	.167*	.063	.004	.748	.015	(497)
II–III	4 months	.852*	.844	.700	.091	.038	.001	.719	.003	(413)
I–II	5 months	.713*	.686	.447	−.070	−.026	.001	.467	.002	(364)
II–IV	7 months	.843*	.770	.588	.178	.069	.005	.616	.000	(356)
I–III	9 months	.707*	.669	.443	−.046	−.017	.000	.450	.001	(282)
I–IV	1 year	.693*	.627	.389	−.009	−.003	.000	.407	.000	(249)
IV–V	1 year	.723*	.734	.522	−.070	−.026	.001	.533	.002	(301)
V–VI	1 year	.688*	.723	.508	.154	.058	.003	.533	.006	(188)
III–V	1 year/3 months	.730*	.737	.521	.102	.042	.002	.543	.003	(249)
II–V	1 year/7 months	.737*	.665	.430	.104	.043	.002	.448	.003	(187)
I–V	2 years	.680*	.590	.341	.143	.055	.003	.375	.000	(155)
IV–VI	2 years	.618*	.689	.450	.156	.064	.004	.500	.008	(131)
III–VI	2 years/3 months	.618*	.639	.389	.238	.105	.011	.456	.019	(108)
II–VI	2 years/7 months	.759*	.672	.442	−.233	−.101	.010	.510	.019	(89)
I–VI	3 years	.653*	.551	.303	.118	.045	.002	.341	.003	(70)

*Significant at .05 level.

account for a high proportion of possible change in the shorter wave pairs, but not be very important in absolute terms. Conversely, a factor may account for a low proportion of possible change in the longer wave pairs, accounting for an important amount of change in absolute terms.

Second, the significance of a coefficient is influenced by the number of cases available for analysis. There are more boys available for the shorter wave pairs, and fewer in the longer pairs. Thus, any explanatory factor has a greater chance of showing statistical significance in the shorter lags, where there is little to explain. Conversely, where the dependent variable shows the most change, and where the analysts desire the most power to discern what the causes of that change are, their ability to detect small influences is weakest. These limitations have to be considered in the interpretation of the findings.[8]

Findings for Valid Reporters

We turn now to examine the basic causal model findings, first for samples of valid reporters.

It will be recalled that a minority of children gave television data of low or questionable validity (see Chapter 4). Because the inclusion of these data might impair our ability to estimate the true impact of television on children's aggression, "less valid reporters" were excluded from the analyses reported in this section. However, data for the total sample (valid and less valid reporters combined) are presented in the section that follows.

Columns (3a) and (3b) of Tables 6.1 and 6.2 present unstandardized b and standardized β coefficients, respectively, of television's impact on later aggression, arranged from shortest to longest elapsed time, for the 15 panels studied.

The first thing to note is that most of these coefficients are positive. (In Table 6.1, 12 out of the 15 coefficients are positive; in Table 6.2, 10 of the 15.) We conclude that there is no support for the hypothesis that exposure to violence in the media acts as a "catharsis" (i.e., reduces the tendency for children so exposed to be aggressive).

Looking next at the significance of the coefficients in Column (3a), we see that there is no statistically significant support for the hypothesis that television violence increases the aggression of children who are exposed to it.

In Table 6.1, which does not control for intervening television exposure, two of the positive coefficients exceed twice their standard errors—those in the III–IV and II–VI panels. A third, in the III–IV wave pair, closely approaches this cutoff. The two significant coefficients are not independent; the III–IV panel is contained within the II–IV sample.

The need for taking the overlap between wave pairs into account becomes apparent when lags III–IV and II–IV are compared. Obviously, the dependent variables in the two models are identical. The relationships between the independent variables are extremely high: .88 between Aggression II and III, .96 between television exposure II and III (see Tables 3.6 and 4.8). It is not surprising, therefore, that the coefficients in these lags are very similar.

In Table 6.2, which does control for intervening *TV*, only one of the coefficients exceeds twice its standard error, that in the III–IV panel. Following this line of reasoning, it is clear that 1 coefficient out of 15 could easily be significant on the basis of chance.

Significance in statistical terms aside, the importance of television exposure as a predictor of children's aggressiveness is quite small in all panels. This can be seen in terms of variance components from Column 4 in both tables, which present variance in aggression explained by *TV*, controlling for earlier aggression. These "unique contributions"[7] of television exposure range from .015 (wave pair III–VI) to .000 (wave pairs I–III, III–V, and II–V) in Table 6.1. (They are even smaller in Table 6.2, ranging from .000 to .011.) In 13 of the 15 pairs, exposure to violent television has a unique contribution of less than 1% of the later aggression variance; in 12 pairs, less than 0.5%.

However, since the stability of aggression is as high as it is, there is little likelihood that any measure would a be a strong predictor of later aggression once initial aggression is controlled. To get a better idea of the importance of television exposure, we can compute a measure of its impact on that portion of later aggression which was not predicted by earlier aggression.[8] This

---

[7]The unique contribution is the R^2 increment due directly to *TV* in the prediction equation—the difference between the zero-order r^2 coefficient between initial and later aggression and the multiple R^2 coefficient of the prediction of later aggression by both initial aggression and initial television exposure. In the two-predictor case this increment, or unique effect, reduces to

$$\beta_A^2(1 - r_{A_1TV_1}^2),$$

or that part of β^2 equal to the percentage of variance in initial television exposure which is independent of initial aggression.

[8]Since $\beta_A^2(1 - r_{A_1TV_1}^2)$ tells us the amount of variance in the later aggression score accounted for by earlier aggression (Table 6.1, column 2), the quantity $[1 - \beta_A^2(1 - r_{A_1TV_1})]$ represents leftover variance. The extent to which television has an impact on this meaning proportion of later aggression is equal to

$$\frac{\beta_{TV}^2(1 - r_{A_1TV_1}^2)}{1 - [\beta_A^2(1 - R_{A_1TV_1}^2)]}$$

coefficient takes out of consideration the absolute amount of change between a pair of waves and, instead, examines the proportion of this change, however small it may be, which is accounted for by initial television exposure.

Column (6) of the two tables gives these data, roughly a measure of the percentage of variance in change-in-aggression uniquely due to the earlier television score, for each wave pair in the panel. In 11 of the 15 wave pairs in Table 6.1 (12 of the 15 in Table 6.2), the initial exposure score accounts for less than 1% of the portion of later aggression that represents change from earlier aggression. Viewing the results as a whole, even when residual variance in later aggression is the criterion, the impact of variation in television exposure is very small.

The fact that a substantial degree of variation in exposure exists in the sample argues that lack of variation is not masking a truly important causal impact. But it is nonetheless useful to push on beyond an analysis of predictive ability to examine the *potential* causal impact of exposure. This is given by the *b* coefficients of the regression analysis. These coefficients describe the potential impact of altering an individual's score on the dependent variable by 1 point on the scale of the independent variable. Thus they relate the specific metric of the dependent variable (aggression) to the specific metric of the independent variable (violent television exposure). For example, a *b* coefficient of .17 between initial exposure to televised violence and subsequent aggression (as in wave pair III–IV in Table 6.1) indicates that for every 10 points the exposure of a child increases at an earlier time, his aggression score at a later time will on the average increase 1.7 points over what it otherwise would have been. Comparison of these *b* coefficients, then, allows speculation about the potential impact of altering exposure by specified amounts.[9]

The positive *b* coefficients range from .02 (wave pair III–V in Table 6.1) to .31 (wave pair I–VI in Table 6.1). They are, on the average, smaller in Table 6.2 than in Table 6.1, and they are smaller over the shorter than the longer time intervals. In Table 6.1, the average *b* value for the five short panels (under 1 year) is .08 and for the five medium panels (between 1 and 2 years) .04; the average for the long panels (between 2 and 3 years) is .21. In the 15 lags in Table 6.1, the average coefficient is .044; in the five adjacent lags, it is .021.

But what, exactly, does a *b* value of .21, the average value in the longer panels in Table 6.1 and also the largest average value in the two tables, mean? To assess the impact of television exposure indicated by a coefficient of that size, let us imagine that this was a true, significant association and that we could conduct an experiment. If we were to take a child in the lowest decile of violence exposure (a score of approximately 15 points on the scale of

[9]The interpretation of the *b* coefficients is highly tentative because only 1 or 2 of the 15 coefficients in each table is statistically significant.

exposure)[10] and persuade him or her to increase viewing until it is in the highest decile of exposure (a score of approximately 87 points on the scale of exposure), we could expect to increase his or her aggression over the 3-year period by this amount:

$$(87 - 15) \times .21 = 15.1$$

The largest *potential* impact of increasing a child's television exposure would be, then, to increase his aggression score by approximately 15 points on an aggression scale with a range of 400 points and a standard deviation of about 70 points. And this would only be possible among the least exposed children. Among those average viewers who are in the 50th percentile range of exposure, an increase to the highest level of viewing would produce a potential impact of only 7 or 8 points over 3 years.

On a scale of aggression as refined as the scale used here, a difference of 7, or even 15, points is extremely small. Even with a measure of aggressiveness as reliable as that in the present study (and it will be recalled from Chapter 3 that the average reliability across the six waves is approximately .96), had we measured a single child on the aggressiveness scale two times in a single day, we would expect his aggression score to fluctuate by about the same amount, 14 points. (That is, [1−.96] times the range. Since the observed aggression scale's range averages about 350 over the six waves, the expected amount of fluctuation due merely to random error is [.04 × 350], or 14 points.)

Findings for the Total Sample

The exclusion of less valid reporters from the analyses examined so far could have serious effects on the conclusions drawn. Not only do less valid reporters score much higher on the television exposure variable than other children, but they are also rated by their peers as more aggressive on the average than their classmates. By omitting these children from the analyses, then, we are cutting off part of the scatter of consistently highly exposed and aggressive children and are, consequently, reducing the correlation between these two variables.

It turns out, however, that the substantive conclusions drawn earlier in this chapter are not altered by the exclusion of less valid reporters. Tables 6.3 and 6.4 present data for the basic linear regression model computed on the total sample, including less valid reporters. Comparison of these tables with Tables 6.1 and 6.2 shows that the coefficients estimated for valid reporters are very close to those that would have been reported had the less valid reporters been

[10]In Wave I, for valid reporters, the distribution of television scores is as follows: 5th percentile = score of 10; 10th percentile = score of 15; 90th percentile = score of 87; 95th percentile = score of 95.

TABLE 6.3

Basic Model Regression Coefficients Showing the Impact of Violent Television Exposure on Later Aggression for All Wave Pairs (Total Sample)

		EARLIER AGGRESSION COEFFICIENTS		UNIQUE CONTRIBUTION OF EARLIER AGGRESSION TO TOTAL R^2	EARLIER VIOLENT TELEVISION EXPOSURE COEFFICIENTS		UNIQUE CONTRIBUTION OF EARLIER VIOLENT TELEVISION EXPOSURE TO TOTAL R^2	TOTAL R^2	VARIANCE OF CHANGE IN AGGRESSION EXPLAINED BY EARLIER TELEVISION	N
WAVE PAIR	DURATION	b (1a)	β (1b)	(2)	b (3a)	β (3b)	(4)	(5)	(6)	(7)
III–IV	3 months	.897*	.830	.671	.118*	.054	.003	.706	.001	(620)
II–III	4 months	.825*	.835	.685	.108	.037	.001	.713	.010	(571)
I–II	5 months	.646*	.661	.416	−.031	−.014	.000	.433	.000	(505)
II–IV	7 months	.788*	.746	.546	.184*	.091	.008	.584	.018	(559)
I–III	9 months	.641*	.657	.411	−.023	−.011	.000	.429	.000	(486)
I–IV	1 year	.662*	.641	.391	.074	.033	.001	.421	.002	(478)
IV–V	1 year	.723*	.751	.522	−.014	−.006	.000	.562	.000	(360)
V–VI	1 year	.658*	.717	.501	.119	.058	.003	.528	.006	(246)
III–V	1 year/3 months	.756*	.733	.501	.054	.026	.001	.547	.002	(362)
II–V	1 year/7 months	.751*	.701	.465	.059	.030	.001	.501	.002	(328)
I–V	2 years	.634*	.595	.332	.262	.119	.013	.403	.022	(296)
IV–VI	2 years	.625*	.697	.442	.032	.016	.000	.493	.001	(204)
III–VI	2 years/3 months	.639*	.647	.396	.165	.088	.007	.453	.014	(205)
II–VI	2 years/7 months	.660*	.643	.390	.120	.067	.004	.438	.007	(191)
I–VI	3 years	.468*	.484	.221	.164	.082	.006	.260	.009	(178)

*Significant at .05 level.

TABLE 6.4

Basic Model Regression Coefficients Showing the Impact of Violent Television Exposure on Later Aggression for All Wave Pairs with Controls for Intervening Television Exposure (Total Sample)

WAVE PAIR	DURATION	EARLIER AGGRESSION COEFFICIENTS b (1a)	EARLIER AGGRESSION COEFFICIENTS β (1b)	UNIQUE CONTRIBUTION OF EARLIER AGGRESSION TO TOTAL R^2 (2)	EARLIER VIOLENT TELEVISION EXPOSURE COEFFICIENTS b (3a)	EARLIER VIOLENT TELEVISION EXPOSURE COEFFICIENTS β (3b)	UNIQUE CONTRIBUTION OF EARLIER VIOLENT TELEVISION EXPOSURE TO TOTAL R^2 (4)	TOTAL R^2 (5)	VARIANCE OF CHANGE IN AGGRESSION EXPLAINED BY EARLIER TELEVISION (6)	N (7)
III–IV	3 months	.897*	.830	.671	.118*	.054	.003	.706	.001	(620)
II–III	4 months	.825*	.835	.685	.108	.037	.001	.713	.010	(571)
I–II	5 months	.646*	.661	.416	−.031	−.014	.000	.433	.000	(505)
II–IV	7 months	.787*	.744	.542	.079	.040	.001	.586	.004	(526)
I–III	9 months	.638*	.654	.406	−.082	−.040	.002	.430	.003	(453)
I–IV	1 year	.658*	.637	.386	−.065	−.003	.000	.424	.000	(417)
IV–V	1 year	.723*	.751	.522	−.014	−.006	.000	.562	.000	(360)
V–VI	1 year	.658*	.717	.501	.119	.058	.003	.528	.006	(246)
III–V	1 year/3 months	.762*	.739	.509	.127	.062	.004	.548	.009	(339)
II–V	1 year/7 months	.749*	.699	.463	.009	.004	.000	.503	.000	(293)
I–V	2 years	.635*	.596	.338	.286*	.132	.016	.404	.027	(257)
IV–VI	2 years	.625*	.700	.446	.007	.004	.000	.493	.000	(199)
III–VI	2 years/3 months	.652*	.661	.414	.252	.137	.018	.456	.033	(189)
II–VI	2 years/7 months	.661*	.644	.390	−.057	−.032	.001	.452	.002	(170)
I–VI	3 years	.466*	.483	.222	.024	.012	.000	.278	.001	(152)

*Significant at .05 level.

included in the sample.[11] In the short and medium lags, the comparable coefficients differ by only trivial amounts. In the longer lags the differences are somewhat more substantial, but the estimates are still quite close. For example, in the long wave pairs the sample of valid reporters (Table 6.1) produces β estimates larger than those in the total sample (Table 6.3) in three instances, smaller in one instance, the same in one instance; *b* estimates are larger than those in the total sample in four instances and the same in one instance. The 15-wave average for valid reporters is a β of .044; for the total sample it is .045 (Tables 6.1 and 6.3).

Additional tables, comparing results for valid reporters and for the total sample when measurement errors are taken into account, are presented in Appendix C (see the following discussion). These tables lead to the same conclusion: Excluding less valid reporters does not change the inferences drawn on the basis of valid reporters only. If anything, their exclusion results in somewhat larger estimates for the effect of television violence on aggression.

EXTENSIONS OF THE BASIC MODEL

As noted in Chapter 5, the basic analysis model used here rests on a number of assumptions. In the remainder of this chapter we briefly report the results of relaxing some of these assumptions. Detailed findings are reported in Appendices A, B, and C.

Linearity of Relationships

The model just examined assumes the existence of a linear relationship between exposure and aggression. However, there is no reason to rule out the possibility of a curvilinear relationship on a priori grounds. For example, children at the extremes of exposure—both those highly exposed to violence and those unexposed—may be found to increase in aggressiveness through time far more than children exposed to a modicum of violence. If nonlinearity of this type exists, it would surely be missed in the results just reported.

To examine this possibility, we conducted a series of nonlinear regression

[11]Several analyses were carried out for less valid reporters only. For example, we defined as "less valid" those boys who gave inaccurate viewing information in one or more waves but accurate information in at least one wave (the vast majority of less valid reporters as shown in Chapter 4, Table 4.7). The pattern of television effects among such respondents, boys who were valid in at least one of the waves, is very unstable, but offers no support for the hypothesis that television effects are more pronounced among less valid than among valid reporters. The same conclusions are drawn when alternative viewing measures (such as favorite show measures, mother's report on boy's viewing) are substituted for self-report exposure.

analyses which made use of polynomials of the exposure score. However, this series of analyses served only to show that the assumption of a simple linear relationship between violent television exposure and aggression is warranted. A full description of the analysis results is given in Appendix A.

Attrition

Another important potential for bias in the results reported in this chapter derives from the fact that a substantial number of children who were members of the initial Wave I sample dropped out of the study permanently or were absent temporarily at some point before data collection ended. As we demonstrated in Chapter 2, these dropouts differ significantly from those children who remained in the study until its completion, and it is possible that they were affected by exposure to television violence differently than those children who stayed, thereby influencing our findings.

The study, it will be remembered, experienced attrition in three ways. First, we studied students only until they had completed the sixth grade, when they moved to junior high schools. The second source of attrition was the loss of children through geographic mobility. These children also differed in several respects from the children who remained in the study until its completion. Finally, for children who were absent on the day of data collection, no measure of television exposure was available, thus forcing us to omit them from the sample for that wave. Because they were nevertheless rated on aggression by their classmates, it is possible to include most absentees in several panel analyses by relating their aggression scores to earlier exposure scores obtained when they were present.

An additional feature of the study design was that some new children moved into the schools during the course of the study. Since we chose to include these children in the analyses, the effects of their inclusion had to be assessed as well.

There is no completely satisfactory way to examine the possible impact of these complex patterns of attrition, and addition, of study children. This is so because we are required to make inferences about the possible influence of missing data. However, we are fortunate in having information from at least some early waves for all the children who prematurely left the panel. This made it possible for us to create profiles of these children and to carry out two sorts of analyses:

1. We were able to examine the effects on our early analyses of removing the children who we knew would become sample dropouts later.
2. We were able to isolate those children in the complete panel who were like the dropouts in significant ways, and to determine the extent to which the television–aggression relationship among them differed from the same relationship observed in the remaining sample children.

These analyses, which draw on some relatively complex considerations of both analysis strategy and model conceptualization, are discussed in detail in Appendix B. The results can be summarized as follows: (*a*) The impact of new respondents on the estimates of television's structural impact (*b* coefficients) was negligible; (*b*) permanent dropouts caused a slight underestimate of television's impact; (*c*) temporary absentees caused a slight overestimate of television's impact; (*d*) the net effect of attrition and the addition of new respondents on the *TV b* coefficients appears to be extremely small.

On the other hand, it is not nearly so clear that the dropout problem had only a small effect on our estimates of explained variance, the β coefficients. This is true because dropouts led to a change in the variances of the exposure and aggression variables. Therefore, in the analyses we have been careful to place emphasis on the interpretation of *b* coefficients and to be liberal in our assessment of statistical significance, which is influenced by the scatter of points around the regression line, the latter described by the β coefficients.

Measurement Error

The problem of measurement error, although inevitable in any type of survey research, is particularly troublesome in longitudinal analysis. The general problem is that the observed relationship between two variables will be lower than the true relationship because of measurement error. In a panel analysis that includes an earlier measure of one variable as a predictor, an additional problem arises: The errors in the two scores are likely to be correlated, artificially inflating their observed stability—in our case, the observed stability of aggression. This means that there is less variance in later aggression for television exposure to explain. Coupled with the fact that the true impact of television is estimated to be smaller than it really is, this means that we are particularly in danger of underestimating the effect of a predictor like television.

One way to estimate the impact of measurement error is to compute internal consistency estimates of variable reliability and use these estimates to adjust observed regression coefficients to approximate those that might have been obtained had all variables been perfectly measured. However, this simple "random" error model is unlikely to apply to our data because, as already noted, measurement errors are likely to be correlated. If such errors are correlated within a single point in time, reliability is overestimated by the conventional internal consistency formula, and the true change in aggression is underestimated. If errors are correlated across time, reliability is correctly estimated, but stability is incorrectly estimated, either inflated or deflated depending on the sign of the correlated errors.

It is likely that some types of error in the reports of young children are correlated across occasions and across indicators of a construct. For example, a commotion in the classroom on the day of data collection might make all the children less accurate in their answers on that day than at any other data collection time. Or, children might consistently over- or underestimate certain characteristics of deviant children in the classroom and thus cause a systematic error in parameter estimates over time.

Until very recently researchers have been unable to estimate efficiently either the presence or magnitude of complex measurement errors of this type. However, work by Jöreskog (1973) has resulted in a procedure that deals with just this sort of problem. We used this procedure to estimate measurement errors in our basic model. The full results of this series of analyses are presented in Appendix C. We found the adjustments resulted in only small changes in the parameter estimates of interest to us, and consequently did not alter the conclusions drawn from the results in Tables 6.1 and 6.2.

SUMMARY

As the results show, there is no consistent statistically significant relationship between violent television exposure and later aggression in our basic two-wave models. Two of the 15 television coefficients are significant for valid reporters; only 1 remains when we control for the overlap between wave pairs. An overall assessment of the 15 lags shows that such patterns are clearly within the bounds of chance. In the total sample, which includes "less valid reporters," findings are very similar. All of the additional tests to which we subjected the data—tests for nonlinearity, for the effects of panel attrition, and for measurement error—are consistent with the results of the basic model analyses.

At the same time, two patterns in the data suggest the possibility of a small association between television and aggression. First, the few significant coefficients are all positive. Were they due entirely to chance variation we would expect them to be half positive and half negative. Second, most of the insignificant coefficients are positive as well.[12]

It is beyond the capacity of this study to explain such small and insignificant associations with certainty. However, we will present analyses in Chapter 7 suggesting that these associations are at least in part spurious.

The analyses in this chapter employed one specific measure of "violent television exposure" and focused on the sample as a whole. It is possible that more substantial associations between television and aggression would be found

[12]The average size of the samples of valid reporters (about 200) allows us to determine television's effects that are very small indeed: β coefficients of about .10 are significant. Thus, we are really examining the possibility of a "trace effect," not of a substantial association.

if other conceptualizations of exposure are considered. Further, it has been suggested that television does not affect every child in the same way and that, consequently, a thorough investigation of television's effects should examine such effects among specific groups of children. Both analyses are presented in the following chapter.

APPENDIX A: CURVILINEARITY

The model in Chapter 6 assumes a simple linear relationship between exposure and aggression. The possibility of a curvilinear relationship can be evaluated by introducing into the basic linear equation a series of variables representing nonlinear components. Here we used a general scheme of polynomial regression analysis of the form

$$A_t = a + B_j A_{(t-1)} + \sum_{j=1}^{n-2} B_j E^j_{(t-1)} \qquad (2)$$

The subscript i for individuals is suppressed in this equation, as is the individual's prediction error u_i. Where there are n cases, and therefore n points in the observed scatter, we can perfectly define the observed relationship between the scatter of points by a regression of $n - 2$ polynomials. Concretely, this means that $n - 2$ connected lines are needed, at a maximum, to connect all n points in the scatter. The linear regression model simply uses a straight line to connect the points. By using higher-order polynomials we can examine the increments in predictive power associated with successively more refined bends in the predictive line. If it should turn out that a rather low degree of polynomial extrapolation improves the fit of a linear regression, we can plot this line and possibly transform our exposure score to conform to it.

Table A.1 presents results of polynomial regressions for each of the 15 panels studied. Explained variance percentages are presented for polynomials from first- to third-order degree (the latter represents two bend points in the estimation line). Inspection shows that these polynomials have only a small effect on the predictive power of the equations. For most of the panels, even a third-degree polynomial does not substantially improve the predictive fit.

Dummy variable regression equations were also estimated, in each of which the exposure score was divided along its range into discrete categories. This series of analyses, which makes no assumptions whatever about the functional form of the television–aggression relationship, was similarly unable to detect a significant nonlinearity in the relationship between television and later aggression.

TABLE A.1

R^2 Progressions for Polynomial Regressions: Initial Aggression and Polynomials of Violent Television to Predict Subsequent Aggression (Valid Reporters)[a]

		EXPONENTS*			
WAVE PAIR	DURATION	*TV*	TV^2	TV^3	*N*
III–IV	3 months	.748	.748	.751	(497)
II–III	4 months	.719	.720	.720	(413)
I–II	5 months	.467	.467	.468	(364)
II–IV	7 months	.615	.620	.620	(409)
I–III	9 months	.450	.450	.453	(356)
I–IV	1 year	.403	.403	.404	(349)
IV–V	1 year	.533	.533	.533	(301)
V–VI	1 year	.533	.536	.537	(188)
III–V	1 year/3 months	.541	.543	.543	(291)
II–V	1 year/7 months	.446	.449	.449	(240)
I–V	2 years	.369	.369	.370	(211)
IV–VI	2 years	.519	.519	.523	(161)
III–VI	2 years/3 months	.460	.463	.463	(147)
II–VI	2years/7 months	.476	.476	.499	(121)
I–VI	3 years	.315	.315	.317	(112)

[a]The linear equation is of the form

$$A_t = a + b_1A_{t-1} + b_2TV_{t-1}.$$

The polynomial two model is of the form

$$A_t = a + b_1A_{t-1} + b_2TV_{t-1} + b_3TV^2_{t-1}.$$

*All R^2 values are significant at the .05 level. None of the increments over the linear model are significant at the .05 level.

APPENDIX B: EFFECTS OF SAMPLE ATTRITION AND ADDITION OF NEW RESPONDENTS

Another important potential source of bias in the results reported in Chapter 6 comes from the fact that a substantial proportion of the children who were members of the initial Wave I sample dropped out of the study permanently or were temporarily absent at some point before its conclusion. As demonstrated in Chapter 2, these dropouts differ from those children who remained in the study until its completion, and they may have been affected by exposure to television violence differently from those children who stayed, thereby altering the findings. The same is true of new respondents who were added to the sample after Wave I.[13]

[13]For sources of attrition and reasons for new respondents, see Chapter 2.

Possibility of Data Bias

Attrition or the addition of new respondents can affect findings in either of two ways. First, they may affect the distribution of critical variables; second, they may influence the estimate of the impact of television exposure. We discuss each of these problems, and explain their meaning.[14]

Panel loss and addition of new respondents can influence both estimates of central tendency (means, modes, medians) and dispersion (mean deviation, standard deviation). This is exactly what has happened in our study in the case of the two central variables—aggression and violent television exposure.

Boys who dropped out of the study permanently were more aggressive in Wave I (median aggression = 96) than those boys who stayed as long as possible (median Wave I aggression = 67). In addition, leavers reported more exposure to violent television (median Wave I violent television exposure = 74) than those who remained (median Wave I violent television exposure = 57). Boys who entered the sample during the first year of this study, but after Wave I, counterbalance the dropouts to a degree: They, too, are more aggressive (median aggression in Wave IV = 80) than those who were part of the initial sample (median aggression in Wave IV = 74), and they also watched somewhat more violent television (median Wave IV violent television exposure = 57 versus 50).[15]

Biases of this type are critical when the task of analysis is to describe the composition of the sample in terms of average levels of behavior, or average differences in a population over time. However, when the goal of the analysis is to estimate the structural impact of key predictors on a criterion score, these biases need not be critical. As long as there remain sufficient numbers of both aggressive and nonaggressive children in the achieved sample to estimate stable coefficients of bivariate association, biases that affect composition need not have an impact on the estimated results.

The descriptive measures that will interest us in the analyses to follow are the *b* coefficients. As stated in Chapter 6, these measure what we assume to be the true structuring of the causal impact of television, the extent to which unit changes in the independent variable will produce unit changes in the dependent variable, controlling for aggression at Time 1.

It can be shown that the composition of the sample, and whether or not that composition changes from one wave to the next, need not distort the estimate of the true causal relation, even though sample composition does influence the standardized regression coefficient. As Schoenberg (1972) has shown, *b* coefficients are relatively robust in the presence of shifts in sample composition.

[14]Chapter 2 details differences in the sample composition between the various samples with regard to demographic characteristics of the respondents.

[15]We report Wave IV data, since Wave I data are not available for new respondents.

Standardized partial regression coefficients, on the other hand, because they describe the extent to which variance in the independent variable predicts variance in the dependent variable, are more highly influenced by the amount of variance in the specific sample in question. Consequently, any differences that affect the variances in the achieved sample, such as loss of more aggressive boys, will usually have a more pronounced effect on β coefficients than on *b* coefficients.

However, there is an important respect in which sample bias can influence even the *b* coefficients. If television has a different effect on children who are members of the achieved sample than on children who should have been included but were not, the results of the analyses will be different than they would have been had all members of the original sample been retained for the duration of the study. The use of coefficients to overcome the problem of panel attrition is based on the assumption that the aggressive children who remain in the study, although fewer in number, nonetheless are typical of the population of aggressive children. Violation of this assumption will lead to distortion of the coefficient in the achieved sample.

It is not obvious that a problem of this type should occur, even though it is theoretically possible. Consider, however, the following hypothetical example as one among many very real possibilities: Children who drop out of the panel are more likely than panel members to come from broken homes, and children from broken homes may be more influenced by exposure to television violence (higher *b* coefficients) than children from intact homes. Here, *b* coefficients would be biased downward by panel attrition.

Method of Analysis

The critical test is to estimate the *b* coefficients separately for those children who remain in the study until its completion, for those who dropped out, and for the new respondents, and to determine whether these estimates of structural impact differ. If they do not, then we can be relatively secure in assuming that attrition has had no impact on altering the conclusions stated in Chapter 6 from what they might have been had we been able to keep the original target study population intact for the entire 3 years over which the study was in progress.

There is no absolutely conclusive way of conducting this critical test. To be conclusive, we would have to make statements about respondents who left the study permanently, and who did not provide us with the data needed for comparison on one or more waves. What we can study, however, are the data collected from dropouts during the early waves, *before they left*, to see whether they showed noticeable differences from the remainder of the sample at this early point in the study. This analysis is limited by the fact that very few of the dropouts stayed in the study long enough to be measured over long time intervals. Therefore, we can compare them with the stable members of the study population only in the short and medium lags.

The situation is somewhat different for temporary absentees, since they moved in and out of the sample over the course of the entire panel of six waves. It is possible to study them in short, medium, and long lags. New respondents, too, can be studied in all lags.

Findings

Data were analyzed for valid reporters.[16] The three groups under consideration—permanent dropouts, temporary absentees, and new respondents—are quite small in nearly all of the lags—usually around 30. Because the base numbers are small, we will not compare any of the groups with other groups. Rather, our approach will be to start with the groups that stayed in the sample permanently, and successively add each of the groups with which we are concerned—permanent dropouts, temporary absentees, and new respondents—to see whether aggregate estimates are altered by these successive additions of cases.

As shown in Chapter 2, analyses dealing with mobility have to separate children of different ages. This is because the respondent's age—or school grade at the time of Wave I—determines how long he can remain in the sample. In order to present these analyses in a comparable form, findings for temporary absentees and new respondents are also separated by age. We discuss three groups: second and third graders, fourth graders, and fifth graders.

Table B.1 is a summary table that averages the *b* coefficients associated with violent television exposure over the short, medium, and long lags.[17] The table shows average number of cases and *b* coefficients for second and third, fourth, and fifth graders in the short lags, and, where available, in medium and long lags.

Column (1) of Table B.1 shows data for respondents who are present in all waves. Columns (2), (3), and (4) show data for the three groups we want to compare with those respondents. Column (2) adds those who left the study permanently because of mobility to those respondents shown in Column (1). The difference between the *b* coefficients in Columns (1) and (2) tells us

[16]This has the effect of reducing the number of cases available for analysis. It should be noted that the differences between respondents who stay and those who leave, those who are and those who are never absentees, and old and new respondents are very similar between the subsamples of valid reporters analyzed here and the total sample.

[17]Short lags are those of less than 1 year, medium lags are 1 year to less than 2 years, long lags are 2 to 3 years. There are no long lags and only one medium lag for fifth graders (not shown in table), and only one long lag for fourth graders (not shown in table).

TABLE B.1

Impact of Attrition on Findings: Effect of Earlier Violent Television Exposure on Later Aggression, by Status in Sample (Average b Coefficients Over Short, Medium, and Long Lags)

			RESPONDENTS WHO WERE PRESENT IN ALL WAVES (COLUMN 1)					
	RESPONDENTS WHO WERE PRESENT IN ALL WAVES (1)		PLUS RESPONDENTS WHO LEFT PERMANENTLY (2)		PLUS RESPONDENTS WHO WERE TEMPORARILY ABSENT (3)		PLUS NEW RESPONDENTS (4)	
GRADE AND LAG	*N*	*b*	*N*	*b*	*N*	*b*	*N*	*b*
Second/third graders								
Short (5 lags)	(93)	.226	(143)	.233	(117)	.203	(107)	.214
Medium (5 lags)	(100)	.031	(124)	.086	(130)	.021	(117)	.075
Long (5 lags)	(97)	.103	(101)	[.130]	(124)	.127	(118)	.147
Fourth graders								
Short (5 lags)	(68)	.240	(86)	.272	(83)	.208	(78)	.246
Medium (4 lags)	(69)	.117	(71)	[.100]	(85)	.107	(82)	.073
Fifth graders								
Short (5 lags)	(71)	−.211	(74)	[−.242]	(98)	−.191	(82)	−.141

[a]Brackets indicate that the number of cases added is quite small, making comparisons tenuous.

whether the addition of respondents who left the study permanently—in those lags where they were still present—had an impact on the coefficients. Note that coefficients for the long lags for second and third graders and for short lags for fifth graders are in brackets, indicating that the number of respondents added is extremely small and the interpretation of possible differences in the coefficients is therefore tenuous.

The *b* coefficients are slightly larger in Column (2)—that is, when boys who subsequently leave the sample are added—in all three comparisons where there are enough added cases to interpret (short and medium lags for second and third graders, short lags for fourth graders). Thus, if none of these respondents had left, the coefficients in the achieved samples would presumably have been slightly larger, at least in the short and medium lags.

Column (3) shows data for those in Column (1) *plus* temporary absentees. The number of temporary absentees added to the sample in Column (3) is smaller than the number of permanent dropouts added in Column (2) in the short lags, but larger in the medium and long lags. We can make six comparisons that are based on enough cases to interpret. Temporary absentees have the effect of reducing the coefficients somewhat in five of these six comparisons, thus causing a slight overestimate of television's impact in these lags from which they are missing.

Finally, Column (4) adds new respondents, roughly equal numbers in all lags. Although, compared with the other two groups, the number of new respondents is small, all six comparisons can be made. The impact of adding new respondents to the sample is also quite small and not consistent across the lags.

We did not evaluate the within-row differences in Table B–1 across the various samples in terms of formal significance criteria, since the coefficients presented are averages of four or five coefficients in specific wave pairs. However, it is quite clear that the substantive differences within rows are extremely small. If we treat these small differences seriously for a moment, some consistent trends appear: (*a*) since the absolute values of the coefficients are larger in Column (2) than in Column (1), permanent dropouts appear to have caused a slight underestimate of television's impact; (*b*) since the coefficients are generally smaller in Column (2) than in Column (3), temporary absentees caused a slight overestimate of television's impact. However, the major conclusion to take away from this analysis is that the effects of these various types of panel loss were extremely small.

APPENDIX C: MODELS OF MEASUREMENT ERROR

Although the existence of unreliability in the measured scores of a survey is always a problem, this is particularly troublesome in a panel study. The problem is that the sources of unreliability are likely to exert their influence consistently through time, which means that the measures of any construct studied through time will be plagued by correlated error. This error will have the effect of magnifying the stability estimate and quite possibly be mistaken for a sign of good reliability.

In our analysis of television exposure and its influence on aggression over time, the possibility of complex sources of measurement error presents a plausible explanation for the low impact coefficients found in analyses of the raw data. Therefore, we estimated a series of models to capture the influence of this type of error on the results. In this appendix, we describe the procedures used to deal with this problem.

Complex Measurement Models

The basic measurement model estimated is illustrated in Figure C.1. For reasons discussed in the following, we treat the observed index of violent television exposure (tv_t) as a single indicator of the unmeasured true exposure (TV_t), measured with error (e_{tv}). The aggression score, on the other hand, is modeled as a series of indicators (lie, hit, push, say mean things) of unmeasured true aggression (A). The errors of these indicators (e_{ij}) are assumed to be autocorrelated through time; that is, correlated with the errors of the same indicators at the later time point.

This model can be estimated, with certain constraints, to give us values for the impact coefficient between TV_t and A_{t+1}. If the errors are all small, this estimated impact coefficient will be very close to that presented in Table 6.2 for the observed scores themselves. However, depending on the relative magnitudes and signs of the errors and their correlations through time, significant measurement error can drastically alter these impact coefficients and the conclusions we draw from them.

To estimate this model for the 15 wave pairs in our panel, we have used a method which fits the parameters of the model in such a way as to minimize a summary measure of discrepancy between the observed matrix of covariances among the indicators and the expected matrix predicted by the parameter estimates (Jöreskog, 1973).

The fitting function used to solve this model is part of a recently developed general approach to maximum-likelihood linear modeling, due to Jöreskog. The estimation procedure we use is contained in the computer program LISREL IV (Jöreskog & Sörbom, 1979). The existence of four indicators makes it possible to construct and to identify a rather broad class of models. We can examine the impact of various sorts of measurement error by building into the models estimates for correlations among the errors and then seeing whether they improve the fit between the predicted and observed matrices.

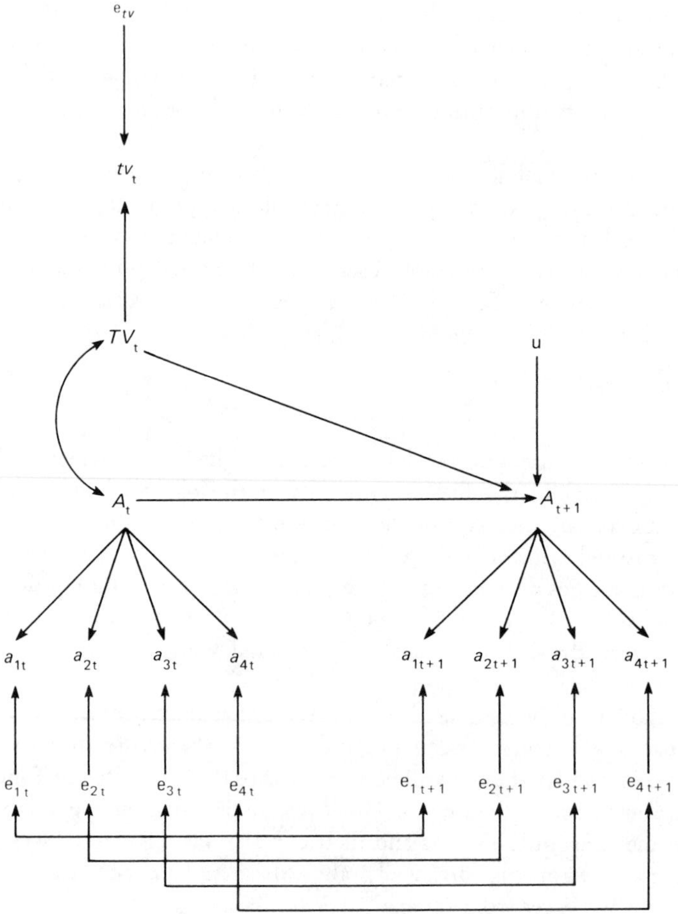

FIGURE C.1. *Basic measurement model for the effect of television exposure on change in aggression.*

There is one indeterminacy in the model in Figure C.1 that had to be resolved before estimation could begin. Because the reliability of the television exposure score is underidentified, it is impossible to estimate a unique value for this reliability within the context of the model. Making use of other data, then, we first developed estimates of the reliability of the exposure scores over the six waves of the panel and used these estimates in the measurement model of television effects. Therefore, before discussing the results of our estimation of the basic measurement model of television impact, we turn in the next section to discuss our estimation of the reliability of the television exposure measure.

Estimating the Reliability of Television Exposure

The model estimated for the television exposure score treats the summed index of exposure as a single indicator, recognizing that our measure is merely a very refined answer to the question: How much television have you watched over the last month? and not really a set of distinct measures.

Conventional reliability estimates of single items require retest after a short period of time. However, given the great complexity of the data collection procedure, we did not consider it feasible to estimate reliability in this fashion. Then, too, we worried that unreliability in the test and retest would be correlated, producing an inflated reliability estimate.

Fortunately, some time after our work began, Jöreskog (1970) and Werts and Linn (1975) described a way to develop models of reliability for single-indicator constructs measured through time. We used this technique to estimate the reliability of our television exposure index. This technique is based on the causal model shown in Figure C.2. In that model, the reported television exposure scores (tv_j) are imperfect indicators of unobserved true exposure scores (TV_j), which change through time, not only because of true shifts in exposure but also because of factors not included in the model (u_j). In the model, the term (e_j) refers to random measurement errors that affect the observed exposure scores (tv_j).

It is never possible to prove a theoretical model such as this one, but it is possible to see how well the actual data fit it. When the fit is good, and when the assumptions are plausible, it is possible to interpret the model results as if they were true estimates of the unobserved variables. The mathematics in the present case are involved and the interested reader is referred to the original papers just cited for a detailed discussion. In brief, with some assumptions to be described in the following, it is possible to estimate the fit of the model in Figure C.2 to the data and also to estimate the correlations between unobserved true scores and the observed scores.

The key assumption implicit in the model is that the true exposure scores change in such a way that exposure at Wave j has a direct causal impact on exposure at the next time point, Wave $j + 1$, but at no subsequent time point. If this assumption is warranted, it is possible to estimate the model unknowns. Fortunately, with six waves there are enough observed data elements both to estimate the model and to test the assumption.

In order to estimate the model, the reliability coefficients at the first and last time points are set to some arbitrary values. Certain algebraic manipulations presented by Jöreskog (1970) show that all parameters can be uniquely identified once this is done. Unfortunately, there is no way to estimate the reliability of Time 1 or Time 6 exposure in this procedure. However, the products of the reliability and the stability coefficients between the outer time-point measures and all other inner time-point measures are identified.

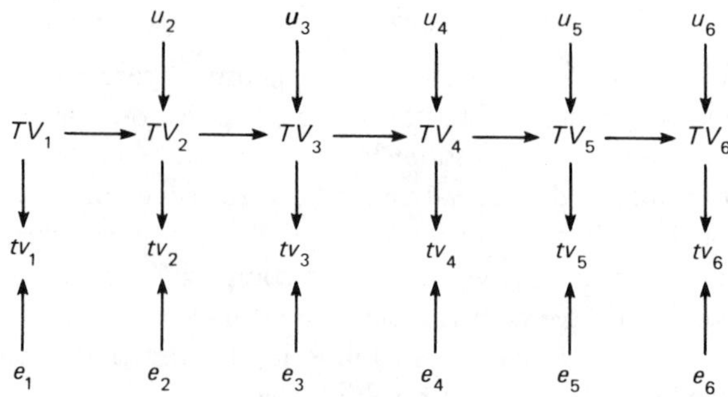

FIGURE C.2. *Basic measurement model of change in television exposure through time.*

When this model was estimated for valid reporters, the value of χ^2 was 3.6 with 6 degrees of freedom (*df*), a very good fit. It is, therefore, reasonable to assume that the model coefficients represent accurate stability and reliability estimates. The estimated correlations between each TV_j and its associated tv_j are given in the first row of Table C.1. These coefficients are all between .77 and .87 and do not show any trend through time. Reliability, the square of these coefficients, is then between .59 and .76; this means that between 59% and 76% of the variance in the violent television exposure score is true variance, and between 24% and 41% is error.

The second row of Table C.1 presents results for the total sample, including less valid reporters. The third and fourth rows repeat the analyses for the measure of total exposure rather than the violence weighted score. Since the total and weighted exposure scores are highly related, it is not surprising to find that the results in rows one versus three and two versus four are very similar.

Details of the parameters in these models are presented in Table C.7 at the end of this appendix.

TABLE C.1
Correlations between True and Observed Exposure Scores

	r_2	r_3	r_4	r_5	χ^2	*df*	*N*
Violence exposure							
Valid reporters	.793	.876	.853	.773	3.648	6	(204)
Total sample	.851	.872	.884	.849	16.253	6	(428)
Total exposure							
Valid reporters	.762	.864	.932	.696	8.883	6	(204)
Total sample	.832	.864	.917	.794	17.203	6	(428)

Two-Wave Measurement Models of Television Effects

Using the estimates of television reliability given in Table C.1, we estimated a number of two-wave models of the effect of television exposure on aggression over time, all based on the general model in Figure C.1. These models were estimated over the full 15 panel wave pairs. The reliability of the exposure score was set at the values estimated earlier by setting the variances of the true exposure scores at $R \times$ (observed variance), where R is the reliability coefficient for each exposure score reported in Table C.1.

Although our method of computing reliability produced no estimate of the reliability of television exposure at Wave I, it did allow us to set upper and lower limits on such an estimate. Since Wave I was the first data collection and the children were younger than at subsequent measurement points, we felt that reliability might be lower in that wave than in the others. Therefore we set the upper limit equal to the estimated reliability in Wave II, reasoning that it was unlikely that children would give better data the first time out than the second. The lower limit was set from an empirical estimate, derived as follows.

Figure C.3 presents the stability and true score-indicator correlations estimated for the violent exposure model of valid reporters, just described in Table C.1, line 1. As noted, the product of the Time 1 correlation and the Time 1 − Time 2 true score stability is uniquely identified in this model. This product is .660. From the model we can see that true score exposure is highly stable over the short time intervals between Waves II–III (4 months) and III–IV (3 months). We can reasonably assume, then, that exposure is equally stable over the interval I–II (5 months). Using this assumption in conjunction with the product $a \times b$ in Figure C.3, we can solve for the reliability coefficient:

$$\text{Stability}^{\,2}_{\text{I--II}} \times \text{Reliability}_{\,\text{I}} = .660^2$$

$$\text{Reliability}_{\,\text{I}} = \frac{.660^2}{\text{Stability}^{\,2}_{\text{I--II}}}$$

If we assume stability over the 5-month interval is .955, then reliability is $.691^2$. If we assume that stability is .990, the reliability is $.667^2$. We can therefore take values of exposure reliability in the vicinity of $.700^2 - .650^2$ as the lower bound of the reliability of TV_1.

The variance of an unmeasured or true score is arbitrary. Therefore, we fixed the variance of true aggression at the beginning of each panel at 300. The subsequent aggression variances have been estimated with this as a base, assuming that the true aggression scores in each pair have constant structural relationships over time with their observed indicators. This assumption assures a constant operational definition of true aggression over time.

The basic measurement error model illustrated in Figure C.1 was used to estimate the impact of television violence exposure for both valid reporters

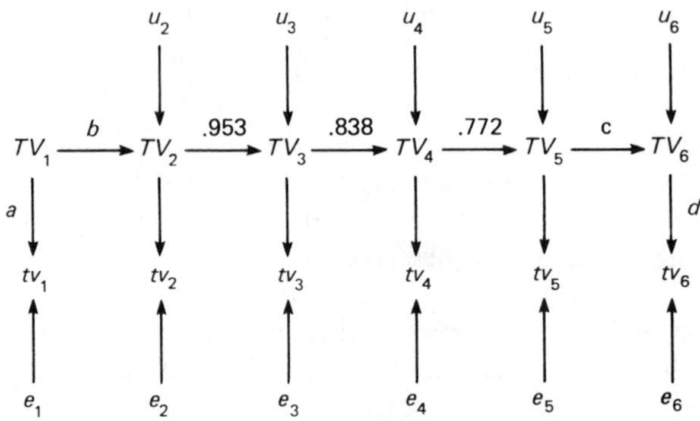

FIGURE C.3. *Basic measurement model of change in television exposure through time with estimated stability and true score indicator correlations.*

and for the total sample under a variety of different specifications of the error terms. We estimated models in which all errors were assumed to be perfectly uncorrelated through time; others in which all autocorrelated errors were allowed; and still others that estimated only selected error correlations. We found that the best-fitting model in most wave pairs was one that allowed only errors of the "lie" indicators to be correlated over time. This indicator showed consistent significant autocorrelations, whereas none of the other indicators did. We suspect that the labeling of a child as a "liar" plays a role in this pattern, because the child's reputation can be more consistent than actual behavior, thus biasing this indicator.

The adjusted regression coefficients derived from this measurement error model are presented in Tables C.2 and C.3 for valid reporters and in Tables C.4 and C.5 for the total sample.[18] Tables C.2 and C.4 utilize the upper limit

[18]The full set of parameter estimates for all wave pair models is given in Table C.8 at the end of this appendix. Each model is estimated on a matrix containing $9 \times 10/2$ or 45 independent variances and covariances. The constraints in this model require the estimation of 16 independent parameters: four *b* coefficients between each true aggression score and its four observed indicators; eight error variances for the observed aggression indicators; an exogenous correlation between violence exposure and aggression at the beginning of the panel; two regression coefficients; and a correlation between the errors of the lie indicators over time. We estimate four rather than eight *b* coefficients between true aggression and its indicators as a way of imposing the assumption that the aggression score we are measuring is exactly the same score through time. Inspection of residuals and partial derivatives shows that this is a warranted assumption in these data. Each model thus has $45 - 16$ or 29 degrees of freedom. The models all have χ^2/df ratios of 5.0 or less, which we judge to be adequate representations of the data. Detailed results of the models with all indicator measurement errors autocorrelated (valid and total errors correlated for the total sample) are available in Documentation 6. This documentation also contains a complete set of the covariance matrices used in these various estimates.

TABLE C.2

Regression Coefficients Showing the Impact of Violent Television Exposure on Later Aggression for All Wave Pairs, LISREL Two-Wave Models, Valid Reporters, Errors of Lie Indicator Correlated, Reliability $TV_1 = TV_2$

		EARLIER AGGRESSION COEFFICIENTS		UNIQUE CONTRIBUTION OF EARLIER AGGRESSION TO TOTAL R^2	EARLIER VIOLENT TELEVISION EXPOSURE COEFFICIENTS		UNIQUE CONTRIBUTION OF EARLIER VIOLENT TELEVISION EXPOSURE TO TOTAL R^2	TOTAL R^2	VARIANCE OF CHANGE IN AGGRESSION EXPLAINED BY EARLIER TELEVISION	X^2/df	N
WAVE PAIR	DURATION	b (1a)	β (1b)	(2)	b (3a)	β (3b)	(4)	(5)	(6)	(7)	(8)
III–IV	3 months	.953*	.885	.767	.059*	.078	.006	.803	.028	4.6	(497)
II–III	4 months	.889*	.876	.761	.035	.046	.002	.777	.009	3.7	(413)
I–II	5 months	.760*	.723	.511	−.036	−.042	.002	.516	.004	2.1	(364)
II–IV	7 months	.868*	.792	.621	.101*	.124	.015	.664	.041	2.5	(409)
I–III	9 months	.765*	.713	.501	−.014	−.016	.000	.506	.001	2.2	(356)
I–IV	1 year	.744*	.669	.440	.032	.035	.001	.455	.002	2.0	(349)
IV–V	1 year	.749*	.759	.549	−.032	−.043	.002	.564	.004	4.1	(301)
V–VI	1 year	.710*	.750	.559	.054	.075	.006	.576	.013	1.3	(188)
III–V	1 year/3 months	.757*	.753	.537	.011	.015	.000	.572	.001	3.2	(291)
II–V	1 year/7 months	.783*	.694	.460	.011	.014	.000	.486	.000	3.6	(240)
I–V	2 years	.735*	.627	.379	.083	.086	.007	.421	.012	2.0	(211)
IV–VI	2 years	.684*	.721	.480	.041	.059	.003	.547	.007	2.2	(161)
III–VI	2 years/3 months	.644*	.663	.410	.087*	.133	.017	.502	.032	2.0	(147)
II–VI	2 years/7 months	.803*	.699	.469	.059	.070	.005	.514	.010	1.7	(121)
I–VI	3 years	.699*	.573	.327	.149	.146	.021	.359	.032	1.7	(112)

*Significant at .05 level.

TABLE C.3

Regression Coefficients Showing the Impact of Violent Television Exposure on Later Aggression for Wave Pairs Beginning with Wave I, LISREL Two-Wave Models, Valid Reporters, Errors of Lie Indicator Correlated, Reliability $TV_1 < TV_2$

WAVE PAIR	DURATION	EARLIER AGGRESSION COEFFICIENTS		UNIQUE CONTRIBUTION OF EARLIER AGGRESSION TO TOTAL R^2	EARLIER VIOLENT TELEVISION EXPOSURE COEFFICIENTS		UNIQUE CONTRIBUTION OF EARLIER VIOLENT TELEVISION EXPOSURE TO TOTAL R^2	TOTAL R^2	VARIANCE OF CHANGE IN AGGRESSION EXPLAINED BY EARLIER TELEVISION	χ^2/df	N
		b (1a)	β (1b)	(2)	b (3a)	β (3b)	(4)	(5)	(6)	(7)	(8)
III–IV	3 months										
II–III	4 months										
I–II	5 months	.763*	.726	.510	−.053	−.051	.003	.516	.005	2.1	(364)
II–IV	7 months										
I–III	9 months	.766*	.714	.500	−.020	−.019	.000	.507	.001	2.2	(356)
I–IV	1 year	.742*	.667	.434	.047	.042	.002	.456	.003	2.0	(349)
IV–V	1 year										
V–VI	1 year										
III–V	1 year/3 months										
II–V	1 year/7 months										
I–V	2 years	.726*	.620	.365	.121	.105	.010	.424	.018	2.0	(211)
IV–VI	2 years										
III–VI	2 years/3 months										
II–VI	2 years/7 months										
I–VI	3 years	.695*	.569	.322	.215	.175	.030	.368	.045	1.7	(112)

*Significant at .05 level.

TABLE C.4

Regression Coefficients Showing the Impact of Violent Television Exposure on Later Aggression for All Wave Pairs, LISREL Two-Wave Models, Total Sample Errors of Lie Indicator Correlated, Reliability $TV_1 = TV_2$

		EARLIER AGGRESSION COEFFICIENTS		UNIQUE CONTRIBUTION OF EARLIER AGGRESSION TO TOTAL R^2	EARLIER VIOLENT TELEVISION EXPOSURE COEFFICIENTS		UNIQUE CONTRIBUTION OF EARLIER VIOLENT TELEVISION EXPOSURE TO TOTAL R^2	TOTAL R^2	VARIANCE OF CHANGE IN AGGRESSION EXPLAINED BY EARLIER TELEVISION	X^2/df	N
WAVE PAIR	DURATION	b (1a)	β (1b)	(2)	b (3a)	β (3b)	(4)	(5)	(6)	(7)	(8)
III–IV	3 months	.933*	.858	.713	.041	.066	.004	.760	.017	5.4	(620)
II–III	4 months	.863*	.871	.741	.031*	.058	.003	.777	.014	5.5	(571)
I–II	5 months	.688*	.698	.456	−.020	−.034	.001	.476	.002	3.8	(505)
II–IV	7 months	.814*	.769	.577	.065*	.113	.012	.632	.031	3.2	(559)
I–III	9 months	.684*	.696	.453	−.016	−.028	.001	.476	.002	3.4	(486)
I–IV	1 year	.695*	.669	.418	.024	.037	.001	.461	.002	2.9	(478)
IV–V	1 year	.751*	.776	.545	−.009	−.015	.000	.595	.001	5.1	(360)
V–VI	1 year	.683*	.745	.544	.039	.070	.005	.575	.011	1.7	(246)
III–V	1 year/3 months	.790*	.756	.522	.017	.029	.001	.585	.002	4.5	(362)
II–V	1 year/7 months	.793*	.730	.493	.016	.027	.001	.544	.002	3.9	(328)
I–V	2 years	.665*	.617	.347	.087*	.135	.017.	.449	.029	2.4	(296)
IV–VI	2 years	.641*	.715	.450	.011	.022	.000	.522	.001	2.3	(204)
III–VI	2 years/3 months	.666*	.668	.415	.056	.103	.010	.493	.019	1.8	(205)
II–VI	2 years/7 months	.696*	.667	.407	.041	.074	.005	.480	.010	2.1	(191)
I–VI	3 years	.496*	.508	.237	.054	.092	.008	.293	.011	1.8	(178)

*Significant at .05 level.

TABLE C.5

Regression Coefficients Showing the Impact of Violent Television Exposure on Later Aggression for Wave Pairs Beginning with Wave I, LISREL Two-Wave Models, Total Sample Errors of Lie Indicator Correlated, Reliability of $TV_1 < TV_2$

WAVE PAIR	DURATION	EARLIER AGGRESSION COEFFICIENTS b (1a)	EARLIER AGGRESSION COEFFICIENTS β (1b)	UNIQUE CONTRIBUTION OF EARLIER AGGRESSION TO TOTAL R^2 (2)	EARLIER VIOLENT TELEVISION EXPOSURE COEFFICIENTS b (3a)	EARLIER VIOLENT TELEVISION EXPOSURE COEFFICIENTS β (3b)	UNIQUE CONTRIBUTION OF EARLIER VIOLENT TELEVISION EXPOSURE TO TOTAL R^2 (4)	TOTAL R^2 (5)	VARIANCE OF CHANGE IN AGGRESSION EXPLAINED BY EARLIER TELEVISION (6)	X^2/df (7)	N (8)
III–IV	3 months										
II–III	4 months										
I–II	5 months	.689*	.699	.452	−.024	−.038	.001	.476	.003	3.8	(505)
II–IV	7 months										
I–III	9 months	.685*	.698	.450	−.020	−.031	.001	.476	.002	3.4	(486)
I–IV	1 year	.693*	.667	.410	.028	.041	.002	.462	.003	2.9	(478)
IV–V	1 year										
V–VI	1 year										
III–V	1 year/3 months										
II–V	1 year/7 months										
I–V	2 years	.656*	.608	.331	.106*	.150	.020	.452	.036	2.4	(296)
IV–VI	2 years										
III–VI	2 years/3 months										
II–VI	2 years/7 months										
I–VI	3 years	.491*	.503	.228	.065	.102	.009	.295	.014	1.8	(178)

*Significant at .05 level.

TABLE C.6
Ratio of Average Potential Impact to Average Range of Aggression Scores for the Estimation Models over the Longest Time Intervals

	RAW	COMPLEX
Impact	15	5
Range	350	88
Impact/Range	.04	.06

reliability estimate of violent television exposure at Time I. Tables C.3 and C.5 present results for wave pairs beginning with Wave I which utilize the lower limit reliability estimate.

The coefficients in these tables are very similar to those presented in Table 6.2, which reports the basic findings of the analysis without adjustment for measurement error. Even when the instability in the coefficients due to measurement imprecision is partialed out, the conclusions stated earlier hold. Exposure to television violence is not a significant predictor of subsequent change in the aggression of boys in this population.

The average *b* coefficient over the longest wave pairs, estimated for the complex measurement model in Tables C.2 and C.3, is about .110,[19] meaning that the maximum possible alteration in aggression due to manipulation of exposure to television is approximately (exposure range) × .110. We have no estimate of the true score exposure range, but we can assume it to be about the same as that estimate for the raw model with the observed exposure score (a range of 72 points from the 10th to 90th percentile in Wave I), multiplied by the reliability of the score (.63 in Wave I), or about 45 points. Thus, if this was a true significant association, the maximum estimated impact of exposure to television on aggression over this 3-year interval would be 45 × .11, or about 5 points.

In the measurement model, the average standard deviation of the aggression scores is approximately 17, which is about one-fourth as large as the average standard deviation estimated in the raw models.[20] We can therefore reasonably

[19]Note that this average *b* coefficient is a good deal smaller than that estimated in Table 6.1 (average of .21), because the scales of these two models are quite different. For example, the standard deviation of the initial aggression score in Table 6.1 is about 70 points; in Table C.2 (the LISREL table), it is approximately 17 points. Thus, even though it is numerically smaller, the average *b* coefficient estimated in the complex measurement model represents a larger proportion of the standard deviation of the aggression score than that estimated in the earlier models.

[20]As just mentioned, the variance of true aggression at the beginning of each panel was arbitrarily set at 300; subsequent aggression variances, estimated with this as a base, were very similar in size.

TABLE C.7

Parameter Estimates for LISREL Six-Wave Measurement Models of Violent and Total Television Exposure, Valid Reporters, and Total Sample

	VIOLENCE EXPOSURE				TOTAL EXPOSURE			
	VALID REPORTERS		TOTAL SAMPLE		VALID REPORTERS		TOTAL SAMPLE	
	M	S	M	S	M	S	M	S
				Epistemic correlations				
tv_1	1.0^f	*	1.0^f	*	1.0^f	.623**	1.0^f	.762**
tv_2	1.0^f	.793	1.0^f	.850	1.0^f	.762	1.0^f	.832
tv_3	1.0^f	.876	1.0^f	.871	1.0^f	.864	1.0^f	.864
tv_4	1.0^f	.853	1.0^f	.885	1.0^f	.932	1.0^f	.917
tv_5	1.0^f	.773	1.0^f	.848	1.0^f	.696	1.0^f	.794
tv_6	1.0^f	*	1.0^f	*	1.0^f	*	1.0^f	*
				Variances				
Var (TV_1)	441.069	1.0	845.535	1.0	30.728**	1.0	85.453**	1.0
Var (TV_2)	527.996	1.0	1022.406	1.0				
Var (TV_3)	617.337	1.0	922.264	1.0	55.531	1.0	93.099	1.0
Var (TV_4)	539.818	1.0	859.992	1.0	57.281	1.0	91.369	1.0
Var (TV_5)	415.485	1.0	739.135	1.0	24.051	1.0	52.867	1.0
Var (TV_6)	267.808	1.0	579.147	1.0	16.086	1.0	46.199	1.0
Var (u_2)	141.503	.268	196.302	.192	0	0	0	
Var (u_3)	56.795	.092	97.760	.106	3.554	.064	8.472	.091

Var (u_4)	160.326	.297	101.479	.118	20.392	.356	13.614	.149
Var (u_5)	167.856	.404	240.958	.326	10.318	.429	13.481	.255
Var (u_6)	85.163	.318	158.107	.273	2.976	.185	9.055	.196
				Covariances				
Cov (tv_1, TV_2)	412.194	.659	835.481	.772				
Cov (TV_5, tv_6)	275.623	.625	558.070	.735	11.872	.403	36.997	.625
				Stability coefficients				
$b_{TV_1TV_2}$	*	*	*	*	1.0**	1.0**	1.0**	1.0
$b_{TV_2TV_3}$	1.032	.953	.899	.946	1.303	.968	.994	.953
$b_{TV_3TV_4}$	.783	.838	.905	.939	.814	.802	.915	.923
$b_{TV_4TV_5}$	.677	.772	.762	.821	.490	.756	.656	.863
$b_{TV_5TV_6}$	*	*	*	*	*	*	*	*
χ^2	3.648		16.253		8.883		17.203	
χ^2/df	.608		2.709		1.481		2.867	
N	(204)		(428)		(308)		(428)	

M = metric coefficients
S = standardized coefficients
f = fixed

*None of these values are individually identified although the terms Cov (tv_1, TV_2) and Cov (TV_5, tv_6) are identified. All other parameters internal to these in the model are individually identified. We estimated these by arbitrarily assigning fixed values to the measurement errors at times 1 and 6.

**Preliminary analysis of this model suggested that the stability between total exposure at times 1 and 2 was perfect. Therefore, we made the following constraints on the model: $b_{TV_1TV_2} = 1.0$ and Var (u_2) = 0. These constraints allowed us to estimate the epistemic correlation of tv_1 and TV_1 uniquely.

TABLE C.8

Parameter Estimates for the LISREL Two-Wave Measurement Models over 15 Wave Pairs, Valid Reporters ($df = 29$), Errors of Lie Indicator Correlated, Reliability $TV_1 = TV_2$

WAVE PAIRS:	I-II		I-III		I-IV		I-V	
	M	S	M	S	M	S	M	S
				Epistemic correlations				
$mean_{1i}$	.899	.857	.912	.862	.890	.859	.802	.847
lie_{2i}	.822	.838	.743	.805	.799	.834	.652	.781
$hits_{3i}$	1.010	.905	1.006	.906	1.014	.908	.972	.882
$push_{4i}$	1.093	.947	1.065	.944	1.051	.940	.947	.919
$mean_{1j}$	.899	.912	.912	.909	.890	.898	.802	.889
lie_{2j}	.822	.880	.743	.886	.799	.878	.652	.832
hit_{3j}	1.010	.938	1.006	.932	1.014	.952	.972	.930
$push_{4j}$	1.093	.949	1.065	.959	1.051	.965	.947	.952
tv_i	1.000^f	.793	1.000^f	.793	1.000^f	.793	1.000^f	.793
				Variances				
Var (A_i)	300.000^f	1.0	300.000^f	1.0	300.000^f	1.0	300.000^f	1.0
Var (A_j)	330.977	1.0	345.374	1.0	371.298	1.0	411.230	1.0
Var (TV_i)	449.806^f	1.0	437.359^f	1.0	424.812^f	1.0	447.528^f	1.0
Var (u_j)	160.378	.484	170.453	.494	202.331	.545	238.204	.579
				Correlated errors				
Covar ($A_i TV_i$)	55.472	.151	42.531	.117	46.906	.131	68.655	.187
Covar ($e_{2i} e_{2j}$)	.258	.296	.120	.157	.197	.215	.266	.272
				Regression coefficients				
$b_{A_i A_j}$	.760	.723	.765	.713	.744	.669	.735	.627
$b_{TV_i A_j}$	−.036*	−.042	−.014*	−.016	.032*	.035	.083*	.086
χ^2	61.73		64.16		58.73		56.94	
	[illegible]		[illegible]		[illegible]		2.0	

WAVE PAIRS::	I–VI		II–III		II–IV		II–V	
	M	S	M	S	M	S	M	S
				Epistemic correlations				
$mean_{1i}$	.802	.905	.981	.927	.958	.925	.893	.925
lie_{2i}	.694	.860	.798	.845	.854	.865	.737	.833
$hits_{3i}$	.897	.839	1.072	.942	1.069	.938	.989	.928
$push_{4i}$	.888	.890	1.119	.948	1.101	.946	1.006	.924
$mean_{1j}$	.802	.916	.981	.921	.958	.924	.893	.900
lie_{2j}	.694	.881	.798	.878	.854	.889	.737	.866
$hits_{3j}$	.897	.936	1.072	.934	1.069	.948	.989	.923
$push_{4j}$	.888	.970	1.119	.957	1.101	.964	1.006	.950
tv_i	1.000^f	.793	1.000^f	.793	1.000^f	.793	1.000^f	.793
				Variances				
Var (A_i)	300.00^f	1.0	300.000^f	1.0	300.000^f	1.0	300.000^f	1.0
Var (A_j)	447.276	1.0	308.822	1.0	360.244	1.0	379.848	1.0
Var (TV_i)	431.629^f	1.0	541.455^f	1.0	548.613^f	1.0	558.378^f	1.0
Var (u_j)	286.994	.641	68.868	.223	121.195	.336	195.921	.514
				Correlated errors				
Covar ($A_i TV_i$)	19.995	.056	37.868	.093	41.195	.103	86.638	.212
Covar ($e_{2i}e_{2j}$)	−.034	−.031	.289	.331	.386	.397	.255	.263
				Regression coefficients				
$b_{A_iA_j}$	.699	.573	.889	.876	.868	.792	.783	.694
$b_{TV_iA_j}$	.149*	.146	.035*	.046	.101	.124	.011*	.014
χ^2	48.99		107.77		71.80		103.30	
χ^2/df	1.7		3.7		2.5		3.6	
N	(112)		(413)		(409)		(240)	

(*Continued next page*)

TABLE C.8 (*continued*)

WAVE PAIRS:	II–VI		III–IV		III–V		III–VI	
	M	S	M	S	M	S	M	S
				Epistemic correlations				
$mean_{1i}$	.848	.917	.984	.912	.959	.898	1.007	.883
lie_{2i}	.765	.850	.807	.871	.771	.863	.801	.859
$hits_{3i}$	.923	.903	1.068	.935	1.066	.952	1.095	.956
$push_{4i}$	.936	.895	1.095	.950	1.057	.956	1.068	.943
$mean_{1j}$	.848	.935	.984	.920	.959	.893	1.007	.913
lie_{2j}	.765	.910	.807	.870	.771	.835	.801	.872
hit_{3j}	.923	.911	1.068	.952	1.066	.924	1.095	.913
$push_{4j}$	.936	.967	1.095	.962	1.057	.947	1.068	.955
tv_i	1.000^f	.793	1000^f	.876	1.000^f	.876	1.000^f	.876
				Variances				
Var (A_i)	300.000^f	1.0	300.000^f	1.0	300.000^f	1.0	300.000^f	1.0
Var (A_j)	395.704	1.0	347.806	1.0	303.702	1.0	283.184	1.0
Var (TV_i)	572.030^f	1.0	613.666^f	1.0	589.183^f	1.0	663.668^f	1.0
Var (u_j)	192.464	.486	68.441	.197	130.003	.428	140.976	.498
				Correlated errors				
Covar $(A_i TV_i)$	82.205	.198	43.162	.101	97.012	.231	115.444	.259
Covar $(e_{2i} e_{2j})$	.273	.324	.431	.398	.326	.287	.177	.193
				Regression coefficients				
$b_{A_i A_j}$	.803	.699	.953	.885	.757	.753	.644	.663
$b_{TV_i A_j}$	.059*	.070	.059	.078	.011*	.015	.087	.133
χ^2	48.26		131.97		93.63		59.40	
χ^2/df	1.7		4.6		3.2		2.0	
N	(121)		(497)		(291)		(147)	

WAVE PAIRS:	IV–V		IV–V		V–VI	
	M	S	M	S	M	S
			Epistemic correlations			
$mean_{1i}$	.986	.922	1.031	.964	1.043	.919
lie_{2i}	.813	.860	.911	.902	.846	.814
$hits_{3i}$	1.137	.954	1.129	.941	1.151	.914
$push_{4i}$	1.144	.966	1.157	.953	1.154	.953
$mean_{1i}$	.986	.902	1.031	.923	1.043	.911
lie_{2j}	.813	.835	.911	.890	.846	.872
hit_{3j}	1.137	.922	1.129	.925	1.151	.920
$push_{4j}$	1.144	.947	1.157	.959	1.154	.951
tv_i	1.000^f	.853	1.000^f	.853	1.000^f	.773
			Variances			
Var (A_i)	300.000^f	1.0	300.000^f	1.0	300.000^f	1.0
Var (A_j)	292.133	1.0	270.159	1.0	269.254	1.0
Var (TV_i)	519.874^f	1.0	561.333^f	1.0	513.560^f	1.0
Var (u_j)	127.373	.436	122.414	.453	114.066	.424
			Correlated errors			
Covar $(A_i TV_i)$	84.899	.215	113.621	.277	30.799	.078
Covar $(e_{2i} e_{2j})$	.337	.307	.262	.259	.209	.280
			Regression coefficients			
$b_{A_i A_j}$	.749	.759	.684	.721	.710	.750
$b_{TV_i A_j}$	−.032*	−.043	.041*	.059	.054*	.075
χ^2	119.72		65.24		39.01	
χ^2/df	4.1		2.2		1.3	
N	(301)		(161)		(188)	

M = metric coefficients.
S = standardized coefficients.
f = fixed.
*Coefficient does *not* exceed twice its standard error.

TABLE C.9

Parameter Estimates for the LISREL Two-Wave Measurement Models over 15 Wave Pairs, Valid Reporters ($df = 29$), Errors of Lie Indicator Correlated, Reliability $TV_1 < TV_2$

WAVE PAIRS:	I-II		I-III		I-IV		I-V		I-VI	
	M	S	M	S	M	S	M	S	M	S
					Epistemic correlations					
$mean_{1i}$	.899	.857	.912	.862	.890	.859	.802	.847	.802	.905
lie_{2i}	.822	.838	.743	.805	.799	.834	.652	.781	.694	.860
$hits_{3i}$	1.101	.905	1.006	.906	1.014	.908	.972	.882	.897	.839
$push_{4i}$	1.093	.947	1.065	.944	1.051	.940	.947	.919	.888	.890
$mean_{1j}$	.899	.912	.912	.909	.890	.898	.802	.889	.802	.897
lie_{2j}	.822	.880	.743	.886	.799	.878	.652	.832	.694	.862
hit_{3j}	1.101	.938	1.006	.935	1.014	.952	.972	.930	.897	.915
$push_{4j}$	1.093	.949	1.065	.959	1.051	.965	.947	.952	.888	.948
tv_i	1.000^f	.660	1.000^f	.660	1.000^f	.660	1.000^f	.660	1.000^f	.660

					Variances					
Var (A_i)	300.000^f	1.0	300.000^f	1.0	300.000^f	1.0	300.000^f	1.0	300.000^f	1.0
Var (A_j)	330.970	1.0	345.387	1.0	371.292	1.0	411.236	1.0	427.652	1.0
Var (TV_i)	311.789^f	1.0	303.161^f	1.0	294.464^f	1.0	310.210^f	1.0	299.190^f	1.0
Var (u_j)	160.119	.484	170.419	.493	202.138	.544	236.839	.576	282.745	.632
					Correlated errors					
Covar ($A_i TV_i$)	55.475	.181	42.521	.141	46.903	.158	68.665	.225	19.967	.067
Covar ($e_{2i} e_{2j}$)	.258	.296	.120	.157	.197	.215	.266	.272	−.034	−.031
					Regression coefficients					
$b_{A_i A_j}$	.763	.726	.766	.714	.742	.667	.726	.620	.695	.569
$b_{TV_i A_j}$	−.053*	−.051	−.020*	−.019	.047*	.042	.121*	.105	.215*	.175
χ^2	61.73		64.16		58.73		56.94		48.99	
χ^2/df	2.1		2.2		2.0		2.0		1.7	
N	(364)		(356)		(349)		(211)		(112)	

M = metric coefficients.
S = standardized coefficients.
f = fixed.
*Coefficient does *not* exceed twice its standard error.

assume that the range of this score is about 88, or one-fourth the average range of the earlier scales scores used in the simple attenuation models. As before, we can think of a potential impact of 5 points as a percentage of the range, and this perspective can be used to compare the coefficients showing violent television's maximum potential impact in the raw data model and the complex measurement model.

Table C.6 gives the comparable numbers for the two estimation procedures. In the raw model the greatest potential impact of exposure to television violence occurred over the five longest wave pairs. As we reported earlier, over the five pairs this impact was estimated to average about 15 points on a scale with a range of 350 points. That is, by taking an unexposed child and exposing him to a very great deal of violent television fare we can expect, at most, to increase his aggressiveness over long time periods (between 2 and 3 years) by about 15 points, or 4% of the range. In the complex measurement model, exposure to television violence has a maximum potential of 5 points on a range of 88 points, for a 6% increase in terms of the range. Thus, the potential impact estimated for the complex measurement model is somewhat higher than for the raw model, although the basic conclusion remains the same—that even the greatest potential impact of exposure estimated by these models is small in substantive terms.

Finally, Tables C.7, C.8, and C.9 are shown to provide comparable data for different LISREL models.

CHAPTER 7

ADDITIONAL ANALYSES

If we had found a substantial, significant causal association between television exposure and aggression in the previous chapter, much of the analysis reported in this chapter would have been superfluous. However, since we did not find such an association, we undertook a variety of additional analyses to make sure this finding was not due to shortcomings in our measures or methods of analysis.

The first of these additional analyses explores whether our findings are replicated when violent television exposure is conceptualized in different ways—for example, as relative exposure to violence and to other programs.

Next we examine the relationship between television and aggression in subgroups of the sample. This analysis tests the hypothesis that exposure effects are more likely to appear among children who are predisposed to act aggressively or are in situations that might facilitate aggression.

The next two analyses are smaller in scope. The first examines whether the analysis model used to explore causal relationships between television and aggression is able to detect significant associations between variables other than television exposure and aggression. The purpose of that analysis is to show that the basic model employed in the previous chapter would have shown significant associations between television and later aggression if they existed.

The final analysis reported here examines mutual causes of television and aggression that were not controlled in the basic analysis model. As described in Chapter 5, there is a limited class of variables not controlled by this model. The analysis examines the effect of some of these variables on the findings reported in the previous chapter. All these analyses confirm the conclusions in Chapter 6.

OTHER CONCEPTUALIZATIONS OF TELEVISION EXPOSURE AND THEIR EFFECT ON AGGRESSION

In the preceding chapter, we assessed the effect of exposure on aggression through analyses using a measure of exposure to "violent" television programs. Here we consider the possibility that this conceptualization of the independent variable was not optimal in showing the full extent of television's effect on later aggression by replicating the analysis with six alternative conceptualizations of television exposure.[1] (Data in the tables are based on valid reporters; findings based on total samples are summarized.[2])

Relative Amount of Exposure to Television Violence

The violence exposure measure used so far ignores exposure to nonviolent programs. It is possible, however, that television violence affects aggressive behavior only when the television "diet" consists of a large proportion of violent programs.

There are at least three possible reasons why this may be so.

First, the effect of exposure to violence may be neutralized by exposure to programs with nonviolent themes. Thus, a viewer who watches a lot of violent and nonviolent programs may not be affected. But a viewer with an equally high score on the violence exposure measure who watches only violent programs is getting a more concentrated dose, and therefore may be influenced more.

Second, a viewer who watches a very high proportion of violent programs overselects those programs, and this may be an indication of enthusiasm for and receptiveness to violence on television. It is reasonable to hypothesize that children who like violent programs may become more involved in them, may

[1]To review briefly, our measure of exposure to violent television programs was computed by multiplying respondents' viewing reports by weights based on public perceptions of violence content. Discrepancies between the public's perceptions and the true amount of violence in these programs could affect the measure's power. Also, since the weighting system assigns a 0 to programs perceived as nonviolent by the public, the violence exposure measure does not take exposure to such shows into account.

[2]Additional details of the analyses (e.g., descriptions of the measures used, correlations between measures, detailed tables for total samples) are available on request.

identify more with the characters, and may be more impressed by the violent actions.

Finally, in our data, total exposure and violence exposure are highly correlated—about .92. This is partly true because we oversampled violent programs. However, it also reflects the fact that, on the average, heavy viewers of violent programs also watch many nonviolent programs. It may be that some of these heavy viewers are very passive, unaggressive children and that this serves to mask the effect of exposure to violent programs among other children.

To test these possibilities, we computed a measure of relative amount of exposure to violent programs. This is the ratio of the violence exposure score to the total exposure score. However much they watched in total, those scoring low on this measure watched proportionately little violence, and those scoring high watched proportionately much. In other words, this measure tells us how much violence (in terms of the 0–7 weighting scale) a child was exposed to per program watched.[3]

The cross-sectional correlations between this measure and the violence exposure measure vary between .19 and .55 (see Table A.1).[4] These weak to moderate correlations show that we have, in fact, found a different way to conceptualize television exposure.

The violence ratio was used in basic model regressions, replacing the violence exposure measure. Standardized partial regression coefficients for the 15 lags are shown in Table 7.1. To permit easy comparison between the new measure and the old one, coefficients based on both variables are presented.

The comparison shows that relative exposure to violent television is not a better predictor than violence exposure. Indeed, the number of statistically significant coefficients drops from almost 3 to 1. Only 2 of 15 coefficients are slightly larger; 12 are smaller; and 1 is the same as comparable coefficients

[3]The measure of relative exposure has a possible range from 0 to 7. The observed scores range from 0 to between 5.2 and 7.0, depending on the wave. In other words, there was at least one child watching only programs rated 0 in each wave, but in some of the waves there was nobody who watched only programs rated 7 or 6. Most watched a mixture of program types. Other statistics give additional indications that most respondents watched a mixture of programs with different violence weights. The means and medians are close to 3.0 and the standard deviations are quite small, .7 to .9. On the average, then, the boys watched programs rated 3 on the 0–7 scale. Since very few programs had violence weights of 3 (or 2 or 4, for that matter), these means and medians indicate that respondents watched a mixture of shows rather than predominantly programs rated 3 (see Appendix A in Chapter 4).

[4]The table, which includes all the exposure measures used in this chapter, also shows cross-sectional correlations with aggression.

Note that this measure, as well as most other conceptualizations of television exposure discussed in the following, was computed for Waves I–V only. Wave VI data were not computed because they are not used in our basic model analyses.

TABLE 7.1
Standardized Partial Regression Coefficients Showing the Net Effect of Exposure to Violent Television and of Relative Amount of Exposure to Violent Television on Aggression (Valid Reporters)

	β		
WAVE PAIR	EXPOSURE TO VIOLENT TELEVISION	RELATIVE AMOUNT OF EXPOSURE TO VIOLENT TELEVISION[a]	*N*
III–IV	.063*	.068*	(497)
II–III	.038	.011	(413)
I–II	−.026	−.064	(364)
II–IV	.094*	−.015	(409)
I–III	−.006	−.048	(356)
I–IV	.023	−.033	(349)
IV–V	−.026	−.032	(301)
V–VI	.058	−.000	(188)
III–V	.007	−.016	(291)
II–V	.016	−.036	(240)
I–V	.067	−.007	(211)
IV–VI	.049	.005	(161)
III–VI	.121(*)	.040	(147)
II–VI	.065	.091	(121)
I–VI	.113	−.060	(112)

[a]Violent television score/total television score = "amount" of violence per program watched.

*Significant at .05 level.

(*)Close to significant at .05 level.

obtained with the violence exposure measure.[5] Findings for total samples are almost identical: the number of significant coefficients drops from 2 to 1.

[5]It can be argued that the measure of relative exposure to television violence is inadequate because it ignores the absolute amount of violence viewed. We therefore reestimated the basic model with both the violent exposure score and the relative exposure measure as independent variables, hypothesizing that together they might predict aggression significantly. We also computed a multiplicative term of violence exposure × violence ratio, hypothesizing that those who were high viewers and watched relatively more violent than nonviolent programs might be influenced to behave aggressively. (The same method of analysis is used below for "Liking TV.")

Table A.2 shows the coefficients of multiple determination for these various equations. There is no systematic improvement over the model containing only the violent television measure as a predictor. In only one instance of the 15 wave pairs is the violence ratio a significant improvement over the violence exposure score (wave pair III–IV) and in only one is the interaction significant (wave pair V–VI). In a set of 15 trials these results could easily have occurred by chance.

Exposure over Longer Time Periods

In each wave, we asked children to indicate how often they watched the programs on the checklists during the past 4 weeks (in the case of weekly prime-time and weekend programs) or during the past week (in the case of daily weekday programs). It may be that a measure reflecting viewing patterns over a longer period of time is necessary to detect an effect on television.

The second conceptualization of television exposure examines this possibility by studying exposure over periods of more than 4 weeks—in fact, up to 2 years.

As we do not know the child's viewing behavior prior to Wave I, we cannot consider additional information about "previous viewing" for the 5 lags starting with the first wave. However, we do have information about previous viewing for the other 10 lags, and this is the information used for this analysis. In time lags starting with Wave II, we were able to add viewing information from one additional wave. In lags starting with later waves, we are able to add viewing data from more than one wave. Since it may be important how many exposure measures are entered in a given regression, we proceeded by adding each wave of available prior exposure data cumulatively, one at a time. As shown in Table A.3, there are 10 ways of using 2 consecutive waves of data, 3 ways of using 4, and 1 way of using 5, making 20 tests in all.

To determine whether adding television exposure information in this manner increases the power to predict aggression, we compared results from these regressions with results using only one exposure variable. There is multicollinearity among television measures from different waves. Consequently we do not examine the predictive ability of each exposure measure, but the coefficient of multiple determination, R^2, adjusted for the number of variables in the regressions.

In Table 7.2, the 20 lags are arranged according to the number of exposure measures entered. R^2s are shown for all lags with two, three, and four/five exposure measures. The first column shows coefficients for regressions with aggression and one exposure variable, the second, coefficients for regressions with aggression and several measures.[6] A comparison of the coefficients shows clearly that measures of exposure over longer time periods are not better predictors of later aggression. There is only one significant increase in R^2 in the 20 lags examined.[7]

Apparently, then a simple additive model of exposure over multiple waves fails to improve the predictive power of television exposure on aggression. However, we speculated that *consistency* of exposure to violence over a long

---

[6]The models with several exposure measures also pick up linear effects of change in exposure (between the earliest and latest exposure measures) on aggression. For more on this interpretation, see Kessler and Greenberg (1981, Chapter 2).

[7]When total samples are analyzed, there are two significant increases in R^2 in the 20 lags.

TABLE 7.2
Effect of Exposure over Longer Time Periods (Valid Reporters)

NUMBER OF WAVES OF TELEVISION MEASURE	LAGS	ADJUSTED R^2 ONE TELEVISION VARIABLE[a]	CUMULATIVE	CONSISTENCY	N
Two	I,II–III	.741	.740	.741	(282)
	I,II–IV	.646	.648	.647	(277)
	I,II–V	.461	.467	.465	(174)
	I,II–VI	.464	.457	.453	(83)
	II,III–IV	.767	.768	.768	(356)
	II,III–V	.525	.523	.524	(212)
	II,III–VI	.529	.524	.523	(102)
	III,IV–V	.590	.588	.587	(249)
	III,IV–VI	.527	.534	.531	(122)
	IV,V–VI	.605	.606	.602	(131)
Three	I,II,III–IV	.801	.801	.799	(249)
	I,II,III–V	.559	.566	.565	(155)
	I,II,III–VI	.536	.533	.534	(70)
	II,III,IV–V	.586	.582	.594	(187)
	II,III,IV–VI	.545	.549	.539	(89)
	III,IV,V–VI	.608	.627*	.621	(108)
Four	I,II,III,IV–V	.598	.606	.620*	(139)
	I,II,III,IV–VI	.540	.530	.541	(63)
	II,III,IV,V–VI	.626	.625	.623	(82)
Five	I,II,III,IV,V–VI	.614	.602	.599	(58)

[a]R^2 coefficients in this column are based on prediction equations using one television exposure variable and all the aggressive scores associated with the time lags for which cumulative television effects are going to be assessed. for example, the R^2 value in the first row is based on the multiple regression of A_3 on A_1, A_2, and TV_2. The R^2 value of .801 in the 11th row is obtained by regressing A_4 on A_3, A_2, A_1, and TV_3.

*R^2 increments significant at .05 level.

period of time might influence the behavior of children in a way that exposure over a period of a few weeks could not. To test this possibility, we added a series of interaction terms to the prediction equations.[8] These are shown in the third column of the table. Only 1 of these 20 coefficients significantly increases the R^2 in the second column.

[8]These terms are all multiplicative functions of the form $TV_i \times TV_j$, for time periods i and j. They represent the consistency of exposure over and above the additive influence of exposure at each of the waves separately. These regressions were again compared with those containing only one television measure and additional aggression terms. For example, we compared the effects of A_1, A_2 and TV_2 on A_3 with the effects of A_1, A_2, TV_1, TV_2, $TV_1 \times TV_2$ on A_3.

Alternative Violence Weighting Systems

The two conceptualizations of television exposure discussed so far both used the public perception violence weights that were part of the original violence exposure measure. To investigate the possibility that this weighting system is flawed, we estimated regressions in which exposure to programs with different violence weights were treated as separate variables. In other words, instead of entering one single measure of violence exposure, we entered one variable that represented the amount of exposure to programs weighted "0", another that represented "1" programs, and so on.[9] Instead of assigning fixed violence weights ahead of time, we let the regressions determine these weights on the basis of the relative ability to predict aggression.[10]

Table 7.3 shows the R^2 coefficients associated with this set of exposure scores as well as those for the regressions reported in Table 6.1. To take into consideration the greater number of exposure scores used in the new set of equations, we present adjusted R^2 values in both columns of the table. As we see from a comparison of the two sets of coefficients, the adjusted coefficients are very similar in the medium and long lags, but are somewhat larger for the set of several measures in the short lags. Coefficients that represent a significant increase over the basic model results are indicated by an asterisk.

Further analysis of the results presented in Table 7.3 shows that the three sets of weights that are significantly better predictors than the 0–7 scheme are not similar to each other and, when applied individually to the complete set of 15 wave pairs, they do not produce R^2 coefficients consistently higher than the set produced by the 0–7 weighting scheme.[11]

On the basis of these results, we conclude that no alternative weighting

---

[9]The individual programs and their weights are listed in Chapter 4, Appendix A. Cross-sectional correlations between television exposure and aggression are shown in Table A.1. All the measures of exposure to programs with different violence weights are positively correlated (most correlations are between about .20 and .50), indicating that respondents who tend to watch one kind of program also watch the others.

[10]In multiple regressions, the raw regression "weights" are identical to the weights that would be applied to the predictors in a composite measure of overall, additive influence. The weights produce the best linear–additive composite. It should be pointed out that this is only one of a very large number of possible tests of the weighting system. The approach just described tells us whether groups of programs derived from public perceptions of the amount of violence can be weighted in a better way. This approach was chosen over one in which all programs in the checklists are entered separately into regressions. Because this would have resulted in regressions with up to 50 independent variables, such analyses would not have been conclusive given our sample sizes.

[11]Increases in R^2 are about the same in analyses with total samples, averaging .011 in the 15 lags (versus .009 with valid reporters in Table 7.3). Five increases are significant, however, no consistent pattern could be detected.

TABLE 7.3

Variance in Later Aggression (Adjusted R^2) Explained by Prior Aggression and Exposure to Television, Measured in One Violence Exposure Variable or in Several Variables Based on the "Violence Weights" of Programs Watched (Valid Reporters)

	R^2		
WAVE PAIR	EXPOSURE TO VIOLENT TELEVISION	SEVEN MEASURES OF EXPOSURE TO TELEVISION BASED ON "VIOLENCE WEIGHTS"	*N*
III–IV	.747	.751	(497)
II–III	.717	.733*	(413)
I–III	.464	.505*	(364)
II–IV	.613	.658*	(409)
I–III	.446	.454	(356)
I–IV	.399	.400	(349)
IV–V	.530	.533	(301)
V–VI	.528	.540	(188)
III–V	.538	.543	(291)
II–V	.442	.450	(240)
I–V	.363	.356	(211)
IV–VI	.513	.530	(161)
III–VI	.453	.445	(147)
II–VI	.467	.456	(121)
I–VI	.302	.317	(112)

*Significant increase in R^2 (.05 level).

scheme would consistently improve our ability to predict aggression from violent television exposure.[12]

Context of Televised Violence

The violence exposure measure uses weights that appear to rank programs primarily according to the amount of perceived violence. However, the *quantity* of violence may not be the decisive factor. It may be the *context* in which televised violence occurs that has the decisive effect on whether or not exposure to a program with violent content influences the viewer's aggressiveness.

[12]Although we have not stated so much in the text, it should be clear that our measure of total television exposure, introduced first in Chapter 4, is implicitly included here as one weighting scheme. Since this measure simply adds together total exposure without weighting of any kind, it is equivalent to giving a weight of "1" to each of the various exposure categories.

Because total exposure and violent exposure scores are correlated over .9 in each wave, it is not surprising to find that analysis of the 15 coefficients produced by estimation equations using the total exposure measure are virtually identical to those obtained by the violence exposure equations (data not shown).

To evaluate this, we grouped programs in the checklists according to the context in which violent and nonviolent action occurred, and constructed measures of exposure to these program clusters.

Our search for ways of conceptualizing the context in which television violence is portrayed began with a literature review. The role of violence context has been examined in experimental studies by several investigations, and most recently by Belson (1978) in a cross-sectional survey.[13] Researchers have investigated the following contextual dimensions: realistic versus unrealistic violence context (Belson, 1978; Berkowitz & Green, 1966; Feshbach, 1972; Lieberman Research 1975); cartoon versus live portrayals (Bandura, Ross & Ross, 1961; Belson, 1978); exciting versus unexciting violence (Zillmann, 1971); dramatic versus humorous violence (Belson, 1978; Lieberman Research, 1975). Belson analyzed many additional dimensions, including violence performed by "good guys" and "in a good cause"; "glorified," "gruesome," and "slap-stick" violence; violence in westerns, science fiction, and sports programs.

We did not test all the contextual dimensions investigated by other researchers. First, some program types (such as sports) were not listed regularly in the program checklists; we stipulated that a program type had to appear in at least four of the six waves in order to be analyzed. Second, we felt classifications such as "violence in a good cause" or "violence performed by good guys" could not be made reliably and decided to restrict ourselves to less subjective classifications.

Based on the research evidence and the considerations just mentioned, we computed the following exposure variables: (exposure to) realistic crime dramas, adventure programs (non- or semirealistic context), westerns, cartoons, slapstick, news documentaries, sitcoms, variety, educational, and miscellaneous. Appendix A has detailed descriptions of these categories.[14]

These exposure measures are interrelated: viewing one kind of program is related to viewing others. (The average correlation is close to .30, the highest is .58.)

---

[13]A good summary of research in this area can be found in Comstock (1976).

Belson (1978) tried to pinpoint which of 25 types of "violent" programs were more or less "likely to stimulate" aggression. Most of these program types were related over .8 to the total exposure measure and about .7 to each other. This kind of overlap can easily cause multicollinearity and, thus, produce erroneous findings.

Because of the overlap between viewing of different program types in Belson's as well as in our data, we believe that attempts to determine exactly which program types are associated with aggression and which are not cannot be successful. The analysis strategies applied in this chapter are designed to avoid erroneous conclusions as a result of multicollinearities.

[14]Note that movies are excluded as—in contrast to television series—movie series have a different content week after week.

TABLE 7.4
Variance in Later Aggression (Adjusted R^2) Explained by Prior Aggression and Exposure to Television, Measured in One Violence Exposure Variable or Measured in Several Variables Based on the Context in Which Violent and Nonviolent Action Occurs (Valid Reporters)

	R^2		
WAVE PAIR	EXPOSURE TO VIOLENT TELEVISION	7–10 MEASURES OF EXPOSURE TO TELEVISION BASED ON "CONTEXT OF VIOLENCE"	*N*
II–IV	.747*	.751*	(497)
II–III	.717	.726*	(413)
I–II	.464	.480*	(364)
II–IV	.613*	.643*	(409)
I–III	.446	.439	(356)
I–IV	.399	.385	(349)
IV–V	.530	.528	(301)
V–VI	.528	.555*	(188)
III–V	.538	.533	(291)
II–V	.442	.453	(240)
I–V	.363	.355	(211)
IV–VI	.513	.520	(161)
III–VI	.453(*)	.438	(147)
II–VI	.467	.467	(121)
I–VI	.302	.302	(112)

*Significant R^2 component associated with television exposure (.05 level).

The analysis proceeds by evaluating the R^2 increments associated with the context of exposure scores, as compared to the basic model $A_t = \beta_1 A_{t-1} + \beta_2 TV_{t-1}$.[15] To facilitate comparison of overall R^2 values, the basic model results from Table 6.1 are presented as well in Table 7.4. As we see, five coefficients contain significant components due to television exposure in the violence context models, as compared to almost three such coefficients in the basic model. In the short lags, there appears to be some evidence that the context measures outperform the basic violence exposure measure in accounting for variance. (Four of the five significant television components can be found in these short lags.) However, as in the previous analysis of measures with different weights, there is no consistency in which of the exposure measures contribute significantly to the increase in R^2: Significant contributors include

[15]This method, rather than an analysis of increases in R^2 as in Table 7.3, is appropriate here, since we do not simply separate the regular violence exposure measure into its components (programs rated 0, 1, etc.) but compute entirely different measures.

exposure to adventure shows, westerns, variety, and miscellaneous.[16] Thus, on balance, this finding does not support the hypothesis that different kinds of violent portrayals have differential effects on boys' aggression.

Empirical Viewing Patterns

None of the conceptualizations examined so far were based on empirically occurring viewing patterns. The analysis in the present section examines patterns of this sort, delineated by factor analyses of program-by-program viewing information.[17] Our initial interest is in the kinds of programs that group together in a factor.

Boy's viewing does form some patterns: There are instances where programs of a similar nature are viewed more or less selectively. Many of these viewing patterns occur in several waves and some are, in fact, characterized by exposure to violent programs.

We found between seven and nine factors in each of the waves, which together explain between 44% and 56% of the variance in boys' viewing reports—suggesting that about half of the boys' viewing is differentiated by distinct viewing patterns.

Table 7.5 summarizes the kinds of factors found in the six waves.[18] Listed first are those that appear to indicate viewing of specific program types; then come those that indicate viewing patterns according to dayparts and networks; and finally, unclassifiable factors. Action/adventure factors and sitcom factors appear in all waves. News, Saturday morning cartoon, and weekday factors as well as unclassifiable factors appear in five waves; other factors appear less frequently. Note that there are many instances where more than one factor in a

[16]In analyses with total samples, we find two significances with the usual exposure measure, three with the "context" measures.

[17]Programs analyzed were television series shown in both cities of the study. The procedure used was a principal factor solution. Both orthogonal and oblique rotations were performed, with essentially the same factors appearing in both solutions.

The measures include only those programs that contribute to a factor according to the following criteria: Arbitrarily, a television program was considered to contribute significantly to a particular factor if the absolute value of its factor loading was greater than .3, and if its factor loading on all other factors was low in comparison. Each factor solution involved only factors whose eigenvalues were greater than 1.0. Each solution explained approximately 50% of the overall variation.

[18]The factors listed in the table are labeled in terms of what we considered the common element of the programs described as important contributors. As is always the case with factor analysis, identifying a common element is an inductive process that is not always clear-cut. In fact, such an identification was not possible in some cases, and those factors are labeled "unclassified."

TABLE 7.5
Number and Kinds of Factors in Each Wave

FACTOR LABEL	NUMBER OF FACTORS IN WAVE I	II	III	IV	V	VI	TOTAL
Action/Adventure	1	1	1	1	1	2	7
Westerns/*Hee Haw*	1	0	1	0	0	0	2
News/Documentary	1	1	1	1	1	0	5
Saturday morning cartoons	1	2	2	3	2	0	10
Sitcoms	1	2	2	2	1	1	9
Saturday–Sunday	1	1	1	0	0	0	3
Weekday	2	0	1	1	1	1	6
ABC	1	0	0	0	0	0	1
Unclassified factors	0	0	0	1	2	4	7
Total number of factors in wave	9	7	9	9	8	8	(50)

wave has the same label. In some instances, we were able to find a differentiating element between these factors (such as ABC and other sitcoms); in others we were not.[19]

From our examination of the factor structure we concluded that identifiable viewing patterns exist, but that they are not very strong or tightly knit and usually do not sharply delineate one type of viewing from another. In general, it seems that children, like adults, watch what is available during the time they have for watching television. The viewing diets of heavy and light viewers differ more in quantity than in quality.

By looking at the amount of aggression variance explained, we can see

[19]Table A.4 shows cross-sectional correlations between the factors and violent television exposure and aggression.

Closer examination of the factor loadings (available on request) shows that there are a number of instances where the dominant programs in a factor are not the only ones with high factor loadings, indicating that a factor is not very sharply defined. For example, in Wave I, the dominant programs in Factor 1 have loadings of .55 and .47. The next highest program has a loading of .42, but it is not regarded as a dominant program because it has a loading of .37 on the ABC factor as well.

There are instances where a factor appears to be "impure" with regard to the dimension underlying the viewing pattern ("unclassified factors"). Factor 1, Wave V is an example. The dominant programs are *Gunsmoke*, *Mod Squad*, *Eddie's Father*, *FBI*, *Bonanza*, *Dr. Dolittle*, and *Jackson 5*. Those programs include two westerns, two action–adventure shows, one situation comedy, and two cartoons. They are shown at different times and on different channels. Since there is no identifiable dimension underlying these programs, we cannot explain any possible effects of this viewing pattern.

whether the different factors together are better predictors of aggression than the measures we have examined so far. If they are, we can examine each factor separately to see which kinds of viewing patterns caused the increase in R^2.

Table 7.6 presents the results of this analysis. The right-hand side of the table shows the amount of variance explained through regressions with the measures based on factors; that explained by regressions with the violence exposure measure is shown on the left. Regressions with one violence exposure measure produce only two (almost three) significant coefficients; regressions with exposure measures based on factors produce four significant coefficients. A comparison of the average R^2s shows that they are very similar; there is little improvement in prediction with these measures.[20]

We examined which factors are significantly related to aggression in these analyses. The data show that there is no consistency: Across the 15 wave pairs sitcoms appear as significant contributors in four lags—three times with a positive and once with a negative sign. Cartoons and other Saturday–Sunday programs also appear with positive and negative signs in different lags. Further, measures of exposure to "violent" programs (crime, adventure, westerns) do not appear as significant contributors in any of the 15 lags. (See Table A.5.)

LIKING VIOLENT TELEVISION

Finally, we investigated whether a measure of liking to watch violent television programs would be useful in detecting an effect of television exposure.

This conceptualization of exposure is different from the ones discussed above, because it does not directly measure either amount or kind of viewing. Instead, it assesses the effect of the respondent's enjoyment of violent television programs in conjunction with the amount of his or her exposure to such programs.

Using data on viewer preferences in this way follows a line of thought laid down by Eron *et al.* (1972), Lefkowitz *et al.* (1972), McIntyre and Teevan (1972), Weigel and Jessor (1973), and Jessor and Jessor (1977), as well as research by Ekman (1972). All of these authors suggest that television violence is more likely to have an effect on those who like it, because they may watch it more attentively, become more involved in it, and may identify with the characters more closely.

Our measures of liking violence are based on "favorite show" measures similar to the one used in the 10-year longitudinal study by Lefkowitz, Eron,

[20]In analyses with total samples, very similar results were obtained.

TABLE 7.6

Variance in Later Aggression (Adjusted R^2) Explained by Prior Aggression and Exposure to Television, Measured in One Violence Exposure Variable or Measured in Several Variables Based on Factor Analyses (Valid Reporters)

	R^2		
WAVE PAIR	EXPOSURE TO VIOLENT TELEVISION	7–9[a] MEASURES OF EXPOSURE TO TELEVISION BASED ON FACTOR ANALYSES	N
III–IV	.747*	.743*	(497)
II–III	.717	.723	(413)
I–II	.464	.480*	(364)
II–IV	.613*	.622*	(409)
I–III	.446	.449	(356)
I–IV	.399	.393	(349)
IV–V	.530	.548*	(301)
V–VI	.528	.542	(188)
III–V	.538	.541	(291)
II–V	.442	.443	(240)
I–V	.363	.358	(211)
IV–VI	.513	.520	(161)
III–VI	.453(*)	.453	(147)
II–VI	.467	.441	(121)
I–VI	.302	.332	(112)

[a]See Table 7.5 for number of factors in waves.
*Significant R^2 component associated with television exposure (.05 level).

and their colleagues (1972). In the last three waves we asked children to name their three favorite programs, and in the interview with mothers (at the time of Waves III and IV), we asked them to name their boys' three favorite programs. We thus have two different measures, one self-reported by the children, the other reported by the mothers.

To create a measure of the violence content of the favorite programs, we summed the violence weights for the three programs mentioned as favorites, separately for the self-reported measure and the one based on mothers' reports. The higher the score, the higher the violence content of the child's best-liked programs.

The violence weights used here are a truncated, 3-point version (with the values 0–2) of those used in constructing the violence exposure measure.[21] If a

[21]As explained in Chapter 4, not all programs used in our checklists were rated in the research on which the violence weight system was based, but we extrapolated from the rated programs to unrated ones, by following specific rules. It was often not possible to follow this procedure with

respondent or his mother reported three violent favorites, the score on the favorite measures is 6; if all three were nonviolent, the score is 0. The correlation between self-reported (Wave IV) and mother-reported favorite scores is .33, indicating considerable disagreement between mothers and children.[22]

Table 7.7 shows the results of the analysis.[23] Column 1 of the table shows the adjusted R^2 in aggression from the model in Table 6.1 for those with favorite show data. In Column 2, we present the R^2 from an equation that adds the favorite-show measure to this basic equation. This equation shows no particular improvement over Column 1; none of the coefficients are significantly larger than those from the basic model equations. In Column 3, we show the results of adding an interaction term between liking and exposure, which is crucial to testing this hypothesis. However, none of the coefficients in Column 3 is significantly larger than the corresponding coefficient in column 2.[24]

The analysis shown in Table 7.7 was repeated with favorite-show measures obtained from mothers' reports, with no change in the results reported here (see Table A.6).[25]

Summary

In this section, we have examined six alternative conceptualizations of television viewing: relative exposure to television violence; exposure over

programs mentioned as favorites, as these included imprecise terms such as "sports programs." In addition, several programs were listed with whose content we were less familiar than we were with the series included in the program checklists. Because of these ambiguities, we were not able to extrapolate using the original 8-point scale. It was possible, however, to assign a 3-point rating scale to all programs, and this simplified scale is the one that was used. Programs that had been rated by the Greenberg/Gordon/Murray samples, or, based on that research, by us for the violence exposure measure, were rated in the following way: 0 remained 0, 1–3 programs were rated 1, 4–7 programs were rated 2.

[22]For cross-sectional relationships between these measures and aggression and violent television exposure, see Table A.1. See Chapter 15 for a discussion of use of this kind of measure in the Lefkowitz/Eron study (1972).

[23]Wave IV data were analyzed for all lags in order to use the largest number of cases available. Similar findings are obtained if the Wave V measure is used even though the two measures are only related .27.

[24]The same results were obtained with total samples.

[25]It should be emphasized that we believe this finding does not warrant a rejection of hypotheses concerning the importance of attentiveness, involvement, and liking television content for detecting effects of television. First, this test addresses only one issue—namely, whether liking a certain kind of program content, namely violent content, affects *aggression*. Preferences for violent or other programs may well affect attitudes or other kinds of behavior. Second, we do not think that a favorite show measure of this kind by itself is necessarily sufficient to determine what kinds of programs a viewer likes, what programs he or she attends to from start to finish, which action he or she gets involved in, or what characters he or she identifies with, and further research along these lines is clearly in order.

TABLE 7.7

Variance in Later Aggression (Adjusted R^2) Explained by Prior Aggression and Exposure to Television, Measured in One Violence Exposure Variable or Measured by Adding a Favorite Show Measure[a] or Measures by Adding a Favorite Show Measure and an Interaction Term (Valid Reporters)[b]

	R^2			
WAVE PAIR	EXPOSURE TO VIOLENT TELEVISION	FAVORITE SHOW MEASURE ADDED	FAVORITE SHOW MEASURE AND INTERACTION TERM ADDED	N^c
III–VI	.762	.763	.763	(426)
II–III	.716	.716	.716	(346)
I–II	.420	.424	.423	(292)
II–IV	.624	.626	.629	(348)
I–III	.469	.470	.468	(294)
I–IV	.442	.441	.439	(295)
IV–V	.535	.534	.538	(283)
V–VI	.548	.548	.542	(141)
III–V	.573	.572	.572	(255)
II–V	.477	.479	.483	(210)
I–V	.411	.408	.406	(182)
IV–VI	.518	.515	.512	(154)
III–VI	.421	.421	.417	(126)
II–VI	.482	.481	.485	(108)
I–VI	.294	.289	.283	(98)

[a]Violence rating of programs mentioned in "self-reported favorite show" measure. The Wave IV measure was used for all lags.

[b]Based on respondents with "favorite show" data in Wave IV.

[c]This is smaller than the number of respondents with valid exposure data used in earlier analyses. As a result, R^2 coefficients in the first column (basic model results comparable to those in Table 6.1) were recomputed on the smaller samples and so differ from the coefficients presented in earlier tables in this chapter.

longer time periods; alternative violence weighting systems; violence contexts; empirical viewing patterns; and liking violent programs. All these analyses failed to uncover a measure of viewing that is consistently or significantly a better predictor of aggression than the violence exposure measure initially used. The measures using alternative violence weights and those based on context of violence seemed to be somewhat better predictors in the short lags. However, a close look at the data showed there was no consistency in which measures contributed to the R^2 increase. Measures based on empirical viewing patterns (factors) caused small but significant R^2 increases in four lags. But again, there was no consistency in which viewing patterns caused the increase.

Finally, there is no evidence in any of the tests that exposure to programs generally considered violent predicts aggression better than does exposure to other kinds of programs. Because of the overlap between different exposure measures, it is impossible to isolate the association between a specific program or program type and aggression. However, the various analyses conducted here consistently failed to show significant associations between aggression and any kind of program, including police and detective dramas, adventure shows, westerns, and cartoons—the types of programs many researchers have mentioned as those most likely to influence aggression. These tests also found that exposure to the most violent program types was no more strongly associated with later aggression than exposure to nonviolent programs. It is clear, then, that these results are essentially the same as those reported in Chapter 6.

EFFECTS OF EXPOSURE TO TELEVISION VIOLENCE AMONG SAMPLE SUBGROUPS

Up to this point, we have focused on the total sample, frequently excluding the less valid reporters of television viewing, but otherwise studying the relationship between television exposure and aggression among all the boys who gave us information at any particular point in time. On the basis of this analysis, we concluded that the aggressiveness of the average boy in the sample was not influenced in a meaningful way by the dimensions of television exposure measured in this study.

However, certain children may be influenced by the television programs they watch, even though the average child is not. This possibility was expressed in a conclusion of the Surgeon General's Report, which stated, "The evidence does indicate that televised violence may lead to increased aggressive behavior in certain subgroups of children who might constitute a small portion or a substantial portion of the total population of young television viewers [1972:7]." As Eleanor Maccoby has put it, we should be less concerned with asking whether the media have any effect than with asking "*how much* or *what kind* of children" will be affected, and under what circumstances (1964:327). The following analyses address these questions.

Theoretical Perspective

There are different ways of conceptualizing an interaction effect in the present context. One is that television acts as a reinforcer of predispositions to act aggressively, that greater exposure to television violence only leads to increased aggression when other conditions conducive to acting aggressively are present.

This possibility is consistent with social psychological research concerning the effects of mass communication, which emphasizes that the media are more likely to reinforce existing predispositions than to alter them significantly (e.g., Klapper, 1960; Kraus & Davis, 1976; Liebert & Schwartzberg, 1977). Given the limited ability of mass media to change behavior radically, it would seem more likely that television violence would cause aggressive behavior among those already leaning in that direction than among those not generally inclined to act aggressively.

This possibility is also consistent with findings in the experimental literature. In virtually all experiments where exposure to television violence has been shown to have an effect, children have been frustrated prior to measuring the behavioral effects of exposure. Thus, these experiments suggest that it is a combination of exposure and frustration that leads to the impact of television.[26]

So far, we have discussed one possible type of interaction effect between television and children's characteristics—namely, the role of television as a *reinforcer* of predispositions to aggression. However, we can also envision a different way in which television and children's characteristics might interact to produce aggressive behavior. Certain characteristics may act as *facilitators* of television's effects. Unlike predisposing factors, facilitators do not produce aggression in and of themselves. Instead, they make it easier for other factors to do so. In this sense, a "black-out" and the consequent silencing of burglar alarms can be considered a facilitating condition for theft, but not a predisposing or motivating cause of it. Facilitators increase the possibility that people who may be inclined to be aggressive by virtue of their exposure will actually act more aggressively. Such variables as physical size, or the absence of parental supervision and controls, may function in this way.

Method of Analysis

Analyses were done in a manner similar to those for the entire sample in Chapter 6. After subgroups had been defined in terms of attributes that could predispose to, or facilitate, communication effects, regressions were computed for each of the subgroups across all of the available 15 wave pairs.[27]

We have noted that attrition from the panel makes it more difficult to find significant television effects in the longer than in the shorter lags. This becomes more pronounced when we begin examining subsamples. In a few instances a

[26]This reasoning is also consistent with one of the major conclusions of the Surgeon General's Report, which stated: "Any such causal relation [that is, between TV violence and aggression] operates only on some children (who are predisposed to be aggressive)[1972:11]."

The report did not define the phrase "predisposed to be aggressive." It did, however, give two examples of "predisposed" groups: those highly aggressive to start with, and those who like to see violent acts (1972:75). Such predispositions might be defined narrowly, as limited to characteristics of the child himself, or more broadly, as including characteristics of his social environment. We view predisposition in the broader sense, assuming that any pressures, internal or external, which themselves tend to make children act aggressively, may be predisposing factors.

[27]Given the small samples in the subgroups, we did not control intervening television scores. Thus, the analysis model is identical to that used in Table 6.1.

subsample was so small that we decided not to analyze it. In other instances we were able to analyze only the short wave pairs.[28] Because of small sample sizes, results from these analyses are tentative: β coefficients below .20 are not significant in many of the regression equations. On the other hand, our power to discover effects among subgroups is increased by the fact that we have examined a large number of conceptually related groups. As a result, we almost always have several indicators of a behavior or attitude under consideration.

Overview of Findings

The sample was divided on the basis of 43 different variables that tap the sorts of factors which might play a role in the television–aggression relationship. Most of these are characteristics that may predispose the child to act aggressively: a history of aggressiveness, having aggressive friends, living in a family in which aggression is common or in which aggressive behavior is condoned. We also examined a few characteristics that might facilitate aggressive behavior, for example, lack of supervision.

The 43 measures are reported in Table 7.8. (More detailed information about the question wording of the measures can be found in Appendix C.) Most of the 43 variables were dichotomized, some were divided into more refined categories, one at a time, to form a total of 95 overlapping subgroups. For each of these, 15 wave-pair models were estimated; in all, 1228 separate equations were calculated. (Tables are shown in Appendix B.)

Before considering this massive amount of data in detail, a global assessment is necessary. The reason is that statistical theory tells us that even if the associations in all subgroups are identical, some will show stronger and others weaker associations. In the many replications, the significant coefficients are not evenly, but randomly, distributed, and the criterion established for statistical significance (three or more significant coefficients out of 15 wave pairs) might be reached by chance in some of these groups. As discussed in the following, the criterion was, in fact, reached in a few subgroups.

A global assessment of the results requires an assessment of the baseline of chance expectation. In a set of overlapping subgroups, each examining 15 overlapping two-wave models, there is no rigorous way to estimate this baseline. But a rough evaluation is possible if we focus on adjacent wave pairs (I–II, II–III, III–IV, IV–V, and V–VI) where we do not have the overlap that makes inferences ambiguous. When we do this we find that about 9% of the coefficients in these subgroup analyses are statistically significant at the .05 level. Of the 95 subgroups, 61% have no significant adjacent wave pair

[28]Equations were estimated only when at least 30 cases were available for analysis. Hence, in some of the tables, analyses are based on fewer than 15 wave pairs. (The exact number of wave pairs analyzed is indicated in each table.)

TABLE 7.8
Summary of Measures Used in Subgroup Analysis

Sociocultural characteristics	Mother's occupation (1)[a]
	Family income (1)
	Race (1)
	City (1)
Family structure	Family type ["intact" versus "broken" home] (1)
	Family size (1)
Family relationships	
Early years:	Parents' attitudes toward pregnancy (2)
	Parents' feelings about raising boy (2)
	Father's activities with boy (5)
Current period:	Number of activities shared by family (4)
	Family religiosity (4)
	Mother's dissatisfaction with son (4)
Parental control and supervision	Mother's current work status (1)
	Number of rules
	— Mother has (17)
	— Father has (1)
	Strictness [in enforcing rules]
	—Of mother (1)
	—Of father (1)
	Mother's attempts to influence boy (6)
Parental use of punishment	Mother's use of physical punishment (6)
	Father's use of physical punishment (6)
	Mother's use of verbal punishment (1)
	Father's use of verbal punishment (6)
	Taking privileges away [as punishment by mother] (1)
Parental attitudes toward aggression	Mother's support for physical aggression (2)
	Father's support for physical aggression (4)
	Both parents' support for physical aggression (6)
Aggression of peers	Classroom aggression (1)
	Aggression of closest friends (1)
	Classroom and friends' aggression (2)
Boy's behavior, attitudes, and characteristics	
Aggressive predisposition:	Initial Aggression (1)
	Altruism (2)
Attitudes toward aggression:	Machismo (4)
	Gentleness (4)
	Enjoyment of real-life violence in films (6)
Other behavior characteristics:	Fantasy behavior
	— Teacher nominations (1)
	— Peer ratings (1)
	Emotional instability (5)
	Shyness (1)
	Size [large/small for age] (1,1)
	Age [grade in school] (1)
	Scholastic ability (1)
Exposure to other media:	Exposure to comic books (12)
	Exposure to theater movies (about 5)

[a]Numbers in parentheses indicate how many items the measure consists of. (For example, "(4)" indicates that the measure is a four-item index.) For additional details see Appendices B and C.

coefficients, 35% have exactly one, and 4% have exactly two. None has as many as three significant coefficients. On the basis of chance expectations, distributing an average of 9% significant coefficients across 95 subgroups, we would expect to find a distribution very close to this[29]: 64% with no significant coefficients, 30% with exactly one, 6% with two, and 1% with more than two. The discrepancy between the observed distribution and chance expectation has a χ^2 of 1.86, well within the bounds of chance.[30]

On the basis of this global assessment, then, there is no evidence that the relationship between television and aggression differs from one subgroup to another in any systematic way. The discrepancies we find in the data, where some subgroups have no significant coefficients and others have one or two, are consistent with chance expectations.

At the same time, it is useful to consider the patterns of association in the individual subgroups to see whether a substantive interpretation might be applied to these patterns despite the negative global assessment just described. For example, if practically all significant coefficients occurred in groups that have conditions facilitating aggressiveness, this might be interpreted as indicating a television effect among these groups. Therefore, in this section we summarize the patterns of association found within specific subgroups.

Results in Individual Subgroups

In 4 of the 95 subgroups examined, four significant coefficients occurred among the 15 wave pairs; in 1 subgroup there were five.[31] Only one of these groups consists of "predisposed" boys: Four coefficients reached significance in a group of boys rated "not shy" by their teachers (see Table B.8). No significant patterns were found among boys with clearly predisposing characteristics, such as violent surroundings either at home, in their school classes, or among their friends. Likewise, the boy's own initial aggression or his liking of violence in films was not a modifier of television exposure effects.

Four significant coefficients were also found among boys who are altruistic (see Table B.7), who do not enjoy watching violence (see Table B.7), and who

---

[29]There are 475 coefficients (95 subgroups times 5 coefficients in each) in these lags, of which 9% are significant. We generated a model to calculate the distribution of the number of significant coefficients in each set of 5 lags that would occur if these 475 were separated into 95 random groupings. This chance distribution closely corresponds to the distribution of the number of significant coefficients actually observed over all the groups studied.

[30]Chi-square was computed on the number of subgroups with 0, 1, and 2 or more significant lags. (The categories 2, 3, etc. were collapsed to meet the expected frequency requirements of the χ^2 test.)

[31]Note that coefficients in overlapping lags are included in this count. Summary tables for valid reporters and, separately, for total samples are shown in Appendix B. Detailed tables are in Documentation 7, "Subgroups Findings," available on request.

have little exposure to violent theater movies (see Table B.10). These are groups with below-average aggression scores. Thus, one might speculate that exposure effects are more likely to occur among those *not* predisposed. However, this is a proposition, which, to our knowledge, has never been suggested in the literature on television exposure effects and, as we have already noted, the overall distribution of significant coefficients agrees with a random model.

Finally, five significant coefficients were found among respondents rated as "low" in fantasy behavior by the teacher (see Table B.8). Coefficients in this subgroup are very small and the pattern of significance is not replicated in a "low fantasy" subgroup based on peer nominations (see Table B.8). It is not clear whether this group should be regarded as predisposed or not predisposed.[32]

Thus, the review of subgroups with several significant positive coefficients tends to confirm the findings of the global test. Since the overall distribution of significant coefficients does not differ from a random model, and since the patterns of significant coefficients do not conform to theoretical expectations, no substantive meaning should be applied to those patterns unless they are corroborated by future research.[33] Also, the groups in which significant coefficients were found are least likely to be affected by attrition. This indicates that there is no impact on the basic findings because television effects were mediated in groups lost through attrition. (See Chapter 2 for discussion.)

SENSITIVITY OF THE ANALYSIS MODEL

The failure to find a significant television–aggression relationship in the lagged models we have examined in the last two chapters may not reflect the lack of such associations in the data, but rather a shortcoming of the analysis

[32]J. L. Singer (1971) has suggested that children with a poor fantasy life are more predisposed to act aggressively than children who can act out their aggressions in imagination. However, we found those nominated as engaging in "make-believe play" (by their peers or teachers) to be more aggressive than those who are not.

[33]The same inconsistent pattern emerges when groups in which three or more coefficients are significant are considered.

There were eight groups with three significant positive coefficients in the 15 lags. Further, three out of six coefficients in the "very strict" group were significant. If these groups are considered in addition to the five with four or more coefficients, the following pattern emerges: three predisposed groups, five not predisposed, five ambiguous. (The latter group includes cases where the middle group produced significances, but the high and low groups did not.)

TABLE 7.9

Impact on Aggression of Exposure to Violence in Television and of Respondent's Socioeconomic Background and Personal Characteristics among Boys (Based on Basic Model Regressions)

	AVERAGE β	NUMBER OF SIGNIFICANT β COEFFICIENTS IN 15 LAGS
Violent television (high)	.04	2[a]
Aggression of class (increase/high)[b]	.33	15
Mother's occupation (low)	.09	5
Feelings about raising boy when young (difficult)	.06	2
Father hits son (often)	.11	5
Average grade in school (low)	.04	3

[a]An additional coefficient approaches significance.

[b]Combined: "aggression of class" at earliest time (t_1) and change in "aggression of class" (between t_1 and t_2). β coefficients for "aggression of class" alone average .13 for boys, .04 for girls; beta coefficients for change scores average .39 for boys, .23 for girls.

model: the model may be too insensitive to detect causal associations over the range of time lags studied. Or the aggression score may be so stable that no significant predictors could possibly be found. To evaluate this possibility empirically, we explored whether analyses using the same basic model and the same aggression measure are sensitive enough to reveal significant associations between variables other than television exposure and our aggression measures. Variables selected for the analysis were those measured more than once that were consistently related to aggression in the cross-sectional analysis.[34]

From the correlates of aggression among boys, shown in Table 5.5, we selected five of the strongest correlates: aggressiveness of the boy's classmates,[35]

[34]Table 5.5, in Chapter 5, lists all significant correlates of aggression.

[35]Preliminary analyses with the measure of classmates' aggressiveness indicated that not only the level of past aggression but also the change between the two waves is an important factor. The model in this analysis is $A_t = b_1 A_{t-1} + b_2 CC_{t-1} + b_3 \Delta CC$, where CC = current classroom aggression context and CC_{t-1} = classroom aggression context at time $t-1$. It should be remembered that this measure is quite different from other measures considered in that it undergoes drastic changes at several points during the study. Each time the class changes, the aggressiveness of the classmates changes. This model to study change in classroom aggression is equivalent mathematically to one that examines the cumulative effects of CC_{t-1} and CC_t on A_{t+1} (Kessler & Greenberg, 1981: Chapter 2). It will be recalled that a model to study the cumulative effects of television was presented in Table 7.2.

average scholastic grade in school, mother's occupation, parents' feelings about raising child when young, and father hits son.[36]

Results of the analyses are summarized in Table 7.8. (All measures are coded to give the high value to the characteristic with the hypothesized effect of increasing aggressiveness.)

Table 7.9 shows that three of the five measures examined for boys have a consistent and significant association with aggression. The associations are strongest for "aggression of class": βs average .33 and are significant in all 15 lags. Another significant predictor is "father hits son," where the βs average .11 and 5 out of the 15 coefficients are significant, and "mother's occupation," where the βs average .09, also with 5 significant coefficients. In other words, these analyses suggest that boys who are in classrooms with a lot of aggressive children, whose fathers often hit them, and whose mothers have blue collar occupations tend to become more aggressive over time relative to their counterparts without these background characteristics.[37]

Cautious interpretation of the meaning of the results for the imputation of causality is in order, as the variables available for this analysis were not as carefully or as frequently measured as the television and aggression variables. Nor can we be sure that significant predictors reveal the existence of a causal effect, as outside factors may have produced the results. Testing for spuriousness would be a necessary first step toward clarifying the causal issue. Other steps would include tests for measurement error, nonlinearities, and nonadditivities. Still, the results demonstrate the ability of the basic model to detect meaningful associations, and we conclude that failure to detect consistently significant effects of television on aggression is not due to problems with the analysis model or the aggression measures.

BASIC MODEL CONTROLS

The supplementary analyses reported thus far aimed at ensuring that the absence of significant associations between exposure to television violence and

[36]The measure of the aggressiveness of the boy's classroom friends, a strong correlate of the respondent's aggression, was not used here because it is highly related to the aggression of class measure. Also, the ambiguity in the direction of causal influences appears greater with the friend than the class measure.

[37]We also collected data on exposure to theater movies in all waves and exposure to comic books in four waves. Although these measures are not as precise and elaborate as the television exposure measure, we felt it was appropriate to find out whether basic model analyses—identical to those performed with violent television exposure as the independent variable—would reveal significant associations of these variables with aggression.

The findings for these two media are almost identical: average βs in the 15 lags are .04 for comic book exposure and .05 for theater movies. The number of significant coefficients for theater movies is four, for comic books it is three.

later aggression reported in Chapter 6 accurately reflected the relationships in the data. The final analysis reported here takes a different perspective.

Although the earlier analyses show that there is no consistent statistically significant relationship, they also show that most of the coefficients have a positive sign.[38] This requires the consideration of the possibility that television influences aggression to a small extent.

The coefficients that measure the extent to which television exposure predicts later aggression are small and mostly insignificant. Therefore it is not possible to explain their origin with absolute certainty. However, we conducted analyses that do suggest an explanation: The greater number of positive than negative coefficients stems from third variables that are not controlled in the basic model analyses.

As discussed in Chapters 5 and 6, the basic model analyses do not control for all possible outside influences. Such uncontrolled factors form a restricted class; they have to influence viewing levels and cause change in aggression over the interval of the panel lag. However, a number of variables exist that could easily cause the small associations. For example, having emotional problems as well as a variety of events in the respondent's family, among friends, and in the larger society could cause some respondents to turn to television for thrills, escape, or for other reasons, and also increase aggressive behavior during the time interval measured in the model.

A review of the mutual correlates that reduced cross-sectional correlations between television and aggression (Chapter 5) led us to 19 variables that were clear causal antecedents of both exposure and aggression. They were introduced one at a time as control variables in basic model regressions.

Most of the variables we examined did not affect the sign of the coefficients and many had small effects on their size, giving testimony to the power of the basic model to control for most outside variables. However, several variables did affect the relations between exposure and aggression; summary findings are reported in Table 7.10.[39] For each variable, data are shown for regressions without and with controls. The first column gives the number of significant coefficients in the 15 lags, the second the pattern of signs, the third the average β coefficient. The next two columns indicate how many of the 15 lags were reduced and how many were increased through the control variable. Finally, the last column gives the average sample size, which differs depending on the availability of the control variable.

[38]For example, 12 of the 15 coefficients in Table 6.1 are positive. When intervening television exposure measures are controlled, the number of positive coefficients is reduced to 10 (Table 6.2).

[39]In all, we found that 14 of the 19 variables reduced the number of positive signs, none increased it. Further, 16 variables reduced the size of the average β, 2 increased it.

TABLE 7.10
Basic Model Controls

	SIGNIFICANT COEFFICIENTS	PATTERN OF SIGNS	AVERAGE β	β COEFFICIENTS CHANGED THROUGH CONTROLS		AVERAGE N
				REDUCED	INCREASED	
School SES						
Sample						
without control	3p[a]	12p 3n	.044			(277)
with control	2p	11p 4n	.025	12	3	
SES of family						
Sample						
without control	1p	10p 5n	.013			(142)
with control	1p	8p 7n	.004	11		
Race						
Sample						
without control	3p	12p 3n	.044			(277)
with control	2p	10p 5n	.025	12	2	
Family religiosity						
Sample						
without control	1p	11p 4n	.027			(132)
with control	1p	8p 7n	.010	12		

[a] p = positive coefficient; n = negative coefficient.

Variables measuring socioeconomic background ("School SES," which is available for the entire sample, "SES of family," which is available for part of the sample, and "race") have a consistent effect on the association between television exposure and later aggression. Most pronounced is the effect on the average β, which is reduced to about half its size compared to analyses without any controls. It appears, then, that SES not only affects viewing and aggression levels, it also has a continuous effect on change in aggression, increasing the aggression level of boys from low-SES backgrounds. In this manner, SES tends to increase television effect coefficients in the basic model.[40]

The table also shows that the number of religious activities in a family influences the television–aggression relationship: High religiosity is associated with decreasing aggressiveness. We do not know the mechanisms by which religion or related factors measured by the index have this effect, but it appears that this index taps a continuous influence on aggression, affecting change in aggression over the time period studied.

As we have said, we are dealing here with very small, insignificant associations, which makes it impossible to draw absolutely firm conclusions. But this supplementary analysis provides evidence for the existence of uncontrolled factors that tend to inflate the small associations between television exposure and aggression found in our basic analyses. Thus, this analysis provides further corroboration for these findings.

APPENDIX A: OTHER CONCEPTUALIZATIONS OF TELEVISION EXPOSURE

CONTEXT OF VIOLENCE MEASURES

Realistic Crime Drama

This category contains programs dealing with crime in a realistic, contemporary United States setting. In addition, these programs contain exciting portrayals of violent actions; most of them are rated high on the violence exposure scale. An inference from the research just mentioned is that such programs are more likely to increase aggressive response than are other types (examples: *F.B.I.; Ironside*).

[40]Very similar results were obtained with other measures of SES (e.g., mother's occupation, family income), not shown here.

TABLE
Cross-Sectional Correlations of All Measures with Violent

	WAVE I		WAVE II	
	VIOLENCE EXPOSURE	AGGRESSION	VIOLENCE EXPOSURE	AGGRESSION
Total exposure	.94	.10	.93	.04
Relative exposure to violent television	.33	.11	.19	.13
Alternative violence weights				
7,6 Weight	.89	.11	.86	.10
5 Weight	.83	.15	.81	.09
4 Weight	.42	.06	.53	.12
3 Weight } 2 Weight }	.35	−.05	.36	.02
1 Weight	.63	.03	.67	.01
0 Weight	.59	.06	.36	.02
Context of violence				
Realistic crime	.72	.13	.44	.04
Adventure	.86	.09	.82	−.04
Westerns	.61	.07	.76	.12
Cartoons	.57	.05	.62	.03
Slapstick	.39	.05	.29	.05
News/Documentary	.28	−.01	.34	.02
Sitcoms	.46	.02	.38	.03
Variety	.49	.06	.26	−03
Education	.36	.04	.40	.00
Miscellaneous	.11	−.02	.42	.08
Favorite show violence				
Self-report				
Comparison				
Regular measure of violence exposure	*	.13	*	.08
N^a	(553)		(428)	

[a]Number of cases is smaller for "Favorite show" measures.

Adventure (Non/Semirealistic)

This category includes programs with exciting action in nonrealistic settings, including science fiction adventures such as *Star Trek*. Because of the more remote settings, it is assumed that behavior effects (such as imitation) are less likely than with portrayals of similar acts in realistic settings. Exluded from this category are westerns, which are grouped separately.[41]

[41]The category includes *Emergency*, which does have a realistic and contemporary setting but does not deal with crimes. It does, however, portray very exciting work by paramedics responding to accidents and disasters, which may lead excited viewers to aggressive responses.

vision Exposure and Aggression (Valid Reporters)

WAVE III		WAVE IV		WAVE V	
)LENCE POSURE	AGGRESSION	VIOLENCE EXPOSURE	AGGRESSION	VIOLENCE EXPOSURE	AGGRESSION
.92	.08	.93	.07	.93	.09
.37	.12	.50	.09	.55	.08
.82	.09	.86	.12	.89	.11
.77	.07	.59	−.01	.83	.07
.55	.05	.75	.07	.56	.08
.58	.11	.51	.07		
.55	.05	.58	−.00	.44	−.08
.38	−.00	.53	.01	.53	.01
.57	.10	.73	.14	.51	.10
.81	.07	.72	.08	.60	.06
.53	.06	.74	.03	.69	.05
.62	.08	.51	.06	.54	.08
.02	−.01	.41	−.07	.16	−.05
.20	−.01	.24	−.01	.20	−.06
.28	.02	.52	−.01	.44	.08
.17	.00	—	—	.34	.08
.54	.03	.23	.04	.18	.05
		.11	.01	.17	.01
*	.11	*	.10	*	.10
(510)		(546)		(414)	

Westerns

Westerns are separated from the adventure category because they are a form with specific characteristics. Most important in this context, westerns contain rather ritualized fistfights and shootouts in which the "good guys" win. It can be argued that the ritualization and predictability of the violent action makes harmful effects less likely.

Cartoons

It seems appropriate to list cartoons separately because of their special features. Animated programs are far removed from reality and hardly seem

TABLE A.2

Variance in Later Aggression (Adjusted R^2) Explained by Prior Aggression and Exposure to Television Measured in One Violence Exposure Variable, and Measured by Adding a Violence Ratio Measure (Valid Reporters)

	R^2			
WAVE PAIR	EXPOSURE TO VIOLENT TELEVISION	VIOLENCE RATIO MEASURE ADDED	INTERACTION TERM ADDED	*N*
III–IV	.748	.750*	.750	(494)
II–III	.716	.715	.715	(411)
I–II	.464	.466	.465	(364)
II–IV	.612	.611	.611	(407)
I–III	.446	.447	.447	(356)
I–IV	.399	.399	.398	(349)
IV–V	.532	.531	.530	(295)
V–VI	.509	.507	.516**	(186)
III–V	.549	.547	.546	(290)
II–V	.442	.441	.439	(240)
I–V	.363	.361	.362	(211)
IV–VI	.513	.511	.508	(161)
III–VI	.453	.450	.458	(147)
II–VI	.467	.468	.476	(121)
I–VI	.302	.304	.327*	(112)

*Significant increase in R^2 (.05 level) compared to the model with the violence exposure measure.
**Significant increase in R^2 (.05 level) compared to the model with the main effects.

likely to encourage imitation of violent behavior, at least as far as adults are concerned. Whether this is true of children—that is, whether children regard the cartoons as unrealistic fantasies without relevance for their own actions—is a different question. There are data indicating that even children of kindergarden age recognize cartoons as "make-believe" (Dorr, 1982). On the other hand, as reported, some researchers, such as Bandura and Ross (1963) and Stein and Friedrich (1972), feel their evidence suggests that children can be affected by cartoon violence.[42]

[42]We computed only one cartoon measure. Depending on one's definition of "violent action," it could be argued that this measure combines cartoons with different levels of violence. However, we feel that most cartoons included in our program checklists were quite similar, featuring primarily accidents and slapstick-type action in a humorous context. (There were only two nonhumorous action–adventure cartoons: *Johnny Quest* and *Hot Wheels*. These two programs were not listed separately but combined with the other cartoons.)

TABLE A.3
Lags for Examination of Exposure over Longer Time Periods

	LAGS	ADDITIONAL PRIOR TELEVISION VARIABLE(S)
Two television variables (one additional television variable)	II–III	Wave I
	II–IV	Wave I
	II–V	Wave I
	II–VI	Wave I
	III–IV	Wave II
	III–V	Wave II
	III–VI	Wave II
	IV–V	Wave III
	IV–VI	Wave III
	V–VI	Wave IV
Three television variables (two additional television variables)	III–IV	Waves II, I
	III–V	Waves II, I
	III–VI	Waves II, I
	IV–V	Waves III, II
	IV–VI	Waves III, II
	V–VI	Waves IV, III
Four television variables (three additional television variables)	IV–V	Waves III, II, I
	IV–VI	Waves III, II, I
	V–VI	Waves IV, III, II
Five television variables (four additional television variables)	V–VI	Waves IV, III, II, I

Slapstick

Slapstick comedies show nonlethal violent action in a humorous context. Presumably, that makes antisocial aggression a much less likely consequence than exposure to such actions in a serious, dramatic context (examples: *Little Rascals; Laugh-In*).

News/Documentaries

This is the only category of nonentertainment programs. News programs have been accused of increasing the level of aggression in society, and Feshbach (1972) found that riot scenes described as part of a news documentary did increase aggressive responses in a laboratory setting (examples: local and network news programs; also *Wild Kingdom*).

TABLE A.4
Cross-Sectional Correlations of All Factors with Violent Television Exposure and Aggression[a] (Valid Reporters)

	WAVE I	
	VIOLENCE EXPOSURE ($N = 553$)	AGGRESSION ($N = 553$)
1. Action/Adventure	.51	.02
2. Weekday	.33	.06
3. Saturday morning cartoons	.26	−.02
4. Weekday	.42	.03
5. ABC variety, *Dark Shadows*	.59	.09
6. Sitcoms	.22	−.02
7. News/Documentary	.11	−.04
8. Westerns, *Hee Haw*	.34	.06
9. Saturday–Sunday (noncartoon)	.12	−.06
Comparison		
Regular measure of violence exposure		.13

	WAVE II	
	VIOLENCE EXPOSURE ($N = 463$)	AGGRESSION ($N = 428$)
1. Saturday morning cartoons (CBS)	.37	.04
2. News	.27	.02
3. Action/Adventure	.46	.02
4. Saturday–Sunday	.19	.01
5. Saturday–Sunday Cartoons (NBC)	.27	.00
6. Sitcoms (CBS)	−.19	−.09
7. Sitcoms/Other	.55	.08
Comparison		
Regular measure of violence exposure		.08

	WAVE III	
	VIOLENCE EXPOSURE ($N = 525$)	AGGRESSION ($N = 510$)
1. Weekday	.50	.07
2. Action/Adventure	.54	.11
3. News	.12	−.04
4. Sitcoms/*Bonanza*	.11	−.02
5. Westerns/*Hee Haw*	.25	.03
6. Saturday morning cartoons (CBS)	.35	.04

(Continued)

TABLE A.4 (*continued*)

	WAVE III	
	VIOLENCE EXPOSURE ($N = 525$)	AGGRESSION ($N = 510$)
7. Saturday morning cartoons/ *Julia* (NBC)	.23	.01
8. Sitcoms (ABC)	.27	.01
9. Unclassified	.21	−.06
Comparison		
Regular measure of violence exposure		.11

	WAVE IV	
	VIOLENCE EXPOSURE ($N = 546$)	AGGRESSION ($N = 546$)
1. Action/Adventure	.53	.03
2. Saturday morning cartoons	.26	.04
3. Sitcoms (ABC)	.23	.05
4. Weekday	.54	.06
5. News/Documentary	.19	−.02
6. Unclassified	.30	−.03
7. Sitcoms (CBS)	.02	−.08
8. Saturday morning cartoons (CBS)	.15	−.02
9. Saturday morning cartoons (ABC)	.44	.05
Comparison		
Regular measure of violence exposure		.10

	WAVE V	
	VIOLENCE EXPOSURE ($N = 416$)	AGGRESSION ($N = 406$)
1. Unclassified	.40	.11
2. Action/Adventure	.43	−.05
3. Sitcom	.10	−.07
4. Saturday morning cartoons (CBS)	.33	.06
5. Saturday morning cartoons	.16	−.08
6. Unclassified	.40	.02
7. Weekday	.38	.14
8. News	.15	−.06
Comparison		
Regular measure of violence exposure		.10

[a]Wave VI factors are not included, as they are not used in the analysis.

TABLE A.5

Factors Significantly Related to Aggression in Regressions with Measures Based on Factor Analyses

WAVE, FACTOR NO., FACTOR LABEL	DOMINANT PROGRAMS	SIGN	LAGS IN WHICH SIGNIFICANT
Wave I			
2. Weekday	*Sesame Street, Mr. Rogers, General Hospital*	[−]	I–II
4. Weekday	*Flintstones*	[−]	I–II
6. Sitcoms	*Doris Day, Family Affair, Brady Bunch*	[+]	I–II, I–III, I–IV
9. Saturday–Sunday (Noncartoon)	*Discovery 70, Amateur Hour*	[+]	I–II, I–VI
Wave II			
4. Saturday–Sunday	*Johnny Quest, Discovery 70, Wild Kingdom*	[−]	II–III, II–IV
6. Sitcom	*Doris Day, Arnie*	[−]	II–IV
Wave III			
7. Saturday morning cartoons (NBC)/ *Julia*	*Julia, Dolittle. H.R Pufnstuf*	[+]	III–V
Wave IV			
2. Saturday morning cartoons	*Bugaloos, Dolittle, Pufnstuf, Sesame Street*	[−]	IV–V
Wave V			
7. Unclassified	*Link Lancelot, Dragnet*	[+]	V–VI

TABLE A.6

Variance in Later Aggression (Adjusted R^2) Explained by Prior Aggression and Exposure to Television, Measured in One Violence Exposure Variable, and Measured by Adding a Favorite Show Measure (Reported by Mother)[a] (Valid Reporters)

	R^2			
WAVE PAIR	EXPOSURE TO VIOLENT TELEVISION	FAVORITE SHOW MEASURE ADDED	FAVORITE SHOW MEASURE AND INTERACTION TERM ADDED	*N*
III–IV	.761	.760	.759	(195)
II–III	.761	.760	.759	(182)
I–II	.533	.534	.540	(193)
II–IV	.703	.703	.708	(181)
I–III	.492	.493	.494	(189)
I–IV	.439	.436	.440	(187)
IV–V	.473	.470	.469	(127)

(Continued)

TABLE A.6 (*continued*)

	R^2			
WAVE PAIR	EXPOSURE TO VIOLENT TELEVISION	FAVORITE SHOW MEASURE ADDED	FAVORITE SHOW MEASURE AND INTERACTION TERM ADDED	N
V–VI	.564	.501	.562	(70)
III–V	.509	.505	.501	(119)
II–V	.480	.475	.479	(113)
I–V	.451	.446	.442	(110)
IV–VI	.417	.438	.434	(73)
III–VI	.541	.533	.534	(61)
II–VI	.528	.526	.528	(59)
I–VI	.367	.368	.360	(58)

[a]Violence rating of programs mentioned by mother as boy's favorites.
[b]Based on respondents with "Favorite show" data (reported by mother).

Nonviolent Context Measures

The following program categories are all nonviolent and are hypothesized to have no effect on aggressiveness: *situation comedies*, such as *Mary Tyler Moore* and *The Partridge Family; variety* shows such as *Tom Jones*, *Flip Wilson; educational* programs such as *Sesame Street*.

APPENDIX B: EFFECTS OF EXPOSURE TO TELEVISION VIOLENCE AMONG SAMPLE SUBGROUPS

The 95 subgroups are organized, as we shall see, into the following categories: sociocultural characteristics, family structure, indicators of family relations and of parental control, supervision and use of punishment, aggression of the boys' peers, aggression behavior and attitudes of the boys' themselves, and other characteristics of the boys.

The summary findings for subgroups based on valid reporters in each of these categories are shown in Tables B.1–B.10. In each table the number of lags in which at least 30 cases were available for analysis is shown in Column 1. The number of significant positive television effects for each subgroup is shown in Column 2; significant negative effects are shown in Column 3; and the average size of the standardized partial regression coefficients is shown in Column 4.

Findings for total samples are in Tables B.11–B.20.

The wordings of the questions used for the subgroup measures are shown in Appendix C.

TABLE B.1
Net Effect of Exposure to Violent Television on Later Aggression for Subgroups Based on Sociocultural Characteristics (Valid Reporters)

SUBGROUP	NUMBER OF LAGS ANALYZED[a]	NUMBER OF SIGNIFICANT β COEFFICIENTS: POSITIVE β COEFFICIENTS	NUMBER OF SIGNIFICANT β COEFFICIENTS: NEGATIVE β COEFFICIENTS	AVERAGE β
Mother's occupation:				
Blue collar	10	0	0	.012
White collar				
Nonprofessional	15	1	2	−.022
Professional	6	0	0	−.035
Family income				
Low[b]	10	1	0	.049
High	15	1	0	.016
Race[c]				
Blacks	13	0	0	.039
Whites	15	3	0	.018
City				
Fort Worth	15	0	2	.020
Minneapolis	15	1	0	.039

[a] Lags with fewer than 30 cases have been excluded from analysis in Tables B.1–B.10.
[b] Low = under $10,000; high = $10,000 and over (see Appendix C for more details on the measures.)
[c] Races other than black and white (3% of sample) are excluded.

TABLE B.2
Net Effect of Exposure to Violent Television on Later Aggression for Subgroups Based on Characteristics of Family Structure (Valid Reporters)

SUBGROUP	NUMBER OF LAGS ANALYZED[a]	NUMBER OF SIGNIFICANT β COEFFICIENTS: POSITIVE β COEFFICIENTS	NUMBER OF SIGNIFICANT β COEFFICIENTS: NEGATIVE β COEFFICIENTS	AVERAGE β
Family type				
"Broken homes"[a]	4	0	0	−.090
"Intact" homes	15	0	0	.026
Family size				
Large (6–10 members living at home)	12	2	1	.061
Medium (5)	10	0	1	−.036
Small (2–4)	10	1	0	.076

[a] The category of "broken homes" consists of families with only one parent as well as those with one natural parent and a stepparent.

TABLE B.3

Net Effect of Exposure to Violent Television on Later Aggression for Subgroups Based on Indicators of Family Closeness, Warmth, and Support, in Current Period and during Early Years (Valid Reporters)

SUBGROUP	NUMBER OF LAGS ANALYZED	NUMBER OF SIGNIFICANT β COEFFICIENTS: POSITIVE β COEFFICIENTS	NEGATIVE β COEFFICIENTS	AVERAGE β
A. *Early years*				
Parents' attitudes toward pregnancy[a]				
Upset	11	1	0	−.019
Not upset	13	0	0	.040
Parents' feelings about raising boy[b]				
Very difficult	7	0	1	−.061
So-so	10	0*	0	.031
Not difficult	10	1	0	.097
Father's activities with boy[c]				
Not involved	13	0*	0	.022
Involved	13	1	0	.008
B. *Current period*				
Number of activities shared by family[d]				
Few shared	12	0	0	.029
Many shared	15	1	1	.017
Family religiosity[e]				
Low	10	0	0	.007
High	15	0	0	.040
Mother's dissatisfaction with son[f]				
Dissatisfied	10	0	0	.010
Satisfied	15	1	1*	−.012

*One additional coefficient closely approaches significance.

[a] A two-item index measuring mother's and father's feelings when learning that she was pregnant with her son. Scores on the index range from 2 (not upset) to 10 (very upset).

[b] A two-item index measuring mother's and father's feelings about raising the boy, ranging from 2 (not difficult) to 8 (difficult).

[c] A five-item index indicating father's involvement in activities with his son when very young, ranging from 1 (involved) to 5 (uninvolved).

[d] A four-item index measuring preference for doing things together versus separately, and the number of activities done together by the family members, ranging from 0 to 4.

[e] An index based on four related measures of involvement with church affairs.

[f] A four-item index measuring mother's dissatisfaction with son's friends, school work, etc.

TABLE B.4

Net Effect of Exposure to Violent Television on Later Aggression for Subgroups Based on Parental Control and Supervision (Valid Reporters)

SUBGROUP	NUMBER OF LAGS ANALYZED	NUMBER OF SIGNIFICANT β COEFFICIENTS: POSITIVE β COEFFICIENTS	NUMBER OF SIGNIFICANT β COEFFICIENTS: NEGATIVE β COEFFICIENTS	AVERAGE β
Mother's current work status[a]				
Works	4	1	0	−.082
Does not work	15	0	0	.037
Number of Rules				
—Of mother[b]				
Few rules	15	1	0	.049
Many rules	12	0	0	.008
—Of father[c]				
Few rules	10	2	0	.097
Many rules	15	0	0	.035
Strictness (in enforcing rules)				
—Of mother[d]				
Not/moderately strict	15	0	0	.003
Very strict	6	3	0	.137
—Of father[d]				
Not/moderately strict	15	1	1	.024
Very strict	10	0	0	.032
Mother's attempts to influence boy[e]				
Few attempts	13	0	0	.092
Many attempts	15	2	0	−.005

[a]Based on single item in the first mother questionnaire.

[b]Measure is based on 17 questions in the first mother questionnaire about specific rules. The measure was dichotomized at the median for this analysis.

[c]Measure is based on a single item in the first mother questionnaire. The four-category measure was dichotomized; the two subgroups are unequal in size due to the distributions of the answers.

[d]Both measures are based on single items in the first mother questionnaire. In both cases the "very strict" group is much smaller than the other when the measures are dichotomized.

[e]The measure is based on 6 questions in the first mother questionnaire exploring in which areas of the boy's life the mother seeks influence. It has 19 categories; here it is dichotomized at the median.

TABLE B.5

Net Effect of Exposure to Violent Television on Later Aggression for Subgroups Based on Parental Use of Punishment and Attitudes toward Aggression (Valid Reporters)

SUBGROUP	NUMBER OF LAGS ANALYZED	NUMBER OF SIGNIFICANT β COEFFICIENTS: POSITIVE β COEFFICIENTS	NUMBER OF SIGNIFICANT β COEFFICIENTS: NEGATIVE β COEFFICIENTS	AVERAGE β
A. *Parental use of punishment*				
Mother's use of physical punishment[a] (frequency plus propensity to hit)				
High	14	0	0	.041
Low	13	1	0	.025
Father's use of physical punishment[b] (frequency plus propensity to hit)				
High	10	1	1	−.062
Low	10	0	0	.020
Mother's use of verbal punishment[c] (mother's yelling)				
High	10	1	0	.001
Low	15	0	0	.045
Father's use of verbal punishment[d] (frequency plus propensity to yell)				
High	13	2	1	−.024
Low	10	0	0	.046
Mother's taking away privileges[e]				
Often/sometimes	15	1	0	.016
Rarely	10	0	0	.028
B. *Parental attitudes toward aggression*				
Mother's support for physical aggression[f] (second interview)				
High	14	1	0	.017
Low	15	2*	0*	.085
Father's support for physical aggression[g] (first questionnaire)				
High	10	0	0	−.000
Low	10	0	0	.024

(Continued next page)

TABLE B.5 (*continued*)

SUBGROUP	NUMBER OF LAGS ANALYZED	NUMBER OF SIGNIFICANT β COEFFICIENTS: POSITIVE β COEFFICIENTS	NEGATIVE β COEFFICIENTS	AVERAGE β
Both parent's support for physical aggression[h] (first interview/ questionnaire)				
High	14	1	0	−.007
Low	9	0	1	−.050

*One additional coefficient closely approaches significance.

[a]This six-item index combines the frequency with which the mother hit, slapped, or spanked her son during the past year, and the likelihood of her using physical punishment in different hypothetical situations.

[b]This six-item index combined the frequency with which the father hit, slapped, or spanked his son during the past year, and the likelihood of his using physical punishment in different hypothetical situations.

[c]Frequency with which mother yells or screams at her son (one item).

[d]This index combines frequency with likelihood as, for fathers, the combined index proved to be more strongly related to son's aggression than the estimate of frequency alone (six items).

[e]Measured by responses to a single question.

[f]This index consists of two items in the second mother questionnaire concerning the use of violence in hypothetical situations, as retaliation and as a means of defense.

[g]Index based on four items in the first father questionnaire.

[h]Six-item index that combines responses to *g* and a similar two-item index regarding mother's attitudes, based on the first mother questionnaire.

TABLE B.6

Net Effect of Exposure to Violent Television on Later Aggression for Subgroups Based on Aggression of Boy's Peers (Valid Reporters)

SUBGROUP	NUMBER OF LAGS ANALYZED	NUMBER OF SIGNIFICANT β COEFFICIENTS: POSITIVE β COEFFICIENTS	NEGATIVE β COEFFICIENTS	AVERAGE β
Classroom aggression[a]				
High	15	0	0	.050
Medium	15	3	0	.058
Low	14	2	0	.009
Aggression of closest friends[b]				
High	14	0	0	.047
Medium	14	1	0	.040
Low	14	1	0	.042
Classroom and friends' aggression[c]				
High	14	1	0	.057
Medium	14	3	0	.098
Low	14	0	0	.013

[a]Average aggression score of other boys in class, excluding boy's own score.

[b]Average aggression score of reciprocally chosen close friends. Wave IV data used for Waves II and III.

[c]Based on the addition of scores in *a* and *b*, above.

TABLE B.7

Net Effect of Exposure to Violent Television on Later Aggression for Subgroups Based on Aggressive Behavior and Aggression-Related Attitudes (Valid Reporters)

SUBGROUP	NUMBER OF LAGS ANALYZED	NUMBER OF SIGNIFICANT β COEFFICIENTS: POSITIVE β COEFFICIENTS	NEGATIVE β COEFFICIENTS	AVERAGE β
A. *Aggressive behavior* (aggressive predisposition)				
Initial aggression[a]				
High	15	0	0	.028
Low	15	3	0	.084
Altruism[b]				
Low	14	0	0	.013
High	15	4*	0	.073
B. *Attitudes toward aggression*				
Machismo[c]				
Favorable	15	3*	0	.084
Unfavorable	15	1	0	.060
Gentleness[d]				
Unfavorable	15	2	0	.086
Favorable	15	2	0	.069
Enjoyment of real-life violence[e]				
High	15	1	0	.037
Low	15	4	0	.121

*One additional coefficient closely approaches significance.

[a]Aggressiveness at the beginning of the lag under consideration. (Subgroups were defined by dichotomizing the range of aggression scores in such a way as to yield approximately equal numbers of boys in each subgroup.)

[b]Index based on two highly interrelated items appearing in all six waves, asking "Who says nice things to people to make them feel good?" and "Who helps other people?"; dichotomized at median.

[c]The four-item index of machismo was based on responses indicating how happy–unhappy the boy would feel about being good at fighting, strong-willed, strong, and brave. The five-item index, with a theoretical range of 4–20, was highly skewed: almost a third of the boys had a score of 4 (most favorable); one-third scored 5–6, and one-third, 7–17. Wave V responses are used for all waves.

[d]The four-item index of gentleness was based on responses indicating how happy–unhappy the boy would feel about being gentle, lovable, quiet, and tender; scores were spread fairly evenly across the 4 (most favorable) to 20 range. Wave V responses are used for all waves.

[e]The index consists of responses to six items asking how enjoyable or disgusting boys had found motion picture scenes of real-life violence. Scores on the index ranged from 6 to 30. Wave V data were used for all waves.

TABLE B.8

Net Effect of Exposure to Violent Television on Later Aggression for Subgroups Based on Fantasy Behavior, Emotional Instability, and Shyness (Valid Reporters)

SUBGROUP	NUMBER OF LAGS ANALYZED	NUMBER OF SIGNIFICANT β COEFFICIENTS: POSITIVE β COEFFICIENTS	NUMBER OF SIGNIFICANT β COEFFICIENTS: NEGATIVE β COEFFICIENTS	AVERAGE β
Fantasy behavior[a] (teacher nominations)				
High	7	0	0	.021
Low	15	5	0	.055
Fantasy behavior[b] (peer ratings)				
High	15	2	0	.020
Low	15	2	0	.060
Emotional instability[c]				
High	15	2	0	.040
Low	15	2*	0	.074
Shyness[d]				
Not shy	15	4	0	.067
Shy	5	0	0	.031

*Two additional coefficients closely approach significance.

[a]Based on teacher nominations of children who "daydream" (Wave II) or who "often tell make-believe stories or play make-believe games" (other waves).

[b]Based on peer nominations in Wave III of those who "often tell make-believe stories or play make-believe games"; the measure was dichotomized at the median.

[c]Based on teacher nominations on five items: Who is moody? Sulks or pouts? Is overly sensitive to criticism? Cries or weeps easily? Is often unhappy? Scores ranged from 0 to 5. Wave IV data are used for Waves I–IV; Wave V data for Wave V.

[d]Based on teacher nominations in Wave IV.

TABLE B.9

Net Effect of Exposure to Violent Television on Later Aggression in Subgroups Defined on the Basis of Physical Size and Age (Valid Reporters)

SUBGROUP	NUMBER OF LAGS ANALYZED	NUMBER OF SIGNIFICANT β COEFFICIENTS: POSITIVE β COEFFICIENTS	NEGATIVE β COEFFICIENTS	AVERAGE β
Physical size[a]				
Large for age	3	0	0	.012
Small for age	9	0	0	.047
Grade in school[b]				
Second	15	1	1	.009
Third	15	2*	0	.083
Fourth	10	1	0	.061
Fifth	6	0	3	−.079

*Two additional coefficients closely approach significance.

[a]Based on teacher nominations of those who were large for their age and small for their age, obtained in Waves I, II, and III.

[b]This measure is used as a substitute for age. The measure indicates grade in school in Wave I.

TABLE B.10

Net Effect of Exposure to Violent Television on Later Aggression in Subgroups Defined on the Basis of Scholastic Ability and Exposure to Other Media (Valid Reporters)

SUBGROUP	NUMBER OF LAGS ANALYZED	NUMBER OF SIGNIFICANT β COEFFICIENTS: POSITIVE β COEFFICIENTS	NEGATIVE β COEFFICIENTS	AVERAGE β
Scholastic ability[a]				
Low	9	0	0	−.041
Medium	14	3	1	.046
High	15	2	0	.062
Exposure to comic books[b]				
High	15	1	0	.022
Low	15	0	1	.054
Exposure to theater movies[b]				
High	15	1	0	.011
Low	15	4	0	.050

[a]Average grade in school year ending at time of Wave I.

[b]Both measures score the number of violent items (comic books and theater movies, respectively) the boy marks. Those who report exposure to nonexisting items are excluded. The variables are dichotomized at the median for this analysis. Exposure data for comic books were not available in Wave II, Wave III data were used for lags starting with Wave II.

Tables for Total Sample

TABLE B.11
Net Effect of Exposure to Violent Television on Later Aggression for Subgroups Based on Sociocultural Characteristics (Total Sample)[a]

SUBGROUP	NUMBER OF SIGNIFICANT β COEFFICIENTS (OF 15)		AVERAGE β
	POSITIVE β COEFFICIENTS	NEGATIVE β COEFFICIENTS	
Mother's occupation			
Blue collar	0	0	.054
White collar			
Nonprofessional	2	1	.012
Professional	0	0	.029
Family income			
Low	2	0	.090
High	2	0	.006
Race			
Blacks	2	0	.012
Whites	0	0	.014
City			
Fort Worth	2	1	.064
Minneapolis	1	0	.023

[a] For details on variables in this and following tables, see corresponding Tables B.1–B.10. For total samples, all lags, disregarding the number of cases, were analyzed.

TABLE B.12
Net Effect of Exposure to Violent Television on Later Aggression for Subgroups Based on Characteristics of Family Structure (Total Sample)

SUBGROUP	NUMBER OF SIGNIFICANT β COEFFICIENTS (OF 15)		AVERAGE β
	POSITIVE β COEFFICIENTS	NEGATIVE β COEFFICIENTS	
Family type			
Broken homes	1	0*	−.060
Intact homes	2	0	.044
Family size			
Large	3	0	.097
Medium	0	0	.010
Small	2	0	.066

*One additional coefficient closely approaches significance.

TABLE B.13

Net Effect of Exposure to Violent Television on Later Aggression for Subgroups Based on Indicators of Family Closeness, Warmth, and Support, in Current Period and during Early Years (Total Sample)

SUBGROUP	NUMBER OF SIGNIFICANT β COEFFICIENTS (OF 15) POSITIVE β COEFFICIENTS	NEGATIVE β COEFFICIENTS	AVERAGE β
A. *Early years*			
Parents' attitudes toward pregnancy			
Upset	2	0	.003
Not upset	1	0	.065
Parents' feelings about raising child			
Very difficult	0	3	−.056
So-so	0	0	.034
Not difficult	0*	0	.096
Father's involvement with son			
Not involved	0	0	.058
Involved	0	0	.015
B. *Current period*			
Number of shared activities			
Few shared	2	0	.079
Many shared	2	1	.021
Religiosity			
Low	1	0	.037
High	1	0	.076
Mother's dissatisfaction with son			
Dissatisfied	2	0	.077
Satisfied	2	0	.017

*One additional coefficient closely approaches significance.

TABLE B.14

Net Effect of Exposure to Violent Television on Later Aggression for Subgroups Based on Parental Control and Supervision (Total Sample)

SUBGROUP	NUMBER OF SIGNIFICANT β COEFFICIENTS (OF 15) POSITIVE β COEFFICIENTS	NEGATIVE β COEFFICIENTS	AVERAGE β
Mother's current work status			
Works	2	0	.076
Does not work	2	0	.046
Number of rules			
—Of mother			
Few rules	2	0	.073

(Continued next page)

TABLE B.14 *(continued)*

SUBGROUP	NUMBER OF SIGNIFICANT β COEFFICIENTS (OF 15)		AVERAGE β
	POSITIVE β COEFFICIENTS	NEGATIVE β COEFFICIENTS	
Many rules	0	0	.019
—Of father			
Few rules	3	1	.075
Many rules	0	0	.037
Strictness (in enforcing rules)			
—Of mother			
Not/moderately strict	1	0	.026
Very strict	3	0	.121
—Of father			
Not/moderately strict	2	0	.056
Very strict	0	0	.033
Mother's attempts to influence boy			
Few attempts	4	0	.123
Many attempts	2	2	−.003

TABLE B.15

Net Effect of Exposure to Violent Television on Later Aggression for Subgroups Based on Parental Use of Punishment and Attitudes toward Aggression (Total Sample)

SUBGROUP	NUMBER OF SIGNIFICANT β COEFFICIENTS (OF 15)		AVERAGE β
	POSITIVE β COEFFICIENTS	NEGATIVE β COEFFICIENTS	
A. *Parental use of punishment*			
Mother's use of physical punishment (frequency plus propensity to hit)			
High	2	0	.057
Low	2	1	.031
Father's use of physical punishment (frequency plus propensity to hit)			
High	0	0	−.029
Low	0	0	.030
Mother's use of verbal punishment (mother's yelling)			
High	1	0	.039
Low	0	0	.046
Father's use of verbal punishment (frequency plus propensity to yell)			
High	0	0	−.022
Low	0	0	.009

(Continued)

TABLE B.15 (*continued*)

SUBGROUP	NUMBER OF SIGNIFICANT β COEFFICIENTS (OF 15): POSITIVE β COEFFICIENTS	NEGATIVE β COEFFICIENTS	AVERAGE β
Mother's taking away privileges			
Often/sometimes	2	0	.015
Rarely	4	0	.163
B. *Parental attitudes toward aggression*			
Mother's support for physical aggression (second interview)			
High	2	0	.025
Low	3	0	.117
Father's support for physical aggression (first questionnaire)			
High	0	0	−.033
Low	0	0	.043
Both parents' support for physical aggression (first interview/ questionnaire)			
High	0	1	−.047
Low	1	0	.026

TABLE B.16

Net Effect of Exposure to Violent Television on Later Aggression for Subgroups Based on Aggression of Boy's Peers (Total Sample)

SUBGROUP	NUMBER OF SIGNIFICANT β COEFFICIENTS (OF 15): POSITIVE β COEFFICIENTS	NEGATIVE β COEFFICIENTS	AVERAGE β
Classroom aggression			
High	0	0	.021
Medium	3	0	.057
Low	2	0	.047
Aggression of closest friends			
High	2	0	.044
Medium	2	0	.043
Low	4*	0	.084
Classroom and friends' aggression			
High	3	0	.061
Medium	3	0	.097
Low	1	0	.027

*One additional coefficient closely approaches significance.

TABLE B.17
Net Effect of Exposure to Violent Television on Later Aggression for Subgroups Based on Aggressive Behavior and Aggression-Related Attitudes (Total Sample)

SUBGROUP	NUMBER OF SIGNIFICANT β COEFFICIENTS (OF 15) POSITIVE β COEFFICIENTS	NEGATIVE β COEFFICIENTS	AVERAGE β
A. *Aggressive behavior*			
Initial Aggression			
High	1	0	.005
Low	6	0	.127
Altruism			
Low	1	0	.013
High	6	1	.075
B. *Attitudes toward aggression*			
Machismo			
Favorable	4	0	.075
Unfavorable	2*	0	.073
Gentleness			
Unfavorable	1	0	.082
Favorable	6	0	.010
Enjoyment of real-life violence			
High	1*	0	.058
Low	7	0	.120

*One additional coefficient closely approaches significance.

TABLE B.18
Net Effect of Exposure to Violent Television on Later Aggression for Subgroups Based on Fantasy Behavior, Emotional Instability, and Shyness (Total Sample)

SUBGROUP		NUMBER OF SIGNIFICANT β COEFFICIENTS (OF 15) POSITIVE β COEFFICIENTS	NEGATIVE β COEFFICIENTS	AVERAGE β
Fantasy behavior (teacher nominations)	High	1	1	.022
	Low	5	0	.053
Fantasy behavior (peer ratings)	High	1	0	.017
	Low	6	0	.090
Emotional instability	High	1	0	.019
	Low	6	0	.085
Shyness	Not shy	5	0	.055
	Shy	1	0	.119

TABLE B.19
Net Effect of Exposure to Violent Television on Later Aggression in Subgroups Defined on the Basis of Physical Size and Age (Total Sample)

SUBGROUP	NUMBER OF SIGNIFICANT β COEFFICIENTS (OF 15)		AVERAGE β
	POSITIVE β COEFFICIENTS	NEGATIVE β COEFFICIENTS	
Physical size			
Large for age	2	0	.025
Small for age	2	0	.122
Grade in school			
Second	0	0	.024
Third	3	0	.067
Fourth	1[a]	0[a]	.061[a]
Fifth	0[b]	2[b]	−.055[b]

[a]Only 10 wave pairs available for analysis.
[b]Only 6 wave pairs available for analysis.

TABLE B.20
Net Effect of Exposure to Violent Television on Later Aggression in Subgroups Defined on the Basis of Scholastic Ability and Exposure to Other Media (Total Sample)

SUBGROUP	NUMBER OF SIGNIFICANT β COEFFICIENTS (OF 15)		AVERAGE β
	POSITIVE β COEFFICIENTS	NEGATIVE β COEFFICIENTS	
Scholastic ability			
Low	1	0	−.040
Medium	2	1	.044
High	1	0	.057
Exposure to comic books			
High	3	0	.034
Low	2	0	.047
Exposure to theater movies			
High	0	0	.073
Low	4	0	.067

APPENDIX C: WORDING OF QUESTIONNAIRE ITEMS USED FOR SUBGROUP MEASURES IN TABLES B.3–B.5, B.7, AND B.10[42]

Table B.3[43]

PARENTS' ATTITUDES TOWARD PREGNANCY

MI[44]Q13 When you found out you were pregnant with [name], what statement on this card best describes what your feelings were? (Very upset, Upset, Neither upset nor pleased, Pleased, Very pleased)

Q14 What about [name]'s father? What number on the card best describes how *he* felt when he found out you were pregnant? (Very upset, etc.)

PARENTS' FEELINGS ABOUT RAISING BOY

MII Q17 Most parents would agree that raising children brings both pleasures and difficulties. Which statement on this card best describes your overall experience raising [name]? (Mostly all pleasures, A lot of pleasure, some difficulties, About half pleasure, and half difficulties, A lot of difficulties, some pleasures, Mostly all difficulties)

Q18 How would [name]'s father describe this? (Mostly all pleasures, etc.)

FATHER'S ACTIVITIES WITH BOY

MII (Q21) I'd like to find out how often [name] did certain things with his father when he was between the ages of 2 and 5. As I mention each thing, please try to remember how often it happened.

Q21B Have stories read or told him by his father. (Almost every day, A few times a week, About once a week, Once or twice a month, Less often or never, I'm not sure)

Q21C Play with his father. (Almost every day, etc.)

Q21D Go somewhere with him without you along. (Almost every day, etc.)

Q21E Taken care of by just his father. (Almost every day, etc.)

Q21F Put to bed by him. (Almost every day, etc.)

[42]Measures based on demographic information (e.g., race, city) and those fully described in Appendix B are not described in this appendix.

[43]Table in which results for measure are reported.

[44]MI = Mother interview I; MII = Mother interview II; FI = Father interview I; this is followed by the question number.

NUMBER OF ACTIVITIES SHARED BY FAMILY

MI (Q13) Now, Mrs. ______, I'd like to find out about some of the activities that you and your family have done *in the past 4 weeks*, and which members of your family did them. As I mention each activity, please tell me the statements on this card that indicate which members of your family, if any, did that activity.

Q13C Spent time with any of [name]'s grandparents.

Q13D Spent time with other family relatives or friends.

Q13G Went out to a restaurant, diner, or drive-in to eat.

Q13H Went for a drive.

FAMILY RELIGIOSITY

(Same introduction as items used for "Activities shared by family")

MI Q13A Attended religious service in past *4 weeks*?

Q13B Attended a church, school, or neighborhood social activity in the past 4 weeks?

(Q16) I am going to read the names of different clubs and organizations. As I mention each one, please tell me whether or not you (or your husband/other male) happen to belong to it.

Q16B Church group.

Q37D And do you have a rule: That he go to church regularly?

MOTHER'S DISSATISFACTIONS WITH SON

MI Q29A How satisfied are you with what [name] does with his leisure time?

Q29B How satisfied are you with who his friends are? (Very satisfied, etc.)

Q29C How about how well he is doing in school? (Very satisfied, etc.)

Q29D How satisfied are you with what he believes? (Very satisfied, etc.)

Table B.4

NUMBER OF RULES—OF MOTHER

MI Q30A Do you have any rule that [name] do chores around the house such as taking the trash out, keeping his room clean and neat, or picking up after himself? (No, Yes)

Q31A Do you have a rule that [name] not be fresh or sassy to his parents? (No, Yes)

Q32A Do you have a rule that [name] not harmfully tease other children? (No, Yes)

Q33A Do you have a rule that [name] not hit or hurt other children? (No, Yes)

Q34A Do you have a rule that [name] keep his parents informed about where he is when he is away from home? (No, Yes)

Q35A Do you have a rule that [name] be home from school by a certain time? (No, Yes)

Q36A Do you have a rule that [name] come home by a certain time at night? (No, Yes)

Q37A Do you have a rule that [name] not spend his money on certain things? (No, Yes)

Q37B Do you have a rule that [name] take a bath or shower regularly? (No, Yes)

Q37C Do you have a rule that [name] keep his hair combed? (No, Yes)

MI Q37D Do you have a rule that [name] goes to church regularly? (No, Yes)

Q37E What about rules that [name] always say "please" and 'thank you"? (No, Yes)

Q37F What about a rule that he address adults in special ways like "sir," "madame," or "Mr." or "Mrs."? (No, Yes)

Q37G Do you have a rule that [name] not use bad language? (No, Yes)

Q37H Do you have a rule that [name] take part in school clubs or activities? (No, Yes)

Q37I Do you have a rule that [name] join nonschool clubs and organizations like Boy Scouts? (No, Yes)

Q37J Do you have a rule that [name] not smoke cigarettes? (No, Yes)

NUMBER OF RULES—FATHER

MI Q42 Overall, how many rules would you say your husband/other male requires [name] to follow? (Many, A moderate number, A few rules, Very few rules)

STRICTNESS (IN ENFORCING RULES)—OF MOTHER

MI Q39 How *strict* would you say that you are in keeping after [name] to follow these rules? (Very strict, Moderately, Slightly, Not strict)

STRICTNESS (IN ENFORCING RULES)—OF FATHER

MI Q43 How *strict* would you say your husband/other male is in keeping after [name] to follow thee rules? (Very strict, etc.)

MOTHER'S ATTEMPTS TO INFLUENCE BOY

MI Q28A To what extent do *you* try to influence or not influence what [name] does with *his leisure time*? (Try very hard to influence this; Try fairly hard to influence this; Try a little to influence this but don't really push it; Leave it pretty much up to him)

MI Q28B To what extent do *you* try to influence or not influence what programs [name] watches on television? (Try very hard to influence this, etc.)

Q28C To what extent do *you* try to influence *who his friends ae*? (Try very hard to influence this, etc.)

Q28D To what extent do *you* try to influence [name] *to do well in school*? (Try very hard to influence this, etc.)

Q28E How much will you try to influence what [name] will do for a living when he grows up? (Try very hard to influence this, etc.)

Q28F To what extent do you try to influence [name] to believe the things that you believe? (Try very hard to influence this, etc.)

Table B.5

MOTHER'S USE OF PHYSICAL PUNISHMENT

MI Q54 About how many times would you say that you hit, slapped, or spanked [name] in the past year? (Number of times)

Q30D How likely were you to *hit, slap,* or *spank* him for not doing a good job in tending to his chores? (Very likely, Likely, 50–50 chance, Unlikely, Very unlikely)

Q31C And how likely were you to *hit, slap*, or *spank* him for being fresh or sassy to his parents? (Very likely, etc.)

Q32C And how likely were you to *hit, slap*, or *spank* him for harmfully teasing other children? (Very likely, etc.)

Q33C How likely were you to *hit, slap*, or *spank* him for hitting or hurting other children? (Very likely, etc.)

Q34C How likely were you to *hit, slap,* or *spank* him for not keeping his parents informed about where he is when he is away from home? (Very likely, etc.)

FATHER'S USE OF PHYSICAL PUNISHMENT

FI Q3D Please indicate about how often in the *past year* you hit, slapped, or spanked "your son." (Never, Hardly ever, Occasionally, Often, Very often)

Q5A How likely were you to hit, slap, or spank "your son" when he was not doing a good job tending to his chores around the house. Very likely, Likely, A 50–50 chance, Unlikely, Very unlikely)

Q5B How were you to hit, slap, or spank "your son" when he was fresh or sassy to his parents. (Very likely, etc.)

Q5D How likely were you to hit, slap, or spank "your son" when he was harmfully teasing other children. (Very likely, etc.)

Q5E How likely were you to hit, slap, or spank "your son" when he did *not* keep his parents informed about where he was when away from home. (Very likely, etc.)

MOTHER'S USE OF VERBAL PUNISHMENT

MI Q51I How often in the past year did you yell or scream at [name]? (Never, Hardly ever, Occasionally, Often, Very often)

FATHER'S USE OF VERBAL PUNISHMENT

FI Q3B How often in the past year did you yell or scream at "your son"? (Never, etc.)

Q4A How likely were you to get really angry and yell at "your son" when he was *not* doing a good job tending to his chores around the house? (Very likely, Likely, A 50–50 chance, Unlikely, Very unlikely)

Q4B How likely were you to get really angry and yell at "your son" when he was fresh or sassy to his parents? (Very likely, etc.)

Q4C How likely were you to get really angry and yell at "your son" when he was harmfully teasing other children? (Very likely, etc.)

FI Q4D How likely were you to get really angry and yell at "your son" when he was hitting or hurting other children? (Very likely, etc.)

Q4E How likely were you to get really angry and yell at "your son" when he did *not* keep his parents informed about where he was when away from home? (Very likely, etc.)

MOTHER'S TAKING AWAY PRIVILEGES

MI Q51K How often in the past year did you take a privilege away from [name]? (Never, Hardly ever, Occasionally, Often, Very often)

MOTHER'S SUPPORT FOR PHYSICAL AGGRESSION

MII Q34A In a situation where someone [name] hardly knows comes up and starts a fist fight with him, what best describes the *first* thing you would want him to do? (Show he's ready to fight; Try and talk him out of it; Hit him back; Refuse to fight and walk away.)

Q34B In a situation where he sees a boy his age trying to steal something of his like a bicycle or sports equipment, what is the *first* thing you would want him to do? (Yell for help; Threaten to hurt him unless he gives it back; Fight him to get it back; Angrily yell at him to give it back.)

FATHER'S SUPPORT FOR PHYSICAL AGGRESSION

FI Q1G A child should be taught to physically fight other children when necessary to protect his rights. (Agree, Disagree)

Q6I It is sometimes necessary to use force when fighting for something one strongly believes in. (Strongly agree, Mildly agree, Mildly disagree, Strong disagree)

Q9A How would you feel if "your son" hit a boy who cursed you or your wife? (Very pleased, Pleased, Neither pleased nor upset, Upset, Very upset)

Q9B How would you feel if "your son" hit a boy who hit him first? (Very pleased, etc.)

BOTH PARENTS' SUPPORT FOR PHYSICAL AGGRESSION

FI Q1G A child should be taught to physically fight other children when necessary to protect his rights. (Agree, Disagree)

Q6I It is sometimes necessary to use force when fighting for something one strongly believes in. (Strongly agree, Mildly agree, Mildly disagree, Strong disagree)

Q9A How would you feel if "your son" hit a boy who cursed you or your wife? (Very pleased, Pleased, Neither pleased nor upset, Upset, Very upset)

Q9B How would you feel if "your son" hit a boy who hit him first? (Very pleased, etc.)

MI Q19A A child should sometimes "turn the other cheek" when he gets into fist fights with other children. (Agree, Disagree)

Q19E A child should be taught to physically fight other children when necessary to protect his rights. (Agree, Disagree)

Table B.7

MACHISMO: PEER QUESTIONNAIRE, WAVE V, Q27

(1) How would someone like you feel about being good at fighting? (Very happy, A little happy, Not happy—not unhappy, A little unhappy, Very unhappy)

(2) How would someone like you feel about being strong-willed? (Very happy, etc.)

(3) How would someone like you feel about being strong? (Very happy, etc.)

(4) How would someone like you feel about being brave? (Very happy, etc.)

GENTLENESS: PEER QUESTIONNAIRE, WAVE V, Q27

(1) How would someone like you feel about being gentle? (Very happy, A little happy, Not happy—not unhappy, A little unhappy, Very unhappy)

(2) How would someone like you feel about being loveable? (Very happy, etc.)

(3) How would someone like you feel about being quiet? (Very happy, etc.)

(4) How would someone like you feel about being tender? (Very happy, etc.)

ENJOYMENT OF REAL-LIFE VIOLENCE: PEER QUESTIONNAIRE, WAVE V, Q26

How would you feel while looking at motion pictures of things that really have happened, like:

(1) People very angrily yelling or screaming at each other? (Enjoy it very much, Like it, No feeling either way, Dislike it, Find it disgusting)

(2) Soldiers burning enemy villages? (Enjoy it very much, etc.)

(3) A fist fight between two men? (Enjoy it very much, etc.)

(4) A man getting shot? (Enjoy it very much, etc.)

(5) Places that have been bombed? (Enjoy it very much, etc.)

(6) A knife fight between two men? (Enjoy it very much, etc.)

Table B.10

EXPOSURE TO COMIC BOOKS: PEER QUESTIONNAIRE, WAVES I–VI (QUESTION NUMBER VARIED)

Which of the following funny books of comic books do you read lots of times? (Violent comics noted: *Amazing Spiderman, Batman, Bugs Bunny, Captain America, Famous Monsters, Fantastic Four, Iron Man, Incredible Hulk, Popeye, Superman, Tomahawk, Tales from the Tomb.*)

EXPOSURE TO THEATER MOVIES: PEER QUESTIONNAIRE, WAVES I–VI (QUESTION NUMBER AND MOVIES ASKED VARIED). EXAMPLE: WAVE IV, MINNEAPOLIS

Here is a list of movies which have been playing in movie theaters. I will read each one, if you have seen the movie draw a line through the name of the *movie*. If you have not seen the movie, *do not do anything*. (Violent movies noted: *House of Dark Shadows, Kelly's Heroes*—starring Clint Eastwood, *Valdez Is Coming*—starring Burt Lancaster, *When Dinosaurs Ruled the Earth.*)

CHAPTER 8

THE EFFECT OF TELEVISION VIOLENCE ON AGGRESSION AMONG GIRLS

DESIGN

Because information about television viewing and aggressive behavior was obtained in classrooms from the entire class, data for girls were obtained at the same time and in the same way as those for boys. Table A.1 on p. 256 shows the number of girls in the initial sample in each city by grade and race.

As a product of collecting peer data in school classrooms, complete information was available on girls' aggression and television exposure. Therefore, the same basic analysis could be conducted for girls as for boys. Since girls were not the focus of the study, we did not collect data pertaining to girls from other sources, such as from parents, and school record data were collected only for a small portion of the girls included in the study. Therefore, we cannot conduct some of the analyses (e.g., the role of ethnic or family backgrounds) that we were able to conduct for boys.

Table 8.1 shows the size of the girls' sample in each of the six waves. The total sample sizes are very similar to those for boys.[1] As was true of the boys, some of the girls entered the sample after Wave I. Table A.2 on p. 257 shows how many of the girls in the six waves were part of the initial sample and how many were added in later waves. Again, the numbers for boys and girls are very similar.

---

[1]As in the initial boys' sample, respondents who do not have complete data (aggression and television expsosure) in Wave I and never enter the study again are excluded from the initial girls' sample ($N = 40$). (See Chapter 2 for more details.)

TABLE 8.1
Size of Sample in Each of Six Waves[a]

WAVE	DATE	TOTAL SAMPLE OF GIRLS IN WAVE
I	May–June 1970	(741)
II	October–November 1970	(703)
III	February 1971	(723)
IV	May 1971	(682)
V	May 1972	(523)
VI	May 1973	(285)

[a]If a comparable table exists for boys, this is indicated in the lower left corner of all tables in this chapter.
Boys: Table 2.4.

As for boys, the sample sizes also reflect attrition due to the graduation of sixth graders, mobility, and temporary absenteeism (see Tables A.3, A.4, and A.5). The effect of attrition on sample composition is not large, despite the reduction in sample size. Those who stay and those who leave are similar with regard to city and socioeconomic background. There is a tendency for those who leave to be less valid reporters of their television viewing, which is indicative of a lower IQ and lower scholastic grades. (We found that mobility reduced the number of boys in the sample who had low school grades and who did not live with both natural parents.) As in the boys' sample, respondents who entered the study after Wave I were more likely to be residents of Minneapolis and more likely to be white; see Table A.6.[2]

AGGRESSION MEASURE

Aggression for girls was measured using the same peer-nominating procedure and the same questions as for boys (see Chapter 3).

According to traditional sex role definitions, one would expect girls to score considerably lower on an aggression measure than boys. This expectation is fulfilled: On the average, girls' aggression scores are half those of boys. Those scores are summarized in Table 8.2. Whereas girls score lower on all aggression items, they score especially low on items tapping physical aggression and

[2]The differences in aggression between the initial and later samples are quite small. Subgroup analyses below indicate that television characteristics affected by attrition were not modifiers of television effects, suggesting that attrition did not distort the basic findings.

TABLE 8.2
Average Means of Aggression Items for Girls and Boys

ITEM	GIRLS	BOYS
Pushes and shoves	12.5	25.5
Says mean things	14.8	24.0
Hits or punches	9.5	23.3
Makes up stories or lies	12.1	18.2
Takes things[a]	9.3	18.4
Breaks things[a]	5.8	12.3
Pushed and shoved yesterday[b]	6.7	12.4
Said mean things yesterday[b]	8.3	13.7
Hit or punched yesterday[b]	4.5	10.2
Made up stories or lied yesterday[b]	5.6	8.3

[a]Available in four waves only.
[b]Available in three waves only.
Boys data summarized from Table 3.1.

damaging property. This finding, too, agrees with expectations based on traditional sex roles.[3]

Despite the large differences between boys and girls in the amount of aggression reported, factor analyses revealed that we are again dealing with only one aggression factor. As among the boys, all items, general and yesterday items, load on one factor: physical and verbal aggression, and also stealing and damaging property, appear as one type of aggression among all elementary school children in this sample. (The factor loadings are slightly lower than for boys; see Table A.7.)

The aggression index for girls was constructed in the same manner as for boys, by adding scores on the four general aggression items asked in all six waves. The distribution of this index is shown in Figure 8.1; the statistics in Table 8.3.

There are very few highly aggressive girls. The J-shape of the distribution of the aggression index is even more pronounced than that for boys. The means and medians for girls are half the size of those for boys and the range is 10–20% smaller.

Reliability coefficients based on the internal consistency of the items were

[3]If girls are much less aggressive than boys, does that mean they engage in more prosocial behavior? According to our findings, they do. In all waves, we asked: "Who says nice things?" and "Who helps others?" In the six waves, girls score 43% higher than boys.

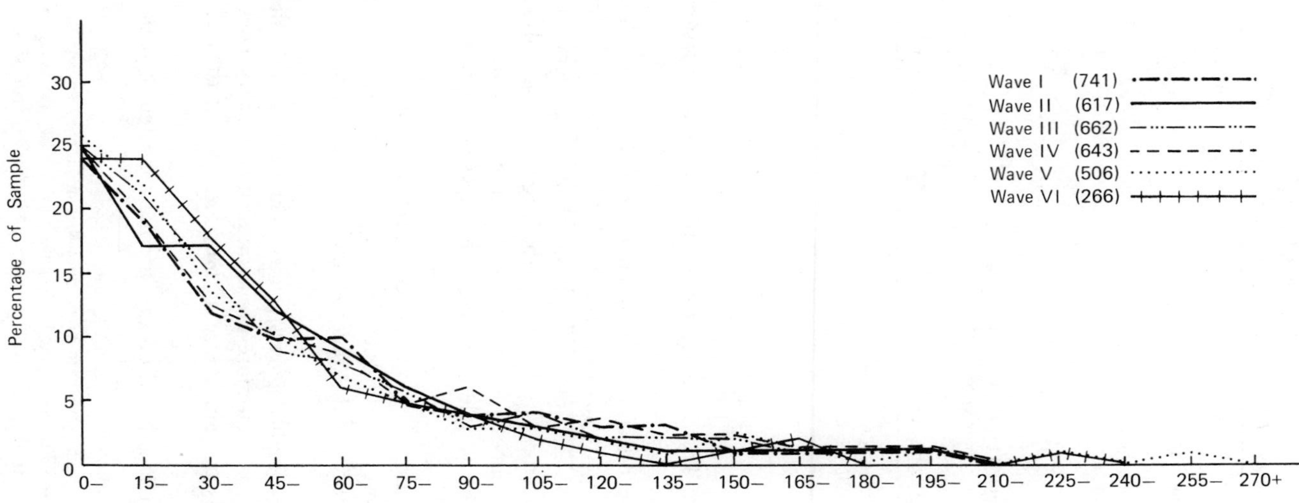

FIGURE 8.1. *Distribution of aggression in all six waves.*

TABLE 8.3
Aggression Descriptive Statistics for All Six Waves

STATISTIC	WAVE I	II	III	IV	V	VI
Median	38.1	34.7	33.3	36.6	31.8	30.3
Mean	52.7	47.8	48.0	53.4	48.7	43.6
Mode	0	0	0	0	0	0
Standard deviation	49.4	45.5	47.4	52.2	52.3	45.9
Range	0–274	0–338	0–276	0–292	0–305	0–300
Skewness	1.4	1.8	1.7	1.5	2.0	2.3
N	(741)	(617)	(662)	(643)	(506)	(266)

Boys: Table 3.4.

computed for the aggression measure. The average reliability for girls is .93, almost as high as that for boys (.95).

The average correlation between the aggression measure and aggression ratings provided by the respondents' teachers in the six waves is .54, just slightly lower than the average for boys, .56. Based on these findings, we conclude that the aggression data for girls are about as reliable and valid as those for boys. The total impact of different kinds of measurement error will be discussed in connection with the findings.

TABLE 8.4
Aggression Stability (Autocorrelations) and Length of Time between Waves

WAVE PAIRS	DURATION	AUTOCORRELATION	*N*
III–IV	3 months	.809	(625)
II–III	4 months	.792	(584)
I–II	5 months	.671	(514)
II–IV	7 months	.692	(554)
I–III	9 months	.639	(506)
I–IV	1 year	.640	(482)
IV–V	1 year	.541	(368)
V–VI	1 year	.644	(207)
III–V	1 year/3 months	.626	(373)
II–V	1 year/7 months	.598	(334)
I–V	2 years	.531	(309)
IV–VI	2 years	.659	(178)
III–VI	2 years/3 months	.556	(181)
II–VI	2 years/7 months	.557	(172)
I–VI	3 years	.584	(158)

Boys: Table 3.7.

The aggression stability for girls, shown in Table 8.4,[4] is lower than for boys in most lags. However, the differences are quite small; the average of all 15 lags is .64 for girls and .70 for boys (based on observed correlations). In other words, over a 3-year period, there is somewhat more relative change in girls' aggressive behavior than in boys'. This finding is in agreement with data reported by Kagan and Moss (1964).

TELEVISION EXPOSURE MEASURE

Girls filled out the same program checklists as boys, and the television exposure measures were computed in the same manner as for boys (see Chapter 4).

Statistics for the violence exposure measure are shown in Table 8.5.[5] The

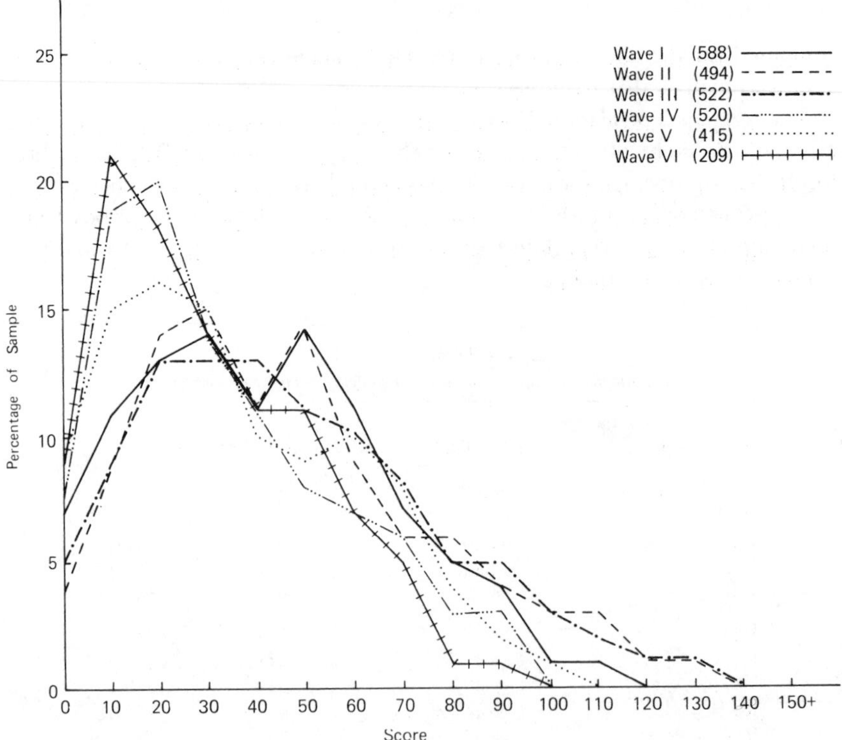

FIGURE 8.2. *Violent television exposure measure: Score distribution in Waves I–VI. (Based on data obtained from valid reporters only.)*

[4]Correlations are not adjusted for measurement error. However, as just noted, the reliability averages .93 over the six waves, which means that adjusted correlations are only about 7% higher than the observed correlations shown in Table 8.4. (See Appendix C for discussion of multiwave reliability estimates.)

[5]The correlations between the measures of total and violence exposure in the six waves average .93 (.92 among boys).

TABLE 8.5
Violent Television Exposure Measure: Descriptive Statistics for All Six Waves[a]

STATISTIC	WAVE I	II	III	IV	V	VI
Median	43.5	47.5	47.0	36.0	31.4	32.1
Mean	45.4	51.7	51.0	40.7	37.2	35.6
Mode	29	37	32	18	16	19
Standard deviation	25.7	29.7	29.9	25.6	24.3	22.4
Range	0–116	0–133	0–138	0–120	0–116	1–111
Skewness	.3	.6	.6	.5	.7	.8
N	(588)	(494)	(522)	(520)	(415)	(209)

[a]Based on data obtained from valid reporters only.
Boys: Table 4.3.

distributions in the six waves are shown in Figure 8.2. (All data are based on valid reporters.) The amount of viewing reported by boys and girls, and the distribution of the scores, are quite similar.

The reliability for the exposure measures was estimated using a maximum-likelihood regression model. The coefficients were similar to those obtained for boys, ranging from .60 to .81 and averaging .72.[6]

Systematic bias in the reporting of television viewing occurred among girls to about the same extent as among boys. Table 8.6 shows the number and percentages of valid and less valid reporters among girls in the six waves. As mentioned in Chapter 4, most of those classified as less valid reporters are valid in other waves and are included in some of the analyses based on valid reporters only.

Since the validity analyses reported in Chapter 4 were carried out on a sample consisting of boys and girls, the conclusions of those analyses apply to girls, too.

TABLE 8.6
Number of Valid and Less Valid Reporters in the Six Waves[a]

	TOTAL SAMPLE		VALID REPORTERS		LESS VALID REPORTERS	
WAVE	*N*	%	*N*	%	*N*	%
I	698	100	588	84	110	16
II	571	100	446	78	125	22
III	612	100	516	84	96	16
IV	598	100	514	86	84	14
V	487	100	410	84	77	16
VI	259	100	204	79	55	21

[a]Aggression and television data available for all respondents.
Boys: Table 4.4.

[6]Details on the computation of the reliability coefficients are reported in Appendix C.

TABLE 8.7
Comparison of Viewing Reports by Girls and Boys (Prime-Time Programs in Waves II and V) (Valid Reporters)

	GIRLS		BOYS	
	MEAN	(RANK)	MEAN	(RANK)
Wave II				
Bewitched	2.8	(2)	2.1	(1)
Brady Bunch	2.9	(1)	2.1	(1)
Adam 12	1.2	(10)	1.9	(3)
Mission Impossible	1.5	(6)	1.8	(4)
Bonanza	1.5	(6)	1.7	(5)
Mod Squad	1.7	(5)	1.7	(5)
Wrestling (local)	1.0	(12)	1.7	(5)
Family Affair	2.3	(3)	1.6	(8)
Doris Day	2.2	(4)	1.4	(9)
Gunsmoke	1.1	(11)	1.3	(10)
Hee Haw	1.5	(6)	1.3	(10)
Young Rebels	.9	(13)	1.2	(12)
Arnie	1.4	(9)	1.1	(13)
Headmaster	.7	(14)	.8	(14)
Don Knotts	.7	(14)	.7	(15)
Mat Lincoln	.4	(16)	.2	(16)
N	(522)		(463)	
Wave V				
Partridge Family	2.7	(1)	2.1	(1)
Adam 12	1.3	(6)	1.8	(2)
All in the Family	2.0	(2)	1.6	(3)
Emergency	1.3	(6)	1.6	(3)
Hawaii 5-O	1.1	(10)	1.5	(5)
Cade's County	.9	(12)	1.4	(6)
Flip Wilson	1.7	(4)	1.4	(6)
Bonanza	1.3	(6)	1.2	(8)
Mary Tyler Moore	1.8	(3)	1.2	(10)
Alias Smith & Jones	.9	(12)	1.0	(10)
Laugh-In	1.4	(5)	1.0	(10)
Mod Squad	1.2	(9)	1.0	(10)
FBI	.8	(14)	.9	(13)
Eddie's Father	1.0	(11)	.6	(14)
Gunsmoke	.6	(15)	.6	(14)
N	(415)		(414)	

No comparable table for boys.

One of the validity tests analyzed sex differences in viewing. Table 8.7 provides additional details. Shown are the means indicating the amount of prime-time viewing reported in Waves II and V.[7] In brackets are the programs' rank orders for easy comparison between girls and boys. There are some interesting differences: Girls watch situation comedies, especially those focusing on female characters (such as Doris Day and Mary Tyler Moore) more than boys, and they watch police dramas (such as *Adam 12*) less than boys. (Note that a police drama starring a female along with two males, *Mod Squad*, is equally popular with boys and girls.) These findings not only have face validity; they are also corroborated by commercial ratings.

The stability of the violence exposure measure is higher for girls than for boys. As shown in Table 8.8, the adjusted[8] autocorrelations are between .58 and 1.00; they average .73 (average for boys, .56). Thus, although there is somewhat more change in girls' aggression over the 3 years of the study, there is less change in violent television exposure among girls than among boys during that period.

CROSS-SECTIONAL CORRELATIONS

Table 8.9 presents the cross-sectional correlations between television exposure and aggression for the total sample of girls. The first column shows correlations with the measure of total exposure; the second column, correlations with the violence exposure measure. As noted for boys, less valid

TABLE 8.8

Stability of Violent Television Exposure: Adjusted and Unadjusted Autocorrelations between all Wave Pairs[a]

WAVES	I	II	III	IV	V	VI
I		.581 (329)	.541 (326)	.489 (319)	.455 (199)	.564 (96)
II	.772		.707 (417)	.597 (407)	.384 (231)	.503 (111)
III	.696	.909		.693 (441)	.505 (256)	.509 (120)
IV	.667	.815	.908		.528 (268)	.524 (126)
V	.682	.576	.727	.806		.596 (146)
VI	.846	.754	.733	.800	1.000	

[a]The autocorrelations are based on data obtained from valid reporters only. The unadjusted autocorrelations are given above the diagonal. The autocorrelations adjusted for measurement unreliabilities are give below the diagonal. See Appendix C for a discussion of the methods used.

Boy: Table 4.6.

[7]A mean of .0 would indicate that nobody reported any viewing; a mean of 4.0, that every respondent reported watching the program four times out of four telecasts during the last month. Waves II and V were selected to provide examples from the earlier and later parts of the study.

[8]See Appendix C for a discussion of the methods used.

TABLE 8.9
Cross-Sectional Correlations between Measures of Total and Violent Television Exposure and Aggression

	TOTAL SAMPLES		
WAVE	TOTAL TELEVISION EXPOSURE	VIOLENT TELEVISION EXPOSURE	*N*
I	.372*	.373*	(698)
II	.300*	.297*	(571)
III	.308*	.322*	(612)
IV	.245*	.267*	(598)
V	.213*	.214*	(487)
VI	.275*	.302*	(259)

*Significant at .05 level.
Boys: Table 5.1.

reporters exaggerate the amount of television they watch and, as shown in Table 8.10, also score higher on the aggression measure. As a result, the cross-sectional correlations in Table 8.9 are higher than they would be if less valid reporters were excluded. Table 8.11 shows the extent to which this is true. The correlations between total exposure and aggression for valid reporters average .22, about 30% less than in the total sample. The correlations between violence exposure and aggression average .23, again about 30% less than in the total sample. The same phenomenon was noted for the boys' cross sectional correlations.

Returning to Table 8.9, we note that the correlations reported there for girls are substantially higher than those in Table 5.1 for boys, indicating that there is

TABLE 8.10
Median Aggression Scores by Validity of Television Reporting in All Six Waves

	VALID REPORTERS		LESS VALID REPORTERS		TOTAL	
WAVE	MEDIAN	*N*	MEDIAN	*N*	MEDIAN	*N*
I	30	(588)	70	(110)	37	(698)
II	30	(446)	59	(125)	34	(571)
III	30	(516)	63	(96)	34	(612)
IV	33	(514)	67	(84)	37	(598)
V	27	(410)	50	(77)	30	(487)
VI	26	(204)	52	(55)	30	(259)

Boys: Table 5.2.

TABLE 8.11

Cross-Sectional Correlations between Measures of Total and Violent TV Exposure and Aggression by Validity of Television Reporting, in all Six Waves

	VALID REPORTERS			LESS VALID REPORTERS		
WAVE	TOTAL TELEVISION EXPOSURE	VIOLENCE TELEVISION EXPOSURE	*N*	TOTAL TELEVISION EXPOSURE	VIOLENCE TELEVISION EXPOSURE	*N*
I	.341*	.335*	(588)	.077	.067	(110)
II	.257*	.259*	(466)	−.101	−.107	(125)
III	.246*	.259*	(516)	−.043	.019	(96)
IV	.176*	.204*	(514)	−.068	.015	(84)
V	.127*	.147*	(410)	.137	.094	(77)
VI	.170*	.183*	(204)	−.114	.010	(55)

*Significant at .05 level.
Boys: Table 5.3.

a stronger relationship between violence on television and aggressive behavior for girls than for boys. The average size of the coefficients in the first column is .29; the average in the second column is .30, whereas the comparable coefficients for boys are .16 and .17.[9] As we shall see in the following, the cross-sectional correlations between aggression and other media variables used in this study are also higher for girls than boys.

Other Correlates of Aggression

The analysis of the correlates of aggression among girls was restricted by the lack of data based on mother and father questionnaires and school record data. Nevertheless, we have 40 measures available for girls and boys, including most of those found to be most strongly correlated with aggression in the boys' sample (Chapter 5).

Table 8.12 shows the rank order of 25 selected correlates of aggression among girls and boys.[10] (Measures with the highest rank are most strongly correlated with aggression.) The table permits an assessment of the relative

[9]In Chapter 5, the cross-sectional correlations between television and aggression are adjusted for measurement unreliability. As discussed in Appendix C, measurement models for girls' aggression did not provide a good fit to the data in the short wave pairs. Hence, similar adjusted correlations are not presented for girls.

[10]Fifteen additional measures available for boys and girls are not included here because they are correlated with measures listed in Table 8.12. All these measures are related to aggression among girls with approximately the same relative strength as among boys.

TABLE 8.12

Relative Importance of Correlates of Aggression among Girls and among Boys (25 Measures Available for Boys and Girls)[a]

	RANK AMONG GIRLS	RANK AMONG BOYS
Socioeconomic composition of school[b]	9	20
City	24	23
Class aggressiveness	2	3
Aggression of closest friends	1	1
Large for age	18	12
Small for age	23	24
Silly	6	6
Shy or withdrawn	16	8
Plays make believe (peer nominations)	4	5
Prosocial behavior (peer nominations)	5	2
Emotional instability	3	3
Need for approval		
—from teacher	11	12
—from other children	7	7
Most friends	16	21
Least friends	12	19
Peer nominations as closest friend	21	16
Slow reader	18	10
First to learn	14	16
Machismo	25	16
Gentleness	22	24
Enjoyment of "real life" violence	13	9
Violent comic books	8	12
Violent magazines	14	15
Violent books	18	22
Violent theater movies	10	11

[a] Highest rank indicates that the measure is most strongly related to aggression in the sample.

[b] Categories are black lower class, white lower class, white middle class.

No comparable table for boys.

importance of these measures within each of the subsamples as well as a comparison of boys and girls.

Overall, the similarity of the correlates for girls and boys is remarkable; indeed, the correlation between the two rank-orders is .79. But there are also differences. For example, the measure of socioeconomic composition of the school attended by the respondent correlates moderately with aggression among girls, but only weakly among boys. (However, a measure of mother's occupation, which is not available for girls, would rank at number 7 for boys—similar to the position of the substitute SES measure for girls.)

All measures of exposure to media rank higher among girls than among boys. This is true for television exposure (not included in Table 8.12) and for comic books as well.[11]

Mutual Correlates of Television Exposure and Aggression

In Chapter 5, we reported that the correlations between exposure to television and aggression among boys were reduced by partialing out a number of mutual correlates of television exposure and aggression: mother's occupation, family income, race, and, for the total sample, quality of reporting of television exposure (discussed in Chapter 4). For girls, the quality of reporting measure is available; there are no race data, but substitute measures for socioeconomic status are available, which turn out to be mutual correlates of television and aggression among girls.

The findings of the analysis are summarized in Table 8.13, which shows that partialing out socioeconomic composition of the school and quality of reporting reduces the size of the average correlation between television and aggression by 50%, from .30 to .15. We assume that, if race and better measures of socioeconomic status were available, the size of the partial correlation coefficients would be reduced further. The next section will address the issue whether the cross-sectional correlations reported here are indicative of a causal influence of television on aggression.

---

[11]The sizes of the zero-order correlations between "other characteristics and aggressions among girls are very similar to those among boys: for example, six measures of aggression among friends, classmates, etc., average .40 among girls, .41 among boys. Eleven measures of behavior traits average .20 among girls, .21 among boys. In contrast, 8 measures of media exposure average .15 for girls, .09 for boys. (All correlations are six-wave averages.)

TABLE 8.13

Zero-Order and Partial Correlations between Exposure to Violent Television and Aggression (Total Sample)

	WAVE						SIX-WAVE AVERAGE
	I	II	III	IV	V	VI	
Zero-order correlations							
Complete total sample (as shown in Table 8.9)	.37* (698)	.30* (571)	.32* (612)	.27* (598)	.21* (487)	.30* (259)	.30
Partial correlations							
Controlling for quality of reporting and SES[a,b]	.27* (694)	.15* (567)	.17* (608)	.14* (594)	.07 (483)	.12* (256)	.15

[a] Quality of reporting of television exposure data. See Chapter 4 for details.
[b] SES measure is socioeconomic composition of the school.
*Significant at .05 level.
Boys: Table 5.6.

FINDINGS FROM THE BASIC MODEL

As with the analysis of the boys' data, the basic model analyzing the effect of television violence on girls' aggression is:

$$A_{t_i} = a + b_1 A_{(t-1)_i} + b_2 TV_{(t-1)_i} + u_i \tag{1}$$

in which aggression at a later time is predicted from earlier levels of exposure, controlling for earlier aggression. (The logic of this analysis is explained in Chapters 5 and 6.)

Only 58 boys had usable data for all six waves. Similarly, and for the same reasons of attrition, only 60 girls have usable data for all six waves. Consequently, we again analyze the causal effect of television on aggression by examining the 15 wave pairs. As the two-wave models cause overlap between the wave pairs, the model was estimated twice—without controls (Table 8.15) and with controls for intervening television variables (Table 8.16). These models, based on valid reporter samples, are discussed first. Subsequently, data based on total samples, including less valid reporters, are presented.

Limitations Imposed by the Stability of Aggression and the Number of Cases

First examining Column (1b) of Tables 8.14 and 8.15, we see that aggression among valid reporters is fairly stable, although less stable than for boys. As with boys, the longer the elapsed time between waves, the less stable the aggression scores.

Because of the stability of aggression, there is little possibility for television exposure or any other predictor to have a very large effect. Furthermore, an explanatory factor may account for a large proportion of change in the shorter wave pairs, but do so only because of the total amount of change is small. Therefore, the effect of the explanatory factor in absolute terms would be small. Conversely, in the longer wave pairs, where there is more change to explain, a factor may account for a small proportion of that change, but be very important in absolute terms.

The number of cases available for each wave pair is given in Column (7) of both tables. As the lags between waves increase in length, the number of cases diminishes, until there are only about 100 cases or fewer in the longest wave pairs. This same trend was noted for boys, and in Chapter 6 we pointed out that the larger samples in the shorter wave pairs, where aggression is more stable, make statistical significance of television's effect easier to detect exactly in those cases where there is less change to explain.

Findings for Valid Reporters

Television's impact on aggression is given by the metric *b* and standardized β coefficients in Columns (3a) and (3b) of Tables 8.14 and 8.15.

The coefficients in Table 8.14 are very similar to those for boys (in Table 6.1). Most are positive (10 out of 15), 5 are negative. They are very small (βs range from .157 to −.037 and average .042 in the 15 lags), and only 3 are significant.[12] (Among boys we found that 12 out of 15 coefficients were positive; they averaged .044, and 2 were significant with a third approaching significance.)

The significant coefficients are in overlapping lags (III–IV, II–IV, and II–VI). Consequently, as among boys, we computed a model that controls for intervening exposure variables, shown in Table 8.15. The control adds one significant coefficient with a positive sign (III–VI) and one with a negative sign (I–III). At the same time, the control eliminates one of the significances in the

[12]The range in adjacent lags is .101 to −.037, the average .003.

overlapping lags (II–III). The net result of the control for intervening exposure variables, then, is 3 positive significances, 1 significant negative coefficient, and 11 insignificant coefficients. This pattern is inconsistent and thus has equivocal meaning for a causal interpretation. Further analyses, to be reported in more detail, suggested that the pattern is spurious. When we controlled for common causes of television and aggression, the number of positive significant coefficients reduced from 3 to 1. Thus, there is no reason to infer that the cross-sectional correlation between television exposure and aggression reported in Table 8.13, which were higher for girls than for boys, are due to exposure causing aggression.

Aside from statistical significance, the impact of television exposure is quite small in all panels. Column (4) in Table 8.14 lists the "unique contribution" of television exposure to predicting the later aggression score. This quantity is the R^2 increment due directly to television, and ranges from .000 to .024. In 12 of the 15 pairs, the unique contribution is less than 1% of the variance in later aggression. (Results in Table 8.15 are similar.)

As the stability of aggression is so high, we also computed the percentage of variance in later aggression explained by television after the effect of earlier aggression has been accounted for. These percentages are given in Column (6) of Tables 8.14 and 8.15. In 10 of the 15 wave pairs (9 in Table 8.15), the initial exposure score accounts for less than 1% of that portion of later aggression that represents change from earlier aggression. (The average is .9% in Table 8.14 and 1.5% in Table 8.15.)

Finally, as we did among boys, we can examine the potential causal impact of television exposure if the coefficients did, in fact, reflect a true causal association. In Table 8.14, the average of the positive *b* coefficients for the shorter lags (less than 1 year) is .13. For the medium lags (between 1 and 2 years) the average is .08; the average for the long lags (between 2 and 3 years) is .15.[13] Let us assume a girl's violence exposure is in the lowest decile (approximately 9 points on the exposure scale), and she is persuaded to increase her viewing until it is in the highest decile of exposure (approximately 76 points on the exposure scale). With an average *b* coefficient of .15 for the long wave pairs, this increase in exposure would result in an increase in her aggression score by this amount: $(76 - 9) \times .15 = 10.1$. As the aggression scale has a possible range of 400 points and a standard deviation of about 50 points, an increase of 10 points is very small, especially if we consider this is possible for

[13]These averages follow the trend for the boys—the largest *b* coefficients are generally found in the longer time intervals.

TABLE 8.14

Basic Model Regression Coefficients Showing the Impact of Violent Television Exposure on Later Aggression for All Wave Pairs (Valid Reporters)

		EARLIER AGGRESSION COEFFICIENTS		UNIQUE CONTRIBUTION OF EARLIER AGGRESSION TO TOTAL R^2	EARLIER VIOLENT TELEVISION EXPOSURE COEFFICIENTS		UNIQUE CONTRIBUTION OF EARLIER VIOLENT TELEVISION EXPOSURE TO TOTAL R^2	TOTAL R^2	VARIANCE OF CHANGE IN AGGRESSION EXPLAINED BY EARLIER TELEVISION	N
WAVE PAIR	DURATION	b (1a)	β (1b)	(2)	b (3a)	β (3b)	(4)	(5)	(6)	(7)
III–IV	3 months	.891*	.784	.575	.138*	.081	.006	.654	.017	(491)
II–III	4 months	.754*	.762	.541	.082	.060	.003	.607	.009	(426)
I–II	5 months	.616*	.676	.403	−.062	−.037	.001	.441	.005	(391)
II–IV	7 months	.766*	.662	.410	.168*	.105	.010	.486	.020	(408)
I–III	9 months	.555*	.634	.355	−.008	−.005	.000	.400	.000	(384)
I–IV	1 year	.612*	.636	.356	.036	.020	.000	.413	.001	(369)
IV–V	1 year	.504*	.501	.237	.120	.062	.004	.270	.005	(296)
V–VI	1 year	.499*	.585	.338	.153	.101	.010	.365	.016	(153)
III–V	1 year/3 months	.694*	.614	.346	−.043	−.028	.001	.369	.001	(292)
II–V	1 year/7 months	.672*	.602	.330	.005	.004	.000	.363	.000	(245)
I–V	2 years	.437*	.484	.205	.103	.062	.003	.259	.005	(236)
IV–VI	2 years	.573*	.679	.444	−.017	−.011	.000	.458	.000	(134)
III–VI	2 years/3 months	.659*	.616	.343	.135	.094	.008	.425	.014	(133)
II–VI	2 years/7 months	.622*	.606	.351	.215*	.157	.024	.433	.039	(123)
I–VI	3 years	.541*	.596	.321	−.049	−.029	.001	.346	.001	(113)

*Significant at .05 level.
Boys: Table 6.1.

TABLE 8.15

Basic Model Regression Coefficients Showing the Impact of Violent Television Exposure on Later Aggression for All Wave Pairs with Controls for Intervening Television Exposure (Valid Reporters)

WAVE PAIR	DURATION	EARLIER AGGRESSION COEFFICIENTS *b* (1a)	EARLIER AGGRESSION COEFFICIENTS β (1b)	UNIQUE CONTRIBUTION OF EARLIER AGGRESSION TO TOTAL R^2 (2)	EARLIER VIOLENT TELEVISION EXPOSURE COEFFICIENTS *b* (3a)	EARLIER VIOLENT TELEVISION EXPOSURE COEFFICIENTS β (3b)	UNIQUE CONTRIBUTION OF EARLIER VIOLENT TELEVISION EXPOSURE TO TOTAL R^2 (4)	TOTAL R^2 (5)	VARIANCE OF CHANGE IN AGGRESSION EXPLAINED BY EARLIER TELEVISION (6)	*N* (7)
III–IV	3 months	.891*	.784	.575	.138*	.081	.006	.654	.017	(491)
II–III	4 months	.754*	.762	.541	.082	.060	.003	.607	.009	(426)
I–II	5 months	.616*	.676	.403	−.062	−.037	.001	.441	.003	(391)
II–IV	7 months	.767*	.663	.411	.176*	.111	.012	.486	.020	(362)
I–III	9 months	.541*	.619	.338	−.173*	−.105	.010	.422	.018	(321)
I–IV	1 year	.601*	.624	.343	−.121	−.067	.004	.429	.007	(281)
IV–V	1 year	.504*	.501	.237	.120	.062	.004	.270	.005	(296)
V–VI	1 year	.499*	.585	.338	.153	.101	.010	.365	.016	(153)
III–V	1 year/3 months	.694*	.614	.346	−.043	−.028	.001	.369	.001	(259)
II–V	1 year/7 months	.687*	.615*	.339	.161	.116	.006	.377	.009	(198)
I–V	2 years	.430*	.475	.197	.025	.015	.000	.263	.000	(174)
IV–VI	2 years	.375*	.444	.190	−.019	−.013	.001	.493	.001	(111)
III–VI	2 years/3 months	.684*	.640	.370	.335*	.235	.048	.447	.094	(96)
II–VI	2 years/7 months	.609*	.594	.337	.125	.091	.008	.471	.013	(87)
I–VI	3 years	.515*	.568	.288	−.129	−.076	.005	.360	.009	(75)

*Significant at .05 level.
Boys: Table 6.2.

only the least exposed girls. For a girl whose violence exposure is at the fiftieth percentile, an increase to the highest level of viewing would yield a potential impact of only 5 or 6 points over the 3-year span of the study.

The effects of errors on the basic model findings for boys were discussed in appendices to Chapter 6. The same procedure is followed here in Appendices B and C.[14]

As mentioned in the analysis of television exposure and aggressive behavior among boys, we are not able to explain the origin of the small positive associations between television and aggression. However, later in this chapter we present evidence that the associations are due to antecedent variables and are at least partly spurious.

Findings for the Total Sample

The exclusion of less valid reporters from the analyses just given presents the same issues as it did for boys: Results for the entire sample may be different from those for valid reporters alone.

Tables 8.16 and 8.17 present the basic linear regression model computed for valid and less valid reporters combined. (The tables correspond to Tables 8.14 and 8.15 for valid reporters.) Comparison of the *b* coefficients in Column (3a) in the two tables shows that most are larger for the total sample than those in Table 8.14. The coefficients average .062, compared to .042 in the analyses based on valid reporters only.

Although this increase is quite small, 5 of the 15 *b* coefficients for television's effect are statistically significant, whereas only 3 of the 15 coefficients were significant for valid reporters. The 3 significant coefficients in the short lags are largely overlapping (lags II–III, II–IV, and III–IV).

Table 8.17 controls for the overlap between lags and reduces the number of significant coefficients to 3. This number of significances could hardly have

[14]Appendix B in Chapter 6 discusses the effects of attrition and addition of new respondents on the sample of boys. The girls' sample experienced attrition for the same three reasons as the boys: graduation from sixth grade, residential mobility, and temporary absenteeism. Clearly, sex is not a determinant of any of these causes of attrition in elementary school. In fact, the rates of graduation and temporary absenteeism were seen earlier to be very similar for girls and boys. For these reasons, we did not repeat an analysis of attrition for girls. Appendix B deals with curvilinearity; C with measurement error.

TABLE 8.16

Basic Model Regression Coefficients Showing the Impact of Violent Television Exposure on Later Aggression for All Wave Pairs (Total Sample)

WAVE PAIR	DURATION	EARLIER AGGRESSION COEFFICIENTS		UNIQUE CONTRIBUTION OF EARLIER AGGRESSION TO TOTAL R^2	EARLIER VIOLENT TELEVISION EXPOSURE COEFFICIENTS		UNIQUE CONTRIBUTION OF EARLIER VIOLENT TELEVISION EXPOSURE TO TOTAL R^2	TOTAL R^2	VARIANCE OF CHANGE IN AGGRESSION EXPLAINED BY EARLIER TELEVISION	N
		b (1a)	β (1b)	(2)	*b* (3a)	β (3b)	(4)	(5)	(6)	(7)
III–IV	3 months	.858*	.784	.548	.115*	.078	.005	.660	.016	(583)
II–III	4 months	.789*	.770	.539	.102*	.081	.006	.637	.016	(542)
I–II	5 months	.604*	.680	.405	−.033	−.025	.001	.451	.001	(477)
II–IV	7 months	.739*	.659	.394	.158*	.115	.012	.493	.023	(517)
I–III	9 months	.569*	.625	.344	.052	.037	.001	.408	.002	(467)
I–IV	1 year	.639*	.633	.352	.058	.038	.001	.419	.002	(447)
IV–V	1 year	.486*	.525	.247	.080	.052	.002	.296	.004	(346)
V–VI	1 year	.570*	.604	.340	.167*	.125	.015	.420	.025	(201)
III–V	1 year/3 months	.659*	.632	.336	−.033	−.024	.000	.389	.001	(350)
II–V	1 year/7 months	.651*	.583	.299	.101	.080	.006	.378	.010	(315)
I–V	2 years	.477*	.500	.225	.116	.084	.006	.284	.009	(286)
IV–VI	2 years	.508*	.647	.371	.046	.036	.001	.436	.002	(165)
III–VI	2 years/3 months	.490*	.521	.220	.083	.070	.004	.308	.007	(169)
II–VI	2 years/7 months	.519*	.518	.253	.214*	.186	.033	.349	.047	(164)
I–VI	3 years	.514*	.574	.303	−.010	−.007	.000	.328	.000	(144)

*Significant at .05 level.
Boys: Table 6.3.

occurred by chance (the probability is only 3%). The size of the average coefficient, however, is quite small, .039 (Column (3b) in Table 8.17), and 5 out of 15 are negative.

In short, analyses with samples that include less valid reporters produced results similar to those obtained with valid respondents. The number of significant coefficients is higher, but because the increase is caused by the addition of respondents with less accurate viewing reports, caution is in order in interpreting this finding as evidence for a consistent and significant television effect among girls.

OTHER CONCEPTUALIZATIONS OF TELEVISION EXPOSURE

Is the measure of violence exposure used in the analyses just reported the best predictor of later aggression, or will other conceptualizations of television violence produce larger coefficients in basic model analyses?

The following measures were computed and used in basic model regressions instead of the violence exposure measure[15]:

1. *Relative amount of exposure to television violence*. As expected, we found that girls watch relatively few violent television programs compared to boys. Otherwise, the analyses resulted in the same finding as those for boys: The measure of relative amount of exposure to television violence is a poorer predictor of later aggression than the exposure measure usually used. (The analyses conducted were the same as those for boys: first a comparison of regressions with the television violence measure and regressions with the new "relative amount of violence" measure; then a comparison of regressions with the television violence measure, both measures, and regressions with an interaction term added.) Data are shown in Tables D.2 and D.3.

2. *Exposure over longer time periods*. This analysis, too, was conducted in the same way as that for boys and brought the same result, that is, measures of cumulative exposure are not better predictors than a violence exposure measure based on data from one wave (see Table D.4).

[15]Table D.1 shows cross-sectional correlations of all measures with the violence exposure measure and aggression. Analyses based on total samples led to essentially the same results as those with samples of valid reporters presented here. Additional details are available on request.

TABLE 8.17

Basic Model Regression Coefficients Showing the Impact of Violent Television Exposure on Later Aggression for All Wave Pairs with Controls for Intervening Television Exposure (Total Sample)

		EARLIER AGGRESSION COEFFICIENTS		UNIQUE CONTRIBUTION OF EARLIER AGGRESSION TO TOTAL R^2	EARLIER VIOLENT TELEVISION EXPOSURE COEFFICIENTS		UNIQUE CONTRIBUTION OF EARLIER VIOLENT TELEVISION EXPOSURE TO TOTAL R^2	TOTAL R^2	VARIANCE OF CHANGE IN AGGRESSION EXPLAINED BY EARLIER TELEVISION	N
WAVE PAIR	DURATION	b (1a)	β (1b)	(2)	b (3a)	β (3b)	(4)	(5)	(6)	(7)
III–IV	3 months	.858*	.784	.548	.115*	.078	.005	.660	.016	(583)
II–III	4 months	.789*	.770	.539	.102*	.081	.006	.637	.016	(542)
I–II	5 months	.604*	.680	.405	−.033	−.025	.001	.451	.001	(477)
II–IV	7 months	.729*	.651	.386	.047	.034	.001	.498	.002	(485)
I–III	9 months	.559*	.614	.332	−.012	−.008	.000	.411	.000	(436)
I–IV	1 year	.621*	.615	.333	−.020	−.013	.000	.427	.000	(393)
IV–V	1 year	.486*	.525	.247	.080	.052	.002	.296	.004	(346)
V–VI	1 year	.570*	.604	.340	.167*	.125	.015	.420	.025	(201)
III–V	1 year/3 months	.660*	.634	.338	−.021	−.016	.000	.389	.000	(329)
II–V	1 year/7 months	.657*	.588	.204	.179	.141	.018	.381	.030	(280)
I–V	2 years	.460*	.482	.209	.028	.020	.000	.289	.001	(253)
IV–VI	2 years	.513	.655	.380	.078	.061	.003	.437	.007	(156)
III–VI	2 years/3 months	.507*	.540	.234	.072	.061	.003	.311	.005	(149)
II–VI	2 years/7 months	.508*	.507	.242	.134	.117	.013	.354	.018	(144)
I–VI	3 years	.482*	.539	.267	−.156	−.119	.013	.348	.020	(127)

*Significant at .05 level.

Boys: Table 6.4.

3. *Alternative violence weighting system*. We computed alternative measures of exposure based on "violence weights," identical to those computed for boys. Findings for girls are shown in Table D.5. In four lags, there is a significant increase in R^2 when the alternative measures are used. However, as among the boys, the average increase in the 15 lags is quite small: .011 (.010 among boys), and there is no consistency in which of the measures contribute to the R^2 increase.[16]

4. *Context of televised violence*. The same measures of the different contexts in which television violence occurs used in the analysis of the boys' data were used for girls. Among boys, these measures were not significantly and consistently better predictors of the later aggression than the basic measure.

Findings for girls are reported in Table D.6. The measures based on violence context explain significantly more variance than regressions with the regular television measure in four lags. (The amount of variance explained is .011 larger with these measures than with one exposure measure.) However, the significant R^2 components are not caused by a consistent set of contexts. Six measures are significant contributors in the four lags with significant R^2 components, and only one (adventure shows) appears more than once as significant—once with a positive and once with a negative sign. Thus, on balance, we conclude that these television exposure measures are not superior predictors of subsequent aggression.

5. *Empirical viewing patterns*. Factor analyses of program-by-program viewing data were conducted in the same manner as for boys. Table 8.18 compares the number and the kind of factors found among girls and boys. There are somewhat fewer factors among girls, but otherwise the similarity is remarkable. The factors also explain about the same amount of variance in viewing for boys and girls, close to 50%.

As predictors of later aggression, measures based on factors produced four significant R^2 components among boys, but there was no consistency in the measures that led to significance. Among girls, results are similar. As shown in Table D.7, factors are significant predictors of later aggression in 6 lags, and there is a .012 increase in the amount of variance explained. Table D.8 shows which factors were significant contributors in these six regressions. The lack of consistency is apparent: As in the previous analyses (measures based on

[16]We also computed basic model regressions with the measure of total exposure, which applies equal weights to all programs. The measure is a slightly weaker predictor of later aggression than the violence exposure measure.

TABLE 8.18
Comparison of Viewing Factors Found among Girls and among Boys (Six-Wave Summary)

	NUMBER OF FACTORS FOUND IN SIX WAVES	
	GIRLS	BOYS
Action/Adventure	6	7
Westerns/*Hee Haw*	1	2
News/Documentary	6	5
Saturday morning cartoons	9	10
Educational children's programs	1	
Sitcoms	7	9
Variety	1	
Black shows	1	
Saturday–Sunday	2	3
Weekday	3	6
ABC	1	1
Unclassified factors	7	7
Total number of factors	45	50

Boys data summarized from Table 7.5.

context), no measure is significant in more than 2 of the 15 lags. Again, we conclude that these measures are not superior to the basic exposure measure.

6. *Liking violent television*. Finally, we looked at the violence content of the self-reported favorite shows. The interaction between this measure and violence exposure was a poor predictor of later aggression among boys, and Table D.9 shows that the same is true for girls.

Summary

The analyses of other conceptualizations of television exposure produced the same results among girls as among boys: None of the other conceptualizations turned out to be consistently and significantly better predictors of later aggression. Further, measures of exposure to programs usually regarded as most "violent" were not significantly more strongly associated with later aggression than measures of exposure to "nonviolent" programs.

TABLE 8.19
Summary of Measures Used in Subgroup Analysis[a]

Sociocultural characteristics	Socioeconomic composition of school (1)[b]
	City (1)
Aggression of peers	Classroom aggression (1)
	Aggression of closest friends (1)
	Classroom and friends' aggression (2)
Girl's behavior, attitudes, and characteristics	
Aggressive predisposition:	Initial aggression (1)
	Altruism (2)
Attitudes toward aggression:	Machismo (5)
	Gentleness (5)
	Enjoyment of real-life violence (6)
Other behavior/characteristics	Fantasy behavior
	—Teacher nominations (1)
	—Peer ratings (1)
	Emotional instability (5)
	Shyness (1)
	Size [large/small for age] (1,1)
	Age [Grade in school] (1)
	Scholastic ability [first to learn] (1)
Exposure to other media:	Exposure to comic books (17)
	Exposure to theater movies (about 8)

[a]All measures except "Socioeconomic composition of school and "first to learn" were used in analyses with boys; see Table 7.8 and Appendices B and C in Chapter 7.

[b]Numbers in brackets indicate how many items the measure consists of. (For example, "(4)" indicates that the measure is a four-item index.)

EFFECTS OF TELEVISION EXPOSURE AMONG SUBGROUPS

After having investigated possible television exposure effects in the girls' sample considered as a whole, we continue to follow the pattern of data analysis used for boys and turn to the analysis of subgroups.

In Chapter 7, we analyzed subgroups of boys based on 43 different attributes. Many of those were derived from mother and father data, which are not available for girls. Thus, the subgroups analysis for girls is based on 20 attributes as compared to 43 for boys. Table 8.19 lists the measures.[17]

[17]Eighteen of the measures used in this analysis are identical to measures used for boys; the two remaining, socioeconomic composition of school and "first to learn," are substitute measures for the socioeconomic and scholastic ability measures used for boys. For details on the 18 measures, see Appendices B and C in Chapter 7. The other two measures are described in Appendix E (see Tables E.1 and E.4).

The 20 attributes available for girls produced 46 subgroups and a total of 600 regressions.

As the subgroup analyses for girls are all based on the entire sample of valid reporters (about 200 cases in the short and 50 in the long lags), we are generally able to detect smaller effects of television exposure among girls than among boys. In most of the short lags, we obtained significance with coefficients less than .1; in the long lags, with coefficients of about .2.

The data were analyzed in the same way as for boys. The analyses for the valid reporter samples are summarized in Tables E.1–E.4; data for total samples (including the less valid reporters) are reported in Tables E.5–E.8.

The analyses produced findings quite similar to those reported for boys. Significant associations between television exposure and later aggression were found in a few subgroups, but an overall assessment of the patterns of significance in all subgroups shows that these agree with a random model. Also, the groups in which significant coefficients were found are different from those among boys. In other words, the patterns of significant coefficients do not support the hypothesis that some groups are more affected by television than others.[18]

Forty-six subgroups were analyzed, and four or more significant coefficients were found in six of them. Three occurred in groups defined by "predisposing" conditions: girls nominated as "not shy" (see Table E.3), and those with high exposure to comic books and theater movies (Table E.4). As discussed in Chapter 7, the status of the "low in fantasy" group is ambiguous (Table E.3). Among girls, four coefficients were found in the group based on peer ratings; this was not replicated when the teacher was the rater. (Among boys, it was the reverse.) The significances in the Fort Worth group were also ambiguous (Table E.1).

The strongest evidence for a possible television effect was found among girls "low in initial aggression," probably the most clearly and most reliably defined "not predisposed" group of all subgroups analyzed (Table E.2).[19] However,

[18]As among the boys, the overall assessment was based on the coefficients in adjacent lags. Of the 46 subgroups, 30% have no significant coefficient in those lags, 52% have one, 13% two, 2% three, and 2% four (out of five). The model that randomly distributes the significant coefficients found in the regression predicts that 35% of the subgroups will have no significant coefficient, 41% have one, 19% have two, 4% have three and 1% have four or five coefficients. The χ^2 for the correspondence between the two distributions is 2.29 with $df = 4$—well within the bounds of chance differences.

[19]Similar inconsistent patterns also emerge when subgroups with three or more significant associations are considered. There were 12 such groups, including the "not shy" (4 out of 15 coefficients) and the "shy" (3 out of 5 coefficients) groups. Of the 12 groups, 5 are "predisposed," 4 are "not predisposed," and 3 are ambiguous.

because the finding goes counter to theoretical prediction, is not replicated in other groups of "not predisposed" girls, and does not violate a random model of overall significance, we are inclined to regard this as a chance result.[20]

SENSITIVITY OF THE ANALYSIS MODEL

Table 7.9 showed that among boys, several measures—other than television exposure—were significant predictors of later aggression in basic regressions. We concluded from that finding that our failure to detect associations between television exposure and later aggression was not due to problems with the analysis model or the aggression measure.

The same analysis for girls corroborated the findings reported for boys. Only two of the variables were available for girls, but both are highly significant predictors of aggression: "Aggression of class," with an average β of .30 and significant coefficients in all 15 lags, and "socioeconomic composition of school, average β of .11 and significant coefficients in 10 lags.[21]

BASIC MODEL CONTROLS

As among boys, we found that most of the television coefficients in the basic model analysis were insignificant, but positive. Therefore, we performed a series of analyses to see whether the small positive associations resulted from third variables that are not controlled in the basic model, or whether there were indications that the associations resulted from a true causal influence of exposure on aggression.

We were able to examine 19 causal antecedents of the television exposure and aggression among boys and found that measures of socioeconomic background and the "Religious family" variable reduced the associations between television and aggression in basic model analyses (Table 7.10). For girls, only five variables are available for such a test, and only one of these had

[20]As just mentioned, the groups in which significant coefficients were found were not affected by attrition.

[21]See Chapter 7 for details on the analysis with the classroom measure. The note of caution regarding the interpretation of these findings in causal terms applies here as well. Finally, we also analyzed exposure to comic book and theater movie violence for girls and found significant associations with the comic book measure.

an effect on the associations among boys: "School SES."[22] This finding is replicated among girls. In basic model regressions, the introduction of School SES reduced the number of significant coefficients in the girls' samples from three to one (in samples with identical number of cases) and reduced the size of the average β from .042 to .024. (The pattern of signs remained 10 positive, 5 negative.) Thus, this very limited test supports our interpretation that the small positive associations found for girls are at least partly caused by uncontrolled third variables.

BASIC MODEL FINDINGS FOR BOYS AND GIRLS COMBINED

Up to this point, we have looked separately at boys and girls because fewer data are available for girls than boys. As we have just seen, the basic model results for girls are very much like those for boys: predominantly positive television effect coefficients that are too small to be significant with the sample size available to us.

We also can ask what the results would be if we combined the boys and girls in a basic model analysis. The pooled model would double the sample size and this would provide more power to evaluate whether or not the television coefficients are indicative of an effect.

It is appropriate to estimate this pooled model only if there are no differences in the patterns of significance between boys and girls in the television and/or aggression effects in the 15 lags. We tested a model that showed that the two samples can be combined. The model is:

$$A_t = a + b_1 A_{t-1} + b_2 TV_{t-1} + b_3 S + b_4(A_{t-1}) \times (S) + b_5(TV_{t-1}) \times (S),$$

where S is a dummy variable for the sex of the respondent (boys coded 1, girls coded 0), $(A_{t-1}) \times (S)$ is an interaction between aggression and sex, and $(TV_{t-1}) \times (S)$ is an interaction between television exposure and sex. The coefficient b_3 in this model can be interpreted as the difference in the intercept of the aggression regression lines between boys and girls. The key coefficients that must be nonsignificant to allow pooling the data are b_4 and b_5. These can be interpreted as the differences in the influences of aggression and television between boys and girls (Cleary & Kessler, 1982).

Thirty models were estimated, one for each wave pair separately for valid reporters and the total sample. None of the 60 estimates for the interaction terms b_4 and b_5 obtained in this way was found to be statistically significant.

[22]The other measures available for girls are city, age, scholastic grade, big for age. None of these had a pronounced or consistent effect on the associations between television and aggression in basic model analyses.

TABLE 8.20

Basic Model Regression Coefficients Showing the Impact of Violent Television Exposure on Later Aggression for All Wave Pairs among Boys and Girls Combined (Valid Reporters)

WAVE PAIR	DURATION	EARLIER AGGRESSION COEFFICIENTS b (1a)	EARLIER AGGRESSION COEFFICIENTS β (1b)	UNIQUE CONTRIBUTION OF EARLIER AGGRESSION TO TOTAL R^2 (2)	EARLIER VIOLENT TELEVISION EXPOSURE COEFFICIENTS b (3a)	EARLIER VIOLENT TELEVISION EXPOSURE COEFFICIENTS β (3b)	UNIQUE CONTRIBUTION OF EARLIER VIOLENT TELEVISION EXPOSURE TO TOTAL R^2 (4)	TOTAL R^2 (5)	VARIANCE OF CHANGE IN AGGRESSION EXPLAINED BY EARLIER TELEVISION (6)	N (7)
III–IV	3 months	.912*	.844	.610	.130*	.056	.003	.748	.009	(988)
II–III	4 months	.825*	.814	.579	.037	.018	.000	.731	.000	(839)
I–II	5 months	.684*	.672	.402	−.040	−.017	.000	.517	.000	(755)
II–IV	7 months	.822*	.743	.481	.125*	.056	.003	.631	.006	(817)
I–III	9 months	.655*	.642	.368	−.041	−.018	.000	.494	.000	(740)
I–IV	1 year	.668*	.627	.350	.028	.012	.000	.453	.000	(718)
IV–V	1 year	.638*	.642	.323	−.038	−.015	.000	.497	.000	(597)
V–VI	1 year	.636*	.701	.340	.129	.055	.003	.555	.005	(341)
III–V	1 year/3 months	.711*	.700	.388	−.048	−.023	.000	.548	.000	(583)
II–V	1 year/7 months	.700*	.623	.330	−.056	−.028	.001	.496	.002	(485)
I–V	2 years	.569*	.530	.244	.018	.008	.000	.399	.000	(447)
IV–VI	2 years	.621*	.664	.349	.013	.006	.000	.569	.000	(295)
III–VI	2 years/3 months	.603*	.622	.296	.156	.077	.005	.522	.007	(280)
II–VI	2 years/7 months	.677*	.613	.317	.093	.048	.002	.526	.004	(244)
I–VI	3 years	.544*	.503	.221	−.041	−.018	.000	.420	.000	(225)

*Significant at .05 level.

TABLE 8.21

Basic Model Regression Coefficients Showing the Impact of Violent Television Exposure on Later Aggression for All Wave Pairs among Boys and Girls Combined with Controls for Intervening Television Exposure (Valid Reporters)

WAVE PAIR	DURATION	EARLIER AGGRESSION COEFFICIENTS		UNIQUE CONTRIBUTION OF EARLIER AGGRESSION TO TOTAL R^2	EARLIER VIOLENT TELEVISION EXPOSURE COEFFICIENTS		UNIQUE CONTRIBUTION OF EARLIER VIOLENT TELEVISION EXPOSURE TO TOTAL R^2	TOTAL R^2	VARIANCE OF CHANGE IN AGGRESSION EXPLAINED BY EARLIER TELEVISION	N
		b (1a)	β (1b)	(2)	b (3a)	β (3b)	(4)	(5)	(6)	(7)
III–IV	3 months	.912*	.844	.610	.130*	.056	.003	.748	.008	(988)
II–III	4 months	.825*	.814	.579	.037	.018	.000	.731	.002	(839)
I–II	5 months	.684*	.672	.402	−.040	−.017	.000	.517	.000	(755)
II–IV	7 months	.822*	.743	.481	.133	.060	.002	.631	.012	(718)
I–III	9 months	.648*	.635	.357	−.125	−.054	.002	.498	.006	(603)
I–IV	1 year	.660*	.619	.337	−.081	−.033	.001	.460	.000	(530)
IV–V	1 year	.638*	.642	.340	−.038	−.015	.000	.497	.000	(597)
V–VI	1 year	.636*	.701	.381	.129	.055	.003	.555	.009	(341)
III–V	1 year/3 months	.713*	.702	.393	.006	.003	.000	.549	.000	(508)
II–V	1 year/7 months	.705*	.628	.333	.082	.040	.001	.500	.003	(385)
I–V	2 years	.566*	.527	.238	−.005	−.002	.000	.401	.000	(329)
IV–VI	2 years	.621*	.664	.344	.016	.007	.000	.569	.000	(242)
III–VI	2 years/3 months	.611*	.630	.301	.247	.122	.008	.529	.020	(204)
II–VI	2 years/7 months	.671*	.608	.309	−.039	−.020	.000	.538	.000	(176)
I–VI	3 years	.531*	.492	.192	−.086	−.037	.001	.427	.002	(145)

*Significant at .05 level.

TABLE 8.22

Basic Model Regression Coefficients Showing the Impact of Violent Television Exposure on Later Aggression for All Wave Pairs among Boys and Girls Combined (Total Sample)

WAVE PAIR	DURATION	EARLIER AGGRESSION COEFFICIENTS		UNIQUE CONTRIBUTION OF EARLIER AGGRESSION TO TOTAL R^2	EARLIER VIOLENT TELEVISION EXPOSURE COEFFICIENTS		UNIQUE CONTRIBUTION OF EARLIER VIOLENT TELEVISION EXPOSURE TO TOTAL R^2	TOTAL R^2	VARIANCE OF CHANGE IN AGGRESSION EXPLAINED BY EARLIER TELEVISION	N
		b (1a)	β (1b)	(2)	b (3a)	β (3b)	(4)	(5)	(6)	(7)
III–IV	3 months	.885*	.822	.572	.096*	.050	.002	.720	.009	(1203)
II–III	4 months	.818*	.813	.571	.058*	.034	.000	.730	.005	(1113)
I–II	5 months	.635*	.656	.368	−.016	−.008	.000	.501	.000	(982)
II–IV	7 months	.779*	.726	.456	.103*	.057	.003	.607	.008	(1076)
I–III	9 months	.618*	.635	.345	−.009	−.005	.000	.488	.000	(953)
I–IV	1 year	.653*	.633	.342	.046	.023	.000	.473	.000	(925)
IV–V	1 year	.643*	.669	.359	−.007	−.003	.000	.527	.000	(706)
V–VI	1 year	.626*	.690	.379	.091	.050	.002	.552	.003	(447)
III–V	1 year/3 months	.719*	.697	.379	−.034	−.019	.000	.552	.000	(712)
II–V	1 year/7 months	.712*	.650	.354	.000	.000	.000	.529	.000	(643)
I–V	2 years	.574*	.547	.250	.115	.059	.003	.446	.005	(582)
IV–VI	2 years	.576*	.654	.337	.003	.002	.000	.538	.000	(369)
III–VI	2 years/3 months	.579*	.598	.270	.072	.043	.001	.480	.002	(374)
II–VI	2 years/7 months	.593*	.575	.277	.075	.047	.001	.492	.002	(355)
I–VI	3 years	.449*	.471	.183	−.014	−.008	.000	.404	.000	(322)

*Significant at .05 level.

TABLE 8.23

Basic Model Regression Coefficients Showing the Impact of Violent Television Exposure on Later Aggression for All Wave Pairs among Boys and Girls Combined with Controls for Intervening Television Exposure (Total Sample)

WAVE PAIR	DURATION	EARLIER AGGRESSION COEFFICIENTS		UNIQUE CONTRIBUTION OF EARLIER AGGRESSION TO TOTAL R^2	EARLIER VIOLENT TELEVISION EXPOSURE COEFFICIENTS		UNIQUE CONTRIBUTION OF EARLIER VIOLENT TELEVISION EXPOSURE TO TOTAL R^2	TOTAL R^2	VARIANCE OF CHANGE IN AGGRESSION EXPLAINED BY EARLIER TELEVISION	N
		b (1a)	β (1b)	(2)	b (3a)	β (3b)	(4)	(5)	(6)	(7)
III–IV	3 months	.885*	.822	.572	.096*	.050	.002	.720	.002	(1203)
II–III	4 months	.818*	.813	.571	.058*	.034	.001	.730	.001	(1113)
I–II	5 months	.635*	.656	.368	−.016	−.008	.000	.501	.000	(982)
II–IV	7 months	.776*	.723	.450	.020	.011	.000	.608	.000	(1011)
I–III	9 months	.614*	.630	.334	−.056	−.029	.000	.489	.000	(889)
I–IV	1 year	.647*	.627	.327	−.020	−.010	.000	.475	.000	(810)
IV–V	1 year	.643*	.669	.360	−.007	−.003	.000	.527	.000	(706)
V–VI	1 year	.626*	.690	.379	.091	.050	.002	.552	.003	(447)
III–V	1 year/3 months	.722*	.701	.375	.013	.007	.000	.553	.000	(668)
II–V	1 year/7 months	.713*	.652	.353	.028	.016	.000	.529	.001	(573)
I–V	2 years	.576*	.550	.245	.135	.070	.002	.447	.003	(510)
IV–VI	2 years	.576*	.655	.338	.035	.019	.000	.539	.000	(355)
III–VI	2 years/3 months	.586*	.605	.268	.138	.083	.003	.482	.005	(338)
II–VI	2 years/7 months	.590*	.572	.273	−.041	−.026	.000	.499	.001	(314)
I–VI	3 years	.442*	.463	.170	−.067	−.037	.001	.409	.002	(281)

*Significant at .05 level.

Thus, there is no evidence that the influence of either TV_{t-1} or A_{t-1} on A_t differs by the sex of the respondent.

This analysis also showed that b_3 in the equation was consistently significantly positive, indicating that boys are typically more aggressive than girls. Therefore, it is necessary to include the respondent's sex as a predictor variable in the pooled basic model equation. We also included socioeconomic status as a predictor in the pooled analysis because, as shown for both boys and girls, it appears to be a causal antecedent of television exposure and aggression that is not fully controlled in the basic model and inflates TV effect coefficients.[23]

Table 8.20 presents basic model results and the aggression and television predictors for valid reporters without controls for intervening *TV* variables, Table 8.21 with controls. (The coefficients for the sex and the SES variables are not reported in these tables. The R^2 coefficients include the contributions of these two variables along with those of earlier *TV* and aggression.)

In the tables, television's impact on aggression is given by the metric *b* and standardized β coefficients in Columns (3a) and (3b). The coefficients in Table 8.20 are very similar to those found earlier for boys (in Table 6.1) and girls (in Table 8.14) in the separate analyses. Most are positive, 6 out of 15 are negative; they are all small (β coefficients ranging from .077 to −.028). The two significant positive coefficients are in overlapping lags (II–IV and III–IV).

The model that controls for intervening *TV* variables, in Table 8.21, shows that only one significant coefficient remains when we control in this way for the overlap among waves. A single significant coefficient in 15 replications could easily have occurred on the basis of chance alone (as discussed in Chapter 6). Taking the set of 15 estimates as a whole, then, there is no evidence for a significant influence of television violence on the aggression of these boys and girls.

Much the same conclusion can be drawn from an analysis of the same models estimated with the total sample rather than restricted to valid reporters of their television viewing, shown in Tables 8.22 and 8.23. Without controls for intervening TV there are 10 positive and 5 negative television coefficients.

Three of the positive coefficients are significant, all of them in overlapping wave pairs (II–III, II–IV, and III–IV). When we control for the overlap among lags, the coefficient in the II–IV wave pair becomes insignificant. Those in the adjacent lags II–III and III–IV remain significant, but they are small in substantive terms (β coefficients of .034 and .050). In short, these analyses confirm our previous findings from the basic models.

[23]"Socioeconomic composition of school" is the measure used for this analysis, since it is available for all children.

APPENDIX A: SUPPLEMENTARY TABLES FOR SECTIONS ON DESIGN, AGGRESSION, AND TELEVISION EXPOSURE

TABLE A.1

Number of Girls in Initial Sample in Each City by Grade and Racial Composition of School[a]

	FORT WORTH				MINNEAPOLIS		
	RACIAL COMPOSITION OF SCHOOL				RACIAL COMPOSITION OF SCHOOL		
GRADE	WHITE	PREDOMINANTLY BLACK	BLACK	TOTAL NUMBER OF GIRLS	WHITE	PREDOMINANTLY BLACK	TOTAL NUMBER OF GIRLS
2	71			71	93		93
3	34		26	60	39	56	95
4	74			74	76		76
5	43		19	62	32	46	78
6	37	41		78	56		54
Total	259 (75%)	41 (12%)	45 (13%)	345 (100%)	296 (74%)	102 (26%)	396 (100%)

[a]Individual race data are not available for girls. As a substitute, data on the racial composition of the school were used.

Boys: See Table 2.3B.

TABLE A.2

Number of Girls from Initial Wave I Sample and Number of New Respondents in Each of Six Waves[a]

WAVE	TOTAL SAMPLE OF GIRLS IN WAVE		TOTAL NUMBER OF GIRLS IN WAVE WHO WERE IN WAVE I SAMPLE		TOTAL NUMBER OF GIRLS IN WAVE WHO ENTERED THE SAMPLE AFTER WAVE I	
	N	%	*N*	%	*N*	%
I	741					
II	703	100	538	77	165	24
III	723	100	537	74	186	26
IV	682	100	503	74	179	25
V	523	100	315	60	208	40
VI	285	100	163	57	122	43

[a]For example, in Wave IV, the total sample size is 682. Of these girls, 503 had been part of the Wave I sample; 179 had not been part of the Wave I sample but entered the study in Wave II, III, or IV.

Boys: Table 2.5.

TABLE A.3

Loss of Respondents Due to Graduation of Sixth Graders[a] *(Initial Sample in Wave I, N = 741)*

LOSS BETWEEN WAVES	*N*
I and II	132
II and III[b]	0
III and IV[b]	0
IV and V	140
V and VI	150
Total	422

[a]Figures indicate loss according to study design and include those who left the sample before graduation.

[b]Both waves conducted during the same school year.

Boys: Table 2.8.

TABLE A.4

Loss of Respondents Due to Mobility (Initial Sample in Wave I, N = 741)

WAVES	NUMBER OF RESPONDENTS LOST BETWEEN WAVES
I and II	66
II and III[a]	4
III and IV[a]	34
IV and V	71
V and VI	47
Total	222

[a]Both waves conducted during the same school year.

Boys: Table 2.9.

TABLE A.5

Loss of Television Exposure Data Due to Temporary Absenteeism[a]

WAVE	TELEVISION AND AGGRESSION DATA AVAILABLE (*N*)	NO TELEVISION DATA AVAILABLE BECAUSE OF TEMPORARY ABSENTEEISM (*N*)
I	698	43
II	571	46
III	612	50
IV	598	45
V	487	19
VI	259	7

[a]A small number of refusals is included.

Boys: Table 2.10.

TABLE A.6
Characteristics of Respondents Who Were in the Initial Sample and New Respondents

CHILD CHARACTERISTICS	INITIAL SAMPLE IN WAVE I (%) (1)	NEW RESPONDENTS WITH AGGRESSION DATA FOR FIRST TIME IN WAVE (%)				
		II (2)	III (3)	IV (4)	V (5)	VI (6)
City of residence						
Fort Worth	47	46	33	22	20	39
Minneapolis	53	54	67	78	80	62
Racial composition of school						
White	75	76	72	67	80	85
Predominantly black	19	20	22	33	19	15
Black	6	4	6	0	1	0
N	(741)	(103)	(18)	(9)	(124)	(52)

Boys: Table 2.11.

TABLE A.7
Factor Loadings of Aggression Items

ITEM	WAVE I	II	III	IV	V	VI
Says mean things	.84	.87	.86	.87	.86	.81
Said mean things yesterday	.81	.82	.77			
Makes up stories or lies	.84	.87	.84	.92	.89	.77
Made up stories or lies yesterday	.79	.82	.76			
Pushes and shoves	.90	.86	.88	.93	.93	.94
Pushed and shoved yesterday	.85	.85	.79			
Hits or punches	.84	.81	.86	.90	.87	.89
Hit or punched yesterday	.80	.79	.79			
Takes things			.82	.87	.86	.83
Breaks things			.84	.89	.91	.84
N	(741)	(601)	(635)	(643)	(506)	(266)

Boys: Table 3.3

APPENDIX B: TESTS FOR CURVILINEARITY

The procedure to examine whether nonlinearities exist is to fit higher-order polynomials to the data and determine whether any of these explain significantly more variation in aggression than the basic causal model. Table B.1 presents the R^2 values associated with models that successively add TV^2 and TV^3 to the basic linear model.

Significance testing of the R^2 increments shows that in wave pairs III–IV, IV–V, and I–VI the cubic equations provide a better fit than the linear model, and we therefore explored the possibility of fitting a general cubic model to the data.

The cubic equations in these three wave pairs are as follows:

Wave Pair I–VI:

$$A_6 = 48.481 + .506A_1 - 2.427TV_1 + .04035TV_1^2 - .000192TV_1^3$$

Wave Pair III–IV:

$$A_4 = 4.038 + .892A_3 + .976TV_3 - .01987TV_3^2 - .000197TV_3^3$$

TABLE B.1

R^2 Progressions for Polynomial Regressions: Initial Aggression and Polynomials of Violent Television Exposure to Predict Subsequent Aggression (Valid Reporters)

		EXPONENTS			
WAVE PAIR	DURATION	TV	TV^2	TV^3	N
III–IV	3 months	.654	.656	.664*	(491)
II–III	4 months	.607	.608	.608	(426)
I–II	5 months	.441	.443	.444	(391)
II–IV	7 months	.486	.487	.488	(408)
I–III	9 months	.400	.401	.402	(384)
I–IV	1 year	.413	.414	.418	(369)
IV–V	1 year	.270	.271	.287*	(296)
V–VI	1 year	.365	.381*	.381	(153)
III–V	1 year/3 months	.369	.374	.377	(292)
II–V	1 year/7 months	.363	.363	.364	(245)
I–V	2 years	.259	.259	.260	(236)
IV–VI	2 years	.458	.461	.467	(134)
III–VI	2 years/3 months	.425	.428	.441	(133)
II–VI	2 years/7 months	.433	.443	.454	(123)
I–VI	3 years	.346	.366	.375*	(113)

*Multiple R^2 is significantly greater than the R^2 for the basic causal model at the .05 level.

Boys: See Chapter 6, Table A.1.

Wave Pair IV–V:

$$A_5 = 30.627 + .500A_4 - 1.37TV_4 + .03788TV_4^2 - .000254TV_4^3$$

Graphs of these three equations are shown in Figure B.1. From these, it can be seen that the models for wave pairs I–VI and IV–V are similar in that aggression levels first decrease, then increase, and then decrease again as television exposure values increase, but the change in direction occurs at different levels of television exposure. The graph for wave pair III–IV shows the opposite, or mirror-image, trend: As television exposure increases, aggression first increases, then decreases, and then increases again.

The differences among the three cubic models can also be seen by using the three equations to compute predicted values of aggression at selected deciles of earlier television exposure. These predicted aggression values are shown in Table B.2, with mean aggression in the ealier wave used to compute predicted aggression in the later wave.

From this analysis of the three cubic models, we conclude that the equations are different in the three wave pairs and that there is no indication of a *consistent* cubic relationship between television exposure and aggression. Thus, although the cubic equations provide a better fit to the data in three specific lags, the process cannot be represented adequately by a general cubic model.

APPENDIX C: MODELS OF MEASUREMENT ERROR

In Appendix C of Chapter 6, the method for estimating parameters and fitting models to account for measurement error is discussed. Exactly the same method, conceptually and practically, is used for the girls' data.

Models of Change in Television Exposure

The basic measurement model of television exposure, shown in Chapter 6, Figure C.2, was estimated for girls' violent television exposure scores. However, unlike the boys' data, we found that this model provided a very poor fit, with a χ^2 of 42.3 and only 6 *df*.

Examining the discrepancies between the estimated and observed values in this model, we found that the basic error in the model's assumptions was that they did not include direct causal relationships between TV_1 and later measures (TV_5 and TV_6) and between TV_2 and later measures (TV_6). As we saw earlier in our discussion of the girls' data, the stability of television exposure is a good deal higher among girls than boys in our sample. Failure to fit a simplex model to the girls' *TV* data probably reflects the fact that this greater stability comes about through a long-term pattern of consistent exposure.

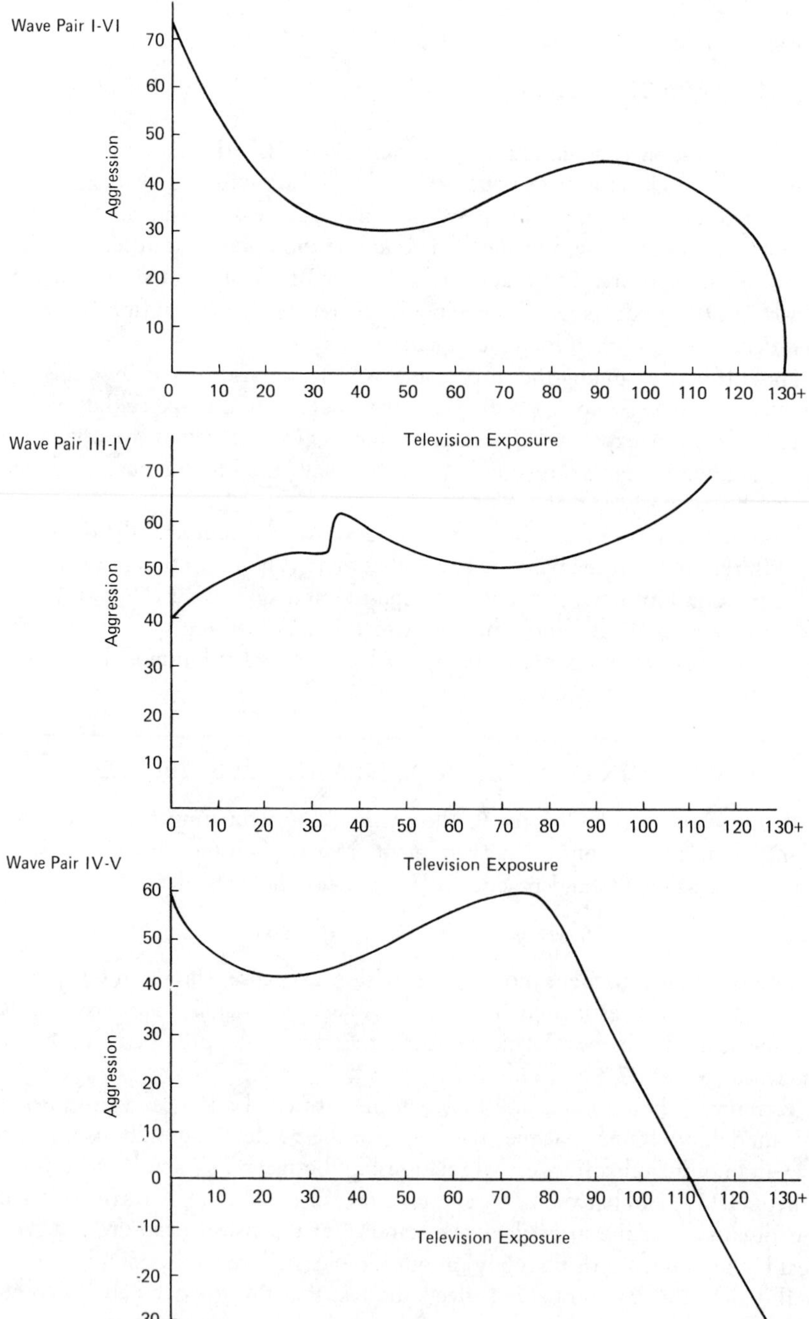

FIGURE B.1. *Graphs of the cubic regression equations using mean aggression values in earlier waves.*

TABLE B.2

Predicted Levels of Aggression at Selected Deciles of Violent Television Exposure and Mean Aggression Values in the Earlier Wave (Based on Cubic Regression Models, Valid Reporters)

DECILES OF TELEVISION EXPOSURE	EARLIER TELEVISION VALUE	PREDICTED AGGRESSION LEVEL
	Wave pair I–VI	
10	4	66.072
20	12	51.502
30	19	42.284
50	37	30.867
70	66	35.559
90	123	29.981
	Wave pair III–IV	
10	4	43.260
20	11	47.269
30	17	50.216
50	33	53.649
70	59	51.778
90	111	66.001
	Wave pair IV–V	
10	4	52.437
20	11	46.503
30	18	43.461
50	38	46.050
70	66	59.003
90	128	−29.245

No comparable table for boys.

In order to develop accurate estimates of *TV* reliability, then, we were forced to estimate submodels. As inspection of the errors in our six-wave model showed that Waves I and II behaved as a simplex with respect to Waves III and IV, but not with respect to Waves V and VI, we estimated a four-wave model for Waves I–IV, and another for Waves III–VI.

As shown in Table C.1, the Wave I–IV model provides a good fit ($\chi^2/df = 1.2$), estimating the Wave II correlation between true and observed scores for valid reporters at .864 (reliability = .746) and the Wave III correlation at .900 (reliability = .810). Similarly, the Wave III–VI model is a good fit ($\chi^2/df = 1.2$) and estimates the Wave IV correlation for valid reporters

TABLE C.1
Correlations between True and Observed Violent Exposure Scores

	r_2	r_3	r_4	r_5	χ^2	*df*	N
			Valid reporters				
Waves I–IV	.864	.900			1.2	1	(437)
Waves III–VI			.848	.772	1.2	1	(302)
			Total sample				
Waves I–IV	.913	.920			1.1	1	(551)
Waves III–VI			.899	.858	1.2	1	(376)

Boys: See Chapter 6, Table C.1.

at .848 (reliability = .719) and the Wave V correlation at .772 (reliability = .596). These values are comparable in size to those estimated for boys. Details of the parameters in these models are presented in Table C.2.

Wave I reliabilities, which cannot be estimated directly, were taken to be the same as for Wave II for one set of analyses, and the value of .460 was set as a lower bound for another set.

Two-Wave Measurement Models of Television Effects

To approach the problem of measurement error in the basic model of television effects on girls' aggression, models in which the error terms of all indicators are autocorrelated were fit to the 15 wave pairs. The diagram of this model was shown in Chapter 6, Figure C.1. Reliability of the exposure score was set at the values estimated earlier. For the Wave I reliability, upper and lower bounds were used.

This model was used as a starting point because it provided a good fit to the boys' data. If a multivariate measurement model exists for boys, one might assume that it will also hold true for girls.

Unfortunately, this model failed to provide as good a fit as it had for the boys. The χ^2/df ratio averaged 3.7 over the 15 wave pairs, compared with 2.6 for boys.[24] In addition, inspection of the residual matrices (observed–predicted covariances) showed substantially more misspecification for girls than for boys. However, further inspection of these results showed that the failures were limited for the most part to the shortest wave pairs—those under one year in

[24]For the comparison, we have used the boys' model with only the error of the lie indicator correlated, which in fact provided a somewhat better fit to the data than the model that assumed all errors to be correlated (cf. Chapter 6, Appendix C).

TABLE C.2

Parameter Estimates for LISREL Measurement Models of Violent and Total Television Exposure for Valid Reporters and Total Sample

	VIOLENT EXPOSURE							
	VALID REPORTERS				TOTAL SAMPLE			
	WAVES I–IV		WAVES III–VI		WAVES I–IV		WAVES III–VI	
	M	S	M	S	M	S	M	S
Epistemic correlations								
tv_1	1.0^f	*			1.0^f	*		
tv_2	1.0^f	.863			1.0^f	.913		
tv_3	1.0^f	.900	1.0^f	*	1.0^f	.920	1.0^f	*
tv_4	1.0^f	*	1.0^f	1.000	1.0^f	*	1.0^f	.899
tv_5			1.0^f	.772			1.0^f	.858
tv_6			1.0^f	*			1.0^f	*
Variances								
Var (TV_1)	361.057	1.0			743.478	1.0		
Var (TV_2)	657.023	1.0			1144.938	1.0		
Var (TV_3)	723.017	1.0	594.078	1.0	1104.013	1.0	1005.160	1.0
Var (TV_4)	551.923	1.0	652.644	1.0	936.896	1.0	797.311	1.0
Var (TV_5)			353.530	1.0			723.366	1.0
Var (TV_6)			401.553	1.0			929.169	1.0
Var (u_2)	113.665	.173			277.075	.242		
Var (u_3)	128.697	.178			164.498	.149		
Var (u_4)	165.025	.299	0^f	0	243.593	.260	35.879	.045
Var (u_5)			125.503	.355			162.034	.224
Var (u_6)			103.199	.257			241.584	.260
Covariances								
Cov(tv_1, TV_2)	442.872	.672			803.380	.735		
Cov(TV_3, tv_4)	528.937	.770			875.232	.839		
Cov(tv_3, TV_4)			622.186	.815			874.232	.857
Cov(TV_5, tv_6)			324.779	.771			705.370	.838
Stability coefficients								
$b_{TV_1TV_2}$	*	*			*	*		
$b_{TV_2TV_3}$	.950	.907			.906	.922		
$b_{TV_3TV_4}$	*	*	*	*	*	*	*	*
$b_{TV_4TV_5}$			.696	.803			.840	.881
$b_{TV_5TV_6}$			*	*			*	*
χ^2	1.2203		.0546		1.1349		1.1709	
χ^2/df	1.2203		.0546		1.1349		1.1709	
N	(437)		(302)		(551)		(376)	

M = metric coefficients.
S = standard coefficients
f = fixed.

*None of these values are individually identified although the terms Cov(tv_1,TV_2) and Cov(TV_3,tv_4) in the Wave I–IV models and the terms Cov(tv_3,TV_4) and Cov(TV_5,tv_6) in the Wave III–VI models are identified. All other parameters internal to these in the models are individually identified. We estimated these by arbitrarily assigning fixed values to the measurement errors at times 1 and 4 in the Wave I–IV models and at times 3 and 6 in the Wave III–VI models.

Boys: Table C.7.

duration. The comparable χ^2/df ratios for boys and girls across the short, medium, and long wave pairs were as follows:

Average χ^2/df Ratios

SHORT WAVE PAIRS		MEDIUM WAVE PAIRS		LONG WAVE PAIRS	
GIRLS	BOYS	GIRLS	BOYS	GIRLS	BOYS
5.0	3.0	3.4	2.8	2.8	1.9

The poor fit for girls in the short wave pairs led us to inspect several complex indicators of model misspecification and to estimate a variety of alternative measurement models. Some of these included specifications in which the true television exposure score was assumed to be directly correlated to some of the aggression error terms, others in which errors of one indicator were assumed correlated with errors of another indicator, and even models in which the true aggression score was assumed directly related to one or more of the error terms. None of these changes produced an acceptable model of the observed data for the short wave pairs.

We considered the possibility of estimating unique models for each of the 15 wave pairs, for some of the special models did provide good fits in particular cases. However, we concluded that this would limit our ability to generalize findings from any one wave pair to another, let alone from our data to the processes that generated the specific sample we obtained. Lacking consistency over time, the models and their resulting estimated parameters could safely be said to be true for only one point in time.

Even though the two-wave models incorporating earlier exposure, earlier aggression, and later aggression with errors of the aggression indicators autocorrelated do not provide a good fit in the short wave pairs, the resulting estimates from the model are presented in Tables C.3 through C.6 at the end of this appendix for the sake of completeness and symmetry with the boys' Chapter 6. (Detailed parameter estimates for valid reporters appear in Table C.7.) Comparable results for the total samples, accompanied by the covariance matrices for both valid reporters and total samples, are available in Documentation 6. The estimates in Table C.3 correspond to those in Table 8.14. Examination of Column (3a) in both tables reveals that the LISREL estimates are slightly lower in 11 of the 15 wave pairs. In addition, the LISREL model yields four significant *b* coefficients for television's effect. Three of these coefficients are in the same wave pairs that yielded significant *b* coefficients in the nonmeasurement error model of Table 8.14.

Thus, although the basic causal model presented in the body of this chapter does not take measurement error into account and the measurement error model of Table C.1 is not an adequate representation of the data in the short waves, the two models are fairly similar in results. Because the measurement model is a poor fit, it does not seem reasonable to explore its results further. (For example, even though the coefficients are small, the number of significant coefficients in some analyses could not have occurred by chance. Most of these occur in the short wave pairs, where the measurement model is most inadequate Thus, a substantive interpretation of these findings is impossible.)

TABLE C.3

Regression Coefficients Showing the Impact of Violent Television Exposure on Later Aggression for All Wave Pairs, LISREL Two-Wave Models, Valid Reporters, Girls, All Errors Correlated, Reliability $TV_1 = TV_2$

WAVE PAIR	DURATION	EARLIER AGGRESSION COEFFICIENTS		UNIQUE CONTRIBUTION OF EARLIER AGGRESSION TO TOTAL R^2	EARLIER VIOLENT TELEVISION EXPOSURE COEFFICIENTS		UNIQUE CONTRIBUTION OF EARLIER VIOLENT TELEVISION EXPOSURE TO TOTAL R^2	TOTAL R^2	VARIANCE OF CHANGE IN AGGRESSION EXPLAINED BY EARLIER TELEVISION	χ^2/df	N
		b (1a)	β (1b)	(2)	b (3a)	β (3b)	(4)	(5)	(6)	(7)	(8)
III–IV	3 months	.954*	.825	.615	.052*	.068	.004	.720	.014	6.0	(491)
II–III	4 months	.791*	.801	.584	.058*	.087	.007	.692	.021	6.1	(426)
I–II	5 months	.675*	.736	.450	−.052	−.074	.005	.503	.000	3.1	(391)
II–IV	7 months	.785*	.676	.414	.102*	.132	.016	.529	.032	4.9	(408)
I–III	9 months	.599*	.688	.393	−.013	−.019	.000	.463	.001	5.0	(384)
I–IV	1 year	.660*	.683	.388	.005	.007	.000	.471	.000	2.7	(369)
IV–V	1 year	.507*	.513	.241	.059	.074	.005	.291	.007	3.7	(296)
V–VI	1 year	.562*	.650	.412	.085	.109	.012	.456	.021	3.6	(153)
III–V	1 year/3 months	.738*	.657	.382	−.032	−.043	.002	.414	.000	3.7	(292)
II–V	1 year/7 months	.714*	.638	.354	−.004	−.006	.000	.404	.000	3.2	(245)
I–V	2 years	.461*	.508	.211	.043	.063	.003	.289	.005	3.4	(236)
IV–VI	2 years	.600*	.723	.493	−.014	−.022	.000	.515	.000	3.2	(134)
III–VI	2 years/3 months	.669*	.610	.323	.098	.141	.017	.454	.032	2.2	(133)
II–VI	2 years/7 months	.634*	.601	.337	.141*	.213	.042	.474	.071	2.2	(123)
I–VI	3 years	.595*	.648	.358	−.013	−.020	.000	.410	.000	2.9	(113)

*Significant at .05 level.

Boys: See Chapter 6, Table C.2.

TABLE C.4

Basic Model Regression Coefficients Showing the Impact of Violent Television Exposure on Later Aggression for All Wave Pairs LISREL Two-Wave Models, Valid Reporters, Girls, Errors of All Indicators Correlated, Reliability $TV_1 < TV_2$

WAVE PAIR	DURATION	EARLIER AGGRESSION COEFFICIENTS b (1a)	β (1b)	UNIQUE CONTRIBUTION OF EARLIER AGGRESSION TO TOTAL R^2 (2)	EARLIER VIOLENT TELEVISION EXPOSURE COEFFICIENT b (3a)	β (3b)	UNIQUE CONTRIBUTION OF EARLIER VIOLENT TELEVISION EXPOSURE TO TOTAL R^2 (4)	TOTAL R^2 (5)	VARIANCE OF CHANGE IN AGGRESSION EXPLAINED BY EARLIER TELEVISION (6)	χ^2/df (7)	N (8)
III–IV	3 months										
II–III	4 months										
I–II	5 months	.699*	.762	.420	−.096	−.107	.008	.506	.027	3.1	(391)
II–IV	7 months										
I–III	9 months	.605*	.694	.348	−.023	−.028	.001	.463	.002	5.0	(384)
I–IV	1 year	.658*	.681	.336	.010	.010	.000	.471	.009	2.7	(369)
IV–V	1 year										
V–VI	1 year										
III–V	1 year/3 months										
II–	1 year/7 months										
I–V	2 years	.440*	.484	.165	.081	.093	.006	.292	.001	3.4	(236)
IV–VI	2 years										
III–VI	2 years/3 months										
II–VI	2 years/7 months										
I–VI	3 years	.601*	.654	.325	−.024	−.028	.001	.410	.001	2.9	(113)

*Significant at .05 level.

Boys: See Chapter 6, Table C.3.

TABLE C.5

Regression Coefficients Showing the Impact of Violent Television Exposure on Later Aggression for All Wave Pairs, LISREL Two-Wave Models, Total Sample, Girls, All Errors Correlated, Reliability $TV_1 = TV_2$

WAVE PAIR	DURATION	EARLIER AGGRESSION COEFFICIENTS b (1a)	EARLIER AGGRESSION COEFFICIENTS β (1b)	UNIQUE CONTRIBUTION OF EARLIER AGGRESSION TO TOTAL R^2 (2)	EARLIER VIOLENT TELEVISION EXPOSURE COEFFICIENTS b (3a)	EARLIER VIOLENT TELEVISION EXPOSURE COEFFICIENTS β (3b)	UNIQUE CONTRIBUTION OF EARLIER VIOLENT TELEVISION EXPOSURE TO TOTAL R^2 (4)	TOTAL R^2 (5)	VARIANCE OF CHANGE IN AGGRESSION EXPLAINED BY EARLIER TELEVISION (6)	χ^2/df (7)	N (8)
III–IV	3 months	.912*	.818	.573	.040*	.069	.004	.717	.014	6.523	(583)
II–III	4 months	.828*	.811	.584	.051*	.098	.009	.721	.028	7.936	(542)
I–II	5 months	.653*	.735	.454	−.027	−.053	.002	.511	.006	2.975	(477)
II–IV	7 months	.774*	.685	.416	.072*	.126	.014	.544	.030	5.669	(517)
I–III	9 months	.611*	.671	.381	.016	.030	.001	.467	.002	5.468	(467)
I–IV	1 year	.688*	.676	.386	.016	.028	.001	.473	.001	3.287	(447)
IV–V	1 year	.489*	.536	.248	.034	.062	.003	.316	.005	4.159	(348)
V–VI	1 year	.619*	.640	.365	.082*	.142	.018	.490	.034	4.542	(203)
III–V	1 year/3 months	.699*	.673	.358	−.022	−.041	.001	.430	.003	3.461	(352)
II–V	1 year/7 months	.692*	.614	.317	.045	.082	.006	.424	.011	4.516	(317)
I–V	2 years	.509*	.531	.244	.045	.083	.006	.321	.010	3.942	(288)
IV–VI	2 years	.523*	.664	.375	.014	.032	.001	.459	.002	3.310	(166)
III–VI	2 years/3 months	.480*	.487	.182	.052	.105	.008	.297	.014	3.358	(170)
II–VI	2 years/7 months	.525*	.506	.237	.115*	.224	.046	.369	.067	3.360	(165)
I–VI	3 years	.558*	.621	.349	.002	.003	.000	.387	.000	3.915	(145)

*Significant at .05 level.

Boys: See Chapter 6, Table C.4.

TABLE C.6

Basic Model Regression Coefficients Showing the Impact of Violent Television Exposure on Later Aggression for All Wave Pairs, LISREL Two-Wave Models, Total Sample, Girls, Errors of All Indicators Correlated, Reliability $TV_1 < TV_2$

WAVE PAIR	DURATION	EARLIER AGGRESSION COEFFICIENTS b (1a)	β (1b)	UNIQUE CONTRIBUTION OF EARLIER AGGRESSION TO TOTAL R^2 (2)	EARLIER VIOLENT TELEVISION EXPOSURE COEFFICIENTS b (3a)	β (3b)	UNIQUE CONTRIBUTION OF EARLIER VIOLENT TELEVISION *EXPOSURE* TO TOTAL R^2 (4)	TOTAL R^2 (5)	VARIANCE OF CHANGE IN AGGRESSION EXPLAINED BY EARLIER TELEVISION (6)	χ^2/df (7)	N (8)
III–IV	3 months										
II–III	4 months										
I–II	5 months	.666*	.749	.426	−.045	−.073	.004	.513	.012	2.975	(477)
II–IV	7 months										
I–III	9 months	.604*	.663	.337	.026	.040	.001	.468	.003	5.468	(467)
I–IV	1 year	.680*	.669	.343	.027	.038	.001	.474	.003	3.287	(447)
IV–V	1 year										
V–VI	1 year										
III–V	1 year/3 months										
II–V	1 year/7 months										
I–V	2 years	.490*	.511	.208	.073	.111	.010	.325	.017	3.942	(288)
IV–VI	2 years										
III–VI	2 years/3 months										
II–VI	2 years/7 months										
I–VI	3 years	.558*	.621	.330	.003	.004	.000	.387	.000	3.915	(145)

*Significant at .05 level.

Boys: See Chapter 6, Table C.5.

TABLE C.7

Parameter Estimates for the LISREL Two-Wave Measurement Models over 15 Wave Pairs, Valid Reporters (df = 26) Errors of All Aggression Indicators Correlated, Reliability|$TV_1 = TV_2$

WAVE PAIR:	I–II		I–III		I–IV		I–V	
	M	S	M	S	M	S	M	S
				Epistemic correlations				
$mean_{1i}$	.685	.863	.723	.879	.709	.876	.734	.884
lie_{2i}	.708	.849	.680	.837	.691	.842	.633	.809
$hits_i$	.578	.867	.594	.876	.591	.876	.618	.871
$push_{4i}$	.720	.911	.713	.903	.743	.919	.713	.894
$mean_{1j}$	.685	.894	.723	.841	.709	.867	.734	.901
lie_{2j}	.708	.900	.680	.837	.691	.884	.633	.829
hit_{3j}	.578	.864	.594	.855	.591	.885	.618	.835
$push_{4j}$	.720	.880	.713	.910	.743	.941	.713	.915
tv_i	1.000^f	.864	1.000^f	.864	1.000^f	.864	1.000^f	.864
				Variances				
Var (A_i)	300.000^f	1.0	300.000^f	1.0	300.000^f	1.0	300.000^f	1.0
Var (A_j)	252.561	1.0	228.056	1.0	279.633	1.0	247.259	1.0
Var (TV_i)	513.054	1.0	509.621	1.0	514.664	1.0	530.486	1.0
Var (u_j)	125.523	.497	122.466	.537	147.926	.529	175.801	.711
				Correlated errors				
Covar $(A_i TV_i)$	161.336	.411	161.576	.413	161.545	.411	169.751	.426
Covar $(e_{1i} e_{1j})$	.022	.028	.037	.036	−.011	−.011	−.035	−.042
Covar $(e_{2i} e_{2j})$	.044	.062	.070	.081	.075	.094	.127	.150
Covar $(e_{3i} e_{3u})$	.238	.255	.157	.163	.234	.254	.204	.193
Covar $(e_{4i} e_{4j})$	.205	.186	−.114	−.136	−.062	−.077	.019	.023
				Regression coefficients				
$b_{A_i A_j}$	.675	.736	.599	.688	.660	.683	.461	.508
$b_{TV_i A_j}$	−.052	−.074	−.013*	−.019	.005*	.007	.043*	.063
χ^2	79.825		129.308		70.194		89.496	
χ^2/df	3.1		5.0		2.7		3.4	
N	(391)		(384)		(369)		(236)	

TABLE C.7 (*continued*)

WAVE PAIR:	I–VI		II–III		II–IV		II–V	
	M	S	M	S	M	S	M	S
				Epistemic correlations				
$mean_{1i}$	.748	.880	.630	.907	.613	.904	.597	.897
lie_{2i}	.637	.833	.589	.900	.593	.909	.559	.898
$hits_{i}$	.700	.881	.521	.859	.524	.856	.520	.863
$push_{4i}$	.772	.904	.596	.856	.615	.865	.582	.858
$mean_{1j}$	.748	.821	.630	.859	.613	.880	.597	.900
lie_{2j}	.637	.837	.589	.846	.593	.893	.559	.878
hit_{3j}	.700	.982	.521	.858	.524	.906	.520	.869
$push_{4j}$	.772	.967	.596	.909	.615	.947	.582	.914
tv_i	1.000^f	.864	1.000^f	.864	1.000^f	.864	1.000^f	.864
				Variances				
Var (A_i)	300.000^f	1.0	300.000^f	1.0	300.000^f	1.0	300.000^f	1.0
Var (A_j)	253.037	1.0	292.643	1.0	405.378	1.0	376.522	1.0
Var (TV_i)	553.118	1.0	670.518	1.0	680.427	1.0	780.971	1.0
Var (u_j)	149.292	.590	90.134	.308	190.933	.471	224.407	.596
				Correlated errors				
Covar $(A_i TV_i)$	156.687	.385	134.222	.299	137.591	.305	175.385	.362
Covar $(e_{e_{1i}e_{1j}})$	.191	.161	−.126	−.099	.184	.141	.149	.135
Covar $(e_{e_{2i}e_{2j}})$	.160	.177	.154	.120	.146	.114	.027	.022
Covar $(e_{e_{3i}e_{3j}})$	.162	.198	.391	.393	.264	.293	.117	.108
Covar $(e_{e_{4i}e_{4j}})$	−.203	−.398	−.015	−.020	.040	.059	.029	.035
				Regression coefficients				
$b_{A_iA_j}$	.595	.648	.791	.801	.785	.676	.714	.638
$b_{TV_iA_j}$	−.013*	−.020	.058	.087	.102	.132	−.004*	−.006
χ^2	76.104		160.038		128.347		82.627	
χ^2/df	2.9		6.1		4.9		3.2	
N	(113)		(426)		(408)		(245)	

(*Continued next page*)

TABLE C.7 (*continued*)

WAVE PAIR:	II–VI		III–IV		III–V		III–VI	
	M	S	M	S	M	S	M	S
				Epistemic correlations				
$mean_{1i}$	.582	.858	.619	.846	.595	.852	.591	.871
lie_{2i}	.569	.877	.584	.823	.523	.817	.469	.740
$hits_i$	.588	.872	.563	.861	.517	.878	.547	.879
$push_{4i}$	.641	.856	.658	.929	.592	.921	.595	.924
$mean_{1j}$	.582	.828	.619	.883	.595	.870	.591	.795
lie_{2j}	.569	.811	.584	.883	.523	.843	.469	.773
$hit3_j$	.588	.906	.563	.785	.517	.872	.547	.906
$push_{4j}$	.641	.977	.658	.817	.592	.924	.595	.982
tv_i	1.000[f]	.864	1.000[f]	.900	1.000[f]	.900	1.000[f]	.900
				Variances				
Var (A_i)	300.000[f]	1.0	300.000[f]	1.0	300.000[f]	1.0	300.000[f]	1.0
Var (A_j)	333.605	1.0	400.936	1.0	378.903	1.0	361.681	1.0
Var (TV_i)	761.156	1.0	670.624	1.0	699.175	1.0	744.001	1.0
Var (u_j)	175.476	.526	112.262	.280	222.037	.586	197.478	.546
				Correlated errors				
Covar ($A_i TV_i$)	124.101	.260	141.621	.311	156.160	.339	171.527	.363
Covar ($e_{1i}e_{1j}$)	.183	.154	.099	.102	.264	.256	−.026	−.018
Covar ($e_{2i}e_{2j}$)	.175	.126	.277	.311	.333	.328	.343	.346
Covar ($e_{3i}e_{3j}$)	.145	.164	.394	.435	.305	.263	.275	.291
Covar ($e_{4i}e_{4j}$)	−.030	−.078	−.021	−.021	−.194	−.176	.033	.067
				Regression coefficients				
$b_{A_iA_j}$	.634	.601	.954	.825	.738	.657	.669	.610
$b_{TV_iA_j}$	.141	.213	.052	.068	−.032*	−.043	.098*	.141
χ^2	57.948		156.889		96.158		58.201	
χ^2/df	2.2		6.0		3.7		2.2	
N	(123)		(491)		(292)		(133)	

TABLE C.7 (*continued*)

WAVE PAIR:	IV–V		IV–VI		V–VI	
	M	S	M	S	M	S
			Epistemic correlations			
$mean_{1i}$	.723	.893	.692	.894	.641	.864
lie_{2i}	.654	.891	.640	.881	.560	.810
$hits_i$	.623	.917	.622	.898	.574	.853
$push_{4i}$	.744	.954	.736	.930	.667	.921
$mean_{1j}$	.723	.887	.692	.771	.641	.769
lie_{2j}	.654	.875	.640	.809	.560	.779
hit_{3j}	.623	.866	.622	.865	.574	.876
$push_{4j}$	.744	.932	.736	.977	.667	.959
tv_i	1.000^f	.848	1.000^f	.848	1.000^f	.772
			Variances			
Var (A_i)	300.000^f	1.0	300.000^f	1.0	300.000^f	1.0
Var (A_j)	292.815	1.0	206.967	1.0	224.425	1.0
Var (TV_i)	462.264	1.0	517.533	1.0	374.523	1.0
Var (u_j)	207.606	.709	100.379	.485	122.087	.544
			Correlated errors			
Covar $(A_i TV_i)$	107.828	.290	94.345	.239	51.786	.154
Covar $(e_{1i} e_{1j})$	.282	.276	.272	.199	.120	.098
Covar $(e_{2i} e_{2j})$	.181	.168	.204	.181	.133	.138
Covar $(e_{3i} e_{3j})$	.314	.239	.241	.245	.183	.235
Covar $(e_{4i} e_{4j})$	−.018	−.015	−.212	−.473	−.067	−.111
			Regression coefficients			
$b_{A_i A_j}$	.507	.513	.600	.723	.562	.650
$b_{TV_i A_j}$	.059*	.074	−.014*	.022	.085*	.109
χ^2	96.235		82.388		94.326	
χ^2/df	3.7		3.2		3.6	
N	(296)		(134)		(153)	

M = metric coefficients
S = standardized coefficients
f = fixed.
*Coefficient is *not* significant at the .05 level.
Boys: See Chapter 6, Table C.8.

APPENDIX D: SUPPLEMENTARY TABLES FOR SECTION ON

TABL

Cross-Sectional Correlations of All Measures with Viole

	WAVE I		WAVE II	
	VIOLENT EXPOSURE	AGGRESSION	VIOLENT EXPOSURE	AGGRESSIO
Total exposure	.93	.34	.94	.26
Relative exposure to violent television	.50	.07	.68	.15
Alternative violent weights				
7,6 Weight	.86	.27	.89	.24
5 Weight	.77	.26	.87	.21
4 Weight	.41	.16	.50	.13
3 Weight 2 Weight	.44	.13	.33	.07
1 Weight	.66	.24	.64	.18
0 Weight	.59	.30	.34	.16
Context of violence				
Realistic crime	.71	.23	.45	.18
Adventure	.86	.26	.84	.20
Westerns	.60	.21	.78	.19
Cartoons	.58	.20	.62	.20
Slapstick	.28	.28	.42	.13
News/Documentary	.27	.05	.33	.06
Sitcoms	.48	.20	.46	.14
Variety	.42	.21	.26	.07
Education	.34	.20	.43	.12
Miscellaneous	.28	.10	.49	.10
Favorite show violence (Self-report)				
Comparison				
Regular measure of violence exposure		.34		.26
N^a	(588)		(446)	

[a]Number of cases is smaller for "Favorite show" measures.
Boys: Chapter 7, Table A.1.

OTHER CONCEPTUALIZATIONS OF TELEVISION EXPOSURE

.1

levision Exposure and Aggression (Valid Reporters)

WAVE III		WAVE IV		WAVE V	
VIOLENT XPOSURE	AGGRESSION	VIOLENT EXPOSURE	AGGRESSION	VIOLENT EXPOSURE	AGGRESSION
.94	.25	.92	.18	.92	.13
.64	.18	.60	.13	.60	.06
.88	.23	.88	.22	.88	.11
.82	.25	.58	.06	.90	.16
.58	.08	.71	.13	.57	.11
.53	.07	.45	.09		
				.44	−.05
.62	.19	.66	.11		
.42	.12	.40	.04	.55	.10
.63	.22	.73	.18	.68	.07
.86	.19	.76	.18	.64	.04
.60	.15	.72	.12	.73	.16
.64	.18	.58	.11	.59	.12
−.05	−.00	.35	−.06	.12	−.02
.31	.06	.29	.01	.24	−.10
.47	−.17	.43	.10	.49	.10
.20	−.02			.28	.03
.35	.09	.29	.05	.25	.07
				.15	.03
	.26		.20		.15
(514)		(520)		(415)	

TABLE D.2

Standardized Partial Regression Coefficients Showing the Net Effect of Exposure to Violent Television and of Relative Amount of Exposure to Violent Television (Valid Reporters)

	β		
WAVE PAIR	EXPOSURE TO VIOLENT TELEVISION	RELATIVE AMOUNT OF EXPOSURE TO VIOLENT TELEVISION[a]	N
III–IV	.081*	.055*	(491)
II–III	.060	.055	(426)
I–II	−.037	−.037	(391)
II–IV	.105*	.075	(408)
I–III	−.005	−.028	(384)
I–IV	.020	−.017	(369)
IV–V	.062	.005	(296)
V–VI	.101	−.051	(153)
III–V	−.028	−.027	(292)
II–V	.004	.060	(245)
I–V	.062	.016	(236)
IV–VI	−.011	−.018	(134)
III–VI	.094	.039	(133)
II–VI	.157*	.122	(123)
I–VI	−.029	−.086	(113)

[a]Violent television score/total television score = "amount" of violence per program watched.

*Significant at .05 level.

Boys: Table 7.1.

TABLE D.3

Variance in Later Aggression (Adjusted R^2) Explained by Prior Aggression and Exposure to Television, Measured in One Violence Exposure Variable, and Measured by Adding a Violence Ratio Measure (Valid Reporters)

	R^2			
	EXPOSURE TO VIOLENT TELEVISION	VIOLENCE RATIO MEASURE ADDED[a]	INTERACTION TERM ADDED[b]	N
III–IV	.652	.651	.651	(490)
II–III	.605	.605	.605	(425)
I–II	.419	.417	.418	(388)
II–IV	.482	.481	.480	(407)
I–III	.377	.376	.376	(381)
I–IV	.391	.389	.389	(366)
IV–V	.265	.263	.261	(292)

(Continued)

TABLE D.3 (*continued*)

	R^2			
	EXPOSURE TO VIOLENT TELEVISION	VIOLENCE RATIO MEASURE ADDED[a]	INTERACTION TERM ADDED[b]	*N*
V–VI	.360	.366	.363	(152)
III–V	.363	.361	.363	(291)
II–V	.358	.361	.367	(245)
I–V	.230	.227	.224	(234)
IV–VI	.455	.453	.449	(132)
III–VI	.416	.412	.407	(133)
II–VI	.423	.419	.424	(123)
I–VI	.281	.275	.277	(112)

[a]None of the coefficients in this column is a significant increase in R^2 (.05 level) over the model with only the violence exposure measure.

[b]None of the coefficients in this column is a significant increase in R^2 (.05 level) over the model with the main effects.

Boys: Chapter 7, Table A.2.

TABLE D.4

Effect of Exposure over Longer Time Periods (Valid Reporters)

		ADJUSTED R^2		
NUMBER OF WAVES OF TELEVISION MEASURE	LAGS	ONE TELEVISION VARIABLE	CUMULATIVE[a]	*N*
Two	I,II–III	.627	.630	(320)
	I,II–IV	.534	.537	(309)
	I,II–V	.386	.383	(194)
	I,II–VI	.437	.436	(92)
	II,III–IV	.617	.616	(362)
	II,III–V	.380	.383	(217)
	II,III–VI	.483	.481	(106)
	III,IV–V	.369	.367	(259)
	III,IV–VI	.497	.503	(115)
	IV,V–VI	.369	.365	(111)
Three	I,II,III–IV	.632	.630	(280)
	I,II,III–V	.370	.368	(175)
	I,II,III–VI	.475	.465	(78)
	II,III,IV–V	.396	.397	(198)
	II,III,IV–VI	.544	.539	(96)
	III,IV,V–VI	.365	.361	(96)

(*Continued next page*)

TABLE D. 4 (*continued*)

NUMBER OF WAVES OF TELEVISION MEASURE	LAGS	ADJUSTED R^2: ONE TELEVISION VARIABLE	ADJUSTED R^2: CUMULATIVE[a]	N
Four	I,II,III,IV–V	.380	.377	(160)
	I,II,III,IV–VI	.541	.524	(73)
	II,III,IV,V–VI	.381	.368	(80)
Five	I,II,III,IV,V–VI	.358	.380	(62)

[a]None of the coefficients in the column is a significant increase in R^2 (.05 level) compared to the model with one television variable.

Boys: Table 7.2.

TABLE D.5

Variance in Later Aggression (Adjusted R^2) Explained through Prior Aggression and Exposure to Violent Television, Measured in One Violence Exposure Variable or Measured in Several Variables Based on the "Violence Weight" of Programs Watched (Valid Reporters)

WAVE PAIR	R^2: EXPOSURE TO VIOLENT TELEVISION	R^2: SEVERAL MEASURES OF EXPOSURE TO TELEVISION BASED ON "VIOLENCE WEIGHTS"	N
III–IV	.652	.658	(491)
II–III	.605	.610	(426)
I–II	.438	.463*	(391)
II–IV	.483	.516*	(408)
I–III	.397	.393	(384)
I–IV	.410	.413	(369)
IV–V	.265	.290*	(296)
V–VI	.357	.348	(153)
III–V	.364	.376	(292)
II–V	.358	.372	(245)
I–V	.253	.245	(236)
IV–VI	.450	.491*	(134)
III–VI	.416	.429	(133)
II–VI	.423	.419	(123)
I–VI	.334	.349	(113)

*Significant increase in R^2 (.05 level) as compared to the basic model.

Boys: Table 7.3.

TABLE D.6

Variance in Later Aggression (Adjusted R^2) Explained through Prior Aggression and Exposure to Television, Measured in One Violence Exposure Variable or Measured in Several Variables Based on the Context in Which Violent and Nonviolent Action Occurs (Valid Reporters)

	R^2		
WAVE PAIR	EXPOSURE TO VIOLENT TELEVISION	SEVERAL MEASURES OF EXPOSURE TO TELEVISION BASED ON "CONTEXT OF VIOLENCE"	*N*
III–IV	.652	.664*	(491)
II–III	.605	.604	(426)
I–II	.438	.466*	(391)
II–IV	.483*	.505*	(408)
I–III	.397	.393	(384)
I–IV	.410	.406	(369)
IV–V	.265	.276	(296)
V–VI	.357	.386	(153)
III–V	.364	.379	(292)
II–V	.358	.360	(245)
I–V	.253	.258	(236)
IV–VI	.450	.493*	(134)
III–VI	.416	.447	(133)
II–VI	.423*	.422*	(123)
I–VI	.334	.324	(113)

*Significant R^2 component associated with television exposure (.05 level).
Boys: Table 7.4.

TABLE D.7

Variance in Later Aggression (Adjusted R^2) Explained through Prior Aggression and Exposure to Television, Measured in One Violence Exposure Variable or Measured in Several Variables Based on Factor Analyses (Valid Reporters)

	R^2		
WAVE PAIR	EXPOSURE TO VIOLENT TELEVISION	SEVERAL MEASURES OF EXPOSURE TO TELEVISION BASED ON FACTOR ANALYSIS	*N*
III–IV	.652*	.656*	(491)
II–III	.605	.606	(426)
I–II	.438	.445	(391)
II–IV	.483*	.493*	(408)
I–III	.397	.391	(384)

(Continued next page)

TABLE D.7 *(continued)*

WAVE PAIR	R^2: EXPOSURE TO VIOLENT TELEVISION	R^2: SEVERAL MEASURES OF EXPOSURE TO TELEVISION BASED ON FACTOR ANALYSIS	N
I–IV	.410	.410	(369)
IV–V	.265	.278*	(296)
V–VI	.357	.420*	(153)
III–V	.364	.361	(292)
II–V	.358	.355	(245)
I–V	.253	.265	(236)
IV–VI	.450	.459	(134)
III–VI	.416	.412	(133)
II–VI	.423*	.439*	(123)
I–VI	.334	.388*	(113)

*Significant R^2 component associated with television exposure.
Boys: Table 7.6.

TABLE D.8
Factors Significantly Related to Aggression in Regressions with Measures Based on Factor Analyses

WAVE, FACTOR LABEL	DOMINANT PROGRAMS	SIGN	LAG(S)
Wave I			
Saturday morning cartoons	*Here Comes the Grump, Penelope Pitstop*	[−]	I–V
Educational children's programs	*Sesame Street, Mr. Rogers*	[−]	I–II, I–VI
Wave II			
News	NBC, CBS, *10 O'clock News*	[+]	II–IV
Action/Adventure	*Mod Squad, Mission Impossible, Young Rebels, Mat Lincoln*	[+]	II–VI
Sitcom	*Don Knotts, Arnie*	[−]	II–III
Wave III			
Action/Adventure	*Ironside, Gunsmoke, Bonanza, Mission Impossible, FBI, Name of the Game, Men from Shiloh*	[+]	III–VI
Unclassified	*Sesame Street, Dark Shadows, Mod Squad*	[+]	III–IV
Wave IV			
Wave V			
Action/Adventure–Western	*Gunsmoke, FBI, Bonanza, Hawaii 5-O, Alias Smith & Jones, Cade's County*	[+]	V–VI

Boys: Chapter 7, Table A.6.

TABLE D.9

Variance in Later Aggression (Adjusted R^2) Explained by Prior Aggression and Exposure to Television, Measured in One Violence Exposure Variable or Measured by Adding a Favorite Show Measure or Measured by Adding a Favorite Show Measure and an Interaction Term (Valid Reporters)

	R^2			
WAVE PAIR	EXPOSURE TO VIOLENT TELEVISION	FAVORITE SHOW MEASURE ADDED	FAVORITE SHOW MEASURE AND INTERACTION TERM ADDED	*N*
III–IV	.568	.568	.569	(274)
II–III	.617	.619	.621	(230)
I–II	.429	.426	.434	(212)
II–IV	.482	.480	.479	(229)
I–III	.450	.448	.454	(215)
I–IV	.448	.449	.454	(213)
IV–V	.263	.266	.264	(276)
V–VI	.371	.368	.381	(147)
III–V	.372	.371	.369	(271)
II–V	.357	.355	.357	(228)
I–V	.268	.265	.273	(216)
IV–VI	.493	.493	.492	(120)
III–VI	.441	.441	.437	(121)
II–VI	.451	.449	.464	(114)
I–VI	.390	.389	.387	(101)

[a]Violence rating of programs mentioned in "self-reported favorite show" measure. The Wave V measure was used for all lags, Wave IV data were not available for girls.

[b]Based on respondents with "Favorite show" data in Wave V.

Boys: Table 7.6.

APPENDIX E: GIRLS' SUBGROUPS

TABLE E.1

Net Effect of Exposure to Violent Television on Later Aggression for Subgroups Based on Sociocultural Characteristics and on Aggression of Girls' Peers (Valid Reporters)

SUBGROUP	NUMBER OF LAGS ANALYZED[a]	NUMBER OF SIGNIFICANT β COEFFICIENTS: POSITIVE β COEFFICIENTS	NUMBER OF SIGNIFICANT β COEFFICIENTS: NEGATIVE β COEFFICIENTS	AVERAGE β
A. *Sociocultural characteristics*				
Socioeconomic composition of school[b]				
Lower class				
—Black	11	1	0	−.042
—White	8	0	0	−.052
Middle class (White)	15	2	0	.072
City				
Fort Worth	15	4	0	.078
Minneapolis	15	1	1	.017
B. *Aggression of peers*				
Classroom aggression				
High	15	2	0	.070
Medium	15	1	0	.018
Low	14	1	0	.087
Aggression of closest friends				
High	11	0	0	.067
Medium	11	0	0	−.005
Low	7	2	0	.048
Classroom and friends' aggression				
High	9	0	0	.075
Medium	10	1	0	.034
Low	10	2	1	.003

[a] Lags with fewer than 30 cases have been excluded from analysis in Tables E.1–E.4.

[b] Schools were classified according to the composition of the student body. At the time of the data collection, these schools were poorly integrated. Therefore, this measure can also be regarded as a substitute measure of race. See boys tables (Chapter 7, Tables B.1–B.10) and Chapter 7, Appendix C for details of variables, categories, and question wording.

Boys: Chapter 7, Tables B.1 and B.6.

TABLE E.2

Net Effect of Exposure to Violent Television on Later Aggression for Subgroups Based on Aggressive Behavior and Aggession-Related Attitudes (Valid Reporters)

SUBGROUP	NUMBER OF LAGS ANALYZED	NUMBER OF SIGNIFICANT β COEFFICIENTS: POSITIVE β COEFFICIENTS	NEGATIVE β COEFFICIENTS	AVERAGE β
a. *Aggressive behavior* (aggressive predisposition)				
Initial aggression				
High	15	2	0	.031
Low	15	7	0	.115
Altruism				
Low	15	2	0	.062
High	15	2	0	.036
b. *Attitudes toward aggression*				
Machismo				
Favorable	15	1	0	.017
Unfavorable	15	2	0	.079
Gentleness				
Unfavorable	15	3	0	.059
Favorable	15	1	0	.023
Enjoyment of real-life violence				
High	15	1	0	.031
Low	15	0	0	.061

Boys: Chapter 7, Table B.7.

TABLE E.3

Net Effect of Exposure to Violent Television on Later Aggression for Subgroups Based on Fantasy Behavior, Emotional Instability, and Shyness (Valid Reporters)

SUBGROUP	NUMBER OF LAGS ANALYZED	NUMBER OF SIGNIFICANT β COEFFICIENTS: POSITIVE β COEFFICIENTS	NEGATIVE β COEFFICIENTS	AVERAGE β
Fantasy behavior (teacher nominations)				
High	6	0	0	.122
Low	15	3	0	.026
Fantasy behavior (peer ratings)				
High	15	1	0	.037
Low	15	4	0	.077

(Continued next page)

TABLE E.3 (*continued*)

SUBGROUP	NUMBER OF LAGS ANALYZED	NUMBER OF SIGNIFICANT β COEFFICIENTS: POSITIVE β COEFFICIENTS	NUMBER OF SIGNIFICANT β COEFFICIENTS: NEGATIVE β COEFFICIENTS	AVERAGE β
Emotional instability				
High	15	2	1	.040
Low	15	3	0	.070
Shyness				
Not shy	15	4	0	.050
Shy	5	3	0	.260

Boys: Chapter 7, Table B.8.

TABLE E.4

Net Effect of Exposure to Violent Television on Later Aggression in Subgroups Defined on the Basis of Physical Size, Age, Scholastic Ability, and Exposure to Other Media (Valid Reporters)

SUBGROUP	NUMBER OF LAGS ANALYZED	NUMBER OF SIGNIFICANT β COEFFICIENTS: POSITIVE β COEFFICIENTS	NUMBER OF SIGNIFICANT β COEFFICIENTS: NEGATIVE β COEFFICIENTS	AVERAGE β
Physical size				
Large for age	7	1	0	.111
Small for age	9	0	1	−.014
Grade in school				
Second	15	0	0	.060
Third	15	2	0	.029
Fourth	10	3*	0	.080
Fifth	6	1	0	−.007
First to learn[a] (scholastic ability)				
Not first	15	1	0	.027
First	15	3	0	.086
Exposure to comic books[b]				
High	15	4	0	.072
Low	15	0	0	−.024
Exposure to theater movies[b]				
High	15	5	0	.071
Low	15	1	0	.022

[a]Substitute measure for scholastic ability. Based on teacher nominations of "Who are the first to learn something new?" in Waves I–III. Wave III data were used for Waves III–V.

[b]Based on exposure to violent items.

*One additional coefficient closely approaches significance.

Boys: Chapter 7, Tables B.9 and B.10.

Tables for Total Samples

TABLE E.5[a]

Net Effect of Exposure to Violent Television on Later Aggression for Subgroups Based on Sociocultural Characteristics and on Aggression of Girls' Peers (Total Sample)

SUBGROUP	NUMBER OF SIGNIFICANT β COEFFICIENTS (OF 15): POSITIVE β COEFFICIENTS	NUMBER OF SIGNIFICANT β COEFFICIENTS (OF 15): NEGATIVE β COEFFICIENTS	AVERAGE β
a. *Sociocultural characteristics*			
Socioeconomic composition of school			
Lower class			
—Black	1	0	.050
—White	0	1	−.120
Middle class (white)	1	0	.059
City			
Fort Worth	7	0	.123
Minneapolis	4	1	.035
b. *Aggression of peers*			
Classroom aggression			
High	4	0	.106
Medium	4	0	.033
Low	4	0	.075
Aggression of closest friends			
High	2*	0	.091
Medium	0	0	.026
Low	1*	0	.105
Classroom and friends' aggression			
High	2	0	.108
Medium	1*	0	.057
Low	1*	0	.101

[a]For total samples, all lags, disregarding the number of cases, were analyzed. Boys tables are in Chapter 7, Tables B.11–B.20.

*One additional coefficient closely approaches significance.

TABLE E.6

Net Effect of Exposure to Violent Television on Later Aggression for Subgroups Based on Aggressive Behavior and Aggression-Related Attitudes of Girls (Total Sample)

SUBGROUP	NUMBER OF SIGNIFICANT β COEFFICIENTS (OF 15)		AVERAGE β
	POSITIVE β COEFFICIENTS	NEGATIVE β COEFFICIENTS	
a. *Aggressive behavior*			
Initial aggression			
High	1	0	.065
Low	5	0	.096
Altruism			
Low	4	0	.072
High	3	0	.055
b. *Attitudes toward aggression*			
Machismo			
Favorable	0	0	.020
Unfavorable	5	0	.101
Gentleness			
Unfavorable	2	0	.073
Favorable	3	0	.053
Enjoyment of real-life violence			
High	3	0	.086
Low	1	0	.026

TABLE E.7

Net Effect of Exposure to Violent Television on Later Aggression for Subgroups Based on Fantasy Behavior, Emotional Instability, and Shyness (Total Sample)

SUBGROUP	NUMBER OF SIGNIFICANT β COEFFICIENTS (OF 15)		AVERAGE β
	POSITIVE β COEFFICIENTS	NEGATIVE β COEFFICIENTS	
Fantasy behavior (teacher nominations)			
High	3	0	.141
Low	5	0	.057
Fantasy behavior (peer ratings)			
High	0	0	.028
Low	4	0	.099

(Continued)

TABLE E.7 (*continued*)

SUBGROUP	NUMBER OF SIGNIFICANT β COEFFICIENTS (OF 15) POSITIVE β COEFFICIENTS	NEGATIVE β COEFFICIENTS	AVERAGE β
Emotional instability			
High	3	1	−.005
Low	3	0	.076
Shyness			
Not shy	3	0	.073
Shy	3	0	.063

TABLE E.8

Net Effect of Exposure to Violent Television on Later Aggression for Subgroups Defined on the Basis of Physical Size, Age, Scholastic Ability, and Exposure to Other Media (Total Sample)

SUBGROUP	NUMBER OF SIGNIFICANT COEFFICIENTS (OF 15) POSITIVE β COEFFICIENTS	NEGATIVE β COEFFICIENTS	AVERAGE β
Physical size			
Large for age	3	0	.075
Small for age	0	0	−.007
Grade in school			
Second	2	0	.053
Third	4*	0	.084
Fourth	2[a]	0[a]	.073[a]
Fifth	2[b]	0[b]	.085[b]
First to learn			
Not first	0	0	.029
First	5	0	.113
Exposure to comic books			
High	5	0	.068
Low	1	0	.010
Exposure to theater movies			
High	5	0	.096
Low	0	0	.027

[a]Only 10 wave pairs available for analysis.
[b]Only 6 wave pairs available for analysis.
*One additional coefficient closely approaches significance.

PART II

TEENAGE BOYS: ANALYSES AND FINDINGS

CHAPTER 9

DESIGN OF THE STUDY OF TEENAGE BOYS

We now turn to the report of our study of teenage boys. Elementary school children and teenagers differ greatly in their intellectual development as well as in their television viewing patterns and aggressive behavior. These differences required the use of separate methods of data collection and analysis for the two samples.

The youngest respondents in the elementary school sample were age 7; the oldest teenagers sampled were 19 years of age. It is clear that valid information cannot be obtained from such disparate groups with the same standardized instrument. For example, special administrative procedures were designed to help the young respondents answer questions about their televison viewing accurately. These procedures would have been clearly inappropriate for teenagers. Similarly, our pretests showed that a measure that teenagers could handle easily would not have been understood by many younger respondents.

Further, most children like and watch television a lot until they reach the age of 11 or 12. Then viewing usually starts to drop and other interests gain more prominence: Teens do watch television, but they tend to watch less than any other age group. This trend may suggest that television is less likely to have an effect among adolescents. However, there is a trend that suggests the opposite hypothesis: Adolescents are more likely than younger children to view adult-oriented programs with violent content. In most homes, it is much easier for a teenage boy to view crime shows and movies during the late evening hours or at night than for younger children. At the same time, children almost never engage in aggressive acts of a criminal nature while teenagers are more likely to do so. Thus, television might promote serious acts of aggression, violence, and theft among teenagers, whereas television's potential to affect that kind of behavior among younger children is very remote.

These differences reduce the researcher's ability to make comparisons between the younger and the older respondents, but this was considered the necessary price to pay for increasing the validity of the data.[1]

The analyses conducted for teenage boys were very similar to those for the younger children, and this report follows the form of presentation for elementary school children very closely.

BASIC DESIGN

Like elementary school children, teenage boys were studied in a longitudinal panel survey. The field work was conducted by outside companies under the auspices of NBC's Research Department. The study was conducted in the same two cities during the same time period. Administrative reasons led to a reduction of data collection waves from six to five.[2]

Table 9.1 shows the dates of the five data collection waves for teenage boys, which span the May 1970–May 1973 period. Spring, fall, and winter are represented; as in the study of elementary school children, only summer—when school is not in session and many respondents were on vacation—is not represented.

The five waves with their purposely varied time intervals produced 10 wave pairs for overtime analysis. As shown in Table 9.2, the duration of the lags ranges from 5 months to 3 years.

SAMPLING

Sampling in the study involved three steps: selection of the cities, of respondents, and of parents for the mother and father interviews. The cities

[1]At the same time, the option of using more than two instruments, each tailored to the needs of more narrowly defined age groups, or other groups, was rejected. The advantages of that procedure would be outweighed by the disadvantage of restricted comparability between groups.

[2]The first two waves of data were collected almost simultaneously for the younger and the older samples. This put considerable strain on the field organization. Therefore, it was decided to conduct the waves separately and to conduct only five waves for teenagers. This allowed us to conduct the data collection with great care, spending a lot of time on assisting the very young children and on editing questionnaires that were answered incorrectly.

The last wave (Wave VI, elementary school children; Wave V teens) was again conducted simultaneously for both samples, as the size of the elementary school sample was very small by then.

TABLE 9.1
Dates of the Five Data Collection Waves for Teenage Sample

WAVE	DATE	
I	May	1970
II	October–November	1970
III	May	1971
IV	December	1972
V	May	1973

were the same as in the children's study. (The reasons for and the process of selection of Fort Worth and Minneapolis were described in Chapter 2.)

The two other steps, selection of respondents and their parents, are quite different in this part of the study, as described in the following sections.

Selection of Respondents

We selected classes from a number of elementary schools for our study of young children. For the teenage study, we conducted the interviews outside of school. We used school system lists to recruit our initial sample. Enrollment lists were obtained from the junior high schools fed by the elementary schools we used in our study of children. From these lists a core sample of 100 seventh, eighth, and ninth graders (50 in each city) was selected.

The selection was made according to a stratified random procedure to ensure adequate representation of the age groups and of boys from different socioeconomic backgrounds, including a relatively high proportion of blacks.[3]

The target boys were contacted and asked for the names of up to eight neighborhood friends with whom they spent a lot of their free time; these friends were also recruited. This procedure allowed us to obtain data from each boy as well as from his neighborhood peer group.

Since we fell short of our target of 100 teenage boys for the original sample, we drew an additional sample of 100 from the enrollment lists and selected enough boys from that second list to achieve our target. The 101 boys recruited in this manner brought 266 friends to the Wave I interview session. We also recruited 36 sixth-grade boys who were part of the elementary school sample.[4]

[3]Specifically, as in the case of elementary school children we wanted about equal representation of the two cities and of the three grades; about half of the sample was to be middle class, the other half low SES; up to half of the low-SES boys were to be black.

[4]As detailed below (Table 9.5), this was the first phase in an ongoing strategy of recruiting graduates from the elementary school sample into the study of teens. This made it possible to compare scores based on the elementary school and teenage aggression measures (see Chapter 3, footnote 2).

TABLE 9.2
Duration of Time Lags between Wave Pairs

NUMBER OF WAVE PAIRS	DURATION	WAVE PAIR
2	5 months	I–II, IV–V
1	7 months	II–III
1	1 year	I–III
1	1 year/7 months	III–IV
1	2 years	III–V
1	2 years/1 month	II–IV
2	2 years/7 months	I–IV, II–V
1	3 years	I–V

This provided a sample of 403 boys for the first data collection wave. Table 9.3 shows the composition of the initial sample with regard to the sampling characteristics—city, age, SES (family income), and race.

In order to increase the size of the sample, we made special efforts to recruit more boys in subsequent waves. All boys interviewed in Wave I were asked to bring neighborhood friends to the Wave II interview sessions. Additional boys who were part of the elementary school sample were recruited to join the teenage sample after their graduation. As a result of these efforts, the Wave II sample size increased to 569.

We considered the size of the Wave II sample satisfactory and made no further efforts to increase it. However, we continued recruiting members of the elementary school sample after their graduation from sixth grade.[5] Table 9.4 shows the sizes of the sample in all five data collection waves. The increase in Wave II is due to the recruitment efforts described above. The increase in Wave IV resulted from a large number of elementary school boys entering the teenage sample at that time.

Tables 9.5 and 9.6 provide details on the addition of elementary school children to the sample as well as the recruitment of new respondents in Wave II.

Table 9.5 shows that the initial sample contained 36 boys who had been part of the elementary school sample. The percentage of such boys in the teens sample increased from 9% in Wave I to 33% in Waves IV and V. Table 9.6 shows how many of the respondents in Waves I–V were in the initial sample,

[5]Initially, we attempted to recruit friendship groups of sixth graders from the elementary school sample. However, we found that there were really not many large groups of friends who saw each other frequently outside of school. Thus, we recruited small groups and "isolates" as well. As our sample design stressed friendship groups and tended to underrepresent small groups, "couples," and isolated boys, this change probably increased the representativeness of the sample. (See the discussion of sample representativeness and "isolates" that follows.)

TABLE 9.3
Composition of Wave I Sample

	%
City:	
Fort Worth	45
Minneapolis	55
Age:	
Under 13	10
13	23
14	30
15	28
Over 15	10
Family Income:	
Low third[a]	37
Middle third	33
Top third	30
Race:	
White	81
Black/other	19

[a]$N = 325$; low third; under $8000; middle third: $8000–11,999; top third: $12,000 and up.

and how many were added in later waves. For example, in Wave IV, the total sample size is 675. Of these boys, 311 had been part of the Wave I sample; 344 had not been part of the initial sample but had entered the study in Wave II, III, or IV. The table shows that the percentage of respondents who were not part of the initial sample increased until the last two waves, when the samples consisted of about 50% old and 50% new respondents.

A total of 824 boys took part in at least one of the five interview session; 807 boys provided usable aggression and television data in at least one wave. 302 respondents—75% of the initial sample—provided data in all five waves.

TABLE 9.4
Size of Sample in Each of Five Waves[a]

WAVE	DATE		TOTAL SAMPLE OF BOYS IN WAVE
I	May	1970	403
II	October–November	1970	569
III	May	1971	568
IV	December	1972	675
V	May	1973	644

[a]Includes boys with usable data on both aggression and television measures.

TABLE 9.5
Boys from Elementary School Sample Who Became Part of Teenage Sample

WAVE	*N*: TOTAL SAMPLE OF TEENAGE BOYS	*N*: NUMBER OF BOYS PRESENT IN ELEMENTARY SCHOOL SAMPLE	PERCENTAGE OF ELEMENTARY SCHOOL SAMPLE BOYS IN TEENS SAMPLE (%)
I	(403)	(36)	9
II	(569)	(73)	13
III	(568)	(87)	15
IV	(675)	(220)	33
V	(644)	(215)	33

The samples of both teenage boys and younger children are purposive rather than random samples.[6]

We were sensitive to the possible drawbacks of our sample selection procedures. One of these possible drawbacks was that the focus on friendship groups may have excluded social isolates from the sample, and the role of television may be different among social isolates. We investigated this possibility and found practically no evidence that a sample bias of that kind exists.[7]

[6]By recruiting friendship groups, we were able to obtain data directly from boys' friends. This procedure probably decreased attrition. Friends went to the sessions together, spent some time there, selected a gift, and were brought back to their neighborhood. All this would have been a much less interesting experience if the boys had been with strangers instead of friends or if the data had been collected individually.

[7]The target sample, selected from school rolls, respresents the universe of friendship patterns one would expect had our entire sample been selected at random. An analysis of how friendship patterns among target boys differ from those in the remaining sample would therefore reveal the extent to which our recruiting friends of target boys has led to an underrepresentation of social isolates.

We were able to examine differences in friendship patterns between target boys and their neighborhood friends because we included a number of questions on friendship in the Wave I questionnaires. We found relatively small differences. At the point of maximum difference, 54% of the target boys had four or fewer "close" boy friends ($N = 104$) compared to 47% of the friends ($N = 258$). At points presumably indicating more social isolation, the differences between targets and friends were even smaller. Comparing the percentage of either three or fewer or two or fewer "close" friends, differences between targets and friends were only 4 percentage points.

A similar pattern emerged when we examined either the number of "ordinary" friends or a combination of "close" and "ordinary" friends. Thus the maximum difference between target boys and friends in the number of both "close" and/or "ordinary" friends is at 8 or fewer, where

TABLE 9.6
Number of Boys in Each of Five Waves, Number of Boys from Initial Wave I Sample, and Number of New Respondents in Each of Five Waves

WAVE	TOTAL NUMBER OF BOYS IN WAVE		TOTAL NUMBER OF BOYS IN WAVE WHO WERE IN WAVE I SAMPLE		TOTAL NUMBER OF BOYS IN WAVE WHO ENTERED THE SAMPLE AFTER WAVE I	
	N	%	*N*	%	*N*	%
I	(403)					
II	(569)	100	(375)	66	(194)	34
III	(568)	100	(369)	65	(199)	35
IV	(675)	100	(331)	49	(344)	51
V	(644)	100	(320)	50	(324)	50

We also compared our sample to the population of United States teenage boys. A comparison of 12 important sample characteristics with national data showed rather high agreement with respect to family structure (presence of natural parents), family income, mother's employment, and father's and mother's occupations. By design, our sample has more blacks than the United States average. Further, the teenage sample overrepresents boys from large families, homeowners, and families who own a color television set, and as a result of the study locations, it underrepresents Catholics and overrepresents Lutherans.[8]

New Respondents and Attrition

As already mentioned, we increased the sample size after the initial wave by recruiting new respondents and by collecting data from respondents who had been part of the elementary boys sample. Whereas these additions increased the

the differential is 10 percentage points. At five or fewer, the difference is only 2 percentage points.

An examination of these data also indicates that extreme social isolation among teenagers is very rare. Only two boys in either group had no male friends at all; 97% of the boys in both groups had four or more friends.

We concluded from this that the range of friendship we find in our total sample is similar to the range one would expect to find were our whole sample randomly selected. As social isolates were only slightly underrepresented, it seemed unlikely that they could affect our results had they been represented in proper proportion.

[8]Details are contained in Documentation 2B (available on request), which also reports the analysis for elementary school boys.

sample size considerably over that of the initial wave, there were also some reductions due to attrition. This section examines the extent of attrition and the way in which the addition of new respondents and attrition affected the sample composition.

In the study of teenage boys, attrition was not a major problem. The only sources of attrition were mobility and refusals, and neither resulted in much panel "mortality."[9]

Table 9.7 shows the number of new respondents and the number of respondents lost because of attrition from wave to wave. Overall, 404 respondents were added to the original Wave I sample. During the course of the study 163 were lost—about half from the Wave I sample, the other half from respondents added after Wave I.

Attrition and the addition of new respondents did not materially change the composition of the sample during the 3 years of the study. Table 9.8A presents the sample composition on four important respondent characteristics; Table 9.8B presents three family characteristics. Examining the effect of attrition, we see that both the losses and the differences between the Wave I sample and the five-wave sample are quite small. The latter has a higher proportion of whites and teens who live with their natural parents. Teenage boys who left the study tended to have somewhat lower school grades. These findings agree with the study of young boys.

The composition of the new respondent samples is very similar to that of the initial sample. Moreover, the differences that do exist are such as to neutralize the effects of attrition. New respondents, too, are more likely to be black, from "broken" homes, and they also tend to be below average students.[10] Thus, as in the study of elementary school students, the net effect of attrition and new respondents is minimal.[11]

DATA SOURCES

The basic data for the teenage study—measures of aggression and television exposure—were obtained from the respondents themselves. The boys filled out

[9]The elementary school study experienced more attrition resulting from mobility because the sample unit was the entire class, not the individual, and respondents had to be part of the class, in order to obtain usable aggression data about him/her. Thus, there was no point in following those who moved.

[10]According to the measures discussed in the following chapters, they also tend to be slightly more aggressive.

[11]Subgroup analyses (Chapter 14) indicate that groups affected by attrition did not modify television effects. Thus, it appears that the small changes in sample composition did not affect the findings of the causal analyses in a significant or systematic way.

TABLE 9.7
New Respondents and Attrition

	NEW RESPONDENTS	ATTRITION	TOTAL SAMPLE
Initial sample (Wave I)			403
Change between waves			
I and II	194	28	569
II and III	37	38	568
III and IV	169	62	675
IV and V	4	35	644
Total	404	163	

self-administered questionnaires in which they reported their aggressive behavior and television viewing.[12] The questionnaires took 1 hr or more to complete and contained items about many aspects of the boys' lives other than aggression and television viewing.

Methods of Data Collection

The questionnaires were filled out during interview sessions on weekends. Teens were picked up by bus and driven to a location provided by the local public television station in one city, a university in the other city.[13] Boys from the same neighborhood attended the sessions together; each group was supervised by two male interviewers of college age.[14] After completion of the questionnaire, discussions were held about a topic related to the study.[15] Each teenager who attended the interview session received a record album as a gift.

The questionnaires for teenage boys included a variety of questions, many of which were of a sensitive nature: serious forms of aggression, fighting with parents and siblings, and drug use. Together, these design features were intended to minimize response bias. It was felt that a neutral location away from homes or schools would help obtain honest responses to questions like

[12]For details, see Chapters 10 and 11, respectively.

[13]When respondents were not able to attend the session, interviews were conducted at school or at home.

[14]We found in our pretests that males of that age were best able to establish good rapport with the respondents.

[15]Often the topic was reporting honesty. Also, boys were asked whether the questionnaire covered all areas of importance in a boy's life. (The study was described as a study of all aspects of teenage boys' lives.) Many boys pointed out that the questionnaire did not cover sex adequately. As a result, we added a number of items dealing with dating and sexual behavior in later waves.

TABLE 9.8

A: Comparison of Characteristics of Respondents in Initial Sample, of Respondents Present in all Five Waves, and of New Respondents[a]

	INITIAL SAMPLE (%)	PRESENT IN ALL FIVE WAVES (%)	NEW RESPONDENTS IN WAVE II (%)	NEW RESPONDENTS IN WAVE IV (%)
City				
Fort Worth	45	48	43	54
Minneapolis	55	52	57	46
Age when enter				
Under 13	10	10	24	36
13	23	26	25	35
14	30	29	21	16
15	28	26	24	4
Over 15	10	9	6	9
Race				
White	81	85	83	79
Black/other	19	15	17	20
Average scholastic grade[b]				
Low	22	17	30	20
Low middle	28	29	33	23
High middle	28	31	24	21
High	21	23	12	36
N	(403)	(302)	(194)	(169)

B: Comparison of Family Data of Respondents in Initial Sample, of Respondents Present in all Five Waves, and of New Respondents[c]

	INITIAL SAMPLE (%)	PRESENT IN ALL FIVE WAVES (%)	NEW RESPONDENTS IN WAVE II (%)	NEW RESPONDENTS IN WAVE IV (%)
Family income[d]				
Low third	37	34	33	46
Middle third	33	35	40	26
Top third	30	32	26	28
Family structure				
Lives with natural mother and father	71	76	66	75
Does not live with natural mother and father	30	24	34	25
Previous residential mobility				
Has lived in 1–3 homes	61	62	67	58
Has lived in 4 or more homes	39	38	33	42

(Continued)

TABLE 9.8 (*continued*)

	INITIAL SAMPLE	PRESENT IN ALL FIVE WAVES	NEW RESPONDENTS	
			IN WAVE II	IN WAVE IV
Total N	(403)	(302)	(194)	(169)
Family data available N	(325)	(266)	(92)	(111)

[a] Thirty-seven new respondents in Wave III are excluded from this analysis.

[b] For new respondents in Wave II, data are available for only $N = 33$; for new respondents in Wave IV, $N = 138$.

[c] Thirty-seven new respondents in Wave III are excluded from this analysis. (No family data are available for this group.)

[d] Low third: under $8000; middle third: $8000–11,999; top third: $12,000 and up.

this. In addition, the confidentiality of the information was stressed, names did not appear on the questionnaires (only ID numbers), and the issue of honest reporting was discussed with the teens (see also Chapter 10).

Each questionnaire contained about 50 questions, many of which included several subquestions. The aggression and television exposure items were interspersed with items covering other areas of the boy's life considered relevant for the analysis. Aggression and television questions were included in all five questionnaires; most of the other questions were asked in one or two waves.[16]

Additional Data Sources

As in the study of younger children, data were obtained not only from the respondents themselves, but from other sources as well.

FRIENDS

During the interview sessions, boys were asked a few questions dealing mainly with friends' aggressiveness. This information turned out to be less

[16] After a review of the literature as well as talks with experts, we decided to develop most items ourselves. Items taken from the work of other researchers included the Rosenberg Self-Esteem scale, Blumenthal Aggression Attitudes items, and the Rokeach Dogmatism scale.

Wave V contained a large number of items related to proprietary and illicit drug use. Those items were included for a special analysis unrelated to the main purpose of the study: the relationship between television drug advertising and proprietary and illicit drug use (Milavsky, Pekowsky, & Stipp, 1976).

TABLE 9.9
Availability of Mother and Father Data for Various Samples

	INITIAL SAMPLE		PRESENT IN ALL FIVE WAVES		NEW RESPONDENTS			
					IN WAVE II		IN WAVE IV	
	N	%	*N*	%	*N*	%	*N*	%
Total sample	(403)	100	(302)	100	(194)	100	(169)	100
Mother questionnaire I available	(325)	81	(266)	88	(92)	47	(111)	66
Father questionnaire I available	(205)	51	(181)	60	(48)	25	(52)	31
Mother questionnaire II available	(288)	71	(251)	83	(85)	44	(104)	62
Father questionnaire II available	(154)	38	(143)	47	(38)	20	(55)	33

useful than anticipated and little emphasis was put on obtaining this type of data toward the end of the study.[17]

SCHOOL RECORDS

Because teachers in high school spend relatively little time with each student, we did not ask them to rate the respondents. We did, however, have access to the boys' school-records data which were almost identical with those for elementary school boys, described in Chapter 2. The most important items are the respondent's average scholastic grade, IQ score, and his tardiness. The school record also contained teacher comments.

PARENTS

Parents of most teenagers were interviewed twice. The questionnaire used was practically the same as that used for the younger children.[18]

Interviews with mothers and fathers provided data on family background and family life for the younger children. The teenage boys provided much of that information themselves. Thus, interviews with parents were somewhat less important as a source of new information. They did, however, serve as a source of "second opinions"—the parents' perspective on questions the boy himself had commented on. For example, we have data on aggressiveness in the family and on the relationship between boy and parents from the boy as well as from the mother or father.

---

[17]Friends' reports on the respondents' aggressiveness appeared to be of questionable validity (see Chapter 11).

[18]See Chapter 2 for additional details; see section below on sample sizes.

TABLE 9.10
Comparison of Characteristics of Respondents with and without Data from Mother Questionnaire (Wave I)

	WITH MOTHER DATA (%)	WITHOUT MOTHER DATA (%)	INITIAL SAMPLE WAVE I (%)
City			
Fort Worth	47	48	45
Minneapolis	53	52	55
Race			
White/other	82	82	81
Black/other	18	18	19
Average scholastic grades[a]			
High	23	8	21
Medium	31	16	36
Low	46	77	44
N	(534)	(290)	(403)

[a]Not available for all respondents.

The nature of the parental interviews was essentially the same for the elementary school and the teenage samples. There was one difference, though: the way the parents were selected.

In the teenage study, we tried to obain data from all mothers and fathers, rather than from a sample of parents (as in the study of elementary school children). We were able to conduct interviews with 325, that is 81%, of the mothers of the 403 boys in the initial sample, and with 205 of their fathers. The latter figure represents 51% of the Wave I boys and 64% of the boys' fathers/stepfathers, since about 20% of these boys lived without an adult male in the home.

In the second wave of parental interviews we tried to get data from all parents who had been interviewed in the first wave. We obtained 288 interviews from the mothers of Wave I boys (71%) and 154 interviews from their fathers (38%).

We also interviewed a large proportion of the mothers and fathers of boys who entered the study after Wave I. First, we tried to get interviews from parents of boys who were recruited in Wave II. Second, many boys who had been part of the elementary school sample brought parental data with them.

All this information is detailed in Table 9.9. The table shows how many interviews were obtained from mothers and fathers in the two data collection waves in these four groups: boys in the initial sample; those who were present in all five waves (which means they were also part of the initial sample); new respondents who entered in Wave II; and new respondents who entered in Wave IV.[19]

In Table 9.10 we examine the extent to which respondents for whom maternal interviews were obtained are representative of the total initial sample of boys on three important measures: city of residence, race, and average scholastic grade. The data show that we were successful in obtaining data from the mothers of black respondents. At the same time, it is apparent that many mothers of students with low grades did not agree to be interviewed. The difference is more pronounced than among younger boys, where the same tendency was noted (see Table 2.7).[20]

---

[19]Only 37 new respondents entered the study in Wave III, and only 4 in Wave V. Consequently, no data are presented for new respondents in those waves.

[20]Respondents without mother questionnaires also tended to be somewhat more aggressive.

CHAPTER 10

AGGRESSION MEASURE

As discussed in Chapter 3, we defined aggression as "physical or verbal acts known in advance to cause injury to others." Intention to harm is the central distinguishing feature of this definition; other related constructs that do not include this element of intent are excluded. The one exception is that we included stealing. Although intent to harm others is not necessarily involved, it is a kind of antisocial behavior that television may influence. With all items, the focus is on behavior rather than on attitudes or self-image.

We expected that the same sorts of aggressive behavior patterns found in the elementary school sample would also be found among teens. But, in addition, we expected that more serious "delinquent" aggression would be found in this sample of adolescents. Therefore, the measures of aggression in the teen questionnaire were designed to cover a broader array of behaviors than those obtained in the elementary school sample.

MEASURING AGGRESSION

Exploratory Work

A review of the literature as well as our own pretests revealed that the aggression of elementary school children can be assessed more accurately by peer ratings than by self-reports. To study adolescent aggression, we concluded that self-reports are the best method after examining the possibility of using peer ratings.

In a pretest, peer ratings were obtained from 180 boys in 18 friendship groups. These groups were purposefully drawn from different socioeconomic strata, from different age groups, and from both white and black populations. In each group boys were asked to report their own levels of involvement in a variety of aggressive activities and also the aggressiveness of each of the other boys in the group. A comparison of self and friend reports showed that when there was disagreement, it resulted from one of the friends rating the boy as nonaggressive, not from the boy denying involvement in aggressive acts reported by his friends.

As the groups of friends were small, their average ratings were easily influenced by one rater's inaccuracies. As a result, we concluded that peer ratings of this kind are not as reliable and valid as those obtained from the adolescents themselves. The fact that the boys' self-reports of aggressive behavior were usually corroborated by at least one of his friends and that these boys did admit to serious forms of aggression encouraged us to concentrate on that measure in the pretests.[1]

A review of the literature showed that our assessments agreed with judgments of researchers in the field of juvenile delinquency. Hirschi, for example, feels that self-report measures are usually the best for studying aggression among teenagers. At the same time, he points out that self-reports are subject to bias, not only through underreporting, but also through overreporting.[2] As discussed in the following, we developed special procedures to minimize dishonest reporting and to identify inaccurate reports.

Administrative Procedures and Aggression Items

Each of the five questionnaires for the five waves of the study contained questions about 14 different acts of aggression. These can be classified into the following four groups:

1. Items involving aggression against other persons: arguing, threatening to hurt someone, fighting, pushing, shoving or hitting someone.

---

[1]In our pretest work, we also considered teachers and parents as sources of information about the boys' aggressive behavior. Teacher ratings were rejected as main sources of information as teachers are poor reporters of the boys' behavior outside of the classroom. We found teacher comments useful in our study of elementary school children as the aggression measure used there focused on behavior at school. When we obtained ratings from parents of elementary school children, we found that they severely underreport the aggressive behavior of their children. (We did obtain teacher and mother comments as well as peer nominations on some aggression items for comparison purposes; see the section "Validity.")

[2]Although we would expect a tendency to underreport serious acts, Hirschi (1969) found that some respondents exaggerated their delinquent activities. Hirschi also found that self-reports of delinquent acts are more reliable than police records: many delinquents do not come to the attention of the police, and those that do disproportionately respresent the lower social strata.

2. Items involving aggression toward teachers: being rude to a teacher and making fun of a teacher to his/her face.
3. Items involving aggression against property: stealing and damaging property.
4. Items about serious aggression (delinquent acts): being beaten up, being arrested, participating in a gang fight, knifing, stealing a car, and mugging. (Some of these questions were not asked in Wave I. Being "badly beaten up" was included as an indicator of involvement in serious fights. The factor analyses below indicate that this item does measure just that, nor positive victimization.)

As we show in the following, the self-reports do, in fact, cluster into these four groups.

Questions about many of these acts were asked in two ways: *how often* the act had been committed during the last four weeks; and *how recently* the act had been committed (from "within the past 3 months" to "never"). If an act occurred fairly frequently, the former question formulation provided the most precise information; if the act occurred rarely, the latter question provided the best data.

It turned out that the items asking about the frequency of the behavior were the most appropriate for the first three groups of acts; questions about recency were the most appropriate for the fourth group, since those kinds of delinquent acts were reported much less frequently than others. These questions, which were interspersed with prosocial items, are listed in the following.

1. Items involving aggression against other persons.

Here are some activities that boys your age may occasionally do at home, in school, in the streets, and in other places. For each of these activities, please circle the number that indicates the *number of times you* did this activity during the past 4 weeks, anywhere.

(CIRCLE CORRECT NUMBER)

Item A. Threatened to hurt someone

0 1 2 3 4 5 6 7 8 9 10 or more times

Item B. Got into a physical fight with someone

0 1 2 3 4 5 6 7 8 9 10 or more times

Item C. Pushed, shoved or hit someone and were *not* fooling around

0 1 2 3 4 5 6 7 8 9 10 or more times

Item D. Got into a heated argument in which people got really angry

0 1 2 3 4 5 6 7 8 9 10 or more times

2. *Items involving aggression toward teachers*

In the *past 4 weeks*, about how many different times have you done the following:

(PLEASE CIRCLE THE NUMBER)

Item A. Talked back rudely to any teacher
0 1 2 3 4 5 6 7 8 9 10 or more times

Item B. Tried to get back at any teacher by making fun of him/her in any way to his/her face?

0 1 2 3 4 5 6 7 8 9 10 or more times

3. *Items involving property aggression.*

Here are some activities that boys your age may occasionally do at home, in school, in the streets, and in other places. For each of these activities, please circle the number that indicates the *number of times you* did this activity during the past 4 weeks, anywhere.

(CIRCLE CORRECT NUMBER)

Item A. Stole something (for example, took things from homes, stores, cars, on your job; not paying bills at restaurants; sneaking into places, or anything else)

0 1 2 3 4 5 6 7 8 9 10 or more times

Item B. Damaged in any way someone else's property (public or private) purposely

0 1 2 3 4 5 6 7 8 9 10 or more times

4. *Items about serious aggression (delinquent acts).*

SOME HAPPENINGS

Here is a list of things which may have happened to boys your age at home, in school, in the streets, and in other places. For each of these things please indicate the *last time* this took place. (CHECK ONE BOX FOR EACH ITEM.)

	WITHIN THE PAST 3 MONTHS	4–6 MONTHS AGO	7–12 MONTHS AGO	MORE THAN 12 MONTHS AGO	NEVER
Item A. You were badly beaten up	1	2	3	4	5
Item B. You were arrested	1	2	3	4	5
Item C. You participated in a gang fight	1	2	3	4	5
Item D. You went for a joy ride in a stolen car	1	2	3	4	5
Item E. You hurt someone to get his money	1	2	3	4	5
Item F. You purposely hurt someone with a knife	1	2	3	4	5

As reported in the previous chapter, the importance of honest reporting and the confidentiality of the material were strongly stressed to the boys.[3] The effort to ensure data accuracy included questionnaire design and administrative procedures to detect inconsistent responses, many of which were found in Wave I. Beginning in Wave II, an immediate edit of each questionnaire was conducted, before the boys left the interviewing location, and they were asked to correct any inconsistencies found in their reports. (See "Reliability of specific items" to come.) Further, as reported in the following, special procedures were used to correct inconsistencies in reports of delinquent acts.

CONSTRUCTION OF AGGRESSION MEASURES

Exploratory Factor Analysis

As in the construction of the aggression measure for elementary school children, the first step in this process for adolescents was an exploratory factor analysis.

Table 10.1 presents the results of the first exploratory factor analysis, separately for the cross-sectional samples in the five waves.[4] An inspection of the rotated factor loadings shows that the prosocial items are clearly differentiated from the aggression items. At the same time, it is apparent that the aggression items do not all factor together (as had been the case among elementary school children) but that four distinct sets of aggression items factor into separate dimensions. The factor analysis results for the separate items in each of the dimensions are presented in Table 10.2.

Aggression Index Construction

Based on the factor analyses we constructed four different measures of aggression. The first was labeled "Personal aggression," a measure of physical

[3]Male interviewers between the ages of 18 and 30 were chosen rather than older adults or women. Names did not appear on the questionnaires. Identification numbers were used to keep track of respondents over time. In nearly all cases, questionnaires were answered on weekends in a place away from home or school. In some of the waves, discussions about the honesty of reporting were held after the boys had answered the questionnaires. Here again, the necessity for honesty was stressed and the boys were encouraged to express their thoughts about it. Relatively few indicated fears of revealing deviant behavior, and during these discussions the moderators reassured the boys about confidentiality.

[4]The factor analyses were based on an iterative principal factors procedure. One item in the beginning analyses, "got into a heated argument," was dropped when we found that it was weakly associated with the other items. This means that only 13 rather than 14 aggression indicators are considered in the remainder of the analysis.

TABLE 10.1
Varimax Rotated Factor Loadings of Aggression and Prosocial Items[a]

FACTOR	1	2	3	4
	Wave I (N = 402)			
Fought with someone	.14	.64	.13	−.04
Pushed, shoved or hit someone	.03	.67	.07	.33
Got into a heated argument	.13	.59	.20	.27
Threatened to hurt someone	.19	.43	.26	.23
Talked rudely to a teacher	.74	.18	.03	.28
Made fun of a teacher	.82	.10	.01	.13
Stole something	.33	.22	.04	.42
Damaged property purposely	.26	.21	.07	.68
Were badly beaten up				
Were arrested				
Were in a gang fight	(not asked in Wave I)			
Knifed someone				
Mugged someone				
Stole a car				
Helped someone with schoolwork	−.04	.12	.50	−.01
Gave advice about personal problems	.10	.14	.66	.10
Tried to cheer someone up	.02	.08	.72	.04

FACTOR	1	2	3	4	5
	Wave II (N = 568)				
Fought with someone	.51	.08	.05	−.02	.13
Pushed, shoved or hit someone	.76	.12	.12	.09	−.09
Got into a heated argument	.65	−.05	.23	.18	.07
Threatened to hurt someone	.47	.06	.13	.21	−.08
Talked rudely to a teacher	.28	.10	.03	.71	.07
Made fun of a teacher	.29	.16	.10	.67	.02
Stole something	.39	.04	−.06	.27	.12
Damaged property purposely	.56	.04	−.05	.20	.10
Were badly beaten up	.07	.22	−.02	.01	.52
Were arrested	.05	.48	.04	.13	.26
Were in a gang fight	.06	.22	−.06	.05	.41
Knifed someone	.05	.76	−.03	.05	.24
Mugged someone	.05	.69	−.09	.10	.08
Stole a car	.10	.79	−.04	.02	.09
Helped someone with schoolwork	.02	−.00	.52	−.12	−.17
Gave advice about personal problems	.12	−.05	.59	.18	.06
Tried to cheer someone up	.13	−.06	.75	.06	.01

TABLE 10.1 (*continued*)

FACTOR	1	2	3	4	5
			Wave III (N = 568)		
Fought with someone	.22	.63	−.04	.12	.05
Pushed, shoved or hit someone	.10	.85	.01	.07	.16
Got into a heated argument	.00	.58	.27	.22	.12
Threatened to hurt someone	.08	.53	.05	.23	.18
Talked rudely to a teacher	.08	.25	.01	.73	.18
Made fun of a teacher	.10	.24	−.02	.70	.14
Stole something	.14	.24	.05	.23	.63
Damaged property purposely	.08	.41	.00	.18	.50
Were badly beaten up	.51	.16	.00	.01	.10
Were arrested	.61	.08	.04	.01	.03
Were in a gang fight	.52	.15	.03	.13	.06
Knifed someone	.75	.05	−.01	−.05	.02
Mugged someone	.67	−.06	−.02	.04	.01
Stole a car	.61	.05	−.03	.13	.03
Helped someone with schoolwork	−.02	−.00	.45	−.09	−.08
Gave advice about personal problems	−.06	.06	.68	.11	.10
Tried to cheer someone up	.11	.09	.78	.02	.07

FACTOR	1	2	3	4	5
			Wave IV (N = 670)		
Fought with someone	.05	.13	.62	.10	.20
Pushed, shoved or hit someone	.15	.08	.80	.03	.04
Got into a heated argument	.21	.08	.56	.28	.08
Threatened to hurt someone	.24	.03	.41	.28	.17
Talked rudely to a teacher	.67	.15	.23	.06	.22
Made fun of a teacher	.88	.19	.12	.01	.16
Stole something	.18	.09	.14	.05	.73
Damaged property purposely	.23	.14	.32	.06	.56
Were badly beaten up	−.00	.14	.16	.00	.07
Were arrested	.18	.24	.10	−.01	.06
Were in a gang fight	.17	.41	.11	−.05	.09
Knifed someone	.00	.65	.06	.06	−.04
Mugged someone	.08	.69	.06	.14	.06
Stole a car	.06	.56	.02	.02	.06
Helped someone with schoolwork	−.03	.04	.01	.45	−.03
Gave advice about personal problems	.02	.04	.12	.72	.05
Tried to cheer someone up	.10	.01	.20	.74	.10

(*Continued next page*)

TABLE 10.1 (*continued*)

FACTOR	1	2	3	4	5
		Wave V (N = 644)			
Fought with someone	.33	.09	.59	.04	.04
Pushed, shoved or hit someone	.08	.16	.70	.04	.15
Got into a heated argument	.14	.16	.53	.18	.16
Threatened to hurt someone	.15	.20	.53	.10	.20
Talked rudely to a teacher	.09	.68	.30	.06	.21
Made fun of a teacher	.10	.81	.17	.09	.13
Stole something	.14	.15	.30	.01	.52
Damaged property purposely	.08	.22	.33	.02	.48
Were badly beaten up	.16	−.10	.23	.11	.20
Were arrested	.34	.13	.04	−.04	.51
Were in a gang fight	.37	.08	.15	.03	.23
Knifed someone	.37	−.00	.15	−.04	.02
Mugged someone	.79	.06	.18	.07	.07
Stole a car	.62	.12	.05	.01	.30
Helped someone with schoolwork	−.01	.01	.05	.39	−.09
Gave advice about personal problems	.03	.08	.04	.77	.07
Tried to cheer someone up	.00	.04	.12	.72	.11

[a] Varimax rotation of all factors with eigenvalues greater than or equal to 1.0 The same basic structure appeared when an oblique rotation was used.

and verbal aggression against others. The second, "Teacher aggression," is a measure of primarily verbal aggression against teachers. "Property aggression" is a measure of stealing and damaging property. (These three measures will be discussed first.) "Delinquency," the fourth index is made up of six serious antisocial acts.

PERSONAL, TEACHER, AND PROPERTY AGGRESSION

The first three measures are additive scales based on items asking about the frequency of the behaviors during the last 4 weeks. Since each item going into these indexes ranges from 0 to 10, the scales range from 0 to 20 (for the property and teacher aggression scales) or 0 to 30 (for the personal aggression scale). The distributions of the scales in all waves, grouped into 5-point intervals, are shown in Figures 10.1, 10.2, and 10.3. Descriptive statistics based on ungrouped data are shown in Table 10.3.

The distributions are distinctively J-shaped, with most boys scoring low and the modal values always being 0. All three are much more J-shaped than the distributions of the elementary school children's aggression measures.

As the indices are composed of different numbers of items, it is not possible

TABLE 10.2
Factor Loadings of Aggression Items[a]

	WAVE				
	I	II	III	IV	V
Personal aggression items:					
Fought with someone	.62	.52	.66	.65	.64
Pushed, shoved, or hit someone	.67	.83	.84	.78	.73
Got into a heated argument	.71	.68	.62	.62	.62
N	(400)	(562)	(565)	(673)	(643)
Teacher aggression items[b]*:*					
Talked rudely to a teacher	.81	.77	.78	.82	.80
Made fun of a teacher	.81	.77	.78	.82	.80
N	(401)	(568)	(562)	(649)	(616)
Property aggression items[b]*:*					
Stole something	.65	.66	.68	.72	.67
Damaged property purposely	.65	.66	.68	.72	.67
N	(402)	(569)	(568)	(674)	(644)
Delinquency items:					
Were badly beaten up		.51	.62	.49	.45
You were arrested		.66	.67	.54	.61
Were in a gang fight		.46	.59	.60	.58
Knifed someone		.68	.70	.63	.52
Mugged someone		.67	.72	.64	.63
Stole a car		.72	.69	.66	.76
N		(567)	(565)	(665)	(640)

[a] Single factor solution for cross-sectional analyses of items in the separate dimensions.
[b] Factor loadings here are the square roots of the observed cross-sectional correlations between the two indicators.

to compare their relative frequencies. For this purpose, Table 10.4 presents means for the number of times (out of a maximum 10) each type of aggression was reported.

It is apparent that property aggression is reported less frequently than the other two kinds of aggression. (The difference between the means for personal and teacher aggression is negligible.) Comparing the means across the five study waves, it appears that reporting of aggressive behavior—particularly personal aggression—decreases slightly with age.

DELINQUENCY

The measure of delinquency is somewhat different from the three others. As we just mentioned, the items used for this measure do not ask about the frequency of the acts, but whether they had occurred at all.

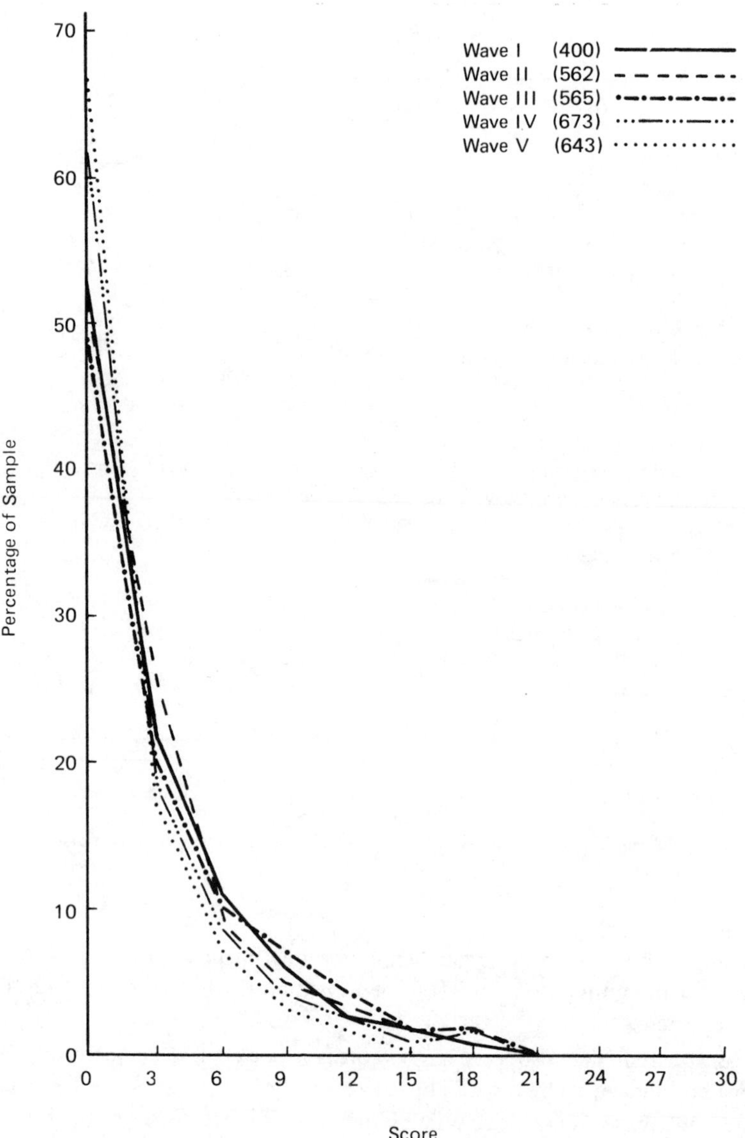

FIGURE 10.1. *Distribution of personal aggression scores in all five waves.*

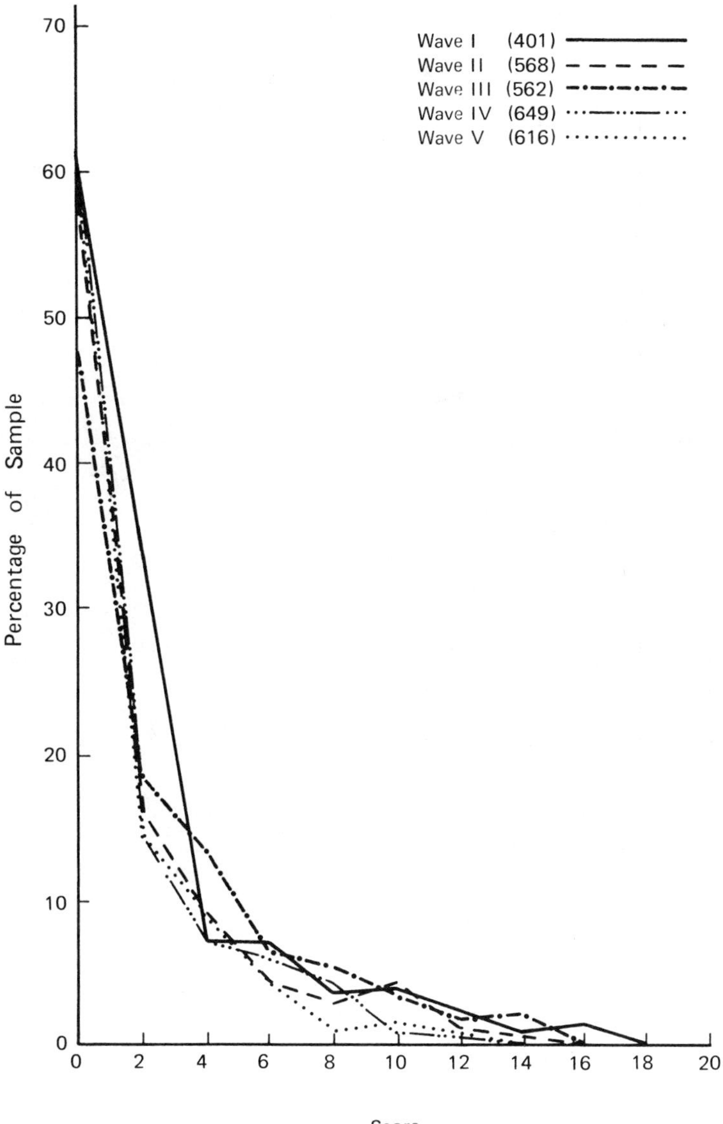

FIGURE 10.2. *Distribution of teacher aggression scores in all five waves.*

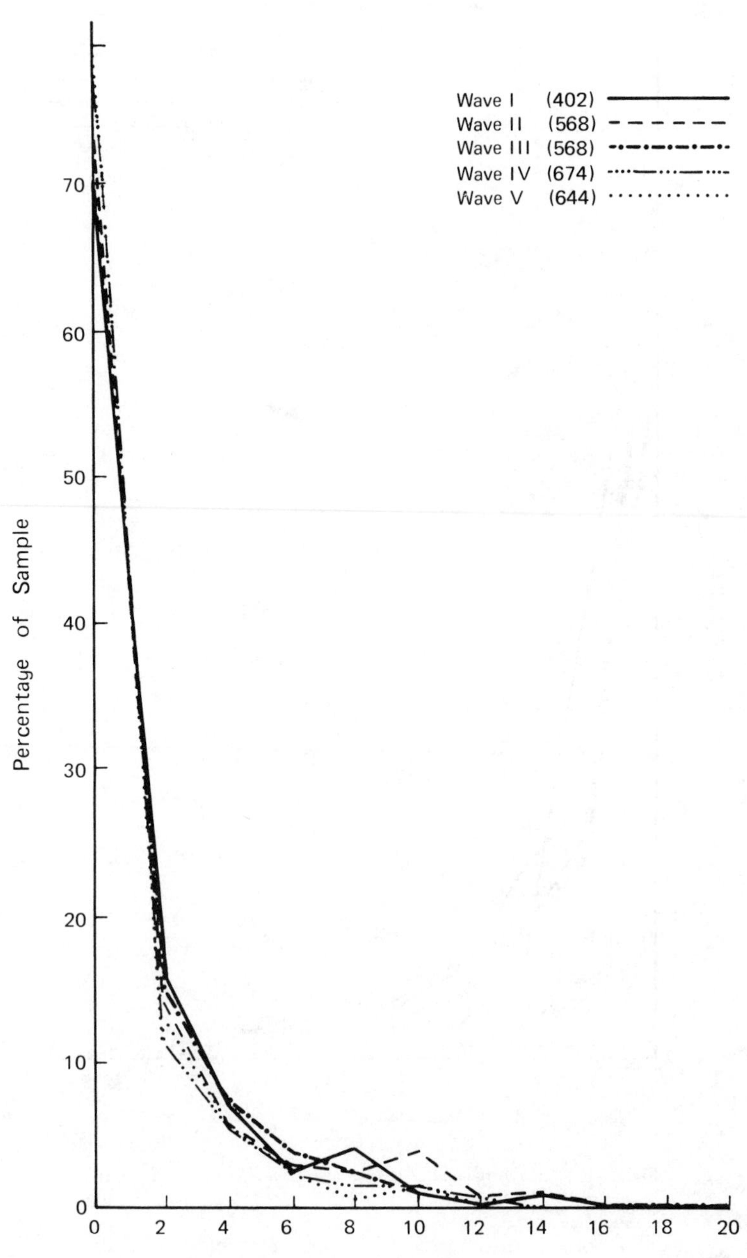

FIGURE 10.3. *Distribution of property agression scores in all five waves.*

TABLE 10.3
Aggression Measures: Descriptive Statistics for All Five Waves

	MEAN	MEDIAN	MODE	RANGE	STANDARD DEVIATION	SKEWNESS	*N*
Personal aggression							
Wave I	3.7	2.3	0	0–24	4.4	1.8	(400)
Wave II	4.0	2.4	0	0–30	5.0	2.1	(562)
Wave III	4.0	2.4	0	0–30	4.9	2.0	(565)
Wave IV	3.2	1.6	0	0–30	4.6	2.6	(673)
Wave V	2.6	1.2	0	0–25	3.9	2.4	(643)
Teacher aggression							
Wave I	2.4	.7	0	0–16	3.7	1.9	(401)
Wave II	2.7	1.0	0	0–20	4.2	2.2	(568)
Wave III	3.3	1.7	0	0–20	4.2	1.8	(562)
Wave IV	2.2	.6	0	0–20	3.7	2.4	(649)
Wave V	2.3	.7	0	0–20	3.8	2.6	(616)
Property aggression							
Wave I	1.7	.4	0	0–16	2.9	2.4	(402)
Wave II	2.0	.4	0	0–20	3.5	2.3	(568)
Wave III	2.0	.5	0	0–20	3.3	2.4	(568)
Wave IV	1.5	.3	0	0–20	3.1	3.0	(674)
Wave V	1.4	.3	0	0–20	2.9	3.2	(644)

Table 10.5A shows descriptive statistics for the six individual delinquent acts. Wave I data are presented for only three of six items because the other three were not asked in the first wave.

The items shown earlier in this chapter were recoded so that a respondent was credited with a "1" if he reported committing an act "within the past 3 months"; he was credited with a "0" for any other response. Thus, "Number who committed the act" in Table 10.5A gives the number of boys who reported each behavior during the 3 months preceding the wave.

Table 10.5B shows the statistics for a measure of delinquency that combines all six measures. (As only three items were available in Wave I, no measure was computed in that wave.) The distribution of that measure is shown in Figure 10.4.

The data show, as we might expect, that delinquent behavior is considerably rarer than the other forms of aggression we have considered. On average, each activity was reported by about 5% of the boys in each of the waves. (Being in a gang fight in Wave II is the only item reaching 10%). Between 13% and 19% of the boys in any one wave reported involvement in at least one of these acts in the past *3 months*; very few respondents reported more than one act. These percentages are a good deal smaller than the 70% who reported acts of personal

TABLE 10.4
Means of Aggression Items

	WAVE[a]				
	I	II	III	IV	V
Personal aggression items					
Fought	.76	.75	.77	.58	.52
Shoved	1.49	1.57	1.41	1.10	.84
Argued	1.49	1.64	1.90	1.53	1.26
Personal aggression	1.25	1.32	1.36	1.07	.87
Teacher aggression items					
Rude to teacher	1.58	1.68	1.99	1.35	1.40
Sassed teacher	.86	1.06	1.28	.89	.89
Teacher aggression	1.22	1.37	1.64	1.12	1.14
Property aggression items					
Stole	.93	1.19	1.16	.97	.91
Damaged	.75	.85	.83	.54	.53
Property aggression	.84	1.02	1.00	.76	.72

[a]In Waves I–V, N = 401–403, 566–569, 562–568, 649–674, 616–644, respectively.

aggression, about 60% who reported teacher aggression, and about 40% who reported property aggression during the last *4 weeks* in a given wave.

There is a small tendency for fewer delinquent acts to be reported in the later waves. This trend is also present when the same boys are examined over time and it agrees with research by Sutherland and Cressey (1970), who found this kind of behavior occurs most often in early adolescence.[5]

The chapters dealing with the causal analyses show that the rarity of the acts reported suggests an analysis approach that focuses on initiation of behavior patterns. It was necessary to compute special measures of delinquency for those analyses.[6] The measures differentiate among those who committed the act for the first time during the course of the study (after Wave I), those who had previously been involved in delinquency, and those who remained uninvolved throughout the study.

Initiation of delinquency was assessed by comparing a boy's report in a given wave with his report in previous waves. Obviously, this was only possible when prior data were available, not in Wave I or for new respondents.[7]

[5]See Documentation 12 "Correlates of Aggression Among Teenage Boys".

[6]Models assessing effects on continuation of delinquent behavior could not be estimated because of the rarity of the acts.

[7]A limited check was available in Wave II as only three delinquency items were asked in Wave I.

TABLE 10.5

A: Delinquency Items: Descriptive Statistics

	DURING THE LAST 3 MONTHS			
	NUMBER WHO COMMITTED THE ACT	NUMBER WHO DID NOT COMMIT THE ACT	PERCENTAGE WHO COMMITTED ACT	*N*
Badly beaten up				
Wave I	19	382	4.7	(401)
Wave II	38	531	6.7	(569)
Wave III	35	533	6.2	(568)
Wave IV	33	640	4.9	(673)
Wave V	24	620	3.7	(644)
Arrested				
Wave I	14	386	3.5	(400)
Wave II	46	522	8.1	(568)
Wave III	33	535	5.8	(568)
Wave IV	44	625	6.6	(669)
Wave V	42	602	6.5	(644)
In a gang fight				
Wave I	18	382	4.5	(402)
Wave II	51	518	9.0	(569)
Wave III	45	523	7.9	(568)
Wave IV	27	644	4.0	(671)
Wave V	30	610	4.7	(640)
Stole a car				
Wave II	25	544	4.6	(569)
Wave III	24	545	4.2	(567)
Wave IV	24	649	3.6	(673)
Wave V	21	623	3.3	(644)
Mugged				
Wave II	24	545	4.2	(569)
Wave III	16	552	2.8	(568)
Wave IV	12	661	1.8	(673)
Wave V	6	638	.9	(643)
Knifed				
Wave II	18	550	3.2	(568)
Wave III	16	550	2.8	(566)
Wave IV	13	658	1.9	(671)
Wave V	5	639	.8	(644)

(Continued next page)

TABLE 10.5 (*continued*)
B. Delinquency: Descriptive Statistics

	NUMBER OF ACTS COMMITTED DURING THE LAST 3 MONTHS								
	0	1	2	3	4	5	6	MEAN	*N*
Wave II[a]	460	57	28	9	6	4	3	.36	(567)
Wave III	469	66	14	5	2	3	6	.30	(565)
Wave IV	564	71	21	2	4	3	0	.23	(665)
Wave V	556	60	12	8	1	2	1	.20	(640)

[a]No Wave I measure was computed, as only three of the six items were available.

The comparison of responses in one wave with those in other waves was also used to correct inconsistencies between different waves.[8]

The large differences in the number of boys who report committing an act for the first time between waves is noteworthy. The explanation is simple: The number is large when the interval between waves is large and small when two waves are only a few months apart.[9]

The second column in Table 10.6 lists the number of respondents who never committed the act; the total number of cases in the last column is the sum of

---

[8]For example, if a boy reported at Time III that he had never committed an act, but had admitted to such behavior in the previous wave, it was assumed that he did in fact commit it.

In the same way, corrections were applied through inspection of later waves. (Again an example: If a boy reported at Time II that he did not commit an act, but admitted at Time III that he had committed it a year ago, he was credited with that act at Time II.) Such retrospective edits were possible in Waves II and IV, but not in Wave III as Wave IV was more than a year after Wave III.

The data items were coded in a manner that corrects for those inconsistencies that were not corrected by the editors of the questionnaires. All corrections of this kind assumed the "I did it" reports to be correct. It was reasoned that a boy who had never committed such an act would not report that he had done it some time ago. On the other hand, it is quite plausible that some boys did not admit such behavior soon after it happened, but a year or so later did report that it happened some time ago.

These corrections increased the number of boys coded as having committed one or more delinquency acts considerably. In Wave IV, for example, 51% reported never having committed any such act. The inspection of reports in the previous waves and in Wave V reduces that percentage by 20% to 31%. In other waves, the reductions are similar (ranging from 17% in Wave II to 24% in Wave V).

[9]The longest lag is between Waves III and IV (1 year, 7 months), the shortest between Waves IV and V (5 months). Consequently, the highest "did act for the first time" figures are in Wave IV, the lowest in Wave V. In contrast, few boys reported delinquency for the first time in Wave V, since the IV–V lag is only 5 months. (In addition, Wave V data could not be corrected by inspection of a later wave, which would probably have increased the number of "initiators" in Wave V. This is also true of Wave III data.)

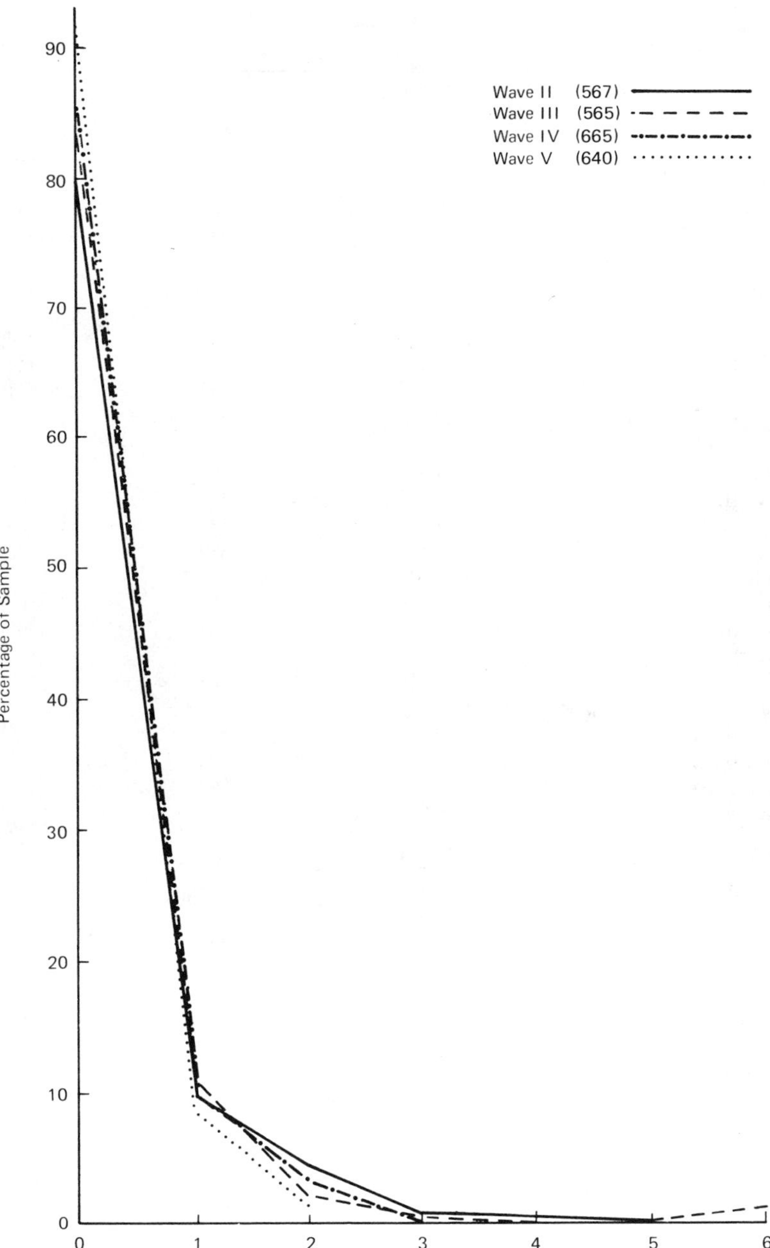

FIGURE 10.4. *Number of delinquent acts committed in past three weeks (Waves II–V).*

TABLE 10.6
Special Measures of Delinquency for Causal Analyses: Descriptive Statistics

	NUMBER WHO COMMITTED THE ACT FOR FIRST TIME	NUMBER WHO NEVER COMMITTED ACT	N^a
Badly beaten up			
Wave II	91	364	(455)
Wave III	40	340	(380)
Wave IV	109	366	(475)
Wave V	16	337	(353)
Arrested			
Wave II	74	445	(519)
Wave III	44	410	(454)
Wave IV	96	445	(541)
Wave V	19	419	(438)
In a gang fight			
Wave II	85	392	(477)
Wave III	55	352	(407)
Wave IV	103	385	(488)
Wave V	14	359	(373)
Stole a car			
Wave II	75[b]	494	(569)
Wave III	33	467	(500)
Wave IV	60	529	(589)
Wave V	6	503	(509)
Mugged			
Wave II	46[b]	523	(569)
Wave III	32	493	(525)
Wave IV	44	569	(613)
Wave V	6	543	(549)
Knifed			
Wave II	63[b]	505	(568)
Wave III	24	483	(507)
Wave IV	46	558	(604)
Wave V	4	535	(539)
Delinquency aggression: (all six measures combined)			
Wave II	163	226	(389)
Wave III	54	198	(252)
Wave IV	144	206	(350)
Wave V	15	185	(200)

[a]Excluded are those who have done act previously (delinquency aggression: one or more acts).
[b]No Wave I data available.

TABLE 10.7
Correlations between Aggression Measures (Average of Five Waves)

	PERSONAL AGGRESSION	TEACHER AGGRESSION	PROPERTY AGGRESSION
Teacher aggression	.28		
Property aggression	.27	.30	
Delinquency	.21	.22	.19

Columns 1 and 2. Excluded from these samples are respondents who have committed the act previously and, of course, those with missing data. These samples, then, are considerably smaller than those in Table 10.5 because boys who committed an act are excluded from all following samples. The sample sizes do not shrink from wave to wave, though, because new respondents are included in the table.[10]

Relationships among Measures

Table 10.7 shows the cross-sectional correlations among the four aggression measures.[11] As this table shows, the measures are not completely independent. But average correlations are small, ranging from .30 for teacher and property aggression to .19 for property and delinquency aggression.

PROPERTIES OF THE AGGRESSION MEASURES

Reliability of the Personal, Teacher, and Property Aggression Indexes

RELIABILITY OF SPECIFIC ITEMS

To help increase our ability to assess consistency, we repeated some of the questions about involvement in aggression. As just noted, these involved two different question formats—one asking respondents the number of times they had engaged in a particular activity in the past 4 weeks, the other asking them to report the last time they had engaged in this activity.

[10]See Table 9.5 on respondents who were added to the sample after Wave I. Sample sizes are smallest for delinquency aggression, since a boy who was involved in any one of the six acts in a previous wave was excluded from all samples. In this case, sample sizes do shrink over the course of the study.

[11]The measure of delinquency used is the one shown in Table 10.5, not the special measure that was computed for the causal analyses (Table 10.6).

TABLE 10.8
Reliability of Report: Engaged in Act in Recent Months (Yes–No)

	PERCENTAGE MAKING ERRORS (*N*)		
	FOUGHT	DAMAGED	STOLE
Wave I error	13% (51)	18% (70)	19% (75)
Wave II error			
First type[a]	5% (28)	6% (31)	6% (32)
Second type	1% (5)	3% (14)	1% (4)
Wave III error	5% (27)	7% (39)	7% (38)
Wave IV error	2% (16)	3% (18)	3% (19)
Wave V error	4% (25)	4% (23)	3% (20)

[a]In Waves I and III-V the "last time" responses could be, at the most recent, sometime in the past 3 months. This means that only one type of inconsistency could be detected—that associated with a report that a particular act had been committed at least once in the last 4 weeks and a report that the last time was longer than 3 months ago. In Wave II the "last time" question included a response for involvement in the past month. This new category allowed for a second kind of inconsistency—that associated with a report that the last time was within the past month and that the act was committed 0 times in the past 4 weeks.

The Wave I test–retest results for the dichotomous measure, "Was the boy involved in this activity at all during the past month?" were disappointing. Between 13% and 19% of teens who reported that they had stolen, damaged property, or fought at least once in the past 4 weeks also reported that the last time they had been involved in one of these acts was more than 3 months ago.

We considered this inconsistency a serious problem and, as a result, we revised our data collection procedures after Wave I. Beginning in Wave II a group of coders checked for inconsistencies of this sort immediately after the questionnaires had been filled out. If discrepancies were found, the boy was asked for the correct answer and the questionnaire was edited to correct the initial inaccuracy.

Table 10.8 shows the number and percentage of inconsistencies for the three repeated questions in each of the five waves. It is clear here that the editing in Waves II, III, IV, and V was successful in reducing inconsistent responses. In Wave I, inconsistency ranged from 13% to 19%. In later waves inconsistency was never higher than 7% and was in two instances as low as 1%.[12]

[12]When the items were edited, both the original and changed responses were recorded, thus allowing for some analysis of the types of changes made. The changes are not heavily biased

TABLE 10.9
Reliabilities of Individual Aggression Items[a]

	FOUGHT	DAMAGED	STOLE
Wave I	.555	.361	.340
Wave II	.864	.799	.860
Wave III	.843	.762	.781
Wave IV	.901	.877	.897
Wave V	.814	.833	.885

[a]Reliability estimates are ϕ coefficients between dichotomous responses about involvement in each activity in the past month. Responses about this involvement for the "last time" question are available only in Wave II, where inconsistencies associated with this response are approximately 50% as large as those associated with the frequency question. In the computation of the reliability coefficients, it is assumed that this ratio of errors holds in the other waves as well.

The reliabilities of reported involvement in fighting, damaging property, and stealing are reported in Table 10.9. As shown there, the Wave I reliabilities are all quite low, ranging from .34 to .56. However, beginning with Wave II the field editing had the effect of increasing reliabilities of these items dramatically, to between .76 and .90.

RELIABILITY OF THE INDEXES

Although the reliabilities of individual aggression items after Wave I appears quite high, internal consistency reliability estimates for the indexes made up of these items are low. Table 10.10 presents these estimates. Across the five waves, personal aggression has a reliability between .70 and .75, teacher aggression has a reliability between .60 and .68, and property aggression has a reliability between .43 and .52.

These reliabilities are considerably lower than those found for the aggression measures for boys and girls. Initially, we had designed the study in such a way that 13 indicators would go into a single aggression scale for teens. However, when the factor analysis showed that four distinct dimensions of aggression exist among these 13 indicators, we were forced to create multiple scales, each

toward one item or the other, indicating that no item is consistently incorrect. When changes were made in the "4 weeks" item, they were most often from having done the act to not having done it. When a boy chose to change the "last time occurred" items, it was usually from the act not occurring in the last 3 months to its having occurred. Thus, the changes in these items are generally split evenly between "doing" and "not doing."

TABLE 10.10
Reliability of Teen-Aggression Measures[a]

	WAVE				
	I	II	III	IV	V
1. *Personal aggression items (Heise-Bohrnstedt reliability measure)*					
Fought with someone					
Pushed, shoved, or hit someone	.71	.75	.75	.73	.70
Got into a heated argument	(400)	(562)	(565)	(673)	(643)
2. *Teacher aggression items (correlations)*					
Talked rudely to a teacher	.66	.60	.61	.68	.64
Made fun of a teacher	(401)	(568)	(562)	(649)	(616)
3. *Property aggression items (correlations)*					
Stole something	.43	.44	.47	.52	.45
Damaged property purposely	(402)	(569)	(568)	(674)	(644)

[a]*N*s are given in parentheses.

containing only a few indicators. As a result, each turned out to have a lower reliability than we would have preferred.[13]

Given the differentiation of adolescent aggression into multiple factors, and the good test–retest reliability of the items, we first suspected that these low reliabilities reflected inadequacies in the reliability formulas rather than the data. We consequently estimated more complex measurement models, taking into consideration the longitudinal as well as cross-sectional data. For each scale separately a series of five-wave measurement models was estimated. (The detailed results of these analyses are presented in Appendix B in Chapter 13.)

Although every effort was made to develop an accurate model of the scale reliabilities, two discouraging results were obtained. First, no plausible measurement model was found to fit the observed data well for any of the three sets of items—personal, teacher, or property aggression. Second, the reliability estimates for the best-fitting models were no larger than those reported in Table 10.10.

These low reliabilities reflect not only the fact that the factor structures in Table 10.2 are more diverse (multidimensional rather than unidimensional) than

[13]Much of the previous research that obtained self-reports on adolescents' aggression failed to report data on the reliability of aggression scales (e.g., Belson, 1978; Lefkowitz *et al.*, 1977). Hirschi (1969) reported pairwise correlations of .20 to .48 between his aggression items, which are somewhat lower than the reliabilities of our two-item teacher and property aggression measures. Donovan (1974, 1977), on the other hand, reported very high reliabilities (Cronbach's α of about .85) with scales consisting of 12 and 26 items.

the comparable elementary school data, but also that the factor loadings are not nearly as high as those reported for the elementary students (where the loadings averaged well over .8).

Two different interpretations of this weaker factor structure come to mind. One is that the items in the teen questionnaire are comparatively weak indicators of behavior dispositions toward the different types of aggression (personal, property, teacher) in which teens engage. The other is that aggression among teenagers is simply too diverse to be captured adequately in a few factors.

As the reliabilities of the individual items are high after Wave I, the latter interpretation is the more plausible of the two. Nonetheless, in the interpretation of the causal models presented in subsequent chapters, these low reliabilities are taken at face value as reflecting imprecise measurement rather than differentiation of accurately reported behaviors. This decision to underestimate reliability maximizes our chances of detecting a significant association between television and aggression.

Reliability of the Delinquency Measure

Table 10.2 shows that the six delinquency questions have moderate factor loadings; if we had worked with these original questions, we could, in fact, assume that this dimension had a reliability somewhat larger than .6. However, as noted above, the analysis to be presented in Chapter 13 makes use of a dichotomous version of the original response: one that simply records whether or not the respondent reports involvement in any of the delinquent activities during the preceding 3 months.

We have no way of knowing the precise reliability of this modified dichotomous measure, although it is likely that the reliability of the original version is its lower bound. In our interpretation of substantive associations between delinquency and television exposure, in Chapter 13, we consider this issue in more detail.

Validity

Given the low reliabilities, it is not possible for the aggression scales to have high validity. But it is important to assure ourselves that what systematic variation does exist in the scales is associated with real aggression rather than with bragging or aggressive attitudes or some other influence only tangentially related to aggressive behavior. Several indications that the scales validly measure aggression have already been reported. We noted that the prosocial behavior items are differentiated from aggression items in exploratory factor analyses and that the aggression indexes form J-shaped distributions. In addition, we found that the indexes correlate with other variables, such as involvement with aggressive friends, in meaningful and expected ways. This is further evidence for validity.

More direct tests, reported in the following, add support to these inferential ones.[14]

1. The most direct validity test came at the end of the Wave II questionnaire, when boys were asked how honest they were in answering the questionnaire ("completely honest" 46%; "very honest" 40%, "moderately honest" 12%, "not very/not at all honest" 2%). The correlations between this question and teacher, property, and delinquency aggression are not significantly different from 0. The correlation between the question and personal aggression is significant, but still only .11. Thus, the overall evidence indicates that the stated degree of honesty is not related to the level of self-reported aggression.

2. School records in both cities were examined for comments by teachers on social behavior in the 1969–1970 school year.[15]

Teachers' comments on social behavior were only available in Minneapolis. For prosocial comments, records were categorized into actively prosocial, passively prosocial, neutral, and no mention, and the means of Wave I aggression and Wave II delinquency were computed for each of these categories. (Wave I data are used because the first wave corresponds most closely in time to the 1969–1970 school year. For delinquency, Wave II data were used because there is no such measure in Wave I.) Here, the expectation is that higher mean aggression will appear in the "neutral" and "no mention" categories, based on the obvious reasoning that those who report more aggressive behavior are less likely to be perceived by teachers as being prosocial in school. Table 10.11(a) shows that this expectation is upheld for personal and property aggression. On teacher aggression and delinquency, the means for the "neutral" and "no mention" categories are among the highest,

[14]As we discussed in the earlier section on validity, though, totally convincing proof of the validity of a measure is usually not possible in the social sciences because criteria of known validity against which to compare a measure rarely exist. In light of this, validity checks must be conducted by comparing the measure to other measures whose validity is also unknown but which seem to be similar and valid on intuitive grounds. The checks presented in the following are of this sort.

[15]This source cannot be expected to replicate exactly the reports of aggressive behavior by the adolescents themselves because the school environment does not represent the total reality of behavior for a teenage boy and because school records encompass the unknown variable of the teachers' perceptions. Additionally, the school data are not available for the entire sample, and in some cases the sample sizes for subgroups is too small to be certain of conclusions. Nevertheless, some correspondence should be seen between these data and the self-reports of aggression. As detailed in the following, there is in fact a reasonable degree of correspondence between the school record data and the aggression measures.

TABLE 10.11
Teacher Comments and Aggression Measures in Minneapolis

	PERSONAL AGGRESSION		TEACHER AGGRESSION		PROPERTY AGGRESSION		DELINQUENCY AGGRESSION	
	MEAN	*N*	MEAN	*N*	MEAN	*N*	MEAN	*N*
a. Actively prosocial	3.3	(32)	2.6	(33)	1.2	(33)	.03	(33)
Passively prosocial	3.7	(79)	2.2	(80)	1.2	(79)	.15	(81)
Neutral	3.8	(31)	2.6	(31)	2.4	(31)	.13	(30)
No mention	4.0	(66)	4.0	(66)	2.7	(66)	.22	(69)
b. Actively antisocial	4.6	(14)	4.3	(14)	1.6	(14)	.27	(11)
Passively antisocial	5.3	(30)	5.6	(31)	2.9	(31)	.16	(32)
Has improved	2.5	(10)	5.5	(10)	3.7	(10)	.25	(8)
Emotional problems	6.6	(20)	2.3	(20)	2.4	(20)	.21	(24)
No mention	3.0	(134)	2.0	(135)	1.4	(134)	.12	(138)
c. Mean for entire sample	3.7	(214)	3.0	(210)	1.9	(209)	.16	(216)
Violent/Problem behaviors	7.8	(16)	5.2	(16)	3.1	(16)	.50	(12)
No mention	3.1	(123)	2.3	(124)	1.4	(123)	.94	(128)

but they are not as clearly distinguished from the aggression means in the prosocial categories.

3. Another set of teachers' comments was categorized into activity antisocial, passively antisocial, has improved, emotional problems, and no mentions. Here, the hypothesis was that the "no mention" category would exhibit lower mean aggression scores than the antisocial categories. The "has improved" group may not necessarily have low aggression means since an improvement does not always imply an absence of aggression. As shown in Table 10.11(b) for all aggression measures, the means are lower for the "no mention" group and the antisocial groups generally have higher means. The "improved" category is too small for comparison. We did not have a hypothesis for those classified as having emotional problems, because those problems may or may not manifest themselves in aggressive behavior. As it turned out, the group with emotional problems was high in personal aggression.

4. In a miscellaneous group of teachers' comments, four categories were identified as possibly being related to aggressive behavior: emotional problems, attendance problems, exhibiting violent behavior, and special school problems. Unfortunately, the sample sizes are too small for analysis with emotional, attendance, and special school problems. However, some information can still be obtained: as seen in Table 10.11(c), if a teenager was *not* mentioned as having one of the miscellaneous problems, the mean aggression score of all types except delinquency is significantly lower than the overall mean. The "violent/problem behaviors" category, while small, most closely corresponds

to the self-report aggression measures, and this category also shows means higher than the overall means.

5. In addition to comments on behavior by teachers, the school records contained citizenship grades for some students. In Minneapolis, these grades correlated −.19 with personal aggression, −.36 with property aggression, −.36 with teacher aggression, and −.22 with delinquency. Clearly, one would not expect very high correlations between citizenship grades and self-reported aggressive behavior because different concepts are being measured in different ways. However, these observed correlations show a reasonable degree of correspondence between the two measures in the expected direction, especially given the relatively low reliabilities of the aggression scales.

Although the sample sizes in Fort Worth are too small for definitive conclusions, there, too, the highest aggression scores are obtained by those with the worst citizenship grades.

6. Another indication of the validity of the aggression measures is the correlation between them and mothers' reports about the boys' aggression. Mothers were questioned about how often their sons had gotten into fights with children outside the family: "often," "occasionally," "seldom," or "never." This measure correlated .33 with Wave I personal aggression, .19 with Wave II personal aggression, and .39 with Wave II delinquency.[16]

7. We obtained friends' reports on some aggression items, which makes it possible to examine the relationship between friends' and self-reports.[17] In Wave I the correlation between these two types of reports (for boys with at least four friends reporting on their aggression) are .13 for stealing, .30 for damaging property, and .25 for fighting.[18]

8. The distribution of delinquent acts in this study is similar to that reported by Belson for "very violent" acts committed by his sample of London adolescents (1978: 356).[19] It should be noted, however, that not only his sample but also the aggression items used by Belson are quite different from ours, making strict comparisons impossible.[20]

---

[16]These aggression measures were the most appropriate ones for comparison because they are closest in time and type of aggression to the question asked of mothers.

[17]Since it would have increased the length of the questionnaire greatly to have each boy report in detail on the aggression of each of his friends, only a sample of aggression items were replicated through friends' reports.

[18]We found that the correlations between self-reports and friends' reports decreased in later waves. Further analysis of this, though, showed that it reflects the fact that boys who were friends at Wave I tended to lose touch with each other over the course of the study.

[19]Belson's data are based on the number of acts committed during a 6-month period. We computed delinquency scores based on the same time interval. (The data in Table 10.5B and Figure 10.4 are based on 3 months.)

[20]Comparisons with studies of delinquency in this country are also difficult because of differences in methodology. Studies by Hirschi (1969) and Donovan (1974, 1977), for example, used items that tap less serious acts than our items. (E.g., "Have you ever taken a car for a ride

Stability of Aggression

The fact that this is a panel study makes it important to see how much aggression itself changes over time. The more stable aggression is, the less change there is for television or any other variable to explain.

PERSONAL AGGRESSION

Table 10.12 shows, above the diagonal, the correlations between personal aggression in an earlier wave with personal aggression in each later wave. These correlations tend to be slightly higher in the short wave pairs than in the long wave pairs. Correlations for the elementary school measure of aggression were higher than these.

Below the diagonal of Table 10.12 are presented the same correlations adjusted for the reliabilities estimated in Table 10.9. Although our earlier discussion shows that we have little faith in these reliability estimates, we accept them as lower bounds on the reliability of the aggression indexes. For purposes of assessing if there is observable change in aggression over the time interval of the panel, then, they are acceptable. As we see from the table, these adjusted autocorrelations are still not very high.

TEACHER AGGRESSION

Table 10.13 presents data on the stability of teacher aggression. The autocorrelations are somewhat higher in the short and lower in the long lags compared with those for personal aggression. The adjusted autocorrelations range from .35 to .91.

PROPERTY AGGRESSION

The autocorrelations for property aggression are presented above the diagonal in Table 10.14. They have a range similar to teacher aggression: .36 to .54 in the short wave pairs to .18 in the longest wave pair.

The fact that property aggression is less reliable than teacher aggression is reflected in the larger increases for property aggression autocorrelations when they are adjusted for measurement unreliability. The adjusted correlation for wave pair IV–V is greater than 1.0, reflecting the fact that our reliability estimates are lower bounds on the true reliability of these indexes.

DELINQUENCY

The measure of delinquency consists of more serious and rarer behaviors than the other types examined. In addition, it is measured on an occur/not occur basis, and the causal analysis (presented in Chapter 13) does not examine

without the owner's permission," Hirschi, 1969. In our study the most similar item is: "You went for a joy ride in a stolen car.") The frequencies of these milder kinds of behavior in Hirschi's and Donovan's research are higher than those reported in our study.

increases or decreases from one value of the variable to another. For this reason, the stability of the variable itself is not relevant here. Nonetheless, delinquency is a rather stable phenomenon. The large majority of adolescents who have not committed a delinquent act in one wave continue not to commit the act in the later waves. Conversely, many of those who committed an act previously do so again.

TABLE 10.12
Stability of Personal Aggression: Adjusted and Unadjusted Autocorrelations between all Wave Pairs[a]

WAVES	I	II	III	IV	V
I		.45 (369)	.40 (365)	.27 (327)	.40 (316)
II	.62		.48 (512)	.32 (464)	.40 (455)
III	.55	.64		.44 (481)	.40 (468)
IV	.38	.43	.60		.49 (622)
V	.57	.55	.55	.69	

[a]Unadjusted autocorrelations are given above the diagonal; autocorrelations adjusted for measurement unreliabilities below.

TABLE 10.13
Stability of Teacher Aggression: Adjusted and Unadjusted Autocorrelations between all Wave Pairs[a]

WAVES	I	II	III	IV	V
I		.54 (372)	.43 (366)	.36 (317)	.23 (302)
II	.86		.49 (516)	.33 (452)	.40 (438)
III	.68	.81		.38 (463)	.37 (448)
IV	.54	.51	.59		.60 (590)
V	.35	.65	.59	.91	

[a]Unadjusted autocorrelations are given above the diagonal; autocorrelations adjusted for measurement unreliabilities below.

TABLE 10.14
Stability of Property Aggression:
Adjusted and Unadjusted Autocorrelations between all Wave Pairs[a]

WAVES	I	II	III	IV	V
I		.42 (373)	.35 (368)	.25 (329)	.18 (319)
II	.96		.36 (579)	.34 (468)	.28 (459)
III	.78	.79		.42 (484)	.43 (471)
IV	.53	.71	.85		.54 (624)
V	.41	.63	.93	1.12	

[a] Unadjusted autocorrelations are given above the diagonal; autocorrelations adjusted for measurement unreliabilities below. See discussion in text.

CHAPTER 11

TELEVISION EXPOSURE MEASURE

Television exposure was measured through self-administered program checklists quite similar to those used for the elementary school sample. The measure for the younger sample had been made simple and short, and special administrative procedures had been designed to meet the needs of those respondents. No such problems were anticipated with adolescents, and therefore the checklists were somewhat longer and more complex.

In this chapter, the checklists and the program samples are discussed first. A description of the computation of the exposure indices follows. The issue of reporting validity, a major problem in the study of elementary school children, is also discussed.

DEVELOPMENT AND PRETEST

The television exposure measures for elementary school children and adolescents were developed at the same time. A program checklist method used by the Brand Rating Index research service seemed to fit our needs, but had to be simplified for the younger respondents. Teenagers, however, experienced very few problems with it. A small pretest with less than a dozen boys indicated this to us initially, and the validity analyses reported in the following show that only a very small group of the teenage sample had problems filling out the exposure checklists. Still, we included "dummy" programs in the checklists for the teens, as we had for younger respondents, in order to be able to check on poor reporting.

PROGRAM CHECKLISTS

The television programs were listed in a section of the self-administered questionnaire. In each wave the checklists were presented in four parts, starting with prime-time programs. The second section listed programs shown every weekday,[1] the third Saturday and Sunday daytime programs (which include children's programs), and the last section, movies shown on television. Figure 11.1 is an example of a checklist for prime-time shows.[2]

Almost half of the programs listed are prime-time shows (about 26). The larger proportion of prime-time programs for teenagers than for elementary school respondents reflects the different viewing habits of the older boys. The number of daily programs averages 12; close to 9 weekend daytime shows and 11 movies were also listed. For a listing of all programs samples, see Appendix A.[3]

Each group of programs contained a dummy program in addition to the sampled programs. (See Appendix A for a listing of all dummy items.)

CONSTRUCTION OF EXPOSURE MEASURES

The television viewing information was converted into two exposure indices; one measures total amount of viewing the other viewing of violent

[1]The weekday list covered 2 weeks, other program lists referred to the last 4 weeks. In the elementary school children study, the daily program list referred to the last week, other lists to the last 4 weeks.

[2]The number of programs listed was slightly larger in the first wave than in the following waves. However, Wave I program lists for one of the study cities were printed in all questionnaires by mistake and, as a result, only the programs listed shown in both cities could be used for analysis. The net outcome is that the number of programs in the five waves is very similar; it averages about 57. (In Wave I, 63 programs were listed; 5 were shown in only one of the cities.)

[3]The program checklists did not contain all programs aired, but samples, for three reasons. First, time considerations precluded asking the boys about hundreds of programs. Second, listing that many programs would have been confusing even to the older respondents. Third, ratings told us that many programs were not watched by teenagers; thus, it was decided to include only programs watched by at least some teens. For example, programs shown during school hours were excluded.

A number of other decisions about the program samples, identical to those made for the elementary school samples, were made: Violent programs were overselected, but all kinds of programs were represented in the sample; the samples in the two cities were matched, and the samples from wave to wave were made comparable.

Complex program selection procedures were designed to ensure that the samples would meet the objectives listed. These procedures were identical to those used in selecting the program samples for elementary school children, except that programs seen by at least 2% of teenagers (rather than 2% of 6- to 11-year-olds) were selected and there was no limit on the number of programs per checklist.

TELEVISION VIEWING

15. Below is a list of nighttime television programs that are shown once a week. Next to each program, please check the box that describes how many times your personally watched this program in the last four weeks.

IF YOU DO NOT WATCH THE PROGRAM, CHECK THE FIRST BOX.

IF YOU WATCH THE PROGRAM NOW AND THEN BUT HAVE NOT WATCHED IT IN THE LAST FOUR WEEKS, CHECK THE NEXT BOX.

IF YOU HAVE WATCHED THE PROGRAM IN THE LAST FOUR WEEKS, THEN CHECK THE BOX THAT TELLS HOW MANY OF THE LAST 4 SHOWS YOU HAVE WATCHED.

Please be sure to check only one box next to each program.-

We have listed the nights that the programs are shown in most places. Even if you watch the program on a different night, please be sure to check the number of times you have watched it.

Nighttime Television Shows	Do Not Watch Program	Watch Program Now And Then But Not In Last 4 Weeks	In The Last 4 Weeks I Watched 1 Show	2 Shows	3 Shows	4 Shows	
	0	X	1	2	3	4	
MONDAY NIGHT							
Bird's Eye View	☐	☐	☐	☐	☐	☐	(11)
Gunsmoke	☐	☐	☐	☐	☐	☐	(12)
Laugh-In	☐	☐	☐	☐	☐	☐	(13)
TUESDAY NIGHT							
Mod Squad	☐	☐	☐	☐	☐	☐	(14)
Julia	☐	☐	☐	☐	☐	☐	(15)
All in the Family . . .	☐	☐	☐	☐	☐	☐	(16)
WEDNESDAY NIGHT							
Eddie's Father	☐	☐	☐	☐	☐	☐	(17)
Room 222	☐	☐	☐	☐	☐	☐	(18)
Tough Twosome	☐	☐	☐	☐	☐	☐	(19)
THURSDAY NIGHT							
Ironside	☐	☐	☐	☐	☐	☐	(20)
Bewitched	☐	☐	☐	☐	☐	☐	(21)
Dan August	☐	☐	☐	☐	☐	☐	(22)
	0	X	1	2	3	4	

FIGURE 11.1. *Example of program checklist page (reduced from 8½ × 11 page).*

programs. The methods used to construct these indices were very similar to those used for the elementary school samples.

Total Television Exposure Index

The reported frequency of viewing each weekly show (prime-time and Saturday/Sunday daytime programs) during the last 4 weeks was multiplied by its duration, hour shows counting twice as much as half-hour shows. A similar procedure was followed for daily (Monday–Friday) shows. The reported frequency of viewing these shows during the last 2 weeks was multiplied by their duration, and that score was doubled to make it comparable with the weekly shows' score, based on a 4-week period. The movie information was standardized to represent hours of exposure in a 4-week period and was added to the program exposure scores. The total score was divided by 10 to make figures less cumbersome.[4]

Table 11.1 shows the descriptive statistics of the total exposure measure for the five waves. The distributions of scores are presented in Figure 11.2.[5]

Wave I, III, and V data were collected in the spring (May), Wave II in October/November, and Wave IV in December. According to television ratings, we should expect higher viewing reports for fall and winter than for spring. Table 11.1, in fact, shows higher means and medians for Waves II and IV. Otherwise, there is not much variation from wave to wave.

A comparison of ratings for children and adolescents shows that teens view considerably less television than children.[6] The differences between the measures for elementary school children and teenage boys do not allow an exact comparison. But, even though the program samples for teens are somewhat larger—which would result in higher scores, all other things being equal—means and medians are smaller for teens in all waves.[7]

---

[4]Reports of viewing a show "now and then, but not in the last 4 (2) weeks" were ignored, because the total exposure scores with and without that information were correlated almost perfectly.

[5]The data shown are based on the total sample of teenage boys in each wave. In the equivalent table for elementary school children, "less valid" reporters were excluded.

[6]For example, a Nielsen report for December 1972 (the time of Wave IV) estimates 27 hr of viewing per week for 6- to 11-year-olds, 21 hr for teenage boys (Nielsen NAC report, December 1972).

[7]As discussed in the section on validity which follows, this indicates lower viewing levels for adolescents, a finding which is corroborated by the rating services. (Because of the larger samples, the range is larger for teens. Standard deviations are similar. In interpreting the range and standard deviation, it should be remembered that scores are divided by 10.)

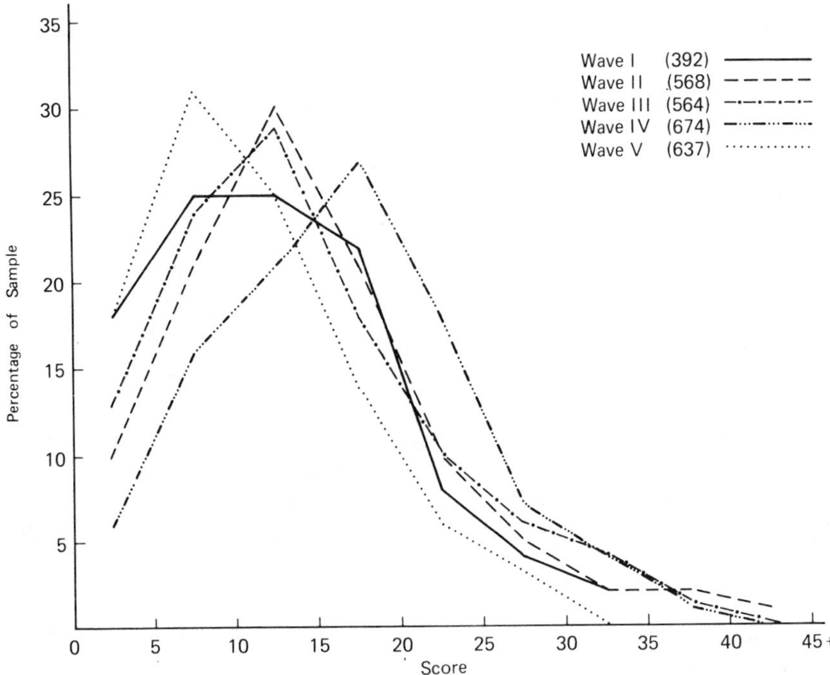

FIGURE 11.2. *Total television exposure measure: Score distribution in Waves I–V.*

Violent Television Exposure Index

The violent television exposure index was constructed in basically the same way as that for elementary school children described in Chapter 4: Individual programs were weighted by violence weights and then added according to the computation procedures for the total exposure measure. Appendix A lists the violence weights of all programs in all waves.

TABLE 11.1
Total Television Exposure Descriptive Statistics for All Five Waves

	WAVE				
	I	II	III	IV	V
Median	10.8	12.5	11.5	16.0	9.7
Mean	11.4	13.6	12.9	16.3	11.1
Mode	11	11	10	18	6
Standard deviation	6.7	7.8	8.1	8.0	7.7
Range	0–33	1–52	0–61	0–48	0–54
Skewness	.6	1.4	1.2	.6	1.4
N	(392)	(568)	(564)	(674)	(637)

TABLE 11.2
Violent Television Exposure Descriptive Statistics for All Five Waves

	WAVE				
	I	II	III	IV	V
Median	31.3	38.2	30.4	46.1	21.8
Mean	34.6	42.9	35.8	47.1	26.6
Mode	26	37	25	37	19
Standard deviation	22.4	25.5	25.3	24.8	21.0
Range	0–109	2–158	0–163	0–144	0–134
Skewness	.7	1.2	1.2	.6	1.5
N	(392)	(568)	(564)	(674)	(637)

Table 11.2 summarizes the descriptive statistics and Figure 11.3 shows the distribution of the scores of the violence exposure measure in all five waves. Total exposure and violence exposure are highly related among adolescents, as they are among elementary school boys.[8] The correlations average .90 in the five waves.[9]

PROPERTIES OF THE VIOLENT TELEVISION EXPOSURE INDEX

Reliability

As the television exposure measure is a sum of reported behaviors, the use of conventional internal consistency reliability estimates is conceptually inappropriate. In order to assess reliability, then, we estimated longitudinal models of test–retest reliability. This was done in two separate longitudinal samples: (*a*) the sample of respondents who were part of the study in all five waves ($N = 293$); and (*b*) the sample of boys who entered the study in Wave II and remained for the next four waves ($N = 134$). The methodology used to estimate these models is detailed in the measurement appendix of Chapter 6. The reliability coefficients for the five-wave model average .75; for the four-

[8]Violence exposure scores (like total exposure scores) are highest in Waves II and IV, which were conducted during the fall and winter, respectively, when viewing is higher.

There is more variation in the violence exposure scores than in total exposure. This is not surprising because the former scores depend not only on the total amount of viewing but also which kind of programs happened to be most popular at the time of the survey. For example, in Wave II, the wave with the highest violence exposure scores, the most popular programs were *Monday Night Football, Hawaii 5-O,* and *Mannix*; *The Dirty Dozen* was one of the most watched movies on television. Three of these programs received the highest violence weight (see Appendix A). In Wave V, which has the lowest violence exposure scores, the most popular shows were *Kung Fu*, *Sanford & Son*, *Emergency*, and *All in the Family*. Three of these shows received low violence weights.

[9]The Pearson correlations in the five waves are: Wave I .88 ($N = 392$); Wave II .92 (568); Wave II .91 (564); Wave IV .90 (674); Wave V .89 (637).

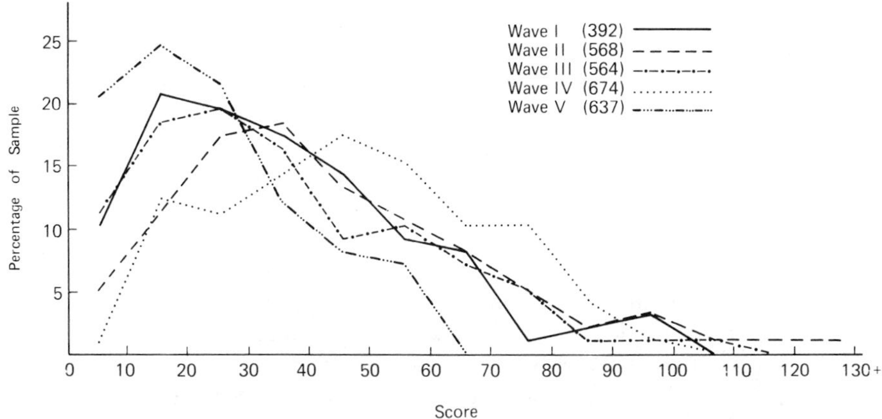

FIGURE 11.3. *Violent television exposure measure: Score distribution in Waves I–V.*

wave model .74. These coefficients are slightly higher than the comparable estimates for the valid elementary school boys (.68), suggesting that older boys report their viewing more accurately.

There was an opportunity to collect some additional data on the test–retest reliability of the television exposure measure in Wave IV, when a sample of boys was asked to fill out a one-page exposure report containing questions about six prime-time, four daily daytime, and four television movies.[10] This was done immediately after completion of the regular questionnaire. These same programs were part of the regular exposure question, thus making it possible to examine short-term reliability in detail.

There was total agreement in the responses for 73% of the prime-time and 68% of the daily programs. Twenty percent of the responses to prime-time and 28% of the responses to daily programs were off by 1 point (e.g., indicated seeing a program once every 4 weeks in one questionnaire and twice every 4 weeks in the other). In 7% of the prime-time and 4% of the daily programs there was substantial disagreement. Answers about seeing television movies were identical 96% of the time. (Since the movie list had a "seen–not seen" format, this means that 4% gave conflicting reports.)[11]

[10]The sheet also contained aggression questions. As the television questions were in the middle of the regular questionnaire, it seems likely that most respondents were not able to give identical answers based on correct recall of their previous answers.

[11]It should be remembered that the respondents are a subsample—those respondents who completed the regular questionnaire first. Included are many good students who probably give more accurate responses. On the other hand, the sample is likely to include a good proportion of those who filled out the questionnaire somewhat sloppily to complete it fast. Overall, about two-thirds of the subsample are above, one-third below average in IQ.

Additional indications of the reliability of the television exposure data could be obtained from analyses of the reports by small groups of respondents who were part of both the elementary school and the adolescent sample, and were given both measurement instruments within 2 weeks. During the course of the study this happened twice; in May/June 1970 (Wave I for both samples) and in May 1972 (Wave V elementary school sample; no regular teens wave; teens were interviewed specifically to allow this comparison). Thirty-four respondents were part of the first; 60 of the second subsample.

As mentioned, exposure data for elementary school children and teenagers were obtained with different methods: The checklists were not the same, programs were sampled separately, and the administration of the methods was completely different. Further, it must not be overlooked that the data were collected a couple of weeks apart at a time when viewing tends to drop as the weather gets warmer. Nonetheless, the correlation between the violence exposure scores in the first sample is .74; in the second sample it is .54. These are substantial evidence of reliability, since they represent lower bounds on the consistency of reporting.

Validity

A substantial minority of the youngest respondents, and a number of older children, had given television viewing reports of questionable validity. We did not expect problems of this sort among our teenage respondents. The pretests had indicated, and the later analyses corroborated, that "less valid" reporting was related to reading and writing problems and other age-related skills. Still, it was decided not only to investigate the validity of the teenage viewing reports in general, but also to ascertain whether the assumption that only a few of the teenage respondents are "less valid" reporters is correct.

LESS VALID REPORTING

Chapter 4 describes how we arrived at the classification of "valid" and "less valid" reporting. In short, we developed three indicators of less valid reporting—each indicative of likely inaccuracies in the viewing report—and classified those scoring high on at least two of the three indicators as less valid.

One of the indicators was already mentioned: marking "dummy" programs. The assumption here is that those who report regular viewing of nonexistent programs may have given erroneous reports regarding actual programs as well. As shown in Table 11.3, only about 5% of the teenagers reported any viewing of nonexistent programs in the five waves; less than 2% marked more than one of the three "dummies" in each of the waves.[12] Among elementary school children, over 20% reported viewing of "dummy" shows.

[12]The lists of television movies also contained "dummy" items. However, they appeared to be poor indicators of less valid reporting because they confused many otherwise accurate

The other two indicators of less valid reporting are an "extremity response pattern" and claiming regularly to watch programs televised simultaneously. Both patterns are quite rare among teenagers. As a result, when the same definition of "less valid" reporters used for elementary school children is applied to teens, we find that, in the five waves, only between 1 and 4% of the respondents are "less valid" reporters (see lower part of Table 11.3).[13] In short, as expected, there were hardly any "less valid" reporters among adolescents, and it was decided not to separate less valid reporters from more valid respondents.[14]

VALIDITY TESTS

In the absence of a comparison measure of known validity, there are only limited possibilities for testing validity. In Table 11.4 we report two tests that give some estimate of the aggregate validity of the data; both are based on comparisons with ratings data.

The upper part of Table 11.4 compares the seasonal variations in the viewing reports of the boys in our sample with the variations in Nielsen samples of male adolescents at the times of our study waves. The agreement is quite remarkable, indicating that, at least in the aggregate, the reports of our respondents accurately reflect seasonal changes in the amount of viewing from wave to wave.

The second test compares reports on viewing of individual prime-time shows with ratings of those shows in Waves II, III, and IV. In all instances the correlations are quite high; they average .62. This result indicates a satisfactory degree of validity, even though correlations for elementary school children were higher than that.[15]

---

respondents. Considering the hundreds of movies shown on television every month, that is not surprising. In Wave I we made up a dummy title which really sounded like an actual movie: "Battle of the Space Monsters." Fifteen percent of the teenage boys reported seeing it, more than for two of the actually televised movies listed. Still, this is a good result compared to the elementary schoolchildren: 30% reported seeing "Battle of the Space Monsters." The overwhelming majority of the teens who marked that item did not mark any other dummies and had no other indications of less valid reporting.

[13]The percentage of less valid reporters is lowest in Wave I, presumably because one of the indicators of less valid reporting was less powerful in that wave. We have no explanation for the relatively high percentage of less valid reporters in Wave II.

[14]There are, however, two instances in which we discuss the effect of less valid reporting. See Chapters 12 and 14.

[15]See Table 4.4; those correlations are close to .90. We do not expect to find correlations of that magnitude between different sets of data on teenagers for two reasons. First, the sample size of ratings services for male teenagers is less than 250, considerably smaller than the sample of 6- to 11-year-olds they survey (450–500). As a result, data on viewing of individual programs, especially those seen by few people, are subject to relatively large sampling errors. (Data on the

(Continued next page)

TABLE 11.3
Validity of Television Exposure Data (Amount of Less Valid Reporting)

	WAVE				
	I	II	III	IV	V
Marking of dummy television programs					
Respondents who did not mark any dummy television programs	96%	91%	96%	96%	98%
Respondents who marked					
—one dummy television program	3%	7%	2%	3%	1%
—two or three dummy television programs	1%	2%	1%	1%	1%
Indications of less valid reporting					
Respondents who score low on indicators of less valid reporting	99%	96%	98%	98%	98%
Less valid reporters (Respondents who score high on indicators of less valid reporting)	1%	4%	2%	2%	2%

As mentioned, ratings data indicate that viewing depends very much on the weather. Viewing of children and adolescents drops significantly during the spring, especially during daytime hours. Are those trends reflected in our data? Looking at those programs listed on both exposure measures, we find that significantly less viewing is reported in Wave II; this is especially true of programs shown during the day.

Also, ratings data show that teens watch less television than elementary school children, especially during the afternoon and on Saturday morning. Only late night viewing (after prime-time 10 P.M. central time) is higher for teens. Although differences in the measurement of exposure do not allow a precise comparison between the two samples in this study, the viewing reports clearly show the same trends as those reflected in commercial ratings: a drop in overall viewing as the child enters his teens, most pronounced in afternoon and Saturday morning viewing. At the same time, adolescents do not report a drop in late night viewing.[16]

---

overall amount of viewing—those used for the other test just reported—are much more reliable.) Thus, discrepancies between our data and ratings data may be primarily due to sampling error. The second reason is that teens find a larger number of programs that suit their taste during prime-time than young children. As a result, there is more differentiation in their viewing behavior, and sample composition etc. can affect the popularity of individual programs more than among children.

[16]In May 1971, for example, 27% of the elementary school boys, but only 6% of the teenage boys reported watching the popular *Archie* cartoon (at least three out of four times). Fifty-nine percent of the adolescents watched the *Tonight Show* at least sometimes; this was not asked of

TABLE 11.4
Comparison of Viewing Reports with Ratings Data

	WAVE				
	I MAY 1970	II OCT./NOV. 1970	III MAY 1971	IV DEC. 1972	V MAY 1973
Seasonal variations in viewing					
Viewing index (total exposure May 1970 = 100)					
—according to viewing reports	100	118	113	143	97
—according to Nielsen ratings[a]	100	123	108	142	106
Comparison of prime-time viewing					
Correlations between viewing reports of prime-time programs and Nielsen ratings[a] of the same programs		.65	.65	.57	
(Number of programs compared)		(25)	(22)	(24)	

[a]NTI/NAC reports, male teens (12–17).

Finally, we also conducted a test of concurrent validity, which compares the correlates of television exposure among our teenage respondents with findings obtained in other studies on the viewing behavior of teens. These analyses showed that relationships found in our data agree with those found by other researchers.[17]

Stability of Exposure over Time

The third property of the violent television exposure measure examined is its stability over the 3-year duration of the study.

Correlations between violence exposure scores are presented in Table 11.5. Unadjusted autocorrelations are shown above the diagonal. The coefficients below the diagonal are adjusted for measurement unreliability; adjustments are based on complex models discussed in Appendix D in Chapter 13. The observed coefficients range from .56 in the short Wave IV–V lag to .37 in the Wave I–IV lag, which covers about 2½ years.[18]

younger boys. The teenagers' viewing of the 10 o'clock news is about as frequent as the viewing levels reported by the younger boys. Thus, their viewing is relatively higher than young boys' viewing of evening programs.

[17]Details are provided in "Correlates of Exposure to Television Among Teenage Boys" (Documentation 4C), available on request.

[18]It is interesting to note that the correlation is slightly higher in the three-year lag I–V. It appears that because of seasonal viewing patterns, viewing is more stable between identical points in time during the year, such as from May to May. The I–III lag is also more stable than the shorter I–II lag. Again, the former is a May to May, the latter a May to October lag.

TABLE 11.5
Stability of Violent Television Exposure: Adjusted and Unadjusted Autocorrelations between all Wave Pairs[a]

WAVES	I	II	III	IV	V
I		.510 (364)	.477 (362)	.374 (325)	.410 (313)
II	.892		.466 (516)	.420 (468)	.407 (455)
III	.844	.825		.471 (481)	.457 (463)
IV	.663	.744	.845		.557 (618)
V	.726	.721	.820	.974	

[a]Unadjusted autocorrelations are given above the diagonal; autocorrelations adjusted for measurement unreliabilities below. Adjusted autocorrelations are based on Heise-Bohrnstedt Ω; see Chapter 13, Appendix D for a discussion.

Adjusted autocorrelations are considerably higher: the coefficients below the diagonal range from .66 to .97.

In general, autocorrelations for teens are somewhat higher than for the elementary school children. This may reflect greater stability in viewing patterns among the older respondents. However, the findings may, at least in part, be due to greater reporting accuracy among teens. In any case, the amount of change exhibited by television exposure enhances the ability to see whether changes in exposure are followed by changes in aggression.

APPENDIX A: LISTING OF PROGRAMS AND VIOLENCE WEIGHTS (TEENS)

TABLE A.1
Prime-Time Programs[a]—Teens

	WAVE					VIOLENCE WEIGHTS
	I	II	III	IV	V	
FBI	X	X	X	X	X	7
Hawaii 5-O	X	X		X	X	7
Mannix	X	X	X	X	X	7
Mod Squad	X	X	X	X	X	7
Mission Impossible	X	X	X	X	X	6
Bonanza	X	X	X			5
High Chaparral	X		X			5
Wagon Train	X					5
Wrestling	X	X	X			5
Adam 12	X	X		X	X	4
Then Came Bronson	X					4
Here Come the Brides	X					2
Laugh-In	X	X	X	X	X	1
Medical Center	X					1
Room 222	X	X	X	X	X	1
Andy Williams	X	X	X			0
Bewitched	X	X	X			0
Bill Cosby	X	X				0
Carol Burnett	X	X				0
Governor & J.J.	X	X				0
Dean Martin	X	X				0
Flying Nun	X					0
Glen Campbell	X	X	X			0
Eddie's Father	X		X			0
Ed Sullivan	X	X				0
Englebert Humperdinck	X					0
Let's Make a Deal	X	X		X		0
Mayberry RFD	X	X				0
Silent Force		X				5
McCloud (Four in One)		X				5
The Immortal		X				5
Monday Night Football		X				4
Young Rebels		X				4
Odd Couple		X				0
Partridge Family		X	X	X	X	0
Dan August			X			6
Gunsmoke			X		X	5
Ironside			X	X		5
Name of the Game			X			5

(Continued next page)

TABLE A.1 (*continued*)

	WAVE					VIOLENCE WEIGHTS
	I	II	III	IV	V	
All in the Family			X	X	X	1
Bird's Eye View			X			0
Brady Bunch			X			0
Julia			X			0
Mary Tyler Moore			X	X	X	0
Cannon				X	X	6
Banyon				X		5
Rookies				X	X	5
Search				X	X	5
Streets of San Francisco				X		5
Marcus Welby, M.D.				X	X	1
Maude				X	X	1
Paul Lynde				X	X	1
Sanford & Son				X	X	1
Bill Cosby (Variety)				X	X	0
Flip Wilson				X		0
Sandy Duncan				X		0
Kung Fu					X	5
Emergency					X	2
M.A.S.H.					X	2
Waltons					X	1
Number of programs listed in wave	28	27	23	25	25	

[a]All programs are listed in both cities.

TABLE A.2

"Daily" Programs—Teens (Monday–Friday)

<table>
<tr><th></th><th colspan="5">WAVE</th><th rowspan="2">VIOLENCE WEIGHTS</th></tr>
<tr><th></th><th>I</th><th>II</th><th>III</th><th>IV</th><th>V</th></tr>
<tr><td>Star Trek**[a]</td><td>X</td><td>X</td><td>X</td><td>X</td><td>X</td><td>6</td></tr>
<tr><td>Big Valley*,[a]</td><td>X</td><td>X</td><td></td><td>X</td><td></td><td>5</td></tr>
<tr><td>Dark Shadows</td><td>X</td><td></td><td>X</td><td></td><td></td><td>5</td></tr>
<tr><td>Perry Mason[b]</td><td>X</td><td>X</td><td>X</td><td></td><td></td><td>4</td></tr>
<tr><td>Gomer Pyle[c]</td><td>X</td><td>X</td><td>X</td><td>X</td><td></td><td>1</td></tr>
<tr><td>News (CBS)</td><td>X</td><td>X</td><td rowspan="2">X</td><td rowspan="2">X</td><td rowspan="2">X</td><td>1</td></tr>
<tr><td>News (NBC)</td><td>X</td><td>X</td><td>1</td></tr>
<tr><td>10 O'Clock News</td><td>X</td><td>X</td><td>X</td><td>X</td><td>X</td><td>1</td></tr>
<tr><td>Flintstones</td><td>X</td><td>X</td><td>X</td><td>X</td><td>X</td><td>1</td></tr>
<tr><td>I Love Lucy[d]</td><td>X</td><td>X</td><td>X</td><td></td><td>X</td><td>1</td></tr>
<tr><td>Tonight Show</td><td>X</td><td>X</td><td>X</td><td>X</td><td>X</td><td>0</td></tr>
</table>

(*Continued next page*)

TABLE A.2 (*continued*)

	WAVE					VIOLENCE
	I	II	III	IV	V	WEIGHTS
Mike Douglas Show	X		X			0
Tonight Show	X	X	X	X	X	0
Batman[e]		X	X			6
*Have Gun—Will Travel**		X	X			5
Daniel Boone		X	X			4
It Takes a Thief[f]			X		X	6
*McHale's Navy***			X			1
*Leave It to Beaver**			X			0
*Munsters**			X			1
*Mr. Ed***			X			0
Wild Wild West[g]				X	X	6
*Dragnet***				X		4
*Popeye**				X	X	4
*Hogan's Heroes**				X		2
Gilligan's Island				X	X	1
Dick Van Dyke				X	X	0
I Dream of Jeannie				X	X	0
Merv Griffin				X	X	0
*Petticoat Junction**[h]				X		0
Truth or Consequences				X	X	0
*Rifleman**					X	6
*High Chaparral***					X	5
Number of programs listed in wave	12	11	14	13	13	

[a] Both cities in Wave I.
[b] Only in Fort Worth in Wave II.
[c] Only in Minneapolis in Wave IV.
[d] Only in Minneapolis in Wave V.
[e] Only in Fort Worth in Wave III.
[f] Heartland in Wave III, Fort Worth in Wave V.
[g] Fort Worth in Wave IV, Minneapolis in Wave V.
[h] Both cities in Wave V.
*Only in Fort Worth.
**Only in Minneapolis.

TABLE A.3

Saturday–Sunday Programs (Exclusive Prime-Time)—Teens

	WAVE					VIOLENCE WEIGHTS
	I	II	III	IV	V	
Hockey	X					5
Dastardly & Mutley	X					4
Perils of Penelope Pitstop	X		X			4
H.R. Pufnstuf	X					1
Wild Kingdom	X	X	X	X	X	1
Amateur Hour	X					0
Bowling	X					0
Discovery 70	X	X	X			0
*The Invaders**		X				6
*Wagon Train***		X				5
Josie and the Pussycats		X				4
Hot Wheels		X				3
Archie		X	X			1
Hot Dog		X				0
*Time Tunnel**			X			6
*The Cat***			X			6
12 O'Clock High			X			6
Wide World of Sports			X		X	3
Sky Hawks			X			2
Dr. Dolittle			X			1
Bugs Bunny				X	X	4
Football (Sunday)				X	X	4
Josie in Outer Space				X	X	3
Here Come the Brides[a]				X	X	2
Fat Albert				X	X	1
The Osmonds				X	X	0
Talking with a Giant				X	X	0
*Rat Patrol***					X	6
Amazing Chan					X	3
Funky Phantom					X	3
Brady Kids					X	0
Number of programs listed in wave	8	7	9	8	11	

[a]Only in Fort Worth in Wave V.

*Programs listed only in Fort Worth.

**Programs listed only in Minneapolis.

TABLE A.4
TV Movies—Teens

Wave I (10 movies)	
Duel of the Titans	6
Khartoum	6
Merrill's Marauders	6
Denver and the Rio Grande	5
Rage	5
Tarzan & His Valley of Gold	5
Destiny of a Spy	4
The Crooked Road	2
Operation Amsterdam	2
The Young Lawyers	2
Wave II (8 movies)	
The Dirty Dozen	7
*Die, Die Darling**	6
*The Killers***	6
None But the Brave	6
Tony Rome	6
The Night of the Following Day	5
The Great Race	3
The Magnificent Men in Their Flying Machines	1
The Russians Are Coming	1
Wave III (11 movies)	
*Border Incident**	6
*Rage of the Bucaneers***	6
*Weapons for Vengeance***	6
Brainstorm	5
Death of a Gunfighter	5
*Gun for a Coward**	5
*Hell Drivers***	5
Tarzan and the Great River	5
The Three Avengers	5
Escape	4
A Countess from Hong Kong	1
The Nutty Professor	1
*Walk Don't Run**	1
1001 Arabian Nights	1
*Rosemarie***	0
Wave IV (11 movies)	
The Green Berets	6
In Cold Blood	6
Once Upon a Time in the West	6
The Vengeance of Fu Manchu	6
Bandolero!	5
Patton	5
True Grit	5
Columbo	4

(Continued next page)

TABLE A.4 (*continued*)

Chitty Chitty Bang Bang	1
All My Darling Daughters	0
Barefoot in the Park	0
Wave V (11 movies)	
The Long Duel	6
The Screaming Woman	5
When Michael Calls	5
The Hired Hand	4
Notorious	4
Don't Make Waves	2
The Secret War of Harry Frigg	2
Situation Hopeless—But Not Serious	2
Oklahoma	1
Three on a Couch	1

*Only in Fort Worth
**Only in Minneapolis

CHAPTER 12

CROSS-SECTIONAL CORRELATIONS AND THE LOGIC OF CAUSAL ANALYSIS

In Chapters 10 and 11, we looked separately at the television exposure and aggression measures. In this chapter we examine the relationship between these two measures at the same point in time. As noted previously, the existence of a correlation does not imply causality. However, if exposure to television violence increases aggressiveness, the two measures should covary cross-sectionally.

In this chapter, we also put the television–aggression correlation into perspective by comparing it with other correlates of aggression. Finally, the logic of our causal analysis will be discussed.

CROSS-SECTIONAL CORRELATIONS

Table 12.1A–D show the cross-sectional correlations between two exposure scores—total exposure and violence exposure—and four measures of aggression—personal, teacher, property, and delinquency aggression—for each wave of the panel. Part E of Table 12.1 summarizes parts A–D.[1]

Part A of Table 12.1 shows that both measures of exposure are positively and weakly correlated with personal aggression. At the .05 level of statistical significance, 8 of the 10 correlations between violent television exposure and personal aggression are significant, and there is a very small but systematic

[1]The samples consist of all respondents who answered both the television and aggression measures at the point in time considered.

TABLE 12.1

A: Cross-sectional correlations between measures of total and violent television exposure and personal aggression

WAVE	TOTAL TELEVISION EXPOSURE	VIOLENT TELEVISION EXPOSURE	*N*
I	.105*	.164*	(389)
II	.125*	.130*	(561)
III	.039	.068	(561)
IV	.152*	.156*	(672)
V	.094*	.119*	(636)

*B: Cross-sectional correlations between measures of total and violent television exposure and teacher aggression**

WAVE	TOTAL TELEVISION EXPOSURE	VIOLENT TELEVISION EXPOSURE	*N*
I	−.090*	−.057	(392)
II	.058	.091*	(567)
III	.029	.076*	(558)
IV	.035	.082*	(648)
V	.110*	.117*	(610)

C: Cross-sectional correlations between measures of total and violent television exposure and property aggression

WAVE	TOTAL TELEVISION EXPOSURE	VIOLENT TELEVISION EXPOSURE	*N*
I	−.015	.030	(391)
II	.023	.035	(568)
III	−.024	.026	(564)
IV	.008	.027	(673)
V	.012	.041	(637)

D: Cross-sectional correlations between measures of total and violent television exposure and delinquency aggression

WAVE	TOTAL TELEVISION EXPOSURE	VIOLENT TELEVISION EXPOSURE	*N*
I			
II	−.001	.010	(567)
III	.050	.068	(561)
IV	.108*	.109*	(664)
V	−.047	−.022	(633)

(Continued next page)

TABLE 12.1 (*continued*)
E: Cross-sectional correlations between measures of total and violent television exposure and aggression measures

	TOTAL TELEVISION EXPOSURE		VIOLENT TELEVISION EXPOSURE	
	AVERAGE CORRELATION	NUMBER OF SIGNIFICANT CORRELATIONS	AVERAGE CORRELATION	NUMBER OF SIGNIFICANT CORRELATIONS
Personal aggression (5 waves)	.103	4	.127	4
Teacher aggression (5 waves)	.028	1p 1n	.062	4
Property aggression (5 waves)	.001	0	.032	0
Delinquency aggression (4 waves)	.022	1	.033	1

*Significant at .05 level.
[a] p = positive coefficient; n = negative coefficient.

difference between the correlations at each point in time when the violence rather than the total exposure score is used. Correlations between exposure and personal aggression average .10 for total exposure and .13 for violence exposure (see Part E of Table 12.1).

As shown in Part B of Table 12.1, teacher aggression does not correlate systematically with the two exposure measures. Correlations are small, averaging .03 for total exposure and .06 for violence exposure, but because of the large number of cases available, four of the five correlations with violence exposure are significant. Nor do we find a meaningful relationship between television and property aggression, shown in Part C of Table 12.1. None of the 10 cross-sectional correlations meets the conventional .05 test of statistical significance. Correlations average .00 for total exposure and .03 for violence exposure.

Part D of Table 12.1 shows correlations with delinquency, the most seriously antisocial of our aggression measures. This measure is available in four waves, in one of which the correlations are significant. However, in the other three waves the correlations are extremely small and in Wave V negative. There is no systematic difference between the correlations with the total and the violence exposure scores. (The average correlations are .03 and .04 for total and violence exposure, respectively.)

Taken as a whole, there is much less evidence in these tables for a consistent cross-sectional relationship between television exposure and aggression for teenage boys than we found in our study of elementary school children, except in the case of personal aggression.

The correlations reported in Table 12.1A–E are not corrected for unreliability of measurement in the television exposure and aggression scales, and hence are smaller than estimates based on true scores. (As detailed in Appendix A in Chapter 13, we have not been able to obtain sufficiently precise estimates of the reliability of the aggression scores to warrant computing adjusted correlations.) However, there is no evidence from our analyses of reliability that the adjusted relationships would be very different from those presented in Table 12.1A–E.[2]

It is difficult to compare these correlations with those reported in previous cross-sectional research, because the measures of television viewing and indicators of aggression used in those studies vary considerably from those used here. The McLeod, Atkin, and Chaffee (1972) study of high school boys is most directly comparable to our teenage data, in that it employed a television exposure score very similar to the one we use here. The correlation between this measure and a scale of "aggressive behavioral delinquency" (consisting of three items: "Been in fights with several people on each side"; "Hurt someone on purpose to get back for something they had done to you"; "Got into a serious fight with another student at school") was .08 for a sample of Maryland junior high school boys, .23 for senior high school boys, and .12 for Wisconsin senior high schoolers. These correlations are roughly similar to those found in the present study between television exposure and personal aggression (the most similar type of aggression we studied to the items contained in their scale).

OTHER CORRELATES OF AGGRESSION

Before turning to the time-lagged analysis we summarize an investigation of the correlations between aggression and background variables that were collected in this study. As explained in Chapter 5, such an analysis enables us to place the television exposure–aggression correlations in perspective.[3]

---

[2]We tried to estimate latent variable models across the five waves in order to obtain consistent reliability coefficients. We were able to construct such models for the television exposure measure; see Chapter 11. However, none of the models for the aggression measures accurately reproduced the observed correlations among the aggression indicators. (For details see Appendix A in Chapter 13.)

Although the complex measurement models of aggression fail to provide good representations of the observed covariances among the aggression indicators in the five waves, cross-sectional reliability estimates based on internal consistency suggest that the reliabilities of the personal aggression scale range from .70 to .75. The correlations between the two items in the property aggression scale range from .43 to .52. Adjusted cross-sectional correlations between television exposure and these aggression scores are still only moderate in magnitude.

[3]Correlates of television exposure are discussed in Documentation 4B and in Chapter 11.

TABLE 12.2
Correlates of Aggression: Summary Table
(Strongest Correlates of Three Aggression Measures)

	AVERAGE CORRELATIONS IN FIVE WAVES AND RANK OF CORRELATION (IN PARENTHESES)[a]					
	PERSONAL AGGRESSION		PROPERTY AGGRESSION		DELINQUENCY AGGRESSION	
Contact with aggressive behavior	.48	(1)	.29	(7)	.17	(7)
Aggressive self-image	.33	(2)	.24	(10)	.20	(4)
Friends' aggressiveness	.31	(3)	.41	(1)	.29	(2)
Father's attitude toward antisocial aggression	.28	(4)	.24	(10)	.16	(–)
Harmony/conflict between family members	.25	(5)	.23	(–)	.20	(4)
Mother's dissatisfaction with son	.20	(7)	.25	(8)	.17	(7)
Use of alcohol/ cigarettes/drugs	.17	(–)	.32	(2)	.21	(3)
Justification for antisocial act	.19	(–)	.30	(3)	.20	(4)
Remorse about antisocial act	–.16	(–)	–.30	(3)	–.14	(–)
Friends' drug use	.17	(–)	.30	(3)	.31	(1)
Expect to spend time in jail	.17	(–)	.30	(3)	.17	(7)

[a](–) indicates not one of 10 strongest correlates.

The findings of that analysis are summarized in Table 12.2, which shows the strongest correlates of personal aggression, property aggression, and delinquency (out of about 130 measures examined). The table shows the strength of the correlations and the rank-order for each of the three aggression measures separately.[4]

As in the analysis of the correlates of aggression among elementary school children, we find that peer measures and characteristics of the respondent are the best predictors of aggressive behavior. Comparing the different rank-orders for the three measures of aggression, we can see many similarities, but also a number of interesting differences. For example, contact with aggressive behavior is strongly related to all three measures, but it is much more strongly

[4]Table 12.2 shows the 5 strongest correlates for each measure, and rank orders from 1 to 10. If a variable is not one of the 10 strongest correlates of one of the aggression measures, the rank is not shown. (Data for teacher aggression are not reported.)

related to personal aggression than to the other measures.[5] Use of alcohol, cigarettes, drugs, and friends' drug use are stronger correlates of property and delinquency than of personal aggression. The portrait of the aggressive teen which emerges from these data is that he lives in a social environment in which aggression occurs often and is condoned, has family members who fight among themselves, and has a mother who rejects him. He uses alcohol and drugs and has friends who do the same. Further, he believes that acts of aggression are justified and feels no remorse about such acts. A realist, he is aware that such behavior will eventually lead to his incarceration. A comparison with the characteristics of elementary school boys (Chapter 5) shows that the social environment of the aggressive teen is much like that of the aggressive younger boy.

Television exposure is not on this list. As shown in Part E of Table 12.1, the highest correlation between exposure to violent television and an aggression measure is .13, with personal aggression. Violent television exposure ranks 40th among correlates of personal aggression. Correlations between television exposure and the other two aggression measures are even weaker.

MUTUAL CORRELATES OF AGGRESSION AND VIOLENT TELEVISION EXPOSURE

Personal aggression correlates with television exposure consistently and significantly. We examined whether this correlation is at least partially due to mutual correlates of aggression and television exposure, limiting our analysis to those factors that antecede both aggression and television exposure to make sure that we do, in fact, control only for spurious relationships.

Table 12.3 shows a small reduction in the cross-sectional correlation between personal aggression and violent television exposure when the effect of three mutual correlates—SES, race, and quality of reporting[6]—is partialed out.

Findings such as this do not put an end to the question of whether or not exposure has a causal effect on aggression. There may be variables that hide such an effect, and there is the possibility that effects exist among segments of the sample that do not show up in the analysis of the sample as a whole. These are issues that will be examined in subsequent chapters.

---

[5]This finding has considerable face validity since the variable measures witnessing acts of personal aggression. This is also true of aggressive self-image, a measure of an image as a fighter, etc. We would expect this to be more strongly related to a measure of personal aggression than to the other aggression measures.

[6]Even though only 1–4% of the samples in the five waves were classified as "less valid reporters" (Table 11.3), the reports of these few boys were found to have a small effect on the correlations.

TABLE 12.3
Zero-Order and Partial Correlations between Exposure to Violent Television and Personal Aggression[a]

	WAVE					FIVE-WAVE
	I	II	III	IV	V	AVERAGE
Zero-order correlations						
All respondents (as shown in Table 14.1A)	.16* (389)	.13* (561)	.07 (561)	.16* (672)	.12* (636)	.13
Respondents with SES, race, and quality of reporting data	.20* (298)	.11* (386)	.06 (374)	.17* (447)	.11* (431)	.13
Partial correlations						
Controlling for SES, and race	.19* (295)	.10* (383)	.04 (371)	.14* (444)	.07 (427)	.11
Controlling for SES, race, and quality of reporting data	.18* (294)	.05 (382)	.03 (370)	.11* (443)	.02 (427)	.08

[a]*N* s given in parentheses.
*Significant at .05 level.

THE BASIC MODEL

For the analyses of the teenage data, we use essentially the same model as that used in the analysis of the children's data. The two-wave linear additive model that serves as our basic model is:

$$A_{t_i} = a + b_1 A_{(t-1)_i} + b_2 TV_{(t-1)_i} + u_i \quad (1)$$

where A_{t_i} represents the ith person's aggression measured at time t, $TV_{(t-1)_i}$ represents his television exposure measured at an earlier time, a represents a regression constant, and u_i represents the error of the prediction equation for that person. The influence of exposure on aggression is assessed by evaluating the parameter b_2 associated with earlier exposure on time t aggression after the predictive influence of earlier aggression has been controlled.[7]

In the panel of elementary school children we decided that the six waves of data could best be analyzed by looking separately at the 15 possible wave pairs, using all the data available for any respondent who remained in the panel for at least two waves. There was a great deal of attrition among these children, thus making the two-wave approach clearly superior to any other. At the same time, we were forced to deal with a troublesome fact that accompanies the use of overlapping wave pair models: the same information is used over and over again, so that the 15 separate wave pairs are not really supplying us with 15

[7]In Chapter 5, it was pointed out that this model goes quite far in reducing the ambiguity caused by rival causal hypotheses. We also reviewed why this model is superior to other analysis models we might have employed to analyze the paired data. (See Chapter 5 for further details.)

different pieces of information. Furthermore, since the numbers of respondents in the various wave pairs differ greatly, we could not say exactly how much overlap there was, thus making the interpretation of findings difficult.

In our study of teenagers we are in a different situation. As described in Chapter 9, there was little attrition in the teenage sample and the sample actually became larger through time as we invited more friends of primary respondents into the panel. The relative advantage of two-wave models, as a way of conserving cases, is here outweighed by the disadvantages that accompany overlapping lags. Consequently, we make use of multiwave panel models in many analyses reported in the next chapter.

Analysis of Personal, Property, and Teacher Aggression

The scales of personal, teacher, and property aggression consist of frequency-of-performance measures. These scales are treated as interval-level measures in the analyses below.[8] The analysis of television effects on these measures of aggression makes use of the same LISREL estimation used in our measurement model analysis of elementary school children. In the teens analysis, however, we estimate five-wave models among the observed scores. The models are described fully in the next chapter.

Analysis of Delinquency

As Chapter 12 showed, we asked respondents if they had ever engaged in each of several types of delinquent behaviors and, if so, how long ago. The questions were asked in this fashion because we knew that very few teens had ever engaged in these activities (mugging, knife fighting, and so forth), and that

---

[8]The scales of personal, teacher, and property aggression are sums of reports about frequency of aggressive acts. Exploratory factor analyses showed that these behaviors do indeed occur together and the internal consistency of the intrascale item correlations is good. However, confirmatory factor analyses discussed in the appendices to Chapter 13 showed that over-time inspection of the items within each scale leaves some doubt about the validity of the scales. We were unable, in fact, to develop measurement models that could describe the over-time correlations among the indicators in any of the scales with great precision.

In the analyses presented in the following chapters, we examine the impact of television exposure on scales of property, personal, and teacher aggression even though we have not been able to develop clean models of theoretical constructs conforming to these scales. We do this because we believe that the exploratory factor analyses uncovered real clusters of aggression. However, we feel that the particular indicators we have of these aggression types are probably weaker than those that we would have preferred.

Each scale has been created by summing the frequency of aggression items. This method of scale construction is very similar in this instance to a scale that would be created by means of factor weights.

a question of the sort "how often do you . . . " would almost always have elicited a response of "never." The question that faced us in the analysis plan was how to deal with this measure in the context of a causal model.

After examining the distributions of the various questions about delinquency it became clear that the basic patterns could be described by transforming the variables into two parts at each wave: (*a*) Have you ever engaged in this behavior? (*b*) Have you engaged in it recently (since the last time of data collection)? Both questions can be coded as dichotomies (Yes = 1; No = 0), which means that the models used to analyze these responses must be appropriate for the analysis of dichotomous measures. A class of models exists that does this, and we have made use of the most common of these, individual-level logit analysis (Nerlove & Press, 1973). This model allows us to estimate a linear model, just like the simple regression model described in (1) above, on a transformed representation of a dichotomy that avoids violation of some technical assumptions of ordinary least-squares regression. These advantages are discussed fully in Nerlove and Press (1973) and less technically in Hanausheck and Jackson (1977).

A disadvantage of the logit procedure is that multiwave panel models cannot be estimated in an easily interpretable fashion. Therefore, in the analysis of delinquency we have returned to two-wave models.

The causal analyses will be presented in the two following chapters. Chapter 13 details the basic model analysis with all aggression measures. Chapter 14 explores whether the television exposure has an effect on aggression when it is conceptualized in different ways or when subgroups are analyzed.

CHAPTER 13

THE EFFECT OF TELEVISION VIOLENCE ON AGGRESSION: FINDINGS FROM THE BASIC MODEL

Four distinct empirical clusters of aggressive behavior were detected among the teenage boys sampled (see Chapter 10). Three of these—personal aggression, aggression against teachers (teacher aggression), and property aggression—consist of relatively common behaviors. They are discussed in the first part of this chapter. Subsequently we discuss delinquency.

PERSONAL, TEACHER, AND PROPERTY AGGRESSION

Since there was little attrition, we were able to employ five-wave models for teens. This is superior to the two-wave approach used in the elementary school analysis as it utilizes all of the panel data simultaneously and eliminates the problem of interpreting findings from overlapping lags.

In the five-wave analysis, we began with a matrix of covariances among the 10 variables TV_1–TV_5 and A_1–A_5 and a set of structural equations to describe the causal influences assumed to connect all these variables. The maximum-likelihood approach contained in LISREL was used to estimate simultaneously the parameters in these equations. As a result, instead of 10 separate wave-pair models with 1 television effect coefficient estimated in each, we have one five-wave model in which all 10 television coefficients are estimated simultaneously.

We were able to work with two additional multiwave models. Because we recruited a sizable number of new respondents in Wave II, we were able to work with a four-wave model (Waves II–V). We also recruited many new respondents in Wave IV, and so were able to work with a two-wave model (Waves IV–V). These four- and five-wave models were independent of the five-wave model and of each other.

Appendix A provides more details on the analysis model and compares it with alternate models.

BASIC MODEL RESULTS

Table 13.1A–C present parameter estimates for the five-, four-, and two-wave models of personal, teacher, and property aggression. In each model, aggression is assumed to depend directly on all earlier measures of aggression and television exposure. Seventeen television effect coefficients are presented for each of the three types of aggression. In the five-wave model there are 10 such coefficients; in the four-wave model there are 6; in the two-wave model there is 1.

Parts A, B, and C of the table show, respectively, parameters for the influence of earlier television and aggression on later aggression (controlling for prior aggression).[1] Each row of the table represents a separate structural equation. For example, the first row in Panel (a) of Table 13.1A shows the effects of A_1 ($b = .591$, $\beta = .530$) and TV_1 ($b = -.005$, $\beta = -.023$) on A_2 in the five-wave sample. The significance of individual coefficients is estimated in relation to their standard errors, and the significance of all the coefficients within an equation by the R^2 increments associated with the set of predictors (Column (9)).

Although the structural equations within a model can be separated for descriptive purposes, they are estimated simultaneously in LISREL. This makes it possible to evaluate the television effects not only in each structural equation, but also in each model. This evaluation is described by the χ^2 increment[2] that results from dropping all television effect coefficients from the model. These χ^2 coefficients have 10 *df* in the five-wave models, because 10 television coefficients are being evaluated simultaneously. In the four-wave models there are 6 *df* (six television coefficients); and in the two-wave models there is 1 *df* (one television coefficient). These χ^2 coefficients are presented in the last row of each panel in the three tables.

---

[1]These parameter estimates are based on an overidentified model in which television exposure is assumed to depend on all earlier measures of television and on aggression at one time point preceding it. Values for χ^2 for these overidentified models can be found in notes to the tables and also in Appendix A, where the procedures used to arrive at the model are described. We do not report half of the coefficients estimated by the model in these various samples—those for the lagged effects of television and aggression on later television viewing patterns.

[2]The χ^2, as mentioned earlier, describes the discrepancy between the observed covariance matrix and the matrix predicted by the model.

When samples are independent, as in the five-, four-, and two-wave samples for each aggression measure, it is possible to add χ^2 values. In panel (d) of each table we have done this as a way of evaluating the total set of 17 (10 in the five-wave, 6 in the four-wave, and 1 in the two-wave models) television coefficients in the three samples combined. These are simply the sums of the χ^2 coefficients of the first three panels.

In all, then, we have four ways to evaluate television effects:

1. Standard errors of individual coefficients
2. R^2 increments of a set of coefficients in one structural equation
3. χ^2 increments for the coefficients in all structural equations of one model
4. χ^2 increments across samples for one particular measure of aggression.

Each of these is considered in the following as we interpret Table 13.1A–C.

We begin with the overall pattern of television effects, shown in Columns (5)–(8) of the tables. These are essentially the same as found in the elementary school sample: All coefficients are small, most are positive, and few are statistically significant. The same is true for the set of coefficients taken as a whole. The R^2 increments associated with the inclusion of all earlier television measures to predict each measure of aggression are presented in Column (9). Only 2 of 24 examined in the tables are statistically significant. Furthermore, the χ^2/df ratios of the multiwave models are all extremely small, varying from 2.901 in the four-wave teacher aggression sample to 0.508 in the four-wave property aggression sample. As a result, the χ^2/df ratios of the 17 television coefficients shown in panel (d) of each table are also small, ranging from 1.315 for personal aggression to 1.875 for teacher aggression.

The findings just reported argue strongly that there is no meaningful lagged association between television exposure and aggression in these data. It is possible, however, that by including all earlier television measures in the models we have divided what would otherwise be a substantial effect into so many parts that each is insignificant. Therefore it is useful to examine the parameter estimates of five-, four-, and two-wave models in which only one television measure is used to predict each aggression measure. Table 13.2 presents the estimates of these adjacent television effect coefficients. The pattern in this table is consistent with what we have so far: All coefficients are small, most are positive, and few are statistically significant. For personal aggression, six of the eight coefficients are positive and one of these is significant; two coefficients are negative. The average β is .019. For teacher aggression, six coefficients are positive and two negative; two positive coefficients are significant. The average β is .057. For property aggression, five coefficients are positive, one of which is significant, three are negative, and the average β is .028. Again, there is no evidence for a consistently significant relationship between television exposure and later aggression.

TABLE 13.1

A: Basic Model Regression Coefficients Showing the Effect of Violent Television Exposure on Later Personal Aggression, LISREL Nonmeasurement Error Models[a]

OUTCOME		PREDICTORS								UNIQUE CONTRIBUTION OF VIOLENT TELEVISION EXPOSURE TO TOTAL R^2	R^2
		A_1 (1)	A_2 (2)	A_3 (3)	A_4 (4)	TV_1 (5)	TV_2 (6)	TV_3 (7)	TV_4 (8)	(9)	(10)
a. *Five-wave model*											
A_2	b	.591				−.005				.001	.279
	β	.530				−.023					
A_3	b	.260*	.417*			−.005	.012			.004	.388
	β	.247	.441			−.023	.069				
A_4	b	.049	.096	.399*		−.009	.003	.018		.011	.329
	β	.053	.115	.452		−.048	.020	.105			
A_5	b	.088	.115*	.238*	.232*	−.012	−.005	.017*	−.001	.010	.409
	β	.107	.149	.291	.150	−.071	−.034	.111	−.004		

$N = 285$
$\chi^2_{10} = 10.905$
$\chi^2/df = 1.090$

b. *Four-wave model*									
A_3	b	.373*			−.002			.000	.124
	β	.353			−.009				
A_4	b	.154*	.404*		.026	−.012		.013	.288
	β	.159	.438		.144	−.057			
A_5	b	.099	.066	.402*	.027*	.003	.005	.029	.396
	β	.119	.083	.470	.172	.015	.031		
$N = 127$									
$\chi^2_6 = 10.234$									
$\chi^2/df = 1.706.$									
c. *Two-wave model*									
A_5	b			.297*			−.012	.004	.120
	β			.348			−.067		
$N = 143$									
$\chi^2_1 = 0.719$									
d. *Overall significance (three models combined)*									
$\chi^2_{17} = 22.358$									
$\chi^2/df = 1.315$									

(*Continued next page*)

TABLE 13.1 (*continued*)

B. Basic Model Regression Coefficients Showing the Effect of Violent Television Exposure on Later Teacher Aggression, LISREL Nonmeasurement Error Models[a]

OUTCOME		PREDICTORS A_1 (1)	A_2 (2)	A_3 (3)	A_4 (4)	TV_1 (5)	TV_2 (6)	TV_3 (7)	TV_4 (8)	UNIQUE CONTRIBUTION OF VIOLENT TELEVISION EXPOSURE TO TOTAL R^2 (9)	R^2 (10)
a. *Five-wave model*											
A_2	b	.636*				.009				.002	.299
	β	.544				.044					
A_3	b	.211*	.394*			−.013	.012			.005	.311
	β	.192	.417			−.073	.070				
A_4	b	.170*	.122*	.192*		−.013	.010	.011		.012	.230
	β	.184	.154	.228		−.081	.068	.079			
A_5	b	−.156*	.247*	.044	.628*	−.005	.004	.006	.009	.013	.489
	β	−.151	.278	.047	.563	−.026	.026	.034	.057		

$N = 272$
$\chi^2_{10} = 13.229$
$\chi^2/df = 1.323$

b. *Four-wave model*								
A_3 b	.292*			−.001			.000	.147
β	.383			−.010				
A_4 b	.160*	.361*		.026	−.015		.022	.196
β	.183	.315		.162	−.078			
A_5 b	.203*	.131	.295*	.017	.018	.010	.067*	.466
β	.292	.144	.371	.134	.124	.072		
$N = 126$								
$\chi^2_6 = 17.405$								
$\chi^2/df = 2.901$								
c. *Two-wave model*								
A_5 b			.632*			.011	.005	.464
β			.678			.070		
$N = 137$								
$\chi^2_1 = 1.249$								
d. *Overall significance (three models combined)*								
$\chi^2_{17} = 31.883$								
$\chi^2/df = 1.875$								

(Continued next page)

TABLE 13.1 (*continued*)

C: Basic Model Regression Coefficients Showing the Effect of Violent Television Exposure on Later Property Aggression, LISREL Nonmeasurement Error Models[a]

OUTCOME		PREDICTORS								UNIQUE CONTRIBUTION OF VIOLENT TELEVISION EXPOSURE TO TOTAL R^2	R^2
		A_1 (1)	A_2 (2)	A_3 (3)	A_4 (4)	TV_1 (5)	TV_2 (6)	TV_3 (7)	TV_4 (8)	(9)	(10)
a. *Five-wave model*											
A_2	b	.524*				−.009				.003	.176
	β	.418				−.059					
A_3	b	.250*	.306*			−.012	.024			.025	.233
	β	.204	.314			.081	.187				
A_4	b	.023	.233*	.355*		.001	−.003	−.002		.001	.347
	β	.022	.277	.412		.012	−.029	−.015			
A_5	b	.003	.021	.130*	.545*	.002	.002	.018*	−.006	.023*	.456
	β	.003	.025	.152	.550	.017	.016	.156	−.156		

$N = 291$
$\chi^2_{10} = 23.063$
$\chi^2/df = 2.306$

b. *Four-wave model*									
A_3	b	.279*			.013			.009	.088
	β	.287			.093				
A_4	b	.131	.406*		.011	−.018		.012	.225
	β	.134	.403		.078	−.110			
A_5	b	.064	.131*	.344*	.009	−.005	.006	.009	.382
	β	.089	.179	.471	.084	−.040	.049		
$N = 130$									
$\chi^2_6 = 5.082$									
$\chi^2/df = 0.508$									
c. *Two-wave model*									
A_5	b			.463*			.007	.003	.233
	β			.477			.052		
$N = 143$									
$\chi^2_1 = 0.494$									
d. *Overall significance (three models combined)*									
$\chi^2_{17} = 28.639$									
$\chi^2/df = 1.685$									

[a] A full description of the overidentifying constraints in the multiwave models used to estimate these coefficients is given in Appendix A. χ^2 values for all models are (a) personal aggression five-wave $\chi^2_6 = 8.839$, four-wave $\chi^2_3 = 7.474$; (b) teacher aggression five-wave $\chi^2_6 = 5.243$, four-wave $\chi^2_3 = 7.618$; (c) property aggression five-wave $\chi^2_3 = 5.330$, four-wave $\chi^2_0 = 0.0$ All two wave models are just-identified.

*Significant at .05 level.

TABLE 13.2

Impact of Violent Television Exposure on Personal, Teacher, and Property Aggression in a Model Considering Only Adjacent Effects[a]

		$TV_1 \rightarrow A_2$	$TV_2 \rightarrow A_3$	$TV_3 \rightarrow A_4$	$TV_4 \rightarrow A_5$
a. *Personal aggression*					
Five-wave model	*b*	−.005	.010	.016*	.001
	β	−.023	.058	.094	.008
Four-wave model	*b*		.002	.000	.016
	β		.009	.000	.092
Two-wave model	*b*				−.012
	β				−.067
b. *Teacher aggression*					
Five-wave model	*b*	.009	.006	.011	.015*
	β	.044	.036	.074	.094
Four-wave model	*b*		−.001	−.002	.023*
	β		−.010	−.012	.158
Two-wave model	*b*				.011
	β				.010
c. *Property aggression*					
Five-wave model	*b*	−.009	.118	−.003	.005
	β	−.059	.144	−.025	.044
Four-wave model	*b*		.013	−.014	.007
	β		.093	−.081	.058
Two-wave model	*b*				.007
	β				.052

[a] The models are identical to those presented in Table 13.1A–C with the exception that only adjacent television effects on aggression are estimated. χ^2 for the models are (*a*) personal aggression five-wave $\chi^2_{12} = 14.495$, four-wave $\chi^2_6 = 16.051$; (*b*) teacher aggression five-wave $\chi^2_{12} = 10.794$, four-wave $\chi^2_6 = 19.775$; (*c*) property aggression five-wave $\chi^2_{12} = 18.392$; four-wave $\chi^2_6 = 1.079$. All two-wave models are just-identified.

*Significant at .05 level.

Table 13.2 also presents several replications of some wave-pair coefficients in the five-, four-, and two-wave models. This allows us to make one additional evaluation: that consistently significant television effects might be found at a particular time even though they do not exist in the set of coefficients as a whole. There are two signs in the table that might be interpreted as evidence of such a television effect. First, the two largest property aggression coefficients are both in the II–III lag (in the five- and four-wave samples). Second, the two significant coefficients in the teacher aggression models are both in the IV–V lag (again, in the five- and four-wave samples). Reviews of television programming immediately prior to Wave II (October, 1970) and Wave IV (December, 1972) were carried out to see if some special broadcasts associated with property or teacher aggression could be detected.. Also other factors, internal as well external to our study, were considered. But these investigations revealed nothing that may have magnified television effects on these particular types of aggression at these particular times.[3] Attempts to replicate the nonlinear association in subgroups showed that it exists both in Minneapolis and Fort Worth among boys coming from both lower and middle socioeconomic status backgrounds.[4] Whereas these replications show that the pattern is robust within the wave, they do not help pinpoint its cause.

EXTENSIONS OF THE BASIC MODEL

Up to this point in the analysis, no evidence for a meaningful causal relationship between violent television exposure and later aggression against one's peers, teachers, or property has been reported. It is conceivable, however, that violation of the model assumptions of linearity, additivity, or perfect measurement has distorted truly significant associations so that they appear to be insignificant here. In the remainder of this section, we report the results of relaxing these assumptions.[5] Detailed findings are reported in Appendices B–F.

Linearity of Relationships

The multiwave models assume the existence of a linear, additive relationship between exposure and aggression. The possibility of nonadditives in the

---

[3]We looked for specials and televised movies shown at or immediately before the data collection waves and for television series that started just prior to the waves under examination and were short-lived. (Programs shown for long time periods would be expected to have lasting effects that reveal themselves in more than just one specific lag.)

With regard to property aggression at Time II, we found a broadcast of the theatrical movie "The Dirty Dozen" (CBS, September 24); the World Series games were shown in the beginning of October; new but short-lived series included *Silent Force, Nancy, The Immortal,* and *The Smokey Bear Show* on Saturday mornings.

We also considered if events in the study cities or aspects of the data collection at those times may have played a role. But we arrived at no plausible explanations for those findings. (See also discussion of nonlinearity below.)

[4]Of the nine quadratic equations (three different regression measures for wave pairs II–III, II–IV, and II–V), in each subgroup, five were significant in Ft. Worth, four in Minneapolis. Among boys whose mother's occupation defined them as middle class, three of the nonlinearities were significant. For boys defined in this way as members of the lower class, two were significant.

[5]The assumptions about linearity and measurement error are discussed in this chapter, with detailed results of our empirical examinations of the validity of the assumptions in the appendices. The assumption about additivity is addressed in two places later in the text. First, in Chapter 14 we consider a special kind of nonadditivity, one in which a series of earlier television measures at times $t-1$, $t-2$, etc., nonadditively influence change in aggression over the time interval $t-1$ to t. A second sort of nonadditivity is also considered in Chapter 14, when we examine the possibility that the influence of earlier television exposure on subsequent aggression is partially a function of initial aggression.

autoregression effects is explored in Chapter 14. Here we are concerned with the possibility of nonlinearities.

It is conceivable that television violence has an influence only if exposure exceeds some critical threshold level. If this is so, we might not expect significant television effects in the linear models considered so far in this chapter.

To explore this possibility, we carried out a series of polynomial regression analyses in which bend points in the regression line were allowed by including in the set of predictors not only earlier aggression and television exposure scores but also exponents of television. These models were estimated for all 10 wave pairs for each of the three aggression measures.

Of the 90 polynomial models estimated, 9 produced significant estimates of nonlinear television exposure effects. (Detailed tables of R^2 progressions are given in Appendix B.) There is a suggestive pattern in the significant relationships: all 9 involve Wave II as the earlier wave in the pair (the significant nonlinearities occurred in wave pairs II–III, II–IV, and II–V).[6]

Some idea of the strength of these nonlinear relationships can be obtained by using the hypothetical experiment approach we have employed earlier. The five equations for the quadratic relationships are as follows[7]:

Personal aggression

$$A_4 = 2.81 + .11A_1 + .21A_2 - .08TV_2 + .00081TV_2^2$$

Teacher aggression

$$A_3 = 2.17 + .23A_1 + .43A_2 - .05TV_2 + .00053TV_2^2$$

$$A_4 = 1.42 + .26A_1 + .12A_2 - .04TV_2 + .00063\,TV_2^2$$

Property aggression

$$A_3 = 1.57 + .23A_1 + .27A_2 - .05TV_2 + .00059TV_2^2$$

$$A_4 = 1.04 + .07A_1 + .24A_2 - .02TV_2 + .00031TV_2^2$$

The fact that these nonlinearities are quadratic means that the effect of television varies along the path of the regression curve, depending on where the function is evaluated. Since the quadratic term is positive in these equations, aggression is expected to increase more by increasing television exposure at the upper end of the scale than at the lower end.

[6]The lengths of the wave pairs II–III, II–IV, and II–V are 7 months, 2 years 1 month, and 2 years 6 months, respectively. Other wave pairs of similar duration did not show significant nonlinearities for any of the three aggression measures.

[7]Three of the nine significant nonlinearities were cubic and one was quartic, but we present only the quadratic equations here.

TABLE 13.3
Quadratic Regressions of Aggression on Earlier Violent Television Exposure

	INCREASE IN AGGRESSION IF TELEVISION IS INCREASED		
	FROM FIFTH TO NINETY-FIFTH PERCENTILE	FROM TENTH TO THIRTIETH PERCENTILE	FROM FIFTIETH TO SEVENTIETH PERCENTILE
Quadratic models			
Personal II–IV	.016	−.952	.344
Teacher II–III	.205	−.570	.272
Teacher II–IV	1.857	−.806	.712
Property II–III	.698	−.528	.416
Property II–V	.887	−.152	.344
Linear models			
Personal II–IV	1.029	.161	.174
Teacher II–III	.822	.129	.139
Teacher II–IV	2.208	.346	.372
Property II–III	1.245	.195	.210
Property II–V	1.071	.168	.181

Predicted values of aggression in these quadratic models are shown in Table 13.3. If we increased the violent television exposure of a teen from the 5th to 95th percentile and used the quadratic equations as our basis of estimation, we would expect to increase Wave IV personal aggression by .016 point, Wave III teacher aggression by .205 point, and so on as shown in Table 13.3. In each of these cases, the quadratic estimates are smaller than they would be had a linear model been used. If television exposure is increased at the lower end of the scale, from the 10th to 30th percentile, we would decrease each aggression score whereas the linear model increases them. On the other hand, increasing exposure at the upper end of the scale, from the 50th to 70th percentile, increases the aggression scores, and does so more than the linear model would.

We see from these hypothetical manipulations that linear and nonlinear predictions give substantially different results. What is puzzling is that this nonlinearity occurs only when Wave II is the early wave in a pair, no matter what the time lag, rather than across a series of comparable lags irrespective of the initial time point. This pattern raises the possibility that some special conditions in our data collection or a unique influence either in the environments of the boys or in the nature of a particular television program broadcast shortly before our November 1970 data collection is responsible for the nonlinear relationship. However, after extensive analysis of the possible internal and external factors, including the television fare offered in the two cities during this time period, we were unable to detect any special influence of this sort.

Measurement Error

Appendix C shows that no consistent longitudinal measurement model for teen aggression could be developed. In our analysis of aggression among elementary school boys and girls we found that individual aggression items formed tight clusters with the other items at a point in time and that changes in the individual items over time had a high degree of consistency. None of the three teen aggression measures exhibits these properties.

This situation makes it difficult to estimate the effect of measurement error on our results in any conventional fashion. We cannot use an internal consistency reliability estimate because we know that the measurement model on which this estimate is based is not consistent with the aggression data. However, the complex models needed to describe changes in the aggression measure are so internally inconsistent (for instance, estimating positively correlated errors across one wave pair and negatively correlated errors across another wave pair) that we can have little faith in the generalizability of findings based on them.

With these cautions in mind, we estimated a series of measurement models for the influence of violent television on our various aggression measures, using the results only as rough indicators of the possible influence of measurement imprecision on our results. The full set of results is presented in Appendix E. The adjustments made only small changes in the parameter estimates of interest to us, and consequently did not alter the conclusions just drawn.

Summary: Personal, Teacher, and Property Aggression

On the basis of global significance tests evaluating simultaneously a group of coefficients for linear models linking television with later aggression, we found no statistically significant evidence that violent television exposure has an effect on either teacher, personal, or property aggression. Analyses of individual coefficients supported this general conclusion.

Two pieces of information, though, are consistent with the possibility that television has some effect that has not been captured in this series of significance tests. The first is similar to the evidence reported in Chapters 6 and 8 for elementary school boys and girls, that most of the television coefficients are positive even though they are not statistically significant, and that all of the significant coefficients are positive as well.

This pattern could mean that television has a consistently small positive effect on aggression but one that is beyond the power of our design to detect. It is also possible that common causes of television viewing and aggressive behavior explain the pattern. Chapter 14 reports the results of exploratory analyses indicating that the preponderance of positive signs is at least in part caused by common causes of television viewing and aggression.

There is evidence of a nonlinear association in wave pairs that begin with Wave II. A full third of the nonlinearities having Wave II as the earlier time point are significant in Tables B.1–B.3. These significant associations appear for all three measures of aggression. In addition, there were significant coefficients in Wave II in the basic model for property aggression reported in Table 13.2. However, efforts to trace down a substantive explanation, such as a historical effect, failed. We could find nothing special about the television fare offered in the fall of 1970, the time of Wave II, that would lead us to expect a special effect of exposure during this time period. Nor could we discover anything in the historical happenings that might magnify the causal influence of television on teenage behavior patterns. (This was also true of the significances found with teacher aggression in Wave IV.)

DELINQUENCY

As discussed in Chapter 10, teens were questioned about six different delinquent acts. In any single wave, about 20% of the respondents admitted to involvement in at least one of these acts in the previous *3 months*. This is much fewer than the 70% who reported acts of personal aggression, 60% who admitted involvement in teacher aggression, and 40% who reported property aggression during the last *4 weeks*.

Given this rarity, our analysis focused on *initiation* of delinquency among teens who had, as of the first time point of the panel, never engaged in any of the six delinquent acts in our battery. A complete analysis of the relationship between television and delinquency would also assess the effects of television violence on continuation among boys who had initially been involved in delinquency. But so few of the study boys had a history of delinquent acts that an analysis of this sort was not possible.[8]

The Basic Model

Our decision to focus on initiation of delinquency required that we abandon the multiwave analysis approach used for the other teen's aggression data. This is because we were concerned only with those boys who at a point in time had

[8]For example, only 9 boys reported committing delinquent acts (during the last 3 months) in three consecutive waves (III, IV, and V).

never previously engaged in delinquency. This sample of boys, obviously, changes with each additional data collection. Therefore, we returned to the two-wave model approach used in our analysis of elementary school children. Among teens, we have five waves of data, giving us a total of 10 wave pairs for analysis. This use of partially overlapping wave pairs introduces a degree of ambiguity into the interpretation of results that was avoided in the multiwave models. But this is a necessary problem that accompanies the conceptualization we feel is appropriate to analyze these rare types of aggression. Our basic model is like that used in the analysis of elementary school children, with two exceptions. The reader will recall from Chapters 5 and 6 that the model used there was:

$$A_{t_i} = a + b_1 A_{(t-1)_i} + b_2 TV_{(t-1)_i} + u_i$$

Here, in contrast, we no longer include a measure of prior aggression, since we have controlled that by limiting ourselves to boys who have previously not been involved in delinquency. So, our model uses only the measure of earlier television exposure to predict initiation to delinquency.

The other exception follows from technical reasons associated with the fact that the delinquency measure is a dichotomy. It is possible to treat a dichotomous variable as if it were an interval level score, simply by assigning delinquents a score of "1" and all others a score of "0" on the "scale." When this is done, a regression analysis comparable to that presented for the elementary school sample can be performed. However, when the proportion of the sample engaged in the delinquent behavior is small, this approach runs afoul of certain technical problems of estimation that should be avoided. Fortunately, a class of models has been developed to deal with these technical problems. One of them, known as logit analysis (Nerlove & Press, 1973), will be used in our analysis. This approach makes use of a transformation of the dichotomous dependent variable of the following form (expressed in terms of means):

$$\ln (p/1 - p) = a + bX \tag{1}$$

which makes the model linear in log-odds. This equation can be solved iteratively to obtain maximum-likelihood estimates of p, the probability of initiating delinquency. Although we will not go into a technical discussion of the model (the reader is referred to Nerlove and Press, 1973, or to Hanushek and Jackson, 1978), we note that a reexpression of this equation in terms of the probability of initiating delinquency gives:

$$p = \frac{1}{1 + e^{-a-bX}} \tag{2}$$

This distribution ranges from 0 to 1 as $-a-bX$ ranges from $-\infty$ to $+\infty$. An ordinary least squares estimation procedure does not have this desirable property.

The Influence of Television Exposure on Delinquency

Table 13.4 reports the findings obtained through logit regression analysis. Respondents who reported delinquency in a wave were excluded from the following waves, since the analysis compares those who have never performed a delinquent act with those doing so for the first time.[9] The lagged relationship between earlier television exposure and later initiation of delinquency was estimated across all nine possible wave pairs in the five waves of the model.[10] (The I–II lag was not computed, because data to assess initiation of delinquency in Wave II were not adequate in Wave I; see footnote to table.) The three adjacent lags are shown in the upper part, the remaining six overlapping lags in the lower part of the tables.

These results might seem somewhat more complex than those presented in earlier analyses of basic relationships between television and aggression. But actually we have only used a more detailed format of presenting the data due to the fact that the *b* coefficients in the logit models have interpretations far less intuitive than those of linear regression coefficients. Rather than present the coefficients themselves, we have calculated the expected probabilities of involvement in delinquency for boys who view various amounts of television violence. These probabilities are generated from the logit regression coefficients. They are smoother than the observed data and are monotonic, because they are generated by a mathematical model. But they do describe the general shape of the television–aggression relationship in each wave pair.[11]

The ratios defining the significance of these relationships are also presented in Table 13.4. Four ratios are positive, five are negative, and one (a positive one) is significant. As in our earlier analysis we applied a global test and found that one wave pair out of the nine could be statistically significant by chance alone.[12] On the basis of this evaluation we conclude that there is no meaningful impact of television violence on initiating delinquency.

---

[9]As a result, sample sizes are smaller than they would be in ordinary two-wave analyses. The sample sizes range from 389 to 200 in the four waves used for the analysis.

[10]Table 13.4 shows results for only 9 lags; in the II–V lag, no analysis was possible because only one boy reported the delinquent behavior.

[11]The percentage of boys reporting delinquency for the first time in the various lags (fiftieth percentile in Table 13.4) is comparatively large in lags ending with Wave IV, as the time lag between Waves III and IV is the longest between adjacent waves (1 year, 7 months). In contrast, few boys reported delinquency for the first time in Wave V, as the IV–V lag is only 5 months. (In addition, Wave V data could not be corrected by inspection of a later wave, which would probably have increased the number of "initiators" in Wave V. This is also true of Wave III data.)

[12]The nine wave pairs considered here are not independent. All wave pairs ending at the same time contain respondents who reported involvement with delinquency for the first time in that

(*Continued next page*)

TABLE 13.4

Results of Logit Analysis for the Impact of Violent Television Exposure on Initiating Delinquency

	PREDICTED PROBABILITY OF INITIATING BEHAVIOR AMONG TEENS WITH EARLIER TELEVISION SCORES OF						
	FIFTH PERCENTILE	TENTH PERCENTILE	FIFTIETH PERCENTILE	NINTIETH PERCENTILE	NINETY-FIFTH PERCENTILE	RATIO OF *b* TO ITS STANDARD ERROR (*b/SE*)	*N*
Adjacent wave pairs							
I–II (5 months)							
II–III (7 months)	.091	.096	.117	.155	.177	1.19	(209)
III–IV (1 year 7 months)	.264	.273	.319	.410	.440	1.40	(175)
IV–V (5 months)	.058	.058	.062	.067	.068	.18	(192)
Nonadjacent wave pairs							
I–III (1 year)	.169	.159	.129	.095	.084	−.87	(143)
I–IV (2 years 7 months)	.296	.295	.293	.291	.290	−.04	(116)
I–V (3 years)	.117	.097	.049	.017	.012	−1.03	(80)
II–IV (2 years 1 month)	.212	.229	.304	.436	.508	2.01*	(172)
II–V (2 years 7 month)	.115	.097	.048	.016	.009	−1.16	(115)
III–V (2 years)	.165	.126	.031	.002	.001	−1.62	(113)

[a]Boys in Wave I were asked only about three of the six acts that made up the delinquency scale, so we were unable to assess initiation by Wave II. However, separate models were estimated for these three acts and none of these was significantly related to Wave I television exposure. The three were: "was arrested" (b/SE = .681); "participated in a gang fight" (b/SE = .869); and "was badly beaten up" (b/SE = −.044).

*Significant at .05 level

Extensions of the Basic Model

NONLINEARITY OF RELATIONSHIPS

The reader referring back to the basic logit equation will see that the cumulative distribution estimated in our various models is inherently nonlinear. Still, we estimated a series of polynomial logits to examine the possibility that various complex forms of nonlinearity are present in the data. The detailed results of this analysis are presented in Appendix F. There is no evidence there for a nonlinear relationship of this complex sort between television and delinquency.

MEASUREMENT ERROR

As in earlier chapters, when we have been concerned with causal relationships between television exposure and aggression, we asked ourselves if the relationships found between television and delinquency might be artificially low due to errors of measurement in the television exposure and delinquency items.

The issue of measurement error begins when we ask ourselves whether or not we can believe the teenagers when they tell us that they did or did not engage in any of several types of delinquent behavior. In Chapter 10 we discussed various ways in which we examined this question, all of which searched for internal inconsistencies in responses. Although it is true that some of our respondents were either mixed up in their estimates of the timing of their first involvement in delinquency, checked the wrong columns in answering our interview self-report forms, or lied, problems of this sort seemed quite rare. As detailed in Chapter 10, certain decisions were made to resolve the inconsistencies. On the basis of this work, we believe that the problem of measurement imprecision is small and does not distort the findings.

Given our belief in the basic soundness of the delinquency measures, the problem of measurement imprecision reduces to a concern with the television exposure index. We estimated the reliability of this index in Appendix D and found that the true relationships between exposure and delinquency might be as much as a third higher than we have estimated them to be in Table 13.4, even if our respondents perfectly reported their delinquency. No formal means exist of incorporating this reliability estimate into a measurement model for logits, which means that we cannot reestimate the models as we did in earlier analyses. But it is possible to return to Table 13.4 and inspect the pattern of relationships

---

wave. Therefore, a precise probability distribution for chance expectation cannot be calculated. However, as before, we can use the independence model to provide a rule of thumb. In a set of nine independent and nonoverlapping wave pairs, each of which has a 95% chance of being found statistically insignificant at the .05 level, the probability of actually finding all nine insignificant is only $.95^9 = .63$ (63%). The probability of finding at least one of the coefficients significant by chance is, then, 37%.

with the thought in mind that relationships might actually be a third larger than they appear to be there.

Going back and performing a mental exercise of this sort results in two conclusions, both of which argue against the importance of measurement error masking a truly important causal connection between television and delinquency. First, in all instances where a relationship exists of such a magnitude that we might imagine it would be significant were we to have available a perfect measure of television exposure, at least one relationship in a wave pair of comparable temporal duration is negative. Since measurement error in the television exposure scale acts to attenuate relationships, not to change signs, these negative relationships must also be assumed larger in reality than they appear to be in our estimations. As a result, improved measurement would leave us with a basic pattern of findings that argues against a consistent positive relationship between television and delinquency.

Furthermore, most relationships are so small that even an inflation by a third would still leave them insignificant in statistical terms. Again, this argues that more precise measures would not produce a pattern of consistent or significant relationships between television exposure and delinquent behavior.

APPENDIX A: PROCEDURES USED TO FIT THE FIVE- AND FOUR-WAVE MODELS

As described in Chapter 13, the parameter estimates in Table 13.1A, B, and C were obtained from overidentified cross-lagged models in which television was assumed to depend on all earlier measures of television exposure and on aggression at one time point preceding it. Aggression was assumed to depend on all earlier measures of both television and aggression. Cross-sectional correlations among the prediction errors of television and aggression were allowed. But serial correlations were assumed to be absent.

This appendix provides data indicating that this model is empirically reasonable. Table A.1 shows χ^2 values and degrees of freedom associated with several alternative models which we also estimated.

Model 1 in the table is the baseline. With each television and aggression measure assumed to depend on all earlier television and aggression measures and with cross-sectional correlations allowed among the prediction errors (a feature common to all models we estimated) there are no *df* in the model and the χ^2 value is 0.

Model 2 imposes the constraint that the effects of aggression on later nonadjacent television are zero. This model has 6 *df* in the five-wave case,

TABLE A.1

Multiwave Models of the Relationship between Violent Television Exposure and Aggression

	FIVE-WAVE			FOUR-WAVE		
	PERSONAL χ^2/df	TEACHER χ^2/df	PROPERTY χ^2/df	PERSONAL χ^2/df	TEACHER χ^2/df	PROPERTY χ^2/df
1. All lagged true score effects included	0/0	0/0	0/0	0/0	0/0	0/0
2. Nonadjacent $A \rightarrow TV$ effects deleted from (1)	8.839/6	5.243/6	5.330/6	7.474/3	7.618/3	16.185/3
3. Nonadjacent $TV \rightarrow TV$ effects deleted from (1)	107.030/6	100.424/6	101.597/6	13.732/3	14.774/3	26.230/3
4. Nonadjacent $TV \rightarrow A$ effects deleted from (2)[a]	14.495/12	10.794/12	18.390/12	16.051/6	19.725/6	2.079/3
5. Adjacent $TV \rightarrow A$ effects deleted from (2)[a]	19.844/16	18.452/16	28.393/16	17.708/9	25.023/9	5.082/6
N	(285)	(272)	(291)	(127)	(126)	(130)
6. χ^2 components due to $TV \rightarrow A$ effects in Model (2)[a]						
Model 5–Model 2[a] (total)	10.905/10	13.229/10	23.063/10	10.234/6	17.405/6	5.082/6
Model 4–Model 2[a] (nonadjacent)	5.554/6	5.571/6	13.060/6	8.577/3	12.107/3	2.079/3
Model 5–Model 4 (adjacent)	5.349/4	7.658/4	10.003/4	1.657/3	5.298/3	3.003/3

[a] In the case of four-wave property aggression, Model (1).

corresponding to the following constraints: $b_{TV_3A_1} = b_{TV_4A_1} = b_{TV_5A_1} = b_{TV_4A_2} = b_{TV_5A_2} = b_{TV_5A_3} = 0$. The four-wave variant of this model has 3 *df*.

The χ^2 values for this model are small with the exception of the four-wave property aggression model, where there are apparently significant nonadjacent influences of aggression and television. Therefore our final model includes the assumption that nonadjacent $A \rightarrow TV$ effects are 0 and that TV depends only on aggression measures in the wave directly preceding them. A model which allows nonadjacent $A \rightarrow TV$ effects is used for four-wave property aggression.

Model 3 imposes the constraint that TV depends on TV lagged by one time unit, but not on measures of TV earlier than this. This model, like Model 2, has 6 *df* for the five-wave and 3 *df* for the four-wave cases. Unlike Model 2, though, these constraints are inconsistent with the observed data. The χ^2 values are all extremely large, demonstrating that there are significant nonadjacent relationships between earlier and later TV in each of the samples. Therefore, our final model assumes that each TV measure depends on all earlier TV measures.

The three models we have considered thus far allowed us to determine the structure of influence in two ($A \rightarrow TV$ and $TV \rightarrow TV$) parts of the final model. We want to include some possibility for aggression to influence television viewing patterns, but nonadjacent effects of this sort are clearly unimportant. So we allowed A_t to influence TV_{t+1} in the final model. We found that empirical considerations dictate that we allow all earlier television scores to influence TV_{t+1}.

A third part of the final model links A_{t+1} with earlier measures of A. An analysis of the stability of aggression, reported in Appendix C, showed that we should allow all earlier measures of A to influence A_{t+1} in the final model.

This leaves us only with one remaining part of the final model, the causal effect of TV on A. Here we evaluated three different possibilities: including all possible links between A_{t+1} and earlier measures of TV (10 coefficients in the five-wave and 6 coefficients in the four-wave models); estimating only adjacent $TV \rightarrow A$ coefficients; estimating a model in which all $TV \rightarrow A$ coefficients are set to zero. These three possibilities, with our preferred assumptions about the other parts of the model ($A \rightarrow A$, $TV \rightarrow A$, $TV \rightarrow TV$) are built into Models 4 and 5.

The parameter estimates in Table 13.1A, B, and C are all taken from Model 2 in Table 13.1, with the exception of the four-wave property aggression model, which is taken from Model 1. The parameter estimates in Table 13.2 are taken from Model 4 in Table A.1. The χ^2 increments in Table 13.1A, B, and C are obtained by subtracting the χ^2 values of Models 2 or 4 from those of Models 4 or 5. The details of how this is done are shown in the last three rows of Table A.1.

APPENDIX B: NONLINEAR TELEVISION EFFECTS FOR PERSONAL, TEACHER, AND PROPERTY AGGRESSION

TABLE B.1
R^2 Progressions for Polynomial Regressions: Initial Aggression and Polynomials of Violent Television Exposure to Predict Later Personal Aggression

	EXPONENTS				
WAVE PAIR	*TV*	*TV^2*	*TV^3*	*TV^4*	*N*
I–II	.217	.218	.218	.224	(359)
I–III	.168	.169	.171	.171	(358)
I–IV	.079	.086	.087	.087	(321)
I–V	.166	.167	.168	.169	(309)
II–III	.358	.364	.370	.372	(350)
II–IV	.132	.168*	.179*	.179	(314)
II–V	.260	.264	.269	.270	(302)
III–IV	.259	.262	.262	.262	(308)
III–V	.363	.364	.365	.366	(298)
IV–V	.404	.406	.406	.408	(291)

*Significant increase (.05 level) in R^2 from the model with the exponent of *TV* one degree less.

TABLE B.2
R^2 Progressions for Polynomial Regressions: Initial Aggression and Polynomials of Violent Television Exposure to Predict Later Teacher Aggression

	EXPONENTS				
WAVE PAIR	*TV*	*TV^2*	*TV^3*	*TV^4*	*N*
I–II	.288	.289	.289	.290	(364)
I–III	.192	.198	.199	.206	(359)
I–IV	.133	.135	.137	.137	(311)
I–V	.054	.055	.055	.056	(295)
II–III	.330	.345*	.346	.347	(353)
II–IV	.193	.222*	.232*	.235	(306)
II–V	.197	.205	.205	.210	(291)
III–IV	.221	.222	.226	.226	(301)
III–V	.217	.225	.226	.228	(288)
IV–V	.484	.488	.488	.492	(278)

*Significant increase (.05 level) in R^2 from the model with the exponent of *TV* one degree less.

TABLE B.3
R^2 Progressions for Polynomial Regressions: Initial Aggression and Polynomials of Violent Television Exposure to Predict Later Property Aggression

WAVE PAIR	EXPONENTS				
	TV	TV^2	TV^3	TV^4	*N*
I–II	.190	.191	.199	.199	(363)
I–III	.133	.133	.133	.134	(361)
I–IV	.062	.062	.064	.069	(323)
I–V	.040	.046	.048	.048	(312)
II–III	.212	.250*	.260*	.261	(356)
II–IV	.164	.172	.177	.180	(318)
II–V	.125	.139*	.145	.162*	(307)
III–IV	.298	.300	.300	.301	(312)
III–V	.246	.248	.252	.252	(303)
IV–V	.430	.430	.430	.433	(296)

*Significant increase (.05 level) in R^2 from the model with the exponent of *TV* one degree less.

APPENDIX C: MEASUREMENT MODELS OF AGGRESSION

As a preliminary to estimating measurement models of the television–aggression relationship, we estimated a series of longitudinal models of change in aggression comparable to those presented for the elementary school sample in Appendix C of Chapter 6. All of these models have as their base a simple measurement model like that diagrammed in Figure C.1, where we assume the existence of true aggression scores (A_t) indicated imperfectly by our measures of aggression (a_{it}). All of the models we estimated assume that the true aggression scores are completely autocorrelated; that aggression at a point in time has a direct causal connection to all later measures of aggression.

As described in Chapter 10, the index of personal aggression contains three indicators, whereas the teacher aggression and property aggression indexes each contain only two indicators. With only these differences in mind, we began our analysis of measurement error by estimating a series of four equivalent models for the different index sets. The results are presented in Table C.1.

The first model estimated is identical to the model diagrammed in Figure C.1, where the measurement errors of the indicators are all assumed to be independent of each other and of the true scores. This model, which has 25 *df* for property and teacher aggression and 80 *df* for personal aggression, is not an adequate fit for any of the aggression measures. The χ^2/df ratio for property aggression is 7.6, that for teacher aggression is 5.7, and that for personal

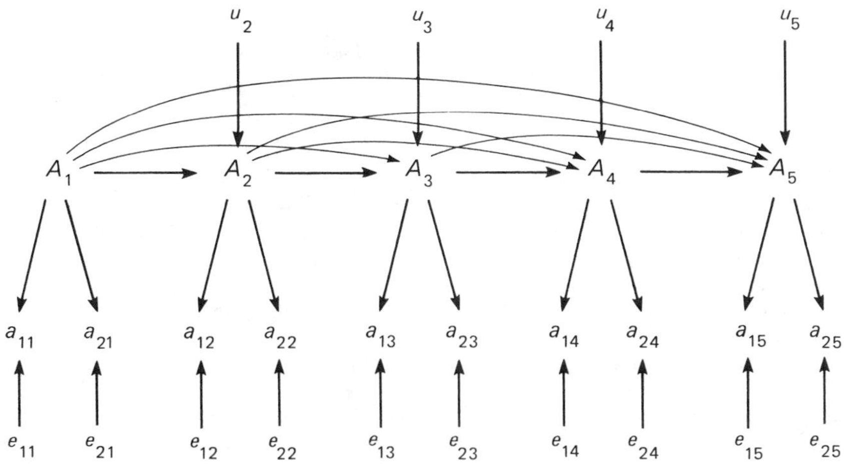

FIGURE C.1. *A basic measurement model of change in aggression.*

aggression is 3.7. As we are dealing with samples somewhat smaller than 300, we require ratios between 2.0 and 2.5 for an adequate model.

We next estimated a model in which the factor loadings for a particular indicator were constrained to be equal across all time points of the panel. For teacher and property aggression, this model has 33 *df*; for personal aggression, 92 *df*. Although this specification improved the fit somewhat for property and teacher aggression (χ^2/df ratios of 6.6 and 4.5, respectively), the improvement was not enough to make the fits acceptable. The fit deteriorated somewhat for the personal aggression model (χ^2/df was 3.8).

Up to this point, our baseline models failed to fit the data with complete accuracy, but nonetheless were close enough to make us optimistic about developing specialized models with good fit. However, as we progressed in our attempts to fit correlated error models, we were stymied by an inability to estimate consistent patterns of error correlation that would improve the overall fits.

The third and fourth equivalent models included correlated errors across one wave of data. That is, we assumed that the measurement error of each indicator was causally related to the measurement error of that same indicator one time point after it. This meant that we estimated 8 additional parameters for the two-indicator teacher and property aggression models and 12 additional parameters for the three-indicator personal aggression models. These models appear to fit well on a global basis. When the factor loadings are constrained to be equal across waves, the χ^2/df ratios for the teacher, property, and personal aggression models are, respectively, 1.9, 2.4, and 3.1. When these constraints are relaxed, the comparable ratios are 2.5, 2.5, and 3.3. An inspection of the residual

TABLE C.1
Several Five-Wave Measurement Models of Aggression

	PERSONAL AGGRESSION ($N = 291$)			TEACHER AGGRESSION ($N = 278$)			PROPERTY AGGRESSION ($N = 296$)		
MODEL	*df*	χ^2	χ^2/df	*df*	χ^2	χ^2/df	*df*	χ^2	χ^2/df
I. All true aggressions correlated. No errors correlated.	80	293.382	3.667	25	142.732	5.709	25	189.405	7.576
II. All true aggressions correlated. Factor loadings fixed to be equal. No errors correlated.	92	345.684	3.757	33	147.104	4.458	33	216.779	6.569
III. All true aggressions correlated. Factor loadings fixed to be equal. Errors correlated across one wave.	80	246.791	3.085	25	47.986	1.919	25	59.507	2.380
IV. All true aggressions correlated. Errors correlated across one wave.	68	225.382	3.314	17	42.701	2.512	17	42.724	2.513

covariance matrices shows that there are no important discrepancies between observed and predicted values.

However, this global support for the models masks important patterns within the models that are incongruous: namely, that the parameter estimates are in some cases implausible. This is true for the most part in the case of the correlated errors themselves, which are estimated to be substantial in magnitude and positive in one wave pair and negative in another—the magnitude and sign patterns having no consistency whatever. For instance, in Model III for teacher aggression with a χ^2/df ratio of 1.9, the correlation between the measurement error of the second indicator at times 1 and 2 is −.51, whereas the correlation at times 3 and 4 is +.25. We attempted to resolve this inconsistency by constraining the error correlations to be equal across the various wave pairs. This effort failed, probably in part because the time intervals separating the various wave pairs are very different.

These efforts were followed by others attempting to develop more specialized models for each of the aggression indexes separately: sometimes entirely dropping parameters connecting certain error terms, at other times imposing various plausible constraints. In each instance, though, we failed to develop a model that was either (*a*) as good a fit as the general models III and IV, or (*b*) more plausible substantively than Models III and IV. The models we estimated either contained relatively consistent patterns of error correlation and fit poorly, or implausible patterns of correlation and better fits.

The estimates of error correlations in these various refined measurement models were obviously confounded in some way. It is not clear to us just why or how this is the case. But we do know that with as few as two or three indicators per wave the likelihood of improved fit by capitalization on chance is high. In fact, there are several ways in which the error correlation models, even of the simple sort estimated in Models III and IV of the table, are indeterminate. For instance, we cannot identify the individual parameters at either Waves I or V in Model IV although once these are constrained, the model as a whole is identified. We therefore presume that the improved fit that seemingly results in an acceptable model on the global level represents overfitting.

On the other hand, we do know from the results in Models I and II that a simple uncorrelated error approach fails to fit any of these data matrices, suggesting that there are confounding errors of some importance. It is therefore not possible to proceed with simple attenuation corrections for cross-sectionally estimated unreliability.

APPENDIX D: MEASUREMENT MODELS OF TELEVISION EXPOSURE

To estimate the reliability of the television exposure score, we used the same technique used for the boys' data. This technique is based on the causal model shown in Figure C.2 in the appendix to Chapter 6. In that model the reported television exposure scores (tv_j) are imperfect indicators of unobserved true exposure scores (TV_j), which change through time not only because of true shifts in exposure, but also because of factors not included in the model (u_j). In the model, the term (e_j) refers to random measurement errors that affect the observed exposure scores.

For the teen sample, there are two sets of data for which we estimated television reliability: the group that entered in Wave I and stayed for all five waves and the group that entered in Wave II and stayed for the remaining four waves. Also, as there are not separate samples of valid and less valid reporters for the teens, we do not have different measures of reliability for the valid reporters and the total sample as we did for the elementary school sample.

When the causal model was estimated for the five-wave sample, the value of

TABLE D.1
Correlations between True and Observed Exposure Scores

	r_2	r_3	r_4	χ^2	*df*	N
Violent exposure						
Five-wave sample	.756	.747	.747	1.636	3	(293)
Four-wave sample		.693	.783	.495	1	(134)
Total exposure						
Five-wave sample	.721	.721	.793	7.093	3	(293)
Four-wave sample		.674	.797	1.247	1	(134)

TABLE D.2
Parameter Estimates for LISREL Measurement Models of Violent Television Exposure for Five-Wave and Four-Wave Samples

	FIVE-WAVE		FOUR-WAVE	
	M	S	M	S
	Epistemic correlations			
tv_1	1.0^f	*		
tv_2	1.0^f	.756	1.0^f	*
tv_3	1.0^f	.747	1.0^f	.693
tv_4	1.0^f	.747	1.0^f	.783
tv_5	1.0^f	*	1.0^f	*
	Variances			
Var (TV_1)	*	1.0		
Var (TV_2)	327.316	1.0	*	1.0
Var (TV_3)	283.810	1.0	290.047	1.0
Var (TV_4)	306.306	1.0	338.704	1.0
Var (TV_5)	*	1.0	*	1.0
Var (u_2)	*	*		
Var (u_3)	61.303	.216	*	*
Var (u_4)	49.009	.160	148.691	.439
Var (u_5)	*	*	*	*
	Stability coefficients			
$b_{TV_1TV_2}$	*	*		
$b_{TV_2TV_3}$	.825	.886	*	*
$b_{TV_3TV_4}$	.952	.917	.810	.749
$b_{TV_4TV_5}$	*	*	*	*
	Covariances			
Cov (tv_1, TV_2)	252.222	.665		

(*Continued next page*)

TABLE D.2 *(continued)*

	FIVE-WAVE		FOUR-WAVE	
	M	S	M	S
	Covariances			
Cov (tv_2, TV_3)			240.260	.538
Cov (TV_4, tv_5)	269.896	.864	213.826	.634
χ^2	1.636		.495	
χ^2/df	.545		.495	
N	(293)		(134)	

M = metric coefficients
S = standardized coefficients
f = fixed
*None of these values is individually identified although the terms Cov (tv_1, TV_2) and Cov (TV_4, tv_5) in the five-wave model and Cov (tv_2, TV_3) and Cov (TV_4, tv_5) in the four-wave model are identified. All other parameters internal to these in the models are individually identified. We estimated these by arbitrarily assigning fixed values to the measurement errors at times 1 and 5 in the five-wave model and at times 2 and 5 in the four-wave model.

χ^2 was 1.636 with 3 df, representing a very good fit.[13] The estimated correlations between each TV_j and its associated tv_j are given in the first row of Table D.1. These coefficients are all near .75 and do not show any trend through time. Reliability, the square of these coefficients, is then near .56; this means that about 56% of the variance in the violent television exposure score is true variance and 44% is error.

The second row of Table D.1 presents results for the four-wave sample. Here the correlations between true and observed violent exposure scores are .69 and .78, corresponding to reliabilities of .48 and .61. Thus, between 48% and 61% of the variance is true variance and between 39% and 52% is error.

Details of the parameters in these models are presented in Table D.2.

---

[13]This result might seem counterintuitive in light of the previous demonstration that nonadjacent autoregressive terms linking earlier and later television measures were needed to fit the five- and four-wave models on which Table 13.1 is based (see Appendix A). It tells us that nonadjacent true exposure score correlations are not needed to fit the five- and four-wave television exposure stability models. The apparent discrepancy is explained by the fact that the models on which Table D.1 is based are *measurement* models, whereas Table 13.1 is based on *observed* score models. In the measurement models we find that there is no net impact of TV_{t-2} on TV_t when the intervening influence of TV_{t-1} is controlled. However, since the observed measure tv_{t-1} is only an imperfect indicator of TV_{t-1}, we do not entirely remove the intervening influence of the latter by controlling the former. This is why there is a net effect of tv_{t-2} on tv_t when tv_{t-1} is controlled.

APPENDIX E: MEASUREMENT MODELS OF TELEVISION'S INFLUENCE ON AGGRESSION

Although we concluded in Appendix C that no consistent longitudinal measurement models for aggression could be developed, it is still important to take measurement error into account in examining the influence of violent television exposure on adolescent aggression. To achieve this, we decomposed the aggression measures into their indicators and estimated a series of models for each until the χ^2/df ratio approached a value near 2.0, and the residual errors of estimation did not exceed 10% of the observed covariances. Then models incorporating the television variable were estimated. The results of these analyses are presented in the following, separately for each of the aggression measures.

Aggression Measurement Models

The best-fitting measurement models for the three aggression measures are quite distinct. For personal aggression, the measurement errors of each indicator are autocorrelated over two subsequent waves. For teacher aggression, the measurement errors are autocorrelated over only one subsequent wave. And for property aggression, the errors of the "damaging" indicator are correlated over two later waves, while the errors of the "stealing" indicator are independent. All of these specifications fit the data well. The χ^2/df ratio for the personal aggression model is 1.5, for the teacher aggression model is 2.1, and for the property aggression model is 1.2. (Five-wave models only were used in this model trimming phase of the analysis.)

Overall χ^2 Evaluations

Table E.1 presents the overall χ^2 coefficients of the five- and four-wave measurement models in which the effects of television on aggression are assessed. In each of these, the initial television–aggression relationship is assumed to be exogenous to the model, the prediction errors of the television and aggression true scores are allowed to be cross-sectionally correlated, the measurement model for television estimated in Appendix D is assumed to hold for the television measures, and the correlated measurement errors described in the last section are estimated for the aggression indicators.

The models in Table E.1 differ only in the number of television effect coefficients estimated. In the first row the χ^2 coefficients are those for models in which all earlier television scores are assumed to influence all later aggression scores. In the five-wave models, this means that 10 television coefficients are estimated; in the four-wave models there are 6 such coefficients. In the second row, the χ^2 coefficients are for models that assume all effects of television on later aggression are 0.

TABLE E.1

χ^2 Coefficients Associated with Measurement Models of the Relationship between Violent Television Exposure and Later Aggression

		FIVE-WAVE			FOUR-WAVE		
		PERSONAL	TEACHER	PROPERTY	PERSONAL	TEACHER	PROPERTY
1. All television effects included	χ^2	194.703	113.764	76.379	171.415	55.516	34.889
	df	118	51	52	70	29	30
2. No television effects included	χ^2	207.408	124.610	95.024	184.470	70.731	39.190
	df	128	61	62	76	35	36
3. χ^2 increments due to television effects Model 1	χ^2	12.705	10.846	18.645	13.055	15.215	4.301
	df	10	10	10	6	6	6
4. χ^2 increments from Table 13.1	χ^2	10.905	13.229	23.063	10.234	17.465	5.082
	df	10	10	10	6	6	6

Subtracting the χ^2 coefficients in the first two rows yields an incremental χ^2 coefficient associated with television effects. These increments can be compared directly to the increments presented in Table 13.1 for the models in which perfect measurement was assumed. This provides us with a quick overall assessment of the implications of the measurement error adjustment for our estimates of the impact of television on aggression. The third row of the table presents these increments and the fourth row presents, for comparative purposes, the increments from Table 13.1. Comparison of the third and fourth rows shows that the increments for the measurement error models are smaller than those from Table 13.1 for teacher and property aggression. The measurement model increments are somewhat larger for personal aggression. On an overall basis, then, the measurement error adjustment had very little effect on our estimate of television's importance in predicting aggression.

Detailed Parameter Estimates

Table E.2 reports regression coefficients for the measurement models. The results reported here are for models in which only adjacent television effects are estimated; that is, the effects of TV_t on A_{t+1}, where t goes from 1 to 4. This is done because the models containing estimates for television effects on all later aggression measures produced highly collinear television effect estimates.

Inspection of the television coefficients in these models shows them to be similar in magnitude to those in Table 13.1. For personal aggression, the two largest coefficients in Table E.2 correspond to the two significant television effects in Table 13.1, although only one remains significant when we adjust for measurement error. For teacher aggression, the significant R^2 increment associated with television in predicting A_5 in the four-wave model in Table 13.1 is again significant here. And for property aggression the largest coefficients in Table E.2 correspond to those in Table 13.1. Here, though, the one television effect coefficient that was significant in Table 13.1 is no longer significant when measurement error is removed from the estimation equation.

Detailed parameter estimates for these models are presented in Tables E.3 (for the five-wave models), E.4 (for the four-wave models), and E.5 (for the two-wave models).

TABLE E.2

A: Basic Model Regression Coefficients Showing the Effect of Violent Television Exposure on Later Personal Aggression, LISREL Measurement Models

		PREDICTORS								
		A_1	A_2	A_3	A_4	TV_1	TV_2	TV_3	TV_4	R^2
OUTCOME		(1)	(2)	(3)	(4)	(5)	(6)	(7)	(8)	(9)
a. *Five-wave model*										
A_2	b	.477				−.003				
	β	.708				−.073				.487
A_3	b	.153	.745*				.001			
	β	.174	.570				.021			.501
A_4	b	.064	−.034	.514*				.004		
	β	.087	−.031	.615				.086		.439
A_5	b	.191	.219	.231	.375*				.000	
	β	.205	.158	.218	.295				−.005	.522
$N = 285$										
$\chi^2_{124} = 204.831$										
$\chi^2/df = 1.7$										
b. *Four-wave model*										
A_3	b		.392*				.001			
	β		.399				.019			.162
A_4	b		.222	.384*				.001		
	β		.256	.437				.021		.350
A_5	b		.114	.041	.832*				.009*	
	β		.104	.036	.654				.206	.577
$N = 127$										
$\chi^2_{73} = 179.763$										
$\chi^2/df = 2.5$										

(Continued next page)

TABLE E.2 (*continued*)

B: Basic Model Regression Coefficients Showing the Effect of Violent Television Exposure on Later Teacher Aggression, LISREL Measurement Models

OUTCOME		A_1 (1)	A_2 (2)	A_3 (3)	A_4 (4)	TV_1 (5)	TV_2 (6)	TV_3 (7)	TV_4 (8)	R^2 (9)
		PREDICTORS								
a. *Five-wave model*										
A_2	b	.698*				.009				
	β	.678				.072				.464
A_3	b	.176	.520*				−.004			
	β	.169	.513				−.035			.399
A_4	b	.174	.227*	.120				.007		
	β	.199	.268	.143				.075		.283
A_5	b	−.306*	.405*	.091	.688*				.012	
	β	−.308	.421	.096	.607				.108	.656
$N = 272$										
$\chi^2_{37} = 118.288$										
$\chi^2/df = 2.1$										
b. *Four-wave model*										
A_3	b		.430*				−.001			
	β		.379				−.010			.143
A_4	b		.602*	.233				.012		
	β		.406	.178				.094		.263
A_5	b		.387*	.226*	.371*				.029*	
	β		.367	.243	.521				.315	.867
$N = 126$										
$\chi^2_{32} = 61.805$										
$\chi^2/df = 1.9$										

C: *Basic Model Regression Coefficients Showing the Effect of Violent Television Exposure on Later Property Aggression, LISREL Measurement Models*

OUTCOME		PREDICTORS								
		A_1 (1)	A_2 (2)	A_3 (3)	A_4 (4)	TV_1 (5)	TV_2 (6)	TV_3 (7)	TV_4 (8)	R^2 (9)
a. *Five-wave model*										
A_2	b	.559*				−.007				
	β	.536				−.084				.292
A_3	b	.214	.474*				.011			
	β	.185	.428				.131			.332
A_4	b	−.017	.330*	.514*				−.006		
	β	−.015	.299	.515				−.062		.504
A_5	b	−.046	.096	.052	.798*				.010	
	β	−.036	.078	.047	.722				.106	.640
$N = 291$										
$\chi^2_{58} = 88.536$										
$\chi^2/df = 1.5$										
b. *Four-wave model*										
A_3	b		.222				.014			
	β		.293				.119			.092
A_4	b		.122	.444*				−.013		
	β		.141	.388				−.083		.207
A_5	b		.046	.254*	.408*				.004	
	β		.056	.235	.432				.025	.350
$N = 130$										
$\chi^2_{33} = 37.399$										
$\chi^2/df = 1.1$										

*Significant at .05 level.

TABLE E.3

Parameter Estimates for the LISREL Five-Wave Measurement Models

	PERSONAL AGGRESSION		TEACHER AGGRESSION		PROPERTY AGGRESSION	
	M	S	M	S	M	S
			*Epistemic correlations***			
a_{11}	1.000^f	.662	1.000^f	.883	1.000^f	.853
a_{21}	1.365	.670	.695	.747	.522	.515
a_{31}	1.024	.565				
a_{12}	1.000^f	.583	1.000^f	.789	1.000^f	.766
a_{22}	2.719	.782	.870	.793	.834	.654
a_{32}	2.398	.772				
a_{13}	1.000^f	.772	1.000^f	.864	1.000^f	.815
a_{23}	1.798	.892	.761	.732	.609	.582
a_{33}	1.650	.681				
a_{14}	1.000^f	.703	1.000^f	.854	1.000^f	.843
a_{24}	1.873	.849	.807	.826	.429	.547
a_{34}	1.544	.558				
a_{15}	1.000^f	.735	1.000^f	.884	1.000^f	.892
a_{25}	1.022	.719	.778	.776	.276	.398
a_{35}	1.284	.688				
tv_1	1.000^f	.756	1.000^f	.756	1.000^f	.756
tv_2	1.000^f	.757	1.000^f	.750	1.000^f	.763
tv_3	1.000^f	.748	1.000^f	.755	1.000^f	.749
tv_4	1.000^f	.744	1.000^f	.741	1.000^f	.746
tv_5	1.000^f	.827	1.000^f	.756	1.000^f	.757
			Variances			
Var (A_1)	.925	1.000	3.430	1.000	1.794	1.000
Var (u_{A_2})	.215	.513	1.950	.536	1.384	.708
Var (u_{A_3})	.358	.499	2.250	.601	1.606	.668

Var (u_{A_4})	.282	.561	1.884	.717	1.186	.496
Var (u_{A_5})	.387	.478	1.160	.344	1.051	.360
Var (TV_1)	250.693[f]	1.000	245.542[f]	1.000	246.054[f]	1.000
Var (u_{TV_2})	72.493	.225	77.922	.282	77.708	.228
Var (u_{TV_3})	69.029	.246	70.625	.242	61.122	.219
Var (u_{TV_4})	47.009	.158	39.125*	.147	30.482*	.100
Var (u_{TV_5})	.000[f]	.000	.000[f]	.000	.000[f]	.000
			Covariances			
Cov (A_1TV_1)	2.794	.184	−.361*	−.012	.467*	.022
Cov (u_{A_2}, u_{TV_2})	1.459*	.125	5.598	.176	2.548*	.099
Cov (u_{A_3}, u_{TV_3})	1.011*	.071	−.364*	−.011	1.668*	.064
Cov (u_{A_4}, u_{TV_4})	−.457*	−.037	−.305*	−.012	.967*	.036
Cov (u_{A_5}, u_{TV_5})	.235*	.017	−1.303*	−.050	−2.001*	−.079
			Correlated errors			
Cov (e_{11}, e_{12})	.019*	.019	−.022*	−.015		
Cov (e_{11}, e_{13})	.264	.347				
Cov (e_{21}, e_{22})	.362	.177	.244*	.167	.452	.288
Cov (e_{21}, e_{23})	.234	.208			.468	.305
Cov (e_{31}, e_{32})	.183*	.099				
Cov (e_{31}, e_{33})	.637	.295				
Cov (e_{12}, e_{13})	.199	.316	.685	.409		
Cov (e_{12}, e_{14})	.111	.172				
Cov (e_{22}, e_{23})	.016*	.015	.075*	.043	.623	.350
Cov (e_{22}, e_{24})	.077*	.066			.452	.330

(Continued next page)

TABLE E.3 (*continued*)

	PERSONAL AGGRESSION		TEACHER AGGRESSION		PROPERTY AGGRESSION	
	M	S	M	S	M	S
	Variances (continued)					
Cov (e_{32}, e_{33})	.492	.255				
Cov (e_{32}, e_{34})	−.015*	−.007				
Cov (e_{13}, e_{14})	.128	.256	.284	.255		
Cov (e_{13}, e_{15})	.153	.264				
Cov (e_{23}, e_{24})	−.179	−.281	.351	.286	.514	.384
Cov (e_{23}, e_{25})	.115*	.167			.363	.253
Cov (e_{33}, e_{34})	.368	.150				
Cov (e_{33}, e_{35})	.491	.268				
Cov (e_{14}, e_{15})	.225	.378	.173*	.181		
Cov (e_{24}, e_{25})	−.088*	−.120	.353	.340	.550	.498
Cov (e_{34}, e_{35})	.569	.287				
	Stability coefficients					
$b_{A_1A_2}$	.477	.708	.698	.678	.559	.536
$b_{A_1A_3}$	.153*	.174	.176*	.169	.214*	.185
$b_{A_1A_4}$	.064*	.087	.174*	.199	−.017*	−.015
$b_{A_1A_5}$	.191*	.205	−.306	−.308	−.046*	−.036
$b_{A_2A_3}$	.745	.570	.520	.513	.474	.428
$b_{A_2A_4}$	−.034*	−.031	.227	.268	.330	.299
$b_{A_2A_5}$	.219*	.158	.405	.421	.096*	.078
$b_{A_3A_4}$	.514	.615	.120*	.143	.514	.515
$b_{A_3A_5}$	.231*	.218	.091*	.096	.052*	.047
$b_{A_4A_5}$	.375	.296	.688	.607	.798	.722
$b_{TV_1TV_2}$	.969	.854	.898	.846	.028	.874
$b_{TV_2TV_3}$	.835	.896	.928	.905	.801	.885
$b_{TV_3TV_4}$	.903	.876	.882	.924	.994	.950
$b_{TV_4TV_5}$	.940	1.028	.877	1.002	.845	.998

			Regression coefficients			
$b_{A_1TV_2}$	2.033*	.109	.576*	.064	.975*	.071
$b_{A_2TV_3}$	−5.220	−.202	−2.023	−.226	−1.273*	−.107
$b_{A_3TV_4}$	3.881	.190	.549*	.065	−.056*	−.005
$b_{A_4TV_5}$	−5.242	−.235	−.716*	−.081	−1.121*	−.117
$b_{TV_1A_2}$	−.003*	−.073	.009*	.072	−.007*	−.084
$b_{TV_2A_3}$	.001*	.021	−.004*	−.035	.011*	.131
$b_{TV_3A_3}$	.004*	.086	.007*	.075	−.006*	−.062
$b_{TV_4A_5}$	.000*	−.005	.012*	.108	.010*	.106
χ^2	204.831		118.288		88.536	
df	124		57		58	
N	(285)		(272)		(291)	

M = metric coefficients

S = standardized coefficients.

f = fixed.

*Coefficient *not* significant at .05 level.

**a_{1i}, a_{2i}, and a_{3i} refer to fighting, pushing, and arguing, respectively, in the personal aggression measure. In the teacher aggression measure, a_{1i} refers to being rude and a_{2i} refers to sassing. In the property aggression measure, a_{1i} refers to stealing and a_{2i} refers to damaging property. For teacher and property aggression there is no a_{3i}.

TABLE E.4

Parameter Estimates for the LISREL Four-Wave Measurement Models

	PERSONAL AGGRESSION		TEACHER AGGRESSION		PROPERTY AGGRESSION	
	M	S	M	S	M	S
			*Epistemic correlations***			
a_{11}						
a_{21}						
a_{31}						
a_{12}	1.000^f	.412	1.000^f	.545	1.000^f	1.159
a_{22}	3.105	.840	1.358	.824	.252	.401
a_{32}	2.041	.594				
a_{13}	1.000^f	.460	1.000^f	.771	1.000^f	.907
a_{23}	3.215	.879	.841	.714	.418	.585
a_{33}	2.262	.562				
a_{14}	1.000^f	.415	1.000^f	.817	1.000^f	1.014
a_{24}	3.604	1.043	.692	.751	.391	.654
a_{34}	2.315	.594				
a_{15}	1.000^f	.551	1.000^f	.771	1.000^f	1.306
a_{25}	2.337	.913	.759	.658	.151	.250
a_{35}	1.378	.511				
tv_1						
tv_2	1.000^f	.756	1.000^f	.756	1.000^f	.756
tv_3	1.000^f	.745	1.000^f	.743	1.000^f	.741
tv_4	1.000^f	.725	1.000^f	.739	1.000^f	.754
tv_5	1.000^f	.754	1.000^f	.744	1.000^f	.733
			Variances			
Var (A_1)						
Var (A_2)	.433	1.000	2.114	1.000	8.871*	1.000
Var (u_{A_3})	.351	.838	2.330	.857	4.596	.908

Var (u_{A_4})	.211	.650	3.422	.737	5.242	.793
Var (u_{A_5})	.223	.423	.314*	.133	3.833*	.650
Var (TV_1)						
Var (TV_2)	384.411	1.000	376.892	1.000	373.740	1.000
Var (u_{TV_3})	120.176	.435	126.466	.465	144.046	.535
Var (u_{TV_4})	86.660	.324	117.454	.408	139.444	.465
Var (u_{TV_5})	5.346*	.027	.000[f]	.000	.000[f]	.000
			Covariances			
Cov (A_1TV_1)						
Cov (A_2TV_2)	2.673*	.207	2.593*	.092	−7.053*	−.122
Cov (u_{A_3}, u_{TV_3})	.582*	.054	5.789*	.213	−.402*	−.011
Cov (u_{A_4}, u_{TV_4})	.862*	.092	−.038*	−.001	.947*	.021
Cov (u_{A_5}, u_{TV_5})	−.452*	−.044	.826*	.039	.215*	.007
			Correlated errors			
Cov (e_{11}, e_{12})						
Cov (e_{11}, e_{13})						
Cov (e_{21}, e_{22})						
Cov (e_{21}, e_{23})						
Cov (e_{31}, e_{32})						
Cov (e_{31}, e_{33})						
Cov (e_{12}, e_{13})	.684	.377	.284*	.093		
Cov (e_{12}, e_{14})	.679	.374				
Cov (e_{22}, e_{23})	−.274*	−.184	.741	.402	.257*	.115
Cov (e_{22}, e_{24})	−1.253	g			.183*	.092

(Continued next page)

TABLE E.4 (*continued*)

	PERSONAL AGGRESSION		TEACHER AGGRESSION		PROPERTY AGGRESSION	
	M	S	M	S	M	S
*Epistemic correlations***						
Cov (e_{32}, e_{33})	1.441	.368				
Cov (e_{32}, e_{34})	.668	.205				
Cov (e_{13}, e_{14})	1.000	.641	1.027	.497		
Cov (e_{13}, e_{15})	−.034*	−.025				
Cov (e_{23}, e_{24})	−.850	g	.395*	.222	.614	.405
Cov (e_{23}, e_{25})	−.045*	−.053			.332*	.179
Cov (e_{33}, e_{34})	1.341	.347				
Cov (e_{33}, e_{35})	.991	.274				
Cov (e_{14}, e_{15})	.293	.213	−.174*	−.091		
Cov (e_{24}, e_{25})	−.506*	g	−.260*	−.149	.358	.216
Cov (e_{34}, e_{35})	1.036	.345				
Stability coefficients						
$b_{A_1A_2}$						
$b_{A_1A_3}$						
$b_{A_1A_4}$						
$b_{A_1A_5}$						
$b_{A_2A_3}$	.392	.399	.430	.379	.222*	.293
$b_{A_2A_4}$	.222*	.256	.602	.406	.122*	.141
$b_{A_2A_5}$	.114*	.104	.387	.367	.046*	.056
$b_{A_3A_4}$	.384	.437	.233*	.178	.444	.388
$b_{A_3A_5}$	.041*	.036	.226	.243	.254	.235
$b_{A_4A_5}$	.832	.654	.371	.521	.408	.432
$b_{TV_1TV_2}$						
$b_{TV_2TV_3}$	.641	.756	.623	.733	.579	.682

$b_{TV_3TV_4}$	.798	.811	.803	.781	.773	.732
$b_{TV_4TV_5}$	.819	.953	.810	.995	.761	.989
			Regression coefficients			
$b_{A_1TV_2}$						
$b_{A_2TV_3}$	−.605*	−.024	−1.293*	−.114	.023*	.004
$b_{A_3TV_4}$	−6.718	−.266	−2.167*	−.211	−.283*	−.037
$b_{A_4TV_5}$	5.476	.222	.588*	.092	−.554*	−.107
$b_{TV_1A_2}$						
$b_{TV_2A_3}$	.001*	.019	−.001*	−.010	.014*	.119
$b_{TV_3A_4}$	.001*	.021	.012*	.094	−.013*	−.083
$b_{TV_4A_5}$	.009	.206	.029	.315	.004*	.025
χ^2	179.763		61.805		37.399	
df	13				33	
N	(127)		(126)		(130)	

M = metric coefficients.

S = standardized coefficients.

f = fixed.

g = covariance undefined because error variance was estimated as less than zero. A situation of this sort, known as a Haywood case, can be rectified (the error variance can be forced to be greater than or equal to zero) by reparametrizing the model so that e_{ij} is conceptualized as a true score that influences the observed a_{ij}. Then the square root of the error variance is estimated, which effectively imposes the desired constraint. We did not make this adjustment though. As discussed in the text, these measurement models have a number of substantively implausible features, other than this one, which we have not been able to correct. In light of this, adjustment for the Haywood case did not seem worthwhile.

*Coefficient *not* significant at .05 level.

**a_{1i}, a_{2i}, and a_{3i} refer to fighting, pushing, and arguing, respectively, in the personal aggression measure. In the teacher aggression measure a_{1i} refers to being rude and a_{2i} refers to sassing. In the property aggression measure a_{1i} refers to stealing and a_{2i} refers to damaging property. For teacher and property aggression there is no a_{3i}.

TABLE E.5

Parameter Estimates for the LISREL Two-Wave Measurement Models

	PERSONAL AGGRESSION		TEACHER AGGRESSION		PROPERTY AGGRESSION	
	M	S	M	S	M	S
			*Epistemic correlations***			
a_{14}	1.000^f	.645	1.000^f	.953	1.000^f	.936
a_{24}	1.209	.565	.842	.805	.458	.640
a_{34}	1.260	.701				
a_{15}	1.000^f	.655	1.000^f	.996	1.000^f	.847
a_{25}	1.336	.702	.499	.603	.635	.699
a_{35}	1.199	.747				
tv_4	1.000^f	.746	1.000^f	.746	1.000^f	1.000
tv_5	1.000^f	.746	1.000^f	.746	1.000^f	1.000
			Variances			
Var (TV_4)	331.452	1.000	293.501	1.000	331.452	1.000
Var (u_{TV_5})	57.294	.190	25.358	.084	60.614	.201
Var (A_4)	1.417	1.000	3.872	1.000	4.653	1.000
Var (u_{A_5})	.789	.686	2.103	.434	2.045	.632
			Covariances			
Cov (u_{TV_5}, u_{A_5})	1.583	.085	−.345	−.009	1.762	.011
			Correlated errors			
Cov (e_{14}, e_{15})	−.069*	−.079	−.319*	−1.000		
Cov (e_{24}, e_{25})	−.139*	−.201	.474	.398	.012*	.013
Cov (e_{34}, e_{35})	.239	.319				

$b_{A_4A_5}$	.520	.577	.840	.751	.498	.597
$b_{TV_4TV_5}$	.830	.871	.969	.957	.851	.894
			Regression coefficients			
$b_{A_4TV_5}$	1.322*	.091				
$b_{TV_4A_5}$	−.014*	−.236	.015*	.119	.008*	.082
χ^2	13.309		2.478		9.041	
χ^2/df	.951		.413		1.507	
N	(143)		(137)		(143)	

M = metric coefficients.

S = standardized coefficients.

f = fixed.

*Coefficient *not* significant at .05 level.

**a_{1i}, a_{2i}, and a_{3i} refer to fighting, pushing, and arguing, respectively, in the personal aggression measure. In the teacher aggression measure a_{1i} refers to being rude and a_{2i} refers to sassing. In the property aggression measure a_{1i} refers to stealing and a_{2i} refers to damaging property. For teacher and property aggression there is no a_{3i}.

APPENDIX F: LOGISTIC REGRESSION TABLE OF NONLINEAR TELEVISION EFFECTS

TABLE F.1
Logistic Regression of Nonlinear Television Effects: Delinquency (All Six Measures Combined)

SOURCE	*df*	I–II	*df*	I–III	*df*	I–IV	*df*	I–V	*df*	II–III
Total χ^2	187	213.6070	142	108.2417	115	140.3385	79	31.7624	208	157.0028
Linear *TV*	1	2.0722	1	.7997	1	.0015	1	1.2769	1	1.3378
Quadratic *TV*	1	1.5252	1	1.6569	1	.1396	1	.2624	1	3.1424
Cubic *TV*	1	2.2170	1	.3592	1	2.2687	1	.0183	1	.9813
Quartic *TV*	1	.7754	1	5.0880*	1	.1425	—	—	1	.0442
Error	183	207.0172	138	100.3379	111	137.7862	76	30.2048	204	151.4971

SOURCE	*df*	II–IV	*df*	II–V	*df*	III–IV	*df*	III–V	*df*	IV–V
Total χ^2	171	215.5827	114	47.1194	174	222.3150	112	40.9549	191	89.7760
Linear *TV*	1	4.1085*	1	1.6057	1	1.9478	1	4.1379*	1	.0341
Quadratic *TV*	1	.3792	1	.6505	1	1.1672	1	1.7566	1	.0104
Cubic *TV*	1	.1564	1	.3132	1	.4180	—	—	1	1.2653
Quartic *TV*	1	.0024	1	.5469	1	1.0690	—	—	—	—
Error	167	210.9362	110	44.0031	170	217.7130	110	35.0604	188	88.4662

Note: Blank table entries signify that a solution to the logistic model was not possible either because of one occurrence of the act or because of prohibitively large exponents in the iterative phase.

*Significant at .05 level.

CHAPTER 14

ADDITIONAL ANALYSES

This chapter reports on analyses conducted to supplement the basic analyses in the previous chapter. The same plan used in the study of elementary school children is followed here. We first examine the predictive power of alternative conceptualizations of exposure to television violence. Then we report subgroup analyses to examine the hypothesis that television influences only certain types of teenage boys. Finally, we test the sensitivity of the analysis model and examine variables that may not have been controlled in the basic model.

OTHER CONCEPTUALIZATIONS OF TELEVISION EXPOSURE AND THEIR EFFECT ON AGGRESSION

Several variables reflecting attitudes toward television were added to the same alternative measures of television that were analyzed for the elementary school sample (Chapters 7 and 8). In each case, the ability of a particular index to predict personal, property, and delinquency aggression is compared to the predictive power of the violent television exposure index.[1]

Because several different conceptualizations of television exposure are tested, different comparisons are used. When a new measure is *substituted* for

[1]Analyses with teacher aggression, which we consider less important than the other aggression measures, are not reported.

violent television exposure, we compare the relative predictive powers of the two statistical models with each other or to a model with no television predictor variable. When new measures are *added* to the usual measure, we examine the increase in predictive power with the additional variables.

To anticipate the results of the analyses, none of the alternative measures tested are consistently better predictors of aggressive behavior than violent television exposure. Further, measures of exposure to violent program types are not significantly more strongly associated with aggression than measures of exposure to nonviolent television content, and we found no evidence that exposure interacts with attitudes toward television to predict aggression.

Relative Amount of Exposure to Television Violence

As noted previously, the violent television exposure measure ignores the amount of exposure to the least violent programs. In Chapter 7, three hypotheses were described that suggest that the relative amount of violent television exposure might be a better predictor of aggressive behaviors than the absolute amount of exposure to violent programs. First, any effect of exposure to violent programs may be neutralized by exposure to nonviolent programs. Second, overselection of violent programs may indicate a person's receptivity to violence. Third, high correlations between total exposure and violent exposure suggests that most heavy viewers of violent programs are also heavy viewers of nonviolent programs. Some of these heavy viewers may have characteristics that lead them to exhibit fewer aggressive behaviors, and their data may mask the effects of television violence on other boys.

The same measure of relative amount of exposure to violent programs was computed as described in Chapter 7.[2]

Table A.1 shows that the correlations between the violence ratio and violent television exposure range from .28 to .38.[3] Apparently this measure of relative violence does tap different information than the violent television exposure measure does. We examined whether respondents with a high proportion of

---

[2]The measure is the ratio of violent television exposure to total television exposure; it ranges from 0 to 7. A score of 0 indicates that only the least violent programs were watched. A score of 7 indicates exposure to only the most violent programs, that is, the higher the score, the greater the proportion of violent to nonviolent exposure. The observed violence ratios range from 0 to 7 with means between 2.7 and 3.2. (Medians and means are virtually identical in the four waves.) Since our interest is in the predictive power of alternatives, all measures reported in this chapter were computed for only the first four of the five waves.

[3]See Table A.1 also for cross-sectional correlations between other television concepts and television experience and aggression.

violent programs in their television diet are affected: those data are shown in Table 14.1. (We also took the absolute amount of viewing into account: Table A.2 compares regressions with and without an interaction term.[4])

The top half of Table 14.1 shows data for personal and property aggression. For these aggression measures the basic model was estimated with the violence ratio replacing the violent television exposure score in the set of predictor variables. Presented in the table are the average of the standard regression coefficients (βs) and the number of significant coefficients for the 4 adjacent lags and for all 10 lags. Summaries for violence exposure are presented on the left and for the violence ratio on the right.

The lower half of Table 14.1 shows the data for delinquency. Here are presented the number of lags for which a significant television–aggression association was found. Again results for both the model with violence exposure and the model with the violence ratio are shown for the adjacent as well as for all 10 lags.[5]

The measure of relative exposure is a better predictor of personal aggression, but a poorer predictor of property and delinquency aggression than the standard violence exposure measure (see Table 14.1); analyses with an interaction term added lead to the same result (see Table A.2).

Exposure over Longer Time Periods

The cumulative effects of exposure to violence on television were assessed by entering a teenager's previous scores on the violence exposure measure into the prediction model.[6] This is the same approach used in the elementary school analysis.

To examine the effects of consistent exposure, we added the interaction of the television exposure measures to the cumulative effects models. For example, the television variables for the cumulative effects model for the III–V lag (with two additional variables) are TV_1, TV_2, and TV_3. The consistency

[4]The analysis approach is detailed in the "Attitudes toward Television" section.

[5]Table A.2 shows results for relative exposure among respondents with low and high levels of exposure to television. Otherwise, the table is set up in the same way as Table 14.1.

[6]For example, we can examine whether a model with both Wave I and Wave II exposure scores predicts future aggression better than a model with Wave II scores only. Furthermore, we can examine how much additional prior information is needed to improve the prediction model substantially; only one additional prior television variable is available to augment Wave II, but three additional variables are available with Wave IV. Constraining the additional variables to those waves immediately prior, one variable can be added to six of the lags, two variables to three of the lags, and three variables can be added to lag IV–V.

TABLE 14.1
Standardized Partial Regression Coefficients Showing the Net Effect of Exposure to Violent Television and of Relative Amount of Exposure to Violent Television on Aggression

	EXPOSURE TO VIOLENT TELEVISION		RELATIVE AMOUNT OF VIOLENT TELEVISION		
	AVERAGE β	NUMBER OF SIGNIFICANT COEFFICIENTS*	AVERAGE β	NUMBER OF SIGNIFICANT COEFFICIENTS	AVERAGE N
		Personal aggression			
4 adjacent lags	.034	0	.071	2	(327)
All 10 lags	.036	1	.070	4	(321)
		Property aggression			
4 adjacent lags	.026	1	.019	0	(332)
All 10 lags	.040	3	.043	0	(325)
		Delinquency			
	EXPOSURE TO VIOLENT TELEVISION (NUMBER OF SIGNIFICANT COEFFICIENTS		RELATIVE AMOUNT OF VIOLENT TELEVISION (NUMBER OF SIGNIFICANT COEFFICIENTS)		
4 adjacent lags	0		0		(191)
All 10 lags	1		0		(150)

[a]Violent television score/total television score = "amount" of violence per program watched.
*Significant at .05 level.

model for this lag (with two additional variables) includes the same set of variables as the cumulative model and $TV_1 \times TV_2$, $TV_1 \times TV_3$, $TV_2 \times TV_3$, and $TV_1 \times TV_2 \times TV_3$ added. (Table A.3 shows the 10 lags and additional variables.)

Since each model builds on the basic model for that lag, our measure of improvement is the increase in R^2 over the basic model with one television variable. The first part of Table 14.2 presents the adjusted R^2 for regressions predicting personal aggression. The results are grouped by the number of additional variables in the model. Adjusted R^2s are presented for the regressions with one television variable, the cumulative effects model, and the consistency model. Neither the cumulative nor the consistency models provide any improvement over the basic model in predicting personal aggression. There are no significant increases in R^2 for either of the models.

The second part of Table 14.2 shows that prediction of property aggression is also not improved by taking into account prior exposure. In both the cumulative and the consistency models, only 1 out of 10 coefficients is a significantly better predictor than the preceding model.

TABLE 14.2
Effect of Exposure over Longer Time Periods[a]

NUMBER OF TELEVISION MEASURES	LAGS	ADJUSTED R^2: ONE TELEVISION VARIABLE	CUMULATIVE	CONSISTENCY	N
		Personal aggression			
Two	I,II–III	.372	.370	.370	(343)
	I,II–IV	.128	.126	.125	(308)
	I,II–V	.246	.247	.261	(295)
	II,III–IV	.238	.236	.246	(307)
	II,III–V	.352	.352	.350	(297)
	III,IV–V	.394	.395	.395	(291)
Three	I,II,III–IV	.238	.235	.240	(302)
	I,II,III–V	.352	.356	.358	(291)
	II,III,IV–V	.392	.396	.394	(290)
Four	I,II,III,IV–V	.388	.392	.404	(285)
		Property aggression			
Two	I,II–III	.219	.222	.234*	(349)
	I,II–IV	.160	.158	.159	(312)
	I,II–V	.119	.117	.120	(300)
	II,III–IV	.289	.287	.288	(312)
	II,III–V	.236	.233	.231	(303)
	III,IV–V	.421	.436*	.435	(296)
Three	I,II,III–IV	.299	.295	.293	(307)
	I,II,III–V	.244	.239	.238	(297)
	II,III,IV–V	.421	.435	.435	(296)
Four	I,II,III,IV–V	.424	.440	.441	(291)

NUMBER OF TELEVISION MEASURES	LAGS	SIGNIFICANT INCREASE IN MAXIMUM-LIKELIHOOD χ^2 RATIO (.05 LEVEL) COMPARED TO MODEL WITH ONE TELEVISION VARIABLE: CUMULATIVE	CONSISTENCY	N
		Delinquency		
Two	I,II–III	No	Yes	(137)
	I,II–IV	No	Yes	(110)
	I,II–V	No	No	(75)
	II,III–IV	No	No	(165)
	II,III–V	No	No	(108)
	III,IV–V	No	No	(112)
Three	I,II,III–IV	No	Yes	(109)
	I,II,III–V	No	No	(75)
	II,III,IV–V	No	No	(107)
Four	I,II,III,IV–V	No	No	(74)

[a]See footnote to Table 7.2 for a full description of the model.
*Significant increase in R^2 (.05 level).

The third part of Table 14.2 presents findings for delinquency. Here we simply show whether or not the use of cumulative or additional consistency measures produces a significant improvement or not. There is no improvement in the cumulative model. In the consistency model we find a significant improvement in 3 out of 10 lags. However, because there is much overlap in these 3 lags, this model does not appear to represent a consistent or pronounced improvement over the basic model

Alternative Violence Weighting Systems

Obviously, there are many possible weighting systems. Rather than selecting these arbitrarily, we tested a model in which the regressions define the optimal weight for each program category. To arrive at these weights, we estimated regression models in the same way as in the elementary school analysis, entering the exposure data for each violence category as a separate unweighted variable. There are seven television exposure variables in this model,[7] and the "weights" are the regression coefficients.

To test for an improvement with this measure we compared the model with the seven television exposure variables to the model with the usual violence measure. Table 14.3 presents the average value of the adjusted R^2s and the number of lags showing a significant increase in R^2 when the violence categories are used as predictors.

For personal aggression and property aggression, none of the regressions resulted in a significant improvement over the model with only one television variable. The average adjusted R^2s are practically unchanged between the two models, nor were any of the logit models using the unweighted categories significant in any of the lags for delinquency. Therefore, we conclude that this alternative violence weighting system yields no better prediction of aggression than the violence exposure index.

Context of Televised Violence

Because the context in which violence is portrayed may be important, we grouped programs into the following types: realistic crime drama, adventure, westerns, cartoons, slapstick, news/documentaries, sitcoms, variety, sports, and miscellaneous (see Appendix A in Chapter 7 for details).

To evaluate this measure, regressions were computed with exposure to each program type used instead of the violent television exposure variable. Table

[7]Programs with weights 0, 1, 2 or 3, 4, 5, 6, 7 in the violence exposure measure. (Categories 2 and 3 were combined for these analyses because of the small number of programs in each category.)

TABLE 14.3
Variance in Later Aggression (Adjusted R^2) Explained by Prior Aggression and Exposure to Television, Measured in One Violence Exposure Variable or Measured in Several Variables Based on the "Violence Weight" of Programs Watched

	EXPOSURE TO VIOLENT TELEVISION AVERAGE R^2	SEVEN MEASURES OF EXPOSURE TO TELEVISION BASED ON "VIOLENCE WEIGHTS": AVERAGE R^2	SEVEN MEASURES OF EXPOSURE TO TELEVISION BASED ON "VIOLENCE WEIGHTS": NUMBER OF SIGNIFICANT R^2 INCREASES	AVERAGE N
		Personal aggression		
4 adjacent lags	.302	.303	0	(327)
All 10 lags	.234	.238	0	(321)
		Property aggression		
4 adjacent lags	.275	.272	0	(332)
All 10 lags	.183	.179	0	(321)
		Delinquency		
	VIOLENT TELEVISION (NUMBER OF SIGNIFICANT COEFFICIENTS)		VIOLENCE WEIGHTS (NUMBER OF SIGNIFICANT COEFFICIENTS)	
4 adjacent lags	0		0	(191)
All 10 lags	1		0	(150)

14.4 presents the average R^2 and the number of regressions showing a significant increase over a model with no television variables. On the left-hand side of the table the same information is presented for models with the usual violence exposure measure.

There is no consistent improvement in predicting either personal aggression or property aggression. Both television exposure measures have only one significant prediction model for delinquency, and in both the amount of exposure is inversely related to aggression.

Empirical Viewing Patterns

Thus far we have tested television measures based on different classifications of program content, but not on actual patterns of viewing behavior. In this section we examine whether empirical viewing patterns are causally related to aggressive behavior.

To determine the empirical viewing patterns, we factor-analyzed the

TABLE 14.4

Variance in Later Aggression (Adjusted R^2) Explained by Prior Aggression and Exposure to Television Measured in One Violence Exposure Variable or Measured in Several Variables Based on the Context in Which Violent and Nonviolent Action Occurs

	EXPOSURE TO VIOLENT TELEVISION		TEN MEASURES OF EXPOSURE BASED ON "CONTEXT OF VIOLENCE"		
	AVERAGE R^2	NUMBER OF SIGNIFICANT R^2 COMPONENTS*	AVERAGE R^2	NUMBER OF SIGNIFICANT R^2 COMPONENTS*	AVERAGE N
			Personal aggression		
4 adjacent lags	.301	0	.302	0	(327)
All 10 lags	.232	1	.237	1	(321)
			Property aggression		
4 adjacent lags	.273	1	.270	0	(332)
All 10 lags	.182	3	.182	0	(325)
			Delinquency		
	VIOLENT TELEVISION (NUMBER OF SIGNIFICANT COEFFICIENTS)		VIOLENCE WEIGHTS (NUMBER OF SIGNIFICANT COEFFICIENTS)		
4 adjacent lags	0		1		(191)
All 10 lags	1		1		(150)

*Significant R^2 component associated with television exposure (.05 level).

program-by-program exposure data.[8] The results show that there are some consistent patterns: between five and seven factors appeared in each wave, accounting for approximately half of the variance in overall viewing. (Among elementary school boys we found an average of eight factors, which also explained about half of the variance.)

Table 14.5 summarizes the kinds of factors found in each wave.[9] First listed

[8]A screening procedure was used to constrain the number of programs in the final solution. First a principal factor solution was obtained on the full set of programs. Then for each wave only factors with an eigenvalue greater than 1.5 were selected. From these factors all programs with a loading of at least .3 were selected.

A second principal factor solution was then obtained using only this constrained set of programs. The resulting factors are presented in Appendix A.

Movies and programs shown in only one of the two study cities were excluded from this analysis.

[9]Table A.4 shows cross-sectional correlations between the measures and television violence and aggression. Note that practically all are below .10. The exception is Saturday morning

TABLE 14.5
Number and Kinds of Factors in Each Wave

	NUMBER OF FACTORS IN WAVE				
	I	II	III	IV	TOTAL
Action/Adventure	0	1	1	1	3
Sitcoms/sitcoms–variety	0	1	1	0	2
Saturday morning cartoons	1	1	1	1	4
Black shows	0	0	0	1	1
News/Talk	1	1	1	1	4
Weekday programs (daily, Mon.–Fri.)	1	0	0	1	2
ABC (prime-time)	1	0	1	0	2
CBS (prime-time)	1	0	0	0	1
Unclassified factors	2	1	0	0	3
Total number of factors in wave	7	5	5	5	22

in the table are factors described by program type, next is a factor based on time of day, and then two factors based on the network watched. Only three unclassified factors appear, and these are in the first two waves. The factors are similar to those obtained for elementary school boys but there are some differences: For example, we get fewer Saturday morning factors for teens than for young boys. On the other hand, news factors are almost identical. Action/adventure factors appear among both samples, but we have somewhat fewer factors for teens.

To test the effectiveness of these factors in predicting aggression, we substituted the factor scores for the violence exposure measure in the prediction models.

Table 14.6 presents the average R^2 values and the number of significant coefficients for the personal and property aggression measures and the number of significant models for delinquency. Both the average values and the number of significant regressions are similar for violence exposure and the factors when used to predict personal aggression. For property aggression the usual measure yields three significant regressions, the factors yield none. The results for delinquency, in the lower part of Table 14.6, also suggest the absence of television effects. (The factors produce one significant model, but the direction of the relationship is opposite to expectations.)

The associations between individual factor measures and aggression are

cartoons in Wave IV. Saturday morning factors in other waves (I, II, III), however, are very weakly related to the aggression measures.

TABLE 14.6

Variance in Later Aggression (Adjusted R^2) Explained by Prior Aggression and Exposure to Television, Measured in One Violence Exposure Variable or Measured in Several Variables Based on Factor Analyses

	EXPOSURE TO VIOLENT TELEVISION		FIVE OR SEVEN[a] MEASURES OF EXPOSURE BASED ON FACTOR ANALYSES		
	AVERAGE R^2	NUMBER OF SIGNIFICANT R^2 COMPONENTS	AVERAGE R^2	NUMBER OF SIGNIFICANT R^2 INCREASES*	AVERAGE N
Personal aggression					
4 adjacent lags	.301	0	.306	0	(327)
All 10 lags	.232	1	.240	1	(321)
Property aggression					
4 adjacent lags	.273	1	.270	0	(332)
All 10 lags	.182	3	.182	0	(325)
Delinquency					
	VIOLENT TELEVISION (NUMBER OF SIGNIFICANT COEFFICIENTS)		FACTORS (NUMBER OF SIGNIFICANT COEFFICIENTS)		
4 adjacent lags	0		0		(191)
All 10 lgas	1		1		(150)

[a]Seven factors in Wave I, five in other waves (see Table 14.5).
*Significant R^2 component associated with television exposure (.05 level).

summarized in Table A.5. Such an analysis is possible in this case because the factors are quite independent of one another. (In the two preceding analyses, exposure measures were highly correlated and could not be analyzed separately because of possible collinearity.) The data clearly show the lack of consistency in the kind of factors that are significantly associated with later aggression.[10] It is also apparent that factors with primarily violent programs are under-represented

In sum, these analyses corroborate those conducted on the children's data.

[10]The significant model with delinquency occurs in lag I–V. However, none of the individual measures are significantly related to later aggression in that lag. One measure is related significantly in lags II–III and II–IV (shown in Table A.5), but the overall model for those lags is not significant.

Although we have not exhausted all possible ways of conceptualizing television exposure, the failure to find a better television measure than the one we have employed lends strong support to the conclusions based on the violent television exposure measure.

Attitudes toward Television

In Chapter 7, we noted that several researchers (e.g., Weigel & Jessor, 1973) have suggested that violence on television may have its most significant effect among people who are positively disposed to television violence in some fashion. In this section of the chapter we investigate this possibility by examining seven indicators of attitudes about television. However, the conclusiveness of the analysis is limited by the fact that six of these measures were obtained in only one wave, and most were measured late in the study. (The boy's favorite shows were asked about in two waves.)

The measures and their means, medians, and ranges are presented in Table A.6, along with cross-sectional correlations between these measures and television viewing and aggression. With the exception of the "favorite show" measure, these measures were not available for elementary school children.

It is important to recognize that attitudes toward televised violence can influence aggression in two ways. First, the attitudes themselves may be causally related to aggressive behavior, either as causes or as effects. Second, the attitudes may modify the impact of television exposure on aggression.

These two different types of influence are both captured in the following expression:

$$A_t = a + b_1ATT + b_2TV_{t-1} + b_3ATT \times TV_{t-1},$$

where the symbol $ATT \times TV$ represents the multiplication of the attitude and the television exposure variables (variables are expressed as deviations from their mean values). The coefficient b_3 represents the modifying effect of the attitude on the relationship between television and aggression, and the b_2 coefficient represents the main effect of the attitude on aggression ("attitude effect"). Our interest is primarily in the coefficient b_3 ("interaction effect"), which describes the modifying effect of the attitude on the television–aggression relationship.

ATTITUDE TOWARD TELEVISION

The Wave II questionnaire included a question asking respondents to evaluate television on a 10-point scale anchored by "very good right now" and "needs much improvement." Scores range from 1 to 10, with 10 indicating a positive attitude. The mean is 7.1, indicating that most boys like television.

Results from these analyses are presented in Table 14.7. For both personal and property aggression there is very little change in the average adjusted R^2

TABLE 14.7

Variance in Later Aggression (Adjusted R^2) Explained by Prior Aggression and Exposure to Television, Measured in One Violence Exposure Variable or Measured by Adding a Measure of Boy's Attitude toward Television[a] and an Interaction Term

	EXPOSURE TO VIOLENT TELEVISION AVERAGE R^2	MEASURE OF ATTITUDE TOWARD TELEVISION ADDED		MEASURE OF ATTITUDE TOWARD TELEVISION AND INTERACTION TERM ADDED		
		AVERAGE R^2	NUMBER OF SIGNIFICANT R^2 INCREASES*	AVERAGE R^2	NUMBER OF SIGNIFICANT R^2 INCREASES*	AVERAGE N
			Personal aggression			
4 adjacent lags	.309	.311	0	.314	1	(327)
All 10 lags	.242	.245	0	.247	1	(318)
			Property aggression			
4 adjacent lags	.276	.277	0	.279	0	(330)
All 10 lags	.195	.197	0	.200	1	(321)

Delinquency

	EXPOSURE TO VIOLENT TELEVISION[b] (NUMBER OF SIGNIFICANT COEFFICIENTS)	MEASURE OF ATTITUDE TOWARD TELEVISION ADDED (NUMBER OF SIGNIFICANT COEFFICIENTS)	MEASURE OF ATTITUDE TOWARD TELEVISION AND INTERACTION TERM ADDED (NUMBER OF SIGNIFICANT COEFFICIENTS)	
4 adjacent lags	0	1	1	(168)
All 10 lags	1	3	1	(139)

[a]Wave II measure; high score: television is very good.
[b]Based on respondents with information on attitude measure.
*Significant increase in R^2 (.05 level).

when the attitude measure and its interaction with violent television exposure are added as predictors.[11]

The lower part of Table 14.7 shows data for delinquency. Here we find that 3 out of 10 coefficients in the attitude model are significant, indicating that boys who like television differ in aggressiveness from those who do not. However, in the models with the interaction term only one coefficient is significant. This means that this attitude toward television does not modify the impact of television exposure on aggressiveness. In other words, the relationship between television and aggression is the same among boys who are favorable, neutral, and negative about television.

VIOLENCE OF FAVORITE SHOWS

As in the study of younger children, respondents were asked to name their three favorite television programs. In both Waves III and IV, an index was constructed by summing the violence scores of the three programs.[12]

As shown in Table 14.8, only two interactions between overall television exposure and this measure of favorite shows significantly predict personal aggression. Only one significantly predicts property aggression; none predict delinquency.

IDENTIFICATION WITH VIOLENT TELEVISION CHARACTERS

Teenage boys may be more likely to behave aggressively if they identify with or admire the aggressor in television programs they watch. To test this possibility, the boys in Wave IV were asked to name the two television characters they would most like to be and to indicate how much they would like to be each of these characters on a 3-point scale. If the respondent named a character who frequently engaged in violent activity, he was given a score of 1; if not, 0.[13] That score was then multiplied by 1 if the respondent said he wanted to be that character "only a little," by 2 if he said "to some extent," and by 3 if he replied "very much." Since two characters were listed, the index can range from 0 to 6.[14]

Table 14.9 shows that this measure produced no significant interactions for either personal or property aggression. There were two for delinquency.

---

[11] R^2s are shown in the first, second, and fourth column. Differences between the first and second columns indicate attitude effects, differences between the second and fourth columns indicate interaction effects.

[12] For details see Chapter 7. The 3-point violence weight scale was used in Wave III, the full 0–7 scale was used in Wave IV. See Table A.6 for descriptive statistics.

[13] Nearly all characters starring in programs rated 4–7 (see Chapter 11) were classified as "frequently engaged in violent activity." Peter Falk as *Columbo* is the exception: he was not involved in violence depicted in the program.

[14] See Table A.6 for descriptive statistics.

TABLE 14.8

Variance in Later Aggression (Adjusted R^2) Explained by Prior Aggression and Exposure to Television, Measured in One Violence Exposure Variable or Measured by Adding a Favorite Show Measure[a] and an Interaction Term

	EXPOSURE TO VIOLENT TELEVISION[b] AVERAGE R^2	FAVORITE SHOW MEASURE ADDED: AVERAGE R^2	FAVORITE SHOW MEASURE ADDED: NUMBER OF SIGNIFICANT R^2 INCREASES*	FAVORITE SHOW MEASURE AND INTERACTION TERM ADDED: AVERAGE R^2	FAVORITE SHOW MEASURE AND INTERACTION TERM ADDED: NUMBER OF SIGNIFICANT R^2 INCREASES*	AVERAGE N
			Personal aggression			
4 adjacent lags	.265	.265	0	.275	1	(277)
All 10 lags	.198	.199	0	.205	2	(268)
			Property aggression			
4 adjacent lags	.279	.279	0	.285	0	(279)
All 10 lags	.203	.205	0	.210	1	(270)

Delinquency

	EXPOSURE TO VIOLENT TELEVISION[b] (NUMBER OF SIGNIFICANT COEFFICIENTS)	FAVORITE SHOW MEASURE ADDED (NUMBER OF SIGNIFICANT COEFFICIENTS)	FAVORITE SHOW MEASURE AND AND INTERACTION TERM ADDED (NUMBER OF SIGNIFICANT COEFFICIENTS)	AVERAGE N
4 adjacent lags	0	0	0	(171)
All 10 lags	1	0	0	(132)

[a]Measured in Waves III and IV (Wave III measure used for lags starting with Wave I, II, III); high score: likes violent shows.
[b]Based on respondents with information on favorite show measure.
*Significant increase in R^2 (.05 level).

TABLE 14.9

Variance in Later Aggression (Adjusted R^2) Explained by Prior Aggression and Exposure to Television, Measured in One Violence Exposure Variable or Measured by Adding a Measure of Boy's Identification with Violent Television Characters[a] and an Interaction Term

	EXPOSURE TO VIOLENT TELEVISION[b] AVERAGE R^2	IDENTIFICATION MEASURE ADDED		IDENTIFICATION MEASURE AND INTERACTION TERM ADDED		AVERAGE N
		AVERAGE R^2	NUMBER OF SIGNIFICANT R^2 INCREASES*	AVERAGE R^2	NUMER OF SIGNIFICANT R^2 INCREASES*	
			Personal aggression			
4 adjacent lags	.308	.311	0	.313	0	(301)
All 10 lags	.244	.246	0	.247	0	(302)
			Property aggression			
4 adjacent lags	272	.274	0	.275	0	(306)
All 10 lags	.186	.187	0	.188	0	(306)

Delinquency

	EXPOSURE TO VIOLENT TELEVISION[b] (NUMBER OF SIGNIFICANT COEFFICIENTS)	IDENTIFICATION MEASURE ADDED (NUMBER OF SIGNIFICANT COEFFICIENTS)	IDENTIFICATION MEASURE AND INTERACTION TERM ADDED (NUMBER OF SIGNIFICANT COEFFICIENTS)	
4 adjacent lags	0	0	1	(179)
All 10 lags	1	0	2	(143)

[a]Wave IV measure; high score: wants to be like violent characters.
[b]Based on respondents with information on identification measure.
*Significant increase in R^2 (.05 level).

REALISM OF TELEVISION

Another possibility is that modeling aggressive behaviors is more likely to occur if the viewer believes the situation depicted on television is "real" or somehow relevant to his life.

Respondents in Wave IV were asked to indicate on a 4-point scale how "real-life" they considered the following portrayals on television:

1. Private-eye work
2. How poor people live
3. What it is like to be black
4. What happens to criminals in the end
5. What it is like to act hard and tough
6. How much crime there is all around us

A score of 1 was assigned an item if the response was "not at all like real life"; a score of 4 if the response was "very much like real life." The scores for the six items were summed to give a scale ranging from 6 to 24. (See Table A.6 for descriptive statistics.)

Data in Table 14.10 show that there is only one significant interaction (with property aggression) associated with this variable out of 30 examined.

INVOLVEMENT WITH TELEVISION

Some people watch television just to kill time or pay scant attention to programs or work on other tasks when viewing. Others become actively involved with programs and characters and emotionally participate in the events portrayed. Weigel and Jessor (1973) and Jessor (1977) suggest that involvement with television is essential for television to influence behavior.

To test whether a person's involvement modified the effect of exposure on aggressive behavior, Wave IV respondents were presented with a series of statements characterizing an actively participating and involved viewer. On a 3-point scale, they rated the extent to which each statement characterized their own reactions to adventure programs.[15]

A review of Table 14.11 shows that there is no consistent interaction between involvement with television and violent television exposure in predicting any of the aggression measures. The evidence of interaction for delinquency is marginal: 2 of 10 interactions are significant.

---

[15]A 3 was assigned if the person said the statement sounded a "lot like me" and a 1 if "not at all like me." Five statements were rated, yielding an index of involvement from 5 to 15 (see Table A.6 for statistics). The statements were: (*a*) "I often get involved and carried away when watching this kind of show." (*b*) "When I watch these shows I pay very close attention to them." (*c*) "Sometimes I get really angry at some of the characters." (*d*) "Sometimes I feel really sad about some of the things that happen to people in these shows." (*e*) "I often see characters I would like to meet personally."

TABLE 14.10

Variance in Later Aggression (Adjusted R^2) Explained by Prior Aggression and Exposure to Television, Measured in One Violence Exposure Variable or Measured by Adding a Measure of Realism of Television (as Perceived by Boy)[a] and an Interaction Term

	EXPOSURE TO VIOLENT TELEVISION[b]	MEASURE OF REALISM OF TELEVISION ADDED		MEASURE OF REALISM OF TELEVISION AND INTERACTION TERM ADDED		
	AVERAGE R^2	AVERAGE R^2	NUMBER OF SIGNIFICANT R^2 INCREASES*	AVERAGE R^2	NUMBER OF SIGNIFICANT R^2 INCREASES*	AVERAGE N
Personal aggression						
4 adjacent lags	.308	.311	2	.311	0	(303)
All 10 lags	.243	.250	2	.252	0	(304)
Property aggression						
4 adjacent lags	274	.275	0	.277	0	(304)
All 10 lags	.187	.190	0	.194	1	(307)

Delinquency

	EXPOSURE TO VIOLENT TELEVISION (NUMBER OF SIGNIFICANT COEFFICIENTS)	MEASURE OF REALISM OF TELEVISION ADDED (NUMBER OF SIGNIFICANT COEFFICIENTS)	MEASURE OF REALISM OF TELEVISION AND INTERACTION TERM ADDED (NUMBER OF SIGNIFICANT COEFFICIENTS)	
4 adjacent lags	0	0	0	(180)
All 10 lags	1	0	0	(144)

[a] Wave IV measure; high score: boy thinks television is realistic.
[b] Based on respondents with information on measure of reality of television.
*Significant increase in R^2 (.05 level).

TABLE 14.11

Variance in Later Aggression (Adjusted R^2) Explained by Prior Aggression and Exposure to Television, Measured in One Violence Exposure Variable or Measured by Adding a Measure of Boy's Involvement with Television Programs[a] and an Interaction Term

	EXPOSURE TO VIOLENT TELEVISION AVERAGE R^2	MEASURE OF INVOLVEMENT WITH TELEVISION ADDED		MEASURE OF INVOLVEMENT WITH TELEVISION AND INTERACTION TERM ADDED		AVERAGE N
		AVERAGE R^2	NUMBER OF SIGNIFICANT R^2 INCREASES*	AVERAGE R^2	NUMBER OF SIGNIFICANT R^2 INCREASES*	
			Personal aggression			
4 adjacent lags	.307	.310	0	.312	0	(303)
All 10 lags	.243	.249	2	.250	0	(304)
			Property aggression			
4 adjacent lags	271	.273	0	.276	1	(309)
All 10 lags	.186	.187	0	.190	1	(308)

Delinquency

	EXPOSURE TO VIOLENT TELEVISION (NUMBER OF SIGNIFICANT COEFFICIENTS)	MEASURE OF INVOLVEMENT WITH TELEVISION ADDED (NUMBER OF SIGNIFICANT COEFFICIENTS)	MEASURE OF INVOLVEMENT WITH TELEVISION AND INTERACTION TERM ADDED (NUMBER OF SIGNIFICANT COEFFICIENTS)	
4 adjacent lags	0	0	0	(181)
All 10 lags	1	0	2	(144)

[a]Wave IV measure; high score: gets very involved.
[b]Based on respondents with information on measure of boy's involvement.
*Significant increase in R^2 (.05 level).

PERCEPTION OF TELEVISION MESSAGES

Another part of the questionnaire in Wave IV listed several behaviors and attitudes and asked whether television teaches that these are right or wrong on a scale of 1–5. Three of the items listed were aggressive attitudes or behaviors: hate someone, physically hurt someone, break things belonging to others. Responses to these three questions were summed to create a scale of attitudes about the teaching of aggression on televison.[16]

Table 14.12 shows the results of using this scale to predict aggression in combination with the violent television exposure measure. Two patterns are readily apparent in the table: that the attitude is consistently associated with property aggression and that there are marginal indications of a television–aggression modifying effect for both personal and property aggression. There is no consistent relationship between the attitude, either as a main effect or in interaction with television exposure, and delinquency.

The main effect of the attitude on property aggression means that there is an association between believing that television teaches aggression and engaging in property aggression. If this is a causal association it is an effect of an attitude on aggression, not an effect of television exposure. Also, the attitude questions were asked in Wave IV and seven of the eight lags in which there is a significant association between attitudes and aggression start with a wave that precedes the measurement of the attitude questions. Thus the causal direction is unclear.

The four significant interaction effects for personal aggression and the three for property aggression, however, represent the possibility of a modifying effect on the television–aggression relationship. Analysis of the individual equations shows that the impact of television on aggression approximately doubles when the interactions are significant as we move from teens who believe strongly that television does not teach aggression to those who believe strongly that it does.[17]

---

[16]Summed together these three items create a scale from 3 to 15. As shown in Table A.6, the mean of this measure is 7.

[17]The strongest interaction for personal aggression occurs in wave pair II–IV. The equation there is:

$$A_4 = .090A_1 + .162A_2^* + .164TV_2^* - .515TVTH^* + .013TV \times TVTH^*.$$

The strongest interaction for property aggression occurs in wave pair II–V. The equation there is:

$$A_5 = .044A_1 + .193A_2^* + .119TV_2^* - .203TVTH + .010TV \times TVTH^*.$$

Coefficients with asterisks in these equations are significant at the .05 level. The personal aggression equation implies that the impact of television on aggression ranges from .203 (.164 + 3 × .013) to .359 (.164 + .15 × .013) as the attitude (*TVTH*) ranges from its minimum

(*Continued next page*)

TABLE 14.12

Variance in Later Aggression (Adjusted R^2) Explained by Prior Aggression and Exposure to Television, Measured in One Violence Exposure Variable or Measured by Adding a Measure of Boy's Perception of Television Messages[a] and an Interaction Term

	EXPOSURE TO VIOLENT TELEVISION[b]	MEASURE OF PERCEPTION OF TELEVISION ADDED		MEASURE OF PERCEPTION OF TELEVISION AND INTERACTION TERM ADDED		
	AVERAGE R^2	AVERAGE R^2	NUMBER OF SIGNIFICANT R^2 INCREASES*	AVERAGE R^2	NUMBER OF SIGNIFICANT R^2 INCREASES*	AVERAGE N
			Personal aggression			
4 adjacent lags	.267	.269	0	.276	1	(300)
All 10 lags	.211	.216	2	.224	4	(301)
			Property aggression			
4 adjacent lags	248	.255	2	.260	0	(305)
All 10 lags	.170	.189	8	.198	3	(305)

Delinquency

	EXPOSURE TO VIOLENT TELEVISION (NUMBER OF SIGNIFICANT COEFFICIENTS)	MEASURE OF PERCEPTION OF TELEVISION ADDED (NUMBER OF SIGNIFICANT COEFFICIENTS)	MEASURE OF PERCEPTION OF TELEVISION AND INTERACTION TERM ADDED (NUMBER OF SIGNIFICANT COEFFICIENTS)	
4 adjacent lags	0	1	0	(180)
All 10 lags	0	3	0	(144)

[a] Wave IV measure; high score: boy thinks television teaches aggression.
[b] Based on respondents with information on measure of perception of television messages.
*Significant increase in R^2 (.05 level).

The evidence for a main effect is not clear since, as mentioned, the measure was obtained in Wave IV and the interactions are not significant in the IV–V lag, the only lag where the causal order is unequivocal. Also, the significances occur in overlapping lags, which means they are not independent replications.[18]

This is the first time in the analyses of television attitudes that we found some indication of a connection between attitudes and the effect of television on aggression. However, the findings are ambiguous because the attitude measure was obtained in only one wave, toward the end of the study, whereas the significant interactions occurred in the early waves. Research with a better attitude measure is needed to clarify this finding.

INTEREST IN VIOLENT PROGRAM ELEMENTS

In Wave V respondents were asked to indicate on a 4-point scale how strongly they agreed with this statement: "I am more interested in the action on a TV show than in the story." (Table A.6 shows descriptive statistics.)

In the main effect regressions with personal and property aggression we find inconsistent evidence for a small attitudinal effect (Table 14.13). Again, the fact that the attitude measure was collected only once, at the end of the study, makes the findings less than conclusive. In the interaction models only 1 of 30 coefficients increases significantly.

EFFECTS OF EXPOSURE TO TELEVISION VIOLENCE AMONG SAMPLE SUBGROUPS

We examined the possibility that television affects only certain types of boys by analyzing groups based on 26 predisposing and facilitating factors. Variables that are theoretically interesting, correlate significantly and systematically with aggression, appear to be reliable and valid, and yield adequate sample sizes formed the basis for subgroups. Most of the subgroups used in the children's analysis were replicated among teenagers, and a few additional subgroups were analyzed as well. Table 14.14 lists the 26 measures.[19]

---

value of 3 to its maximum of 15. The property agression equation implies a television effect ranging from .149 (.119 + 3 × .010) to .269 (.119 + 15 × .010).

The personal aggression interactions that were significant appear in lags II–III, II–IV, I–IV, and II–V. Significant property aggression interactions appear in lags I–IV, I–V, and II–V. See discussion in Chapter 6 on overlap and independence between lags.

[18]The analysis was also conducted with teacher aggression. There were significant interactions in one adjacent and three overlapping lags starting with Waves I and II. The average R^2 increase was .005.

[19]The measures are described in Appendices B and C in Chapter 7 and B and C in this chapter.

TABLE 14.13

Variance in Later Aggression (Adjusted R^2) Explained by Prior Aggression and Exposure to Television, Measured in One Violence Exposure Variable or Measured by Adding a Measure of Boy's Interest in Violent Program Elements [a] and an Interaction Term

	EXPOSURE TO VIOLENT TELEVISION (AVERAGE R^2)	MEASURE OF INTEREST IN VIOLENT TELEVISION PROGRAMS ADDED		MEASURE OF INTEREST IN VIOLENT TELEVISION PROGRAMS AND INTERACTION TERM ADDED		AVERAGE *N*
		AVERAGE R^2	NUMBER OF SIGNIFICANT R^2 INCREASES*	AVERAGE R^2	NUMBER OF SIGNIFICANT R^2 INCREASES*	
Personal aggression						
4 adjacent lags	.341	.343	0	.346	1	(293)
All 10 lags	.266	.270	3	.273	1	(296)
Property aggression						
4 adjacent lags	284	.290	1	.291	0	(297)
All 10 lags	.194	.203	4	.204	0	(300)

Delinquency

	EXPOSURE TO VIOLENT TELEVISION[b] (NUMBER OF SIGNIFICANT COEFFICIENTS)	MEASURE OF INTEREST IN VIOLENT TELEVISION ADDED (NUMBER OF SIGNIFICANT COEFFICIENTS)	MEASURE OF INTEREST IN VIOLENT TELEVISION PROGRAMS AND INTERACTION TERM ADDED (NUMBER OF SIGNIFICANT COEFFICIENTS	
4 adjacent lags	0	0	0	(174)
All 10 lags	0	0	0	(140)

[a] Wave V measure; high score: boy is more interested in action than in plot of program.

[b] Based on respondents with information on measure of interest in violent television.

*Significant increase in R^2 (.05 level).

TABLE 14.14
Summary of Measures Used in Subgroups Analysis

Sociocultural characteristics	Family income (1)[a]
	Family type (1)
	Family size (1)
Parental control and supervision	Father's strictness (1)
	Supervision (1)
	Mother's use of physical punishment (6)
	Father's use of physical punishment (6)
Other family characteristics	Father's activities with boy as child (5)
	Mother's dissatisfaction with son (4)
	Boy's arguments with family (4)
	Mother's irritability (5)
	Father's support for son's aggression (2)
Aggression of peers	Friends' aggressiveness (4)
	Contact with aggressive behavior (2)
Boy's behavior/attitudes and characteristics	
Scholastic measures	Average grade (1)
	Attitude toward school (1)
Aggressive predisposition	Earlier childhood aggression (1)
	Initial aggression (1)
Attitudes toward aggression	Support for breaking the law (5)
	Machismo (3)
	Enjoyment of real-life violence in films (6)
Other characteristics	Use of alcohol, cigarettes, drugs (3)
	Self-esteem (10)
	Irritability (1)
	Aggressive fantasies (1)
	Exposure to comic books (17)

[a]Numbers in parentheses represent the number of items in the construct.

Method of Subgroup Analysis

ANALYSES WITH PERSONAL AGGRESSION AND PROPERTY AGGRESSION

The analysis of television effects on personal and property aggression among adolescent subgroups was designed to overcome a disadvantage in the analysis of children's subgroups, in which we assessed television effects by calculating regression equations for the 15 possible wave pairs within each subgroup category. A shortcoming of that strategy was a high variation in the size and composition of the wave pairs. In some instances, the number of cases in a wave pair was so small that only a television β as large as .5 or .6 could be reliably discriminated from a random component. In other instances, the wave pair was so large that a very small coefficient could appear as significant. The changing composition of the sample also meant that we were not always comparing the same boys.

In our analysis of personal and property aggression within adolescent subgroups all equations predicting one of the aggression variables within a subgroup are estimated simultaneously. Because of this, the problem of overlapping wave pairs encountered in the analysis of elementary school children is avoided and results can be interpreted with more certainty than those for subgroups of elementary school children.

The simultaneous estimation of equations has the additional advantage of providing us with a test for the significance of a set of television effect coefficients. Testing a group of coefficients all at once allows us to find effects that may not be evident through examination of individual coefficients.

The strength of this test is its global nature. Its weakness is that it is not very powerful in discriminating meaningful from nonmeaningful associations. In large samples this test tends to count as significant most associations, even substantively trivial ones. Furthermore, the χ^2 treats large positive and large negative coefficients both as indications of a significant television effect, whereas we want to focus on magnitude and consistency of coefficients.[20] To compensate for these problems of the χ^2 test, we use it primarily to pinpoint potential television effects, supplementing it with a more rigorous inspection and evaluation of television coefficients. As in the elementary school analysis, we look for effects in adjacent lags. Then, we examine the consistency and direction of the significant relationships.

[20]This can be illustrated by a detailed examination of the data for "Low family income" presented in Table B.1, where we find significant χ^2 ratios, but no other signs of a significant association. The individual coefficients are as follows:

FAMILY INCOME	β				N
	WAVE II	WAVE III	WAVE IV	WAVE V	
Low	−.116	.259*	−.031	.083	(116)

Clearly then, the overall significance is a result of a mixture of positive and negative associations.

ANALYSES WITH DELINQUENCY AGGRESSION

Analysis of the effects of television exposure on delinquency returns to the strategy of estimating coefficients separately for all possible wave pairs. As explained, we employ logit analysis to predict delinquency because of the skewness of the variable (Chapters 12 and 15).

With logit analysis, we are able to calculate for each subgroup the net effect of television at one time period on the probability that a teen will exhibit delinquent behavior at a later time period. We study only boys who had not reported delinquent acts prior to the later wave.

Limiting the pool in this way has the effect of reducing sample sizes, which decline when the time lags are long. The small sample sizes create a problem when predicting a behavior as rare as these serious antisocial acts. In fact, there are several lags in various subgroups where nobody reports a delinquent act at the second time period. For these time lags, we are not able to present any findings. Further, not all items were asked in Wave I. Thus, initiation of delinquent behavior between Waves I and II cannot be assessed with much certainty and the tables report data based on only nine lags.[21]

Our power to distinguish true, but small, effects of television on delinquency is severely limited in lags with few cases, and we have decided to exclude as unreliable lags with less than 30 cases. Even so, the power of the significance test is still low for a few remaining subgroups. We can, however, improve the certainty of our conclusions by comparing results for delinquency with those for subgroups conceptually related to each other and also by comparisons with the other two aggression variables.

Findings of Subgroup Analysis

Between 46 and 52 subgroups were examined for each of the personal, property, and delinquency aggression measures, resulting in some 800 individual regression or logit coefficients.[22] In order to consider this large amount of information, a global assessment is necessary. As discussed in Chapter 7, chance alone can be expected to produce a certain number of statistically significant coefficients in the set of 800, resulting in a few subgroups with seemingly significant television effects. Thus, we consider whether or not the

[21]Detailed tables that include data for the I–II lag are available. Those regressions were computed to utilize all available data and because the I-II lags usually have the largest number of cases. Inspection of these lags confirms the findings in the other regressions.

[22]Personal and property aggression: 52 subgroups each with four nonoverlapping lags analyzed per subgroup, totaling 208 lags for each measure. (Teacher aggression data are not reported. Analyses for key subgroups were conducted, but no effects were found.) Delinquency aggression was analyzed differently; see the following. Forty-six subgroups with 9 lags each produced a total of 331 lags. (Lags were not analyzed when the number of cases was less than 30 or when no or only one boy became delinquent.)

overall patterns of significance differ from a random model before we interpret the findings in individual groups.

For personal aggression, 52 subgroups in all were examined. Of these, 56% had no significant television coefficients, 42% had one, and 2% had two. None had as many as three signficiant coefficients. This overall pattern is very similar to one we would expect if the significant coefficients were distributed on the basis of chance.[23]

The result for property aggression is quite similar: the distribution of significant coefficients does not differ from a random model.[24]

For delinquency we focused on the adjacent wave pairs and found a total of 14 coefficients significant and positive. Of the 46 subgroups, 78% had no significant coefficients, 16% had one, and 6% had two. By chance, we would expect 75% to have none, 23% one, and 2% more than one. The χ^2 here is 5.4, again insignificant.

Thus the overall evaluation shows there is no pattern in the teenage subgroups that indicates that television has a more substantial influence on aggression among some kinds of boys than among others.

As in the case of elementary school children, there were significant associations among a few subgroups (see Appendix B). For personal aggression, as many as two significant coefficients were found in 1 of the 52 groups studied: boys who reported in Wave III that they rarely get into arguments with other members of their families (Table B.3A). For property aggression, as many as two significant coefficients were found in two groups: boys whose fathers were not strict (according to mother reports; Table B.2B) and boys who were not aggressive as children (also according to mother reports; Table B.6A). The interaction of the television–aggression relationship with lenient fathers makes some theoretical sense, but the other two interactions do not.

As in the subgroup analyses of elementary school boys and girls, we find no consistent evidence of television effects among predisposed groups such as aggressive boys, those who enjoy violence in films or those who have aggressive friends and families. Therefore, as a whole the best explanation for the significant coefficients to have occurred in the three groups above is chance. Consistent with this is the fact that none of these groups overlaps with groups showing significant

[23]In a set of 208 (52 × 4) coefficients of which 24 are significant, the chance distribution of grouping these coefficients into 52 sets of 4 each yields the following pattern of significant coefficients: 61% in which no significant television effect is found, 32% in which exactly one significant television effect is found, and 7% in which two or more significant television effects are found. The χ^2 for the discrepancy between the chance and the observed distributions is 3.4, which is not significant.

[24]Fifty-two subgroups were examined. In 50% no television coefficients were significant, in 46% one coefficient was significant, and in 4% two were significant. The chance distribution of the significant coefficients is 56% with none, 35% with one, 8% with two, and 1% with a three or more. The χ^2 for the discrepancy is 3.8, which is insignificant.

associations among elementary school boys or girls and that no signs of significance were detected among teens with similar characteristics (such as boys who are not supervised, or boys scoring low on personal aggression when they were younger). Based on this evidence, we conclude that no meaningful specifications exist.[25]

SENSITIVITY OF THE ANALYSIS MODEL

We conducted the same investigation as that reported for children in Chapters 7 and 8 to assure ourselves that the analysis model used is sensitive enough to show significant associations between aggression and other measures.

Six variables were selected from the strongest correlates of aggression to conduct analyses with personal and property aggression using two-wave models.

Table 14.15 clearly shows that the analysis strategy used here can identify significant predictors of aggression. (Average βs and the number of significant coefficients in the four adjacent lags are reported. For comparison, the results for violent television exposure are included.[26]) Conflict between family members and the aggressiveness of the respondent's friends appear to be the strongest predictors of both personal and property aggression. Contact with aggressive behavior is another strong predictor of personal aggression, and a measure of the extent to which the boy feels he has the right to commit certain antisocial acts, is consistently related to later property aggression.[27] This is to say that the teens who become relatively more aggressive over time are those who live in families in which there is conflict, have aggressive friends, have friends who use drugs, live in environments in which aggression often occurs, and think that they have the right to commit antisocial acts.

As emphasized in the discussion of the same analyses for children, the data should be interpreted carefully: additional measures must be considered and additional analyses conducted before causality can be established. It is clear, though, that a significant influence of a meaningful predictor—be it television or any other variable—could have been found with the methods used here.

BASIC MODEL CONTROLS

The analysis model we have used does not control for all variables that may affect the relationship between television and aggression. In our analysis of the

[25]As mentioned in Chapter 9, the groups in which significant associations were found are not those affected by attrition, indicating that attrition did not distort our findings.

[26]All measures were coded to give the high value to the characteristic with the hypothesized effect of increasing aggression.

[27]Consistent significant relationships with exposure to violence in comic books or theater movies were not found.

TABLE 14.15

Impact of Exposure to Violence in Television and of Respondent Characteristics on Personal and Property Aggression (Basic Model Regressions, Adjacent Lags Only)

	PERSONAL AGGRESSION		PROPERTY AGGRESSION	
	AVERAGE β COEFFICIENTS	NUMBER OF SIGNIFICANT β COEFFICIENTS IN 4 LAGS	AVERAGE β COEFFICIENTS	NUMBER OF SIGNIFICANT β COEFFICIENTS IN 4 LAGS
Violent television [five-wave model] (high)	.03	1	.06	1
Harmony/conflict between family members (mostly conflict)	.14	4	.16	3
Friends' aggressiveness (many friends do aggressive, antisocial things)	.11	3	.14	3
Friends' drug use (many friends use illegal drugs)	.06	2	.08	2
Contact with aggressive behavior (often saw fight)	.14	4	.02	1
Use of alcohol/cigarettes/drugs (boy uses all three)	.07	1	.11	2
Justification for antisocial act (boy thinks he has right to commit them)	.09	2	.14	4

TABLE 14.16
Basic Model Controls (Personal Aggression)

	SIGNIFICANT COEFFICIENTS	PATTERN OF SIGNS	AVERAGE β	β COEFFICIENTS CHANGED THROUGH CONTROLS REDUCED	INCREASED	AVERAGE *N*
Family type						
Sample						
without control		8p 2n	.039			(253)
with control		7p 3n	.025	7	0	
IQ						
Sample						
without control	1p[a]	6p 4n	.024			(296)
with control	1p	6p 4n	.016	8	0	
Less valid reporting						
Sample						
without control	1p[a]	8p 1n[b]	.039			(322)
with control		8p 1n[b]	.018	7	0	

[a]p = positive coefficient; n = negative coefficient.
[b]No less valid reporters in one lag.

elementary school data, we examined whether the preponderance of small positive television coefficients was caused by such uncontrolled variables (Chapters 7 and 8). The adolescent data reveal a similar pattern of small positive associations between television and milder forms of aggression. Therefore, we conducted the same kinds of analysis with personal, teacher, and property aggression. The analysis was not conducted with delinquency because the pattern of small positive associations was not found with that measure of serious aggression.

Nineteen antecedents of television exposure and aggression were entered into simple two-wave basic model regressions (identical to those used for the analysis of the childrens' data).[28] We found evidence that some of these mutual correlates were in fact uncontrolled in the basic model analyses and, thus, helped to create a small spurious association between television exposure and aggression. Table 14.16 shows measures that affected the relationship between exposure and personal aggression.[29]

Among children, measures of SES were the best indicators of those factors that influence television exposure levels and have a continuous effect on

[28]As there were only five teenage waves, the number of lags is 10, not 15 as among elementary school children.

[29]Most of those variables also affected relationships with teacher and property aggression. However, the effect was generally smaller than in analyses with personal aggression.

aggression. We find different measures among adolescents, but they are all related to socioeconomic status: family type ("intact" versus "broken" home), IQ (a measure based on various IQ and aptitude tests), and "less valid reporting" (based on the quality of the television viewing reports, discussed in Chapter 11).[30] Although we cannot reach firm conclusions, these analyses suggest that the associations between television exposure and aggression in the adolescent sample were inflated to some extent by spurious factors.

[30]Of the 19 measures, three reduced the number of significant coefficients and the sign pattern, 14 reduced the size of the average β. The measures shown in Table 14.16 had the most pronounced effect.

APPENDIX A: OTHER CONCEPTUALIZATIONS OF TELEVISION EXPOSURE

TABLE A.1

Cross-Sectional Correlations of All Exposure Measures with Violent Television Exposure and Aggression

	WAVE I			WAVE II			
		AGGRESSION			AGGRESSION		
	VIOLENCE EXPOSURE	PERSONAL	PROPERTY	VIOLENCE EXPOSURE	PERSONAL	PROPERTY	DELINQUENCY
Total exposure	.88	.11	−.02	.92	.12	.02	−.00
Relative exposure to violent television	.34	.09	.06	.30	.03	.04	.06
Alternative violent weights							
7 Weight	.62	.13	.08	.73	.14	.05	.01
6 Weight	.69	.11	.03	.71	.12	.07	.02
5 Weight	.78	.13	.01	.77	.08	−.01	.03
4 Weight	.61	.09	−.02	.75	.03	−.01	−.01
3,2 Weight	.41	.07	.06	.40	.10	.02	−.07
1 Weight	.51	−.02	−.09	.60	.07	−.00	−.03
0 Weight	.31	.03	−.03	.45	.11	.03	.01
Context of violence							
Realistic crime	.72	.11	.01	.75	.13	.01	.02
Adventure	.70	.10	.05	.57	.09	.04	.00
Westerns	.69	.10	.00	.76	.04	.00	−.01
Cartoons	.40	.06	−.02	.56	.11	.04	.03
Slapstick	.26	−.03	−.03	.25	.06	.05	−.03
News/Documentary	.16	−.08	−.07	.28	.03	−.10	−.05
Sitcoms	.56	.03	−.06	.56	.07	.08	.00
Variety	.20	.01	−.02	.36	.08	.02	.01
Education	.48	.08	.02	.50	.01	−.01	.03
Miscellaneous	.27	.01	−.06	.23	−.01	−.05	−.04

(Continued next page)

TABLE A.1 (*continued*)

	WAVE I			WAVE II			
		AGGRESSION			AGGRESSION		
	VIOLENCE EXPOSURE	PERSONAL	PROPERTY	VIOLENCE EXPOSURE	PERSONAL	PROPERTY	DELINQUENCY
Comparison							
Regular measure of violence exposure		.16	.03		.09	.01	.01
N	(392)	(389)	(391)	(568)	(561)	(566)	(567)

	WAVE III				WAVE IV			
		AGGRESSION				AGGRESSION		
	VIOLENCE EXPOSURE	PERSONAL	PROPERTY	DELINQUENCY	VIOLENCE EXPOSURE	PERSONAL	PROPERTY	DELINQUENCY
Total exposure	.91	.04	−.02	.05	.90	.15	.01	.11
Relative exposure to violent television	.38	.08	.11	.01	.28	.02	.03	.01
Alternative violent weights								
7 Weight	.69	−.01	.00	.03	.67	.13	.01	.14
6 Weight	.73	.05	.04	.06	.87	.13	.04	.07

5 Weight	.75	.10	.03	.07	.74	.09	.01	.04
4 Weight	.71	.03	.03	.06	.63	.10	.00	.11
3,2 Weight	.46	.01	−.03	.02	.25	−.02	.00	−.01
1 Weight	.65	.02	−.08	−.02	.61	.12	−.03	.09
0 Weight	.43	−.02	−.06	.05	.49	.09	−.01	.07
Context of violence								
Realistic crime	.82	−.01	.00	.08	.70	.18	.01	.16
Adventure	.70	.05	.04	.06	.47	.10	.03	.06
Westerns	.70	.03	.01	.04	.53	.08	.00	.07
Cartoons	.57	.03	.00	.06	.53	.17	.04	.14
Slapstick	.29	.02	−.02	.02	.15	−.04	−.02	−.02
News/Documentary	.26	−.07	−.07	−.05	.23	−.08	−.08	−.02
Sitcoms	.58	.01	−.10	−.01	.64	.19	.04	.10
Variety	.22	−.03	−.04	.05	.23	−.01	−.02	.04
Education	.53	.03	−.04	−.02	.38	−.05	−.06	.01
Miscellaneous	.40	−.02	.03	−.04	.42	.04	−.08	.03
Comparison								
Regular measure of violence exposure		.07	.03	.07		.16	.03	.11
N	(564)	(561)	(564)	(561)	(674)	(672)	(673)	(664)

TABLE A.2

Variance in Later Aggression (Adjusted R^2) Explained by Prior Aggression and Exposure to Television, Measured in One Violence Exposure Variable, or Measured by Adding a Measure of Relative Exposure to Violent Television and an Interaction Term

		MEASURE OF RELATIVE EXPOSURE ADDED		MEASURE OF RELATIVE EXPOSURE AND INTERACTION TERMS ADDED		
	EXPOSURE TO VIOLENT TELEVISION AVERAGE R^2	AVERAGE R^2	NUMBER OF SIGNIFICANT R^2 INCREMENTS	AVERAGE R^2	NUMBER OF SIGNIFICANT R^2 INCREMENTS	AVERAGE N
		Personal aggression				
4 adjacent lags	.303	.309	1	.309	0	(324)
All 10 lags	.234	.237	1	.237	0	(318)
		Property aggression				
4 adjacent lags	.283	.283	0	.281	0	(328)
All 10 lags	.188	.193	1	.189	0	(322)
		Delinquency				
4 adjacent lags	0		0		0	(191)
All 10 lags	1		0		0	(150)

TABLE A.3

Lags for Examination of Effect of Exposure over Longer Time Periods

	LAGS	ADDITIONAL PRIOR TELEVISION VARIABLE(S)
Two television variables	II–III	Wave I
(one additional television variable)	II–IV	Wave I
	II–V	Wave I
	III–IV	Wave II
	III–V	Wave II
	IV–V	Wave III
Three television variables	III–IV	Waves II, I
(two additional television variables)	III–V	Waves II, I
	IV–V	Waves III, II
Four television variables	IV–V	Waves III, II, I
(three additional television variables)		

TABLE A.4
Cross-Sectional Correlations of All Factors with Violent Television Exposure and Aggression

	VIOLENCE EXPOSURE	AGGRESSION		
		PERSONAL	PROPERTY	DELINQUENCY
Wave I				
1. Miscellaneous	.44	.09	.17	.04
2. Weekday (daily, Mon.–Fri.)	.57	.06	−.02	.02
3. CBS (prime-time)	.38	.05	−.04	.00
4. Saturday morning programs	.11	−.02	−.04	−.04
5. Miscellaneous	.31	.10	−.04	−.01
6. ABC (prime-time)	.27	−.01	−.06	.01
7. News/Talk	.05	−.04	−.10	−.04
Comparison				
Regular measure of violence exposure		.16	.03	.04
N	(392)	(389)	(391)	(389)
Wave II				
1. Saturday morning cartoons	.49	.13	.03	.02
2. Sitcom/Variety	.19	.09	.08	−.06
3. Action/Adventure	.67	.12	.05	.02
4. News	.18	.01	−.12	−.07
5. Miscellaneous	.22	.01	−.04	.02
Comparison				
Regular measure of violence exposure		.09	.01	.01
N	(568)	(581)	(566)	(567)
Wave III				
1. ABC (prime-time)	.25	−.02	−.08	.02
2. Saturday morning cartoons	.54	.03	.04	.01
3. Sitcoms	.32	−.03	−.04	.01
4. Action/Adventure	.66	.05	.00	.06
5. News/Talk	.25	−.04	−.04	.02
Comparison				
Regular measure of violence exposure		.07	.03	.07
N	(564)	(561)	(564)	(561)
Wave IV				
1. Action/Adventure	.61	.11	−.02	.12
2. Weekday (daily, Mon.–Fri.)	.39	.10	−.01	.08
3. Black shows	.31	.05	−.04	.05
4. Saturday morning cartoons	.34	.20	.13	.11
5. News/Talk	.15	−.11	−.10	−.04
Comparison				
Regular measure of violence exposure		.16	.03	.11
N	(674)	(672)	(673)	(664)

TABLE A.5

Factors Significantly Related to Aggression in Regressions with Measures Based on Factor Analysis

WAVE, FACTOR NUMBER, FACTOR LABEL	DOMINANT PROGRAMS	SIGN	LAGS IN WHICH SIGNIFICANT
	Personal aggression		
Wave I			
1. Miscellaneous	*Flying Nun, Bewitched, Wagon Train, Gomer Pyle*	[+]	I–IV
Wave III			
2. Saturday morning cartoons	*Sky Hawks, Perils of Penelope, Archie*	[+]	III–IV, III–V
	Property aggression		
Wave I			
1. Miscellaneous	*Flying Nun, Bewitched, Wagon Train, Gomer Pyle*	[+]	I–V
Wave II			
1. Saturday morning cartoons	*Archie, Josie, Hot Dog*	[+]	II–III, II–V
Wave III			
3. Sitcoms	*Partridge Family, Brady Bunch*	[+]	III–V
	Delinquency		
Wave II			
1. Saturday morning cartoons	*Archie, Josie, Hot Dog*	[+]	II–III
5. Miscellaneous	*Wild Kingdom, McCloud*	[−]	II–IV

TABLE A.6

Descriptive Statistics for Attitudes toward Television and Their Correlations with Violence Exposure and Aggression

	DESCRIPTIVE STATISTICS					CROSS-SECTIONAL CORRELATIONS WITH VIOLENT TELEVISION EXPOSURE AND AGGRESSION			
							AGGRESSION		
	MEAN	MEDIAN	RANGE	STANDARD DEVIATION	*N*	VIOLENCE EXPOSURE	PERSONAL	PROPERTY	DELINQUENCY
Attitude toward television, Wave II (television is very good)[a]	7.1	7.1	1–10	2.4	(567)	.15	.00	−.05	.01
Favorite shows (likes violent shows)									
Wave III	2.7	2.8	0–6	1.7	(472)	.17	.03	.09	.06
Wave IV	8.4	8.5	0–18	4.6	(610)	.24	−.03	−.04	−.03
Identification with violent TV characters, Wave IV (wants to be like violent characters)	1.07	.4	0–6	1.4	(670)	.17	.02	−.01	−.01
Realism of television, Wave IV (television is realistic)	15.0	15.0	6–23	3.1	(670)	.19	.09	.01	.07
Involvement with television, Wave IV (gets very involved)	9.9	9.9	5–15	2.3	(674)	.22	.10	.07	.02
Perception of television messages, Wave IV (thinks television teaches aggression)	7.0	6.9	3–15	2.3	(668)	.01	.10	.22	.08
Interest in violent program elements, Wave V (more interested in action than plot)	2.6	2.6	1–4	.9	(641)	.11	.07	.06	.03

[a] High end of scale.

APPENDIX B: EFFECTS OF EXPOSURE TO TELEVISION VIOLENCE AMONG SAMPLE SUBGROUPS

For each subgroup, we present the findings first for personal aggression; second, for property aggression; and third, for delinquency. We begin with sociocultural factors, move on to family characteristics and peer group characteristics, and end with characteristics of the boys themselves. (Detailed tables are available on request.).

The measures that were used for the subgroup analysis of elementary school boys are described in Chapter 7, Appendices B and C. For information on new measures see the footnotes to the tables in this appendix and see Appendix C for question wording.

TABLE B.1A

Net Effect (χ^2 and β) of Exposure to Violent Television on Later Personal Aggression for Subgroups Based on Sociocultural Factors

SUBGROUP	GOODNESS-OF-FIT χ^2/df RATIO	TELEVISION EFFECT χ^2/df RATIO	NUMBER OF SIGNIFICANT β COEFFICIENTS IN ADJACENT LAGS		AVERAGE β COEFFICIENTS	*N*
			POSITIVE β COEFFICIENTS	NEGATIVE[a] β COEFFICIENTS		
a. *Family income*[b]						
Low	1.705	.245	0	0	.017	(114)
High	1.103	1.189	1	0	.058	(145)
b. *Family type*[c]						
Broken homes	1.571	1.124	0	0	−.033	(57)
Intact homes	1.143	1.527	1	0	.035	(198)
c. *Family size*[d]						
Large	1.439	1.213	0	0	.021	(158)
Small	1.120	1.258	0	0	.090	(102)

[a] Out of four possible coefficients (lags I–II, II–III, III–IV, IV–V).

[b] Taken from first mothers' interview; low is at or below the sample median (under $10,000), high is above the sample median ($10,000 and over). See Chapter 7, Appendices B, C, and see this chapter, Appendix C for more details on the measures.

[c] Taken from first mothers' interview. "Intact homes" means the adolescent is living with both natural parents. "Broken homes" includes those with only one parent, those with one natural parent and a stepparent, and those in foster homes.

Number of family members living at home, taken from first mothers' questionnaire.

TABLE B.1B

Net Effect (χ^2 and β) of Exposure to Violent Television on Later Property Aggression for Subgroups Based on Sociocultural Factors

	SUBGROUP	GOODNESS-OF-FIT χ^2/df RATIO	TELEVISION EFFECT χ^2/df RATIO	NUMBER OF SIGNIFICANT β COEFFICIENTS IN ADJACENT LAGS[a]		AVERAGE β COEFFICIENTS	*N*
				POSITIVE β COEFFICIENTS	NEGATIVE β COEFFICIENTS		
a.	*Family income*						
	Low	1.885	3.429*	1	0	.049	(116)
	High	.807	3.124*	0	0	.014	(146)
b.	*Family type*						
	Broken homes	.468	1.348	0	0	.004	(60)
	Intact homes	1.250	2.571*	1	0	.053	(198)
c.	*Family size*						
	Large	.752	4.622*	1	0	.034	(160)
	Small	1.263	.822	0	0	.049	(103)

[a]Out of four possible β coefficients, lags I–II, II–III, III–IV, IV–V.
*Significant at .05 level.

TABLE B.1C

Net Effect of Exposure to Violent Television on the Probability of Becoming Delinquent for Subgroups Based on Sociocultural Factors

SUBGROUP	NUMBER OF LAGS ANALYZED	LOGIT COEFFICIENTS	
		POSITIVE	NEGATIVE
a. *Family income*			
Low	8	1	0
High	6	0	0
b. *Family type*			
Broken homes[a]	0		
Intact homes	9	0	1
c. *Family size*			
Large	8	0	0
Small	8	0	0

[a]No lag had as many as 30 cases.

TABLE B.2A

Net Effect (χ^2 and β) of Exposure to Violent Television on Later Personal Aggression for Subgroups Based on Parental Control Variables

SUBGROUP	GOODNESS-OF-FIT χ^2/df RATIO	TELEVISION EFFECT χ^2/df RATIO	NUMBER OF SIGNIFICANT β COEFFICIENTS IN ADJACENT LAGS: POSITIVE β COEFFICIENTS	NUMBER OF SIGNIFICANT β COEFFICIENTS IN ADJACENT LAGS: NEGATIVE β COEFFICIENTS	AVERAGE β COEFFICIENTS	*N*
a. *Strictness*						
Father's strictness[a] (in enforcing rules)						
Not strict	1.325	2.153	1	0	.055	(168)
Strict	.813	2.381	0	0	.024	(71)
b. *Supervision*						
Supervision[b]						
Low	1.327	.865	0	0	.047	(103)
High	.914	1.452	0	0	.035	(182)
c. *Punishment*						
Mother's use of physical punishment[c] (frequency plus propensity to hit)						
High	1.213	.493	1	0	.072	(94)
Low	1.863	1.345	0	0	.046	(141)
Father's use of physical punishment[d] (frequency plus propensity to hit)						
High	1.213	.207	0	0	.048	(74)
Low	.633	.496	0	0	.020	(93)

[a] A one-time question appearing in the first mothers' questionnaire and asking how strict the father (or other male) is in keeping after the sample teenager to follow rules.

[b] Response to the question, "How much do any of your parents know what you do during your free time on Saturday and Sunday?" Asked of teens in the third wave.

[c] A six-item index combining the frequency with which the mother hit, slapped, or spanked the son in the last year, and her stated likelihood of doing so under specified circumstances (e.g., if the son teased other children). The variable comes from the first mothers' questionnaire.

[d] An index similar to the one above, except that it comes from the fathers' questionnaire (six items).

TABLE B.2B

Net Effect (χ^2 and β) of Exposure to Violent Television on Later Property Aggression for Subgroups Based on Parental Control Variables

SUBGROUP	GOODNESS-OF-FIT χ^2/df RATIO	TELEVISION EFFECT χ^2/df RATIO	NUMBER OF SIGNIFICANT β COEFFICIENTS IN ADJACENT LAGS		AVERAGE β COEFFICIENTS	*N*
			POSITIVE β COEFFICIENTS	NEGATIVE β COEFFICIENTS		
a. *Strictness*						
Father's strictness (in enforcing rules)						
Not strict	1.662	3.680*	2	0	.056	(169)
Strict	.751	.976	0	0	.057	(72)
b. *Supervision*						
Supervision						
Low	.574	2.389	0	1	.011	(106)
High	3.350	2.491	1	0	.053	(185)
c. *Punishment*						
Mother's use of physical punishment (frequency plus propensity to hit)						
High	1.307	3.315*	1	0	.044	(96)
Low	1.139	.500	0	0	.046	(142)
Father's use of physical punishment (frequency plus propensity to hit)						
High	2.763	1.440	0	1	−.021	(73)
Low	.789	2.620*	1	0	.069	(95)

*Significant at .05 level.

TABLE B.2C

Net Effect of Exposure to Violent Television on the Probability of Becoming Delinquent for Subgroups Based on Parental Control Variables

SUBGROUP	NUMBER OF LAGS ANALYZED	NUMBER OF SIGNIFICANT LOGIT COEFFICIENTS	
		POSITIVE	NEGATIVE
a. *Strictness*			
Father's strictness (in enforcing rules)			
Not strict	9	1†	0
Strict	5	0	0
b. *Supervision*			
Supervision			
Low	5	0	0
High	9	0	0
c. *Punishment*			
Mother's use of physical punishment (frequency plus propensity to hit)			
High	6	2†	0
Low	9	0	0
Father's use of physical punishment (frequency plus propensity to hit)			
High	4	0	1
Low	9	0	0

†One additional coefficient closely approaches significance.

TABLE B.3A

Net Effect (χ^2 and β) of Exposure to Violent Television on Later Personal Aggression for Subgroups Based on Other Family Characteristics

SUBGROUP	GOODNESS-OF-FIT χ^2/df RATIO	TELEVISION EFFECT χ^2/df RATIO	NUMBER OF SIGNIFICANT β COEFFICIENTS IN ADJACENT LAGS		AVERAGE β COEFFICIENTS	*N*
			POSITIVE β COEFFICIENTS	NEGATIVE β COEFFICIENTS		
a. *Family warmth*						
Father's activities with boy as child[a]						
Few	1.956	1.249	0	1	−.035	(87)
Many	2.170	1.222	1	0	.093	(84)
Mother's current dissatisfaction with son[b]						
Low	.597	1.602	0	1	.041	(99)
High	2.515	1.913	1	0	.085	(159)
b. *Aggression in family*						
Boy's arguments with family[c]						
Many	.645	1.168	0	0	−.022	(114)
Few	2.190	4.643*	2	0	.100	(152)

(Continued next page)

TABLE B.3A (*continued*)

SUBGROUP	GOODNESS-OF-FIT χ^2/df RATIO	TELEVISION EFFECT χ^2/df RATIO	NUMBER OF SIGNIFICANT β COEFFICIENTS IN ADJACENT LAGS		AVERAGE β COEFFICIENTS	*N*
			POSITIVE β COEFFICIENTS	NEGATIVE β COEFFICIENTS		
Mother's irritability[d]						
Frequently angry	1.263	.292	0	0	.004	(97)
Not frequently angry	1.425	1.212	0	0	.073	(150)
c. *Attitude toward aggression*						
Father's support for son's aggression[e]						
High	.911	.821	0	0	−.034	(90)
Low	1.109	2.384	0	0	.097	(83)

[a] A five-item measure taken from the second mothers' questionnaire. Mothers were asked how often the father did certain things with the son (e.g., eat meals together, read or tell the boy stories) when the son was between the ages of 2 and 5.

[b] From the first mothers' questionnaire, an unweighted sum of responses indicating the mother's dissatisfaction with the son's leisure time activities, friends, progress in school, and beliefs (four items).

[c] A (four-item) index of the frequency of serious arguments between the boy and his siblings, mother, and father; and the frequency of physical fights between the boy and his siblings. Based on the adolescent's self-report in Wave III.

[d] The sum of the frequency with which the mother loses her temper, gets annoyed with her son, goes out of her way to help people outside family (with direction reversed), drinks alcohol, and gets so angry at someone that she feels like hurting them. Asked in the second mothers' questionnaire.

[e] From the father's questionnaire, an index of how pleased he would be if his son "sneaked on a bus or train without paying when he wanted to go someplace." and "threw a rock through a streetlight when having fun with a bunch of boys."

*Significant at .05 level.

TABLE B.3B

Net Effect (χ^2 and β) of Exposure to Violent Television on Later Property Aggression for Subgroups Based on Other Family Characteristics

SUBGROUP	GOODNESS-OF-FIT χ^2/df RATIO	TELEVISION EFFECT χ^2/df RATIO	NUMBER OF SIGNIFICANT β COEFFICIENTS IN ADJACENT LAGS		AVERAGE β COEFFICIENTS	*N*
			POSITIVE β COEFFICIENTS	NEGATIVE β COEFFICIENTS		
a. *Family warmth*						
Father's activities with boy as child						
Few	1.228	2.411	1	0	.035	(89)
Many	1.426	2.197	0	0	.010	(85)
Mother's current dissatisfaction with son						
Low	1.092	2.482	1	0	.020	(101)
High	.638	3.326*	1	0	.093	(160)
b. *Aggression in family*						
Teen's arguments with family						
Many	.824	1.698	0	0	.043	(119)
Few	1.465	2.654*	1	0	.031	(153)
Mother's irritability						
Frequently angry	1.391	4.105*	1	0	.002	(73)
Not frequently angry	1.262	.892	0	0	.042	(95)
c. *Attitude toward aggression*						
Father's support for son's aggression						
High	.929	1.881	0	0	−.005	(91)
Low	1.133	3.268*	1	0	.008	(83)

*Significant at .05 level.

TABLE B.3C

Net Effect of Exposure to Violent Television on the Probability of Becoming Delinquent for Subgroups Based on Other Family Characteristics

SUBGROUP	NUMBER OF LAGS ANALYZED	NUMBER OF SIGNIFICANT COEFFICIENTS	
		POSITIVE	NEGATIVE
a. *Family warmth*			
Father's activities with boy as child			
Few	5	0	0
Many	9	2	0
Mother's current dissatisfaction with son			
Low	5	0	0
High	6	0	0
b. *Aggression in family*			
Adolescent's arguments with family			
Many	9	0	0
Few	5	1	1
Mother's irritability			
Frequently angry	8	2	0
Not frequently angry	8	0	0
c. *Attitude toward aggression*			
Father's support for son's aggression			
High	7	0	1
Low	4	1	0

TABLE B.4A

Net Effect (χ^2 and β) of Exposure to Violent Television on Later Personal Aggression for Subgroups Based on Peer Context Variables

SUBGROUP	GOODNESS-OF-FIT χ^2/df RATIO	TELEVISION EFFECT χ^2/df RATIO	NUMBER OF SIGNIFICANT β COEFFICIENTS IN ADJACENT LAGS		AVERAGE β COEFFICIENTS	*N*
			POSITIVE β COEFFICIENTS	NEGATIVE β COEFFICIENTS		
a. *Friends' aggressiveness*[a]						
High	2.278	1.734	0	0	−.015	(78)
Low	1.066	2.296	1	0	.064	(129)
b. *Contact with aggressive behavior*[b]						
Much	1.103	.903	0	0	−.013	(87)
Little	.842	1.850	1	0	.029	(110)

[a] Based on questions in Waves I and III asking the teenager how many of his close and ordinary friends do a variety of antisocial acts. Teens at or below the median response for both Waves I and III were placed in the low category. Those above the median for the two waves are in the high category (four items).

[b] Derived from two questions in Waves I and II regarding how often the teenager in the last four weeks saw in person a physical fight or an argument. High scorers are those above the median in the first two waves; low scorers are at or below the median in the two waves.

TABLE B.4B

Net Effect (χ^2 and β) of Exposure to Violent Television on Later Property Aggression for Subgroups Based on Peer Context Variables

SUBGROUP	GOODNESS-OF-FIT χ^2/df RATIO	TELEVISION EFFECT χ^2/df RATIO	NUMBER OF SIGNIFICANT β COEFFICIENTS IN ADJACENT LAGS: POSITIVE β COEFFICIENTS	NUMBER OF SIGNIFICANT β COEFFICIENTS IN ADJACENT LAGS: NEGATIVE β COEFFICIENTS	AVERAGE β COEFFICIENTS	N
a. *Friends' aggressiveness*						
High	1.198	2.438	1	0	.070	(82)
Low	1.508	1.305	0	0	−.005	(130)
b. *Contact with aggressive behavior*						
Much	2.879	.988	0	0	.053	(70)
Little	.879	1.242	0	0	−.070	(82)

TABLE B.4C

Net Effect of Exposure to Violent Television on the Probability of Becoming Delinquent for Subgroups Based on Peer Context Variables

SUBGROUP	NUMBER OF LAGS ANALYZED	NUMBER OF SIGNIFICANT LOGIT COEFFICIENTS	
		POSITIVE	NEGATIVE
a. *Friends' aggressiveness*			
High[a]	0		
Low	9	0	0
b. *Contact with aggressive behavior*			
Much[a]	0		
Little	5	0	0

[a] No lag was as large as 30 cases.

TABLE B.5A

Net Effect (χ^2 and β) of Exposure to Violent Television on Later Personal Aggression for Subgroups Based on Scholastic Variables

SUBGROUP	GOODNESS-OF-FIT χ^2/df RATIO	TELEVISION EFFECT χ^2/df RATIO	NUMBER OF SIGNIFICANT β COEFFICIENTS IN ADJACENT LAGS		AVERAGE β COEFFICIENTS	N
			POSITIVE β COEFFICIENTS	NEGATIVE β COEFFICIENTS		
a. *Average grade in Wave I*[a]						
Low	1.515	.223	0	0	.003	(131)
High	1.921	1.816	1	0	.090	(147)
b. *Attitude toward school*[b]						
Does not like school	1.092	.662	0	0	−.017	(142)
Likes school	1.369	.717	1	0	.079	(143)

[a] Taken from school records, the teenage boy's class quartile ranking for grades at Wave I.
[b] Response to the question, "How well do you like school?" Asked in Wave I.

TABLE B.5B

Net Effect (χ^2 and β) of Exposure to Violent Television on Later Property Aggression for Subgroups Based on Scholastic Variables

SUBGROUP	GOODNESS-OF-FIT χ^2/df RATIO	TELEVISION EFFECT χ^2/df RATIO	NUMBER OF SIGNIFICANT β COEFFICIENTS IN ADJACENT LAGS: POSITIVE β COEFFICIENTS	NUMBER OF SIGNIFICANT β COEFFICIENTS IN ADJACENT LAGS: NEGATIVE β COEFFICIENTS	AVERAGE β COEFFICIENTS	*N*
A. *Average grade in Wave I*						
Low	1.223	1.657	0	0	−.009	(136)
High	1.425	.689	1	0	.067	(147)
b. *Attitude toward school*						
Does not like school	1.868	.315	0	0	−.006	(145)
Likes school	1.428	4.285*	1	0	.056	(146)

*Significant at .05 level.

TABLE B.5C

Net Effect of Exposure to Violent Television on the Probability of Becoming Delinquent for Subgroups Based on Scholastic Variables

SUBGROUP	NUMBER OF LAGS ANALYZED	NUMBER OF SIGNIFICANT LOGIT COEFFICIENTS	
		POSITIVE	NEGATIVE
a. *Average grade in Wave I*			
Low	9	0	0
High	9	0	0
b. *Attitude toward school*			
Does not like school	9	1	0
Likes school	5	0	0

TABLE B.6A

Net Effect (χ^2 and β) of Exposure to Violent Television on Later Personal Aggression for Subgroups Based on Prior Aggression

SUBGROUP	GOODNESS-OF-FIT χ^2/df RATIO	TELEVISION EFFECT χ^2/df RATIO	NUMBER OF SIGNIFICANT β COEFFICIENTS IN ADJACENT LAGS		AVERAGE β COEFFICIENTS	*N*
			POSITIVE β COEFFICIENTS	NEGATIVE β COEFFICIENTS		
a. *Earlier childhood aggression*[a]						
High	1.076	.629	0	0	.018	(149)
Low	1.468	1.458	0†	0	.073	(107)
b. *Initial personal aggression*[b]						
High	1.090	.614	1	0	.060	(84)
Low	1.457	5.063*	1	0	.091	(119)

[a]Based on response to question, "What about when ______ was younger, when he was in the first few grades at school . . . how often did he get into physical fights with other children outside the family?"

[b]High scorers are those above the median on this variable for Waves I and II. Those in the low category scored at or below the median in the two waves.

*Significant at .05 level.

†One additional coefficient closely approaches significance.

TABLE B.6B

Net Effect (χ^2 and β) of Exposure to Violent Television on Later Property Aggression for Subgroups Based on Prior Aggression

SUBGROUP	GOODNESS-OF-FIT χ^2/df RATIO	TELEVISION EFFECT χ^2/df RATIO	NUMBER OF SIGNIFICANT β COEFFICIENTS IN ADJACENT LAGS		AVERAGE β COEFFICIENTS	N
			POSITIVE β COEFFICIENTS	NEGATIVE β COEFFICIENTS		
a. *Earlier childhood aggression*						
High	2.118	5.286*	1	0	.031	(152)
Low	.848	3.577*	2	0	.107	(107)
b. *Initial personal aggression*						
High	.739	2.424	1	0	.058	(84)
Low	.505	.643	0	0	−.034	(119)

*Significant at .05 level.

TABLE B.6C

Net Effect of Exposure to Violent Television on the Probability of Becoming Delinquent for Subgroups Based on Prior Aggression

SUBGROUP	NUMBER OF LAGS ANALYZED	NUMBER OF SIGNIFICANT LOGIT COEFFICIENTS	
		POSITIVE	NEGATIVE
a. *Earlier childhood aggression*			
High	5	0†	0
Low	9	0	0
b. *Initial personal aggression*			
High[a]	0		
Low	9	0	0

†One coefficient closely approaches significance.
[a]No lag was as large as 30 cases.

TABLE B.7A

Net Effect (χ^2 and β) of Exposure to Violent Television on Later Personal Aggression for Subgroups Based on Attitudes toward Aggression

SUBGROUP	GOODNESS-OF-FIT χ^2/df RATIO	TELEVISION EFFECT χ^2/df RATIO	NUMBER OF SIGNIFICANT β COEFFICIENTS IN ADJACENT LAGS		AVERAGE β COEFFICIENTS	*N*
			POSITIVE β COEFFICIENTS	NEGATIVE β COEFFICIENTS		
Support for breaking law[a]						
High	2.597	1.005	0	0	.046	(95)
Low	1.635	3.827*	1	0	.036	(97)
Machismo[b]						
High	2.293	1.624	1	0	.067	(130)
Low	.431	2.318	1	0†	−.006	(150)
Enjoyment of violent movie scenes[c]						
High	1.454	1.226	1	0	.108	(98)
Low	.717	3.223*	1	0†	.014	(107)

[a]How right or wrong the teenage boy feels it would be for him to do things, such as: "Knife a boy who threatens to knife you" and "sneak on a bus or train without paying when you want to go somewhere." The series was asked in Waves I and III. We used data only for boys whose score remained stable relative to the median for both time periods (five-item index).

[b]Three items in Wave III relating to boasting about aggression (e.g., agreement with the statement, "If someone were anxious to start a fight I would never back away").

[c]Based on responses to six questions asking for the teenage boy's reaction to scenes in motion pictures taken of actual, violent events (e.g., soldiers burning an enemy village). The questions were asked in each wave. Respondents in the low category scored at or below the median in Waves I and II; in the high category, above the median.

*Significant at .05 level.

†One additional coefficient closely approaches significance.

TABLE B.7B

Net Effect (χ^2 and β) of Exposure to Violent Television on Later Property Aggression for Subgroups Based on Attitudes toward Aggression

SUBGROUP	GOODNESS-OF-FIT χ^2/df RATIO	TELEVISION EFFECT χ^2/df RATIO	NUMBER OF SIGNIFICANT β COEFFICIENTS IN ADJACENT LAGS		AVERAGE β	N
			POSITIVE β COEFFICIENTS	NEGATIVE β COEFFICIENTS		
Support for breaking law						
High	2.194	2.461	1	0	.050	(99)
Low	1.302	.687	0	0	.043	(97)
Machismo						
High	1.296	3.199*	1	0	.077	(135)
Low	1.130	1.089	0	0	−.060	(151)
Enjoyment of violent movie scenes						
High	1.056	.557	0	0	−.001	(103)
Low	1.047	2.152	1	0†	.025	(106)

*Significant at .05 level.

†One additional β coefficient closely approaches significance.

TABLE B.7C

Net Effect of Exposure to Violent Television on the Probability of Becoming Delinquent for Subgroups Based on Attitudes toward Aggression

SUBGROUP	NUMBER OF LAGS ANALYZED	NUMBER OF SIGNIFICANT LOGIT COEFFICIENTS	
		POSITIVE	NEGATIVE
Support for breaking law			
High[a]	0		
Low	3	0	0
Machismo			
High	5	0	0
Low	9	1	0
Enjoyment of violent movie scenes			
High	5	0	0
Low	9	0	0

[a]No lag was as large as 30 cases.

Net Effect (χ^2 and β) of Exposure to Violent Television on Later Personal Aggression for Subgroups Based on Other Personal Characteristics

SUBGROUP	GOODNESS-OF-FIT χ^2/df RATIO	TELEVISION EFFECT χ^2/df RATIO	NUMBER OF SIGNIFICANT β COEFFICIENTS IN ADJACENT LAGS		AVERAGE β COEFFICIENTS	*N*
			POSITIVE β COEFFICIENTS	NEGATIVE β COEFFICIENTS		
a. *Behavior*						
Use of alcohol, cigarettes, drugs[a]						
High	1.779	.286	0	0	−.016	(81)
Low	1.121	1.877	1	0	.017	(120)
b. *Personality*						
Self-esteem[b]						
Low	.622	2.240	1	0	.063	(175)
High	.981	2.682*	0	0	−.024	(107)
Irritability[c]						
Frequently annoyed	2.518	.846	0	0	.057	(76)
Not frequently annoyed	1.550	.189	0	0	.013	(97)
Aggressive fantasies[d]						
High	1.246	1.073	1	1	.039	(126)
Low	.364	1.012	0	0	.029	(154)
c. *Exposure to comics*[e]						
High	1.364	.783	0	0	.006	(169)
Low	.839	1.860	1	0	.077	(113)

[a]Based on Wave I measures asking respondents if they occasionally smoke and drink, and Wave III measures asking about smoking, drinking, and sniffing things to "get you 'high.' " Low scorers were at or below the median in Waves I and III, high scorers were above the median in the two waves.

[b]A 10-item scale of agreement with negative and positive items measuring feelings of self-worth (e.g., "On the whole I am satisfied with myself"). The items were asked in the second wave.

[c]Derived from responses to the question, "About how many different times during an average day do you find yourself annoyed at something or someone?" To be in the low category, respondents had to score at or below the median on Waves I and III. For the high category, scorers were above the median both times.

[d]Response to a Wave V question asking the respondent how much he is like a guy "who often daydreams about exciting action like fighting or wars."

[e]An index of the frequency with which the respondent reads 17 selected comic books (Wave II).

*Significant at .05 level.

TABLE B.8B

Net Effect (χ^2 and β) of Exposure to Violent Television on Later Property Aggression for Subgroups Based on Other Personal Characteristics

SUBGROUP	GOODNESS-OF-FIT χ^2/df RATIO	TELEVISION EFFECT χ^2/df RATIO	NUMBER OF SIGNIFICANT β COEFFICIENTS IN ADJACENT LAGS		AVERAGE β COEFFICIENTS	*N*
			POSITIVE β COEFFICIENTS	NEGATIVE β COEFFICIENTS		
a. *Behavior*						
Use of alcohol, cigarettes, drugs						
High	2.406	2.232	1	0	.040	(84)
Low	.999	.108	0	0	.018	(120)
b. *Personality*						
Self-esteem						
Low	1.228	2.505*	0	1	.031	(180)
High	.650	3.341*	0	0	.004	(108)
Irritability						
Frequently annoyed	2.460	1.352	0	0	.016	(76)
Not frequently annoyed	2.773	.528	0	0	.013	(97)
Aggressive fantasies						
High	2.503	3.087*	1	0	.036	(129)
Low	.489	1.758	0†	0	.000	(157)
c. *Exposure to comics*						
High	1.388	3.060*	1	0	−.037	(116)
Low	1.034	.854	0	0	−.024	(172)

*Significant at .05 level.

†One additional coefficient closely approaches significance.

TABLE B.8C

Net Effect of Exposure to Violent Television on the Probability of Becoming Delinquent for Subgroups Based on Other Personal Characteristics

SUBGROUP	NUMBER OF LAGS ANALYZED	NUMBER OF SIGNIFICANT LOGIT COEFFICIENTS	
		POSITIVE	NEGATIVE
a. *Behavior*			
Use of alcohol, cigarettes, drugs			
High[a]	0		
Low	9	0	0
b. *Personality*			
Self-esteem			
Low	9	0	0
High	8	0	0
Irritability			
Frequently annoyed	5	1	0
Not frequently annoyed	5	0	0
Aggressive fantasies			
High	8	1	0
Low	9	0	0
c. *Exposure to comics*			
High	8	0	0
Low	9	1	0

[a]No lag was as large as 30 cases.

APPENDIX C: WORDING OF QUESTIONNAIRE ITEMS USED FOR SUBGROUP MEASURES IN TABLES B.2A–C, B.3A–C, B.7A–C, AND B.8A–C[31]

Table B.2A–C[32]

FATHER'S STRICTNESS (SEE CHAPTER 7, TABLE C.4)

MOTHER'S USE OF PHYSICAL PUNISHMENT (SEE CHAPTER 7, TABLE C.5)

FATHER'S USE OF PHYSICAL PUNISHMENT (SEE CHAPTER 7, TABLE C.6)

Table B.3A–C

FATHER'S ACTIVITIES WITH BOY AS A CHILD (SEE CHAPTER 7, TABLES C.1 AND C.2)

MOTHER'S CURRENT DISSATISFACTION WITH SON (SEE CHAPTER 7, TABLE C.3)

BOY'S ARGUMENTS WITH FAMILY

TIII[33] Q42A There are serious arguments—that is, times when at least one of you gets really angry—between you and your brother(s) and/or sister(s). (Almost every day, A few times a week, A few times a month, Less often than a few times a month, I'm not living with this person)

Q42B You get into physical fights with your brother(s) and/or sister(s). (Almost every day, etc.)

Q42D You have serious arguments—that is, times when one of you gets really angry, with your mother, step-mother, foster mother, or guardian with whom you are now living. (Almost every day, etc.)

Q42E You have serious arguments—that is, times when one of you gets really angry, with your father, step father, foster father, or

[31]Measures based on demographic information (e.g., race, city) and those described in Chapter 7, Appendix B or C (boys) or Appendix B of this chapter (teens) not described here.

[32]Table in which results for measure are reported.

[33]TI–V = Teens questionnaire Waves I–V; MI = Mother interview I; MII = Mother interview II; FI = Father interview I; this is followed by the question number.

guardian, with whom you are now living. (Almost every day, etc.)

MOTHER'S IRRITABILITY

MII Q46A How often do you lose your temper? (More than once a day, About once a day, A few times a week, A few times a month, Less often than a few times a month)

Q46B How often do you get annoyed with [name]? (More than once a day, etc.)

Q46C How often do you go out of your way to help someone outside your family? (More than once a day, etc.)

Q46D How often do you get into arguments with people? (More than once a day, etc.)

Q46E How often do you drink alcohol? (More than once a day, etc.)

Q46F How often do you get so angry at someone that you feel like hurting them? (More than once a day, etc.)

FATHER'S SUPPORT FOR SON'S AGGRESSION

FI Q9D How pleased or upset would you feel if "your son" sneaked on a bus or train without paying when he wanted to go someplace? (Very pleased, Pleased, Neither pleased nor upset, Upset, Very upset)

Q9E How pleased or upset would you feel if "your son" threw a rock through a streetlight when having fun with a bunch of boys. (Very pleased, etc.)

Table B.7A–C

SUPPORT FOR BREAKING LAWS

TI,III,IV Q–A How right or wrong do you feel it is for you to hit a boy who curses your father or mother? (Very right, Right, Neither right nor wrong, Wrong, Very wrong)

Q–B How right or wrong do you feel it is for you to hit a boy who hits you first? (Very right, etc.)

Q–C How right or wrong do you feel it is for you to knife a boy who threatens to knife you? (Very right, etc.)

Q–E How right or wrong do you feel it is for you to sneak on a bus or train without paying when you want to go somewhere? (Very right, etc.)

Q–I How right or wrong do you feel it is for you to throw a rock through a streetlight when having fun with a bunch of boys?

MACHISMO: PERSONAL ATTITUDES AND TRAITS

TIII Q39B I have often broken the law and gotten away with it. (True or False)

Q39H I would never lose a fist fight against a boy my size and weight. (True or False)

Q39L If someone were anxious to start a fight I would never back away. (True or False)

ENJOYMENT OF VIOLENT MOVIE SCENES

TI–V Q–B How do you (or would you) personally react to seeing a motion picture of people very angrily yelling or screaming at each other? (Enjoy it very much, Like it, No feeling either way, Dislike it, Find it disgusting)

Q–D How do you (or would you) personally react to seeing a motion picture of soldiers burning enemy villages? (Enjoy it very much, etc.)

Q–E How do you (or would you) personally react to seeing a motion picture of a fist fight between two men? (Enjoy it very much, etc.)

Q–F How do you (or would you) personally react to seeing a motion picture of police clubbing rioters? (Enjoy it very much, etc.)

Q–G How do you (or would you) personally react to seeing a motion picture of a man getting shot? (Enjoy it very much, etc.)

Q–I How do you (or would you) personally react to seeing a motion picture of places that have been bombed? (Enjoy it very much, etc.)

Table B.8A–C

USE OF ALCOHOL, CIGARETTES, DRUGS

TIII Q38A Do you occasionally smoke cigarettes? (Yes, No)

Q38B Do you occasionally get drunk on wine, beer, or alcohol? (Yes, No)

Q38C Do you occasionally sniff glue, gasoline or other things in order to get you "high"? (Yes, No)

PERSONALITY SELF-ESTEEM

TII Q35A On the whole, you are satisfied with yourself. (Strongly agree, Agree, Disagree, Strongly disagree)

Q35B At times I think I am no good at all. (Strongly agree, etc.)

Q35C I feel that I have a number of good qualities. (Strongly agree, etc.)

Q35D I am able to do things as well as most other people. (Strongly agree, etc.)

Q35E I feel I do not have much to be proud of. (Strongly agree, etc.)

Q35F I certainly feel useless at times. (Strongly agree, etc.)

Q35G I feel that I am a person of worth, at least on an equal plane with others. (Strongly agree, etc.)

Q35H I wish I could have more respect for myself. (Strongly agree, etc.)

Q35I All in all, I am inclined to feel that I am a failure. (Strongly agree, etc.)

Q35J I take a positive attitude toward myself. (Strongly agree, etc.)

EXPOSURE TO COMIC BOOKS

TII Q8 How often do you read: *Amazing Spiderman; Archie Comics; Batman, Superman, Superboy; Captain America; Devil Kids; Donald Duck; Mickey Mouse, Walt Disney; Fantastic Four; Fightin' Marines; Flintstones; Huckleberry Hound; Iron Man; Incredible Hulk; Popeye; Sadsack; Tarzan; Thor; Tom and Jerry* (Often, Sometimes, Never)

PART III

SUMMARY AND CONCLUSIONS

CHAPTER 15

SUMMARY AND CONCLUSIONS

The research reported in this volume was designed to determine whether continued exposure to violence on television leads to the development of aggressive behavior patterns among elementary school children and adolescent boys. Before attempting to place the findings in perspective, we will summarize what has been reported so far.

STUDY OF ELEMENTARY SCHOOL BOYS AND GIRLS

Design

In this panel survey, exposure to television violence and aggressive behavior among elementary school children were measured in nine different schools in two cities. These measures of television exposure and aggression were obtained on six different occasions beginning in May 1970 and ending in May 1973. During that period, information was also obtained from teachers and, in the case of the boys, from parents and school records as well.

The sample experienced both planned and unplanned attrition during the 3 years of the study. During the same period, the sample was augmented by new children entering the classrooms. In total, over 1200 boys and almost as many girls took part in the research. Because of attrition, however, the number of children for whom data were available for all six measurement waves was quite small.

We assessed the effects of television based on a model that uses regression equations in which later aggression is predicted from earlier levels of television exposure, controlling for earlier aggression. Fifteen wave pairs were formed from the six basic measurement points available.

Findings for Boys

Regardless of how it is measured, the great majority of young boys are not antisocially aggressive. Clearly social controls are generally effective when it comes to aggressive behavior. The problem with aggression lies with a few who do a great deal of it.

Aggression is a highly stable behavior pattern for the elementary school boys studied. This means that we cannot expect to find a strong effect of television exposure or any other predictor on aggression over intervals in this range. Even so, there is enough change in aggression to allow the detection of a television effect if it exists.

Just as other studies have found, we find that there is a statistical association between exposure to violent television and aggressive behavior at single points in time. But the existence of such correlations apparently indicates processes other than a causal connection from television exposure to aggression.

On the basis of the analyses we carried out to test for such a causal connection there is no evidence that television exposure has a consistently significant effect on subsequent aggressive behavior in the sample of boys. This is true both for the total sample and that part of the sample we identified as valid reporters of their television exposure. None of the additional tests to which the data were subjected—tests for curvilinearity, for the effects of attrition and of new respondents, and for measurement error—required any substantial revision of these conclusions.

Most coefficients in these analyses were small and insignificant, but most of them were also positive. There are two implications of this. The first is that there is no evidence to support the catharsis hypothesis—that exposure to violence on television leads to a decrease in real-life aggression (Feshbach & Singer, 1971). The second is that there might be a trace effect of television exposure on aggression. A supplementary analysis examined that issue (Chapter 7) and found that mutual causes of television exposure and aggression that were not controlled in the basic analysis account for a substantial part of this sign pattern. If the remaining part of the sign pattern were due to a television effect, it would be an extremely small effect that could not be detected as significant even with the sophisticated statistical techniques used in this analysis.

Additional analyses were aimed at determining whether alternative ways of conceptualizing and measuring exposure would change the conclusions. We examined six alternative conceptualizations, including cumulative exposure over longer periods of time, alternative violence weighting systems, and empirical viewing patterns.

On balance, the findings based on these alternative conceptualizations argue that the insignificance of television effects in the basic model was not due to the way we conceptualized "television violence" in the regular exposure measure. Indeed, measures of exposure to "violent" television content do not have a consistently stronger relationship to later aggression than do measures of "nonviolent" exposure.

We also examined the effect of exposure to television violence among subgroups of the sample, hypothesizing that an impact might appear if boys were predisposed to aggression by other factors in their environment or if certain facilitating conditions were present. These hypotheses are based on principles of learning theory as well as past research on the effects of television, including several specifications suggested by the Surgeon General's Report (1972).

The relationship between television and aggression was further examined in subgroups defined on the basis of sociocultural variables, family structure, family relations, peer group contacts, and other characteristics of the boy himself—some 43 different attributes in all. The basic 15 wave pair models were estimated in all these subgroups, resulting, for boys, in 1228 separate regression equations.

Obviously, given so many replications, statistical significance could be reached by chance in some of these groups. In fact, the criterion was reached in a few subgroups. However, we found no evidence that television played any role among boys who could be considered predisposed toward aggressive behavior. In fact, the defining characteristics of these subgroups are inconsistent with theoretical assumptions about predisposing and facilitating conditions. For example, statistically significant associations occurred among boys not noted by their teachers for being shy, who could be considered predisposed, but also occurred among those who help others, rather than among those who do not, and among boys who find movies about real-life violence disgusting, rather than among those who enjoy such movies.

Furthermore, the patterns of significance in the subgroups correspond closely to those one would expect if the significances in the various subgroups were distributed at random. In addition, none of these patterns of significance is replicated among girls or teens. Because the results are theoretically implausible and because overall results are consistent with chance model expectations, the results of the subgroup analyses do not provide support for the existence of television influences among predisposed boys.

Although this study was designed to focus on detecting effects of television on aggression, it did uncover factors which are more strongly correlated with aggression than is television. Some of these proved to be predictors of change in aggression over the time periods studied: aggressive boys are in low socioeconomic circumstances, and in classrooms and families where aggression is commonplace. Such children tend to become more aggressive as time goes on, relative to those in other circumstances. They are socially insecure, have other emotional problems, and are not accepted by their parents. Although we are not able to be definitive about whether these other characteristics are truly causes of aggression, they certainly should be considered important leads on which to base further research.

Findings for Girls

Concern about aggressive behavior has in the past focused largely on males. Therefore, most of our research efforts were directed toward discovering whether or not, and to what extent, exposure to television violence was causally related to aggression among boys. Nevertheless, the measurement instruments used to obtain television and aggression data from girls (in the same classes, schools, and cities as the boys) were, for the most part, comparable to those we had available for boys, although data from mothers and school records were not collected.

Girls are considerably less aggressive than boys, but the cross-sectional correlations between aggression and violent television exposure are higher for girls than for boys. As discussed earlier, the existence of cross-sectional correlations between exposure and aggression does not necessarily mean that there is a causal connection between the measures. Findings from our basic model—multiple regression equations that control for some spurious factors—do not show significant indications of a causal influence of television exposure. Coefficients in these analyses are quite similar to those obtained for boys: Most are positive but very small. Additional analyses, controlling for other common causes of television and aggression, reduce the number of positive coefficients. Thus, the lack of consistent statistically significant association found among boys is replicated among the elementary school girls. Again, this is not due to the high stability of aggression among girls; there is sufficient change to detect effects if they exist.

Analyses involving alternative conceptualizations of television exposure were also performed for the girls' sample and showed that there were at best small and inconsistent improvements in prediction with these measures.

We were able to examine effects of televised violence in subgroups of girls based on 20 different characteristics. As among boys, the pattern of significant coefficients showed no substantive consistency, and their distribution agreed with chance expectations.

Finally, a pooled multiple regression analysis of boys and girls together produced essentially the same results as the basic model analyses for the two groups separately.

STUDY OF TEENAGE BOYS

Design

During the 3-year period covered by the study, data were collected five times from teenage boys. Respondents were studied in the same two cities as the elementary school children, but the sampling approaches were different. The sampling and other design differences were a result of the fact that teenage boys rotate among different classrooms rather than spend the entire day in the same class.

Teenage boys were selected from school enrollment lists of the secondary schools that were fed by the elementary schools of the younger respondents. The boys who were selected were then asked to bring neighborhood friends to interview sessions. The boys who attended the first session were asked to bring additional friends for the Wave II session to increase the sample size. During the 3-year study, about 800 boys took part in at least one wave, 302 in all five.

Television exposure data were obtained in much the same way as in the study of elementary school respondents, through program checklists. The aggression measure, however, was quite different. Aggression was measured through self-reports, and we included questions about serious aggression in addition to questions about milder forms of aggression.

We found that there is more differentiation of aggression among teens than among elementary school children. Compared to the unidimensional representation found among boys and girls, factor analysis revealed four separate dimensions of aggression among teenage boys: personal, property, and teacher aggression, and delinquency. We also found the behavior patterns of the teenagers to be considerably less stable than aggression among the younger children. This means that there is more change in teenage aggression to explain, so the effect of television exposure should be more easily detectable.

Even though the measures were different and produced more differentiated types of aggressive behavior among teens, the resulting distributions are J-shaped, indicating that, like the younger boys, most teens are not aggressive. Three of the four measures of aggression were correlated with exposure to violence on television at single points in time; delinquency, a measure of very serious aggression, was not. Nevertheless, we examined whether there might be a causal association with all four types of aggression.

The analysis approach chosen to explore the existence of a causal connection between television exposure and aggression was the same as that used for the younger respondents. However, due to larger sample sizes, it was possible to analyze four- and five-wave models as well as two-wave models.

Findings for Mild Forms of Aggression

Using a maximum-likelihood approach to the estimation of multiwave models, we found no significant global associations between television exposure and personal, teacher, or property aggression. Individual wave-pair parameter estimates, tests for measurement error, nonlinearities, and nonadditivities confirmed the findings of the global model: No evidence of a consistent significant association was found.

The conclusion was corroborated in analyses using different conceptualizations of "violent" television exposure. Further, a limited investigation of whether exposure interacts with positive attitudes toward television to produce aggression using measures that were not available for young respondents also supported the conclusion.

Findings for Delinquency

Because the acts included in the measure of delinquency are extremely rare, a special approach designed for the analysis of rare events was chosen. This approach, logit analysis, requires the use of two-wave models. Also, the rarity of these events forced us to limit the analysis to an examination of television's role in initiating delinquent acts; television's impact on continued involvement in delinquency could not be examined.

The logit analyses showed that the patterns of association between television exposure and serious acts of aggression are clearly within the bounds of chance and provided no evidence of a consistent significant association. Nor did supplementary analyses, based on other conceptualizations of exposure and on subgroups, produce any evidence of television effects. Because of the rarity of delinquent acts, however, these analyses are less conclusive than equivalent analyses for milder forms of aggression.

Finally, the study showed that many of the factors which were more strongly related than television exposure to the aggression of elementary school boys are also similarly related to teen aggression: living in neighborhoods and families where aggression occurs often, and being rejected by their mothers. In addition, the aggressive teen accepts aggression as a proper form of behavior and feels no regret when he is aggressive. He uses alcohol and has friends who use drugs. Most of these factors are predictors of his becoming more aggressive over time relative to teens who do not share such circumstances. These factors, too, deserve attention in future research efforts aimed at understanding the causes of aggressive behavior.

DISCUSSION AND CONCLUSIONS

In the present study, criteria for detecting an effect were not met for elementary school boys and girls or teenage boys. This was true for total samples as well as subgroups considered to be predisposed. In other words this study did not find evidence that television violence was causally implicated in the development of aggressive behavior patterns among children and adolescents over the time periods studied. At the same time, the analysis model used to detect television exposure effects showed that there are social and individual characteristics which are related to significant change in subsequent aggression over the time periods studied. Thus, it is clear that the study findings were produced by an analysis model that is able to detect meaningful effects.

The study was designed to determine whether exposure to violence on television, under the conditions in which such exposure takes place in the real world, leads to developmental changes in aggression. As pointed out in the opening chapter, it was not designed to address the possibility of short-term arousal or modeling effects, nor to study the role of specific depictions in triggering unusual or rare acts of violence.

The study conceptualized aggression as antisocial behavior, and this, too, had implications for what would be included as a focus of study and therefore what could be found. It is possible, for example, that television may stimulate aggressive fantasies. But so long as these fantasies are not translated into overt behavior, our study does not pick them up. Although we do not regard this as a deficiency, the precise meaning of "aggression" ought to be kept in mind in interpreting the results.

Furthermore, it ought to be noted that we studied children and teens in two midwestern cities, not in the United States as a whole. The intent of this selection procedure was to maximize opportunities for the occurrence and detection of television effects on aggression. Thus, we chose cities with their higher crime rates, rather than rural areas; two cities rather than one; and schools within those cities that would draw into the study children with diverse socioeconomic and ethnic backgrounds. It is difficult to imagine that the impact of television violence would be less in this than in other samples.

The fact that we have been unable to detect a clear and pronounced effect on aggressive behavior either in the sample as a whole or among subgroups of the sample does not mean that such effects may not exist for some children. (Children with significant specific psychological problems may be such a group.) However, our subgroup analysis indicates that if such children exist, they constitute such a small portion of the sample that we could not draw conclusions from observing them.

Further, the findings in this study were obtained with a wide variety of programs shown in this country in the early 1970s. We believe, however, that a replication with programs shown in the late 1970s or today would arrive at very similar findings for two reasons. First, the programs shown during our study period were reviewed by the networks' Broadcast Standards departments in order to eliminate portrayals of violence in television programs that may incite imitation as well as excessive or gratuitous violence. Programs shown since the completion of our fieldwork have been reviewed by the same departments who have applied standards restricting the kind of violence in a similar, if not more restrictive, manner than in the early 1970s. Second, we found that the number of action/adventure programs shown in our study cities during times when children watch has decreased about one-third since 1971.

Comparing the results of this study with those found in other research on this topic, we see agreement in some respects and disagreement in others.

Like other real-life correlational studies, ours found a significant positive association between television and aggression at single points in time. It is difficult, however, to be very precise in comparing our cross-sectional results with those of the cross-sectional surveys that have been carried out over the past decade since our measures of television exposure and aggression differ in some respects from those used by others. But in general terms, the sign and size of the correlations found in our samples are similar to those found in previous cross-sectional surveys on television and aggression.

There is a clear contrast between the results reported here and those reported in many experimental studies. Laboratory experiments have demonstrated that exposure to specific filmed segments influences aggression. We found no significant association between violent television exposure and subsequent change in aggression. There is nothing necessarily contradictory between those two findings. Experiments assess short-term arousal and modeling effects. The existence of long-term socialization effects in a real-life context, with which this study deals, is not addressed in experimental research.

However, our results are relevant for understanding the long-term implications of experimentally documented short-term effects. If these short-term effects cumulated and generalized to day-to-day behavior, we would have found clear indications of this in our data. The fact that we did not find evidence of this sort suggests that the short-term effects found experimentally do not lead to stable patterns of aggression in the "real world."

The unique feature of our study is its longitudinal design. Thus, it is most relevant to compare our results with longitudinal surveys. While this is being written, a panel study of elementary school children by Huesman, Fischer, and Eron is being analyzed now. The only published panel study comparable to ours is by Lefkowitz *et al.* (1972). These researchers found a lagged correlation of .31 between their television measure and aggression. There is no association of that size in our data or any other research we know of.

The design of the Lefkowitz study differs from ours in three important respects. Lefkowitz and his colleagues used a "favorite show" rather than a television exposure measure; the measure of later aggression was based on retrospective nominations rather than on ratings of current behavior; and, finally, their measures were taken 10 years apart, whereas our maximum interval is 3 years.[1]

The results of our study seem more compelling than those of Lefkowitz *et al.* because of the greater validity and consistency of the measures, and because of the superior analysis technique employed.

Finally, turning back to the study at hand, we have presented its design, execution, and analysis as completely as possible. We have detailed all the analyses, the criteria for detecting an effect, and the results that led us to the conclusion that this study did not find evidence that, over the periods studied, television was causally implicated in the development of aggressive behavior patterns among children and adolescents.

[1]Lefkowitz *et al.*'s indicator of television exposure was based on mother's reports of their children's three favorite programs when the children were in third grade. The use of that retrospective measure, rather than self-reports of actual exposure, might account for the larger association found in the Lefkowitz study. We used this measure in our study and found it a very poor indicator of the child's television exposure, correlating only .25 with our index of violent television exposure. Furthermore, we found that the cross-sectional relationship between the mother's report of favorite (violent) shows and our aggression measures is much less substantial than that between the child's self-reported exposure and these same aggression measures.

The difference between aggression measures in the two studies might also account for the difference in results. In the Lefkowitz *et al.* study, nominators in the tenth grade were not asked to rate their peers' aggressiveness at that time but according to "the way they acted in school" based on "what you last knew of each person from personal observation and contact [1972, p. 44]." The resultant measure is likely to be reputational. The time reference of the measure is vague and the study does not actually measure a 10-year lag. Finally, as pointed out by Chaffee (1972), differences between the early and the later aggression and television measures in the Lefkowitz study may have distorted the findings. In our study, television and aggression measures were identical at all times.

BIBLIOGRAPHY

Abel, J., & M. Beninson. Perceptions of TV program violence by children and mothers. *Journal of Broadcasting*, 1976, *20*:355–363.

Aberle, D.F., & K.D. Naegele. Middle class fathers' occupational role and attitudes toward children. *American Journal of Orthopsychiatry*, 1952, *22*:366–378.

Ahlstrom, W.M., & R.J. Havighurst. *400 losers*. San Francisco: Jossey-Bass, 1971.

Allport, F.H. The J-curve hypothesis of conforming behavior. *Journal of Social Psychology*, 1934, *5*:141–183.

Alwin, D. The use of factor analysis in the construction of linear composites in social research. *Sociological Methods and Research*, 1973, *2*:191–214.

Bachman, J.G. *Youth in transition*, Vol II: *The impact of family background and intelligence on tenth-grade boys*. Ann Arbor: Institute for Social Research, University of Michigan, 1970.

Baker, R., & S. Ball (Eds.). *Mass media and violence* (staff report). Washington, D.C.: National Commission on the Causes and Prevention of Violence. Vol. IX, 1969.

Bandura, A., D. Ross, & S.A. Ross. Transmission of aggression through imitation of aggressive models. *Journal of Abnormal and Social Psychology*, 1961, *63*:575–582.

Bandura, A., & R.H. Walters. *Adolescent aggression*. New York: Ronald Press, 1959.

Banks, S., & R. Gupta. Television as a dependent variable, for a change. *Journal of Consumer Research*, 1980, 7:327–330.

Banks, S., & R. Gupta. Television as a dependent variable, for a change. *Journal of Consumer Research*, 1980, 7:327–330.

Battin, T. *The use of diary and survey methods involving the questionnaire-interview technique to determine the impact of television on school children*. Unpublished Ph.D. dissertation, University of Michigan, 1952.

Belson, W. *Television violence and the adolescent boy*. London: Saxon House, 1978.

Berelson, B., & G. Steiner. *Human behavior: An inventory of scientific findings*. New York: Harcourt, Brace and Jovanovich, 1967.

Berkowitz, L., & R.G. Green. Film violence and the cue properties of available targets. *Journal of Personality and Social Psychology* 1966, *3*:525–530.

Berkowitz, L., & E. Rawlings. Effects of film violence on inhibitions against subsequent aggression. *Journal of Abnormal and Social Psychology* 1963, *66*:405–412.

Biblow, E. Imaginative play and the control of aggressive behavior. In J. Singer (Ed.), *The child's world of make believe*. New York and London: Academic Press, 1973. Pp. 104–128.

Block, J. *Lives through time*. Berkeley: Bancroft, 1971.

Bloom, B. *Stability and change in human characteristics*. New York: Wiley, 1964.

Bogart, L. *The age of television.* 2nd ed. New York: Ungar, 1958; 3rd ed. New York: Ungar, 1972.

Bohrnstedt, G.W. Observations on the measurement of change. In E.F. Borgatta (Ed.), *Sociological methodology*. San Francisco: Jossey-Bass, 1969.

Bohrnstedt, G.W., & T.M. Carter. Robustness in regression analysis. In Herbert L. Costner (Ed.), *Sociological methodology.* San Francisco: Jossey-Bass, 1971. Pp. 118–146.

Boruch, R., & H. Gomez. Sensitivity, bias, and theory in impact evaluations. *Professional Psychology* 1977, *8*:411–434.

Bossard, J.H.S., & E.S. Boll. *The large family system*. Philadelphia: University of Pennsylvania Press, 1958.

Bower, R. *Television and the public.* New York: Holt, Rinehart, and Winston, 1973.

Bronfenbrenner, U. Socialization and social class through time and space. In E.E. Maccoby, T.M. Newcomb, and E. L. Hartley (Eds.). *Readings in social psychology* (3rd ed.). New York: Holt, Rinehart, and Winston, 1958.

Bronfenbrenner, U. Toward a theoretical model for the analysis of parent-child relationships in a social context. In J.C. Glidwell (Ed.), *Parental attitudes and child behavior.* Springfield, IL: C.C. Thomas, 1961.

Campbell, D. From description to experimentation: Interpreting trends as quasi experiments. In C.W. Harris (Ed.), *Problems in measuring change*. Madison: University of Wisconsin Press, 1963.

Campbell, D., & J. Stanley. *Experimental and quasi-experimental design for research*. Chicago: Rand-McNally, 1966.

Campbell, J. Peer relations in childhood. In M.L. Hoffman and L. W. Hoffman (Eds.), *Review of child development research* (Vol. I). New York: Russell Sage, 1964.

Chaffee, S. Television and adolescent aggressiveness (Overview). In *National Institute of Mental Health, Television and Social Behavior,* Reports and Papers. Washington, D.C., U.S. Gov't Printing Office, Technical Report to Surgeon General's Scientific Advisory Committee on Television and Social Behavior (Vol III), 1972.

Cleary, Paul D. & Ronald C. Kessler. The estimation and interpretation of modified effects. *Journal of Health and Social Behavior* 1982, in press.

Cline, V.B., R.G. Croft & S. Courrir. Desensitization of children to television violence. *Journal of Personality and Social Psychology* 1973, *27*:360–365.

Cloward, R.A., & L.E. Ohlin. *Delinquency and opportunity: A theory of delinquent gangs*. New York: Free Press, 1960.

Coffin, T.E. Television's effects on leisure time activities. *Journal of Applied Psychology* 1948, *32*:550–558.

Coffin, T.E. The Hofstra Study, 1950, Hofstra College, Hempstead, N.Y. National Boradcasting Company, N.Y., N.Y.

Coffin, T.E., & S. Tuchman. Rating television programs for violence: A comparison of five surveys. *Journal of Broadcasting* 1972/1973, *17*:3–20.

Cohen, A. *Delinquent boys: The culture of the gang*. New York: Free Press, 1955.

Comstock, G.A. *The evidence on television violence*. Rand Paper Series P-5730. Santa Monica, CA: Rand Corporation, 1976.

Comstock, G.A., S. Chafee, N. Katzman, M. McCombs, & D. Roberts. *Television and human behavior*. New York: Columbia University Press, 1978.

Comstock, G.A., & E.A. Rubinstein (Eds.). *Television and Social Behavior: A Technical Report to the Surgeon General's Scientific Advisory Committee on Television and Social Behavior.* Vol. I: *Media content and control.* Vol. II: *Television and social learning.* Vol. III: *Television and adolescent aggressiveness*. Vol. IV: *Television in day-to-day life: Patterns of use.* Vol. V: *Television's effects: Further explorations*. Rockville, MD: U.S. Dept. of HEW, National Institute of Mental Health, 1972.

Cook, T.D., & D.T. Campbell. *Quasi-experimentation: Design and analysis issues for field settings*. Chicago: Rand McNally, 1979.

Davis, A. Child training and social class. In R.G. Barber, I.S. Kounin, and H.F. Wright (Eds.), *Child behavior and development*. New York: McGraw-Hill, 1943. Pp. 607–620. *Socialization and adolescent personality.* 1944 Yearbook *National Society for the Study of Education* (Chicago) 1944, *43*:198–242. American status systems and the socialization of the child. In C. Kluckhohn and H.A. Murray (Eds.), *Personality in nature, society, and culture*. New York: Knopf; 1948. Pp. 567–576.

Dollard, J., L.W. Doob, N.E. Miller, O.H. Mowrer, & R.R. Sears. *Frustration and aggression*. New Haven: Yale University Press, 1939.

Donovan, J. Self reported deviance in an adolescent sample: Cross-sectional and longitudinal analyses of personality and social correlates. Unpublished manuscript, Institute for Behavioral Science, University of Colorado, 1974.

Donovan, J. *A typological study of self-reported deviance in a national sample of adolescents*. Unpublished doctoral dissertation, University of Colorado, 1977.

Door, A. No short cuts to judging reality. In D.R. Anderson & J. Bryant. *Watching TV, understanding TV: reseach on children's attention and comprehension.* New York: Academic Press, 1982, in press.

Drabman, R.S., & M.H. Thomas. Does media violence increase children's toleration of real-life aggression? *Developmental Psychology* 1974, *10*:418–421.

Duncan, O.D. Some linear models for two-wave two-variable panel analysis. *Psychological Bulletin* 1969, *72*:177–182.

Duncan, O.D. Unmeasured variables in linear models for panel analysis. In H.L. Costner (Ed.), *Sociological methodology*. San Francisco: Jossey-Bass, 1972. Pp. 36–82.

Duncan, P. Parental attitudes and interactions in delinquency. *Child Development* 1971, *42*:1751–1785.

Efron, B. Regression and ANOVA with zero-one data: Measures of residual variation. *Journal of the American Statistical Association*, 1978, *73*:113–121.

Ekman, P., R.M. Liebert, W.V. Friesen, R. Harrison, C. Zlatchin, E.J. Malmstrom, & R.A. Baron. Facial expressions of emotion while watching television violence as predictors of subsequent aggression. In *National Institute of Mental Health, Television and Social Behavior, Reports and Papers*. Technical Report to Surgeon General's Scientific Advisory Committee on Television and Social Behavior. Vol V. Washington, D.C.: U.S. Gov't. Printing Office, 1972.

Erickson, M.L. & L.T. Empey. Class position, peers, and delinquency. *Sociology and Social Research* 1966, *49*:268–282.

Eron, L.D. Sex, aggression, and fantasy. Paper read at the Annual Meeting, Midwestern Psychological Association. Chicago, May 14, 1979.

Eron, L.D., L.R. Huesmann, M.M. Lefkowitz & L.O. Walder. Does television violence cause aggression? *American Psychologist,* 1972, *27*:253–263.

Eron, L.D. Parent-child interaction, television violence, and aggression of children. *American Psychologist* 1982, *37*:197–211.

Eron, L.D., L. Walder, & M. Lefkowitz. *Learning of aggression in children*. Boston: Little, Brown, 1971.

Federal Bureau of Investigation, U.S. Justice Department. *Uniform Crime Reports, 1969*. Washington, D.C.: U.S. Government Printing Office, 1969.

Fenigstein, A. Does aggression cause a preference for viewing media violence? *Journal of Personality and Social Psychology* 1979, *37*(12):2307–2317.

Feshbach, S. The catharsis hypothesis and some consequences of interaction with aggressive and neutral play objects. *Journal of Personality* 1956, *24*:449–462.

Feshbach, S. Aggression. In Paul Mussen (Ed.), *Carmichael's manual of child psychology* (Vol. 2, 3rd. ed.). New York: Wiley, 1970.

Feshbach, S. Reality and fantasy in filmed violence. In J.P. Murray, E.A. Rubinstein, & G.A.

Comstock (Eds.), *Television and social behavior* (Vol 2). Washington, D.C.: U.S. Government Printing Office, 1972.

Feshbach, S., & R.D. Singer. *Television and aggression: An experimental field study*. San Francisco: Jossey-Bass, 1971.

Furu, T., T. Nakano, K. Furuhata, Y. Akutsu, K. Hirata, & T. Ikutu. *The function of television for children and adolescents.* Tokyo: Monumenta Nipponica, Sophia (Sapporo) University, 1971.

Gastil, R. Homicide and a regional culture of violence. *American Sociological Review* 1971, *36*:413–427.

Gerbner, G. Violence in television drama: Trends and symbolic functions. In *National Institute of Mental Health, Television and Social Behavior, Reports and Papers*. Technical Report to Surgeon General's Scientific Advisory Committee on Television and Social Behavior. Vol. I. Washington, D.C.: U.S. Gov't Printing Office, 1972.

Gerbner, G. & L. Gross. Living with television: The violence profile. *Journal of Communications* 1976, *26*:173–199.

Gerbner, G., L. Gross, M. Eleey, S. Fox, M. Jackson-Beeck, & N. Signorielli. *Violence Profile Number 7: Trends in network television drama and viewer conceptions of social reality, 1967–1975.* Philadelphia: The Annenberg School of Communications, University of Pennsylvania, 1976.

Glueck, S., & E.T. Glueck. *Unraveling juvenile delinquency*. New York: Commonwealth Fund, 1950.

Gold, M., & D. Mann. Delinquency as defense. *American Journal of Orthopsychiatry* 1972, *42*:463–479.

Goldstein, A. Aggression and hostility in the elementary school in low socioeconomic areas. *Understanding the Child* 1955, *24*:20.

Goodman, L.A. Causal analysis of data from panel studies and other kinds of surveys. *American Journal of Sociology* 1973, *78*:1135–1191.

Gordon, R.A. Issues in multiple regression. *American Journal of Sociology* 1968, *73*:592–616.

Greenberg, B.S. British children and televised violence. *Public Opinion Quarterly* 1975, *38*:531–547.

Greenberg, B., P. Ericson, & M. Vlahos. Children's television behaviors as perceived by mother and child. In *National Institute of Mental Health, Television and Social Behavior, Reports and Papers*. Technical Report to Surgeon General's Scientific Advisory Committee on Television and Social Behavior. Vol III. Washington, D.C.: U.S. Gov't Printing Office, 1972.

Greenberg, B., & J. Dominick. Television behavior among disadvantaged children. In B. Greenberg, B. Derrin, J. Dominick, & J. Bowes, *Use of the mass media by the urban poor.* New York: Praeger, 1970. Pp. 51–71.

Greenberg, B., & T. Gordon. Perceptions of violence in television programs: Critics and the public. In *National Institue of Mental Health, Televison and Social Behavior, Reports and Papers*. Technical Report to Surgeon General's Scientific Advisory Committee on Television and Social Behavior. Vol. I. U.S. Gov't Printing Office, 1972.

Greenblum, J., & L. Pearlin. Vertical mobility and prejudice: A socio-psychological analysis. In R. Bendix and S. J. Lipset (Eds.), *Class, status and power* (2nd ed.) New York: Free Press, 1966.

Halloran, J., R. Brown & D. Chaney. *Television and delinquency*. Leicester, England: Leicester University Press, 1970.

Hanratty, M.A., E. O'Neal, & J.L. Sulzer. Effect of frustration upon initiation of aggression. *Journal of Personality and Social Psychology* 1972, *21*:30–34.

Hanushek, E.A., & J. Jackson, *Statistical methods for social scientists.* New York: Academic Press, 1978.

Hartnagel, T.F., J.J. Teevan, Jr., & J.J. McIntyre. Television violence and violent behavior. *Social Forces,* 1975, *54*:341–351.

Havighurst, R.J., & H. Taba. *Adolescent character and personality*. New York: Wiley, 1949.
Hays, W.L. *Statistics for the social sciences* (2nd ed.). New York: Holt, Rinehart, and Winston, 1973.
Heise, D.R. Separating reliability and stability in test-retest correlations. *American Sociological Review* 1969, *34*:93–101.
Heise, D.R. Causal inferences from panel data. In E.F. Borgatta and G.W. Bohrnstedt (Eds.), *Sociological methodology*. San Francisco: Jossey-Bass, 1970. Pp. 3–27.
Heise, D.R., & G.W. Bohrnstedt. Validity, invalidity, and reliability. In E.F. Borgatta and G.M. Borhnstedt (Eds.), *Sociological methodology*. San Francisco: Jossey-Bass, 1970. Pp. 104–129.
Heller, M.S., & S. Polsky. Overview: Five-Year Review of Research Sponsored by the American Broadcasting Company, September 1970 through August 1975. New York: ABC, 1975.
Himmelweit, H., A. Oppenheim, & P. Vince. *Television and the child*. London: The Oxford University Press, 1958.
Hirschi, T. *Causes of delinquency*. Berkeley, Calif.: University of California Press, 1969.
Holmes, T.H., & R.H. Rahe. "The social readjustment rating scale. *Journal of Psychosomatic Research* 1967, *11*:213–218.
Homans, G.C. *Sentiments and activities*. New York: Free Press, 1962.
Jensen, G.F. Parents, peers, and delinquent action: A test of the differential association perspective. *American Journal of Sociology* 1973, *78*:562–575.
Jessor, R., & S.L. Jessor. *Problem behavior and psychosocial development*. New York: Academic Press, 1977.
Johnston, J. *Econometric methods.* (2nd ed.). New York: McGraw-Hill, 1972.
Jöreskog, K.G. A general approach to confirmatory maximum likelihood factor analysis. *Psychometrika* 1969, *34*:183–202.
Jöreskog, K.G. Estimation and testing of simplex models. *British Journal of Mathematical and Statistical Psychology* 1970, *23*:121–145.
Jöreskog, K.G. A general method for estimating a linear structural equation system. In A.S. Goldberger and O.D. Duncan (Eds.), *Structural equation models in the social sciences*. New York: Academic Press, 1973. Pp. 85–112.
Jöreskog, K.G., & D. Sörbom. Statistical Models and Methods for Analysis of Longitudinal Data. Research Report 75-1, Department of Statistics, University of Uppsala, Sweden, 1975. Mimeographed.
Jöreskog, K.G., & D. Sörbom. *Lisrel IV: Estimation of linear structural relationships by the method of maximum likelihood*. Chicago: International Educational Services, 1977.
Kagan, J., & H.A. Moss. *Birth to maturity*. New York: Wiley, 1962.
Kaplan, H.B. Toward a general theory of psychosocial deviance: the case of aggressive behavior. *Social Science and Medicine* 1972, *6*:593–617.
Kaplan, R.M. & R.D. Singer. Television violence and viewer aggression: A reexamination of the evidence. *The Journal of Social Issues* 1976, *32*:35–70.
Katz, E., & D. Foulkes. On the use of the mass media as 'escape'; clarification of a concept. *Public Opinion Quarterly* 1962, *26*:377–388.
Kay, H. Weaknesses in the television-causes-aggression analysis by Eron *et al*. *American Psychologist* 1972, *27*:970–973.
Kenny, D. "Cross-lagged panel correlations: A test for spuriousness. *Psychological Bulletin* 1975, *82*:887–903.
Kessler, R.C., & D.F. Greenberg. *Linear panel analysis: Models of quantitative change.* New York: Academic Press, 1981.
Klapper, J. *The effects of mass communication*. New York: Free Press, 1960.
Kohn, M.L. *Class and conformity: A study of values* (2nd ed.). Chicago: University of Chicago Press, 1977.

Kohn, M.L. & C. Schooler. The reciprocal effects of the substantive complexity of work and intellectual flexibility: A longitudinal assessment. *American Journal of Sociology* 1978, *84*:24–52.

Kohn, M.L. & C. Schooler. Job conditions and personality: A longitudinal assessment of their reciprocal effect. *American Journal of Sociology* 1982, in press.

Kraus, S., & D. Davis. *The effects of mass communication on political behavior.* University Park: Pennsylvania State University Press, 1976.

Krugman, H., & E. Hartley. Passive learning from television. *Public Opinion Quarterly* 1970, *34*:184–190.

Labovitz, S. In defense of assigning numbers to ranks. *American Sociological Review* 1971, *36*:521–522.

Labovitz, S. Statistical usage in sociology. *Sociological Methods and Research* 1972, *1*:13–37.

Lalli, M. & S.H. Turner. Suicide and homicide: A comparative analysis by race and occupation levels. *Journal of Criminal Law, Criminology and Police Science* 1968, *59*:191–200.

Lazarsfeld, P.F. *Mutual effects on statistical variables.* New York: Bureau of Applied Social Research, 1948. Mimeographed.

Lazarsfeld, P.F. Mutual relations over time of two attributes: A review and integration of various approaches. In M. Hammer, K. Salzingo, & S. Sutton (Eds.), *Psychopathology: Contributions from the social, behavioral, and biological sciences.* New York: Wiley, 1973. Pp. 461–479.

Lazarsfeld, P.F., B. Berelson, & H. Gaudet. *The people's choice*. New York. Columbia University Press, 1944.

Lefkowitz, M., L. Eron, L. Walder, & L. Huesmann. Television violence and child aggression: A follow-up study. In *National Institute of Mental Health, Television and Social Behavior, Reports and Papers*. Technical Report to Surgeon General's Scientific Advisory Committee on Television and Social Behavior. Vol. III, 1972.

Lefkowitz, M., L. Eron, L. Walder, & L. Heusmann. *Growing up to be violent.* New York: Pergamon, 1977.

Lesser, G.S. Relationships between various forms of aggression and popularity among lower class children. *Journal of Educational Psychology* 1959, *50*:20–25.

Lewis, D.O., S.S. Shanok, J.H. Pincus, & G.H. Glaser. Violent juvenile delinquents: Psychiatric, neurological, and abuse factors. *Journal of the American Academy of Child Psychiatry* 1979, *18*(2):307–318.

Lieberman Research Inc. Overview: Five Year Review of Research Sponsored by the American Broadcasting Company, September 1970 through August 1975. 1975.

Liebert, R.M., & N.S. Schwartzberg. Effects of mass media. In M. R. Rosenzweig and L. W. Porter (Eds.), *Annual Review of Psychology* 1977, *28*:141–173. Palo Alto, CA: Annual Reviews, Inc.

Lyle, J. Television in daily life: patterns of use (over-view). In *National Institute of Mental Health, Television and Social Behavior, Reports and Papers*. Technical Report to Surgeon General's Scientific Advisory Committee on Television and Social Behavior. Vol IV. U.S. Gov't Printing Office, 1972. Pp. 1–32.

Lyle, J. & H. Hoffman. Explorations in patterns of television viewing by preschool-age children. In *National Institute of Mental Health, Television and Social Behavior, Reports and Papers*. Technical Report to Surgeon General's Scientific Advisory Committee on Television and Social Behavior. Vol IV. U.S. Gov't Printing Office, 1972.

McCandless, B.R. *Children and adolescents* (Rev. ed.), New York: Holt, Rinehart, and Winston, 1967.

McCarthy, E.D., T.S. Langner, J. C. Gersten, J.G. Eisenberg & L. Orzeck. Violence and behavior disorders. *Journal of Communication*, 1975, *25*:71–85.

Maccoby, E.E. Effects of the mass media. In Martin L. Hoffman & L.W. Hoffman (Eds.) *Review of child development research*, Vol. I. New York Russell Sage Foundation, 1964. pp. 323–348.

Maccoby, E.E. Why do children watch television? *Public Opinion Quarterly* 1954, *18*:239–244.

McCord, W., J. McCord, & A. Howard. Familial correlates of aggression in nondelinquent male children. *Journal of Abnormal and Social Psychology* 1961, *62*:79–93.

McKee, J., & F. Leader. The relationship of socioeconomic status and aggression to the competitive behavior of pre-school children. *Child Development* 1955, *26*:135–142.

McIntyre, J.J., & J.J. Teevan. Television violence and deviant behavior. In *National Institute of Mental Health, Television and Social Behavior, Reports and Papers*. Technical Report to Surgeon General's Scientific Advisory Committee on Television and Social Behavior. Vol III. U.S. Gov't Printing Office, 1972. Pp. 383–485.

McLeod, J.M., C. Atkin, & S. Chaffee. Adolescents, parents, and television use: Adolescent self-report measures from Maryland and Wisconsin samples. In *National Institute of Mental Health, Television and Social Behavior, Reports and Papers*. Technical Report to Surgeon General's Scientific Advisory Committee on Television and Social Behavior. Vol. III. U.S. Gov't Printing Office, 1972. Pp. 173–238.

Merrill, I. Broadcast viewing and listening by children. *Public Opinion Quarterly* 1961, *25*:263–276.

Meyerson, L.J. *The effects of filmed aggression on the aggressive responses of high and low aggressive subjects*. Ph.D. dissertation, University of Iowa, 1966.

Milavsky, J.R. The effects of exposure to television violence on aggressive behavior of boys. Paper read at the annual meeting of the American Association for Public Opinion Research (AAPOR), May 20, 1977. (a)

Milavsky, J.R. TV and aggressive behavior of elementary school boys: Eight conceptualizations of TV exposure in search of an effect. Paper read at the annual meeting of the American Psychological Association (APA), August 29, 1977. (b)

Milavsky, J.R. A search for mediators of the effects of TV violence on the aggressive behavior of elementary school boys: results of a longitudinal panel study. Paper read at the annual meeting of the American Sociological Association (ASA), September 7, 1977. (c)

Milavsky, J.R., R. Kessler, H.H. Stipp, & W.S. Rubens. Television and aggression: Results of a panel study. In D. Pearl, L. Bouthilet, and J. Lazar (Eds.), *Television and behavior: Ten years of scientific progress and implications for the eighties*. Washington, D.C.: United States Government Printing Office, 1982.

Milavsky, J.R., & B. Pekowsky. Exposure to TV "violence" and aggressive behavior in boys, examined as process: A status report of a longitudinal study. Paper read at the annual meeting of the American Sociological Association (ASA), August 31, 1972.

Milavsky, J.R., B. Pekowsky, & H. Stipp. TV drug advertising and proprietary and illicit drug use among teenage boys. *Public Opinion Quarterly* 1976, *40*:457–481.

Milgram, S., & L. Shotland. *Television and antisocial behavior: Field experiments*. New York and London: Academic Press, 1973.

Miller, W.B. Lower class culture as a generating milieu of gang delinquency. *Journal of Social Issues* 1958, *14*:5–19.

Mohr, P. *Television, children, and parents*. Wichita, KA: Wichita State University, Dept. of Speech Communication, 1976.

Mortimer, J.T., & J. Lorence. Work experience and occupational value socialization: A longitudinal study. *American Journal of Sociology* 1979, *84*:1361–1385.

Murray, R., R. Cole, & F. Felder. Teenagers and TV violence: How they rate it and view it. *Journalism Quarterly*, 1970, *47*:247–255.

Muson, H. Teenage violence and the telly. *Psychology Today* 1978, *50*:50–54.

Mussen, P.H., J.J. Conger, & J. Kagan. *Child development and personality* (5th ed.). New York: Harper and Row, 1979.

National Broadcasting Company. Why sales come in curves. New York: NBC, 1953.

National Institute of Mental Health: U.S. Department of Health, Education and Welfare. *Tele-*

vision and growing up: The impact of televised violence. From the Surgeon General's Scientific Advisory Committee on Television and Social Behavior. Washington, D.C. U.S. Government Printing Office, 1972.

National Institute of Mental Health: U.S. Department of Health, Education, and Welfare. *Television and social behavior, reports and papers.* Technical Report to Surgeon General's Scientific Advisory Committee on Television and Social Behavior. Vol. I: *Media content and control.* G.A Comstock and E.A. Rubinstein (Eds.). Vol. II: *Television and social learning*. J.P. Murray, E.A Rubinstein, and G.A. Comstock (Eds.). Vol. III: *Television and adolescent aggressiveness*. G.A. Comstock and E.A. Rubinstein (Eds.). Vol. IV: *Television in day-to-day life: Patterns of use.* E.A. Rubenstein, G.A. Comstock, and J.P. Murray (Eds.). Vol. V: *Television's effects: Further explorations*. G.A. Comstock, E.A. Rubinstein, and J.P. Murray (Eds.). Washington, D.C. U.S. Government Printing Office, 1972.

Nerlove, M., & S.J. Press. *Univariate and multivariate log-linear and logistic models.* Santa Monica, CA.: Rand, 1973.

A.C. Nielsen, Co. *Nielsen television index (NTI),* Chicago: A.C. Nielsen Co., 1971. (a)

A.C. Nielsen, Co. *NTI/NAC audience demographics reports*. Chicago: A.C. Nielsen, Co., 1971 (b)

A.C. Nielsen, Co. *Additional demographic dimensions report*. Chicago: A.C. Nielsen, Co., 1974 (a)

A.C. Nielsen, Co. *Nielsen newscast No. 1* Chicago: A.C. Nielsen, Co., 1974. (b)

O'Brian, R.M. Using rank category variables to represent continuous variables: A critique of generally accepted practices. Paper read at the annual meeting of the American Sociological Association, 1980.

Pearl, D., L. Bouthilet, & J. Lazar (Eds.). *Television and behavior: Ten years of scientific progress and implications for the eighties.* Vol. I "Summary Report." Vol. II. "Technical Report." Washington D.C.: United States Government Printing Office, in press.

Pelz, D., & R. Lew. Heise's causal model applied. In E.F. Borgatta and G.W. Bohrnstedt (Eds.), *Sociological methodology*. San Francisco: Jossey-Bass, 1970. Pp. 28–37.

Pokorny, A.D. Human violence: A comparison of homicide, aggravated assault, suicide, and attempted suicide. *The Journal of Criminal Law, Criminology, and Police Science* 1965, *56*:488–497.

Riley, M.W., and J.W. Riley, Jr. A sociological approach to communication research. *Public Opinion Quarterly* 1951, *15*:445–460.

Robins, L.N. *Deviant children grow up*. Baltimore: Williams and Wilkins, 1966.

Robinson, C.R., L.J. Hamernik, & B.K.L. Genova. Viewer definitions of violence. Paper read at the International Communication Association Convention, 1980.

Rogosa, D. Causal models in longitudinal research: Rationale, formulation, and interpretation. In J.R. Nesselrrode and P.B. Baltes (Eds.), *Longitudinal research in human development: Design and analysis.* New York: Academic Press, 1979. Pp. 263–302.

Rogosa, D. A critique of cross-lagged correlation. *Psychological Bulletin* 1980, *88*:245–258.

Schoenberg, R. Strategies for meaningful comparison. In Herbert L. Costner (Ed.), *Sociological methodology*. San Francisco: Jossey-Bass, 1972. Pp. 1–35.

Schramm, W, J. Lyle, & E.B. Parker. *Television in the lives of our children*. Stanford, CA: Stanford University Press, 1961.

Sears, R.R., E.E. Maccoby, & H. Levin. *Patterns of child rearing*. Evanston, IL: Row, Peterson, 1957.

Short, J., R.A. Tennyson, & K.I. Howard. Behavior dimensions of gang delinquency. *American Sociological Review* 1963, *28*:411–428.

Singer, J.L. (Ed.). The influence of violence portrayed in television or motion pictures upon overt aggressive behavior. In J.L. Singer (Ed.), *The control of aggression and violence: Cognitive and physiological factors*. New York: Academic Press, 1971. Pp. 19–56.

Singer, J.L. *The child's world of make-believe: Experimental studies of imaginative play*. New York and London: Academic Press, 1973.

Singer, J.L., & G.D. Singer. Televison viewing, family style, and aggressive behavior in preschool children. In M. Green (ed.), *Violence in the family: Psychiatric, sociological, and historical implications*. Washington, D.C.: AAAS Symposium Series, 1979.

Sletto, R.F. Sibling position and juvenile delinquency. *American Journal of Sociology* 1934, *39*:657–669.

Sörbom, D. Detection of correlated errors in longitudinal data. *British Journal of Mathematical and Statistical Psychology*, 1975, *28*:138–151.

Statistical Abstracts of the United States. Washington, D.C.: U.S. Department of Commerce, 1970 Bureau of Census, 1975.

Stein, A.H., & L.K. Friedrich. Television content and young children's behavior. In *National Institute of Mental Health, Television and Social Behavior, Reports and Papers.* Technical Report to Surgeon General's Scientific Advisory Committee on Television and Social Behavior. Vol II. Washington, D.C.; U.S. Gov't Printing Office, 1972.

Stipp, H.H. *Validity in social research: Measuring children's television exposure.* Unpublished Ph.D. dissertation, Columbia University, 1975.

Stolz, R.E., & M.D. Smith. Some effects of socio-economic, age, and sex factors on chidren's responses to the Rosenzweig Picture-Frustration Study. *Journal of Clinical Psychology* 1959, *15*:200–203.

Surgeon General's Scientific Advisory Committee on Television and Social Behavior. *Television and growing up: The impact of televised violence*. Report to the Surgeon General, United States Public Health Service. HEW Publication No. HSM 72–9090. Rockville, MD: National Institute of Mental Health. U.S. Gov't Printing Office, 1972.

Sutherland, E.H., & D.R. Cressey. Principles of criminology (8th ed.). Philadelphia: J.B. Lippincott, 1970.

Sykes, G.M., & D. Matza. Techniques of neutralization: A theory of delinquency. *American Journal of Sociology* 1957, *22*:664–670.

Tedeschi, J.T., R.B. Smith III, & R. Brown Jr. A reinterpretation of research on aggression. *Psychological Bulletin* 1974, *81*:540–562.

Treiman, D.J. Status discrepancy and prejudice. *American Journal of Sociology* 1966, *71*:651–664.

Tuddenham, R.D. Studies in reputation: I. Sex and grade differences in school children's evaluations of their peers. *Psychological Monograph* 1952, *333*:1–39.

Walder, L., R. Abelson, L. Eron, T. Banta, & J. Laulicht. Development of a peer-rating measure of aggression. *Psychological Reports* 1961, *9*:497–556.

Weigel, R.H., & R. Jessor. Television and adolescent conventionality. *Public Opinion Quarterly* 1973, *37*:76–90.

Wells, W.D. 1973. Television and aggression: Replication of an experimental field study. Unpublished manuscript, Graduate School of Business, University of Chicago.

Werts, C., & R. Linn. Study of Academic Growth Using Simplex Models. U.S. Dept. of Health, Education and Welfare. Washington, D.C.: National Institute of Education, 1975.

Wheaton, B., B. Muthen, D.F. Alwin, & G.F. Summers. Assessing reliability and stability in panel models. In D.R. Heise (Ed.), *Sociological methodology*. San Francisco: Jossey-Bass, 1977. Pp. 84–136.

Wicker, A.W. Attitudes vs. actions: The relationship of verbal and overt behavioral responses to attitude objects. *Journal of Social Issues* 1969, *25*:41–78.

Wicker, A.W. Winter vs. summer viewing. *Broadcasting* 1960, *21*:84–85.

Witty, P. Studies of mass media—1949–1965. *Science Education* 1966, *50*:119–126.

Wolfgang, M. *Patterns of criminal homicide*. Philadelphia: University of Pennsylvania Press, 1958.

Yablonsky, L. The delinquent gang as a near-group. *Social Problems* 1959, 7:108–117.

Zillmann, D. Excitation transfer in communication-mediated aggressive behavior. *Journal of Experimental Social Psychology* 1971, 7:419–434.

INDEX

QUANTITATIVE STUDIES IN SOCIAL RELATIONS
(Continued from page ii)

Bruce Jacobs, **THE POLITICAL ECONOMY OF ORGANIZATIONAL CHANGE:** ***Urban Institutional Response to the War on Poverty***

Ronald C. Kessler and David F. Greenberg, **LINEAR PANEL ANALYSIS:** ***Models of Quantitative Change***

Ivar Berg (Ed.), **SOCIOLOGICAL PERSPECTIVES ON LABOR MARKETS**

James Alan Fox (Ed.), **METHODS IN QUANTITATIVE CRIMINOLOGY**

James Alan Fox (Ed.), **MODELS IN QUANTITATIVE CRIMINOLOGY**

Philip K. Robins, Robert G. Spiegelman, Samuel Weiner, and Joseph G. Bell (Eds.), **A GUARANTEED ANNUAL INCOME:** ***Evidence from a Social Experiment***

Zev Klein and Yohanan Eshel, **INTEGRATING JERUSALEM SCHOOLS**

Juan E. Mezzich and Herbert Solomon, **TAXONOMY AND BEHAVIORAL SCIENCE**

Walter Williams, **GOVERNMENT BY AGENCY:** ***Lessons from the Social Program Grants-in-Aid Experience***

Peter H. Rossi, Richard A. Berk, and Kenneth J. Lenihan, **MONEY, WORK, AND CRIME:** ***Experimental Evidence***

Robert M. Groves and Robert L. Kahn, **SURVEYS BY TELEPHONE:** ***A National Comparison with Personal Interviews***

N. Krishnan Namboodiri (Ed.), **SURVEY SAMPLING AND MEASUREMENT**

Beverly Duncan and Otis Dudley Duncan, **SEX TYPING AND SOCIAL ROLES:** ***A Research Report***

Donald J. Treiman, **OCCUPATIONAL PRESTIGE IN COMPARATIVE PERSPECTIVE**

Samuel Leinhardt (Ed.), **SOCIAL NETWORKS:** ***A Developing Paradigm***

Richard A. Berk, Harold Brackman, and Selma Lesser, **A MEASURE OF JUSTICE:** ***An Empirical Study of Changes in the California Penal Code, 1955–1971***

Richard F. Curtis and Elton F. Jackson, **INEQUALITY IN AMERICAN COMMUNITIES**

Eric Hanushek and John Jackson, **STATISTICAL METHODS FOR SOCIAL SCIENTISTS**

Edward O. Laumann and Franz U. Pappi, **NETWORKS OF COLLECTIVE ACTION:** ***A Perspective on Community Influence Systems***

Walter Williams and Richard F. Elmore, **SOCIAL PROGRAM IMPLEMENTATION**

Roland J. Liebert, **DISINTEGRATION AND POLITICAL ACTION:** ***The Changing Functions of City Governments in America***

James D. Wright, **THE DISSENT OF THE GOVERNED:** ***Alienation and Democracy in America***

Seymour Sudman, **APPLIED SAMPLING**

Michael D. Ornstein, **ENTRY INTO THE AMERICAN LABOR FORCE**

Carl A. Bennett and Arthur A. Lumsdaine (Eds.), **EVALUATION AND EXPERIMENT: *Some Critical Issues in Assessing Social Programs***

H. M. Blalock, A. Aganbegian, F. M. Borodkin, Raymond Boudon, and Vittorio Capecchi (Eds.), **QUANTITATIVE SOCIOLOGY: *International Perspectives on Mathematical and Statistical Modeling***

N. J. Demerath, III, Otto Larsen, and Karl F. Schuessler (Eds.), **SOCIAL POLICY AND SOCIOLOGY**

Henry W. Riecken and Robert F. Boruch (Eds.), **SOCIAL EXPERIMENTATION: *A Method for Planning and Evaluating Social Intervention***

Arthur S. Goldberger and Otis Dudley Duncan (Eds.), **STRUCTURAL EQUATION MODELS IN THE SOCIAL SCIENCES**

Robert B. Tapp, **RELIGION AMONG THE UNITARIAN UNIVERSALISTS: *Converts in the Stepfathers' House***

Kent S. Miller and Ralph Mason Dreger (Eds.), **COMPARATIVE STUDIES OF BLACKS AND WHITES IN THE UNITED STATES**

Douglas T. Hall and Benjamin Schneider, **ORGANIZATIONAL CLIMATES AND CAREERS: *The Work Lives of Priests***

Robert L. Crain and Carol S. Weisman, **DISCRIMINATION, PERSONALITY, AND ACHIEVEMENT: *A Survey of Northern Blacks***

Roger N. Shepard, A. Kimball Romney, and Sara Beth Nerlove (Eds.), **MULTIDIMENSIONAL SCALING: *Theory and Applications in the Behavioral Sciences***, Volume I – Theory; Volume II – Applications

Peter H. Rossi and Walter Williams (Eds.), **EVALUATING SOCIAL PROGRAMS: *Theory, Practice, and Politics***